EXAM✓CRAM

MCTS 70-680
Microsoft Windows 7, Configuring

Patrick Regan

MCTS 70-680 Exam Cram: Microsoft Windows 7, Configuring

ISBN-13: 978-0-7897-4734-1

ISBN-10: 0-7897-4734-0

Library of Congress Cataloging-in-Publication data is on file.

Printed in the United States of America

Second Printing: August 2011

Trademarks

All terms mentioned in this book that are known to be trademarks or service marks have been appropriately capitalized. Pearson cannot attest to the accuracy of this information. Use of a term in this book should not be regarded as affecting the validity of any trademark or service mark.

Warning and Disclaimer

Bulk Sales

Pearson offers excellent discounts on this book when ordered in quantity for bulk purchases or special sales. For more information, please contact

U.S. Corporate and Government Sales

1-800-382-3419

corpsales@pearsontechgroup.com

For sales outside of the U.S., please contact

International Sales

international@pearsoned.com

Associate Publisher
David Dusthimer

Acquisitions Editor
Betsy Brown

Senior Development Editor
Christopher Cleveland

Managing Editor
Sandra Schroeder

Project Editor
Seth Kerney

Copy Editor
The Wordsmithery LLC

Indexer
Tim Wright

Proofreader
Water Crest Publishing

Technical Editor
Chris Crayton

Publishing Coordinator
Vanessa Evans

Multimedia Developer
Dan Scherf

Designer
Gary Adair

Page Layout
Studio Galou, LLC

Contents at a Glance

Table of Contents

About the Author

Patrick Regan has been a PC technician, network administrator/engineer, design architect, and security analyst for the past 17 years since graduating with a bachelor's degree in physics from the University of Akron. He has taught many computer and network classes at Sacramento local colleges (Heald Colleges and MTI Colleges) and participated in and led many projects (Heald Colleges, Intel Corporation, Miles Consulting Corporation, and Pacific Coast Companies). For his teaching accomplishments, he received the Teacher of the Year award from Heald Colleges, and he has received several recognition awards from Intel. Previously, he worked as a product support engineer for the Intel Corporation Customer Service, a senior network engineer for Virtual Alert supporting the BioTerrorism Readiness suite and as a senior design architect/engineer and training coordinator for Miles Consulting Corporation (MCC), a premiere Microsoft Gold partner and consulting firm. He is currently a senior network engineer supporting a large enterprise network at Pacific Coast Companies.

He holds many certifications including the Microsoft MCSE, MCSA, MCT; CompTIA's A+, Network+, Server+, Linux+, Security+ and CTT+; Cisco CCNA; and Novell's CNE and CWNP Certified Wireless Network Administrator (CWNA).

Over the last several years, he has written several textbooks for Prentice Hall, including *Troubleshooting the PC, Networking with Windows 2000 and 2003, Linux, Local Area Networks, Wide Area Networks*, and the Acing Series (*Acing the A+, Acing the Network+, Acing the Security+*, and *Acing the Linux+*). He has also co-authored the *MCSA/MCSE 70-290 Exam Cram: Managing and Maintaining a Microsoft Windows Server 2003 Environment*, Second Edition and has written several *Exam Cram* books for the Windows Vista and Windows Server 2008 certification exams.

You can write with questions and comments to the author at Patrick_Regan@hotmail.com. (Because of the high volume of mail, every message might not receive a reply.)

Dedication

I dedicate this book to the most beautiful woman and most wonderful person, Lidia. She is the best there is.

About the Technical Reviewer

Christopher A. Crayton is an author, technical editor, technical consultant, security consultant, trainer, and SkillsUSA state-level technology competition judge. Formerly, he worked as a computer and networking instructor at Keiser College (2001 Teacher of the Year); as network administrator for Protocol, a global electronic customer relationship management (eCRM) company; and at Eastman Kodak Headquarters as a computer and network specialist. Chris has authored several print and online books, including *The A+ Exams Guide*, Second Edition (Cengage Learning, 2008), *Microsoft Windows Vista 70-620 Exam Guide Short Cut* (O'Reilly, 2007), *CompTIA A+ Essentials 220-601 Exam Guide Short Cut* (O'Reilly, 2007), *The A+ Exams Guide, The A+ Certification and PC Repair Handbook* (Charles River Media, 2005), *The Security+ Exam Guide* (Charles River Media, 2003), and *A+ Adaptive Exams* (Charles River Media, 2002). He is also co-author of *How to Cheat at Securing Your Network* (Syngress, 2007). As an experienced technical editor, Chris has provided many technical edits/reviews for several major publishing companies, including Pearson Education, McGraw-Hill, Cengage Learning, Wiley, O'Reilly, Syngress, and Apress. He holds MCSE, A+, and Network+ certifications.

We Want to Hear from You!

As the reader of this book, *you* are our most important critic and commentator. We value your opinion and want to know what we're doing right, what we could do better, what areas you'd like to see us publish in, and any other words of wisdom you're willing to pass our way.

As an associate publisher for Pearson IT Certification, I welcome your comments. You can email or write me directly to let me know what you did or didn't like about this book—as well as what we can do to make our books better.

Please note that I cannot help you with technical problems related to the topic of this book. We do have a User Services group, however, where I will forward specific technical questions related to the book.

When you write, please be sure to include this book's title and author as well as your name, email address, and phone number. I will carefully review your comments and share them with the author and editors who worked on the book.

Email: feedback@pearsonitcertification.com

Mail: Dave Dusthimer
        Associate Publisher
        Pearson IT Certification
        800 East 96th Street
        Indianapolis, IN 46240 USA

Reader Services

Visit our website and register this book at www.pearsonitcertification.com/register for convenient access to any updates, downloads, or errata that might be available for this book.

Introduction

Welcome to *MCTS 70-680 Exam Cram: Microsoft Windows 7, Configuring*! Whether this book is your first or your fifteenth *Exam Cram* series book, you'll find information here that will help ensure your success as you pursue knowledge, experience, and certification. This book aims to help you get ready to take and pass the Microsoft certification exam "TS: Windows 7, Configuring" (Exam 70-680). After you pass this exam, you will earn the Microsoft Certified Technology Specialist: Windows 7, Configuration certification.

This introduction explains Microsoft's certification programs in general and talks about how the *Exam Cram* series can help you prepare for Microsoft's latest certification exams. Chapters 1 through 16 are designed to remind you of everything you need to know to pass the 70-680 certification exam. At the beginning and end of each main section, you see Cram Saver and Cram Exam questions to review the material. Then, at the end of each chapter, you find 10 review questions, and at the end of the book, you find a practice exam. Read the book, understand the material, and you stand a very good chance of passing the real test.

Based on what you learn from the self-assessment, you might decide to begin your studies with classroom training or some background reading. On the other hand, you might decide to pick up and read one of the many study guides available from Microsoft or third-party vendors. We also recommend that you supplement your study program with visits to http://examcram.com to receive additional practice questions, get advice, and track the Windows certification programs.

The Value of Certification

It is an established fact that computers and networking is a fast-paced environment. Therefore, employees who work in Information Technology (IT) must learn to keep up with the ever-changing technology and have the ability to learn new technology. It is said that a person in IT must be able to learn or retrain him- or herself every 1 to 1 1/2 years.

According to *Certification Magazine* (http://www.certmag.com), the successful IT worker must

- Be proficient in two or more technical specialties.

- Be able to wear multiple hats.

- Be more business-oriented because hiring managers look for employees who see the big picture of profit, loss, competitive advantage, and customer retention and understand that IT fits into this picture.

- Be able to work easily with non-technical personnel.

- Have soft skills of good listening, problem-solving, and effective written and verbal communication.

In addition, there is a demand for those who can demonstrate expertise in IT project management. Those moving to a mid- to high-level position have a mix of academic credentials and industry certifications, as well as increasing levels of responsibility.

Today, technical certifications are highly valuable. Depending on which certification or certifications an individual has, a user can begin as an entry-level technician or administrator. Certifications also demonstrate the knowledge and capabilities of a current technician or administrator. Technical companies see some technical certifications are as valuable as a college degree and non-technical companies see them just a little less than a college degree.

In 2001, researchers from Gartner Consulting surveyed nearly 18,000 IT managers, certified professionals, and certification candidates. They reported that

- IT professionals seek certification to increase compensation, find employment, or boost productivity.

- Of those certified, 66% of certified professionals received an increase in salary after becoming certified, and 83% reported that certification helped them gain a new position.

- Although most certification candidates combine several study methods, printed materials designed for self-study and instructor-led training were reported as the most useful preparation methods.

From the employer's perspective, although many managers (42%) feared that certified employees would move on to another organization, 71% of IT professionals gaining certification stay put. IT managers cited a higher level of service, competitive advantage, and increased productivity as key benefits of having certified staff. Of course, the drawbacks include cost of training and testing.

So as you can see, many people in IT see certification as a valuable tool. You can see that certification is

- ► A demonstration of specific areas of competence with particular technologies.

- ► A credential desired or required by an increasing number of employers.

- ► A tool people use successfully to challenge themselves.

- ► A road map for continuing education.

- ► A potential bridge to a new specialty.

- ► Evidence that you are self-motivated and actively working to stay current.

On the other hand, certification is not a substitute for extensive hands-on experience, and it is not a career cure-all. Lastly, usually a little bit of work and discipline is required to pass these exams.

The Microsoft Certification Program

Microsoft currently offers multiple certification titles, each of which boasts its own special abbreviation. (As a certification candidate and computer professional, you need to have a high tolerance for acronyms.)

Certifications for end-users are

- ► **Microsoft Office Specialists**: Recognized for demonstrating advanced skills with Microsoft desktop software (including Microsoft Office).

The older certifications associated with the Windows Server 2003 operating system and related network infrastructure are as follows:

- ► **Microsoft Certified Professional (MCP)**: For professionals who have the skills to successfully implement a Microsoft product (such as Windows XP or Windows Server 2003) or technology as part of a business solution in an organization.

- ▶ **Microsoft Certified Desktop Support Technician (MCDST)**: For professionals who have the technical and customer service skills to troubleshoot hardware and software operation issues in Microsoft Windows environments.

- ▶ **Microsoft Certified Systems Administrators (MCSAs)**: For professionals who administer network and systems environments based on the Microsoft Windows operating systems. Specializations include MCSA: Messaging and MCSA: Security.

- ▶ **Microsoft Certified Systems Engineer (MCSE)**: For professionals who design and implement an infrastructure solution that is based on the Windows operating system and Microsoft Windows Server System software. Specializations include MCSE: Messaging and MCSE: Security.

The newer certification base on Windows Vista and related server products are

- ▶ **Microsoft Certified Technology Specialist (MCTS)**: For professionals who target specific technologies and to distinguish themselves by demonstrating in-depth knowledge and expertise in the various Microsoft specialized technologies. The MCTS is a replacement for the MCP program.

- ▶ **Microsoft Certified IT Professional (MCITP)**: For professionals who demonstrate comprehensive skills in planning, deploying, supporting, maintaining, and optimizing IT infrastructures. The MCITP is a replacement for the MCSA and MCSE programs.

- ▶ **Microsoft Certified Architect (MCA)**: For professionals who are identified as top industry experts in IT architecture that use multiple technologies to solve business problems and provide business metrics and measurements. Candidates for the MCA program are required to present to a review board—consisting of previously certified architects—to earn the certification.

For database professionals:

- ▶ **Microsoft Certified Database Administrators (MCDBAs)**: For professionals who design, implement, and administer Microsoft SQL Server databases.

For developers and programmers:

▶ **Microsoft Certified Professional Developer (MCPD)**: Professionals who are recognized as expert Windows Application Developer, Web Application Developer, or Enterprise Applications Developer. They demonstrate that you can build rich applications that target a variety of platforms, such as the Microsoft .NET Framework 2.0.

▶ **Microsoft Certified Application Developers (MCADs)**: For professionals who use Microsoft technologies to develop and maintain department-level applications, components, Web or desktop clients, or back-end data services.

For trainers and curriculum developers, there is the

▶ **Microsoft Certified Trainer (MCT)**: For qualified instructors who are certified by Microsoft to deliver Microsoft training courses to IT professionals and developers.

▶ **Microsoft Certified Learning Consultant (MCLC)**: For recognized MCTs whose job roles have grown to include frequent consultative engagements with their customers and who are experts in delivering customized learning solutions that positively affect customer return on investment (ROI).

The best place to keep tabs on all Microsoft certifications is the following website:

http://www.microsoft.com/learning/default.mspx

Because Microsoft changes the website often and this URL might not work in the future, you should use the Search tool on Microsoft's site to find more information on a particular certification.

Microsoft Certified Technology Specialist

Technology Specialist certifications enable professionals to target specific technologies and to distinguish themselves by demonstrating in-depth knowledge and expertise in their specialized technologies. Microsoft Technology Specialists are consistently capable of implementing, building, troubleshooting, and debugging a particular Microsoft technology.

Microsoft Certified IT Professional

The new Microsoft Certified IT Professional (MCITP) credential lets you highlight your specific area of expertise. Now you can easily distinguish yourself as an expert in database administration, database development, business intelligence, or support. Some of the Microsoft Certified IT Professional certifications are

- ▶ IT Professional: Database Developer

- ▶ IT Professional: Database Administrator

- ▶ IT Professional: Business Intelligence Developer

- ▶ IT Professional: Enterprise Support Technician

At the time of this writing, details are just starting to be revealed on the Microsoft Certified Technology Specialist (MCTS) on Windows Server 2008/Windows Server 2008 R2. The MCTS on Windows Server 2008 helps you and your organization take advantage of advanced server technology with the power to increase the flexibility of your server infrastructure, save time, and reduce costs. Transition certifications are available today for Windows Server 2003 certified professionals to Windows Server 2008 Windows Server 2008 R2 product release. For more details about these certifications, visit the following website:

http://www.microsoft.com/learning/mcp/windowsserver2008/default.mspx

If the URL is no longer available, don't forget to search for MCTS and Windows Server 2008 using the Microsoft search tool found on the Microsoft website.

Microsoft Certified Technology Specialist: Windows 7 Configuration

The Microsoft Certified Technology Specialist certifications enable professionals to target specific technologies and distinguish themselves by demonstrating in-depth knowledge and expertise in their specialized technologies. A

Microsoft Certified Technology Specialist in Windows 7, Configuration possesses the knowledge and skills to configure Windows 7 for optimal performance on the desktop, including installing, managing, and configuring the new security, network, and application features in Windows 7.

To earn the Microsoft Certified Technology Specialist: Windows 7, Configuration, you must pass one exam that focuses on supporting end-user issues about network connectivity, security, and applications installation and compatibility, and logon problems that include account issues and password resets:

Exam 70-680 TS: Windows 7, Configuration

If you decide to take Microsoft recognized class, you would take several classes to cover all of the material found on this exam. The preparation guide (including exam objectives) for Exam 70-680 TS: Windows 7, Configuration can be found at

http://tinyurl.com/ye8mjce

Table I.1 outlines the major topic areas, individual exam objectives, and which chapters in the book cover these objectives.

TABLE I.1 **MCTS 70-680 Exam Outline**

Exam Topic Area (Percentage of Exam)	Exam Objective	Exam Objective Description	Chapter Covering Exam Objective
Installing, Upgrading, and Migrating to Windows 7 (14 percent)	Perform a clean installation	This objective might include but is not limited to identifying hardware requirements; setting up as the sole operating system; setting up as dual boot; installation methods; boot from the source of installation, preparing the installation source: USB, CD, network share, WDS.	Chapter 2
	Upgrade to Windows 7 from previous versions of Windows	This objective might include but is not limited to upgrading from Windows Vista; migrating from Windows XP; upgrading from one edition of Windows 7 to another edition of Windows 7.	Chapter 2

TABLE I.1 **Continued**

Exam Topic Area (Percentage of Exam)	Exam Objective	Exam Objective Description	Chapter Covering Exam Objective
	Migrate user profiles	This objective might include but is not limited to migrating from one machine to another; migrating from previous versions of Windows; side-by-side versus. wipe and load.	Chapter 2
Deploying Windows 7 (13 percent)	Capture a system image	This objective might include but is not limited to preparing system for capture; creating a WIM file; automated capture; manual capture.	Chapter 2
	Prepare a system image for deployment	This objective might include but is not limited to inserting an application into a system image; inserting a driver into a system image; inserting an update into a system image; configuring tasks to run after deployment.	Chapter 2
	Deploy a system image	This objective might include but is not limited to automated deployment methods; manually deploying a customized image.	Chapter 2
	Configure a VHD	This objective might include but is not limited to creating, deploying, booting, mounting, and updating VHDs; offline updates; offline servicing.	Chapter 2
Configuring Hardware and Applications (14 percent)	Configure devices	This objective might include but is not limited to updating, disabling, and uninstalling drivers; signed drivers; conflicts between drivers; configuring driver settings; resolving problem device drivers.	Chapter 3

TABLE I.1 **Continued**

Exam Topic Area (Percentage of Exam)	Exam Objective	Exam Objective Description	Chapter Covering Exam Objective
	Configure application compatibility	This objective might include but is not limited to setting compatibility mode; implementing shims; compatibility issues with Internet Explorer.	Chapters 12 and 13
	Configure application restrictions	This objective might include but is not limited to setting software restriction policies; setting application control policies; setting through group policy or local security policy.	Chapter 12
	Configure Internet Explorer	This objective might include but is not limited to configuring compatibility view; configuring security settings; configuring providers; managing add-ons; controlling InPrivate mode; certificates for secure websites.	Chapter 13
Configuring Network Connectivity (14 percent)	Configure IPv4 network settings	This objective might include but is not limited to connecting to a network; configuring name resolution; setting up a connection for a network; network locations; resolving connectivity issues; APIPA.	Chapter 5
	Configure IPv6 network settings	This objective might include but is not limited to configuring name resolution; connecting to a network; setting up a connection for a network; network locations; resolving connectivity issues; link local multicast name resolution.	Chapter 5

TABLE I.1 **Continued**

Exam Topic Area (Percentage of Exam)	Exam Objective	Exam Objective Description	Chapter Covering Exam Objective
	Configure networking settings	This objective might include but is not limited to adding a physically connected (wired) or wireless device; connecting to a wireless network; configuring security settings on the client; setting preferred wireless networks; configuring network adapters; configuring location-aware printing.	Chapters 5 and 6
	Configure Windows Firewall	This objective might include but is not limited to configuring rules for multiple profiles; allowing or denying an application; network-profile-specific rules; configuring notifications; configuring authenticated exceptions.	Chapter 7
	Configure remote management	This objective might include but is not limited to remote management methods; configuring remote management tools; executing PowerShell commands.	Chapter 14
Configuring Access to Resources (13 percent)	Configure shared resources	This objective might include but is not limited to folder virtualization; shared folder permissions; printers and queues; configuring Homegroup settings.	Chapters 10 and 11
	Configure file and folder access.	This objective might include but is not limited to encrypting files and folders by using EFS; configuring NTFS permissions; resolving effective permissions issues; copying files versus moving files.	Chapters 9 and 10

TABLE I.1 **Continued**

Exam Topic Area (Percentage of Exam)	Exam Objective	Exam Objective Description	Chapter Covering Exam Objective
	Configure user account control (UAC)	This objective might include but is not limited to configuring local security policy; configuring admin versus standard UAC prompt behaviors; configuring Secure Desktop.	Chapter 8
	Configure authentication and authorization	This objective might include but is not limited to resolving authentication issues; configuring rights; managing credentials; managing certificates; smart cards with PIV; elevating user privileges; multifactor authentication.	Chapter 8
	Configure BranchCache	This objective might include but is not limited to distributed cache mode versus hosted mode; network infrastructure requirements; configuring settings; certificate management.	Chapter 10
Configuring Mobile Computing (10 percent)	Configure BitLocker and BitLocker To Go	This objective might include but is not limited to configuring BitLocker and BitLocker To Go policies; managing Trusted Platform Module (TPM) PINs; configuring startup key storage; data recovery agent support.	Chapter 9
	Configure DirectAccess	This objective might include but is not limited to configuring client side; configuring authentication; network infrastructure requirements.	Chapter 6

TABLE I.1   **Continued**

Exam Topic Area (Percentage of Exam)	Exam Objective	Exam Objective Description	Chapter Covering Exam Objective
	Configure mobility options	This objective might include but is not limited to configuring offline file policies; transparent caching; creating and migrating power policy.	Chapter 14
	Configure remote connections	This objective might include but is not limited to establishing VPN connections and authentication; enabling a VPN reconnect; advanced security auditing; NAP quarantine remediation; dial-up connections; remote desktop; published apps.	Chapters 6, 8, and 14
Monitoring and Maintaining Systems That Run Windows 7 (11 percent)	Configure updates to Windows 7	This objective might include but is not limited to configuring update settings; determining source of updates; configuring Windows Update policies; reviewing update history; checking for new updates; rolling back updates.	Chapter 2
	Manage disks	This objective might include but is not limited to managing disk volumes; managing file system fragmentation; RAID; removable device policies.	Chapter 4
	Monitor systems	This objective might include but is not limited to configuring event logging; filtering event logs; event subscriptions; data collector sets; generating a system diagnostics report.	Chapters 15 and 16

TABLE I.1 **Continued**

Exam Topic Area (Percentage of Exam)	Exam Objective	Exam Objective Description	Chapter Covering Exam Objective
	Configure performance settings	This objective might include but is not limited to configuring page files; configuring hard drive cache; updated drivers; configuring networking performance; configuring power plans; configuring processor scheduling; configuring desktop environment; configuring services and programs to resolve performance issues; mobile computing performance issues; configuring power.	Chapter 15
Configuring Backup and Recovery Options (11 percent)	Configure backup	This objective might include but is not limited to creating a system recovery disk; backing up files, folders, or full system; scheduling backups.	Chapter 16
	Configure system recovery options	This objective might include but is not limited to configuring system restore points; restoring system settings; last known good configuration; complete restore; driver rollback.	Chapters 3 and 16
	Configure file recovery options	This objective might include but is not limited to configuring file restore points; restoring previous versions of files and folders; restoring damaged or deleted files by using shadow copies; restoring user profiles.	Chapter 16

Taking a Certification Exam

After you prepare for your exam, you need to register with a testing center. At the time of this writing, the cost to take Exam 70-680 is (U.S.) $125, and if you don't pass, you can take each again for an additional (U.S.) $125 for each attempt. In the United States and Canada, tests are administered by Prometric. Here's how you can contact them:

> ▶ **Prometric**: You can sign up for a test through the company's website, http://www.2test.com or http://www.prometric.com. Within the United States and Canada, you can register by phone at 800-755-3926. If you live outside this region, you should check the Prometric website for the appropriate phone number.

To sign up for a test, you must possess a valid credit card or contact either Prometric for mailing instructions to send a check (in the U.S.). Only when payment is verified, or a check has cleared, can you actually register for a test.

To schedule an exam, you need to call the appropriate phone number or visit the Prometric websites at least one day in advance of the test date. To cancel or reschedule an exam in the United States or Canada, you must call before 3 p.m. Eastern time the day before the scheduled test time (or you might be charged, even if you don't show up to take the test). When you want to schedule a test, you should have the following information ready:

> ▶ Your name, organization, and mailing address.

> ▶ Your Microsoft test ID. (In the United States, this means your Social Security number; citizens of other countries should call ahead to find out what type of identification number is required to register for a test.)

> ▶ The name and number of the exam you want to take.

> ▶ A method of payment. (As mentioned previously, a credit card is the most convenient method, but alternate means can be arranged in advance, if necessary.)

After you sign up for a test, you are told when and where the test is scheduled. You should arrive at least 15 minutes early. You must supply two forms of identification, one of which must be a photo ID, to be admitted into the testing room.

How to Prepare for an Exam

Preparing for any Microsoft certification test (including Exam 70-680) requires that you obtain and study materials designed to provide comprehensive information about the product and its capabilities that will appear on the specific exam for which you are preparing. The following list of materials can help you study and prepare:

- ▶ The Windows 7 product DVD-ROM. This disk includes comprehensive online documentation and related materials; it should be one of your primary resources when you are preparing for the test. Currently, you can download a Windows 7 Enterprise 90-day trial from the following website:

  http://technet.microsoft.com/en-us/evalcenter/cc442495.aspx

- ▶ The exam preparation materials, practice tests, and self-assessment exams on the Microsoft Training and Certification site, at http://www.microsoft.com/learning/default.mspx. The Exam Resources link offers samples of the new question types on the Windows Server 2003/2008 Microsoft Certification track series of exams. You should find the materials, download them, and use them!

- ▶ The exam preparation advice, practice tests, questions of the day, and forums at http://www.examcram.com.

In addition, you might find any or all of the following materials useful in your quest for Windows 7 expertise:

- ▶ **Microsoft training kits**: Microsoft Learning offers a training kit that specifically targets Exam 70-680. For more information, visit http://www.microsoft.com/learning/books/. This training kit contains information that you will find useful in preparing for the test.

- ▶ **Microsoft TechNet CD or DVD and website**: This monthly CD- or DVD-based publication delivers numerous electronic titles that include coverage of Windows Server 2003 and Windows Server 2008 and related topics on the Technical Information (TechNet) series on CD or DVD. Its offerings include product facts, technical notes, tools and utilities, and information on how to access the Seminars Online training materials for Windows Server 2003/2008 and the Windows Server System line of products. Visit http://technet.microsoft.com and check out the information for TechNet subscriptions. You can utilize a large portion of the TechNet website at no charge.

▶ **Study guides**: Several publishers—including Pearson—offer Windows Server 2008, Windows Server 2003, Windows 7, Windows Vista, and Windows XP study guides. Pearson offers the following:

   ▶ **The Exam Cram series**: These books give you the insights about the material that you need to know to successfully pass the certification tests.

   ▶ **Pearson Certification Guides**: These books provide a greater level of detail than the *Exam Cram* books and are designed to teach you everything you need to know about the subject covered by an exam. Each book comes with a CD-ROM that contains interactive practice exams in a variety of testing formats.

   Together, these two series make a perfect pair if you are new to Windows.

▶ **Classroom training**: CTECs, online partners, and third-party training companies (such as Wave Technologies, New Horizons, and Global Knowledge) offer classroom training on Windows Server 2008, Windows Server 2003, Windows 7, Windows Vista, and Windows XP. These companies aim to help you prepare to pass Exam 70-680 as well as several others. Although this type of training tends to be pricey, most of the individuals lucky enough to attend find this training to be quite worthwhile.

Although many websites offer information on what to study for a particular exam, few sites offer how you should study for an exam. The study process can be broken down into various stages. However, key to all of these stages is the ability to concentrate. Concentration, or the lack of, plays a big part in the study process.

To be able to concentrate, you must remove all distractions. You should plan for study breaks, but it is the unplanned breaks caused by distractions that do not allow you to concentrate on what you need to learn. Therefore, first, you need to create an environment that's conducive to studying or seek out an existing environment that meets these criteria, such as a library.

First, do not study with the TV on and do not have other people in the room. It is easy for the TV to break your concentration and grab your attention. In addition, if you have people in the room, you have to pretend that you are not there and that they are not causing distractions, including talking with other people. Lastly, there are varying opinions on whether it is better to study with or without music playing. Although some people need to have a little white noise in the background to study, if you do choose to have music, you should keep the volume on a low level and you should listen to music without vocals in it.

After you find a place to study, you must schedule the time to study. You should take into consideration not studying on an empty stomach. You should also not study on a full stomach because it tends to make people drowsy. You might also consider having a glass of water near to sip on.

In addition, make sure that you well rested so that you don't start dozing off when you start. Next, make sure that you find a position that is comfortable and that the furniture that you are using is also comfortable. Lastly, make sure that your study area is well lit. Natural light is best for fighting fatigue.

The first thing that you should do when you study is to clear your mind of distractions. So take a minute or two, close your eyes, and empty your mind.

When you prepare for an exam, the best place to start is to take the list of exam objectives and study them carefully. You can then organize your study keeping these objectives in mind. This narrows down your focus area to individual topics or subtopics. In addition, you need to understand and visualize the process as a whole. This helps in addressing practical problems in real environments as well as some unsuspected questions.

In a multiple-choice type exam, you do have one advantage: The answer or answers are already there, and you have to simply choose the correct ones. Because the answers are already there, you can start eliminating the incorrect answers by using your knowledge and some logical thinking. One common mistake is to select the first obvious-looking answers without checking the other options, so always examine all the options, think, and choose the right answer. Of course, with multiple-choice questions, you have to be exact and should be able to differentiate between very similar answers. This is where a peaceful place of study without distractions helps so that you can read between the lines and so that you don't miss key points.

Day of the Exam

Before you take an exam, eat something light, even if you have no appetite. If your stomach is actively upset, try mild foods such as toast or crackers. Plain saltine crackers are great for settling a cranky stomach. Keep your caffeine and nicotine consumption to a minimum; excessive stimulants aren't exactly conducive to reducing stress. Plan to take a bottle of water or some hard candies, such as lozenges, with you to combat dry mouth. Also, make sure to dress comfortably.

Arrive at the testing center early. If you have never been to the testing center before, make sure that you know where it is. You might even consider taking a test drive. If you arrive between 15 and 30 minutes early for any certification exam, it gives you

▶ Ample time for prayer, meditation, and/or breathing.

▶ Time to scan glossary terms and quick access tables before taking the exam so that you can get the intellectual juices flowing and build a little confidence.

▶ Time to practice physical relaxation techniques.

▶ Time to visit the washroom.

But don't arrive too early.

When you are escorted into the testing chamber, you are usually given two sheets of paper (or laminated paper) with a pen (or wet erase pen). As soon as you hear the door close behind you, immediately unload bits of exam information that you need to quickly recall onto the paper. Then throughout the exam, you can refer to this information easily without thinking about it. This way, you can focus on answering the questions and using this information as reference. Before you actually start the exam, close your eyes and take deep breath to clear your mind of distractions.

Typically, the testing room is furnished with anywhere from one to six computers, and each workstation is separated from the others by dividers designed to keep anyone from seeing what's happening on someone else's computer screen. Most testing rooms feature a wall with a large picture window. This layout permits the exam coordinator to monitor the room, to prevent exam takers from talking to one another, and to observe anything out of the ordinary that might go on. The exam coordinator will have preloaded the appropriate Microsoft certification exam—for this book, that's Exam 70-680 MCTS: Windows 7, Configuring—and you are permitted to start as soon as you're seated in front of the computer.

> **ExamAlert**
>
> Always remember that the testing center's test coordinator is there to assist you in case you encounter some unusual problems, such as a malfunctioning test computer. If you need some assistance not related to the content of the exam itself, feel free to notify one of the test coordinators—after all, they are there to make your exam-taking experience as pleasant as possible.

All exams are completely closed book. In fact, you are not permitted to take anything with you into the testing area, but you receive a blank sheet of paper and a pen or, in some cases, an erasable plastic sheet and an erasable pen. We suggest that you immediately write down on that sheet of paper all the information you've memorized for the test. In *Exam Cram* books, this information appears on the tear-out sheet (Cram Sheet) inside the front cover of each book. You are given some time to compose yourself, record this information, and take a sample orientation exam before you begin the real thing. We suggest that you take the orientation test before taking your first exam, but because all the certification exams are more or less identical in layout, behavior, and controls, you probably don't need to do so more than once.

All Microsoft certification exams allow a certain maximum amount of testing time. (This time is indicated on the exam by an onscreen timer clock, so you can check the time remaining whenever you like.) All Microsoft certification exams are computer generated. In addition to multiple choice, most exams contain select–and-place (drag-and-drop), create-a-tree (categorization and prioritization), drag-and-connect, and build-list-and-reorder (list prioritization) types of questions. Although this format might sound quite simple, the questions are constructed not only to check your mastery of basic facts and figures about Windows Vista, but also to require you to evaluate one or more sets of circumstances or requirements. Often, you are asked to give more than one answer to a question. Likewise, you might be asked to select the best or most effective solution to a problem from a range of choices—all of which are technically correct. Taking the exam is quite an adventure, and it involves real thinking and concentration. This book shows you what to expect and how to deal with the potential problems, puzzles, and predicaments.

Dealing with Test Anxiety

Because a certification exam costs money to take and time to prepare for the exam and failing an exam can be a blow to your self-confidence, most people feel a certain amount of anxiety when they are about to take a certification exam. It is no wonder that most of us are a little sweaty in the palms when taking the exam. However, certain levels of stress can actually help you to raise your level of performance when taking an exam. This anxiety usually serves to help you focus your concentration and think clearly through a problem.

But for some individuals, exam anxiety is more than just a nuisance. For these people, exam anxiety is a debilitating condition that affects their performance with a negative impact on the exam results.

Exam anxiety reduction begins with the preparation process. The first thing that you should think of is if you know the material, there should not be anything that you should be nervous over. It goes without saying that the better prepared you are for an exam, the less stress you will experience when taking it. Always give yourself plenty of time to prepare for an exam; don't place yourself under unreasonable deadlines. But again, make goals and make every effort to meet those goals. Procrastination and making excuses can be just as bad.

There is not hard and fast rule for how long it takes to prepare for an exam. The time required varies from student to student and is dependent on a number of different factors including reading speed, access to study materials, personal commitments, and so on. In addition, don't compare yourself to peers, especially if doing so has a negative effect on your confidence.

For many students, practice exams are a great way to shed some of the fears that arise in the test center. Practice exams are best used near the end of the exam preparation. Be sure to use them as an assessment of your current knowledge, not as a method to try to memorize key concepts. When reviewing these questions, be sure you understand the question and understand all answers (right and wrong). Lastly, set time limits on the practice exams.

If you know the material, don't plan on studying the day of your exam. You should end your studying the evening before the exam. In addition, don't make it a late night so that you can get a full good night's rest. Of course, you should be studying on a regular basis for at least a few weeks prior to the evening of the exam so that you should not need the last-minute cramming.

Additional Resources

A good source of information about Microsoft certification exams comes from Microsoft itself. Because its products and technologies—and the exams that go with them—change frequently, the best place to go for exam-related information is online.

Microsoft offers training, certification, and other learning-related information and links at the http://www.microsoft.com/learning web address. If you haven't already visited the Microsoft Training and Certification website, you should do so right now. Microsoft's Training and Certification home page resides at http://www.microsoft.com/learning/default.mspx.

Coping with Change on the Web

Sooner or later, all the information we've shared with you about the Microsoft Certified Professional pages and the other Web-based resources mentioned throughout the rest of this book will go stale or be replaced by newer information. In some cases, the URLs you find here might lead you to their replacements; in other cases, the URLs will go nowhere, leaving you with the dreaded "404 File not found" error message. When that happens, don't give up.

There's always a way to find what you want on the Web if you're willing to invest some time and energy. Most large or complex websites—and Microsoft's qualifies on both counts—offer search engines. All of Microsoft's web pages have a Search button at the top edge of the page. As long as you can get to Microsoft's site (it should stay at http://www.microsoft.com for a long time), you can use the Search button to find what you need.

The more focused (or specific) you can make a search request, the more likely the results will include information you can use. For example, you can search for the string

```
"training and certification"
```

to produce a lot of data about the subject in general, but if you're looking for the preparation guide for Exam 70-680: Windows 7, Configuring, you'll be more likely to get there quickly if you use a search string similar to the following:

```
"Exam 70-680" AND "preparation guide"
```

Likewise, if you want to find the Training and Certification downloads, you should try a search string such as this:

```
"training and certification" AND "download page"
```

Finally, you should feel free to use general search tools—such as http://www.google.com, http://www.yahoo.com, http://www.excite.com, and http://www.bing.com—to look for related information. Although Microsoft offers great information about its certification exams online, there are plenty of third-party sources of information and assistance that need not follow Microsoft's party line. Therefore, if you can't find something where the book says it lives, you should intensify your search.

Thanks for making this *Exam Cram* book a pivotal part of your certification study plan. Best of luck on becoming certified!

CHAPTER 1

Introduction to Windows 7

This chapter covers the following 70-680 Objectives:

▶ **Supplemental Objective**: List and describe the main differences between Windows 7, Windows Vista, and Windows XP.

▶ **Supplemental Objective**: List the different editions of Windows 7.

▶ **Supplemental Objective**: Describe the difference between the 32-bit and 64-bit versions of Windows 7.

▶ **Supplemental Objectives**: List and describe the main components that make up the graphical user interface used in Windows 7.

Before discussing the exact objectives found in the 70-680 exam, you need to understand how Windows 7 came about and what is different between Windows 7 and older versions of Windows, specifically Windows XP and Windows Vista. Before you decide to install Windows 7, you need to know which editions and versions are available so that you can choose the correct version for you.

Furthermore, if you are new to Windows 7, you will notice the Windows graphical user interface is significantly different than Windows XP and, to a lesser degree, Windows Vista. So before you jump into the "blood and guts" of Windows 7, make sure that you understand the basics of using Windows 7.

The Road to Windows 7

▶ **Supplemental Objective:** List and describe the main differences between Windows 7, Windows Vista, and Windows XP.

▶ **Supplemental Objective:** List the different editions of Windows 7.

▶ **Supplemental Objective:** Describe the difference between the 32-bit and 64-bit versions of Windows 7.

CramSaver

1. Which edition of Windows 7 is aimed at large corporations and includes numerous tools to secure Windows, including BitLocker and AppLocker?

   ○ **A.** Windows 7 Home Premium

   ○ **B.** Windows 7 Professional

   ○ **C.** Windows 7 Enterprise

   ○ **D.** Windows 7 Ultimate

2. You want to access 64 GB of memory. Which edition of Windows 7 should you use?

   ○ **A.** 16 MB

   ○ **B.** 32-bit

   ○ **C.** 32 GB

   ○ **D.** 64-bit

   ○ **E.** 64 GB

Answers

1. **C** is correct. Windows 7 Enterprise provides advanced data protection and information access for businesses. It is targeted for managed environments, mainly large enterprises. It includes BitLocker, BitLocker To Go, AppLocker, Direct Access, and BranchCache. Answer A is incorrect because Windows 7 Home Premium is aimed at home consumers. Answer B is incorrect because Windows 7 Professional is the business-focused edition for small and lower mid-market companies. It does not include BitLocker and AppLocker. Answer D is incorrect because although Windows 7 Ultimate has all the components that Windows 7 Enterprise has, it has additional features that are not needed for an Enterprise environment.

2. **D** is correct. Windows 7 comes in two flavors, 32-bit and 64-bit. If you want to recognize more than 4 GB of memory, you need to use the 64-bit version. Answer B is incorrect because 32-bit Windows only supports up to 4 GB of memory. Answers A, C, and E are incorrect because the 16 MB, 32 GB, and 64 GB editions do not exist.

Windows XP was first released on October 25, 2001. Windows XP grew to be the most widely used operating system, which peaked in December 2006 with more than 400 million copies and an 85.3% market share. Even after the release of Windows Vista, as of July 2010, Windows XP still remains the most widely used operating system with a 54.6% market share. Compared to previous versions of Windows, Windows XP was known for its improved functionality, stability, and flexibility while providing an easy-to-use interface. As a result, Windows XP became the de facto standard for the desktop and laptop operating systems for corporations around the world.

Windows XP was aimed at both the corporate and consumer world. The most common editions of the operating system are Windows XP Home Edition, which was aimed at home users, and Windows XP Professional Edition, which was targeted at power users and corporate clients.

The more popular versions of Windows before Windows XP were partially based on DOS, which was the base operating system that worked underneath Windows. To finally break the limitations imposed by DOS, Windows XP was built on the Windows NT architecture instead of using DOS as a base OS. Although Windows XP could run a DOS virtual machine to run DOS applications, it did not allow DOS programs to communicate directly with the hardware without going through Windows (this is necessary to keep the system secure). As a result, some DOS programs would not operate under Windows XP. Nonetheless, Windows XP ushered in Windows for the masses at home and in the corporate office.

One of the biggest criticisms of Windows XP has been security. The design of Windows XP placed some emphasis on security; however, the security features were not the highest priority. Because Windows XP became the de facto standard for operating systems, it became a popular platform to attack by hackers and programmers who looked for and exploited weaknesses within the operating system, usually using malware such as viruses, Trojan horses, and worms. As a result, Microsoft has released numerous security patches and three service packs to help make Windows XP more secure. In addition, it is highly recommended that your system includes an up-to-date antivirus program that includes anti-spyware software and that the system is protected with some form of firewall. In fact, Windows XP Service Packs 2 and 3 include the Windows Firewall to help make Windows more secure.

Windows XP was such a success that the next major release of Windows did not occur for five years. On January 30, 2007, Windows Vista was released worldwide. Unfortunately, Windows Vista received an overall negative reception based on numerous reasons, including

▶ Confusion over hardware requirements and higher hardware requirements to utilize all features available from Windows Vista, including the new Windows Aero interface, while maintaining decent performance.

▶ Annoying security features, such as User Account Control, that generated too many prompts for you to proceed with common actions.

▶ A new interface that makes it more difficult for corporations to transition to the new version of Windows because of the involved learning curve and the increase in support calls.

▶ Expensive licenses compared to Windows XP and additional cost for corporations who already had an investment in Windows XP and saw no real benefit for paying significant amounts of money to upgrade to Windows Vista.

▶ Although every new operating system has compatibility problems with older applications, Windows Vista had more than its share of popular applications that would not operate under Windows Vista or ran poorly even if using application-compatible settings.

▶ Hardware incompatibility caused by changes in the driver models and requiring 64-bit versions of Windows Vista, allowing only signed drivers to be installed in kernel mode. This caused many hardware devices not to run under Windows Vista or to run very poorly.

▶ Poor game quality and game performance.

▶ Overall slower performance.

▶ Software bloat.

▶ Poor laptop battery life.

Although Microsoft tried to address some of the complaints with Service Pack 1, Windows Vista was not widely accepted. Many people purchased Windows Vista only to use the downgrade license to run Windows XP, particularly within corporations.

After a rocky run for Windows Vista, Microsoft tried to address the concerns of Windows Vista by releasing Windows 7. Although Windows 7 is based on the Windows Vista core, there are many improvements and enhancements, including

▶ Improved thicker taskbar with improved Notification Area and integrated quick launch/application pinning capability and improved taskbar previews.

- ▶ Enhanced desktop, including bigger icons and peek-into-desktop features.

- ▶ Removal of sidebar and integration of gadgets into the desktop.

- ▶ Jump Lists that enable speedy access to your favorite pictures, songs, websites, and documents.

- ▶ Internet Explorer 8, Windows Media Player 12, and DirectX 11.

- ▶ Reduced memory thumbprint and reduced I/O reads.

- ▶ Enhanced power management capabilities.

- ▶ Improved User Access Control (UAC), including fewer prompts and enhanced granularity of notifications.

- ▶ Improved mobile device support, including new power-saving features.

- ▶ Easier wireless networking.

- ▶ Simplified configuration of home networks using HomeGroup.

- ▶ Use of libraries to replace the old documents, pictures, and similar folders.

- ▶ Windows XP mode that enables you to run older Windows XP business software on your Windows 7 desktop using virtual technology.

- ▶ Capability to natively mount Virtual Hard Disk (VHD) files using the diskpart tool and the capability to run Windows 7 from a VHD file.

- ▶ DirectAccess that gives mobile users seamless access to corporate networks without a need to establish a virtual private network (VPN) connection.

- ▶ BranchCache decreases the time branch office users spend waiting to download files across the network.

Because Windows 7 is built on the Windows Vista core, the application and driver compatibility issues should be kept to a minimum.

Defining Windows 7

Windows 7 is the latest version (following Windows XP and Vista) of Microsoft Windows operating system produced by Microsoft for use on personal computers, including home and business desktops, laptops, netbooks, tablet PCs, and media center PCs. It was released to manufacturers on July 22, 2009 and to the general public on October 22, 2009.

Windows 7 is called 7 because it is based on the seventh version of the
Windows Kernel. Table 1.1 outlines the popular versions of Windows based
on the Windows NT kernel.

TABLE 1.1   **Windows Versions**

Windows Operating System	Windows Kernel Version	Date of Release
Windows NT 4.0	4.0	1996
Windows 2000	5.0	2000
Windows XP	5.1	2001
Windows Vista	6.0	2007
Windows 7	7.0	2009

As an operating system, Windows 7 enables you to coordinate hardware and
software and enables you to run business/productivity and entertainment
applications. It also enables you to save and access data usually stored in documents or other data files.

Windows 7 includes many features that enable users to be more productive
while providing an easy-to-use interface. It also provides a more secure desktop environment and a higher level of reliability when compared to the previous versions of Windows.

For more information about Windows 7, visit the following website:

http://www.microsoft.com/windows/windows-7/default.aspx

For more information comparing Windows XP, Windows Vista, and
Windows 7, visit the following website:

http://www.microsoft.com/windows/windows-7/compare/versions.aspx

Windows 7 Flavors

Similar to Windows Vista, Windows 7 is available in many flavors, including
six Windows 7 editions and two platforms (32-bit and 64-bit). You should
choose the edition and platform based on your current hardware and the
desired functionality.

Editions of Windows 7

There are six Windows 7 editions: two editions for mainstream consumers
and business users and four specialized editions for enterprise customers,

technical enthusiasts, emerging markets, and entry-level PCs. They include the following:

▶ **Windows 7 Starter**: This edition is targeted specifically for small form factor PCs (such as cubes and book-size PCs) in all markets. It is only available for 32-bit platforms. It includes an improved Windows taskbar and Jump Lists, Windows Search, ability to join a HomeGroup, Action Center, Device Stage, Windows Fax and Scan, and enhanced media streaming. Initially when Windows 7 Starter was released, it was limited to run three applications at the same time. Microsoft has since removed this restriction and runs as many applications as the hardware can handle.

▶ **Windows 7 Home Basic**: This edition is targeted for value PCs in emerging markets and is meant for accessing the Internet and running basic productivity applications. It includes all features available in Windows 7 Starter, and other features, such as Live Thumbnail previews, enhanced visual experiences, and advanced networking support. It lacks most Aero support, has limited networking capabilities, and does not include the Windows Media Center application.

▶ **Windows 7 Home Premium**: This edition is the standard edition for customers. It provides full functionality on the latest hardware, easy ways to connect, and a visually rich environment. This edition includes all features available in Windows 7 Home Basic and other features, such as Windows Aero, Windows Touch, ability to create a HomeGroup, DVD Video playback and authoring, Windows Media Center, Snipping Tool, Sticky Notes, Windows Journal, and Windows SideShow.

▶ **Windows 7 Professional**: This edition is the business-focused edition for small and lower mid-market companies and users who have networking, backup, and security needs and multiple PCs or servers. It includes all features available in Windows 7 Home Premium, and other features, such as core business features including Domain Join and Group Policy, data protection with advanced network backup and Encrypted File System, ability to print to the correct printer at home or work with Location Aware Printing, Remote Desktop host, and Offline folders.

▶ **Windows 7 Enterprise**: This edition provides advanced data protection and information access for businesses. It is targeted for managed environments, mainly large enterprises. This edition includes all features available in Windows 7 Professional, and other features, such as BitLocker, BitLocker To Go, AppLocker, DirectAccess, BranchCache, Enterprise Search Scopes, all worldwide interface languages, Virtual Desktop Infrastructure (VDI) enhancements, and the ability to boot from a VHD.

▶ **Windows 7 Ultimate**: This edition is targeted for technical enthusiasts who want all Windows 7 features without a Volume License agreement. It includes all of the same features as the Windows 7 Enterprise. Windows 7 Ultimate is not licensed for VDI scenarios.

ExamAlert

Be sure you know what features are available for each edition of Windows 7 so that you can choose the correct edition of Windows 7 if given a scenario.

Microsoft also produces an N edition of Windows 7 Starter, Windows 7 Home Basic, and Windows 7 Professional, mostly aimed at the European market. The N editions of Windows 7 include all of the features as the corresponding editions, but the N editions do not include Microsoft Windows Media Player and related technologies. This enables you to install your own media player and associated components.

For more information about the Windows 7 Editions, visit the following websites:

http://www.microsoft.com/windows/windows-7/compare/default.aspx

http://www.winsupersite.com/win7/win7_skus_compare.asp

32-Bit Versus 64-Bit

A 64-bit processor is a processor with a default word size of 64 bits and a 64-bit external data bus. Most people don't realize that today's processors can already handle 64-bit calculations. But one of the main benefits of 64-bit processors is that they can process significantly more memory than 32-bit processors (4 GB with a 32-bit address bus and 64 GB with a 36-bit address bus). Windows 7 Home Premium edition can recognize up to 16 GB of RAM, and Windows 7 Enterprise and Windows 7 Ultimate editions can recognize up to 192 GB. With more data in memory, a 64-bit processor can work faster because it doesn't have to swap large sets of information in and out of memory the way a 32-bit processor does. Today, just about every computer processor sold is a 64-bit processor.

If an operating system and programs are written to use the larger 64-bit calculations and to use the additional memory, the processing power of a computer can be significantly increased. Most programs designed for a computer running a 32-bit version of Windows work on a computer running 64-bit versions of

Windows. Notable exceptions are many antivirus programs and some hardware drivers. The biggest problem that you might encounter is finding 64-bit drivers for some of your older hardware devices because all drivers must also be 64-bit.

Note two things when using 64-bit Windows 7. You are not able to run legacy 16-bit applications unless you run them under a virtual environment such as XP Mode. Instead, you need to install XP mode to put an instance of x86 Windows XP SP3 on your x64 Windows 7 desktop and run the application from there. In addition, some 32-bit applications might run slightly slower.

Note

IA-32 (Intel Architecture, 32-bit) was the de facto standard for Intel processors and Intel-compatible processors including AMD. Today, IA-32 is often generically called i386, x86-32, and x86. The x86 architecture is the 32-bit architecture used on Intel and Intel-compatible processors, including AMD processors. x64 is today's de facto standard for processors that are built on a 64-bit architecture. Surprisingly, the x64 (also referred to as AMD64 and EM64T, was created by AMD instead of Intel and was later adopted by Intel and other processor manufacturers. It should be noted that x64 is different from Intel Itanium (IA-64 processors), which was Intel's earlier attempt at a mass produced 64-bit processor.

Exam**Alert**

Be sure you understand the differences between the 32-bit and 64-bit versions of Windows 7 and when you should use each one if given a scenario.

Cram Quiz

1. Which of the following was not an improvement of Windows 7 over Windows Vista?

    ○ **A.** Thicker taskbar

    ○ **B.** Gadgets integrated directly into the desktop

    ○ **C.** Use of libraries to replace the old documents, pictures, and similar folders

    ○ **D.** BitLocker

2. Which edition of Windows 7 is the minimum needed to fully support HomeGroups and DVD Video Playback and authoring?

   ○ **A.** Windows 7 Home Basic

   ○ **B.** Windows 7 Home Premium

   ○ **C.** Windows 7 Professional

   ○ **D.** Windows 7 Enterprise

3. How much memory does a 32-bit version of Windows support?

   ○ **A.** 1 GB

   ○ **B.** 2 GB

   ○ **C.** 4 GB

   ○ **D.** 8 GB

Cram Quiz Answers

1. **D** is correct. BitLocker was introduced with Windows Vista. Answers A, B, and C are incorrect because Windows 7 includes a thicker taskbar, gadgets integrated directly into the desktop, and the use of libraries.

2. **B** is correct. HomeGroup and DVD Video Playback and authoring are supported by Windows Home Premium, Windows 7 Professional, and Windows 7 Enterprise. However, the minimum you need would be Windows 7 Home Premium. Therefore, the other answers are incorrect.

3. **C** is correct. The 32-bit version of Windows 7 can only recognize up to 4 GB of memory. It should be noted that not all 32-bit editions of Windows 7 support 4 GB. Therefore, the other answers are incorrect.

Windows 7 Graphical User Interface

▶ **Supplemental Objectives:** List and describe the main components that make up the graphical user interface used in Windows 7.

CramSaver

1. The area where the clock and a few select system icons is located on the taskbar is called what?

   ○ **A.** Start menu

   ○ **B.** The Notification Area

   ○ **C.** The Recycle Bin

   ○ **D.** The Sidebar

2. What do you call a list that provides a shortcut to a program and is used to provide quick access to recently opened and pinned items from this list?

   ○ **A.** Jump List

   ○ **B.** Notification list

   ○ **C.** Quick Launch

   ○ **D.** Window list

3. Which feature in Windows 7 enables you to quickly reveal hidden icons and gadgets?

   ○ **A.** Aero Shake

   ○ **B.** Aero Peek

   ○ **C.** Aero Snap

   ○ **D.** Windows Flip 3D

Answers

1. **B** is correct. The Notification Area is located on the taskbar that has a few system icons that require user attention. Answer A is incorrect because the Start menu is a menu that you open by clicking the Start button to access programs. Answer C is incorrect because the Recycle Bin is used as a temporary area for files that are deleted in Windows. Answer D is incorrect because the Sidebar was a component that held gadgets in Windows Vista but was discontinued in Windows 7.

2. **A** is correct. A Jump List is a list of items you go to frequently. Jump Lists appear on the Start menu next to pinned programs and recently used programs. The Jump Lists can contain recently opened items and items you have pinned to the Jump List. You can also add Jump Lists to the taskbar. Answer B is incorrect because there is no Notification list in the Windows GUI. However, there is a Notification Area located on the taskbar that has a few system icons that require user attention. Answer C is incorrect because the Quick Launch area was used in Windows XP and Windows Vista was replaced with the Jump Lists. Answer D is incorrect because there is no such thing as a Window list.

3. **B** is correct. Aero Peek enables you to peer past all your open windows by making the windows transparent to reveal your hidden icons and gadgets. Answer A is incorrect because Aero Shake enables you to cut through a cluttered desktop so that you can quickly focus on a single window. Answer C is incorrect because Aero Snap is a quick way to resize open windows by dragging them to the edges of your screen. Answer D is incorrect because Windows Flip 3D enables you to flip through all open Windows in a three-dimensional stack without having to click the taskbar.

As with previous versions of Windows, the desktop is the main screen area that you see after you turn on your computer and log on to Windows. Like the top of an actual desk, it serves as a surface for your work. When you open programs or folders, they appear on the desktop. You can also put things on the desktop, such as files and folders, and arrange them however you want, as shown in Figure 1.1.

When you run visible programs or processes in Windows, you run them in a rectangular box called a window. The name *Windows* comes from the ability to run multiple programs or processes at the same time (multitasking) by having multiple Windows open on the desktop.

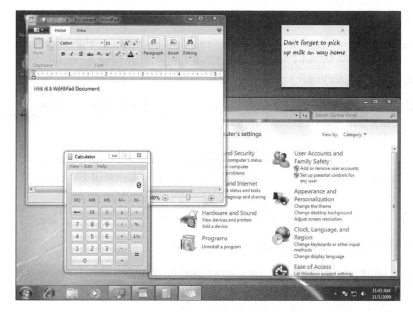

FIGURE 1.1   **Windows desktop with taskbar and several running programs.**

Working with the Desktop

To represent the files, folders, and programs, Windows 7 uses icons. A shortcut is an icon that represents a link to an item, rather than the item itself. You can identify shortcuts by the arrow on their icon. Like Windows XP, double-clicking an icon starts or opens the item it represents. If you double-click the Internet Explorer icon, it starts Internet Explorer. If you double-click a report that was written using Microsoft Word, Microsoft Word starts and the report opens. When you double-click a shortcut, the item opens.

By default, when you first start Windows, you see at least one icon on your desktop—the Recycle Bin. Depending on how your computer is configured, after its initial installation, you might have additional desktop icons including the Control Panel, Internet Explorer, or Computer icon. Of course, depending on the user's preference, you can add or remove icons. Some people like to have a clean, uncluttered desktop with few or no icons, and others like to have their frequently used programs, files, and folders available right from the desktop.

To add a shortcut to the desktop, follow these steps:

1. Locate the item (open the Start menu and browse through the installed programs or use Windows Explorer\Computer to find the executable, data file, or folder) that you want to create a shortcut for.

2. Right-click the item, click **Send To**, and then click **Desktop (create shortcut)**. The shortcut icon appears on your desktop.

To add or remove common desktop icons such as Computer, your personal folder, Network, the Recycle Bin, Internet Explorer, and Control Panel, do the following:

1. Right-click an empty area of the desktop and then click **Personalize**.

2. In the left pane, click **Change desktop icons**.

3. Under Desktop icons, select the checkbox for each icon that you want to add to the desktop, or clear the checkbox for each icon that you want to remove from the desktop, and then click **OK**.

To remove an icon from the desktop, right-click the icon, and then click **Delete**. If the icon is a shortcut, only the shortcut is removed; the original item is not deleted.

To move a file from a folder to the desktop, do the following:

1. Open the folder that contains the file.

2. Drag the file to the desktop.

By default, Windows lines up the icons in columns on the left side of the desktop. However, you can move an icon by dragging it to a new place on the desktop.

You can have Windows automatically arrange your icons. Right-click an empty area of the desktop, click **View**, and then click **Auto Arrange**. Windows lines up your icons starting in the upper-left corner, locking them into place. To unlock the icons so that you can move them again, click **Auto Arrange** again, clearing the check mark next to it.

By default, Windows spaces icons evenly on an invisible grid. To place icons closer together or with more precision, turn off the grid. Right-click an empty area of the desktop, click **View**, and then click **Align to Grid** to clear the check mark. Repeat these steps to turn the grid back on.

To move or delete a bunch of icons at once, you must first select all of them. Click an empty area of the desktop and drag the mouse to surround the icons with the rectangle that appears. Then release the mouse button. Now you can drag the icons as a group or delete them.

> **Note**
>
> In a list of items, you can click on sequential items such as files and folders by clicking the first item, pressing the Shift key, and using the arrows on the keyboard or clicking with the mouse. To select non-sequential items, click and hold down the Ctrl key and use the mouse to select each item.

To temporarily hide all of your desktop icons without actually removing them, right-click an empty part of the desktop, click **View**, and then click **Show Desktop Icons** to clear the checkmark from that option. To get the icons back, click the **Show Desktop Icons** option again.

> **Note**
>
> The very right edge of the taskbar is a hidden Show Desktop button.

Windows 7 Taskbar

The taskbar is the long horizontal bar at the bottom of your screen. Unlike the desktop, which can be obscured by open windows, the taskbar is almost always visible. As shown in Figure 1.2, it has three main sections:

- ► The Start button opens the Start menu.
- ► The middle section shows you which programs and files you have open and enables you to quickly switch between them.
- ► The Notification Area includes a clock and icons (small pictures) that communicate the status of certain programs and computer settings.

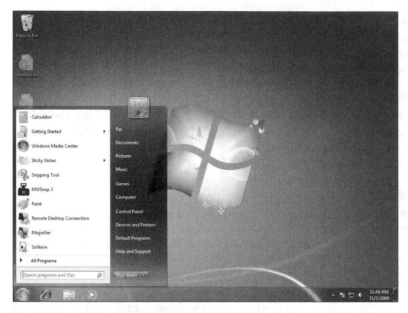

FIGURE 1.2   **Windows taskbar with open Start menu.**

Windows 7 Start Menu

To start programs and open folders, you use the Start menu. As the name implies, the Start menu provides a list of choices of items you can launch. It also enables you to search for files, folders, and programs; adjust computer settings; get help with the Windows operating system; turn off the computer; and log off from Windows or switch to a different user account. To open the Start menu, click the Start button in the lower-left corner of your screen or press the Windows logo key on your keyboard.

The Start menu has three basic parts, as illustrated previously in Figure 1.2:

- ▶ The large left pane shows a short list of programs on your computer. Your computer manufacturer can customize this list, so its exact appearance varies. Clicking **All Programs** displays a complete list of programs.

- ▶ At the bottom of the left pane is the search box, which enables you to look for programs and files on your computer by typing in search terms.

- ▶ The right pane provides access to commonly used folders, files, settings, and features. It's also where you go to log off from Windows or turn off your computer.

If you don't see the program you want, click **All Programs** at the bottom of the left pane. The left pane displays a long list of programs in alphabetical order, followed by a list of folders. Clicking one of the program icons starts the program, and the Start menu closes. You also see programs that are used to organize programs.

Under the Accessories folder, you find a set of useful applications, including the following:

▶ **Calculator**: You can use Calculator to perform simple calculations such as addition, subtraction, multiplication, and division. Calculator also offers the advanced capabilities of a programming, scientific, statistical calculator and converting common number systems, including converting between decimal, binary, and hexadecimal number systems.

▶ **Command Prompt**: An entry point for typing computer commands in the Command Prompt window. By typing commands at the command prompt, you can perform tasks on your computer without using the Windows graphical interface.

▶ **Notepad**: A basic text-editing program that you can use to create documents.

▶ **Paint**: Used to create drawings on a blank drawing area or in existing pictures. Many of the tools you use in Paint are found in the Ribbon, which is near the top of the Paint window.

▶ **Run**: A quick way to open programs, files, folders, and (when you're connected to the Internet) websites. You can also use the search box on the Start menu in place of the **Run** command.

▶ **Sticky Notes**: Used to write a to-do list, jot down a phone number, or do anything else that you'd use a pad of paper for. You can use Sticky Notes with a tablet pen or a standard keyboard. To write a note using a tablet pen, simply start writing on the note where you want the ink to appear. To type a note, click where you want the text to appear, and then start typing.

▶ **Sync Center**: Enables you to check the results of your recent sync activity if you've set up your computer to sync files with a network server. This enables you to access copies of your network files even when your computer isn't connected to the network. Sync Center can tell you if the files synced successfully or if there are any sync errors or warnings.

- **Windows Explorer**: A file manager application that provides a graphical user interface for accessing the file systems. It is sometimes referred to as the Windows Shell, or simply "Explorer"; not to be confused with Internet Explorer, which is an Internet browser. If you open Computer, Documents, or the C drive folder, you are using Windows Explorer.

- **WordPad**: A text-editing program you can use to create and edit documents. Unlike Notepad, WordPad documents can include rich formatting and graphics, and you can link to or embed objects, such as pictures or other documents.

- **Ease of Access folders**: Several programs and settings that can make the computer easier and more comfortable to use. You can add other assistive technology products to your computer if you need more accessibility features. It includes the Ease of Access Center, Magnifier, Narrator, On-Screen Keyboard, and Windows Speech Recognition.

- **System Tools folder**: A set of tools used to provide many system functions including Character Map (character/font selection tool), Control Panel, Disk Cleanup, Disk Defragmenter, Internet Explorer (No Add-ons), Resource Monitor, System Restore, Task Scheduler, and Windows Easy Transfer.

- **Windows PowerShell folder**: A command-line shell and associated scripting language that enables you to execute system commands that might not be executable in a graphical interface.

Under the Maintenance folder, you find

- **Backup and Restore**: Used to back up and restore Windows.

- **Create a System Repair Disc**: A system recovery option that can help you repair Windows if a serious error occurs. To use system recovery options, you need a Windows installation disc or access to the recovery options provided by your computer manufacturer. If you don't have either of those choices, you can create a system repair disc to access system recovery options.

- **Help and Support**: A built-in help system for Windows. It's a place to get quick answers to common questions, suggestions for troubleshooting, and instructions for how to do things. You can access it by clicking the Start button and clicking **Help and Support**.

- **Windows Remote Assistance**: A tool that can be used to give remote access to your machine to assist in fixing or overcoming a problem.

The right pane of the Start menu contains links to parts of Windows that you're likely to use frequently. Here they are, from top to bottom:

▶ **Personal folder**: Opens your personal folder, which is named for whoever is currently logged on to Windows. For example, if the current user is Patrick Regan, the folder is named Patrick Regan. This folder, in turn, contains user-specific files, including the Desktop, My Documents, My Music, My Pictures, and My Videos folders.

▶ **Documents**: Opens the Documents library, where you can access and open text files, spreadsheets, presentations, and other kinds of documents.

▶ **Pictures**: Opens the Pictures library, where you can access and view digital pictures and graphics files.

▶ **Music**: Opens the Music library, where you can access and play music and other audio files.

▶ **Games**: Opens the Games folder, where you can access all of the games on your computer.

▶ **Computer**: Opens a window where you can access disk drives, cameras, printers, scanners, and other hardware connected to your computer.

▶ **Control Panel**: Opens Control Panel, where you can customize the appearance and functionality of your computer, install or uninstall programs, set up network connections, and manage user accounts.

▶ **Devices and Printers**: Opens a window where you can view information about the printer, mouse, and other devices installed on your computer.

▶ **Default Programs**: Opens a window where you can choose which program you want Windows to use for activities such as web browsing.

▶ **Help and Support**: Opens Windows Help and Support, where you can browse and search Help topics about using Windows and your computer.

At the bottom of the right pane is the Shut down button. Click the **Shut down** button to turn off your computer. Clicking the arrow next to the Shut down button displays a menu with additional options for switching users, logging off, locking, restarting, or sleep.

The Notification Area

In Windows 7, the Notification Area of the taskbar has been returned to the user's control. By default, only a select few system icons are shown. When Windows 7 determines that a specific condition requires the user's attention, a new icon appears in the Notification Area. Click the icon to access a menu to address the issue or to open the Action Center for more details.

Users can control the notification experience by dragging icons on or off the taskbar. Better yet, every balloon tip that appears in the system has a little wrench icon that enables you to view the cause of the notification and a direct way to disable it.

A popular change to the Notification Area is about showing more information. The default taskbar now reveals both the time and the date. Only system icons appear by default, and users can customize the area to their liking.

You can customize the icons and notifications that appear in the Notification Area by performing either of the following steps:

▶ Click the arrow on the left side of the Notification Area to access its Jump List and then click **Customize**.

▶ In Control Panel, click **All Control Panel Items**, and then click **Notification Area Icons** for the resulting window shown in Figure 1.3. Customizing the Notification Area enables you to consolidate notifications and reduce the number of icons that present notification balloons to users.

You can customize the following icons and their behaviors:

▶ Action Center

▶ Power

▶ Network

▶ Windows Explorer

▶ Windows Activation Client

▶ Volume

▶ Windows Update Automatic Updates

FIGURE 1.3   **Customizing the Notification Area.**

For each icon, you can set its display behavior to one of the following options:

▶ Show icon and notifications

▶ Hide icon and notifications

▶ Only show notifications

Windows 7 enables you to control the number of system icons displayed in the system tray. In Control Panel, click **All Control Panel Items** and then click **System Icons**. This displays the following list of system icons, each of which has an On/Off option that controls whether the icon appears in the system tray:

▶ Clock

▶ Volume

▶ Network

▶ Power

▶ Action Center

> **Note**
>
> Turning off a system icon not only removes the icon from the system tray, but also turns off displaying any notifications for the icon.

Customizing the Taskbar and Start Menu

In previous versions of Windows, Windows used a Quick Launch shortcut to quickly start commonly used programs or open commonly used folders or files. Sometimes, an additional icon appeared in the Notification Area to represent running programs, including some programs running in the background. In Windows 7, you can use a single icon for a program on the taskbar, which enables you to start the program and open more program windows. Additionally, Windows 7 helps to provide quick access to recently opened and pinned items from the program's Jump List.

A shortcut enables you to access a program, folder, or document quickly, but a Jump List is a list of items you go to frequently. On the taskbar, Jump Lists appear for programs that you've pinned to the taskbar and programs that are currently running, as shown in Figure 1.4.

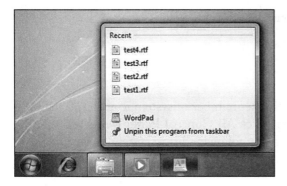

FIGURE 1.4   **A Jump List coming from a running program.**

For example, if you are working on a large report, which takes you several weeks to write, you can pin the report to your taskbar, work on it day after day, and unpin it when the report is complete. This way, you can quickly access the report each day. If you log off or reboot the computer, the pinned item is still on the taskbar when you log on next time.

To pin something to the taskbar, do one of the following:

▶ If the program is already running, right-click the program's icon (or drag the icon toward the desktop) to open the program's Jump List, and then click **Pin to taskbar**.

▶ If the program is not running, click **Start**, browse to the program's icon, right-click the icon, and then click **Pin to taskbar**, as shown in Figure 1.5.

▶ You can also pin a program's shortcut from the desktop to the taskbar by simply dragging the shortcut to the taskbar. If the shortcut is to a file, then the program used to open it is pinned to the desktop, and the file is pinned to the program's Jump List.

FIGURE 1.5   **By right-clicking a program, you can pin to the taskbar or Start menu.**

If you right-click the document/program, you can remove it from the taskbar by clicking again to unpin the document or program.

You can also use Jump Lists for the Start menu and programs. You can pin program shortcuts to the top of the Start menu so you can open them quickly and conveniently. There are two methods by which you can pin a program to the Start menu:

▶ Click **Start**, browse to the program, right-click the program, and click **Pin to Start menu**. The program's icon will now always appear at the top of the Start menu.

► Click **Start**, browse to the program, and then drag it to the top left of the Start menu.

Note

You can pin a program from the Start menu to the taskbar, but not from the taskbar to the Start menu.

Jump Lists appear on the Start menu next to pinned programs and recently used programs. The Jump Lists can contain recently opened items and items you have pinned to the Jump List.

Note

Jump Lists don't appear in All Programs on the Start menu.

In previous Windows versions, icons for the default web browser and email program were pinned to the top of the Start menu. In Windows 7, the pinned area of the Start menu remains, but is empty for a cleaner look. However, you can still pin programs to the top of the Start menu just like in previous Windows versions.

In addition, the Connect to and Network links are removed from the Start menu. Instead, use the Network icon on the taskbar to view available connections or open the Networking and Sharing Center. You can also view computers that are accessible on your network in the navigation pane in any Windows Explorer window.

Perform the following steps to turn window arrangement options on and off:

1. Navigate to Control Panel. Click **Ease of Access Center**. Under Explore all settings, click **Make it easier to focus on tasks**.

2. To turn automatic window arrangement off, scroll toward the bottom of the window, and under Make it easier to manage windows, select the checkbox labeled **Prevent windows from being automatically arranged when moved to the edge of the screen**.

3. To turn automatic window arrangement back on, clear the checkbox labeled **Prevent windows from being automatically arranged when moved to the edge of the screen**.

There are many ways to customize the taskbar to suit your preferences. For example, you can drag the entire taskbar to the left, right, or top edge of the screen. You can make the taskbar larger by dragging the edge of the taskbar.

If you right-click the taskbar and select **Properties**, you can use the Taskbar and Start Menu Properties dialog box, shown in Figure 1.6, to lock the taskbar, auto-hide the taskbar, use small icons, or change the location of the taskbar. You can also customize the Notification Area. If you select the **Start Menu** tab and click the **Customize** button, you can choose which links, icons, or menus appear in the Start menu.

FIGURE 1.6   **The Taskbar and Start Menu Properties dialog box.**

Working with Open Windows

Windows 7 automatically resizes the open windows that you drag to the edges of your desktop so you can organize, compare, and read them. This Automatic window arrangement is turned on by default, but you can turn it off and move windows around on the desktop, just as was done with previous Windows versions.

Maximizing a window helps you focus on a single item without the distraction of other open windows.

▶ To maximize a window, drag the title bar of a window to the top of the screen.

▶ To return the window to its original size, drag the title bar away from the top of the screen.

There are additional ways to maximize an open window, including

▶ Double-click the top of an open window just below the top edge. Double-click the top of a maximized window to reduce the window to a smaller size.

▶ Shift + right-click a program's icon, or a thumbnail of an open window, and click Maximize or Minimize. If multiple windows are running for a program, click Maximize all windows or Minimize all windows.

▶ Press the Windows logo key + up arrow to maximize a window. Press the Windows logo key + down arrow to restore the window.

If you minimize a window by pressing the Windows logo key + down arrow, restore it by clicking on its thumbnail on the taskbar or by pressing Shift + right-clicking on the program's icon on the taskbar and then clicking **Restore**.

You can rearrange and organize all program icons on the taskbar (including pinned programs and running programs that are not pinned) so they appear in the order you prefer.

To rearrange the order of program icons on the taskbar, simply drag an icon from its current position to a different position on the taskbar. You can rearrange programs as often as you like. You can also rearrange an icon that appears in the taskbar's Notification Area by dragging the icon to a different position.

All open files from the same program are always grouped together, even if you did not open them one after the other. This is done so that all previews for an open program can be viewed together at the same time.

You can customize how program icons appear and how they group together on the taskbar. You can also change the size of the icons, which changes the height of the taskbar as well. The following options are available for maintaining the icons on the taskbar:

▶ Always combine, hide labels. Each program is a single icon without labels, even when multiple items for a program are open. This is the default setting, resulting in a clean and uncluttered taskbar.

► Combine when taskbar is full. Each open item has an individual, labeled icon.

When the taskbar becomes crowded, programs with multiple open items collapse into a single program icon. Clicking the icon displays a list of the items that are open. Both this and the Never Combine option resemble the look and behavior of earlier Windows versions.

Gadgets

Windows 7 contains mini-programs called *gadgets*, which offer information at a glance and provide easy access to frequently used tools. Although they were originally introduced in Windows Vista, they differ because gadgets can be placed anywhere within the desktop. In Windows Vista, gadgets had to be placed on the Windows Sidebar, which no longer exists in Windows 7. Some examples of gadgets include displaying a picture slide show, viewing continuously updated headlines, or viewing a clock, as shown in Figure 1.7. If you are running Windows Aero, you can use the Aero Peek feature to temporarily view your desktop gadgets without minimizing or closing the windows you're working with.

FIGURE 1.7   **Gadgets (Slide Show, Feed Headlines, and Clock) located on the desktop and an open Desktop Gadget Gallery.**

To add a gadget, do the following:

1. Right-click the desktop and click **Gadgets**.

2. Double-click a gadget to add it.

To remove a gadget, right-click the gadget and then click **Close Gadget**.

You can drag a gadget to a new position anywhere on the desktop. You can also install multiple instances of gadget; for example, to see two time zones for the clock or to get different headlines.

To configure a gadget, right-click the gadget and choose the appropriate option. For example, if you right-click the Clock gadget, you can close the Clock, keeping it on top of your open windows, and changing the Clock's options (such as its name, time zone, and appearance).

Before you can add a gadget, it must be installed on your computer. To see which gadgets are installed on your computer, do the following:

1. Right-click the desktop and click **Gadgets**.

2. Click the scroll buttons to see all the gadgets.

3. To see information about a gadget, click the gadget, and then click **Show details**.

You can download additional gadgets online from the following website:

http://windows.microsoft.com/en-US/windows/downloads/personalize?T1=desktop-gadgets

Aero Desktop Experience

Windows Aero, introduced with Windows Vista, is the premium visual experience of Windows. It features a transparent glass design with subtle window animations and new window colors. Part of the Windows Aero experience is Windows Flip 3D (shown in Figure 1.8), which is a way to arrange your open windows in a three-dimensional stack that you can quickly flip through without having to click the taskbar. The keyboard shortcuts for Windows Flip 3D are the Windows key + Tab.

FIGURE 1.8   **Windows Flip 3D**

Aero also includes taskbar previews for your open windows. When you point to a taskbar button, you see a thumbnail-sized preview of the window, whether the content of the window is a document, a photo, or even a running video. Beyond the new graphics and visual polish, the Windows Aero desktop experience includes smoother window handling, increased graphics stability, and glitch-free visuals, all of which give you a simple, comfortable, and high-quality experience.

Windows 7 includes some new features to work with your desktop applications:

- ▶ **Aero Shake**: If you need to cut through a cluttered desktop and quickly focus on a single window, just click a pane and shake your mouse back and forth. Every open window except that one instantly disappears. Jiggle again—and your windows are back. Note that some windows, such as open dialog boxes, cannot be minimized in this way.

- ▶ **Aero Peek**: Enables you to peer past all your open windows by making all the windows transparent to reveal all your hidden icons and gadgets.

- ▶ **Aero Snap**: A quick way to resize open windows simply by dragging them to the edges of your screen. Depending on where you drag a window, you can make it expand vertically, take up the entire screen, or appear side-by-side with another window.

The following editions of Windows 7 include Aero:

▶ Windows 7 Home Premium

▶ Windows 7 Professional

▶ Windows 7 Enterprise

▶ Windows 7 Ultimate

Aero is not included in Windows 7 Home Basic or Windows 7 Starter.

ExamAlert

Be sure you know what editions of Windows 7 support Windows Aero.

Cram Quiz

1. What do you call the long horizontal bar at the bottom of the screen that includes the running programs, the Start button, and the Notification Area?

   ○ **A.** Desktop

   ○ **B.** Taskbar

   ○ **C.** Windows Explorer

   ○ **D.** Alert Center

2. What replaced the Quick Launch shortcut?

   ○ **A.** Notification Area

   ○ **B.** Alert Center

   ○ **C.** Recycle Bin

   ○ **D.** Jump Lists

3. Which features are new to Windows 7? (Choose all that apply.)

   ○ **A.** Aero Shake

   ○ **B.** Aero Peek

   ○ **C.** Aero Snap

   ○ **D.** Windows Flip 3D

Cram Quiz Answers

1. **B** is correct. The taskbar is the long horizontal bar at the bottom of the screen. Answer A is incorrect because the desktop is the main screen area that you use after you turn on your computer and log on to Windows. Answer C is incorrect because the Windows Explorer is the program that enables you to manage files and folders. Answer D is incorrect because the Alert Center is a program that notifies you of security and maintenance problems.

2. **D** is correct. A Jump List appears for programs that you've pinned to the taskbar and for programs that you are currently running. It helps you quickly access a program, folder, or document quickly. Answer A is incorrect because the Notification Area contains system icons that are alerting you of their status. Answer B is incorrect because the Alert Center notifies you of maintenance and security alerts. Answer C is incorrect because the Recycle Bin is used as a temporary storage area for files and folders that you delete.

3. **A**, **B**, and **C** are correct. If you need to cut through a cluttered desktop and quickly focus on a single window, just click a pane and shake your mouse back and forth (Aero Shake). Every open window except the one instantly disappears. Aero Peek enables you to peer past all of your open windows by making all of the Windows transparent. Aero Snap is a quick way to resize open widows. Answer D is incorrect because Windows Flip 3D was introduced in Windows Vista and enables you to arrange your windows in a three-dimensional stack that you can quickly flip through without having to click the taskbar.

Review Questions

1. Which operating system was the most popular operating system when Windows 7 was released?

   ○ **A.** Windows XP

   ○ **B.** Windows Vista

   ○ **C.** Windows 2003 Workstation

   ○ **D.** Windows 98

2. Which version of the kernel does Windows 7 use?

   ○ **A.** 5

   ○ **B.** 5.1

   ○ **C.** 6

   ○ **D.** 7

3. What is the maximum number of applications you can run concurrently with the Windows 7 Starter?

   ○ **A.** 1

   ○ **B.** 2

   ○ **C.** 3

   ○ **D.** Limited only by the hardware

4. Which editions of Windows 7 include all features that Windows 7 has to offer? (Choose two answers.)

   ○ **A.** Windows 7 Home Premium

   ○ **B.** Windows 7 Professional

   ○ **C.** Windows 7 Enterprise

   ○ **D.** Windows 7 Ultimate

5. Which of the following support added Windows 7 to a Windows domain? (Choose all that apply.)

   ○ **A.** Windows 7 Starter

   ○ **B.** Windows 7 Home Basic

   ○ **C.** Windows 7 Home Premium

   ○ **D.** Windows 7 Professional

   ○ **E.** Windows 7 Enterprise

   ○ **F.** Windows 7 Ultimate

6. What is the disadvantage of using a 64-bit version of Windows 7 when running applications?

○ **A.** You are not able to run legacy 16-bit applications directly on Windows 7.

○ **B.** You are only able to run up to three legacy 16-bit applications.

○ **C.** You need to have 16-bit drivers available to use 16-bit applications.

○ **D.** Your 16-bit applications run slowly.

7. What do you call the main screen area that you see after you turn on your computer and log on to Windows?

○ **A.** Desktop

○ **B.** Taskbar

○ **C.** Windows Explorer

○ **D.** Notification Area

8. Where do you place your gadgets?

○ **A.** Notification Area

○ **B.** Start menu

○ **C.** Desktop

○ **D.** Taskbar

9. What do you call the feature that enables you to shake away the cluttered desktop to quickly focus on a single window?

○ **A.** Aero Shake

○ **B.** Aero Peek

○ **C.** Aero Snap

○ **D.** Windows Flip 3D

10. Which of the following include Windows Aero? (Choose all that apply.)

○ **A.** Windows 7 Home Premium

○ **B.** Windows 7 Home Basic

○ **C.** Windows 7 Professional

○ **D.** Windows 7 Ultimate

Review Question Answers

1. **A** is correct. Although Windows XP was released in 2001, it was still the most popular operating system when Windows 7 was released. Answer B is incorrect because Windows Vista was heavily criticized and never became as popular as Windows XP. Answer C is incorrect because Windows 2003 Workstation does not exist. Answer D is incorrect because although Windows 98 was popular long ago, Windows XP became more popular, and it replaced Windows 98.

2. **D** is correct. Windows 7 uses the 7.0 version of the kernel. Answer A is incorrect because Windows 2000 used the 5.0 kernel. Answer B is incorrect because Windows XP uses the 5.1 kernel. Answer C is incorrect because Windows Vista uses 6.0 kernel.

3. **D** is correct. Windows 7 Starter is an edition targeted specifically for small form factor PCs. It is only available for 32-bit platforms. Initially, Windows 7 Starter edition could only support up to three concurrent programs. Since then, Microsoft has eased this restriction and now enables you to run as many programs as you desire, being limited only by your hardware such as the amount of RAM. Therefore, Answers A, B, and C are incorrect.

4. **C** and **D** are correct. Windows 7 Enterprise is targeted at large Enterprise customers. Windows 7 Ultimate is targeted for technical enthusiasts who want all Windows 7 features. Windows 7 Enterprise edition requires a volume license, but Microsoft Windows 7 Ultimate does not. Answers A and B are not correct because Windows 7 Home Premium and Windows 7 Professional do not include the language packs and do not have some of the more advanced enterprise applications, such as BitLocker, BitLocker To Go, AppLocker, DirectAccess, and BranchCache.

5. **D**, **E**, and **F** are correct. The only versions that support adding to a domain are Windows 7 Professional, Enterprise, and Ultimate. Windows 7 Starter, Home Basic, and Home Premium do not support adding to a domain. Therefore, answers A, B, and C are incorrect.

6. **A** is correct. Although 64-bit versions of Windows 7 can address more memory and can process more at one time, they cannot directly support legacy 16-bit applications. Therefore, the other answers are incorrect. If you have a 16-bit application and you want to run the application on a 64-bit version of Windows 7, you should try using XP Mode.

7. **A** is correct. The desktop is the main screen area that you see after you turn on your computer and log on to Windows. You can think of it as similar to a desk, which serves as a surface for your work. Answer B is incorrect because the taskbar is a long horizontal bar at the bottom of the screen. Answer C is incorrect because the Windows Explorer is the program that enables you to manage files and folders. Answer D is incorrect because the Notification Area is the area on the taskbar that holds system icons to let you know of an event.

8. **C** is correct. Unlike in Windows Vista, Gadgets in Windows 7 can be placed anywhere on the desktop. They cannot be placed on the Start menu, taskbar, or Notification Area; therefore, Answers A, B, and D are incorrect.

9. **A** is correct. If you need to cut through a cluttered desktop and quickly focus on a single window, just click a pane and shake your mouse back and forth. Every open window except the one selected disappears. Answer B is incorrect because Aero Peek enables you to peer past all your open windows by making all the windows transparent. Answer C is incorrect because Aero Snap is a quick way to resize open windows. Answer D is incorrect because Windows Flip 3D enables you to arrange your windows in a three-dimensional stack that you can quickly flip through without having to click the taskbar.

10. **A, C**, and **D** are correct. Windows Aero can be found on Windows 7 Home Premium, Windows 7 Professional, Windows 7 Enterprise, and Windows 7 Ultimate. It is not included in Windows 7 Home Basic or Windows 7 Starter. Therefore, Answer B is incorrect.

CHAPTER 2

Installing, Upgrading, and Migrating to Windows 7

This chapter covers the following 70-680 Objectives:

▶ Installing, Upgrading, and Migrating to Windows 7:

    ▶ Perform a clean installation

    ▶ Upgrade to Windows 7 from previous versions of Windows

    ▶ Migrate user profiles

▶ Deploying Windows 7:

    ▶ Capture a system image

    ▶ Prepare a system image for deployment

    ▶ Deploy a system image

    ▶ Configure a VHD

▶ Monitoring and Maintaining Systems That Run Windows 7:

    ▶ Configure updates to Windows 7

This chapter discusses how to install and deploy Windows 7 so that you can start using it. If you have a new machine, you do a clean installation. If you have an older machine with an operating system already on it, you need to choose between doing a clean installation or upgrading the current installation. Either way, you need to make sure you have the system resources available that allow for some modest growth.

Installing Windows 7

▶ **Installing, Upgrading, and Migrating to Windows 7**

    ▶ **Perform a clean installation**

    ▶ **Upgrade to Windows 7 from previous versions of Windows**

▶ **Monitoring and Maintaining Systems That Run Windows 7**

    ▶ **Configure updates to Windows 7**

Cram**Saver**

1. What is the minimum amount of RAM and processor required for the 64-bit Windows 7 Professional Edition?

    ◯ **A.** 512 MB and 1 GHz processor

    ◯ **B.** 1 GB and 1 GHz processor.

    ◯ **C.** 2 GB and 800 MHz

    ◯ **D.** 2 GB and 1 GHz

    ◯ **E.** 1 GB and 1.2 GHz

2. If you have Windows XP Professional installed, what would it take to upgrade to Windows 7 Professional?

    ◯ **A.** You need to first upgrade to Windows Vista Business and then upgrade to Windows 7 Professional.

    ◯ **B.** You need to install Windows XP SP3 before upgrading to Windows 7 Professional.

    ◯ **C.** You need to migrate the user settings using the Windows Easy Transfer and then perform a clean install of Windows 7.

    ◯ **D.** You need to migrate the user settings using the Windows Easy Transfer and then perform an upgrade to Windows 7.

Answers

1. **D** is correct. For the 64-bit Windows 7 Professional Edition, you need a 1-GHz processor and 2 GB of RAM. Therefore, the other answers are incorrect.

2. **A** is correct. There is not a direct upgrade from Windows XP to Windows 7. Therefore, you need to upgrade to Windows Vista Business first and then upgrade to Windows 7. Of course, this is not recommended and can be very costly if you have to purchase Windows Vista and Windows 7.

Before installing or upgrading to Windows 7, you need to look at the system and verify whether it has the necessary hardware to effectively run Windows 7. Table 2.1 outlines the hardware requirements for installing Windows 7.

TABLE 2.1 **Minimum Hardware Requirements for Installing Windows 7**

Hardware	Starter	Home Basic	Other Versions of Windows 7
Processor	800 MHz	1 GHz	1 GHz
RAM	512 MB	1 gigabyte (GB) RAM (32-bit) or 2 GB RAM (64-bit)	1 gigabyte (GB) RAM (32-bit) or 2 GB RAM (64-bit)
GPU	SVGA	DirectX 9	Aero Capable GPU that supports DirectX 9 with a WDDM driver, Pixel Shader 2.0 and 32 bits per pixel
Video RAM	Not applicable	Not applicable	128 MB
HDD	20 GB	40 GB	40 GB
Free HDD Space	16 GB available hard disk space (32-bit)	16 GB available hard disk space (32-bit) or 20 GB (64-bit)	16 GB available hard disk 20 space (32-bit) or GB (64-bit)
Optical Drive	CD	DVD	DVD

> **Note**
>
> Windows XP Mode requires an additional 1 GB of RAM and an additional 15 GB of available hard disk space.

Of course, like older versions of Windows, if a system has a faster processor or additional RAM, your system runs faster, and it is almost always recommended. In addition, as you patch Windows, the C:\Windows\Winsxs folder can take significant disk space as it holds copies of dynamic linked libraries (DLLs) and other components, all of which are used to make your system more reliable.

Although 32-bit versions of Windows 7 can support up to 4 GB of RAM, the 64-bit versions of Windows 7 can support up to 192 GB. Table 2.2 outlines the maximum memory recognized by Windows 7. In addition, although all editions of Windows 7 can support multiple core CPUs, only Windows 7 Professional, Ultimate, and Enterprise can support dual processors.

> **ExamAlert**
>
> You need to know the minimum memory requirements and the maximum memory recognized by Windows 7.

TABLE 2.2   **Maximum Memory Recognized by Windows 7**

Version	Limit in 32-Bit Windows	Limit in 64-Bit Windows
Windows 7 Ultimate	4 GB	192 GB
Windows 7 Enterprise	4 GB	192 GB
Windows 7 Professional	4 GB	192 GB
Windows 7 Home Premium	4 GB	16 GB
Windows 7 Home Basic	4 GB	8 GB
Windows 7 Starter	2 GB	2 GB

Windows 7 Installation Methods

To start the installation process, you insert the Windows 7 Installation DVD into the drive and boot from the DVD drive. If the system does not boot from the DVD disc, you might need to modify the boot order specified in the BIOS setup program. You can also boot and install from a USB device. All packaged retail editions of Windows 7 (except for Home Basic) include both 32- and 64-bit software.

Similar to Windows Vista, the process to install Windows 7 is pretty straightforward. During the installation, you can choose one of three installation methods:

▶ **Installing a custom version of Windows**: With this method, you perform a clean installation, including installing Windows on a new system with no previous operating system or completely replace your current operating system. You can also use this option to specify which drive or partition on which to install Windows 7 and if you need to establish a multiboot system.

▶ **Upgrading to Windows 7**: Used to keep your files, settings, and programs from your current version of Windows (also known as an in-place upgrade). If your version of Windows can't be upgraded, you need to choose Custom.

▶ **Reinstalling Windows 7**: Choose this method if you want to restore default Windows settings or if you are having trouble with Windows and need to reinstall it by performing a custom installation.

Windows Clean Installation

There are several methods to perform a clean installation of Windows 7.

- ▶ **Running Windows 7 installation from CD/DVD or USB boot device:** Installing from the product CD/DVD is the simplest way to install Windows 7.

- ▶ **Running Windows 7 installation from a Network Share:** Instead of a CD/DVD, the Windows 7 installation files can be stored in a network share. Generally, the network source is a shared folder on a file server. If your computer does not currently have an operating system, start the computer by using Windows Preinstallation Environment (PE). If your computer already has an operating system, you can start the computer with the old operating system.

> **Note**
>
> Windows PE is a minimal 32- or 64-bit operating system with limited services, built on the Windows 7 kernel. Windows PE is used to install and repair a Windows operating system, which is particularly useful if your system does not boot. It can also be used to install Windows on systems over the network that do not support Preboot eXecution Environment (PXE) boot.

- ▶ **Installing Windows 7 by Using an Image:** With this method, you install Windows 7 to a reference computer and prepare the reference computer for duplication. You capture the volume image to a Windows Imaging (WIM) file by using the ImageX tool and then use the deployment tools, such as ImageX, Windows Deployment Services (WDS), or Microsoft Deployment Toolkit (MDT) to deploy the captured image.

Upgrading Windows

You must perform an in-place upgrade when you do not want to reinstall all of your applications. In addition, you can consider performing an upgrade when:

- ▶ You do not have storage space to store your user state.
- ▶ You are not replacing existing computer hardware.
- ▶ You plan to deploy Windows on only a few computers.

Although you can upgrade computers in large enterprises, it is usually recommended that you perform a clean installation by using images followed by migrating user settings and data.

You can upgrade from a similar version of Windows Vista to Windows 7. In all other instances, you have to perform a custom install to replace your previous Windows. For example, you can upgrade Windows Vista Ultimate 32-bit to Windows 7 Ultimate 32-bit or a Windows Vista Business 64-bit to Windows 7 Professional 64-bit. You also need to perform a custom install from Windows XP to Windows 7. Table 2.3 outlines which versions and editions of Windows can be upgraded and which require a custom installation.

TABLE 2.3 **Upgrading to Windows 7**

		Windows 7 Home Premium		Windows 7 Professional		Windows 7 Ultimate	
		32-bit	64-bit	32-bit	64-bit	32-bit	64-bit
Windows XP	32-bit	Custom Install	Custom Install	Custom Install	Custom Install	Custom Install	Custom Install
	64-bit	Custom Install	Custom Install	Custom Install	Custom Install	Custom Install	Custom Install
Windows Vista Starter	32-bit	Custom Install	Custom Install	Custom Install	Custom Install	Custom Install	Custom Install
	64-bit	Custom Install	Custom Install	Custom Install	Custom Install	Custom Install	Custom Install
Windows Vista Home Basic	32-bit	In-Place Upgrade	Custom Install	Custom Install	Custom Install	In-Place Upgrade	Custom Install
	64-bit	Custom Install	In-Place Upgrade	Custom Install	Custom Install	Custom Install	In-Place Upgrade
Windows Vista Home Premium	32-bit	In-Place Upgrade	Custom Install	Custom Install	Custom Install	In-Place Upgrade	Custom Install
	64-bit	Custom Install	In-Place Upgrade	Custom Install	Custom Install	Custom Install	In-Place Upgrade
Windows Vista Business	32-bit	Custom Install	Custom Install	In-Place Upgrade	Custom Install	In-Place Upgrade	Custom Install
	64-bit	Custom Install	Custom Install	Custom Install	In-Place Upgrade	Custom Install	In-Place Upgrade

TABLE 2.3 **Continued**

		Windows 7 Home Premium		Windows 7 Professional		Windows 7 Ultimate	
		32-bit	**64-bit**	**32-bit**	**64-bit**	**32-bit**	**64-bit**
Windows Vista Ultimate	32-bit	Custom Install	Custom Install	Custom Install	Custom Install	In-Place Upgrade	Custom Install
	64-bit	Custom Install	Custom Install	Custom Install	Custom Install	Custom Install	In-Place Upgrade

> **Exam Alert**
>
> One of the criticisms of Windows 7 is that there is no direct upgrade from Windows XP to Windows 7. If you need to upgrade a system, you need to upgrade Windows XP to Windows Vista and then upgrade Windows Vista to Windows 7.

An in-place upgrade does not support cross architecture. This means that you cannot upgrade from 32-bit to 64-bit or vice versa. An in-place upgrade does not support cross language. In both cases, you need to perform a clean installation and the necessary migration.

When you install/upgrade Windows 7, you should follow these guidelines:

▶ Update your antivirus program, run it, and then disable it. After you install Windows, remember to re-enable the antivirus program, or install new antivirus software that works with Windows 7.

▶ Back up your files. You can back up files to an external hard disk, a DVD or CD, or a network folder.

▶ Connect to the Internet. Make sure your Internet connection is working so that you can get the latest installation updates. These updates include security updates and hardware driver updates that can help with installation. If you don't have an Internet connection, you can still upgrade or install Windows.

You can perform an upgrade between two editions of Windows 7 by using Windows Anytime Upgrade. Different from Windows Vista, Windows 7 Anytime Upgrade does not require any discs because no matter which edition is installed, the entire operating system is placed on the computer's local drive.

Upgrading your computer to your new edition of Windows 7 can take between 10 and 90 minutes. You do not have access to your programs and files during this time.

> **Note**
>
> Windows Enterprise is excluded from Windows Anytime Upgrade because it is only available through volume license and it includes all features available for Windows 7.

The steps to perform an upgrade include the following:

1. Insert the Windows 7 DVD.

2. Click **Install now** on the Install Windows screen.

3. Click the **Install Now** button and the computer begins the installation.

4. After some files are copied, choose the **Install** option.

5. When it asks to get important updates for installation, click the **Go online to get the latest updates for installation** option.

6. When it asks you to accept the license terms, click the appropriate checkbox and then click the **Next** button.

7. Toward the end of the installation process, specify a Windows login name and password.

8. Set the time and date.

For more information upgrading to Windows 7, visit the following websites:

http://windows.microsoft.com/en-us/windows7/help/upgrading-from-windows-vista-to-windows-7

http://technet.microsoft.com/en-us/library/ee461274(WS.10).aspx

Windows 7 Upgrade Advisor

In general, if your PC can run Windows Vista, it can run Windows 7. But if you're not running Windows Vista, or are just not sure if your system is ready to run Windows 7, you can use the Windows 7 Upgrade Advisor. The Windows 7 Upgrade Advisor can be found here:

http://www.microsoft.com/windows/windows-7/get/upgrade-advisor.aspx

The only prerequisite to run the Windows 7 Upgrade Advisor is to have .NET 2.0 Framework or higher and MSXML 6.0. After you've downloaded, installed, and run the Windows 7 Upgrade Advisor, the program displays a report telling you if your PC can run Windows 7 and if there are any known compatibility issues. If an issue can be resolved, you get suggestions for next steps.

Troubleshooting an Upgrade or Migration to Windows 7

If you experience problems during an upgrade or migration to Windows 7, you use standard troubleshooting methodology to isolate the problem. Of course, to gather information, you should

- ▶ **Review and research error messages**: When an error message is displayed, use your favorite search engine to research the meaning of the message and how to overcome the problem with the proper solution.

- ▶ **Check logs**: During setup, Windows 7 produces log files (located in Windows\panther) into which it records setup progress and information relating to problems encountered during setup.

- ▶ **Verify system meets minimum requirements**: A common reason for an upgrade to fail is that the computer does not meet the minimum hardware requirements to support the edition of Windows 7 that you are installing.

- ▶ **Check devices and BIOS**: If Windows setup encounters a compatibility problem with a device or with the computer's BIOS, the upgrade might fail.

- ▶ **Verify installation media**: Make sure that the installation media is not damaged or corrupt.

Windows Updates

After installing Windows, check to see if Microsoft has any fixes, patches, service packs, and device drivers and apply them to the Windows system. By adding fixes and patches, you keep Windows stable and secure. If there are many fixes or patches, Microsoft releases them together as a service pack. To update Windows 7, Internet Explorer, and other programs that ship with Windows, go to Windows Update in the Control Panel or click the **Start** button, select **All Programs**, and select **Windows Update**. Windows then scans your system to see what you have installed and gives you a list of suggested components. This system check assures that you get the most up-to-date and accurate versions of anything you choose to download from the site.

To help users with the Windows updates, Windows 7 also offers Dynamic Update and Auto Update. Dynamic Update is a feature built into Windows Setup that automatically checks for new drivers, compatibility updates, and security fixes while Windows is being installed. All that is required is that you have a working connection to the Internet. During installation, you can choose to have Dynamic Update check for updates. Dynamic Update automatically downloads any device or application updates and uses these replacement files instead of the installation files, thereby ensuring you have the latest updates available. By updating your installation files as needed, Windows can quickly integrate new, certified device drivers, critical security fixes, and compatibility updates.

Microsoft routinely releases security updates on the second Tuesday of each month on what is known as "Patch Tuesday." Most other updates are released as needed. After you install Windows, you can use Auto Update to ensure that critical security and compatibility updates are made available for installation automatically, without significantly affecting your regular use of the Internet. Auto Update works in the background when you are connected to the Internet to identify when new updates are available and to download them to your computer. The download is managed so that it does not affect the performance during web surfing, and it picks up where it left off if the download is interrupted.

When the download is completed, you are notified and prompted to install the update. You can install it then, get more details about what is included in the update, or let Windows remind you about it later. Some installations might require you to reboot, but some do not.

To manually install updates, it is recommended that you click the **Start** button, click **All Programs**, and click **Windows Update**. Then in the left pane, click **Check for updates**, as shown in Figure 2.1.

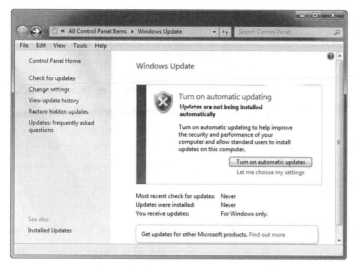

FIGURE 2.1 **Windows Update.**

To change the Windows Update settings, click the **Change settings** option in the left pane to display the window shown in Figure 2.2. The options enable you to specify whether to download and let you specify which ones to install, specify which updates to install and then download, or just disable Windows Updates all together. You can also specify if Windows Update should check for other Microsoft products other than the operating system and also install software that Microsoft recommends.

FIGURE 2.2 **Choose how Windows can install Updates.**

If Windows Update fails to get updates, you should check your proxy settings in Internet Explorer to see if it can get through your proxy server (if any) or firewall. You should also check to see if you can access the Internet, such as accessing the www.microsoft.com website.

To see all updates that have been installed, click the View Update History link in the left pane (shown in Figure 2.1). If you suspect a problem with a specific update, you can then click **Installed Updates** at the bottom of the screen, which opens the Control Panel's Programs. From there, you then see all installed programs and installed updates. If the option is available, you can then remove the update.

Activating Windows 7

While volume license might not require activation, retail versions of Windows 7 need to be activated after installation. In the Welcome Center, the Activation Status entry specifies whether you have activated the operating system. If Windows 7 has not been activated, you can activate the operating system by clicking **More Details** to access the System console and then selecting **Click Here To Activate Windows Now** under Windows Activation.

Unlike in Windows XP, you can easily change the product key used by the operating system except in Original Equipment Manufacturer (OEM) copies of Windows 7. In the System console, click **Change Product Key** under Windows Activation. In the Windows Activation window, type the product key and then click **Next**. As in Setup, you do not need to type the dashes in the product key.

Restore a Computer to a Previous Windows Installation

When you perform a clean installation of Windows 7 on a hard disk partition that contains an existing Windows installation (assuming you did not reformat the hard disk), the previous operating system, user data, and program files are saved to a Windows.OLD folder. If the Windows.OLD folder exists on this drive, files from the previous Windows installation are saved during the Windows 7 installation process. Therefore, you can restore the computer to the previous Windows installation by following the directions from the following Microsoft website:

http://support.microsoft.com/kb/971760

Using BCDEdit

During the boot process, the system ROM BIOS accesses the primary hard drive and reads the master boot record (MBR), which is the first 512 bytes of the hard drive. It contains the disk's primary partition table and a boot loader. A boot loader is a file that contains necessary information that instructs the system how to boot/start an operating system. For Windows Vista and Windows 7, the boot loader starts the Boot Manager (bootmgr), which then reads the partition table to identify the active partition, accesses the Boot Configuration Data (BCD) store, and starts the Windows Boot Manager (winload.exe), which loads Windows.

The active partition or volume that contains the Boot Manager is known as the *system partition/volume*. The partition or volume that contains the Windows operating system files (usually the Windows folder) is called the *boot partition*. It is common for computer systems to have one drive and one partition/volume, which makes the partition both the system partition and the boot partition.

Boot Configuration Data (BCD) is a database store (located in the \Boot\bcd folder on the system volume) that contains the boot-time configuration data used by Microsoft's Windows Boot Manager found with Windows Vista, Windows 7, and Windows Server 2008. To edit the Boot Configuration, you typically use the bcdedit.exe command-line tool.

Note

To run the bcdedit command, you need to run the command from an elevated command prompt.

Before you start making changes using the bcdedit command, you need to look at your configuration and record the identifiers. To list the entries in the store, you would execute the following command:

bcdedit /enum

As you can see in Figure 2.3, the bcdedit command identifies the Windows Boot Manager is located on the D drive and the Windows Boot Loader is located on the C:\Windows\System32\winload.exe.

FIGURE 2.3 **Executing the** bcdedit /enum **command.**

Every drive or partition on the system is identified as one of the following:

- ▶ {**legacy**}: Describes a drive or partition on which a pre-Windows Vista operating system exists

- ▶ {**default**}: Describes the drive or partition containing the current default operating system

- ▶ {**current**}: Describes the current drive or partition one is booted to

Each drive or partition also includes a global unique identifier (GUID). To display the GUIDs, execute the following command:

bcdedit /v

Figure 2.4 demonstrates executing the bcdedit /v command.

FIGURE 2.4 **Executing the** `bcdedit /v` **command.**

In addition, you can add the following parameters to the `bcdedit /enum` command to change the information that is displayed:

- ▶ `Active`: Displays all entries in the boot manager display order (default)

- ▶ `Firmware`: Displays all firmware applications

- ▶ `Bootapp`: Displays all boot environment applications

- ▶ `Bootmgr`: Displays the boot manager

- ▶ `Osloader`: Displays all operating system entries

- ▶ `Resume`: Displays all resume from hibernation entries

- ▶ `Inherit`: Displays all inherit entries

- ▶ `All`: Displays all entries

Because the BCD store is essential for your system to boot properly, it is recommended that you back up the BCD settings before you make any changes. To make a backup of your current BCD registry settings, execute the following command:

```
bcdedit /export name_of_file.bcd
```

To restore your BSD registry settings, execute the following command:

```
bcdedit /import name_of_file.bcd
```

To view the `bcdedit` command options, execute the following command:

```
bcdedit /?
```

These options include the following:

- **/createstore**: Creates a new empty BCD store
- **/export**: Exports the contents of the system BCD store to a specified file
- **/import**: Restores the state of the system BCD store from a specified file
- **/copy**: Makes copies of boot entries
- **/create**: Creates new boot entries
- **/delete**: Deletes boot entries
- **/deletevalue**: Deletes elements from a boot entry
- **/set**: Creates or modifies a boot entry's elements
- **/bootsequence**: Specifies a one-time boot sequence
- **/default**: Specifies the default boot entry
- **/displayorder**: Specifies the order in which Boot Manager displays its menu
- **/timeout**: Specifies the Boot Manager Timeout value
- **/toolsdisplayorder**: Specifies the order in which Boot Manager displays the tools menu
- **/bootems**: Enables or disables Emergency Management Services (EMS) for a specified boot application
- **/ems**: Enables or disables EMS for an operating system boot entry
- **/emssettings**: Specifies global EMS parameters
- **/store**: Specifies the BCD store upon which a command acts

To set a new default boot volume, run the following command:

```
bcdedit /default id
```

where the *id* is the identifier for the new entry.

For example, to configure the Windows Boot Manager to start the previous installation of Windows XP by default (which is identified as {ntldr}), run the following command:

```
bcdedit /default {ntldr}
```

To configure the currently running instance of Windows 7 as the default, run the following command:

```
bcdedit /default {current}
```

To change the timeout on showing boot menu:

```
bcdedit /timeout 5
```

To change the title of the boot menu entry, you would use the /set option. For example, to change the title to Windows XP from Earlier Windows Version, you would type in the following:

```
bcdedit /set {ntldr} description "Windows XP"
```

For more information about the bcdedit command, visit the following websites:

http://technet.microsoft.com/en-us/library/cc709667(WS.10).aspx

http://www.windows7home.net/how-to-use-bcdedit-in-windows-7

Enabling a Dual-Boot System

Sometimes, it might be beneficial to have a single computer have the capability to boot more than one operating system so that you can save on purchasing additional hardware or when you want to test a new operating system. You can configure a computer to boot different copies of Windows, each of which is selected during a Windows boot menu.

If you want to have Windows 7 on the same system as Windows XP, you need to install Windows XP first while leaving room on the same drive or a different drive on the computer to install Windows 7. Then, install Windows 7 using the custom installation and select the partition on which you want to install Windows 7. Windows 7 automatically identifies your previous installation of Windows (XP) and includes it in the boot menu.

To create a dual-boot system between Windows Vista and Windows 7 (or multiple copies of Windows Vista and Windows 7), the procedure is very similar to creating a dual boot system with Windows XP and Windows 7. One difference when you have a Windows Vista or Windows 7 installation is that you can use the Disk Management console (found as part of the Computer

Management console) to shrink a volume if you have free disk space on the volume you want to shrink. It is usually recommended that you defrag the hard drive first. Then right-click the volume you want to shrink and select **Shrink Volume**. After you've allocated the desired amount of space, click the **Shrink** button. Windows creates a new partition out of the free space you've allocated, all without even having to reboot. Of course, because this is a major change to the system, you should make sure that you have a good backup of your data before shrinking the volume.

You can also modify the default operating system and the time the list of operating system appears by right-clicking **Computer**, selecting **Properties**, clicking **Advanced system settings**, selecting the **Advanced** tab, and clicking the **Settings** button in the Startup and Recovery section. You can also specify what type of dump occurs during a system failure.

Cram Quiz

1. Which versions of Windows can be directly upgraded to Windows 7 Home Premium Edition?

    ○ **A.** Microsoft Windows XP Professional

    ○ **B.** Microsoft Windows XP Home

    ○ **C.** Microsoft Windows XP Tablet PC

    ○ **D.** Microsoft Windows 2000 Professional SP3

    ○ **E.** None of the above

2. You work as a helpdesk technician for Acme.com. You have a Windows XP computer that you need to upgrade to Windows 7, but you are not sure if the older sound card and video card are compatible? What should you do?

    ○ **A.** Run the Windows 7 Program Compatibility Assistant tool

    ○ **B.** Run the Windows 7 Upgrade Advisor

    ○ **C.** Run the Windows Update

    ○ **D.** Open the Device Manager and update its drivers

3. What command or utility do you use to configure BCD store, add boot menu options, and change the default boot operating system?

    ○ **A.** System Configuration

    ○ **B.** bcdedit

    ○ **C.** Computer Management Console

    ○ **D.** Windows Boot Manager Console

Cram Quiz Answers

1. **E** is correct. You cannot upgrade Windows XP or Windows 2000 Professional to Windows 7 Home Premium. Therefore, A, B, C, and D are incorrect.

2. **B** is correct. When you want to determine system compatibility with Windows 7, you should run the Windows 7 upgrade Advisor. Answer A is incorrect because it does not check hardware compatibility. Answer C is incorrect because Windows update does not specify if a device is compatible with Windows 7. Answer D is incorrect because updating drivers in Windows XP does not specify if a device is compatible with Windows 7.

3. **B** is correct. `bcdedit` is a command-line tool for managing BCD stores. It can be used for a variety of purposes, including creating new stores, modifying existing stores, adding boot menu options, and so on. Answer A is incorrect because System Configuration is used to manage startup programs and services. Answer C is incorrect because the Computer Management Console includes multiple management tools including the Disk Management MMC, but it does not have any tools to manage the BCD stores. Answer D is incorrect because the Windows Boot Manager is a Windows boot component. It is not a console or tool to configure the Windows BCD stores.

Windows Easy Transfer and Windows User State Migration Tool

▶ **Migrate user profiles.**

Cram**Saver**

1. What are the two tools used to migrate user settings between a Windows Vista computer and Windows 7? (Choose two answers.)

   ○ **A.** Windows migrate.exe tool

   ○ **B.** Windows Easy Transfer

   ○ **C.** Windows User State Migration Tool

   ○ **D.** Windows Disk Migration Tool

2. If you want to migrate user settings from a Windows XP computer, which parameter should you use with the `ScanState.exe` command?

   ○ **A.** `/xp`

   ○ **B.** `/target:xp`

   ○ **C.** `/targetxp`

   ○ **D.** No options are required.

Answers

1. **B** and **C** are correct. Both the Windows Easy Transfer and Windows User Migration Tool can migrate user settings between one Windows computer to another. Although the Windows Easy Transfer is used for a small number of migrations, the User State Migration Tool is a scriptable command-line tool that should be used for large deployments. Answers A and D are invalid and therefore incorrect.

2. **C** is correct. When you want to migrate from a Windows XP computer, you should use the `/targetxp` parameter. Answers A and B have invalid syntax and are therefore incorrect. Answer D is incorrect because C is a valid parameter.

If you cannot do an in-place upgrade, you can still move your data files and settings from one Windows installation (Windows XP, Windows Vista, and Windows 7) to another or from one computer running Windows to another using the Windows Easy Transfer (WET) program or the User State Migration Tool (USMT).

WET is a graphical program that enables you to transfer one user's profile or multiple users' profiles. You cannot use WET to move program files and you cannot transfer any system files such as fonts and drivers. With WET, you can transfer files and settings using a network, a USB flash drive (UFD), or the Easy Transfer cable; however, you cannot use a regular universal serial bus (USB) cable to transfer files and settings using WET. You can purchase an Easy Transfer cable on the Web, from your computer manufacturer, or at an electronics store.

WET (Migwiz.exe) is installed with Windows 7 and is located under **Accessories, System Tools**. It is also available on the Windows 7 DVD in the Support\Migwiz directory.

The User State Migration Tool (USMT) is a scriptable command-line tool that is highly customizable. Because it a scriptable command-line tool, it is usually used to automate migration during large deployments of the Windows operating system.

USMT has been around for several years.

▶ USMT 2.0 was made to migrate to Windows 2000 and Windows XP workstations. USMT 2.6.2 was made available publicly.

▶ USMT 3.0 was made to migrate to Windows XP and Windows Vista. It also migrated EFS files and certificates. USMT 3.01 was made available publicly.

▶ USMT 4.0 was made to migrate to Windows Vista and Windows 7. It is included in the Windows Automated Installation Kit.

USMT includes two components, ScanState and LoadState, and a set of modifiable .xml files:

▶ **MigApp.xml**: Used to migrate application settings to computers running Windows 7

▶ **MigUser.xml**: Used to migrate user folders, files, and file types to computers running Windows 7

▶ **MigDocs.xml**: Used to migrate all user folders and files that are found by the MigXmlHelper.GenerateDocPatterns helper function

In addition, you can use the config.xml file to exclude components from the migration with the `ScanState.exe /genconfig` option.

The **ScanState** command is used to scan the source computer, collect files and settings, and create a store. For example:

```
scanstate \\fileserver\share\mystore /x:migsys.xml /x:migapp.xml
/x:miguser.xml /v:13
```

The **/v:13** option enables verbose, status, and debugger output.

You can also add the following options to the preceding command:

- ▶ **/efs:copyraw**: Used to migrate the EFS-encrypted files and EFS certificates.

- ▶ **/encrypt /key:keystring**: Encrypts the store with the specified key.

- ▶ **/l**: Specifies the location and name of the ScanState log.

- ▶ **/nocompress**: Disables compression of data and saves the files to a hidden folder called "File." Compression is enabled by default.

- ▶ **/p**: Without any additional parameters gives you storage space estimation if used with the /nocompress option.

- ▶ **/targetvista**: Use this option if you are migrating from a Windows Vista computer.

- ▶ **/targetxp**: Use this option if you are migrating from a Windows XP.

- ▶ **/vsc**: Enables the volume's shadow-copy service to migrate files that are locked or in use.

ExamAlert

/efs:copyraw began with USMT 3.0, which is used to copy encrypted EFS files and its certificates.

The **LoadState** command migrates the files and settings from the store to the destination computer. The **LoadState** command has similar options. Of course instead of using the **/encrypt** option to encrypt the store, you would use the **decrypt** option to decrypt the store.

No matter which program you decide to use, WET or USMT, you generally follow the same high-level steps to migrate user settings from one computer to another. These steps include the following:

1. Verify that your system is capable of running of Windows 7 by using the Windows 7 Upgrade Advisor. You also need to determine which applications have compatibility problems with Windows 7 and resolve those compatibility issues.

2. To protect from data loss, make sure to back up any data and personal settings before you start the upgrade.

3. Run WET or USMT to copy user profiles to a network drive or removable drive.

4. Install Windows 7 and perform a clean installation.

5. Use the Microsoft update site to update Windows with the newest patches, fixes, and security packs.

6. Re-install all programs.

7. Use WET or USMT 4.0 to migrate both your program settings and your user-related settings from the network or removable drive to complete the migration process.

For more information about Easy Transfer and USMT, visit the following website:

http://technet.microsoft.com/en-us/library/ee461274(WS.10).aspx

---

Cram Quiz

1. Which command would you use with the USMT to copy user profiles from a source computer?

   ○ **A.** scanstate

   ○ **B.** loadstate

   ○ **C.** copystate

   ○ **D.** migstate

2. You need to migrate the user settings from Windows XP Professional workstations to Windows 7 Enterprise workstations. Because some users use EFS, you
   need to also migrate the EFS files and certificates. You also need to ensure that
   you are able to encrypt the migration store during the migration. What should
   you use?

   ○ **A.** On the Windows XP computers, use the USMT 3.0.

   ○ **B.** On the Windows XP computer, use the USMT 2.6.

   ○ **C.** On the Windows XP computer, use the EFSCopy command.

   ○ **D.** On the Windows XP computer, use the Export certificates using the
   Certificates MMC console. Be sure to select the Export file option.

Cram Quiz Answers

1. **A** is correct. To migrate data from a source computer to a network or removable
   disk, you use `scanstate` to create a store. When the target computer is ready,
   you then use `loadstate` (Answer B) to migrate the data to the target. Answers
   C and D are incorrect because the `copystate` and `migstate` commands are
   not included with Windows 7.

2. **A** is correct. The `/efs:copyraw` option specifies to copy the files in the
   encrypted format. This option was introduced with USMT 3.0; therefore, you
   need to use USMT 3.0 or higher. Answer B is incorrect because USMT 2.6 did
   not support migrating EFS files. Answer C is incorrect because the EFSCopy
   command does not exist. Answer D is incorrect because there is no Export File
   option and using the Certificates MMC console does not move files over.

Deploying Windows 7

▶ **Deploying Windows 7:**

    ▶ **Capture a system image**

    ▶ **Prepare a system image for deployment**

    ▶ **Deploy a system image**

    ▶ **Configure a VHD**

CramSaver

1. You want to establish an automated installation of Windows 7 using the Microsoft Windows 7 DVD. What should you do?

    ○ **A.** Create an answer file called `oobe.xlm` in the C:\ folder of the computer

    ○ **B.** Create an answer file called `winnt.sif` file and copy it to a USB drive

    ○ **C.** Create an answer file called `autounattend.xml` in the C:\ folder of the computer

    ○ **D.** Create an answer file named `autounattend.xml` and copy it to a USB drive

2. You have an offline Windows 7 image. What tool would you use to add updated device drivers to the image?

    ○ **A.** Use the `imagex` command-line utility

    ○ **B.** Use the `pkgmgr.exe` utility

    ○ **C.** Use Windows SIM

    ○ **D.** Use the DISM tool

Answers

1. **D** is correct. To perform an automated installation of Windows 7, the installation process automatically looks for the autounattend.xml file on the DVD or USB drive. Answer A is incorrect because the oobe is an option to use with sysprep, not an answer file. Answer B is incorrect because the winnt.sif file is an answer file used in older versions of Windows. Answer C is incorrect because the autounattend.xml file needs to be put on a USB drive or network drive, not the C:\.

2. **D** is correct. Deployment Image Servicing and Management (DISM) is a command-line tool that is used to service and manage Windows images. You can use it to install, uninstall, configure, and update Windows features, packages, drivers, and international settings. Answer A is incorrect because imagex is used to create and manage a WIM file. Answer B is incorrect because pkgmgr.exe (short for Package Manager) installs, uninstalls, configures, and updates features and packages for Windows. Answer C is incorrect because Windows SIM is used to create or validate answer files.

When you are at home and you need to install a single copy of Windows 7, it is simple enough to boot with the Windows 7 DVD and perform the installation. But when you are with a corporation and you need to perform hundreds of installations, it becomes a bit more challenging to install numerous machines while keeping the machines standardized. Therefore, Microsoft offers several ways to deploy Windows 7.

Windows Automated Installation Kit

The Windows Automated Installation Kit (AIK) is a set of tools and documentation that support the configuration and deployment of Windows operating systems. By using Windows AIK, you can automate Windows installations, capture Windows images with ImageX, configure and modify images using Deployment Imaging Servicing and Management (DISM), create Windows PE images, and migrate user profiles and data with the User State Migration Tool (USMT). Windows AIK also includes the Volume Activation Management Tool (VAMT), which enables IT professionals to automate and centrally manage the volume activation process using a Multiple Activation Key (MAK).

If you have older systems that do not have DVD drives but do have CD-ROM drives, you can use the createspannedshares.cdm script to create spanned media, which then divides the DVD into multiple CDs. The createspannedshares.cdm is part of the Windows AIK.

To install the Windows AIK, you must first download the ISO, write the ISO file to a DVD using a third-party tool, and then install the Windows AIK from the DVD. The Windows AIK for Windows 7 can be found at the following website:

http://www.microsoft.com/downloads/details.aspx?familyid=696DD665-9F76-4177-A811-39C26D3B3B34&displaylang=en

Windows PE

Windows Preinstallation Environment (Windows PE or WinPE) is a lightweight version of Windows that is booted from a network disk, a CD, or a USB flash drive. Windows PE can be used to deploy workstations and servers, restore Windows to manufacturing specifications, and as a tool to fix and troubleshoot a wide variety of problems.

The newest version of Windows PE is Windows PE 3.0, which is built from Windows 7. To create a Windows PE disk, you would run the **copype.cmd** script and then copy the **imagex.exe** file to the iso folder under the

WinPE_x86 directory. Next create the `wimscript.ini` configuration file in Notepad and save the file in the same directory as `imagex.exe`. Lastly, run the `oscdimg` command to create an ISO image of WinPE and burn the image to a CD. For more information, visit the following website:

http://technet.microsoft.com/en-us/library/dd799303(WS.10).aspx

Windows PE 3.0 is available in both 32-bit and 64-bit versions. If you need to install a 32-bit version of Windows 7 using Windows PE, you must boot with the 32-bit version. If you need to install a 64-bit version of Windows 7, you must boot with the 64-bit version.

Original equipment manufacturers (OEMs) such as HP and Dell often include a system recovery disc rather than an operating system installation disc. The system recovery disk (which is sometimes a Windows PE disc) includes an image file so that you can boot with the disc and restore the computer to its original state as it left the manufacturer.

Disk Cloning and the System Preparation Tool

One way to install Windows 7 is to use disk cloning software such as Norton Ghost to create an image file. To use the disk cloning software, you use the installation disc to install Windows onto a master computer (also called reference computer), update and patch the computer, customize Windows, and install any additional software. You then use the cloning software to copy the contents of a hard drive to a file. You use the disk cloning software to copy the contents of the image to a target computer.

If you create a cloned copy of Windows and apply the cloned copy to multiple computers, each copy of Windows cloned to a target computer using the same image has the same parameters, such as the same computer name and security identifier (SID). Unfortunately, for these computers to operate properly on a network, these parameters have to be unique.

To overcome this problem, you run the *System Preparation Tool (Sysprep)*, which removes the security identifiers and all other user-specific or computer-specific information from the computer before you run the disk cloning software to make the cloned disk image. When you copy the cloned image to the disk image, a small wizard runs that enables you to specify the computer name and other computer specific information. The SID and other information is re-created automatically. The Sysprep utility is located in the c:\Windows\System32\sysprep or the c:\Windows\SysWOW64\sysprep folder. The disk structure is explained more in Chapter 9, "Managing Files and Folders."

The syntax for the `sysprep` command is as follows:

```
sysprep.exe [/oobe | /audit] [/generalize] [/reboot | /shutdown |
/quit] [/quiet] [/unattend:answerfile]
```

- ▶ **/audit**: Restarts the computer into audit mode. Audit mode enables you to add additional drivers or applications to Windows. You can also test an installation of Windows before it is sent to an end user. If an unattended Windows setup file is specified, the audit mode of Windows Setup runs the auditSystem and auditUser configuration passes.

- ▶ **/generalize**: Prepares the Windows installation to be imaged. If this option is specified, all unique system information is removed from the Windows installation. The security ID (SID) resets, any system restore points are cleared, and event logs are deleted. The next time the computer starts, a specialize configuration pass runs. A new security ID (SID) is created, and the clock for Windows activation resets, if the clock has not already been reset three times.

- ▶ **/oobe**: Restarts the computer into Windows Welcome mode. Windows Welcome enables end users to customize their Windows operating system, create user accounts, name the computer, and other tasks. Any settings in the oobe system configuration passed in an answer file are processed immediately before Windows Welcome starts.

- ▶ **/reboot**: Restarts the computer. Use this option to audit the computer and to verify that the first-run experience operates correctly.

- ▶ **/shutdown**: Shuts down the computer after Sysprep completes.

- ▶ **/quiet**: Runs Sysprep without displaying onscreen confirmation messages. Use this option if you automate Sysprep.

- ▶ **/quit**: Closes Sysprep after running the specified commands.

- ▶ **/unattend:*answerfile***: Applies settings in an answer file to Windows during unattended installation. The *answerfile* specifies the path and filename of the answer file to use.

The Unattended Installation

An answer file is an XML file that stores the answers for a series of graphical user interface (GUI) dialog boxes. Because the answer file is an XML file, you can use any text editor, such as Notepad, to create and modify the answer file. However, you will find it much easier if you use the Windows System Image Manager.

If you call the answer file *autounattend.xml* and place in a USB flash drive, you can then perform an unattended installation just by rebooting the computer and booting from the Windows 7 installation DVD. Windows 7 setup (`setup.exe`) automatically searches the root directory of all removable media for an answer file called *autounattend.xml* and performs the installation without you replying to any prompts on the screen.

To see more information about basic Windows deployment, visit the following website:

http://technet.microsoft.com/en-us/library/dd349348(WS.10).aspx

Installing Windows Using Windows System Image Manager

Windows System Image Manager (Windows SIM) provides a GUI to create unattended Windows setup answer files. Using Windows SIM, you can:

▶ Create or update existing unattended answer files

▶ Validate the settings of an existing answer file against a WIM file

▶ View all the configurable component settings in a WIM file

▶ Create a configuration set

▶ Add third-party drivers, applications, or other packages to an answer file

> **ExamAlert**
>
> Although you can create an answer file using any text editor, it is recommended that you validate the answer file with the Windows System Image Manager.

To install Windows SIM, you first need to download and install Windows Automated Installation Kit (AIK) for Windows 7 from the Microsoft website. To start Windows SIM, you then click the **Start** button, select **Microsoft Windows AIK,** and select **Windows System Image Manager.**

To deploy Windows 7 by using ImageX, do the following:

1. Install and configure Windows 7 on a source PC.

2. Use **sysprep** on the PC so that the OS can be deployed by removing some computer-specific information such as the workstation's SID, which must be unique.

3. Boot the master with the Windows PE CD.

4. Use ImageX on the master to create the image file.

5. Boot the target with the Windows PE CD.

6. Use Diskpart to format the drive. Diskpart is a PE tool that is used to configure the hard drive on a PC.

7. Use ImageX to apply the image to the target.

For more information, see the Windows 7 Upgrade and Migration Guide, located at the following website:

http://technet.microsoft.com/en-us/library/dd446674(WS.10).aspx

Deploying Windows with WIM Images

The Windows installation files can be distributed within a *Windows Imaging Format (WIM) file*. WIM is the file-based imaging format that Windows Server uses for rapid installation on a new computer. WIM files store copies (known as images) of the operating systems, such as Windows PE, Windows 7, or Windows Server 2008. Maintaining an operating system in a WIM file is easy because you can add and remove drivers, updates, and Windows components offline without ever starting the operating system.

The following are the benefits of using a file-based image format over the typical sector-based image format:

- A single WIM file deals with different hardware configurations.

- WIM can store multiple images within a single file.

- WIM enables compression and single instancing of files. Single instancing enables multiple images to share a single copy of a file.

- WIM allows images to be serviced offline. You can add or remove drivers, files, and patches.

- A WIM image can be installed on partitions of any size, unlike sector-based image formats.

- WIM enables you to boot Windows PE from a WIM file.

You can do the following with WIM files:

- When installing Windows 7 using Windows Deployment Server (WDS), you first boot the system with Windows PE. You then install Windows 7 from a WIM file that contains the Windows image.

- You can mount the WIM image as a new volume under Windows with a drive letter associated to facilitate easier extraction.

- You can mount the WIM image as a new volume and convert the WIM image to an ISO image.

- WIM images can be made bootable, as is the case with the setup DVD for Windows 7. In this case, BOOT.WIM contains a bootable version of Windows PE from which the installation is performed. Other setup files are contained in the file INSTALL.WIM.

- Because Windows PE can be contained within a WIM file, you can start Windows PE directly from a WIM file without copying it to a hard disk.

The image-based installation process consists of five high-level steps. These steps include the following:

1. Build an answer file, which is used to configure Windows settings during installation.

2. Build a reference installation with a customized/configured installation of Windows that you plan to duplicate onto one or more destination computers.

3. Create a bootable Windows PE media by using the `copype.cmd` script so that you can start a computer for the purposes of deployment and recovery.

4. Capture the Installation Image of the reference computer by using Windows PE and the ImageX tool. You can store the captured image on a network share.

5. Deploy the image from a network share onto a destination computer by using Windows PE and ImageX technologies. Follow these steps to deploy the image from a network share:

   a. Start the computer by using Windows PE media.

   b. Format that hard drive.

   c. Connect to your network share and copy the custom image down to the destination computer's local hard drive.

   d. Apply the image by using ImageX.

For high-volume deployments, you can store the image of the new installation to your distribution share and deploy the image to destination computers by using deployment tools, such as Windows Deployment Services (WDS) or Microsoft Deployment Toolkit (MDT).

To create and manage a WIM file, you use the ImageX command-line tool, which is available in several of Microsoft's deployment tools, such as in the Windows Automated Installation Kit (WAIK), Windows OEM Preinstallation Kit (OPK), or in Business Desktop Deployment 2007. By using the ImageX command-line tool, you can do the following:

▶ View the contents of a WIM file

▶ Capture desktop images

▶ Mount images for offline image editing

▶ Store multiple images in a single file

▶ Compress image files

▶ Implement scripts for image creation

The `imagex` command uses the following syntax:

```
imagex [flags] {/append | /apply | /capture | /delete | /dir |
/export
  | /info | /mount | /mountrw | /split | /unmount} [parameters]
```

- ▶ **/append**: Used to add a volume image to an existing WIM file and create a single instance of the file.

- ▶ **/apply**: Used to apply a volume image to a specified drive.

- ▶ **/capture**: Used to capture a volume image from a drive to a new .wim file.

- ▶ **/delete**: Used to remove the specified volume image from a .wim file.

- ▶ **/dir**: Displays a list of the files and folders within a specified volume image.

- ▶ **/export**: Exports a copy of the specified .wim to another .wim file. If you use the /ref splitwim.swm option, it enables you to reference a split .wim file (*.swm).

- ▶ **/info**: Returns information about the WIM file.

- ▶ **/mount**: Used to mount a WIM file with read-only permission.

- ▶ **/mountw**: Used to mount a WIM file with read/write permission, thereby allowing the contents of the file to be modified.

- ▶ **/split**: Splits an existing .wim file into multiple read-only split .wim files (*.swm).

- ▶ **/unmount**: Used to unmount an image from a specified directory.

The *parameters* options vary based on the options that you select. For example, you can use several parameters when you use the /append option; you can use the /boot parameter to mark the volume image as bootable; and use the /check parameter to check the integrity of the WIM file.

For more information about the imagex command, visit the following website:

http://msdn.microsoft.com/en-us/library/ff794852.aspx

Deployment Image Servicing and Management

Deployment Image Servicing and Management (DISM) is a command-line tool that is used to service and manage Windows images. You can use it to install, uninstall, configure, and update Windows features, packages, drivers, and international settings.

DISM can also be used to service Windows PE images. DISM is installed with Windows 7 and is also distributed in Windows OPK and Windows AIK. It is a consolidated tool that replaces several tools such as PEimg, Intlcfg, and Package Manager used in Windows, with added functionalities to improve the experience for offline servicing.

You can use DISM to:

▶ Add, remove, and enumerate packages and drivers

▶ Enable or disable Windows features

▶ Apply changes based on the offlineServicing section of an unattend.xml answer file

▶ Configure international settings

▶ Upgrade a Windows image to a different edition

▶ Prepare a Windows PE image

▶ Take advantage of better logging

▶ Service all platforms (32-bit, 64-bit, and Itanium), service a 32-bit image from a 64-bit host, and service a 64-bit image from a 32-bit host

▶ Use old Package Manager Scripts

The base syntax for nearly all DISM commands is the same. After you have mounted or applied your Windows image so that it is available offline as a flat file structure, you can specify any DISM options, the servicing command that updates your image, and the location of the offline image. You can use only one servicing command per command line. If you are servicing a running computer, you can use the **/Online** option instead of specifying the location of the offline Windows Image.

The base syntax for DISM is the following:

```
DISM.exe {/Image:path_to_image | /Online} [dism_options]
{servicing_command} [servicing_argument]
```

The following DISM options are available for an offline image:

```
DISM.exe /image:path_to_offline_image_directory
[/WinDir:path_to_%WINDIR%] [/LogPath:path_to_log_file.log]
[/LogLevel:n] [SysDriveDir:path_to_bootMgr_file] [/Quiet]
[/NoRestart] [/ScratchDir:path_to_scratch_directory]
```

The following DISM options are available for a running operating system:

```
DISM.exe /online [/LogPath:path_to_log_file] [/LogLevel:n] [/Quiet]
[/NoRestart] [/ScratchDir:path_to_scratch_directory]
```

Before you start working with an image, you need to retrieve information about the OS images that are contained within a WIM file. Do this with the following command:

```
dism /Get-WimInfo /WimFile:d:\sources\install.wim
```

If you add the command-line option **/index** plus the image's index number, you get information about a specific image, such as the OS version, size, installed service pack, and so on:

```
dism /Get-WimInfo /WimFile:d:\sources\install.wim /index:4
```

Before you can work with a WIM image, you have to mount it to a folder with the following command:

```
dism /Mount-Wim /wimfile:c:\wim\install.wim /index:4 /MountDir:c:\img
```

If you need to mount an image onto a DVD or if you want to access the image in read-only mode, you just have to add **/ReadOnly** to the command.

After you have mounted an image, you can navigate through its folder structure using Windows Explorer and make changes to all files and folders. In most cases, however, you use DISM to gather specific information about an image and also to add features, drivers, and packages.

To list all installed third-party drivers in the image mounted to *c:\img*, you execute the following command:

```
dism /image:c:\img /Get-Drivers
```

To add the driver (INF) file to the image in the mount directory, you execute the following command:

```
dism /image:c:\img /add-driver /driver: C:\drivers\driver.INF
```

To dismount the image, execute the following command:

```
dism /unmount-wim /mountdir:c:\img /discard
```

For more information about the Deployment Image Servicing and Management program, visit the following websites:

http://technet.microsoft.com/en-us/library/dd744256(WS.10).aspx

http://technet.microsoft.com/en-us/library/dd744382(WS.10).aspx

Windows Deployment Services

Another way to install Windows is to use the Windows Deployment Services (WDS). You can use it to deploy Windows Vista, Windows 7, and Windows Server 2008. By booting a computer with Windows PE 2.0 or 3.0, you can connect to the WDS server and install Windows from a configured image.

If you choose to install the Deployment Server, you need the following prerequisites available on your network:

▶ Active Directory Domain Services

▶ Dynamic Host Configuration Protocol (DHCP) server

▶ Dynamic Name Services (DNS) server

Unfortunately, installing and configuring the Windows Deployment Services is beyond the scope of this exam.

To install Windows 7 using a Windows Deployment Server, you would

1. Turn on your computer and boot from the network card (PXE).

2. By booting using PXE, you connect to the Windows Deployment Service server and download the customized Windows PE image across the network.

3. The new computer loads Windows PE into memory and launches the configuration script. The script verifies the computer's configuration and hardware requirements.

4. If necessary, the script backs up the user's data to a shared folder on another computer.

5. The script runs the Diskpart tool to partition and format the disk.

The script connects to a shared folder containing the Windows Setup files and runs the Windows Setup program to install the operating system fully unattended.

Cram Quiz

1. You manually create an answer file for a Windows 7 unattended installation. What should you do next?
   - ○ **A.** Use `sysprep.exe` to capture an image on a reference computer
   - ○ **B.** Use `imagex.exe` to capture an image on a reference computer
   - ○ **C.** Use Windows SIM to validate the answer file
   - ○ **D.** Use `sysprep.exe` to validate the answer file

2. What tool can you use to create a bootable media that is used to deploy Windows 7 on non-PXE–supporting client computers?
   - ○ **A.** Use Windows SIM
   - ○ **B.** Use Windows AIK
   - ○ **C.** Use BDD
   - ○ **D.** Use SMS

Cram Quiz Answers

1. **C** is correct. Although you can create an answer file with any text editor, it is recommended you that you use Windows SIM to validate the answer file. Answer A is incorrect because `sysprep.exe` is used to prepare a system for mass deployment by removing the security identifiers and all other user-specific or computer-specific information from the Windows volume before cloning. Answer B is incorrect because `imagex.exe` is used to create and manage WIM files. Answer D is incorrect because Windows SIM is used to validate the answer file.

2. **B** is correct. To create bootable media to deploy Windows 7 on non-PXE–supporting client computers, you need create a WinPE disk, which is done with Windows Automated Installation Kit (AIK). Answer A is incorrect because Windows SIM is used to create and validate answer files. Answer C is incorrect because Business Desktop Deployment (BDD) was a deployment tool mostly used with deploying Windows, but does not include tools to create a WinPE disk. Answer D is incorrect because SMS (short for System Management Server) has been replaced with System Center Configuration Manager to deploy and manage operating systems, patches, and software. It does not help boot a system that cannot PXE boot.

Booting with a VHD Image

▶ **Configure a VHD**

CramSaver

1. When using a virtual system such as Hyper-V, the disk for a virtual system is stored in what file?

   ○ **A.** VMC

   ○ **B.** VHD

   ○ **C.** VSV

   ○ **D.** AVHD

2. What utility would you use to create a VHD file?

   ○ **A.** `bcdboot`

   ○ **B.** `bcdedit`

   ○ **C.** `imagex.exe`

   ○ **D.** Disk Management console.

Answers

1. **B** is correct. The virtual hard disk (.vhd) files store guest operating systems, applications and data for the virtual machine. Answer A is incorrect because the virtual machine configuration (.vmc) file contains the virtual machine configuration information including all settings for the virtual machine. Answer C is incorrect because the saved-state (.vsv) file is used if a virtual server has been placed in a saved state. Answer D is incorrect because the .avhd file is a differencing disk used with Hyper-V.

2. **D** is correct. To create a VHD, you would use the Disk Management console. Answer A is incorrect because `bcdboot` is a command-line tool for initializing the BCD store and copying boot environment files to the system partition. Answer B is incorrect because `bcdedit` is a command-line tool for managing Boot Configuration Data (BCD) stores. Answer C is incorrect because `imageX.exe` is a tool used to create and manage WIM files.

Over the last few years, virtualization has become popular. *Virtual machine* technology enables multiple operating systems to run concurrently on a single machine. This allows for a separation of services while keeping cost to a minimum. In addition, you can easily and quickly create Windows test environments in a safe, self-contained environment. Of course, for a virtual machine to handle such a load, it must have sufficient processing and memory resources.

Previously, Microsoft virtual server included Microsoft Virtual Server and Virtual PC. Starting with Windows Server 2008, Microsoft introduced *Hyper-V*. Hyper-V is based on *hypervisor*, a virtual machine monitor that provides a virtualization platform that allows multiple operating systems to run on a host computer at the same time. To keep each virtual server secure and reliable, each virtual server is placed in its own partition. A partition is a logical unit of isolation, in which operating systems execute.

Each virtual machine uses the following files:

▶ A *virtual machine configuration (.vmc) file* in XML format that contains the virtual machine configuration information, including all settings for the virtual machine.

▶ One or more *virtual hard disk (.vhd) files* to store the guest operating system, applications, and data for the virtual machine. So, if you create a 12 GB partition for the virtual machine's hard drive, the virtual hard disk file is 12 GB.

In Windows 7, a VHD can be used to store an operating system to run on a computer without a parent operating system, virtual machine, or hypervisor. This feature, called *VHD boot*, is a new feature in Windows 7 that eases the transition between virtual and physical environments. It is best used in the following scenarios:

▶ In an organization that has hundreds of users working remotely through Virtual Desktop Infrastructure (VDI) via virtual computers but also needs the same desktop images as the users working onsite using physical computers.

▶ In an organization with users in a highly managed environment that use technologies such as Folder Redirection and Roaming User Profiles so that the user state is not stored in the image.

▶ As dual boot, when you only have a single disk volume as an alternative to running virtual machines.

Windows 7 also enables IT professionals to use the same processes and tools to manage WIM and VHD image files.

The following steps outline Windows 7 deployment on VHD:

1. **Create the VHD**: You can create a VHD by using the DiskPart tool or the Disk Management MMC. The Disk Management MMC also enables you to attach the VHD, so that it appears on the host computer

as a drive and not as a static file. VHD files can then be partitioned and formatted before you install an operating system.

2. **Prepare the VHD**: Install Windows 7 on the VHD by using the `imagex` command with the `/capture` and `/apply` options.

3. **Deploy the VHD**: You can then copy the VHD file to one or more systems, to be run in a virtual machine or for native boot. To configure native-boot, add the native-boot VHD to the boot menu by using `bcdedit` or `bcdboot` tool. `bcdedit` is a command-line tool for managing Boot Configuration Data (BCD) stores and `bcdboot` is a command-line tool for initializing the BCD store and copying boot environment files to the system partition. You can also automate the network deployment of VHD by using WDS. You can use WDS to copy the VHD image to a local partition and to configure the local Boot Configuration Data (BCD) for native-boot from the VHD.

To create a VHD using the Disk Management console, perform the following instructions:

1. In the left pane, right-click **Disk Management** and then click on **Create VHD**. See Figure 2.5.

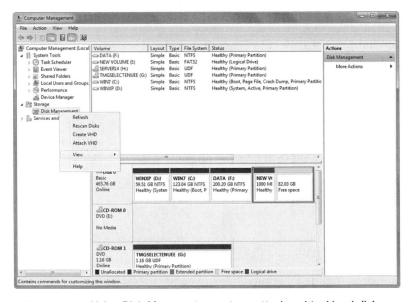

FIGURE 2.5   **Using Disk Manager to create or attach a virtual hard disk.**

2. After choosing to create a VHD, select a location to save your VHD file.

3. Next, enter the maximum size you want the Virtual Hard Disk to be, and select the size type to be used. Choose MB, GB, or TB (see Figure 2.6).

FIGURE 2.6 **Specifying the location and size of the virtual hard disk.**

4. Select whether to let Windows decide the size by choosing **Dynamic** or use a set size by choosing **Fixed** and clicking **OK**.

5. The new disk displays in the right pane as unallocated space. Right-click the new unallocated VHD Disk # and click **Initialize Disk**.

6. Select the **Disk #** from Step 5 for the new VHD. You have to choose if you want the new VHD to have Master Boot Record (MBR) or GUID Partition Table (GPT) partition and click OK.

7. Right-click the new unallocated VHD and click **New Simple Volume**.

8. Type the maximum disk space you want to use for this VHD partition and then click **Next**.

9. Select a FAT or a NTFS file system and enter a name for your VHD. Click the **Perform a quick format** checkbox and click **Next**.

10. When the summary appears, click the **Finish** button and the Disk Management console creates a new simple volume on your VHD, which is already attached.

You can also create a VHD using an open-source tool available on the MSDN Code Gallery called WIM2VHD, which converts the WIM image into a VHD you can use to boot off. You can find it at http://code.msdn.microsoft.com/wim2vhd/.

To install a VHD boot machine:

1. Boot the system with a Windows 7 DVD or USB flash drive.

2. At the setup screen, instead of choosing **Install Now**, press **Shift+F10** to get into command-line mode.

3. Enter diskpart to start the partitioning utility.

4. Create a new VHD file by entering the following command:

```
create vdisk file="d:\path_to-vhd.vhd" type=expandable
maximum=maxsizeInMegabyte
```

5. To select the new VHD and attach it as a physical disk, enter the following command:

```
select vdisk file="D:\pathToVhd.vhd"
```

6. Use Alt+Tab to switch back to the setup screen and start the setup to the attached VDisk.

7. Now proceed with the normal setup.

8. After the installation, Windows 7 displays in the boot menu. If you want to add a VHD manually to the boot menu, use this command sequence:

```
bcdedit /copy {originalguid} /d "New Windows 7 Installation"
bcdedit /set {newguid} device vhd=[D:]\Image.vhd
bcdedit /set {newguid} osdevice vhd=[D:]\Image.vhd
bcdedit /set {newguid} detecthal on
```

9. Open the Computer Management console and open Disk Management.

10. Right-click **Disk Management** and then click **Attach VHD**.

Cram Quiz

1. You have a Virtual Hard Disk with Windows 7. How do you add the VHD to the Windows 7 boot menu?

   ○ **A.** Use `diskpart.exe` to select vdisk

   ○ **B.** Attach to your machine using Disk Management

   ○ **C.** Use the `bcdedit.exe` command and modify the Windows Boot Manager settings

   ○ **D.** Use the `bootcfg.exe` command to modify the Windows Boot Manager settings

2. What utilities do you use to create a VHD file? (Choose all that apply.)

   ○ **A.** `diskpart`

   ○ **B.** Disk Management

   ○ **C.** `bcdedit`

   ○ **D.** `bcdboot`

Cram Quiz Answers

1. **C** is correct. For Windows Vista and 7, the boot menu is configured using the `bcdedit` command, which edits a hidden file called *c:\boot\bcd*. To add a VHD manually to the boot menu, you also use `bcdedit.exe`. Answer A is incorrect because `diskpart` is a PE tool that is used to configure the hard drive on a PC. Answer B is incorrect because adding a machine using Disk Management does not add Windows 7 running on a VHD to the boot menu. Answer D is incorrect because `bootcfg.exe` is used to modify the boot.ini on Windows Server 2003 machines.

2. **A** and **B** are correct. `diskpart` and Disk Management are used to create a VHD file (virtual hard drive). Answer C is incorrect because BCDedit is used to configured using the `bcdedit` command, which edits a hidden file called *c:\boot\bcd* that displays the boot menu. To add a VHD manually to the boot menu, you would also use the `bcdedit.exe` utility. Answer D is incorrect because `bcdboot` is a command-line tool for initializing the BCD store and copying boot environment files to the system partition.

Review Questions

1. You work as a desktop support technician at Acme.com. Because you need to connect to the domain, you need to install Windows 7 Enterprise Edition on a new computer for the graphics department. The new computer has the following specifications:

    ▶ 1.4 GHz Intel processor

    ▶ 512 MB of RAM

    ▶ 50 GB hard drive

    ▶ Super VGA video card with 256 MB of video memory

    ▶ Integrated sound card

    ▶ Intel 10/100 network adapter

    Which hardware does not meet the minimum requirements to install Windows 7?

    ○   **A.** The processor

    ○   **B.** The amount of RAM

    ○   **C.** The hard drive

    ○   **D.** The video card

    ○   **E.** The network adapter

2. You work as the desktop support technician at Acme.com. You have a computer that has a 120 GB hard drive divided into two partitions. Each partition is 60 GB. Windows XP Professional has been installed on the first partition. The second partition has not been defined. You want to set up the computer to dual boot between Windows XP Professional and Windows 7 Professional. What do you need to do to set this up?

    ○   **A.** Format the second partition with the NTFS file system. Boot from the Windows 7 DVD and install Windows 7 on the second partition.

    ○   **B.** Format the first partition with the NTFS file system. Boot from the Windows 7 DVD and install Windows 7 on the first partition.

    ○   **C.** Boot from the Windows 7 DVD and upgrade the Windows XP partition to Windows 7.

    ○   **D.** Install Windows XP on the first partition. Boot from the Windows 7 DVD and install Windows 7 on the second partition.

3. You work as the desktop support technician at Acme.com. Within your corporation, you have new computer with Windows 7 Professional. You need to install the same build and configuration of Windows 7 on 10 other computers. To accomplish this, you burn a bootable Windows PE CD that includes all the required deployment tools. What should you do next with the least amount of administrative effort?

  ○ **A.** Boot the master with the Windows PE CD. Use ImageX on the master to create the image file. Boot each target with the Windows PE CD. Use Diskpart to format the drive. Use ImageX to apply the image to the target.

  ○ **B.** Use Sysprep to seal the master. Boot the master with the Windows PE CD. Use ImageX on the master to create the image file. Boot each target with the Windows PE CD. Use ImageX to apply the image to the target.

  ○ **C.** Boot the master with the Windows PE CD. Use ImageX on the master to create the image file. Boot each target with the Windows PE CD. Use Diskpart to format the drive. Use ImageX to apply the image to the target. Use Sysprep to seal the master.

  ○ **D.** Use Sysprep to seal the master. Boot the master with the Windows PE CD. Use ImageX on the master to create the image file. Boot each target with the Windows PE CD. Use Diskpart to format the drive. Use ImageX to apply the image to the target.

4. You work as the desktop support technician at Acme.com. You have a new computer that has Windows XP on which you want to install Windows 7. You place the DVD into the drive and start the workstation. Unfortunately, it boots to Windows XP without starting the install program. You enter the BIOS program and determine that you are not allowed to boot from the DVD. What do you do next?

  ○ **A.** Install new drivers for the DVD drive

  ○ **B.** Retrieve updates from Microsoft

  ○ **C.** Update the PC's BIOS

  ○ **D.** Boot from a Windows PE disk

5. Which versions of Windows can be upgraded to Windows 7 Home Premium Edition?

  ○ **A.** Microsoft Windows Vista Business

  ○ **B.** Microsoft Windows Vista Home Basic

  ○ **C.** Microsoft Windows Vista Starter

  ○ **D.** Microsoft Windows Vista Ultimate

6. You have several workstations. You want to produce a new Security ID (SID) for each workstation. What should you do?

  ○ **A.** Using the Welcome screen, deactivate the license activation on all the Windows 7 workstations

  ○ **B.** Use the System Properties and remove the computers from the domain

   ○ **C.** Use the sysinfo.exe `/resetID` command on all the Windows 7 workstations

   ○ **D.** Use the sysprep.exe `/oobe` `/generalize` command on all the Windows workstations

7. You are going to migrate the server between two Windows 7 computers. You want to determine the amount of space needed to accomplish the migration. What should you do?

   ○ **A.** Run the `scanstate` command with the `/nocompress` `/p` option on the source computer

   ○ **B.** Run the `scanstate` command with the `/nocompress` `/p` option on the target computer

   ○ **C.** Run the `loadstate` command with the `/nocompress` `/p` option on the source computer

   ○ **D.** Run the `loadstate` command with the `/nocompress` `/p` option on the target command

8. You manually create an answer file for a Windows 7 unattended installation. What can you use to validate the answer file?

   ○ **A.** Use the Setup Manager

   ○ **B.** Use the Sysprep.exe utility

   ○ **C.** Use the Windows System Image Manager tool

   ○ **D.** Use `image.exe`

9. You want to create an image of a Windows 7 computer on multiple CDs. Therefore, you need to use the createspannedshares.cmd script. Where is the createspannedshared.cmd script found?

   ○ **A.** The Package Manager

   ○ **B.** DISM

   ○ **C.** Windows AIK

   ○ **D.** Windows SIM

10. You have a system with both Windows Vista and Windows 7. Which command would you use to configure the system to start Windows Vista by default?

   ○ **A.** Use the `bcdedit.exe` command with the `/default` option

   ○ **B.** Use the `bcdedit.exe` command with the `/Vista` option

   ○ **C.** Modify the `boot.ini` file to boot Vista using a text editor

   ○ **D.** Create the `boot.ini` in the C:\ folder and specify the `/Vista` option

Review Question Answers

1. Answer **B** is correct. The system requirements specify a minimum of 1 GB of RAM. The other requirements are 15 GB hard drive space for the 32-bit edition, 20 GB hard drive space for the 64-bit edition, 1 GHz processor, and a video card with 128 MB of video memory. Therefore, Answers A, C, and D are incorrect. The system requirements do not specify a network card, so Answer E is not correct. Of course, you need a network card to communicate with a network.

2. Answer **A** is correct. To have a system dual boot between Windows XP and Windows 7, you have to install each operating system onto two different partitions. Because Windows XP is already on the first partition, you need to install Windows 7 on the other partition. You do not want to format the first partition because it erases everything on that partition. So, Answer B is incorrect. You don't want to upgrade Windows because Windows XP will not be available. Therefore, Answer C is incorrect. Answer D is incorrect because you don't need to install Windows XP; it already exists.

3. Answer **D** is correct. To install the same configuration on 10 different computers, you have to use images. You already have the source system. Answer D then specifies the rest of the steps to install Windows 7 with images. After you have the source computer, the next step would be to sysprep the system. Therefore, Answers A and C are incorrect. Because you need to create a new partition before installing the image, Answer B is incorrect.

4. Answer **C** is correct. Because the system did not find the DVD disc, you need to fix that problem. The BIOS not allowing you to specify a DVD to boot from indicates that the BIOS is too old to support bootable DVD drives. Therefore, you need to update the system BIOS. Answers A and B are incorrect because drivers and updates do not help boot from the DVD because these load when Windows 7 loads, and to boot from a DVD does not require Windows 7 to load. Answer D is incorrect because you don't need the Windows PE disk to load DVD drivers.

5. Answer **B** is correct. You can only upgrade from Windows Vista Home Basic and Windows Vista Home Premium to Windows 7 Home Premium. If you have Windows Vista Business, Windows Vista Starter, and Windows Vista Ultimate, you have to perform a custom install instead of an in-place upgrade. Therefore, A, C, and D are incorrect.

6. Answer **D** is correct. The System Preparation Tool (Sysprep) removes the security identifiers and all other user-specific or computer-specific information from the computer. Answers A and B are incorrect because the Welcome screen and the System Properties do not produce a new Security ID. Answer C is incorrect because sysinfo.exe does not have a `/resetID` option and cannot be used to reset the SID.

7. Answer **A** is correct. The `scanstate` command is used to scan the source computer, collect files and settings, and create a store. The `/p` option without any parameters gives you a storage space estimation if used with the `/nocompress` option. Answer C is incorrect because the `loadstate` command migrates the files and settings from the store to the destination computer.

Answers B and D are incorrect because you need to run the command on the source computer and not the target computer.

8. Answer **C** is correct. The Windows System Image Manager (Windows SIM) provides a GUI interface to create and validate unattended Windows setup answer files. Answer A is incorrect because the Setup Manager is a Windows XP deployment tool. Answer B is incorrect because the System Preparation Tool removes the security identifiers and all other user-specific or computer-specific information from the computer. Answer D is incorrect because `imagex.exe` is used to create and manage a WIM file.

9. Answer **C** is correct. If you have older systems that do not have DVD drives but do have CD-ROM drives, you can use the createspannedshares.cdm script to create spanned media, which then breaks the DVD to multiple CDs. The createspannedshares.cdm is part of the Windows AIK. Answer A is incorrect because pkgmgr.exe (short for Package Manager) installs, uninstalls, configures, and updates features and packages for Windows. Answer B is incorrect because the Deployment Image Servicing and Management (DISM) is a command-line tool that is used to service and manage Windows images including install, uninstall, configure, and update Windows features, packages, drivers, and international settings. Answer D is incorrect because the Windows System Image Manager (Windows SIM) provides a GUI to create or check unattended Windows setup answer files.

10. Answer **A** is correct. `bcdedit` is a command-line tool for managing Boot Configuration Data (BCD) stores. The `/default` option defines which operating system is the default boot operating system. Answer B is incorrect because you would not use a `/Vista` option. Answers C and D are incorrect because the boot.ini files are used in Windows XP boot menus, not for Windows Vista or 7 boot menus.

CHAPTER 3

System Management

This chapter covers the following 70-680 Objectives:

▶ Supplemental Objective: Manage and configure Windows

▶ Installing, Upgrading, and Migrating to Windows 7:

   ▶ Configure devices

▶ Configuring Backup and Recovery Options:

   ▶ Configure system recovery options

Now that you have learned how to installed Windows, you also need to know how to configure Windows, including installing devices. To configure and manage Windows, you still use the standard tools, including the Control Panel and Administrative Tools, which can be found in most modern versions of Windows. Although these tools have been updated, they still have a lot in common to these tools found in older versions of Windows.

Configuring and Managing Windows

▶ **Supplemental Objectives: Manage and configure Windows**

Cram**Saver**

1. Which of the following is the primary tool to manage and configure Windows 7?

   ○ **A.** Registry Editor

   ○ **B.** Windows Explorer

   ○ **C.** Control Panel

   ○ **D.** System Manager

2. Which applet in the Control Panel do you use to change the computer name?

   ○ **A.** Name

   ○ **B.** System

   ○ **C.** Workgroup

   ○ **D.** Administrative Tools

3. What do you use to enable features so that disabled people can better use Windows 7? (Choose the best answer.)

   ○ **A.** Accessibility applet

   ○ **B.** Ease of Access Center

   ○ **C.** Administrative Tools

   ○ **D.** System applet

Answers

1. **C** is correct. The primary program used to configure Windows is the Control Panel. Answer A is incorrect because the Registry Editor is used to manually change the registry, which should rarely be done. Answer B is incorrect because Windows Explorer is used to manage the files and folders. Answer D is incorrect because there is no System Manager that comes with Windows 7.

2. **B** is correct. To change the name of a computer to add the computer to a domain, you need to use the System applet in the Control Panel. Answers A and C are incorrect because there are no Name or Workgroup applets. Answer D is incorrect because Administrative Tools are more IT-oriented tools used in managing your computer.

3. B is correct. To configure accessibility options, you use the Ease of Access Center. Answer A is incorrect because the Accessibility applet was the name used in Windows XP. Answers C and D are incorrect because the Administrative Tools and System applet are not used for accessibility options.

To simplify the process of setting up a new computer, Windows 7 includes the Welcome Center/Getting Started screen, as shown in Figure 3.1. This screen pulls all the tasks you most likely want to complete when you set up your computer into a single location. Such tasks include adding user accounts for different people, transferring files and settings, backing up your files, personalizing Windows, and changing the size of the text on your screen. You can also use Homegroup to share files and printers with other computers in your home and go online to get Windows Live Essentials. You can also go online to find out what's new in Windows 7.

FIGURE 3.1   **The Windows Welcome Center.**

The *Control Panel* is a graphical tool used to configure the Windows environment and hardware devices, as shown in Figure 3.2. To access the Control Panel, you can click the **Start** button on the taskbar and select **Control Panel**. You can also display the Control Panel in any Windows Explorer view by clicking the leftmost option button in the Address bar and selecting **Control Panel**.

FIGURE 3.2   Windows 7 Control Panel in Category view.

Of the eight categories that are listed, each category includes a top-level link, and under this link are several of the most frequently performed tasks for the category. Clicking a category link provides a list of utilities in that category. Each utility listed within a category includes a link to open the utility, and under this link are several of the most frequently performed tasks for the utility.

As with Windows XP and Windows Vista, you can change from the default Category view to Classic view (Large Icon view or Small Icon view). Icon view is an alternative view that provides the look and functionality of Control Panel in Windows 2000 and earlier versions of Windows, as shown in Figure 3.3.

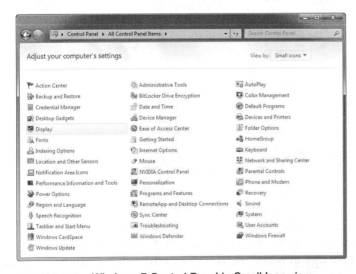

FIGURE 3.3   Windows 7 Control Panel in Small Icon view.

Viewing Basic Information

You can view a summary of important information about your computer by opening System in Control Panel by clicking one of the following:

- ▶ If you are in Category view, click **System and Security** and click **View amount of RAM and processor speed**.

- ▶ If you are in Classic view, double-click the **System** applet.

- ▶ Right-click **Computer** and select **Properties**.

At the top of the screen, you see the Windows edition you have and the system type (32-bit or 64-bit) in the middle of the screen. Toward the bottom of the screen, you see the computer name and domain (if any), the Product ID, and if Windows is activated.

As Figure 3.4 shows, in the System section you find the Windows Experience Index (WEI) base score, which is a number that describes the overall capability of your computer. Your computer's processor type, speed, and quantity (if your computer uses multiple processors) are listed. For example, if your computer has two processors, you see "(2 processors)" displayed. Also displayed is how much random access memory (RAM) is installed and, in some cases, how much of the memory is usable by Windows.

> **ExamAlert**
>
> To see the Windows 7 edition and version, open the System Properties.

FIGURE 3.4 **Computer properties.**

Changing Computer Name and Domain/Workgroup

Every computer should have a unique computer name assigned a network. To change the computer name, you open System in the Control Panel and click the **Change settings** option in the Computer name, domain, and workgroup settings section, which opens the System Properties dialog box, as shown in Figure 3.5. You then click the **Change** button and type in the computer name in the Computer name textbox.

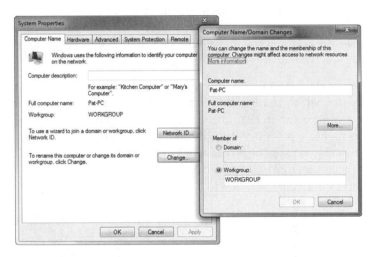

FIGURE 3.5   Changing computer name.

If you need to add a computer to a domain, you then select the Domain option, and specify the name of the domain in the Domain text box. When you click **OK**, you are asked for credentials for an administrative account for the domain. After you enter the credentials (username and password), it shows you a welcome dialog box. When you click **OK** to close the welcome dialog box and when you close the System Properties dialog box, you are prompted to reboot the computer.

To remove a computer from a domain, join an existing workgroup, or create a new workgroup, you select the workgroup option and type in the name of the workgroup. You then click **OK**. If you are removing yourself from the domain, you are asked for administrative credentials.

Windows Features and Programs

Some programs and features included with Windows, such as Internet Information Services (IIS), must be turned on before you can use them. Other features might be on by default and you might want to turn them off if they are not going to be used. To turn on features, do the following:

1. Click **Programs** in the Control Panel.

2. Click **Turn Windows features on or off**.

3. In the screen shown in Figure 3.6, turn a feature on by selecting the checkbox next to the feature. To turn off a Windows feature, clear the checkbox.

4. Click **OK**.

FIGURE 3.6   **Turning Windows features on or off.**

You can uninstall a program from your computer if you no longer use it or if you want to free up space on your hard disk. You can use Programs and Features to uninstall programs or to change a program's configuration by adding or removing certain options.

To uninstall a program or change a program, perform the following:

1. Open the Control Panel.

2. If you are in Category view, click **Programs** and click **Programs and Features**. If you are in Icon view, double-click **Programs and Features**.

3. In the window shown in Figure 3.7, select a program and then click **Uninstall**. Some programs include the option to repair the program in addition to uninstalling it, but many simply offer the option to uninstall. To change the program, click **Change** or **Repair**. If you are prompted for an administrator password or confirmation, type the password or provide confirmation.

If the program you want to uninstall isn't listed, it might not have been written for Windows 7. You should check the documentation for the software.

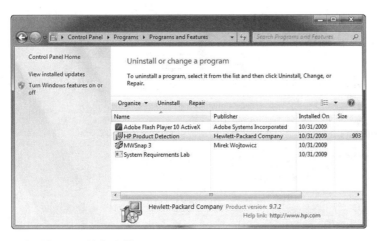

FIGURE 3.7   **Uninstalling a program.**

A default program is used to make a program the default for all file types and protocols it can open. For example, if you have more than one web browser installed on your computer, you can choose one of them to be the default program by using Set Default Programs. Another handy use is configuring a player (Windows Media Player or some other third-party player such as Real Player) to open all audio, music, and movie files.

If a program does not show up in the list or you want more control over which program opens up which files, you can make the program a default by using Set Association, also known as file association. For example, when you install Microsoft Word, Windows is configured so that anytime you double-click a file with a *.doc* or *.docx* filename extension, Microsoft Word automatically opens it.

To change the Set Association, do the following:

1. If you are in Category view, click **Programs** and click **Make a file type always open in a specific program**. If you are in Icon view, double-click **Default Programs** and click **Associate a file type or protocol with a program**. Figure 3.8 shows the resulting window.

2. Click the file type or protocol for which you want the program to act as the default.

3. Click **Change program**.

4. Click the program that you want to use as the default for the file type you selected, or click the arrow next to **Other programs** to show additional programs.

5. Click **OK**.

FIGURE 3.8   Changing the Set Association for a filename extension.

You can also right-click the file and select **Open With**. If the program you want to use to open the program does not appear in the Recommended Programs, you use the Browse button to browse to the program you do want to use. To change the filename association, be sure that the **Always use the selected programs to open this kind of file** checkbox is selected.

ExamAlert

To configure which programs open up a filename as specified by their filename extension, you use either Set Default Programs or Set Association.

Configuring Accessibility

Windows 7 includes accessibility technology, which enables computer users to adjust their computers to make them easier to see, hear, and interact with. The accessibility settings in Windows are particularly helpful to people with visual difficulties, hearing loss, pain in their hands or arms, or reasoning and cognitive issues.

Windows offers several programs and settings that can make the computer easier and more comfortable to use. You can add other assistive technology products to your computer if you need additional accessibility features.

The Ease of Access Center is a central location that you can use to set up the accessibility settings and programs available in Windows. As Figure 3.9 shows, in the Ease of Access Center, you find quick access for setting up the accessibility settings and programs included in Windows. You also find a link to a questionnaire that Windows can use to help suggest settings that you might find useful.

To open the Ease of Access Center, click the **Start** button, click **Control Panel**, click **Ease of Access**, and then click **Ease of Access Center**. Another way to access the Ease of Access Center is to press **Windows key + U**. You can open a mini Ease of Access Center by clicking the **Accessibility** icon, located on the bottom-left corner on the logon page.

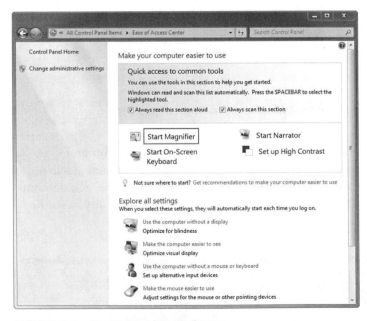

FIGURE 3.9   **The Ease of Access Center.**

The settings that can be adjusted are as follows:

▶ **Use the computer without a display**: Windows comes with a basic screen reader called Narrator that reads aloud text that appears on the screen. Windows also has settings for providing audio descriptions for videos and controlling how dialog boxes appear. For more information, search for **Use the computer without a display** using Windows Help and Support. Additionally, many other programs and hardware are compatible with Windows and available to help individuals who are blind, including screen readers, Braille output devices, and many other useful products.

▶ **Make the computer easier to see**: Several settings are available to help make the information on the screen easier to understand. For example, the screen can be magnified, screen colors can be adjusted to make the screen easier to see and read, and unnecessary animations and background images can be removed.

▶ **Use the computer without a mouse or keyboard**: Windows includes an on-screen keyboard that you can use to type. You can also use Speech Recognition to control your computer with voice commands as well as dictate text into programs.

▶ **Make the mouse pointer easier to use**: You can change the size and color of the mouse pointer, as well as use the keyboard to control the mouse.

▶ **Make the keyboard easier to use**: You can adjust the way Windows responds to mouse or keyboard input so that key combinations are easier to press, typing is easier, or inadvertent key presses are ignored.

▶ **Use text and visual alternatives for sounds**: Windows can replace two types of audio information with visual equivalents. You can replace system sounds with visual alerts and you can display text captions for spoken dialog in multimedia programs.

▶ **Make it easier to focus on reading and typing tasks**: There are a number of settings that can help make it easier to focus on reading and typing. You can have Narrator read information on the screen, adjust how the keyboard responds to certain keystrokes, and control whether certain visual elements are displayed.

> **Note**
>
> To find more information about assistive technology products, see the "Information for Assistive Technology Manufacturers" website at www.microsoft.com/enable/at/atvinfo.aspx.

Parental Controls

As a concerned parent, you want to protect your children. The Internet opens a new world of information gathering, communication, commerce, productivity, and entertainment; however, it also presents new risks for information disclosure, and easy access to inappropriate content in websites, messages, file downloads, games, and audio/video multimedia.

> **ExamAlert**
>
> Remember that Parental Controls are not available if the computer is part of a domain. They also apply only to standard user accounts.

Parental Controls are not available if your computer is connected to a domain. In addition, Parental Controls are only applied to standard user accounts, not administrative accounts. Of course, you need an Administrator user account to enable and configure Parental Controls.

To turn on Parental Controls for a standard user account:

1. Open Parental Controls by clicking the **Start** button, clicking **Control Panel**, and then, under User Accounts, clicking **Set up Parental Controls**. If you are prompted for an administrator password or confirmation, type the password or provide confirmation.

2. Click the standard user account for which you want to set Parental Controls.

3. Under Parental Controls, click **On**.

4. After you've turned on Parental Controls for your child's standard user account, you can adjust the individual settings that you want to control, as shown in Figure 3.10.

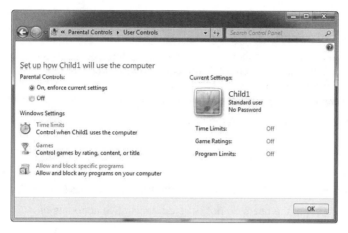

FIGURE 3.10 **Parental Controls.**

You can control the following areas:

▶ **Web restrictions**: You can restrict the websites that children can visit, make sure children only visit age-appropriate websites, indicate whether you want to allow file downloads, and set up which content you want the content filters to block and allow. You can also block or allow specific websites.

▶ **Time limits**: You can set time limits to control when children are allowed to log on to the computer. Time limits prevent children from logging on during the specified hours and, if they are already logged on, they are automatically logged off. You can set different logon hours for every day of the week.

▶ **Games**: You can control access to games, choose an age rating level, choose the types of content you want to block, and decide whether you want to allow or block unrated or specific games.

▶ **Allow or block specific programs**: You can prevent children from running programs that you don't want them to run.

After you've set up Parental Controls, you can set up activity reports to keep a record of your child's computer activity.

Cram Quiz

1. You work as a desktop support technician at Acme.com. The new systems are using Windows 7 Home Basic edition. At Acme.com, you must ensure that users do not use instant messaging applications. What can you do?

   - ○ **A.** Upgrade the systems to Windows 7 Professional. Then configure Parental Controls to disable the use of instant messaging applications.

   - ○ **B.** Configure Parental Controls to only run allowed programs on each system.

   - ○ **C.** Configure Parental Controls to enable the Windows 7 Web Filter.

   - ○ **D.** Make sure that the users do not have administrative accounts on these local systems.

2. What can you use to determine which edition of Windows 7 you have?

   - ○ **A.** Task Manager
   - ○ **B.** Start Menu
   - ○ **C.** Notification Area
   - ○ **D.** System Properties
   - ○ **E.** Welcome Center

3. You want to add Internet Information Services (IIS) to your Windows 7 installation. What should you do?

   - ○ **A.** Use Default Program in the Control Panel
   - ○ **B.** Use Set Association in the Control Panel
   - ○ **C.** Use Windows Features in the Control Panel
   - ○ **D.** Use Web Configuration in the Control Panel

Cram Quiz Answers

1. **B** is correct. You can use the Parental Controls to run only allowed programs that you specify. Answer A is incorrect because Windows 7 Home Basic edition already has Parental Control. Answer C is incorrect because Web filter does not stop messenger. Answer D is incorrect because you should not use administrative accounts to do daily tasks.

2. **D** is correct. To see the version and edition of Windows 7 that you are using, open the System Properties. The quickest way to get there is click the Start button, right-click Computer and select Properties. Answer E is incorrect because although the Welcome Center displayed the Windows Vista edition, this information is not displayed in the Welcome Center in Windows 7. Answers B, C, and D are incorrect because none of them show what version you are using.

3. **C** is correct. To add or remove Windows components, you use the Windows Features in the Control Panel. Answer A is incorrect because the Default Program makes a program the default for all file types and protocols it can open. Answer B is incorrect because Set Association is used to make a file or program always open a specific program. Answer D is incorrect because there is no Web Configuration in the Control Panel.

Device Drivers

▶ **Configure devices.**

▶ **Configure system recovery options**

Cram**Saver**

1. What are the advantages of using signed drivers? (Choose all that apply.)

   ○ **A.** You can verify where the driver came from.

   ○ **B.** You can verify that the driver has not been tampered with.

   ○ **C.** You can limit who has access to the driver.

   ○ **D.** You can verify the driver has been thoroughly tested.

2. In Device Manager, how do you know if a device is disabled?

   ○ **A.** There is a red X.

   ○ **B.** There is an exclamation point.

   ○ **C.** There is a down arrow.

   ○ **D.** It is flashing.

3. You installed a new driver you got from the Internet for your sound card. Now the sound card does not work. What do you do to correct this problem?

   ○ **A.** Enter Safe mode and remove the driver

   ○ **B.** Rollback the driver

   ○ **C.** Disable the device

   ○ **D.** Uninstall the driver

Answers

1. **A, B**, and **D** are correct. It is always recommended that you use signed drivers because you can verify where the driver came from, that the driver has not been tampered with, and that the driver has been thoroughly tested to be reliable. Answer C is incorrect because you cannot control who can access a specific driver.

2. **C** is correct. A down black arrow indicates a disabled device. A disabled device is a device that is physically present in the computer and is consuming resources, but does not have a driver loaded. Answer A is incorrect because a red X indicates a disabled device in Windows XP. Answer B is incorrect because problems with drivers are indicated by an exclamation point. Answer D is incorrect because if the device is having problems in the device manager, the device icon does not flash.

> **3.** **B** is correct. When a new device driver does not function properly, you should roll it back so you can revert to the previous driver. Answers A and D are incorrect because uninstalling the driver means you still need to load the correct one. Answer C is incorrect because disabling the device causes the device not to function at all.

Device drivers are programs that control a device. They each act like a translator between the device and programs that use the device. Each device has its own set of specialized commands that only its driver knows. Most programs access devices by using generic commands, and the driver accepts the generic commands from the program and translates them into specialized commands for the device.

Device drivers are needed for a device to work. These drivers can be retrieved from the following sources:

- ▶ Bundled with Windows 7

- ▶ Supplied with a device

- ▶ Updated with Windows Update

- ▶ Updated from the manufacturer's Internet site

Sometimes, you might have to download an updated driver from Microsoft or the manufacturer's website to fix problems with device functionality caused by poorly written drivers or by changing technology.

The driver store is an extensive library of device drivers. On 32-bit computers, it is located in the \Window\System32\DriverStore folder. On a 64-bit computer, the 32-bit drivers are located in the \Windows\SysWOW64\ DriverStore folder and the 64-bit drivers store is in the \Windows\ System32\DriverStore folder. In the DriverStore folder, you find subfolders with located driver information, such as en-US for U.S. English, have thousands of different drivers. When you add a hardware device, Windows can check the Driver Store for the correct driver.

> **Note**
>
> Although the 64-bit version of Windows has a Windows\SysWOW64\DriverStore to store 32-bit drivers, you cannot use 32-bit drivers on a 64-bit version of Windows. Instead, you find Multilingual User Interface files that are used to display menus and dialog boxes in the designed language folders within the 32-bit DriverStore.

Plug and Play Devices

Plug and play refers to the capability of a computer system to automatically configure expansion boards and other devices. You should be able to plug in a device and play with it, without worrying about setting DIP switches, jumpers, and other configuration elements. If you connect USB, IEEE 1394, and SCSI devices to a Windows 7 system, Windows 7 automatically detects these devices. When you connect a PCI or AGP plug-and-play expansion card and turn on the computer, Windows detects these devices. If Windows 7 does not have a driver available on the device after detection, Windows 7 prompts you to provide a media or path to the driver.

Signed Drivers

To ensure reliable drivers, Microsoft implemented signed drivers starting with Windows 2000. A signed driver is a device driver that includes a digital signature, which is an electronic security mark that can indicate the publisher of the software and information that can show if a driver has been altered. When it is signed by Microsoft, the driver has been thoroughly tested to make sure that the driver will not cause problems with the system's reliability and not cause a security problem.

By default, if a driver is not signed, is signed by a publisher that cannot be properly identified, or has been altered since its release, Windows 7 notifies you. Of course, you should only install drivers that are properly signed.

> **ExamAlert**
>
> A driver that lacks a valid digital signature, or that was altered after it was signed, can't be installed on x64-based versions of Windows Vista or 7.

Device drivers that are included on the Windows 7 installation DVD or downloaded from Microsoft's update website include a Microsoft digital signature (making it a signed driver). If you have problems installing a driver or a device is not working properly, you should check with Microsoft's update website and visit the device manufacturer's support website to obtain an up-to-date digitally signed driver for your device.

You can use the File Signature Verification program (Sigverif.exe) to check if unsigned device drivers are in the system area of a computer. You can obtain a basic list of signed and unsigned device drivers from a command prompt by running the **driverquery** command with the **/si** switch.

ExamAlert

To verify that your drivers are properly signed, you should use the File Signature Verification program (Sigverif.exe).

Devices and Printers Folder

When you want to see all the devices connected to your computer, use one of them, or troubleshoot one that isn't working properly, you can open the Devices and Printers folder found within the Control Panel.

The Devices and Printers folder gives you a quick view of devices connected to your computer, as Figure 3.11 shows.

FIGURE 3.11   **Devices and Printers folder.**

These devices are typically external devices that you can connect to or disconnect from your computer through a port or network connection. Your computer is also displayed. The items displayed include

▶ Portable devices you carry with you and occasionally connect to your computer, such as mobile phones, portable music players, and digital cameras

▶ All devices you plug into a USB port on your computer, including external USB hard drives, flash drives, webcams, keyboards, and mice

▶ All printers connected to your computer, which include printers connected by USB cable, the network, or wirelessly

▶ Wireless devices connected to your computer, including Bluetooth devices and Wireless USB devices

▶ Your computer

▶ Compatible network devices connected to your computer, such as network-enabled scanners, media extenders, or Network Attached Storage devices (NAS devices)

The Devices and Printers folder does not display devices that are installed inside your computer case, such as internal hard drives, disc drives, sound cards, video cards (graphics cards), memory (RAM), processors, and other internal computer components. It does not display speakers connected to your computer with conventional speaker wires but might display USB and wireless speakers. The Devices and Printers folder also does not display legacy devices such as keyboards and mice connected through a PS/2 or serial port.

The Devices and Printers folder enables you to perform many tasks, which vary depending on the device. Here are the main tasks you can do:

▶ Add a new wireless or network device or printer to your computer

▶ View all the external devices and printers connected to your computer

▶ Check to see if a specific device is working properly

▶ View information about your devices, such as make, model, and manufacturer, including detailed information about the sync capabilities of a mobile phone or other mobile device

When you right-click a device icon in the Devices and Printers folder, you can select from a list of tasks that vary depending on the capabilities of the device. For example, you might be able to see what's printing on a network printer, view files stored on a USB flash drive, or open a program from the device manufacturer. For mobile devices that support the new Device Stage feature in Windows, you can also open advanced, device-specific features in Windows from the right-click menu, such as the ability to sync with a mobile phone or change ringtones.

If you have problems with devices, you can right-click a device or computer with the yellow warning icon and click **Troubleshooter** so that Windows can detect the problem. You would then follow the instructions on the screen.

Device Manager

To find devices that are connected to your computer but aren't listed in the Devices and Printers folder, look in Device Manager. Device Manager lists all of the hardware installed inside your computer as well as devices connected externally. Device Manager is primarily for advanced computer users. When a device is added to the system, the device list in Device Manager is re-created.

To access the Device Manager, you must be logged on to the system as an administrator. To open Device Manager, click the **Start** button, click **Control Panel**, click **System and Security**, and then click **Device Manager** in the System section. Figure 3.12 shows the resulting window. If you are prompted for an administrator password or confirmation, type the password or provide confirmation.

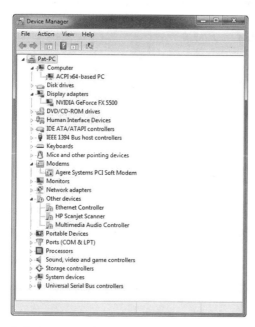

FIGURE 3.12   **Device Manager.**

If you locate and double-click a device, you can view the details of the driver in the General tab including the status of the device. If you select the Driver tab, as shown in Figure 3.13, you are able to do the following:

- **Driver File Details**: Shows the driver file and its location, the provider of the driver, the version of the file, and the digital signer of the file.

- **Uninstall a device**: The Device Manager tool can be used to uninstall the device driver and remove the driver software from the computer.

- **Enable or disable devices**: Instead of uninstalling the driver installer, you can use the Device Manager to disable the device. The hardware configuration is not changed.

- **Update device drivers**: If you have an updated driver for a device, you can use the Device Manager tool to apply the updated driver.

- **Roll back drivers**: If you experience system problems after you update a driver, you can roll back to the previous driver by using driver rollback. This feature enables you to reinstall the last device driver that was functioning before the installation of the current device driver. If there's no previous version of the driver installed for the selected device, the Roll Back Driver button is unavailable.

FIGURE 3.13   **Device properties.**

ExamAlert

If you load a driver and the device fails, it is recommended that you roll back the driver, assuming Windows is functioning well enough for you to access the properties of the device.

A down black arrow indicates a disabled device. A disabled device is a device that is physically present in the computer and is consuming resources but does not have a driver loaded. In Device Manager, a black exclamation point (!) on a yellow field indicates the device is in a problem state. You also need to look to see if any devices are listed under Unknown Device or have a generic name, such as Ethernet Adapter or PCI Simple Communications Controller, which indicates that the proper driver is not loaded.

ExamAlert

Be sure you know how to identify potential problems when using Device Manager, including devices with problems, disabled devices, and unknown devices.

Adding a Device

Today, most modern devices are plug-and-play devices. Therefore, when you add or connect a new device, Windows 7 automatically recognizes the device and loads the appropriate driver. When a driver cannot be found, Windows might ask if you want to connect to the Internet in an attempt to find a driver or to specify the location of a driver such as on a CD. You can also open the **Control Panel**, click **Hardware and Sound**, and select **Add a device** under the Devices and Printers section. Windows then searches for any devices that are not currently recognized by Windows.

For more information about device management and installation for Windows 7, visit the following website:

http://technet.microsoft.com/en-us/library/dd919230(WS.10).aspx

Configuring Keyboard and Mouse

You can configure how the keyboard and mouse respond when using them. For example, if you open the Keyboard properties, you can configure how characters are repeated when you press a key and the rate that the cursor blinks. The mouse Properties (see Figure 3.14) enables you to switch buttons, determine the speed of a double-click, determine what kind of pointer you want to use, and how fast the pointer moves when you move the mouse. In addition, depending on your type of mouse or pointing device, you might have additional options to configure, such as how many lines of a document or web page scroll when you move one notch on the wheel of the mouse or other pointing device.

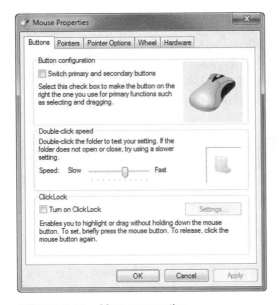

FIGURE 3.14   **Mouse properties.**

> **Note**
>
> If you have a touch pad or track point, install the drivers that come with the touch pad. This gives you more control over your touch pad and automatically disables the track pad while you are typing so that you don't accidently tap the touch pad, causing the cursor to jump to a different spot on the screen. When you stop typing, the track pad reactivates.

Managing Sound

Today, most computers include a sound card, either one that is built into the motherboard or one that is added as an expansion card. You can use Sound in the Control Panel to configure the speakers, microphones, and sound theme.

As Figure 3.15 shows, a sound theme is a set of sounds applied to events in Windows and programs. For example, you can have one sound when you first log on to Windows and another sound when you shut down Windows. You can also modify the beep when an error occurs.

FIGURE 3.15   **Sound properties.**

When playing sound, there are several places that you might need to check when you want to control the volume. First, always check your speaker buttons and knobs. If you are using a laptop computer, you should look for keys on the keyboard to control volume. Second, check the program that you are using. For example, the Windows Media Player has a slider to control volume. Lastly, you should double-click the speaker icon in the notification area to open a slider to modify the volume. You can also click Mixer to give you more volume control such as speaker volume, application volume, and Windows Media Player volume, as shown in Figure 3.16. Of course, if you are getting no sound, make sure that the cables between the speakers (if they are external speakers) and sound card are plugged in properly.

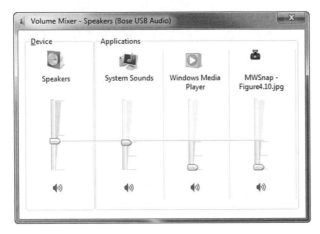

FIGURE 3.16   **Volume Mixer.**

Cram Quiz

1. Different from Windows XP and Windows Vista, where do you manage your plug-in devices, including printers?

   ○ **A.** Device Manager

   ○ **B.** Administrative Tools

   ○ **C.** Devices and Printers Folder

   ○ **D.** Computer Management Console

2. Which driver cannot be installed on a 64-bit version of Windows 7? (Choose two answers.)

   ○ **A.** An unsigned device driver

   ○ **B.** A 32-bit driver

   ○ **C.** AGP drivers

   ○ **D.** Drivers that are not included on the Windows 7 Installation DVD

3. How do you have Windows 7 scan for new devices?

   ○ **A.** Run the `sigverif.exe` command

   ○ **B.** Run the `scandisk.exe` command

   ○ **C.** Click Hardware and Sound in the Control Panel and select Add a device under the Devices and Printers section

   ○ **D.** Run the `scanhw.exe` command

Cram Quiz Answers

1. **C** is correct. The Devices and Printers folder gives you a quick view of devices connected to your computer. These devices are typically external devices that you can connect or disconnect from your computer through a port or network connection. Answer A is incorrect because the Device Manager is a more advanced tool to manage all devices. The Devices and Printers folder enables you to control common settings for the plug-in devices. Answers B and D are incorrect because using the Computer Management Console, which is included in the Administrative Tools, enables you to access the Device Manager.

2. **A** and **B** are correct. A driver that lacks a valid digital signature, or that was altered after it was signed, cannot be installed on x64-based version of Windows Vista or 7. You also cannot load 32-bit drivers on a 64-bit system. Answer C is incorrect because AGP drivers can be loaded on a 64-bit version of Windows assuming they have been signed and are 64-bit drivers. Answer D is incorrect because you can also get device drivers from Microsoft and third-party websites. They just need to be signed by Microsoft.

3. **C** is correct. Often when you connect a device, it is automatically recognized and Windows 7 automatically tries to load the proper driver. If it doesn't, you need to select **Add a device** under the Devices and Printers section in the Control Panel so that Windows scans for hardware changes. Answer A is incorrect because `sigverif.exe` is used to verify the digital certificates for device drivers. Answer B is incorrect because `scandisk.exe` is the command to scan the disk in older versions of Windows. Answer D is incorrect because there is no `scanhw.exe` in Windows 7.

Display Settings

▶ **Configure devices**

Cram**Saver**

1. If you don't see transparent windows on your Windows 7 desktop, what do you need to check?

   ○ **A.** Make sure Windows Aero is enabled

   ○ **B.** Make sure you have an Aero-compatible Super-VGA monitor

   ○ **C.** Make sure you are not using Windows 7 Home Premium, Enterprise, or Ultimate

   ○ **D.** Make sure you are not running with a Windows XP driver

2. You want to use two monitors so that you can double your workspace. What do you need to do?

   ○ **A.** Double the number of colors to display

   ○ **B.** Choose Screen Resolution and click Extend these displays

   ○ **C.** Choose Screen Resolution and click Copy this display

   ○ **D.** Choose Screen Resolution and click Duplicate these displays

3. What do you call a combination of pictures, colors, and sounds that specify the look and feel of your Windows graphical user interface?

   ○ **A.** A color display

   ○ **B.** Display Properties

   ○ **C.** Aero Properties

   ○ **D.** A theme

Answers

1. **A** is correct. You need to make sure that Windows Aero is enabled. That means you have a display adapter that supports Windows Aero and you have to have a color depth of 32 bits per pixel, a refresh rate of 10 hertz or greater, select a Windows Aero theme, and have the Windows frame transparency on. Answer B is incorrect because there is no such thing as an Aero-compatible Super-VGA monitor. The compatibility is in the display adapter. Answer C is incorrect because Windows 7 Professional, Enterprise, Home Premium, and Ultimate support Windows Aero. Answer D is incorrect because you would not be able to load a Windows XP driver.

2. **B** is correct. When you connect another monitor to a desktop PC, the display is set to "extended" by default, and you should be able to drag a window from one screen to the other without changing any settings. Answer A is incorrect because the number of colors do not affect how many monitors you can use and how you can use them. Answer C is incorrect because there is no Copy this display option. Answer D is incorrect because you want to extend these displays, not duplicate these displays.

3. **D** is correct. A theme is a collection of visual elements and sounds for your computer desktop. A theme determines the look of the various visual elements of your desktop, such as windows, icons, fonts, and colors, and it can include sounds. Answer A is incorrect because there is no Color display in Windows 7. Answer B is incorrect because the display properties do not allow you to change your Windows GUI settings. Answer C is incorrect because there is no Aero Properties screen in Windows 7.

As a desktop technician, you are sometimes tasked with adjusting the look and feel of Windows, such as the background, the screen saver, and the display settings. You can find these settings by clicking the **Start** button, clicking **Control Panel**, clicking **Appearance and Personalization**, and clicking **Personalization** for the resulting screen in Figure 3.17. You can also right-click the desktop and select Personalize.

FIGURE 3.17 **Personalizing appearance.**

Desktop Themes

A theme is a combination of pictures, colors, and sounds on your computer. It includes a desktop background, a screen saver, a window border color, and a sound scheme. Some themes might also include desktop icons and mouse pointers.

A theme determines the look of the various visual elements of your desktop, such as windows, icons, fonts, and colors, and it can include sounds. You can choose an Aero theme to personalize your computer, use the Windows 7 Basic theme if your computer is performing slowly, or a High Contrast theme to make the items on your screen easier to see.

To change the desktop theme in Windows 7:

1. Open Theme Settings by clicking the **Start** button, clicking **Control Panel**, clicking **Appearance and Personalization**, clicking **Personalization**, and then clicking **Change the Theme**.

2. In the Theme list, click an Aero Theme if you want to use Windows Aero. Other themes available are basic and high contrast themes.

At the bottom of the screen, you can also change the Desktop Background, the Windows color, sounds, and screen saver.

Windows Aero features windows that are truly translucent. This glass effect enables you to focus on the content of a window while providing better context for the surrounding elements on your desktop. For added personalization and to get exactly the look and feel you want, you can change the

▶ Color of your windows

▶ Saturation of the screen colors

▶ Level of transparency

To turn on window frame transparency, the color scheme must first be set to a Windows Aero theme. Then you must do the following:

1. Open Personalization by clicking the **Start** button, clicking **Control Panel**, clicking **Appearance and Personalization**, and then clicking **Personalization**.

2. Click **Window Color and Appearance**.

3. Select the **Enable transparency** checkbox.

You can also open Window Color and Appearance to change colors of individual components.

To configure Window color and appearance, do the following:

1. Click the **Start** button, click **Control Panel**, click **Appearance and Personalization**, click **Personalization**, and then click **Window Color and Appearance**.

2. You can then change the color of windows, Start menu, and taskbar, and you can enable or disable transparency, as demonstrated in Figure 3.18.

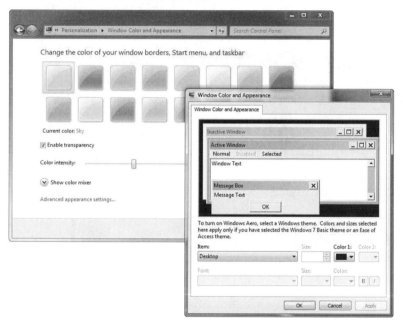

FIGURE 3.18   Configuring the Window Color and Appearance.

Adjusting the Screen Settings

Screen resolution refers to the clarity of the text and images on your screen. At higher resolutions, items appear sharper because more pixels are used to form the images on the screen. Typically when you use a higher resolution, images appear smaller, so more items fit on the screen. At lower resolutions, fewer items fit on the screen, but they are larger and easier to see. At very low resolutions, however, images might have jagged edges.

To change the resolution, click **Display Settings** under **Personalization**.

1. If you are in Category view of Control Panel, click **Appearance and Personalization** and then click **Adjust screen resolution**. If you are in Icon view, you can double-click **Display** and select **Adjust resolution**. You can also right-click the desktop and choose **Screen resolution**.

2. In the resulting window shown in Figure 3.19, under Resolution, select the resolution and click **Apply** or **OK**.

> **Note**
>
> When you change the screen resolution, it affects all users who log on to the computer.

FIGURE 3.19   **Changing resolution.**

If you need to change the color depth (the number of bits that determine the number of possible colors on the screen) or the screen resolution (the frequency at which the screen is redrawn), under the Screen Resolution dialog box, click **Advanced settings** and select the **Monitor** tab, as shown in Figure 3.20. Then select the appropriate screen refresh rate or colors. For the most possible colors, select **True Color (32 bit)** and click **Apply** or **OK**.

> ### Note
>
> Changes to the refresh rate or number of colors affect all users who log on to the computer.

FIGURE 3.20   **Changing colors.**

If you sometimes have trouble seeing items on your screen, you can adjust the settings to make text and images on the screen appear larger, improve the contrast between items on the screen, and hear on-screen text read aloud. You can adjust these settings on the Make the computer easier to see page in the Ease of Access Center:

1. Open the **Make the computer easier to see page** by clicking the **Start** button, clicking **Control Panel**, clicking **Ease of Access**, clicking **Ease of Access Center**, and then clicking **Make the computer easier to see**.

2. Select the options that you want to use:

   ▶ **Choose a High Contrast color scheme**: This option enables you to set a high-contrast color scheme that heightens the color contrast of some text and images on your computer screen, making those items more distinct and easier to identify.

   ▶ **Turn on Narrator**: This option sets Narrator to run when you log on to your computer. Narrator reads aloud on-screen text and describes some events (such as error messages appearing) that happen while you're using the computer.

▶ **Turn on Audio Description**: This option sets Audio Descriptions to run when you log on to your computer. Audio Descriptions describe what's happening in videos.

▶ **Turn on Magnifier**: This option sets Magnifier to run when you log on to your computer. Magnifier enlarges the part of the screen where the mouse is pointing and can be especially useful for viewing objects that are difficult to see.

▶ **Adjust the color and transparency of the window borders**: This option enables you to change the appearance of window borders to make them easier to see.

▶ **Make the focus rectangle thicker**: This option makes the rectangle around the currently selected item in dialog boxes thicker, which makes it easier to see.

▶ **Set the thickness of the blinking cursor**: This option enables you to make the blinking cursor in dialog boxes and programs thicker and easier to see.

▶ **Turn off all unnecessary animations**: This option turns off animation effects, such as fading effects, when windows and other elements are closed.

▶ **Remove background images**: This option turns off all unimportant, overlapped content and background images to help make the screen easier to see.

Multiple Monitors

You can easily extend your Windows desktop across more than one monitor by plugging two or more monitors into a desktop computer or one or more monitors into a laptop. Most laptops allow you to connect one external monitor. A desktop that spans two or more monitors significantly increases your desktop area so that you can drag windows, program icons, and other items to any location on the extended desktop. To move a window from one display to another, click the title bar of the window and then drag the window to a new location.

By default, when you connect an external monitor to a laptop, the same image (mirror image) of your desktop appears on the external monitor. Before you can drag a window from your laptop screen to the external screen, you must extend your display by changing your display settings. By contrast, when you connect another monitor to a desktop PC, the display is set to "extended" by default, and you should be able to drag a window from one screen to the other without changing any settings.

To change your display settings to extended:

1. Right-click the desktop and choose **Screen Resolution**.

2. Click the drop-down list next to Multiple displays, click **Extend these displays**, and then click **OK**.

Your other options is to duplicate these displays, show desktop only on 1, and show desktop only on 2.

Windows Aero

Windows Aero is an enhanced visual experience for Windows Vista and Windows 7. Different from older versions of Windows, Windows Aero supports transparent glass and other graphical enhancements that lead to a cosmetic pleasing display. In addition, you will notice smoother window control when opening, closing, moving, and resizing windows with increased stability.

Remember that the following editions of Windows 7 support Aero:

▶ Windows 7 Professional

▶ Windows 7 Enterprise

▶ Windows 7 Home Premium

▶ Windows 7 Ultimate

In addition to meeting the Windows edition prerequisite, the display adapter must support the following:

▶ DirectX 9, with Pixel Shader 2.0

▶ Windows 7 Display Driver Model (WDDM)

Finally, the system must have the following minimum graphics memory:

▶ **Graphics Memory**: Support single monitor resolution

▶ **64 MB**: Up to 1,310,720 pixels (equivalent to 1280×1024)

▶ **128 MB**: Up to 2,304,000 pixels (equivalent to 1920×1200)

▶ **256 MB**: Greater than 2,304,000 pixels

You must also configure the display system to the following:

▶ A color depth of 32 bits per pixel (bpp)

▶ A refresh rate that is higher than 10 hertz

▶ The theme is set to a Windows Aero theme

▶ Window frame transparency is on

ExamAlert

Be sure to know which editions of Windows 7 include Windows Aero and the requirements for Windows 7 to enable Windows Aero. For Windows Aero to be automatically enabled in Windows 7, you must have a Windows Experience Index of 3.0 or higher.

If your system has a built-in graphics adapter based on the Unified Memory Architecture (UMA), you need 1 GB of dual-channel configured system memory and your system must have 512 MB of RAM available for general system activities after graphics processing.

If you receive a message that some visual elements, such as window frame transparency, have been turned off, if you receive a message that the color scheme has been changed to Windows Basic or Flip 3D does not function, one of the following might have happened:

▶ A program that you're running is incompatible with the Windows Aero color scheme. When you run a program that is incompatible with the Windows Aero color scheme, some visual elements are automatically turned off. When the program is no longer running, the visual elements that were turned off are turned on again automatically.

▶ Verify that your hardware configuration, screen resolution, theme, and color depths have not changed. Another cause could be because your computer does not have enough memory to run all of the programs that you have open and also run the Windows Aero color scheme.

To mitigate these issues, you should try closing some of the applications and retry the Flip 3D feature. If an application is incompatible with the Windows Aero color scheme, some of the visual elements are automatically disabled and then re-enabled after the incompatible application is closed.

Cram Quiz

1. Which of the following does not support Windows Aero?

    ○ **A.** Windows 7 Professional

    ○ **B.** Windows 7 Enterprise

    ○ **C.** Windows 7 Home Basic

    ○ **D.** Windows 7 Home Premium

2. What do you call the option that specifies how many colors you can display at one time?

    ○ **A.** Color width

    ○ **B.** Color length

    ○ **C.** Color depth

    ○ **D.** Color resolution

3. Which of the following is not a requirement for Windows Aero?

    ○ **A.** Display adapter that supports DirectX 9.

    ○ **B.** Display adapter that supports the Windows Display Driver Model (WDDM).

    ○ **C.** A color depth of 32 bits per pixel.

    ○ **D.** Window frame transparency is off.

Cram Quiz Answers

1. **C** is correct. Windows Aero is included with Windows 7 Professional, Enterprise, Home Premium, and Ultimate editions. It is not supported in Windows 7 Home Basic. Therefore, the other answers are incorrect.

2. **C** is correct. The number of colors that can be displayed on a monitor is known as color depth. Answers A, B, and D are incorrect because there is no such thing as color width, length, or resolution. However, the resolution specifies how many pixels make up the screen.

3. **D** is incorrect. Answers A, B, and C are incorrect because although you need to have a display adapter that supports DirectX 9 (Answer A), a display adapter that follows the WDDM (Answer B), and a color depth of 32 bits per pixel (Answer C), you also need to have the Windows frame transparency on. You also need to have a refresh rate of 10 hertz and you must be using a Windows Aero theme.

Advanced Windows Configuration

▶ **Configure devices**

▶ **Supplemental Objectives: Manage and configure Windows**

Cram**Saver**

1. Which program would you use to perform advanced configuration including managing your users and groups, disks, Event Viewer, and shared folders and services?

   ○ **A.** Server Management console

   ○ **B.** Computer Management console

   ○ **C.** Task Scheduler

   ○ **D.** Local Security Policy

2. What do you call a program, routine, or process that performs a specific system function to support other programs?

   ○ **A.** A task

   ○ **B.** A service

   ○ **C.** An applet

   ○ **D.** A local policy

Answers

1. **B** is correct. The Computer Management console enables you to manage local or remote computers by using a single, consolidated desktop tool. Using Computer Management, you can perform many tasks, such as monitoring system events, configuring hard disks, and managing system performance. Answer A is incorrect because the Server Management console is not available in Windows 7. Instead, it can be found on Windows Server 2008 computers. Answer C is incorrect because the Task Scheduler is used to schedule programs or other tasks to run automatically. Answer D is incorrect because the Local Security Policy enables you to view and edit group policy security settings.

2. **B** is correct. A service is a program, routine, or process that performs a specific system function to support other programs. To manage services, use the Services console located under Administrative Tools or the MMC with the Services snap-in. Answer A is incorrect because a task is a program or event that you can schedule with Task Manager. Answer C is incorrect because an applet is an icon found within the Control Panel. Answer D is incorrect because a local policy is used to configure the system settings, including how programs, network resources, and the operating system work for users.

Microsoft Management Console

Microsoft Management Console (MMC) hosts and displays administrative tools created by Microsoft and other software providers. These tools are called snap-ins, and they are used for managing the hardware, software, and network components of Windows. Several of the tools in the Administrative Tools folder in Control Panel, such as Computer Management, are MMC snap-ins. The following section discusses the commonly used Administrative Tools found in Windows.

Administrative Tools

Administrative Tools is a folder in Control Panel that contains tools for system administrators and advanced users. Many of the tools in this folder, such as Computer Management, are *Microsoft Management Console (MMC)* snap-ins that include their own help topics. To view specific help for an MMC tool, or to search for an MMC snap-in that you do not see in the following list, open the tool, click the **Help** menu, and then click **Help Topics**.

To access the Administrative Tools, open the Control Panel, open Administrative Tools by clicking **Start**, **Control Panel**, **System and Security** while in Category view, or double-click the Administrative Tools applet while in Icon view. You can also find it on the Start menu.

Some common administrative tools in this folder include the following:

- ▶ **Computer Management:** Manage local or remote computers by using a single, consolidated desktop tool. As shown in Figure 3.21, using Computer Management, you can perform many tasks, such as monitoring system events, configuring hard disks, and managing system performance.

- ▶ **Data Sources (ODBC)**: Use Open Database Connectivity (ODBC) to move data from one type of database (a data source) to another.

- ▶ **Event Viewer**: View information about significant events, such as a program starting or stopping or a security error, that are recorded in event logs.

- ▶ **iSCSI Initiator**: Configure advanced connections between storage devices on a network.

- ▶ **Local Security Policy**: View and edit Group Policy security settings.

- ▶ **Memory Diagnostics Tool**: Check your computer's memory to see whether it is functioning properly.

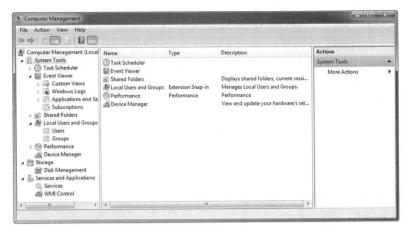

FIGURE 3.21   **Computer Management.**

▶ **Print Management**: Manage printers and print servers on a network and perform other administrative tasks.

▶ **Reliability and Performance Monitor**: View advanced system information about the central processing unit (CPU), memory, hard disk, and network performance.

▶ **Services**: Manage the different services that run in the background on your computer.

▶ **System Configuration**: Identify problems that might be preventing Windows from running correctly.

▶ **Task Scheduler**: Schedule programs or other tasks to run automatically.

▶ **Windows Firewall with Advanced Security**: Configure advanced firewall settings on both this computer and remote computers on your network.

> **Note**
>
> You can access the Computer Management console by right-clicking **Computer** and selecting **Manage**.

Services

A service is a program, routine, or process that performs a specific system function to support other programs. To manage the services, use the Services console located under Administrative Tools or the MMC with the Services snap-in. The Services console is included in the Server Management console and the Computer Management console. To start, stop, pause, or resume services, right-click the service and click the desired option. On the left of the service name is a description.

To configure a service, right-click the service and click the **Properties** option. As shown in Figure 3.22, on the General tab, under the Startup type pull-down option, set the following:

- ▶ **Automatic**: Specifies that the service should start automatically when the system starts.

- ▶ **Automatic (Delayed Start)**: Specifies that a service should be started approximately two minutes after the system has completed starting the operating system. It helps reduce the effect on the system's overall boot performance.

- ▶ **Manual**: Specifies that a user or a dependent service can start the service. Services with manual start-up do not start automatically when the system starts.

- ▶ **Disable**: Prevents the service from being started by the system, a user, or any dependent service.

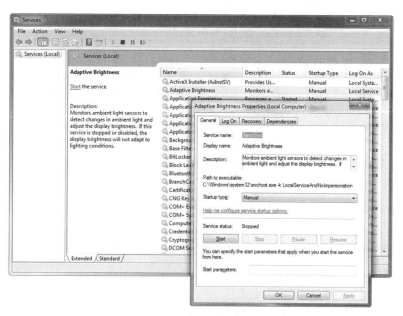

FIGURE 3.22   **The Services Console.**

Local and Group Policies

Group Policy Objects (GPOs) are collections of user and computer configuration settings that specify how programs, network resources, and the operating system work for users and computers in an organization. Settings include the following:

▶ **System settings**: Application settings, desktop appearance, and behavior of system services.

▶ **Security settings**: Local computer, domain, and network security settings.

▶ **Software installation settings**: Management of software installation, updates, and removal.

▶ **Scripts settings**: Scripts for when a computer starts or shuts down and when a user logs on and off.

▶ **Folder redirection settings**: Storage for users' folders on the network.

Group policies can be set locally, on the workstation, or can be set at different levels (site, domain, or organizational unit) within Active Directory. Microsoft's directory service is used for authentication and authorization. If you configure a group policy setting at the site, domain, or organization unit level and that setting contradicts a setting configured at the local policy, the group policy overrides the settings of the local policy.

You can open the Local Group Policy Editor by using the command line or by using the Microsoft Management Console (MMC). To open the Local Group Policy Editor from the command line click **Start**, type **gpedit.msc** in the Start Search box, and then press **Enter**.

To open the Local Group Policy Editor as an MMC snap-in:

1. Open MMC (click **Start**, click in the **Start Search** box, type **mmc**, and then press **Enter**).

2. On the File menu, click **Add/Remove Snap-in**.

3. In the Add or Remove Snap-ins dialog box, click **Group Policy Object Editor** and then click **Add**.

4. With Local Computer already selected, click the **Finish** button.

Most times, you just need to access the security settings that you find in the local policy. You can do this by opening the Local Security Policy from Administrative Tools.

The Registry

The registry is a central, secure database in which Windows stores all hardware configuration information, software configuration information, and system security policies. Components that use the registry include the Windows kernel, device drivers, setup programs, hardware profiles, and user profiles.

You shouldn't need to make manual changes to the registry because programs and applications typically make all the necessary changes automatically. An incorrect change to your computer's registry could render your computer inoperable. However, if a corrupt file appears in the registry, you might be required to make changes or to make a change that does not have a program to change. Typically if you are changing the registry, you are following instructions from a reliable source. The Registry Editor (Regedit.exe) is a tool used to manually view and change settings in the system registry, as shown in Figure 3.23.

FIGURE 3.23   Using Regedit.exe to view the Registry.

The registry contains two basic elements: keys and values. *Registry Keys* are similar to folders; in addition to values, each key can contain subkeys, which may contain further subkeys, and so on. Keys are referenced with a syntax similar to Windows's path names, using backslashes to indicate levels of hierarchy. For example, HKEY_LOCAL_MACHINE\Software\Microsoft\Windows refers to the subkey "Windows" of the subkey "Microsoft" of the subkey "Software" of the HKEY_LOCAL_MACHINE key. Windows 7 has five Root Keys:

- ► **HKEY_CLASSES_ROOT**: Stores information about registered applications, such as file associations.

- ► **HKEY_CURRENT_USER**: Stores settings that are specific to the currently logged-in user.

- ► **HKEY_LOCAL_MACHINE**: Stores settings that are specific to the local computer.

- ► **HKEY_USERS**: Contains subkeys corresponding to the HKEY_CUR-RENT_USER keys for each user profile actively loaded on the machine, though user hives are usually only loaded for currently logged-in users.

- ► **HKEY_CURRENT_CONFIG**: Contains information gathered at run-time. Information stored in this key is not permanently stored on disk, but rather regenerated at boot time.

Registry Values are name/data pairs stored within keys. Values are referenced separately from keys. There are multiple types of values. Some of the common ones include the following:

- ► **REG_SZ**: A string value

- ► **REG_BINARY**: Binary data

- ► **REG DWORD**: A 32-bit unsigned integer (numbers between 0 and 4294967295 decimal)

- ► **REG_MULTI_SZ**: A multi-string value, which is an array of unique strings

Reg files (also known as Registration entries) are text files for storing portions of the registry. They have a .reg filename extension. If you double-click a reg file, it adds the Registry entries into the Registry. You can export any Registry subkey by right-clicking the subkey and choosing **Export**. You can back up the entire Registry to a reg file by right-clicking **Computer** at the top of Regedit and selecting **Export**.

Cram Quiz

1. Where do you find the Windows Firewall with Advanced Security?
   - O **A.** Administrative Tools
   - O **B.** Registry Editor
   - O **C.** Program Manager
   - O **D.** File Manager

2. Which Registry Root Key stores settings that are specific to the local computer?
   - O **A.** HKEY_CLASSES_ROOT
   - O **B.** HKEY_CURRENT_USER
   - O **C.** HKEY_LOCAL_MACHINE
   - O **D.** HKEY_USERS

Cram Quiz Answers

1. **A** is correct. The Administrative Tools include the Computer Management Console, Event Viewer, Local Security Policy, Services console, Task Scheduler, and Windows Firewall with Advanced Security. Answer B is incorrect because the Registry Editor is used to configure the Registry, which is Windows's database of computer and user settings. Answers C and D are incorrect because there is no Program Manager or File Manager in Windows 7 to access the Windows Firewall.

2. **C** is correct. The HKEY_LOCAL_MACHINE stores settings that are specific to the local computer. Answer A is incorrect because the HKEY_CLASSES_ROOT stores information about registered applications, such as file associated. Answer B is incorrect because the HKEY_CURRENT_USER stores settings that are specific to the currently logged-in user. Answer D is incorrect because the HKEY_USERS contains subkeys corresponding to the HKEY_CURRENT_USER keys for each user profile actively loaded on the machine.

Review Questions

1. Which of the following is not a good place to get device drivers? (Choose the best answer.)

   ○ **A.** Using a peer-to-peer search engine

   ○ **B.** Bundled with Windows 7

   ○ **C.** Supplied with a device

   ○ **D.** Updated with Windows Update

   ○ **E.** Updated from the manufacturer's website

2. In the Windows 7 Device Manager, how do you know if there is a problem with a driver? (Choose the best answer.)

   ○ **A.** The driver icon has a red X.

   ○ **B.** The driver icon has an exclamation point.

   ○ **C.** The driver icon has a down arrow.

   ○ **D.** The driver icon is flashing.

3. You work as a desktop support technician at Acme.com. You are tasked to install Windows 7 Enterprise Edition on computers that have been running Windows XP. You verified the video cards are WDDM-compatible. What else do you need to do to support Aero? (Each correct answer presents part of the solution. Choose three.)

   ○ **A.** Set the monitor settings to a refresh rate higher than 10

   ○ **B.** Press the Windows key + Tab

   ○ **C.** Set the resolution to 1280×1024 or higher

   ○ **D.** Set Color to 32 bit

   ○ **E.** Select a Windows Aero theme

   ○ **F.** Set the Color Scheme to Windows Aero

4. You are logged in with an administrator account on each Windows 7 Home Basic Edition. You have enabled Parental Controls, which restricts certain websites and only allows certain programs to run on the machine. You noticed that when you log in, you can access the restricted websites and run any software. What is the problem? (Choose the best answer.)

   ○ **A.** The system must be part of the domain, so the option is not available.

   ○ **B.** You just upgraded to the Windows 7 Ultimate edition.

   ○ **C.** Parental Controls only apply to standard users, and not administrative accounts.

   ○ **D.** Someone disabled the Parental Control on the system.

5. You work as a technician at Acme.com. You need to install a fingerprint reader. What should you do next? (Choose two answers.)

   ○ **A.** Make sure that the application that uses the fingerprint reader is digitally signed

   ○ **B.** Make sure that the driver that you are installing is digitally signed

   ○ **C.** Connect the device before you load the driver

   ○ **D.** Load the driver before you connect the device

6. You were able to download a new printer driver from the Internet. How can you check the driver to make sure it is compatible with Windows 7?

   ○ **A.** Right-click the driver and click Verify signing

   ○ **B.** Run the File Signature verification to verify that the new driver has a Microsoft digital signature

   ○ **C.** Install the driver and click the Verify Certificate button in the Device Manager

   ○ **D.** Install the driver and check the device logs in the Event Viewer

7. You have a report generator that uses .rep filename extensions. You want to modify Windows 7 so that when you double-click a file with the .rep filename extension, Internet Explorer opens with the report being displayed. What do you need to do?

   ○ **A.** Open the Default Programs and select Set Association from the Control Panel

   ○ **B.** Right-click IExplore.exe and select Properties

   ○ **C.** Modify the filename association using registry

   ○ **D.** Modify the filename association using the local security policies

8. You have purchased some devices that have been sitting on the shelf at a store for several months and are about ready to be discontinued. You installed the drivers for those devices and now your system has some sporadic errors. What should you do?

   ○ **A.** Look on the Windows CD for more up-to-date drivers

   ○ **B.** Check with the manufacturer's website and the Windows update website for more up-to-date drivers

   ○ **C.** Upgrade Windows 7 to the Ultimate edition so that it can make proper use of the drivers

   ○ **D.** Disable the prompting of unsigned driver warnings

9. You are a parent who wants your children to only run certain programs that you allow on the computer. What can you do?

    ○   **A.** You should use Parental Controls on your computer to allow only certain programs.

    ○   **B.** You should use Ease of Access on your computer to allow only certain programs.

    ○   **C.** You should adjust your NTFS permissions so that they cannot install applications on your computer.

    ○   **D.** You should configure the firewall to block all ports not being used.

10. What console do you use to manage accessibility technology?

    ○   **A.** Ease of Access Center

    ○   **B.** Accessibility

    ○   **C.** Disability

    ○   **D.** Computer Management

Review Question Answers

1. Answer **A** is correct. Answers B, C, D, and E are recommended places to get drivers. Answer A is not a good place because you cannot verify where the driver came from or if it has been tampered with.

2. Answer **B** is correct. Problems with drivers are indicated by an exclamation point. Answer A is incorrect because a red X indicates a disabled device in Windows XP. Answer C is incorrect because a down arrow indicates a device is disabled. Answer D is incorrect because Device Manager does not flash.

3. Answers **A**, **D**, and **E** are correct. To enable Windows Aero, you must have set the monitor settings to a refresh rate higher than 10, set Color to 32 bit, and select a Windows Aero theme. Answer B is incorrect because the key combination does not enable or disable Windows Aero. Answer C is incorrect because the resolution is not a direct factor for Windows Aero. Different from Windows Vista, you do not have to select the Windows Aero color scheme (Answer F).

4. Answer **C** is correct. Parental Controls only affect standard users, not administrative users. Answer A is incorrect because Parental Controls would not have been enabled if it was part of a domain. Answer B is incorrect because you don't need to upgrade as Parental Controls are available in the Windows 7 Home Basic edition. Answer D requires an administrative account to disable Parental Controls. Therefore, it is unlikely this is correct.

5. Answers **B** and **C** are correct. To load drivers, you must have the device connected first. Then it is always recommended that you use signed drivers. Answer A is incorrect because applications do not have to be digitally signed. Answer D is incorrect because you have to have the device connected before you load the driver.

6. Answer **B** is correct. When you install new software, system files, and device drivers, unsigned or incompatible versions can cause system instability. Therefore, you should use the File Signature Verification to identify unsigned files on your computer, and you should not install drivers that do not have a proper driver signature. Answer A is incorrect because you cannot right-click the driver and click Verify signing. Answer C is incorrect because there is not a Verify Certificate button to click. Answer D is incorrect because there are no device logs in the Event Viewer and such information is not typically found in the Event Viewer.

7. Answer **A** is correct. When you want to change what program opens a particular type of data file, you should use the Control Panel's Default Program and select Set Association. Answer B is incorrect because there is no file associated or related option in the Internet Explorer properties. Answer C is incorrect because you could configure the filename association with the registry, but it is much more complicated than using the Control Panel. Answer D is incorrect because the local security policy cannot be used for filename association.

8. Answer **B** is correct because it is obvious that these drivers are not the newest. Therefore, you should check the Windows update website and manufacturer websites for newer drivers. Answer A is not the best answer because it might not have the newest drivers. Answer C is incorrect because the edition has no effect on how a driver is loaded. Answer D is incorrect because it is always recommended to load only signed drivers whenever possible.

9. Answer **A** is correct because if the computer is not part of the domain, you can use Parental Controls. Answer B is incorrect because you configure access to certain programs with Parental Controls and not Ease of Access. Answer C is incorrect because configuring NTFS is not the best way to configure accessibility options for children in this scenario. Answer D is incorrect because blocking ports is only partially effective and that would only block programs from communicating over the network.

10. Answer **A** is correct because the Ease of Access Center enables you to control the accessibility options. Answers B and C are incorrect because there are no such consoles with those names. Answer D is incorrect because the computer management is a powerful console but does not include accessibility options.

CHAPTER 4

Disk Management

This chapter covers the following 70-680 Objectives:

▶ Monitoring and Maintaining Systems That Run Windows 7:

    ▶ Manage disks

Although most computers that run Windows 7 only have one hard drive, some have two or more hard drives. If your system only has one hard drive, it might be beneficial to take that one hard drive and divide it into multiple volumes so that you can run multiple operating systems or to isolate a data area. Besides using multiple drives and volumes, you also need to know how to optimize the drives. This includes configuring your drives with Redundant Array of Inexpensive Disks (RAID) to increase disk performance and reliability or using disk utilities to make the drives run efficiently. Therefore, as a desktop technician, you need to learn how to manage your disks in Windows 7.

Disk Management Tools

▶ **Manage disks**

1. What two commands or utilities are used to manage your disk volumes? (Choose two answers.)

   ○ **A.** Diskpart

   ○ **B.** Scandisk

   ○ **C.** Disk Management console

   ○ **D.** Shared Folders console

2. You installed Windows 7 on a new computer. You want to expand your C drive to a second hard drive. How should the disk be configured?

   ○ **A.** The disk needs to be a basic disk.

   ○ **B.** The disk needs to be a dynamic disk.

   ○ **C.** The disk needs to use MBR.

   ○ **D.** The disk needs to use GPT.

Answers

1. **A** and **C** are correct. The two main programs or utilities to manage your disks are the Diskpart command and the Disk Management console. The Disk Management console can be found as part of the Computer Management console. Answer B is incorrect because Scandisk is a program found on older versions of Windows to check for errors. Answer D is incorrect because the Shared folders console, which is also part of the Computer Management console, is used to configure your shared folders.

2. **B** is correct. Dynamic disks do not have the same limitations of basic disks (Answer A). For example, you can extend a dynamic disk "on-the-fly" without requiring a reboot. In addition, dynamic disks can contain a virtually unlimited number of volumes, so you are not restricted to four volumes per disk as you are with basic disks. MBR (Answer C) and GPT (Answer D) are partitioning styles and have no bearing on the expanding or shrinking of a volume.

There are two main tools to manage your disks. The most common tool is the Disk Management console, which is part of the Computer Management console, as shown in Figure 4.1. With Disk Management, you can initialize disks, create volumes, and format volumes with the FAT, FAT32, or NTFS file systems.

Disk Management enables you to perform most disk-related tasks without restarting the system or interrupting users. Most configuration changes take effect immediately.

FIGURE 4.1 **Disk Management console.**

The other tool to manage your disks is Diskpart, which is a command-line hard disk partitioning utility included with Windows 2000, Windows Server 2003, Windows Server 2008, Windows XP, Windows Vista, and Windows 7. It replaces fdisk, which was used in MS-DOS–based operating systems. You can use Diskpart to convert a basic disk to a dynamic disk. Diskpart is included as part of the Windows 7 operating system, and it can also be found as part of WinPE. Different from most commands executed at the command prompt, the diskpart command starts a command-based environment specifically used to manage your disks. It can also be used with scripts to automate its usage.

Before performing a specific operation using diskpart, you need to first change the focus or select the specific disk, partition, or volume using the **select** command. All commands except for list, help, rem, exit, or help require focus. To use the select command, you would do one of the following:

▶ **select**: To obtain a list of focus types, execute the select command with no parameters.

▶ **select disk[=n]**: Use the select disk command to set the focus to the disk that has the specified Windows disk number. If you do not specify a disk number, the command displays the current in-focus disk.

▶ `select partition[=n/1]`: Use the `select partition` command to set the focus to the specified partition. If you do not specify a partition, the current in-focus partition is displayed. On basic disks, you can specify the partition by either index, drive letter, or mount point. You can only specify the partition by index on dynamic disks.

▶ `select volume[=n/1]`: Use the `select volume` command to set the focus to the specified volume. If you do not specify a volume, the command displays the current in-focus volume. You can specify the volume by either index, drive letter, or mount point path. On a basic disk, if you select a volume, the corresponding partition is put in focus.

Use the **list** command to display a summary. To display more information, set the focus, and then use the **detail** command. Use the **detail disk** command to obtain the detailed information about the current in-focus disk. Of course, with each of these, you use either disk, partition, or volume (see Figure 4.2). After you have selected your drive, partition, or volume, you then use create partition, delete partition, create volume, or delete volume. Lastly, you use the **exit** command to exit diskpart.

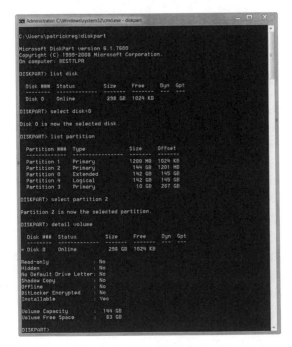

FIGURE 4.2   **Using Diskpart to select and list a volume.**

For more information about the `diskpart` utility, visit the following website: http://support.microsoft.com/kb/300415

> **Note**
>
> To create a fourth primary partition on a basic disk, you must use the `diskpart` utility. It cannot be done with the Disk Management console.

Disk Partitioning

When you prepare any drive or volume to be used by Windows 7, you must first partition the disk and then format the disk. Partitioning is defining and dividing the physical or virtual disk into logical volumes called *partitions*. Each partition functions as if it were a separate disk drive.

Windows 7 supports two types of disk partitioning styles: Master Boot Record (MBR) and GUID partition table (GPT). Therefore, when you install a new drive, you need to choose which type of partition style you want to use.

MBR disks have been used as *standard equipment* on IBM-compatible personal computers since the days of MS-DOS. MBR disks support volume sizes up to two terabytes (TB) and allow up to four primary partitions per disk. Alternatively, MBR disks support three primary partitions, one extended partition, and an unlimited number of logical drive letters created within the extended partition.

Windows 7 includes support for GPT disks in cluster storage. GPT disks were introduced with computers equipped with Intel Itanium-based processors and the Extensible Firmware Interface (EFI) instead of using a Basic Input/Output System (BIOS) as the interface between the computer's hardware devices, its firmware, and the operating system. GPT provides a more flexible mechanism for partitioning disks than the older MBR partitioning scheme that has been common to PCs. GPT disks support volume sizes up to 18 Exabytes (EB) and can store up to 128 partitions on each disk. Eighteen Exabytes are roughly equivalent to 18 billion Gigabytes. Critical system files are stored on GPT partitions, and GPT disks store a duplicate set of partition tables to ensure that partitioning information is retained. Although GPT has been around a while, no x86 version of Windows prior to Windows Vista supported it. Windows XP Professional x64 does support it.

> **ExamAlert**
>
> If you have disks that are greater than 2 TB, you must use GPT.

The *active partition* is the partition or volume that is marked as the partition to boot from. Therefore, it is expected to have the necessary boot files. The active partition or volume that contains the boot file is known as the *system partition/volume*. The partition or volume that contains the Windows operating system (such as the Windows folder) is called the *boot partition*. If a system has only one partition with the initial boot files and the Windows folder, then the partition is both the system partition and the boot partition.

> **ExamAlert**
>
> As strange as it sounds, the system volume contains the Windows boot files and the boot volumes contains the Windows operating system files.

The *%systemroot%* or *systemroot* indicates the folder into which Windows 7 is installed, which is located on the boot partition. By default, the Windows 7 system root directory is C:\Windows.

Disk Storage Management

Windows 7 supports two types of hard disk storage: basic and dynamic. All disks begin as basic disks until an administrator converts them to dynamic status, one physical disk at a time. The biggest advantage that dynamic disks offer when compared to basic disks is that you can create software-based fault-tolerant volumes via the operating system from the volumes stored on dynamic disks using mirrored volumes (RAID 1). Of course, you can always implement a hardware RAID solution using a RAID controller, which supports striping with parity (RAID) 5.

> **Note**
>
> RAID is short for redundant array of inexpensive disks (or redundant array of independent disks). RAID is technology that provides high levels of storage reliability from low-cost and less reliable disk drives.

Basic Disks

A basic disk under Windows 7 is essentially the same as the disk configuration under earlier versions of Windows—it is a physical disk with primary and extended partitions. You can create up to three primary partitions and one extended partition on a basic disk or four primary partitions. Primary partitions are partitions from which you can boot an operating system. You can divide an extended partition into numerous logical drives. Basic disks store their configuration information in the *partition table*, which is stored on the first sector of each hard disk. The configuration of a basic disk consists of the partition information on the disk.

Dynamic Disks

A Windows 7 dynamic disk is a physical disk configuration that does not use partitions or logical drives, and the MBR is not used. Instead, the basic partition table is modified and any partition table entries from the MBR are added as part of the Logical Disk Manager (LDR) database that stores dynamic disk information at the end of each dynamic disk. You can divide dynamic disks into as many as 2,000 separate volumes, but you should limit the number of volumes to 32 for each dynamic disk to avoid slow boot time performance. Of course, this type of configuration is most likely found on servers.

Dynamic disks do not have the same limitations as basic disks. For example, you can extend a dynamic disk "on-the-fly" without requiring a reboot. Dynamic disks are associated with disk groups, which are disks that are managed as a collection. This managed collection of disks helps organize dynamic disks. All dynamic disks in a computer are members of the same disk group. Each disk in a disk group stores replicas of the same configuration data. This configuration data is stored in the 1 MB LDR region at the end of each dynamic disk.

Dynamic disks support four types of volumes: simple, spanned, mirrored, and striped. Although the option for RAID-5 is listed with dynamic disks, the option is not available for desktop operating systems including Windows 7. Therefore, the option is grayed out. Dynamic disks can contain a virtually unlimited number of volumes, so you are not restricted to four volumes per disk as you are with basic disks.

Managing Basic Disks and Dynamic Disks

When you install Windows 7, the system automatically configures the existing hard disks as basic NTFS disks, unless they have been configured as dynamic from a previous installation. Windows 7 does not support dynamic disks on mobile PCs (laptops or notebooks). If you're using an older desktop machine that is not Advanced Configuration and Power Interface (ACPI) compliant, the Convert to Dynamic Disk option is not available. Dynamic disks have some additional limitations. You can install Windows 7 on a dynamic volume that you converted from a basic disk, but you cannot extend either the system or the boot volume on a dynamic disk. Any troubleshooting tools that cannot read the dynamic disk management database work only on basic disks.

> **Exam Alert**
>
> Dynamic disks are supported only on computers that use the Small Computer System Interface (SCSI), Fibre Channel, Serial Storage Architecture (SSA), or Integrated Drive Electronics (IDE). Portable computers, removable disks, and disks connected via Universal Serial Bus (USB) or FireWire (IEEE 1394) interfaces are not supported for dynamic storage. Dynamic disks are also not supported on hard drives with a sector size of less than 512 bytes.

To make a partition active so that it can boot the operating system boot files, you just need to right-click the volume in the Disk Management add-in and select the Mark Partition as Active. If the boot files do not exist, you get a message such as "Non-system disk" or a similar message.

Converting Basic Disks to Dynamic Disks

From the graphical user interface (GUI), you use the Windows 7 Disk Management console (an MMC snap-in) to upgrade a basic disk to a dynamic disk. The Disk Management snap-in is located in the Computer Management console and the Server Management console. You must be a member of the local Administrators group or the backup operators group, or else the proper authority must be delegated to you if you are working within an Active Directory environment to make any changes to the computer's disk-management configuration.

For the conversion to succeed, any disks to be converted must contain at least 1 MB of unallocated space. Disk Management automatically reserves this space when creating partitions or volumes on a disk, but disks with partitions or volumes created by other operating systems might not have this space available. (This space can exist even if it is not visible in Disk Management.) Windows 7 requires this minimal amount of disk space to store the dynamic database, which the operating system that created it maintains. In addition, you cannot convert drives that use an allocation unit size greater than 512 bytes. Before you convert any disks, close any programs that are running on those disks.

If your computer can multiboot between different versions of Windows, you should not convert to dynamic disk because you will not be able to start installed operating systems from any volume on the disk, except the current boot volume. In addition, other operating systems might not be able to read dynamic disks.

To convert a basic disk to a dynamic disk from the Disk Management console, perform the following steps:

1. Open the Disk Management console.

2. Right-click the basic disk that you want to convert to a dynamic disk and then click **Convert to Dynamic Disk**.

When you upgrade an empty basic disk to a dynamic disk, you do not need to reboot. However, if you convert a basic disk that already has partitions on it, or if the basic disk contains the system or boot partitions, you must restart your computer for the change to take effect.

To convert a basic disk to a dynamic disk from the Windows 7 command line, perform these steps:

1. Open a command prompt window, type `diskpart`, and press **Enter**.

2. Type `commands` or `help` to view a list of available commands.

3. Type `select disk 0` to select the first hard disk (`select disk 1` to select the second hard disk, and so on) and press **Enter**.

4. Type `convert dynamic` and press **Enter**.

5. Type `exit` to quit the `diskpart.exe` tool and then restart the computer to have the new configuration take effect.

When you convert a basic disk to a dynamic disk, any existing partitions on the basic disk become simple volumes on the dynamic disk. Any existing mirror sets, stripe sets, stripe sets with parity, or volume sets become mirrored volumes, striped volumes, dynamic RAID-5 volumes, or spanned volumes, respectively. After you convert a basic disk to a dynamic disk, you cannot change the volumes back to partitions.

Because the conversion process from basic to dynamic is per physical disk, a disk has all dynamic volumes or all basic partitions; you won't see both on the same physical disk. Remember, you do not need to restart your computer when you upgrade from an empty basic to a dynamic disk from the Disk Management console. However, you do have to restart your computer if you use the `diskpart.exe` command-line tool for the conversion; if you convert a disk containing the system volume, boot volume, or a volume with an active paging file; or if the disk contains any existing volumes or partitions.

> **ExamAlert**
>
> When you upgrade or convert a basic disk to a dynamic disk, at least 1 MB of free space must be available for the dynamic disk database. Under normal circumstances, this requirement should not be a problem.

Converting Dynamic Disks Back to Basic Disks

You must remove all volumes (and therefore all data) from a dynamic disk before you can change it back to a basic disk. After you convert a dynamic disk back to a basic disk, you can only create partitions and logical drives on that disk. After being converted from a basic disk, a dynamic disk can no longer contain partitions or logical drives, nor can any operating systems other than newer versions of Windows. To revert a dynamic disk to a basic disk, perform the following steps:

1. Back up the data on the dynamic disk.

2. Open Disk Management.

3. Delete all the volumes on the disk.

4. Right-click the dynamic disk that you want to change back to a basic disk and then click **Convert to Basic Disk**.

5. Restore the data to the newly converted basic disk.

The disk structure does not describe how a hard drive or floppy disk physically works, but how it stores files on the disk. In other words, it describes the formatting of the disk (file system, partitions, the root directory, and the directories). A file system is the overall structure in which files are named, stored, and organized. File systems used in Windows 7 include FAT, FAT32, and NTFS. Although FAT and FAT32 were primarily used in older operating systems, NTFS is the preferred file system.

ExamAlert

Converting to a dynamic disk is a one-way process. Yes, you can convert a dynamic disk back to a basic disk, but you lose all your data. Obviously, this loss is a major consideration! If you find yourself needing to do it, first back up your data and then you can delete all the volumes on the disk, convert the disk to basic, and restore your data.

File Systems

An older file system used by DOS was the file allocation table (FAT). FAT is a simple file system that uses minimum memory. Although it is based on file names of 11 characters, which include the 8 characters for the file name and 3 characters for the file extension, it has been expanded to support long filenames. Early DOS used FAT12, which used a 12-bit number for each cluster, but was later expanded to FAT16, which recognized volumes up to 2 GB.

FAT32, which was introduced in the second major release of Windows 95, was an enhancement to the FAT file system. It uses 32-bit FAT entries, which supports hard drives up to 2 TB, although Windows 2000, Windows XP, Windows Vista, Windows 7, Windows Server 2003, and Windows Server 2008 (including R2) support volumes up to 32 GB. FAT32 does not have the security that NTFS provides, so if you have a FAT32 partition or volume on your computer, any user who has access to your computer can read any file on it. Today, the only time you use FAT32 is in the event that you have a computer that can boot to multiple operating systems, and one of the other operating systems (such as Windows 95 or 98) cannot read and write to NTFS. Systems that can load more than one operating system are known as having a *multi-boot configuration*.

NTFS is the preferred file system for Windows XP and later versions. It has many benefits over the FAT and FAT32 file systems, including

- ▶ Improved support for much larger hard disks
- ▶ Some automatic recovery of disk-related errors because it is a journaling file system that keeps track of its transactions to make sure that that entire transaction is completed before being recognized
- ▶ Better security because you can use permissions and encryption to restrict access to specific files to approved users
- ▶ Disk compression
- ▶ Disk quotas

Another file system used in Windows 7 is Extended File Allocation Table (exFAT), sometimes referred to as FAT64. ExFAT is a new file system that is better adapted to the growing needs of mobile personal storage such as USB flash drives that require minimum overhead. Although exFAT can theoretically handle up to 64 ZB (a Zettabtye (ZB) is equal to 1 billion Terabytes), 512 TB is the recommended maximum. It can also handle files that are larger than 4 GB. Unfortunately, exFAT does not support the encryption and permission features found in NTFS.

Cram Quiz

1. You have a new hard drive that has 4 TB. What type of partitioning style do you need to use?

   ○ **A.** GPT

   ○ **B.** MBR

   ○ **C.** Basic

   ○ **D.** Dynamic

2. How do you convert a dynamic disk to basic disk?

   ○ **A.** Right-click the dynamic disk and select **Convert to Basic Disk** in the Disk Management console.

   ○ **B.** Right-click the disk in Windows Explorer and select Format. In the Format dialog box, select **Basic format**.

   ○ **C.** Specify the convert command using `diskpart`.

   ○ **D.** Back up all data on the dynamic disk. Delete the disk. Re-create the disk as a Basic Disk. Restore the data.

Cram Quiz Answers

1. **A** is correct. Partitioning is defining and dividing the physical or virtual disk into logical volumes called partitions. Each partition functions as if it were a separate disk drive. Windows 7 supports two types of disk partitioning styles: Master Boot Record (MBR) and GUID partition table (GPT). If you have disks that are greater than 2 TB, you must use GPT because MBR (Answer B) does not support disks larger than 2 TB. Answers C and D are incorrect because Basic and Dynamic disks describe the type of hard disk storage.

2. **D** is correct. Converting a basic disk to a dynamic disk is a one-way process. Therefore, the only way to convert a dynamic disk back to a basic disk is to delete the old disk and re-create it. Because that loses all data, you need to back up first and restore after you are done; therefore, the other answers are incorrect.

Working with Volumes

▶ **Manage disks**

1. You have a new Windows 7 computer with multiple hard drives. You want to implement RAID1 on the computer. What do you need to do first?

   ○ **A.** Enable write caching on the first disk

   ○ **B.** Enable write caching on the second disk

   ○ **C.** Convert the basic disk to dynamic disks

   ○ **D.** Convert the dynamic disk to basic disks

2. You have a computer running Windows 7. Your system has a large hard drive with one volume that holds the Windows 7 volume. Out of 500 GB, you realize that you are only using approximately 100 GB. You decide you want to create a new volume on disk 0. What should you do?

   ○ **A.** Compress volume C

   ○ **B.** Create a virtual hard disk (VHD)

   ○ **C.** Shrink volume C

   ○ **D.** Configure a disk quota for volume C

3. What is the maximum number of volumes you can add to a striped volume?

   ○ **A.** 2

   ○ **B.** 4

   ○ **C.** 8

   ○ **D.** 16

   ○ **E.** 32

Answers

1. **C** is correct. RAID1 (disk mirroring) needs two disks to implement. Before you can enable RAID1 using Windows 7, you need to convert basic disks to dynamic disks, which converts the partitions into volumes. Answers A and B are incorrect because write caching only improves disk performance and does not help implement RAID1. Answer D is incorrect because to implement RAID1 using Windows 7, you must use dynamic disks.

2. **C** is correct. To make room for the new volume, you can shrink the system drive assuming the disk drive is set to dynamic. Answer A is incorrect because compressing volume C only gives you more disk space on the C drive but does not shrink the volume itself. Answer B is incorrect because a virtual hard disk can be attached to a system, but it does not add a volume to the 500 GB drive. Answer D is incorrect because disk quotas help you manage the disk to make sure users do not use too much disk space.

3. **E** is correct. A striped volume can contain up to 32 volumes. Therefore, the other answers are incorrect.

You can create primary partitions, extended partitions, and logical drives only on basic disks. Partitions and logical drives can reside only on basic disks. You can create up to four primary partitions on a basic disk or up to three primary partitions and one extended partition. You can use the free space in an extended partition to create multiple logical drives. You must be a member of the local Administrators group or the backup operators group, or else the proper authority must be delegated to you (if you are working within an Active Directory environment) to create, modify, or delete basic volumes.

You must first create an extended partition before you can create a new logical drive, if no extended partition exists already. If you choose to delete a partition, all data on the deleted partition or logical drive is lost. You cannot recover deleted partitions or logical drives. You cannot delete the system partition, boot partition, or any partition that contains an active paging file. The operating system uses one or more paging files on disk as virtual memory that can be swapped into and out of the computer's physical random access memory (RAM) as the system's load and volume of data dictate.

ExamAlert

Windows 7 requires that you delete all logical drives and any other partitions that have not been assigned a drive letter within an extended partition before you delete the extended partition itself.

With dynamic disks, you are no longer limited to four volumes per disk (as you are with basic disks). As mentioned before, Windows 7 supports simple, spanned, mirrored, and striped volumes. You must be a member of the local Administrators group or the backup operators group.

Simple Volumes

A simple volume consists of disk space on a single physical disk. It can consist of a single area on a disk or multiple areas on the same disk that are linked together. To create a simple volume using the Disk Management console, perform the following steps:

1. Open Disk Management.

2. Right-click the unallocated space on the dynamic disk where you want to create the simple volume and then click **New Simple Volume**.

3. When the Welcome to the New Simple Volume Wizard appears, click **Next**.

4. Specify the size of the volume and click **Next**.

5. When it asks you to assign a drive letter or path as shown in Figure 4.3, select a drive letter and click **Next**.

6. Choose a file system (NTFS is recommended). You should also specify a name for the volume so that it can be easier to identify. You can then perform a quick format (or a long format if you don't select quick format) and enable file and folder compression if desired.

7. When the summary appears, click the **Finish** button.

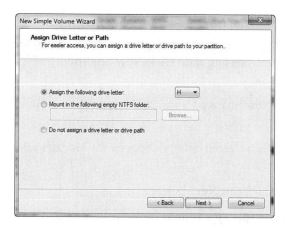

FIGURE 4.3   **Assigning a drive letter or path to a simple volume.**

To create a partition primary of length size and a starting address offset on the current drive using the `diskpart` command prompt, you use the following command:

```
create partition primary size=xxx
```

After the partition is created, the new extended partition gains the focus.

To create a simple volume of length size at the diskpart command prompt, you use the following command:

```
create volume simple size=xxx disk=n
```

If you do not specify a size, the new volume can take up the remaining contiguous free space on the disk. If you do not specify a disk, the current in-focus disk is used. After the volume is created, the disk focus is given to the targeted disk.

Here are some guidelines about simple volumes:

▶ You can create simple volumes on dynamic disks only.

▶ Simple volumes are not fault tolerant.

▶ Simple volumes cannot contain partitions or logical drives.

Spanned Volumes

A spanned volume consists of disk space from more than one physical disk. You can add more space to a spanned volume by extending it at any time. To create a spanned volume, perform the following steps:

1. Open Disk Management.

2. Right-click the unallocated space on one of the dynamic disks where you want to create the spanned volume and then click **New Spanned Volume**.

3. When the Welcome to the New Spanned Volume Wizard appears, click the **Next** button.

4. Add two or more drives on the selected column. Specify the size of each volume. Click the **Next** button.

5. Specify the drive letter and click the **Next** button.

6. Specify NTFS file system and specify a volume label for easier identification. You can also specify a quick format and enable file and folder compression. Click the **Next** button.

7. When the wizard is complete, click the **Finish** button.

Here are some guidelines about spanned volumes:

- ▶ You can create spanned volumes on dynamic disks only.

- ▶ You need at least two dynamic disks to create a spanned volume.

- ▶ You can extend a spanned volume onto a maximum of 32 dynamic disks.

- ▶ Spanned volumes cannot be mirrored or striped.

- ▶ Spanned volumes are not fault tolerant.

Extending Simple or Spanned Volumes

Simple volumes are the most basic volumes on dynamic disks. If you extend a simple volume to another dynamic disk, it automatically becomes a spanned volume. You can extend a simple volume to make it a spanned volume, and you can also further extend a spanned volume to add disk storage capacity to the volume. To extend a simple or a spanned volume, perform the following steps:

1. Open Disk Management.

2. Right-click the simple or spanned volume you want to extend, and click **Extend Volume**.

3. When the Welcome to the Extend Volume Wizard appears, click the **Next** button.

4. Select a disk that has free disk space on the Selected column and specify the amount that you want to expand. Then click the **Next** button.

5. Click the **Finish** button.

You must be a member of the Backup Operators or the Administrators group to extend or shrink any partition or volume.

You should be aware of the many rules about extending a simple or a spanned volume:

- ▶ You can extend partitions on basic disks or volumes in dynamic disks.

- ▶ You can only extend if the volume has been formatted with NTFS or raw (not formatted). You cannot extend volumes formatted using FAT or FAT32.

- ▶ After a volume is extended onto multiple disks (spanned), you cannot mirror the volume, nor can you make it into a striped volume or a RAID-5 volume.

▸ For logical drives, boot, or system volumes, you can extend the volume only into contiguous space and only if the disk can be upgraded to a dynamic disk. For other volumes, you can extend the volume into non-contiguous space, but you are prompted to convert the disk to dynamic.

▸ You can extend a logical drive within contiguous free space in the extended partition that contains it. If you extend a logical drive beyond the free space available in the extended partition, the extended partition grows to contain the logical drive.

▸ After a spanned volume is extended, no portion of it can be deleted without the entire spanned volume being deleted.

▸ You can extend simple and spanned volumes on dynamic disks onto a maximum of 32 dynamic disks.

▸ Spanned volumes write data only to subsequent disks as each disk volume fills up. Therefore, a spanned volume writes data to physical disk 0 until it fills up, then it writes to physical disk 1 until its available space is full, then it writes to physical disk 2, and so on. However, if just one disk fails as part of the spanned volume, *all the data contained on that spanned volume is lost*.

Shrinking Volumes

If you are using dynamic disks, you can also shrink a volume assuming that you have enough space to hold its contents and all files can be moved out of the way if necessary. Different from expanded volumes, you can shrink the system volume.

To shrink a volume:

1. Right-click the volume and select **Shrink volume**.

2. Enter the amount of space to shrink and click the **Shrink** button.

Striped Volumes

A striped volume stores data in stripes on two or more physical disks. Data in a striped volume is allocated alternately and evenly (in stripes) to the disks contained within the striped volume. Striped volumes can substantially improve the speed of access to the data on disk. Striped volumes are often referred to as RAID-0; this configuration tends to enhance performance, but it is not fault tolerant. To create a striped volume, perform the following steps:

1. Open Disk Management.

2. Right-click unallocated space on one of the dynamic disks where you want to create the striped volume and select **New Striped Volume**.

3. When the Welcome to the New Striped Volume screen displays, click the **Next** button.

4. Add two disks to the Selected column, as shown in Figure 4.4. Specify the amount of the striped volume.

5. Assign the appropriate drive letter and click the **Next** button.

6. Specify **NTFS** for the file system. You should also specify a volume label for easier identification in the future. You can also choose to do a quick format and enable file and folder compression. Click the **Next** button.

7. When the wizard is complete, click the **Finish** button.

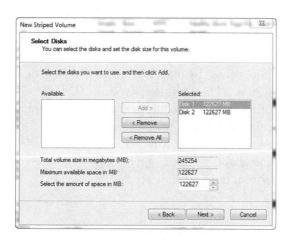

FIGURE 4.4   **Selecting disks for a striped volume.**

Here are some guidelines about striped volumes:

▶ You need at least two physical dynamic disks to create a striped volume.

▶ You can create a striped volume onto a maximum of 32 disks.

▶ Striped volumes are not fault tolerant.

▶ For increased volume capacity, select disks that contain similar amounts of available disk space. A striped volume's capacity is limited to the space available on the disk with the smallest amount of available space.

▶ Whenever possible, use disks that are the same model and from the same manufacturer.

▶ Striped volumes cannot be extended or mirrored. If you need to make a striped volume larger by adding another disk, you first have to delete the volume and then re-create it.

Mirrored Volumes

A mirrored volume uses volumes stored on two separate physical disks to "mirror" (write) the data onto both disks simultaneously and redundantly. This configuration is also referred to as RAID-1. If one of the disks in the mirrored configuration fails, Windows 7 writes an event into the system log of the Event Viewer. The system functions normally (unless the second disk fails) until the failed disk is replaced and then the volume can be mirrored again. Mirrored volumes cost you 50% of your available storage space because of the built-in redundancy. If you mirror two 70 GB disks, you are left with just 70 GB of space rather than 140 GB.

You can make mirrored volumes more robust by installing a separate hard disk controller for each disk; technically, this is known as *disk duplexing*. Disk duplexing is better than disk mirroring because you alleviate the single point of failure by having one controller for each disk. Under Windows Server 2008, disk duplexing is still referred to as disk mirroring. You can create mirrored volumes only by using dynamic disks. To create a new empty mirrored volume from unallocated space, perform the following steps:

1. Open Disk Management.

2. Right-click an area of unallocated space on a dynamic disk and select **New Mirrored Volume**.

3. When the Welcome to the New Mirrored Volume Wizard starts, click **Next**.

4. Add two or more drives to the Selected column. Specify the amount of space and click the **Next** button.

5. Select the appropriate drive letter and click the **Next** button.

4. Click the **Remove Mirror** button.

5. Click **Yes** to confirm the removal action at the Disk Management message box that appears.

Mount Points

When you prepare a volume in Windows 7, you can assign a drive letter to the new volume or you can create a mount point the new volume as an empty NTFS folder. By using volume mount points, you can graft, or mount, a target partition into a folder on another drive. The mounting is handled transparently to the user and applications. With the NTFS volume mount points feature, you can surpass the 26-drive-letter limitation.

To assign a mount-point folder path to a drive by using the Windows interface:

1. In Disk Manager, right-click the partition or volume where you want to assign the mount-point folder path, and then click **Change Drive Letter and Paths**.

2. To assign a mount-point folder path, click **Add**. As shown in Figure 4.7, click **Mount in the following empty NTFS folder**, type the path to an empty folder on an NTFS volume, or click **Browse** to locate it.

To remove the mount-point folder path, click it and then click **Remove**.

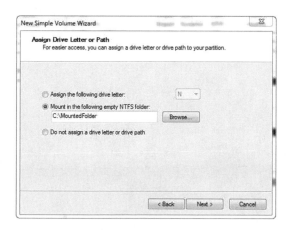

FIGURE 4.7   **Mount points.**

Formatting Disks

Formatting a hard drive is the process of writing the file system structure on the disk so that it can be used to store programs and data. This includes creating a file allocation table (an index listing all directories and files and where they are located on the disk) and a root directory to start with. In addition, formatting creates a volume boot sector, which is used to store the boot files of an operating system. If you format a disk that already has a file system and files or folders, you overwrite with a new file system, which erases all content on the drive.

When you create a volume in the Disk Management console using the Add Volume Wizard, it formats the volume. However, you can format the disk any time if you want to erase all content on a volume by right-clicking the volume in the Disk Management console and selecting **Format**. You then specify a volume label, the file system, the allocation unit size, if you want to perform a quick format, and if you want to enable file and folder compression. Then click **OK**.

To format the disk using a command executed from the command prompt, you can also use the `format` command. To format the drive as D drive with an NTFS file system, you execute the following command:

```
format d: /fs:ntfs
```

Cram Quiz

1. Which of the following is not supported in Windows 7?

   ○ **A.** Simple disk

   ○ **B.** Spanned disk

   ○ **C.** Mirrored disk

   ○ **D.** Striped disk

   ○ **E.** RAID-5

Optimizing the Disk

▶ **Manage disks**

Cram**Saver**

1. Why do you need to keep your drives defragged?

   ○ **A.** To keep your drive from filling up

   ○ **B.** To keep your drive clean from viruses

   ○ **C.** To keep your drive optimized for better performance

   ○ **D.** To keep your drive free from disk errors

2. You have a computer running Windows 7 used by multiple users. You want to ensure that a single user does not use too much disk space on the system. What can you do?

   ○ **A.** Do not assign administrative permissions to the users

   ○ **B.** Enable disk compression

   ○ **C.** Establish disk quotas

   ○ **D.** Run the disk cleanup tool

Answers

1. **C** is the correct because disk fragmentation leads to slow disk perform-ance. Answers A and B are incorrect because defragging your drive does not keep the drive from filling up or clean from viruses. Answer D is incor-rect because keeping a drive free from disk errors is done by `chkdsk`.

2. **C** is correct. To limit how much space a user can use, you can use disk quotas. Answer A is incorrect because not assigning administrative per-missions does not prevent or limit someone who has the write permission to store files on their Desktop or Documents library. Answer B is incorrect because disk compression only provides more disk space but does not limit how much a user can use. Answer D is incorrect because the disk cleanup tool helps free up disk space to remove unnecessary files and compress old files but does not limit how much space a user can use.

2. You have a Windows 7 computer. You want to provide fault tolerance for the volume containing the operating system. Each disk is configured as a basic disk. The operating system is installed on the first disk. What should you do?

   ○ **A.** Configure a new mirrored volume using disk 0 and 1.

   ○ **B.** Convert both disks to a dynamic disk. Configure a new mirrored volume using disk 0 and 1.

   ○ **C.** Convert disk 1 to dynamic disks. Configure a new mirrored volume using disk 0 and 1.

   ○ **D.** Convert the disk 0 and disk 1 to dynamic disks. Configure the two disks as a striped set using disk 0 and 1.

3. Which of the following gives you the best read-access performance?

   ○ **A.** Simple disk

   ○ **B.** Spanned disk

   ○ **C.** Mirrored disk

   ○ **D.** Striped disk

Cram Quiz Answers

1. **E** is correct. Although Windows Server 2008 supports all five that are listed, Windows 7 does not support RAID-5 software RAID using Windows. You can still use hardware RAID to implement RAID-5, but this capability is not Windows 7 native. Therefore, the other answers are incorrect because they are supported in Windows 7.

2. **B** is correct. To use RAID provided by Windows 7, you must use dynamic disks. To provide fault tolerance, you create a mirrored set using disk 0 and 1. Answer A is incorrect because basic disks cannot be used for a mirror or RAID 5 disks. Answer C is incorrect because both disks must be dynamic to support mirroring and RAID-5 sets. Answer D is incorrect because a striped set is not fault tolerant.

3. **D** is correct. Striped volumes can substantially improve the speed of access to the data on disk. Striped volumes are often referred to as RAID-0; this config-uration tends to enhance performance, but it is not fault tolerant. Answer C is incorrect because while mirroring does provide some increased performance and provides fault tolerance, striped disks offer faster read performance. Answers A and B are incorrect because they do not offer any increase in performance.

One of the key components to the system is the disk. In the Windows operating system, your applications and the data come from the hard drive, so you must keep the hard drive optimized to keep your system performing well. Of course, as mentioned earlier, it is important that you use the NTFS file system. You should monitor free disk space, check your drive for errors, and defrag your hard drive on a regular basis.

Monitoring Disk Space

You should closely monitor disk space usage on all system drives. When a system drive fills up, the performance and reliability of Windows can be greatly reduced, particularly if the system runs low on space for storing virtual memory or temporary files. One way to reduce disk space usage is to use the Disk Cleanup tool to remove unnecessary files and compress old files.

Running Check Disk

You should periodically use the Error-checking tool to check the integrity of disks, which examines and corrects many types of common errors. You can run Check Disk (chkdsk.exe) from the command line. However, both methods cannot fix a corrupt file.

To test the C drive with the **chkdsk** command, you first open an elevated command prompt. You then type the following:

```
chkdsk C:
```

Without the **/f** option, Check Disk only reports the status of the C drive and any problems that it finds. To fix the problems, you need to do the following:

```
chkdsk C: /f
```

ExamAlert

To fix errors, you must include the **/f** option with the **chkdsk** command.

To run the graphical interface of Check Disk, you do the following:

1. Click **Start** and then click **Computer**. Under Hard Disk Drives, right-click a drive and then select **Properties**.

2. On the Tools tab, click **Check now**, as shown in Figure 4.8.

FIGURE 4.8   **Disk Tools.**

If you are using the command prompt or the graphical interface, you are prompted to dismount or schedule the disk to be checked the next time you restart the system.

If your machine experiences an abnormal shutdown, there is a specific bit in the registry so that when the operating system boots the next time, it knows that the file system is considered "dirty" and that it needs to be checked for possible errors. The `chkntfs` command displays or modifies automatic disk checking when the computer is started. If used without options, `chkntfs` displays the file system of the specified volume. If automatic file checking is scheduled to run, `chkntfs` displays whether the specified volume is dirty or is scheduled to be checked the next time the computer is started.

Defragging the Hard Drive

When a file is created, it is assigned the number of clusters needed to hold the amount of data. After the file is saved to the disk, other information is usually saved to the clusters following those assigned to the saved file. Therefore, if the original file is changed or more information is added to it, the bigger file doesn't fit within the allocated clusters when it is saved back to the disk. Part of the file is saved in the original clusters and the remaining amount are placed elsewhere on the disk. Over time, files become fragmented as they are spread across the disk. The fragmented files are still complete when they are opened, but it takes longer for the computer to read them, and opening them causes more wear and tear on the hard disk.

To reduce fragmentation, Windows 7 automatically defragments the disk periodically using Disk Defragmenter, as shown previously in Figure 4.6. By default, Windows 7 runs the disk defragmenter automatically at 1:00 A.M. every Wednesday via the Task Scheduler. As long as the computer is on at the scheduled run time, automatic defragmentation occurs. You can cancel automated defragmentation or modify the defragmentation schedule by following these steps:

1. Click **Start** and then click **Computer**.

2. Under Hard Disk Drives, right-click a drive and then select **Properties**.

3. On the Tools tab, click **Defragment Now** to open the Disk Defragmenter dialog box.

4. To cancel automated defragmentation, clear **Run Automatically** and then click **OK** twice. To modify the defragmentation schedule, click **Modify Schedule**. Use the Modify Schedule dialog box to set the desired run schedule.

5. Click **OK** twice to save your settings.

You can manually defragment a disk by completing the following steps:

1. Click **Start** and then click **Computer**.

2. Under Hard Disk Drives, right-click a drive and then select **Properties**.

3. On the Tools tab, click **Defragment Now**.

> **Note**
>
> Depending on the size of the disk, defragmentation can take several hours. You can click **Cancel Defragmentation** at any time to stop defragmentation.

NTFS Disk Quotas

NTFS disk quotas track and control disk usage on a per-user, per-drive letter (partition or volume) basis. You can apply disk quotas only to NTFS-formatted drive letters under Windows 7. Quotas are tracked for each drive letter, even if the drive letters reside on the same physical disk. The per-user feature of quotas enables you to track every user's disk space usage regardless of which folder the user stores files in. To enable disk quotas, open Windows Explorer or Computer, right-click a drive letter and select **Properties**, click the **Quota** tab, and configure the options, as shown in Figure 4.9.

> **ExamAlert**
>
> NTFS disk quotas do not use compression to measure disk-space usage, so users cannot obtain or use more space simply by compressing their own data.

FIGURE 4.9   **Configuring disk quotas.**

After you turn on the disk quota system, you can establish individual disk-quota limits for each user by clicking the **Quota Entries** button at the bottom of the Quota tab. By default, only members of the Administrators group can view and change quota entries and settings. In addition, all members of the Administrators group inherit unlimited disk quotas by default. NTFS disk quotas are based on file ownership; operating system accounts are not immune to disk quotas. System accounts such as the local system are also susceptible to running out of disk space because of disk quotas having been set. From the Quota Entries window, you can change an existing quota entry for a user by double-clicking the quota entry. To set up a new quota entry for a user, click

the **Quota** menu and select the **New Quota Entry** option. When a user no longer stores data on a volume, you should delete the user's disk-quota entries. The catch is that you can only delete the user's quota entries after you remove all the files that the user owns or after another user takes ownership of the files.

Cram Quiz

1. You have a computer running Windows 7 Enterprise. Unfortunately, you notice that the computer is running slowly. When you first look at it, you notice that your system has 2 GB of RAM and approximately 200 MB of free disk space. What should you do to improve performance? (Choose two answers.)

   ○ **A.** Enable your paging file

   ○ **B.** Run the Disk Defragmenter utility

   ○ **C.** Use Disk Cleanup to delete temporary files and unnecessary program files

   ○ **D.** Modify non-essential services to run in the background

2. What option do you have to use with the chkdsk command if you want the chkdsk command to fix problems that it finds?

   ○ **A.** /c

   ○ **B.** /x

   ○ **C.** /f

   ○ **D.** No option is required.

Cram Quiz Answers

1. **B** and **C** are correct. You should run the Disk Defragmenter. A disk tends to become more fragmented when the disk fills up. Disk Defragmenter also helps increase performance. You should also run the Disk Cleanup program to free up additional space. Answer A is incorrect because you most likely already have a paging file. Answer D is incorrect because services already run in the background.

2. **C** is correct. Without the /f option, Check Disk only reports the status of the C drive and any problems that it finds. Answer A is incorrect because the /c option skips checking of cycles within the NTFS folder structure. Answer B is incorrect because the /x option forces the volume to dismount first if necessary. Answer D is incorrect because you have to include the /f option.

Review Questions

1. How many primary partitions does an MBR basic disk support?

   ○ **A.** 2

   ○ **B.** 4

   ○ **C.** 6

   ○ **D.** 16

   ○ **E.** 128

2. How many partitions does a GPT disk support?

   ○ **A.** 2

   ○ **B.** 4

   ○ **C.** 8

   ○ **D.** 16

   ○ **E.** 128

3. You have a Windows 7 computer with two hard drives. What type of RAID can you implement to provide fault tolerance?

   ○ **A.** RAID-0

   ○ **B.** RAID-1

   ○ **C.** RAID-5

   ○ **D.** RAID-1 and -5

4. Which of the following statements are true about basic disks under Windows 7? (Choose two.)

   ○ **A.** Basic disks are not supported under Windows 7.

   ○ **B.** Basic disks that were configured as one disk striping with parity set under Windows NT Workstation 4.0 are mounted automatically after the computer is upgraded to Windows 7.

   ○ **C.** Basic disks can only be formatted as FAT or FAT32.

   ○ **D.** You cannot convert dynamic disks back to basic disks without deleting all data and volumes on the disks first.

   ○ **E.** IEEE 1394 disks can only be basic disks.

5. You have a Windows 7 computer. What command do you use to convert a basic disk to a dynamic disk?

○ **A.** `diskpart basic to dynamic`

○ **B.** `diskpart convert dynamic`

○ **C.** `format c: /fs:dynamic`

○ **D.** `convert c: /fs:dynamic`

6. What command would you use to change a master boot record disk into a GUID partition table disk?

○ **A.** `fdisk`

○ **B.** `format`

○ **C.** `diskpart`

○ **D.** `convert`

7. What is the largest drive that the MBR partitioning style supports?

○ **A.** 1 TB

○ **B.** 2 TB

○ **C.** 4 TB

○ **D.** 16 TB

8. Which of the following is not true when considering extending a volume?

○ **A.** You can extend partitions on basic disks.

○ **B.** You can extend volumes on dynamic disks.

○ **C.** You cannot extend System or boot volumes.

○ **D.** You can only extend a volume if the volume is NTFS or raw (not formatted).

9. What is the maximum number of simple or spanned volumes that you can use on dynamic disks?

○ **A.** 4

○ **B.** 8

○ **C.** 16

○ **D.** 32

10. How can you use volumes beyond the 26 drive letters?

○ **A.** Compress the drive

○ **B.** Assign double letters for the drive letters

○ **C.** Mount the drives

○ **D.** Double format the drives

Review Questions Answers

1. Answer **B** is correct. An MBR basic disk can support up to four primary partitions or three primary partitions and one extended partition. Therefore, the other answers are incorrect.

2. Answer **E** is correct. Although MBR can support up to 4 partitions, GPT can support up to 128 partitions. Therefore, the other answers are incorrect.

3. Answer **B** is correct. RAID-1, disk mirroring, uses two disks to provide fault tolerance. In RAID-1, whatever is written to one disk is written to the other. Answer A is incorrect because RAID-0, disk striping, does enhance performance, but does not provide fault tolerance. Answers C and D are incorrect because RAID-5 (disk striping with parity) needs three disks to implement. In addition, software RAID-5 is not supported on Windows 7.

4. Answers **D** and **E** are correct. To convert dynamic disks back to basic disks, you must remove all volumes on the disk, which means that all data must be removed as well. IEEE 1394 (or FireWire) disks cannot be converted to dynamic; therefore, they can only be basic disks. Answer A is incorrect because basic disks are supported under Windows 7. Answer B is incorrect because you cannot upgrade from Windows NT to Windows 7. Answer C is incorrect because basic disks (and dynamic disks) can be formatted as FAT, FAT32, or NTFS.

5. Answer **B** is correct. To convert a basic disk to a dynamic disk, you use the `diskpart convert dynamic` command. Answer A is incorrect because the proper command is `diskpart convert dynamic`. Answers C and D are incorrect because the `format` and `convert` commands cannot be used to convert basic to dynamic disks.

6. Answer **C** is correct. Diskpart is a powerful disk management tool that can convert an MBR disk to a GUID partition table disk. Answer A is incorrect because `fdisk` is a partitioning tool used in older operating systems. Format is used to format a disk, which would define FAT32 or NTFS. Answer D is incorrect because the convert command could be used to convert a FAT32 volume to a NTFS volume.

7. Answer **B** is correct. The largest drive that MBR partitioning style supports is 2 TB. If you need a larger drive, you have to use the GPT partitioning style.

8. Answer **C** is correct. You can extend a system or boot volume if the drive has contiguous space next to the system or boot volume and only if the disk is upgraded to dynamic disks. Answer A is incorrect because you can extend partitions on basic disks. You cannot extend logical drives, boot, or system volumes unless you convert it to dynamic disk first. Answer B is incorrect because you can extend dynamic disks. Answer D is incorrect because you can only extend NTFS or raw partitions. You cannot extend FAT or FAT32 volumes.

9. Answer **D** is correct. You can extend simple and spanned volumes on dynamic disks onto a maximum of 32 dynamic disks. Therefore, the other answers are incorrect.

10. Answer **C** is correct. When you prepare a volume in Windows 7, you can assign a drive letter to the new volume or you can create a mount point, and then you assign the new volume to an empty NTFS folder. By using volume mount points, you can graft, or mount, a target partition into a folder on another drive. The mounting is handled transparently to the user and applications. With the NTFS volume mount points feature, you can surpass the 26-drive-letter limitation. Answer A is incorrect because compressing the drive only gives you more space on the drive. Answer B is incorrect because you cannot assign double letters. Answer D is incorrect because there is no such thing as double formatting a drive.

CHAPTER 5

Configuring Windows Networking

This chapter covers the following 70-680 Objectives:

▶ Configuring Network Connectivity:

  ▶ Configure IPv4 network settings

  ▶ Configure IPv6 network settings

  ▶ Configure networking settings

A network is two more computers connected to share resources such as files or printers. To function, a network requires a service to share (such as file or print sharing) and access to a common medium or pathway. Today, most computers connect to a wired network using an Ethernet adapter, which in turn connects to a switch or set of switches via a twisted pair cable, or the computers connect to a wireless network using a wireless adapter to connect to a wireless switch. To bring it all together, protocols give the entire system common communication rules. Today, virtually all networks use the TCP/IP protocol suite, the same protocol that the Internet runs.

Introduction to TCP/IP

▶ **Configure IPv4 network settings**

▶ **Configure IPv6 network settings**

▶ **Configure networking settings**

Cram**Saver**

1. What is the default subnet mask for the host address of 172.1.32.4?

   ○ **A.** 255.0.0.0

   ○ **B.** 255.255.0.0

   ○ **C.** 255.255.255.0

   ○ **D.** 255.255.255.255

2. You have the following addresses:

   Server01 (DNS Server): 172.24.1.30

   Server02 (WINS Server): 172.24.2.31

   Server03 (DHCP Server): 172.24.2.60

   Server04 (DC): 172.24.2.61

   Router: 172.24.2.1

   Which address should your default gateway point to?

   ○ **A.** 172.24.1.30

   ○ **B.** 172.24.2.31

   ○ **C.** 172.24.2.60

   ○ **D.** 172.24.2.61

   ○ **E.** 172.24.2.1

3. What do you call the following:

   2001::efd3:934a:42a2

   ○ **A.** MAC address

   ○ **B.** DNS Suffix address

   ○ **C.** WEP key

   ○ **D.** IPv4 address

   ○ **E.** IPv6 address

1. **B** is correct. The 172.1.32.4 address is a Class B address and a private address. The default subnet mask for a Class B address is 255.255.0.0. Answer A is incorrect because the 255.0.0.0 mask is used for a Class A network that has the first octet beginning with 1 to 126. Answer C is incorrect because the 255.255.255.0 mask is used for a Class C network that has the first octet beginning with 192 to 223. Answer D is incorrect because the 255.255.255.255 mask is used to specify that the address is the only one included and is not part of a range.

2. **E** is correct. The default gateway should point to a router so that it knows where to forward packets that need to be sent to remote subnets. Therefore, the other answers are incorrect.

3. **E** is correct. The 2001::efd3:934a:42a2 address is an IPv6 address. This address is short for 2001:0000:0000:0000:0000:efd3:934a:42a2. Therefore, the other answers are incorrect.

Transmission Control Protocol/Internet Protocol (TCP/IP) is an industry suite of protocols on which the Internet is based. It is supported by all versions of Windows and virtually all modern operating systems. The TCP/IP protocol suite operates on top of the networking physical layer, such as Ethernet and 802.11 wireless networks.

The lowest level protocol within the TCP/IP model (not to be confused with the OSI model) is the Internet protocol (IP), which is primarily responsible for addressing and routing packets between hosts. Each connection on a TCP/IP address is called a *host* (a computer or other network device that is connected to a TCP/IP network) and is assigned a unique IP address. A host is any network interface, including each network's interface cards or a network printer that connects directly onto the network. When you send or receive data, the data is divided into little chunks called packets. Each of these packets contains both the sender's TCP/IP address and the receiver's TCP/IP address.

Windows 7 supports both IPv4 and IPv6 through a dual-IP-layer architecture and enables both by default. This architecture enables you to tunnel IPv6 traffic across an IPv4 network in addition to tunneling IPv4 traffic across an IPv6 network.

IPv4 TCP/IP Addressing

When you talk about networking, you have to use addressing to identify a host on the network. All hosts use physical addresses known as Media Access Control (MAC) addresses. Most network interfaces have their MAC addresses burned onto a chip and cannot be changed. These addresses are 48-bits and are expressed in hexadecimal format with colons or dashes:

00-C0-9F-8E-82-00

Much like a host address, you cannot have two hosts with the same MAC address on the same physical network. The Address Resolution Protocol (ARP) translates from logical addresses to the MAC addresses, which can be viewed with the arp.exe command from a command prompt.

The traditional version of the IP protocol is version 4—IPv4. Each connection on a TCP/IP network is assigned a unique IP address. An IPv4 address is a logical address that is managed and organized by a network administrator. The format of the IP address is four 8-bit numbers (octets) divided by periods (.). Each number can be 0 to 255. For example, a TCP/IP address could be 131.107.3.1 or 2.0.0.1.

IP addresses are manually assigned and configured (static IP addresses) or dynamically assigned and configured by a Dynamic Host Configuration Protocol (DHCP) server (dynamic IP addresses). Because the IP address is used to identify the computer, no two connections can use the same IP address; otherwise, one or both of the computers would not be able to communicate, which usually results in a message stating "IP address conflict."

The TCP/IP address is broken down into a network number and a host number. The network number identifies the entire network and the host number identifies the computer or connection on the specified network.

Usually when defining the TCP/IP for a network connection, IT managers also specify a subnet mask. A subnet mask is used to define which address bits describe the network number and which address bits describe the host address. Similar to the IP address, the format of the subnet mask is four 8-bit numbers (octet) divided by periods (.). Each number can be 0 to 255. For example, a subnet mask could be 255.0.0.0, 255.255.255.0, or 255.255.240.0.

For example, if you have an address of 15.2.3.6 and you define a subnet mask of 255.255.255.0, 15.2.3.0 defines the network address where every computer on that network must begin with 15.2.3. Then each computer must have a unique host number, making the entire address unique. Because the first three octets are defined as the network ID, the last octet defines the host ID. Therefore, one host (and only one host) has a host ID of 0.0.0.6 located on the 15.2.3.0 network.

In simple IPv4 networks, the subnet mask defines full octets as part of the network ID and host ID. Table 5.1 lists the characteristics of each IP address class.

TABLE 5.1 **IP Address Classes**

Class	First Octet	Default Subnet Mask	Number of Networks	Number of Hosts per Network
A	1–126	255.0.0.0	126	16,777,214
B	128–191	255.255.0.0	16,384	64,534
C	192–223	255.255.255.0	2,097,152	254

The loopback address (127.0.0.1) is a special designated IP address (127.0.0.1) that is designated for the software loopback interface of a machine and is used to test IP software. In addition, if you access localhost, you are accessing the loopback address of 127.0.01.

Unfortunately, using classes to define networks allows for a lot of wasted addresses. To make use of these wasted addresses, classless addresses, or Classless Inter-Domain Routing (CIDR), was developed to not use the specific Class A, B, and C. Because CIDR does not use assign a Class A network address to a corporation or some other organization, it does not waste 16 million addresses. Instead, what would normally be a Class A address can be divided and given to multiple companies and organizations.

Because there are no classes that have a default subnet mask, CIDR subnetting uses a different notation that defines how many bits are masked. For example, if you had a subnet mask of 255.255.255.0, you use a CIDR notation of /24. The 24 is because the first 24 bits are masked (11111111.11111111.11111111.00000000). Therefore, an address is designated as

192.168.1.1/24

If an individual network is connected to another network and users must communicate with any computers on the other network, they must also define the default gateway, which specifies the local address of the router. If the default gateway is not specified, users are not able to communicate with computers on other networks. If the LAN is connected to more than two networks, users must specify only one gateway, because when a data packet is sent, the gateway first determines if the data packet needs to go to a local computer or onto another network. If the data packet is meant to be sent to a computer on another network, the gateway forwards the data packet to the router. The router then determines the best direction that the data packet must go to reach its destination.

If you are connected to the Internet, you need a default gateway. Because the default gateway address is an address of a host, it also is four 8-bit numbers (octet) divided by periods (.). Each number can be 0 to 255. Because it must be connected on the same network as the host, it must also have the same network address as the host address.

Because TCP/IP addresses are scarce for the Internet (based on the IPv4 and its 32-bit addresses), a series of addresses have been reserved to be used by the private networks. These addresses can be used by many organizations because these addresses are not seen from outside of the local network. The private IPv4 addresses are as follows:

► 10.x.x.x (1 Class A address range)

► 172.16.x.x to 172.31.x.x (16 Class B address ranges)

► 192.168.0.x to 192.168.255.x (256 Class C address ranges)

To allow for these addresses to connect to the Internet, you use a router that supports Network Address Translation (NAT), also known as "IP Masquerading," which translates between the internal private addresses and the public Internet addresses.

IPv6 TCP/IP Addressing

The Internet has grown and continues to grow at an exponential rate. Eventually the Internet will run out of network numbers. Therefore, a new IP protocol called IPv6 is replacing IPv4.

IPv6 provides a number of benefits for TCP/IP-based networking connectivity, including

► **Large address space**: The 128-bit address space for IPv6 potentially provides every device on the Internet with a globally unique address.

► **Efficient routing**: The IPv6 network packet supports hierarchical routing infrastructures, which enables more efficient routing than IPv4.

► **Straightforward configuration**: IPv6 can use both DHCP for IPv6 (DHCPv6) and local routers for automatic IP configuration.

► **Enhanced security**: The IPv6 standard provides better protection against address and port scanning attacks and all IPv6 implementations support IPsec for protection of IPv6 traffic.

IPv4 is based on 32-bit addresses (four 8-bit octets), which allows a little more than 4 billion hosts. IPv6 uses 128 bits for the addresses, which can have up to 3.4×10^{38} hosts. Thus, IPv6 can handle all of today's IP-based machines and allow for future growth while handling IP addresses for mobile devices such as personal digital assistants (PDAs), cell phones, and similar smart devices.

An IPv6 address is divided into groups of 16 bits, written as four hex digits. Hex digits include 0, 1, 2, 3, 4, 5, 6, 7, 8, 9, A, B, C, D, E, and F. The groups are separated by colons. An example of an address is

FE80:0000:0000:0000:02A0:D2EF:FEA5:E9F5

Similar to IPv4, the IPv6 addresses are split in two parts: bits that identify the network and bits that define the host address. Different from IPv4, IPv6 has a fixed prefix that contains specific routing and subnet information. The first 64 bits (four groups of four hex digits) define the network address and the second 64 bits define the host address. For the address of FE80:0000:0000:0000: 02A0:D2EF:FEA5:E9F5, FE80:0000:0000:0000 defines the network bits and 02A0:D2EF:FEA5:E9F5 defines the host bits.

While IPv6 addresses are expressed with hexadecimal digits, a 128-bit address still uses 32 hexadecimal digits. Therefore, in some situations, you can abbreviate an IPv6 address. When an IPv6 address has two or more consecutive eight-bit blocks of zeroes, you can replace them with a double colon, as follows:

42cd:0051:0000:0000:c8ba:03f2:003d:b291

This becomes

42cd:0051::c8ba:03f2:003d:b291

You can also remove the leading zeros in any block. Therefore, for our example, you have

42cd:51::c8ba:3f2:3d:b291

The IPv6 address types include the following:

- ▶ **Unicast**: Used for one-to-one communication between hosts. Each IPv6 host has multiple unicast addresses. The Unicast IPv6 can be further broken down to
    - ▶ **Global Unicast address**: Addresses that are equivalent to IPv4 public addresses so they are globally routable and reachable on the IPv6 portion of the Internet. Global Unicast addresses start with a 2 or 3.
    - ▶ **Link-Local addresses**: Used by hosts when communicating with neighboring hosts on the same link. They are equivalent to IPv4 APIPA addresses and start with FE8.

▶ **Unique local unicast addresses**: Equivalent to IPv4 private address spaces and start with FEC0.

▶ **Multicast**: Used for one-to-many communication between computers that are defined as using the same multicast address.

▶ **Anycast address**: An IPv6 unicast address that is assigned to multiple computers. When IPv6 addresses communicate to an anycast address, only the closest host responds. You typically use this for locating services or the nearest router.

The last 64-bits of an IPv6 address are the interface identifier. This is equivalent to the host ID in an IPv4 address. Each interface in an IPv6 network must have a unique interface identifier. Some network implementations use EIU-64, which derives the last 64-bits based on the MAC address.

Because the interface identifier is unique to each interface, IPv6 uses it rather than media access control (MAC) addresses to identify hosts uniquely. Because the MAC address can partially be used to uniquely identify a computer, some IPv6 implementations generate a unique interface identifier to preserve privacy in network communication rather than using the network adapter's MAC address.

In the next-generation Internet Protocol, IPv6, ARP's functionality is provided by the Neighbor Discovery Protocol (NDP). NDP is responsible for

▶ Address autoconfiguration of nodes

▶ Discovery of other nodes on the link

▶ Determining the Link Layer addresses of other nodes

▶ Duplicate address detection

▶ Finding available routers and Domain Name System (DNS) servers

▶ Address prefix discovery

▶ Maintaining reachability information about the paths to other active neighbor nodes

ExamAlert

If you need to assign a computer directly to the Internet, you should configure the computer with an IPv6 address that is equivalent to a public IPv4 address, which is a global unicast IPv6 address. These addresses are globally routable and can be reached from the Internet. However, computers running Windows 7 are usually connected through your ISP, which is automatically assigned an IPv6 address.

Similar to the loopback address of 127.0.0.1 used for testing, IPv6 uses 0:0:0:0:0:0:0:1. To abbreviate this address, you can write it as ::1.

Because most networks use IPv4, there are several methods that were created to transition from IPv4 to IPv6. Windows 7 and Windows Server 2008 R2 support the following methods:

▶ **IPv4-compatible address**: 0:0:0:0:0:0:w.x.y.z or ::w.x.y.z (where w.x.y.z is the dotted decimal representation of a public IPv4 address) is used by IPv6/IPv4 nodes that are communicating using IPv6. The address format consists of 96 bits of zeroes, followed by an IPv4 address in its standard dotted-decimal notation. As a result, an IPv4-compatible address is used as an IPv6 destination. The IPv6 is automatically encapsulated with an IPv6 header and sent to the destination using the IPv4 infrastructure. An example is ::192.168.1.20.

▶ **IPv4-mapped address**: The IPv4-mapped IPv6 address has its first 80 bits set to zero, the next 16 set to one, and the last 32 bits represent the IPv4 address. For example, ::FFFF:C000:280 is the mapped IPv6 address for 192.0.2.128. Remember, the 192.0.2.128 is written in decimal format, while the C000:280 is written in hexadecimal format. The IPv4-mapped IPv6 addresses always identify IPv4-only nodes. An example is ::ffff:192.168.1.20.

▶ **6to4 address**: A tunneling technology that enables computers to transmit IPv6 packets over an IPv4 network. The 6to4 address is formed by combining the prefix 2002::/16 with the 32 bits of a public IPv4 address, forming a 48-bit prefix. An example using the 192.168.1.20 IPv4 address appears as follows: 2002:C0A8:0114::/16. 6to4 is enabled by default on machines running Windows 7.

▶ **Intra-Site Automatic Tunnel Addressing Protocol (ISATAP) address**: Used between two unicast nodes running both IPv4 and IPv6 over an IPv4 routing infrastructure. ISATAP addresses use the locally administered interface ID ::0:5EFE:w.x.y.z, where w.x.y.z is any unicast IPv4 address, which includes both public and private addresses. The ISATAP interface ID can be combined with any 64-bit prefix that is valid for IPv6 unicast addresses. This includes the link-local address prefix (FE80::/64), site-local prefixes, and global prefixes. ISATAP is enabled by default on machines running Windows 7.

▶ **Teredo address**: Teredo tunneling enables you to tunnel across the IPv4 network when the clients are behind an IPv4 NAT. Teredo was created because many IPv4 routers use NAT to define a private address space for corporate networks. For two Windows-based Teredo clients, the most crucial Teredo processes are those that you use for initial configuration and communication with a different site's peer. Teredo addresses use the prefix 2001:0000::/32. Beyond the first 32 bits, Teredo addresses are used to encode the IPv4 address of a Teredo server, flags, and the encoded version of the external address and port of a Teredo client. An example of a Teredo address is 2001:0000:9d36:b007:8000:82ff:3f57:e00c. Teredo is enabled by default on machines running Windows 7.

Default Gateway

A default gateway is a device, usually a router, that connects the local network to other networks. When you need to communicate with a host on another subnet, you forward all packets to the default gateway. The router then determines the best way to get to the remote subnet and forwards the packets toward the remote subnet.

Name Resolution

Most users find the IPv4 and IPv6 addresses difficult to remember when communicating with other computers. Instead, a user specifies a recognizable name, and the name is translated into an address. For example, when a user opens Internet Explorer and specifies http://www.microsoft.com, the www.microsoft.com is translated into an IP address. The web page is then accessed from the server using the translated IP addresses.

Fully Qualified Domain Names (FQDNs), sometimes referred to as just *domain names*, are used to identify computers on a TCP/IP network. Examples include the following:

www.microsoft.com

www.intel.com

server1.acme.com

One way to translate the FQDN to the IP address is to use a DNS server. DNS is a distributed database (a database contained in multiple servers) containing host name and IP address information for all domains on the Internet. For every domain, there is a single authoritative name server that contains all DNS-related information about the domain. When you configure IP configurations, you need to specify the address of a DNS server so that you use the Internet or log in to a Windows Active Directory domain.

For DNS to keep track of specific information, the DNS server uses resource records to hold the information. The most common resource records are the following:

- **Address record (A)**: Used to resolve host names into a 32-bit IPv4 addresses.

- **IPv6 address record (AAAA)**: Used to resolve host names into a 128-bit IPv6 address.

- **Pointer record (PTR)**: Used to resolve IP address into a host name (reverse DNS lookup.)

- **Mail exchange record (MX)**: Used to identify the mail transfer agent for an organization.

- **Service locator (SRV)**: Used to identify generalized service location record, including finding the domain controllers.

Because an organization could have hundreds or even thousands of hosts, Dynamic DNS was created to register automatically a host name and IP address to a DNS server.

Besides the DNS server, a HOSTS file on each machine can also be used to translate domain/host names to IP addresses. The disadvantage of using HOSTS files is that you must add entries on every machine; however, a HOSTS file can come in handy when you want to connect to a test machine that you do not want to become widely available to everyone else.

Another naming scheme used on TCP/IP networks is using the NetBIOS names (such as that is used to identify share names for files and printers \\COMPUTERNAME\SHARENAME). To translate NetBIOS names to IP addresses, you use a Windows Internet Name Service (WINS) server or the LMHOSTS files.

> **Note**
>
> On Windows machines, the HOSTS and LMHOSTS files are located in the C:\Windows\System32\drivers\etc folder.

If you try to access a network resource by name instead of IP address and the device cannot be found, it is most likely a problem with the DNS server/HOSTS file or the WINS server/LMHOSTS file. Either the servers cannot be contacted, or the servers or files have the wrong address associated with the name. The failure of these servers or files can also affect network applications that need to access various services or resources.

For computers with IPv6 link-local addresses that do not have access to a DNS server, the system uses the Link Local Multicast Name Resolution (LLMNR) protocol. LLMNR automatically transmits name query request messages as multicast to the local network. The computer with the requested name then replies with a message containing its IP address using a unicast packet.

DHCP Services

The Dynamic Host Configuration Protocol (DHCP) is used to automatically configure a host during boot-up on a TCP/IP network and to change settings while the host is attached. DHCP can automatically set many parameters with the DHCP server for IPv4 and IPv6 networks, which prevents network administrators from having to manually configure hundreds or even thousands of computers. Some of the more common parameters include the following:

- ▶ IP address

- ▶ Subnet mask

- ▶ Gateway (router) address

- ▶ Address of DNS server

- ▶ Address of WINS servers

- ▶ WINS client mode

IP Automatic Configuration is a method of assigning an IPv6 address to an interface automatically. It can be stateful or stateless:

- ▶ Stateful addresses are assigned by a DHCP service on a server or other device. The service that allocated the address to the client manages the stateful address.

- ▶ Stateless addresses are configured by the client and are not maintained by a service. The record of the address assignment is not maintained. Instead, the computer configures its own address after transmitting router solicitation multicasts to the routers and receives routing advertisement messages in return.

The link-local address is a stateless address that is automatically generated. It is used by the host to communicate with other hosts on the local network. A link-local address is not routable and cannot be used to communicate with hosts on a remote network. When the host generates the link-local address, the host also performs duplicate address detection to ensure that it is unique.

IP Configuration on Windows 7 Machines

To configure the IP configuration in Windows 7, do the following:

1. Open the Control Panel.

2. While in Category view, click **Network and Internet**, click **Network and Sharing Center**, and click **Change adapter settings**.

3. Right-click the connection that you want to change and then click **Properties**. If you are prompted for an administrator password or confirmation, type the password or provide confirmation.

4. Click the **Networking** tab. Under **This connection uses the following items,** click either **Internet Protocol Version 4 (TCP/IPv4)** or **Internet Protocol Version 6 (TCP/IPv6),** and then click **Properties** to display the resulting window in Figure 5.1.

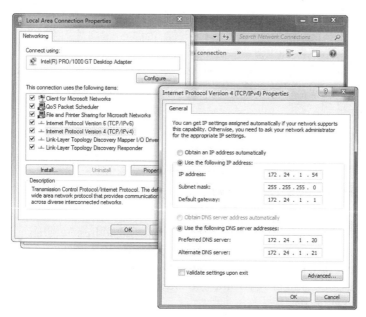

FIGURE 5.1   Configure IPv4 settings in Windows 7.

To specify IPv4 IP address settings, do one of the following:

▶ To obtain IP settings automatically from a DHCP server, click **Obtain an IP address automatically** and then click **OK**.

▶ To specify an IP address, click **Use the following IP address**, and then, in the IP address, Subnet mask, and Default gateway boxes, type the IP address settings.

To specify IPv6 IP address settings, do one of the following (see Figure 5.2):

▶ To obtain IP settings automatically, click **Obtain an IPv6 address automatically** and then click **OK**.

▶ To specify an IP address, click **Use the following IPv6 address**, and then, in the IPv6 address, Subnet prefix length, and Default gateway boxes, type the IP address settings.

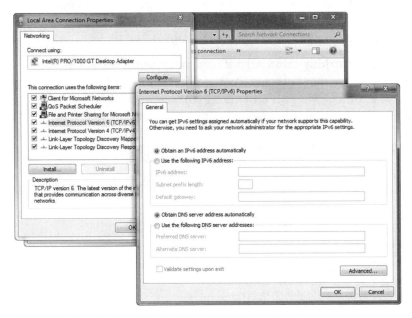

FIGURE 5.2 **Configure IPv6 settings in Windows 7.**

Windows 7 provides the capability to configure alternate IP address settings to support connecting to different networks. Although static IP addresses can be used with workstations, most workstations use dynamic or alternative IP addressing, or both. You configure dynamic and alternative addressing by completing the following steps:

1. Open the Control Panel.

2. While in Category view, click **Network and Internet**, click **Network and Sharing Center**, and click **Manage Network Connections**.

> **Note**
>
> Some versions of Windows 7 use Change Adapter Settings instead of Manage Network Connections.

3. Right-click the connection that you want to change and then click **Properties**.

4. Double-click **Internet Protocol Version 6 (TCP/IPv6)** or **Internet Protocol Version 4 (TCP/IPv4)** as appropriate for the type of IP address you are configuring.

5. Select **Obtain an IPv6 address automatically** or **Obtain an IP address automatically** as appropriate for the type of IP address you are configuring. If desired, select **Obtain DNS server address automatically**. Or select **Use the following DNS server addresses** and then type a preferred and alternate DNS server address in the text boxes provided.

6. When you use dynamic IPv4 addressing with desktop computers, you should configure an automatic alternative address. To use this configuration, from the Alternate Configuration tab, select **Automatic Private IP Address**. Click **OK** twice, click **Close**, and then skip the remaining steps.

7. When you use dynamic IPv4 addressing with mobile computers, you usually want to configure the alternative address manually. To use this configuration, on the Alternate Configuration tab, select **User Configured**. Then in the IP Address text box, type the IP address you want to use. The IP address that you assign to the computer should be a private IP address, and it must not be in use anywhere else when the settings are applied.

8. With dynamic IPv4 addressing, complete the alternate configuration by entering a subnet mask, default gateway, DNS, and WINS settings. When you're finished, click **OK** twice and then click **Close**.

To specify DNS server address settings for IPv4 and IPv6, do one of the following:

▶ To obtain a DNS server address automatically, click **Obtain DNS server address automatically** and then click **OK**.

▶ To specify a DNS server address, click **Use the following DNS server addresses**, and then, in the Preferred DNS server and Alternate DNS server boxes, type the addresses of the primary and secondary DNS servers.

Network and Sharing Center

As shown in Figure 5.3, the Network and Sharing Center provides real-time status information about your network. You can see if your computer is connected to your network or the Internet, the type of connection, and what level of access you have to other computers and devices on the network. This information can be useful when you set up your network or if you have connection problems. You can find more detailed information about your network in the network map, which is accessible from the Network and Sharing Center. You can access the Network and Sharing Center from the Control Panel or from the Notification Area. You can also use the Network and Sharing Center to set up a wireless or VPN connection; create and manage homegroups; and manage a system's sharing options.

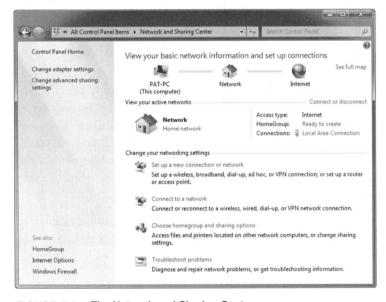

FIGURE 5.3   The Network and Sharing Center.

Using the netsh Command

Netsh.exe is a tool an administrator can use to configure and monitor various networking parameters using the command prompt, including

▶ Configuring IP addresses, default gateway, and DNS servers

▶ Configuring interfaces

▶ Configuring routing protocols

▶ Configuring filters

▶ Configuring routes

▶ Configuring remote access behavior for Windows-based remote access servers that are running the Routing and Remote Access Server (RRAS) Service

▶ Displaying the configuration of a currently running router

▶ Using the scripting feature to run a collection of commands in batch mode against a specified router

To display the available options for the `netsh` command, you enter the following at the command line:

```
netsh /?
```

To view your interfaces, execute the following command:

```
netsh interface ipv4 show interfaces
```

When you view the output of the `netsh` command, you need to note the names of the interfaces for your network adapter.

To set a static IP address and default gateway, you use the following command:

```
netsh interface ipv4 set address name "interface name" source=static
address=preferred IP address mask=SubnetMask gateway=gateway address
```

If you are using and configuring IPv6, you specify **ipv6** instead of **ipv4**. If the interface name includes spaces, you need to surround the name with quotes (""). If you don't want to assign a gateway, you specify **gateway=none**.

To set the static DNS address, use the following command:

```
netsh interface ipv4 add dnsserver name="interface name" address=IP
address of the primary DNS server index=1
```

For each DNS server that you want to set, increment the **index=** `number` each time. Therefore, for the first DNS server, index would be 1. For the second DNS server, index would be 2.

To change a server to the DHCP-provided IP address from a static IP address, use the following command:

```
netsh interface ipv4 set address name="interface name" source=DHCP
```

For more information about using the netsh command, use the following websites:

http://technet.microsoft.com/en-us/library/cc754516(WS.10).aspx

http://technet.microsoft.com/en-us/library/cc770948(WS.10).aspx

Cram Quiz

1. What are the two services that provide name resolution? (Choose two answers.)
   - ○ **A.** DNS
   - ○ **B.** DHCP
   - ○ **C.** WINS
   - ○ **D.** NAT

2. What command do you use to view your IPv4 interfaces on a computer running Windows 7?
   - ○ **A.** netsh interface ipv4 show interfaces
   - ○ **B.** netsh interface ipv4 set address name all
   - ○ **C.** netsh interface ipv4 add interface
   - ○ **D.** netsh interface ipv4 set address name source=DHCP

3. What IPv6 address is used to communicate with neighboring hosts on the same link?
   - ○ **A.** Global unicast
   - ○ **B.** Link-local
   - ○ **C.** Unique local unicast
   - ○ **D.** Multicast

Cram Quiz Answers

1. **A** and **C** are correct. DNS is short for Domain Name System and WINS is short for Windows Internet Name Service. DNS translates from host names/domain names to IP addresses and WINS translates from NetBIOS names/computer names. Answer B is incorrect because DHCP (short for Dynamic Host Configuration Protocol) is used to assign IP addresses automatically. Answer D is incorrect because NAT, short for Network Address Translation, is used to connect a private network through a single public address.

2. **A** is correct. To view your interfaces, execute the following command: `netsh interface ipv4 show interfaces`. Answers B, C, and D are incorrect because the `set` option and `add` option are used to modify or add an address, not view an address.

3. **B** is correct. A link-local address is used by hosts when communicating with neighboring hosts on the same link. Answer A is incorrect because the global unicast addresses are equivalent to IPv4 public addresses, so they are globally routable and reachable on the IPv6 portion of the Internet. Answer C is incorrect because the unique local unicast addresses are equivalent to IPv4 private address spaces. Answer D is incorrect because a multicast address is used for one-to-many communications between computers.

Tools to Help Diagnose Network Problems

▶ **Configure IPv4 network settings**

▶ **Configure IPv6 network settings**

▶ **Configure networking settings**

CramSaver

1. You had to move a well-used server to a different subnet and change the IP address. Now users are complaining that they cannot access the server. What should you do?

   ○ **A.** Have the users run the `ipconfig /all` command

   ○ **B.** Have the users run the `ipconfig /flushdns` command

   ○ **C.** Have the users change their DNS server to the new address of the server they are trying to connect to

   ○ **D.** Have the users run the `netsh interface ip set dns` command

2. You have a computer running Windows 7. You just configured your DHCP server to assign IPv6 addresses. What can you do to verify the addresses? (Choose two answers.)

   ○ **A.** Run the `net config` command at a command prompt

   ○ **B.** Select Details from the network connection status

   ○ **C.** Select Internet Protocol version 6 (TCP/IP) and then properties from network connection properties

   ○ **D.** Run the `NetStat` command at a command prompt

   ○ **E.** Run the `ipconfig /all` command at a command prompt

Answers

1. **B** is correct. The `ipconfig /flushdns` command clears out the users' DNS cache so they can then retrieve the new IP address when they access the server by name. Answer A is incorrect because the `ipconfig /all` command only displays the configuration. Answer C is incorrect because changing the DNS address to the new server prevents the computers from performing DNS resolution, including the name resolution to the server, because the new server is most likely not a DNS server, which would be incapable of providing name resolution for the client PC. Answer D is incorrect because it also changes the DNS settings at a command prompt, which prevents the computer from performing DNS resolution, including the name resolution to the server, because the new server is

most likely not a DNS server, which would be incapable of providing name
resolution for the client PC.

2. **B** and **E** are correct. To see what addresses are assigned to a computer,
you can select Details from the network connection status or use the
`ipconfig /all` command. Answer A is incorrect because the `net
config` command displays the configurable workstation and server
services that are running. Answer C is incorrect because the Internet
Protocol version 6 (TCP/IP) only allows you to specify static addresses or
to use a DHCP address. If you select to use DHCP, it does not show you
the actual TCP/IP address. Answer D is incorrect because the `netstat`
command is used to display protocol statistics and current TCP/IP network connections.

You can use several utilities to test and troubleshoot the TCP/IP network.

If you experience network connectivity problems while using Windows 7, you
can use Window Network Diagnostics to start the troubleshooting process. If
there is a problem, Windows Network Diagnostics analyzes the problem and,
if possible, presents a solution or a list of possible causes. To start the
Windows Network Diagnostics program, right-click the Network and Sharing
Center and select Troubleshoot problems.

Windows Network Diagnostics might be able to complete the solution automatically or might require the user to perform steps in the resolution process.
If Windows Network Diagnostics cannot resolve the problem, you should follow a logical troubleshooting process using tools available in Windows 7.
Table 5.2 outlines some of these tools. Although some of these tools have new
options to accommodate IPv6, these tools have been around for years. The
`ipconfig` command shows a computer's current configuration while `ping`,
`tracert`, and `pathping` are used to test network connectivity. NSlookup is
used to test DNS name resolution.

TABLE 5.2   **Windows 7 TCP/IP Troubleshooting Tools**

Tool	Functionality
ipconfig	The `ipconfig` command displays current TCP/IP configuration as shown in Figure 5.4.
	▶ `ipconfig /all` command displays full TCP/IP configuration information, as shown in Figure 5.5.
	▶ `ipconfig /release` releases the IPv4 address configured by a DHCP server.
	▶ `ipconfig /release6` releases the IPv6 address configured by a DHCP server.

TABLE 5.2 **Continued**

Tool	Functionality
	▶ `ipconfig /renew` renews the IPv4 address configured by a DHCP server. ▶ `ipconfig /renew6` renews the IPv6 address configured by a DHCP server. ▶ `ipconfig /flushdns` purges the DNS resolver cache. ▶ `ipconfig /registerdns` refreshes all DHCP leases and re-registers DNS names.
ping	By using the ICMP protocol, the `ping` command verifies connections to a remote computer by verifying configurations and testing IP connectivity. ▶ The `-t` option pings the specified host until stopped. ▶ The `-a` option resolves address to host name. ▶ The `-S srcaddr` option specifies the source address to use. ▶ The `-4` option forces the ping command to use IPv4. ▶ The `-6` option forces the ping command to use IPv6.
tracert	The `tracert` command traces the route that a packet takes to a destination and displays the series of IP routers that are used in delivering packets to the destination. If the packets are unable to be delivered to the destination, the `tracert` command displays the last router that successfully forwarded the packet. The `tracert` command also uses the ICMP protocol.
pathping	`pathping` traces a route through the network in a manner similar to `tracert`. However, `pathping` also provides more detailed statistics on the individual hops.
nslookup	The `nslookup` command displays information that you can use to diagnose your DNS infrastructure. You can use `nslookup` to confirm connection to the DNS server and the existence of required resource records.

FIGURE 5.4   **Using the** `ipconfig` **command.**

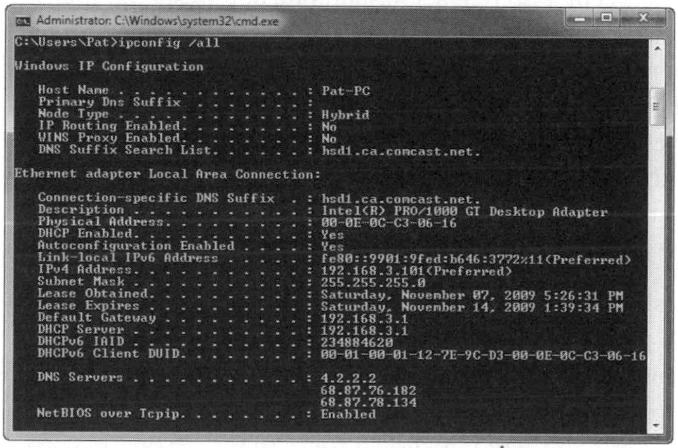

FIGURE 5.5   **Using the** `ipconfig /all` **command.**

A typical troubleshooting process would be

1. Check local IP configuration (`ipconfig`).

2. Use the **ping** command to gather more information on the extent of the problem:

  ▶ Ping the loopback address (127.0.0.1) or ::1.

  ▶ Ping the local IP address.

  ▶ Ping the remote gateway.

  ▶ Ping the remote computer.

3. Identify each hop (router) between two systems using the **tracert** command.

4. Verify DNS configuration using the **nslookup** command.

Using `ipconfig` with the `/all` switch shows you the IP configuration of the computer. If the IP address is invalid, communication might fail. If the subnet mask is incorrect, the computer has an incorrect Network ID and therefore communication might fail, especially to remote subnets. If the default gateway is incorrect or missing, the computer is not able to communicate with remote subnets. If the DNS server is incorrect or missing, the computer might not be able to resolve names and communication might fail.

If the computer is set to accept a DHCP server and one does respond, the computer uses Automatic Private IP Addressing (APIPA), which generates an IP address in the form of 169.254.xxx.xxx and the subnet mask of 255.255.0.0. After the computer generates the address, it broadcasts this address until it can find a DHCP server. When you have an Automatic Private IP Address, you can only communicate with computers on the same network/subnet that has an Automatic Private IP Address.

If you can successfully ping an IP address but not the name, name resolution is failing. If you successfully ping the computer name but the response does not resolve the FQDN name, resolution has not used DNS. This means a process such as broadcasts or WINS has been used to resolve the name, and applications that require DNS might fail. If you encounter a Request Timed Out message, this indicates that there is a known route to the destination computer but one or more computers or routers along the path, including the source and destination, are not configured correctly. A Destination Host Unreachable message indicates that the system cannot find a route to the destination system and therefore does not know where to send the packet on the next hop.

Cram Quiz

1. What command would you use to release the IPv6 address handed out by a DHCP server?

   ○ **A.** `ipconfig /all`

   ○ **B.** `ipconfig /release`

   ○ **C.** `ipconfig /release6`

   ○ **D.** `ipconfig /flushdns`

2. What command can you use to query a DNS server for a name translation to an IP address?

   ○ **A.** `ipconfig`

   ○ **B.** `ipconfig /flushdns`

   ○ **C.** `ipconfig /registerdns`

   ○ **D.** `nslookup`

Cram Quiz Answers

1. **C** is correct. The `ipconfig /release6` command releases the IPv6 address configured by a DHCP server. Answer A is incorrect because the `ipconfig /all` command only displays the IP configuration. Answer B is incorrect because the `ipconfig /release` command releases IPv4 addresses. Answer D is incorrect because the `ipconfig /flushdns` clears out the local DNS cache on a Windows system.

2. **D** is correct. The `nslookup` command displays information that you can use to diagnose your DNS infrastructure. Answer A is incorrect because the `ipconfig` command only displays IP configuration. Answer B is incorrect because the `ipconfig /flushdns` command clears out the local DNS cache on a Windows system. Answer C is incorrect because the `ipconfig /regis-terdns` registers a system with a DNS server.

Review Questions

1. What command would you use to renew the DHCP IPv4 addresses?

   ○ **A.** `ipconfig`

   ○ **B.** `ipconfig /renew`

   ○ **C.** `ipconfig /renew6`

   ○ **D.** `ipconfig /release_and_renew`

   ○ **E.** `ipconfig /registerdns`

2. What command would you use to flush the DNS cache stored on an individual Windows 7 machine?

   ○ **A.** `ipconfig`

   ○ **B.** `ipconfig /renew`

   ○ **C.** `ipconfig /renew6`

   ○ **D.** `ipconfig /registerdns`

   ○ **E.** `ipconfig /flushdns`

3. What command can be used to show network connectivity to a computer?

   ○ **A.** `ipconfig`

   ○ **B.** `arp`

   ○ **C.** `ping`

   ○ **D.** `traceroute`

4. If you want to show IP addresses and their corresponding MAC addresses, what command would you use?

   ○ **A.** `ipconfig`

   ○ **B.** `ipconfig /all`

   ○ **C.** `arp`

   ○ **D.** `ping`

   ○ **E.** `tracert`

5. You are trying to figure out why a computer cannot connect to a file server. You type in `ipconfig` and you get the following output:

```
C:\Users\User>ipconfig
Windows IP Configuration
Ethernet adapter Local Area Connection:
   Connection-specific DNS Suffix  . : acme.com.
   Link-local IPv6 Address . . . . . : fe80::35d3:1958:365b:380a%13
   IPv4 Address. . . . . . . . . . . : 169.254.3.103
```

```
Subnet Mask . . . . . . . . . . : 255.255.0.0
Default Gateway . . . . . . . . . :
```

What is the problem?

- ○ **A.** The computer cannot connect to the DHCP server to get an address.
- ○ **B.** The server was not assigned a default gateway.
- ○ **C.** The subnet mask is wrong.
- ○ **D.** You cannot determine the problem from this example.

6. You can ping a PC using an address but not by name. What is the problem?

- ○ **A.** You are not on the same subnet as the computer.
- ○ **B.** A firewall is blocking access to the computer by name.
- ○ **C.** You need to start the DHCP client service on your PC.
- ○ **D.** You have a DNS name resolution problem.

7. You work as the desktop support technician at Acme.com. You want to assign an address to a computer that will be available on the Internet and it will have the same address for both IPv4 and IPv6. What kind of address is this?

- ○ **A.** A unique private address
- ○ **B.** A multicast local address
- ○ **C.** A site-local address
- ○ **D.** A global unicast address

8. You work as the desktop support technician at Acme.com. You have a user that works between the Sacramento and New York offices. She currently has a static IP addresses assigned to her computer. When she is at the Sacramento office, her system has no problem connecting to the network. When she travels to New York, her system cannot connect to the network. What is the problem?

- ○ **A.** You need to update the drivers for the network card.
- ○ **B.** You need to assign a Public IPv4 address.
- ○ **C.** You need to run the troubleshooting wizard.
- ○ **D.** Within the TCP/IPv4 Properties dialog box, you need to select the Obtain an IP address automatically option.

9. You are assigned a computer to test the IPv6 address of Server01. What command would you use?

- ○ **A.** `ping -s server01`
- ○ **B.** `ping -6 server01`
- ○ **C.** `ping -a server01`
- ○ **D.** `ping -t server01`

10. Which type of IPv6 address is automatically configured and is used to communicate with local network devices such as a neighboring router?

   ○ **A.** Global unicast address

   ○ **B.** Unique local unicast address

   ○ **C.** Link-local address

   ○ **D.** Anycast address

Review Question Answers

1. Answer **B** is correct. To renew IPv4, you have to use the `ipconfig /renew` command. Answer A is incorrect because the `ipconfig` command without any options only displays basic IP configuration information. Answer C is incorrect because the `/renew6` option renews IPv6 IP addresses. Answer D is incorrect because the `/release_and_renew` option does not exist. Answer E is incorrect because the `/registerdns` option is how to get the computer to register itself with the DNS server.

2. Answer **E** is correct. The command to flush local cached DNS information is `ipconfig /flushdns`. Answer A is incorrect because the `ipconfig` command without any options only displays basic IP configuration information. Answer B is incorrect because the `/renew` option renews the IPv4 IP addresses. Answer C is incorrect because the `/renew6` option renews IPv6 IP addresses. Answer D is incorrect because the `/registerdns` option is how to get the computer to register itself with the DNS server.

3. Answer **C** is correct. The two commands that show network connectivity to another computer are the `ping` command the `tracert` command. Answer A is incorrect because the `ipconfig` command without any options only displays basic IP configuration information. Answer B is incorrect because the `arp` command is used to view and manage IP address to MAC address mappings. The `traceroute` command is found on UNIX and Linux machines. Windows machines use **tracert**.

4. Answer **B** is correct. To show all IP configuration information, you must use the `ipconfig /all` command. Answer A is incorrect because the `ipconfig` command without any options only displays basic IP configuration information. Answer C is incorrect because the `arp` command is used to view and manage IP address. Answers D and E are incorrect because `ping` and `tracert` are commands used to test network connectivity.

5. Answer **A** is correct. By looking at the example, the address assigned to the computer is 169.254.3.103, which is an Automatic Private IP address. Automatic Private IP addresses begin with 169.254. Automatic Private IP addresses are assigned to Windows computers when they cannot find a DHCP server from which to get an address. Answer B is incorrect because although a gateway address might be needed to communicate with computers on another network, the gateway was not assigned because it could not find a DHCP server. Answer

C is incorrect because this subnet mask was assigned when it could not find a DHCP server. Answer D is incorrect because you can determine the problem from the information provided in the example.

6. Answer **D** is correct. If you have a name resolution issue, the problem has to be with a DNS or WINS server or you have incorrect entries in your HOSTS or LMHOSTS files. Answer A is incorrect because if you can ping it by address, you have network connectivity to the server. So, it does not matter if the server is on the same subnet or a different subnet. Answer B is incorrect because you cannot block access to a computer by name but keep access by address. Answer C is incorrect because if the DHCP client service was not on, you would not be able to get any address from a DHCP server and are not able to connect to other hosts on the network.

7. Answer **D** is correct. If you want an address to be available from the Internet and be the same address for both IPv4 and IPv6, it must have a global unicast address that can be seen on the Internet. Answer A is incorrect because private addresses cannot be used on the public network such as the Internet. Answer B is incorrect because it has to be a single address assigned to a single computer, and not a multicast, which is used to broadcast to multiple addresses at the same time. Answer C is incorrect because a local address cannot be seen on the outside.

8. Answer **D** is correct. Because this person is traveling between two sites, the user needs to have a local address on each site. Therefore, you should let the local DHCP server hand out the addresses when she connects to each network. Answer A is incorrect because she can connect to one network. Therefore, the driver is working fine. Answer B is incorrect because this means that you are putting this computer directly on the Internet. Answer C is incorrect because running a troubleshooting wizard could be a lengthy process when the solution is simple.

9. Answer **B** is correct. To force the ping command to test a IPv6 connection, you need to use the -6 option. Answer A is incorrect because the -s option is used to specify a source address, which can come in handy when you have a computer with multiple network cards. Answer C is incorrect because the –a option is used to resolve the address to a host name. Answer D is incorrect because the –t option pings the specified host until it is stopped.

10. Answer **C** is correct. Link-local addresses are used by hosts when communicating with neighboring hosts on the same link. Answer A is incorrect because a global unicast address is an address that is equivalent to IPv4 public addresses so they are globally routable and reachable on the IPv6 portion of the Internet. Answer B is incorrect because a unique local unicast address is an IPv6 address that is equivalent to IPv4 private address spaces. Answer D is incorrect because the anycast address is an IPv6 unicast address that is assigned to multiple computers. When IPv6 addresses communication to an anycast address, only the closest host responds.

CHAPTER 6

Configuring Advanced Windows Networking

This chapter covers the following 70-680 Objectives:

▶ Configuring Network Connectivity:

  ▶ Configure networking settings

▶ Configuring Mobile Computing:

  ▶ Configure remote connections

  ▶ Configure DirectAccess

Chapter 5, "Configuring Windows Networking," covered the basics of networking including how to configure your computer to connect to a TCP/IP network. This chapter continues the discussion by looking at different networking technologies that you need to configure to connect to a network, which might include a wireless connection, a dial-up connection, or a VPN connection.

Wireless Connection

▶ **Configure networking settings**

Cram**Saver**

1. You have a wireless access point configured to use Advanced Encryption Standard (AES) security; however, you do not have a pre-shared key. Which option should you use to connect to the wireless access point?

   ○ **A.** Use WPA2-Enterprise

   ○ **B.** Use WPA2-Personal

   ○ **C.** Use WPA-Enterprise

   ○ **D.** Use WPA-Personal

2. You have a laptop that runs Windows 7. At your corporation, the network administrators recently disabled the SSID broadcast. When you try to connect to the wireless network, you fail to connect. What do you need to do?

   ○ **A.** Change the wireless network connection settings on your computer

   ○ **B.** Update your Windows credentials

   ○ **C.** Enable network discovery

   ○ **D.** Install a digital certificate on the laptop

Answers

1. **A** is correct. WPA2 uses AES encryption. Enterprise uses digital certificates instead of a pre-shared key. Answers B and D are incorrect because WPA and WPA2 Personal use a pre-shared key. Answer C is incorrect because WPA-Enterprise uses Temporary Key Integrity Protocol (TKIP) instead of AES.

2. **A** is correct. Because the SSID broadcast is disabled, the wireless network does not show up under the available networks list. Therefore, you need to manually configure the wireless connection. Answer B is incorrect because your Windows credentials are not used to connect to a wireless network. Answer C is incorrect because network discovery only helps you locate other wireless hosts on your wireless network. Answer D is incorrect because the digital certificate is needed to connect using WPA-Enterprise or WPA2-Enterprise; however, because you were able to connect to the network before and the only thing that has changed is that the SSID has been disabled, you most likely already have the appropriate digital certificate if necessary.

A quickly advancing field in networking is wireless technology. Today's computers can have a wireless network adapter to connect to other computers or to a wireless access point, which in turn enables the users to connect to the Internet or the rest of the internal network. Today's wireless adapters include PC cards for notebooks, Peripheral Component Interconnect (PCI)/PCI Express (PCIe) cards for desktops, and universal serial bus (USB) devices (which can be used with laptops or desktops).

Wireless adapters can run in one of two operating modes:

▶ **Ad hoc**: Wireless adapter used to connect directly to other computers with wireless adapters.

▶ **Infrastructure**: Wireless adapter connected to a wireless access point.

The most widely used wireless network adapters and access points are based on the Institute of Electrical and Electronics Engineers (IEEE) 802.11 specifications, as shown in Table 6.1. Most wireless networks used by companies are 802.11b, 802.11g, or 802.11n networks. Wireless devices that are based on these specifications can be Wi-Fi Certified to show they have been thoroughly tested for performance and compatibility.

> **Note**
>
> Because these devices use common public low-powered wireless frequencies, other wireless devices such as wireless phones or handsets might interfere with wireless adapters if they use the same frequency when they are used at the same time.

TABLE 6.1 **Popular Wireless Standards**

Wireless Standard	802.11a	802.11b	802.11g	802.11n
Speed	Up to 54 Mbps	Up to 11 Mbps	Up to 54 Mbps	Up to 240 Mbps
Transmission frequency	5 GHz	2.4 GHz	2.4 GHz	2.4 GHz
Effective indoor range	Approximately 25 to 75 feet	Approximately 100 to 150 feet	Approximately 100 to 150 feet	Approximately 300 to 450 feet
Compatibility	Incompatible with 802.11b and 802.11g.	802.11b wireless devices can interoperate with 802.11g devices (at 11 Mbps).	802.11g wireless devices can operate with 802.11b devices (at 11 Mbps).	802.11n can interoperate with 802.11b and 802.11g devices.

Of course, because a wireless network signal can be captured by anyone within the range of the antennas, it is easy for someone to intercept the wireless signals that are being broadcasted; therefore, it is always recommended that you use some form of encryption.

The most basic wireless encryption scheme is Wireless Equivalent Privacy (WEP). With WEP, you encrypt data using 40-bit, 128-bit, 152-bit, or higher private key encryption. With WEP, all data is encrypted using a symmetric key derived from the WEP key or password before it is transmitted, and any computer that wants to read the data must be able to decrypt it using the key. However, it is easy for someone with a little knowledge or experience to break the shared key because it doesn't change automatically over time. Therefore, it is recommended to use a higher form of wireless encryption then WEP.

Today, it is recommended that you use Wi-Fi Protected Access (WPA) or Wi-Fi Protected Access Version 2 (WPA2). WPA was adopted by the Wi-Fi Alliance as an interim standard prior to the ratification of 802.11i. WPA2 is based on the official 802.11i standard and is fully backward compatible with WPA. 802.11i is another substandard of 802.11 that specifies an encryption standard to be used with wireless networks.

WPA provides strong data encryption via Temporal Key Integrity Protocol (TKIP), and WPA2 provides enhanced data encryption via Advanced Encryption Standard (AES), which meets the Federal Information Processing Standard (FIPS) 140-2 requirement of some government agencies. To help prevent someone from hacking the key, WPA and WPA2 rotate the keys and change the way keys are derived.

WPA-compatible and WPA2-compatible devices can operate in one of the following modes:

▶ **Personal mode**: Provides authentication via a preshared key or password.

▶ **Enterprise mode**: Provides authentication using IEEE 802.1X and Extensible Authentication Protocol (EAP).

802.1X provides an authentication framework for wireless local area networks (LANs), allowing a user to be authenticated by a central authority such as a RADIUS server. EAP is a protocol for wireless networks that expands on authentication methods used by the Point-to-Point Protocol (PPP), which support multiple authentication mechanisms, such as token cards, smart cards, certificates, one-time passwords, and public key encryption authentication.

In personal mode, WPA or WPA2 uses a preshared encryption key rather
than a changing encryption key. The preshared encryption key is programmed
into the access point and all wireless devices, which is used as a starting point
to mathematically generate session keys. The session keys are then changed
regularly so that the same session key is never used twice. Because the key
rotation is automatic, key management is handled in the background.

In WPA or WPA2 Enterprise mode, wireless devices have two sets of keys:

▶ Session keys, which are unique to each association between an access
point and a wireless client. They are used to create a private virtual port
between the access point and the client.

▶ Group keys, which are shared among all clients connected to the same
access point.

Both sets of keys are generated dynamically and are rotated to help safeguard
the integrity of keys over time. The encryption key could be supplied through
a certificate or smart card.

Configuring Wireless Networks

Any wireless access point broadcasting within range should be available to a
computer with a wireless adapter. By default, Windows 7 is set to enable you
to configure the network settings that should be used. This enables you to
configure different authentication, encryption, and communication options as
necessary.

If you haven't previously connected to a wireless network, you can create a
connection for the network by completing the following steps:

1. Open the **Network and Sharing Center**.

2. Click **Connect to a Network**. Select the network to which you want to
   connect. If the SSID is not listed for your network because it is not
   broadcasting, you have to go back to the Network and Sharing Center
   and click **Manage wireless networks** to create a network profile.

3. If it asks for a network security key, type in the security key and click **OK**.

4. Use the Security Type selection list to select the type of security being used. The encryption type is then filled in automatically for you.

You can also create a new wireless connection when the wireless network is not available or is hidden by doing the following:

1. Open the Network and Sharing Center and click **Set up a new connection or network**. Then click **Manually connect to a wireless network**. Click the **Next** button.

2. In the window shown in Figure 6.1, specify the Network Name (SSID), Security type, Encryption type, and Security Key. Then specify if you want to start the connection automatically and if you want to connect even if the network is not broadcasting. Click the **Next** button.

3. Click the **Close** button.

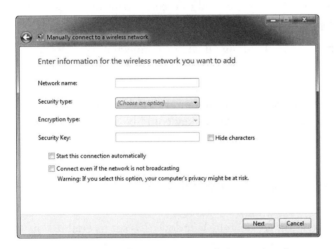

FIGURE 6.1   **Manually connect to a wireless network.**

To connect to a wireless or dial-up connection that you have defined, click the Network and Sharing Center icon in the Notification Area and click the connection to which you want to connect. If you move the mouse over a wireless network connection, you see the signal strength, security strength, radio type, and SSID (if available), as shown in Figure 6.2. You can also open the Network and Sharing Center and click **Connect** or **Disconnect** or click **Connect to a network**. To disconnect from a network connection, click the **Network and Sharing Center icon** in the Notification Area, click the connection from which you want to disconnect, and click the **Disconnect** button.

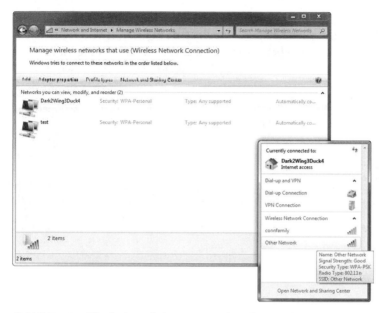

FIGURE 6.2   **Displaying wireless connection characteristics.**

If you open the Network and Sharing Center and double-click an active wireless network connection, you can view the status for the wireless connection including the duration, speed, and signal quality, as shown in Figure 6.3. You can also right-connect a connection from the notification area and click **Status**.

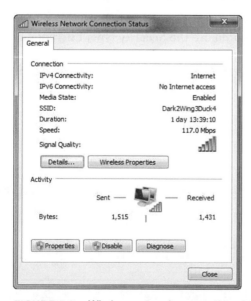

FIGURE 6.3   **Wireless network connection status.**

To manage all of your wireless network connections, just open the **Network and Sharing Center** and click **Manage wireless networks**. If you right-click an active connection and click **Properties** and view the Connection tab, as shown in Figure 6.4, you can specify how you connect to the wireless connection.

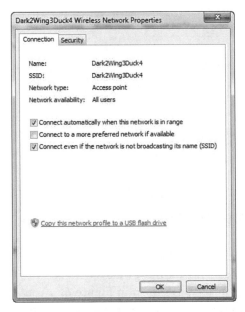

FIGURE 6.4   **Connections options for a wireless connection.**

If you select the Security tab, you can configure the Security type, Encryption type, and Network security key, as shown in Figure 6.5.

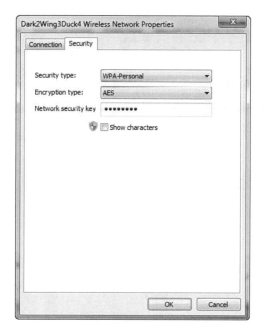

FIGURE 6.5 **Security for a wireless connection.**

If you have multiple computers that need to be configured to connect to a wireless network, you can use a USB flash drive to carry the configuration from computer to computer.

To save your wireless network settings to a USB flash drive, insert a USB flash drive into the computer, and then follow these steps:

1. Open the **Network and Sharing Center**.

2. In the left pane, click **Manage wireless networks**.

3. Right-click the network and then click **Properties**.

4. Click **Copy this network profile to a USB flash drive**. See Figure 6.6.

5. Select the USB device and then click **Next**. If you only have the one device, click the **Next** button. If you don't have a USB device connected, insert the USB device and click the **Next** button.

6. When the wizard is complete, click the **Close** button.

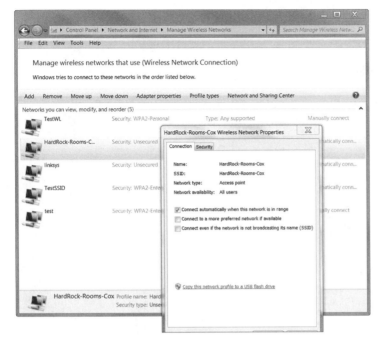

FIGURE 6.6   Copying a network profile to a USB flash drive.

To add a wireless computer running Windows 7 to a network by using a USB flash drive, do the following:

1. Plug the USB flash drive into a USB port on the computer.

2. For a computer running Windows 7, in the AutoPlay dialog box, click **Connect to a Wireless Network**.

3. When it asks if you want to add the network, click the **Yes** button.

4. When it says it was successful, click the **OK** button.

Network Locations

The first time you connect to a network, you must choose a network location (sometimes known as a profile). This automatically sets the appropriate firewall and security settings for the type of network to which you connect. If you connect to networks in different locations, such as work, home, or your favorite coffee shop or hotel, choosing a network location can help ensure that your computer is always set to the appropriate security level.

There are four network locations:

▶ **Home network**: For home networks or when you know and trust the people and devices on the network. Network discovery is turned on for home networks, which enables you to see other computers and devices on the network and enables other network users to see your computer.

▶ **Work network**: For small office or other workplace networks. Network discovery is on by default, but you cannot create or join a homegroup.

▶ **Public network**: Used while you are visiting coffee shops, restaurants, hotels, and airports. This location is designed to keep your computer from being visible to other computers around you and to help protect your computer from any malicious software on the Internet. Homegroup is not available on public networks, and network discovery is turned off. It is recommended that you use this option when you are connected directly to the Internet without using a router, or if you have a mobile broadband connection.

▶ **Domain**: Used for domain networks such as those found in corporations. This type of network location is controlled by your network administrator and cannot be selected or changed.

To change a network location:

1. Click to open the **Network and Sharing Center**.

2. Click **Work network, Home network**, or **Public network**, as shown in Figure 6.7, and then click the network location you want.

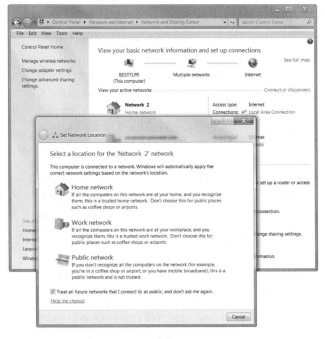

FIGURE 6.7   **Setting network location.**

Cram Quiz

1. You have a wireless access point configured to use TKIP security with a pre-shared key. Which option should you use to connect to the wireless access point?

    ○ **A.** Use WPA2-Enterprise

    ○ **B.** Use WPA2-Personal

    ○ **C.** Use WPA-Enterprise

    ○ **D.** Use WPA-Personal

2. Your network administrator just installed a wireless access point for you to connect to. What do you need to do to connect to the wireless network?

    ○ **A.** Configure the Network Category of the wireless connection to Public

    ○ **B.** Configure the Network Category of the wireless connection to Private

    ○ **C.** Enable Internet Connection Sharing for your wireless network adapter

    ○ **D.** Configure the wireless network adapter to connect to the appropriate wireless network from the Connect to a network list

Cram Quiz Answers

1. **D** is correct. WPA-Personal uses TKIP and uses a pre-shared key. Answers A and B are incorrect because WPA2-Enterprise and WPA2-Personal use AES encryption instead of TKIP. Answer C is incorrect because WPA-Enterprise uses a digital certificate instead of a pre-shared key.

2. **D** is correct. To connect to a wireless network, you need to configure a connection to the wireless network. Assuming that SSID broadcast is enabled, you can then select the wireless network from the available network list. Just select the network and click Connect. Answer A is incorrect because setting it to public disables some network features such as network discovery, making your network connection more secure. Answer B is incorrect because making it Private opens up your network connection including enabling network discovery. In either case, public and private connections do not help you connect to the wireless network. Answer C is incorrect because enabling Internet Connection Sharing enables other people to use your computer to connect to the Internet. It does not help you connect to a wireless network.

Remote Access

▶ **Configure remote connections**

▶ **Configure DirectAccess**

Cram**Saver**

1. You create a VPN connection for your corporate network. Where would you find the VPN connection when you want to connect remotely to your corporation?

   ○ **A.** Check Ease of Access

   ○ **B.** Check the Network and Sharing Center

   ○ **C.** Check in Mobile PC

   ○ **D.** Check the Parental Controls

2. How do you configure split-tunneling when using a VPN connection?

   ○ **A.** Right-click a VPN connection and click Properties. Then, under the Networking tab, open the Advanced options for the Internet Protocol 4 (TCP/IPv4). Lastly, deselect the Use default gateway on remote network option.

   ○ **B.** Right-click the VPN connection and click the Split-tunnel option.

   ○ **C.** Right-click the VPN connection and select Advanced options. Then select the Split-tunnel option.

   ○ **D.** Right-click the VPN connection and select Properties. Then select the Split-tunnel option.

3. What new technology introduced with Windows 7 provides a secure, always-on connection using IPsec and IPv6 that enables authorized users to access corporate shares, view intranet websites, and work with intranet applications without going through a traditional VPN?

   ○ **A.** BitLocker

   ○ **B.** DirectAccess

   ○ **C.** Teredo

   ○ **D.** ISATAP

1. **B** is correct. The Network and Sharing Center is where you would go to view all your network connections, including VPN connections. Answer A is incorrect because Ease of Access is used to configure Windows 7 for disabled people. Answer C is incorrect because Mobile PC enables you to configure most common options necessary for laptop and other mobile computers. Answer D is incorrect because Parental Controls enables you to configure your computer to protect your children.

2. **A** is correct. To create a split tunnel, you need to right-click a VPN connection and click Properties. Then click the Networking tab and double-click the Internet Protocol Version 4 (TCP/IPv4) option. Click the Advanced button and deselect the Use default gateway on remote network. The other answers do not provide the correct instructions for creating a split tunnel.

3. **B** is correct. DirectAccess is a new technology that establishes a secure bi-directional connection to access a corporate network or resources. Answer A is incorrect because BitLocker is a full disk encryption tool introduced with Windows Vista and is included with Windows 7. Answers C and D are incorrect because Teredo and ISATAP are IPv6 technologies that help migrate from IPv4 to IPv6.

As a Windows 7 Technology Specialist, you might be expected to support users in remote locations including being at their homes. Remote connections connect individuals or groups to a network from a remote location. Windows 7 includes three types of remote connections:

- Dial-up
- Broadband
- Virtual private network (VPN)

Dial-Up Connection

A dial-up connection is a nonpermanent point-to-point connection. Traditionally, it used a modem line and phone. A modem over a phone line is considered a legacy device network connection method with extremely slow bandwidth. In either case, you can open the **Network and Sharing Center** and click **Set up a new network or connect to a workplace**, as shown in Figure 6.8.

FIGURE 6.8   **Setting up a connection or network.**

Analog modems use dedicated telephone lines to connect users to the internal network at speeds up to 33.6 kilobits per second (Kbps). Digital modems use channels of an ISDN line to connect users to the internal network at speeds up to 56 Kbps. Communication is typically controlled by a Remote Access Server (RAS), which authenticates the login ID and password and authorizes the user to connect to the Internet or internal network.

If you are using a modem, you need to configure dialing rules so that the modem knows how the phone lines are accessed, what the caller's area code is, and what additional features should be used when dialing connections. Sets of dialing rules are saved as dialing locations in the Phone and Modem Options tool.

To view and set the default dialing location, follow these steps:

1. Click **Start** and then click **Control Panel**.

2. While in Icon view, double-click **Phone and Modem**.

3. The first time you start this tool, you see the Location Information dialog box.

4. Specify the country/region you are in, the area code (or city code), a number to access an outside line, and if the phone uses tone dialing or pulse dialing.

After you configure an initial location and click **OK**, you see the Phone and Modem Options dialog box.

To create a dial-up Internet connection to an ISP, follow these steps:

1. Open the **Network and Sharing Center**.

2. Click the **Set up a new connection or network** option.

3. If you already have an Internet connection, click the **Set up a new connection anyway** option.

4. Click **Dial-up**.

5. Set the phone number to dial for this connection, the user name, and password. You can also rename the connection name. If multiple people use the computer, you can select **Allow other people to use this connection**, as shown in Figure 6.9.

6. Click **Create**.

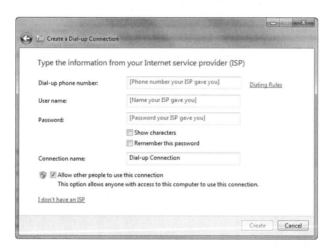

FIGURE 6.9 Create a Dial-up Connection dialog box.

After the connection has been defined, you can connect any time by opening the **Network and Sharing Center** and clicking **Connect to a network**.

You can also set up a connection to your computer from another computer by doing the following:

1. Open the **Control Panel**.

2. Click **Network and Internet**, click **Network and Sharing Center**, and then click **Manage Network Connections**.

Note

Some versions of Windows 7 accidently labeled this link **Change adapter settings**.

3. Open the file menu and select **New Incoming Connection**.

4. Specify who can connect to a computer. If necessary, add someone. When complete, click the **Next** button.

5. From the window shown in Figure 6.10, choose to connect through the Internet or through a dial-up modem. Click the **Next** button.

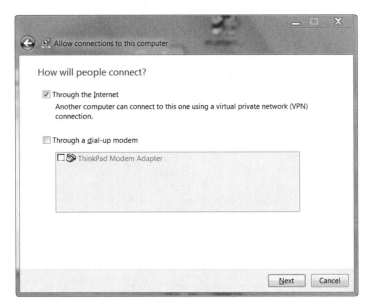

FIGURE 6.10 **Specify how people will connect.**

6. Select which network software you want available for the user and click **Allow access**, as shown in Figure 6.11.

FIGURE 6.11   **Allowing software to connect.**

Broadband Connection

Today, many connections are broadband connections, typically using a cable or DSL connection. Because these connections are always on, you don't need to set up dial-up rules or locations and you don't have to worry about ISP access numbers. Most broadband providers provide users with a router or modem, which users need to connect to the service provider. Most systems then use a network adapter on the computer to connect to a router or modem. In this configuration, the necessary connection is established over the LAN rather than a specific broadband connection. Therefore, it is the LAN that must be properly configured to gain access to the Internet. You won't need to create a broadband connection.

You can, however, create a specific broadband connection if needed. In some cases, you need to do this to set specific configuration options required by the ISP, such as secure authentication, or you might want to use this technique to set the user name and password required by the broadband provider. Although some ISPs might have you install their own software, other ISPs have you manually configure the broadband settings.

A common technology used for broadband is Point-to-Point Protocol over Ethernet (PPPoE). PPPoE is a network protocol for encapsulating Point-to-Point Protocol (PPP) frames inside Ethernet frames. Today, it is typically found with DSL lines that require authentication. To configure a PPPoE connection, you do the following:

1. Open the **Network and Sharing Center**.

2. Click **Set up a new connection or network**.

3. Click **Connect to the Internet**.

4. Click **Broadband (PPPoE)**.

5. Specify a user name, password, and connection name and click the **Connect** button.

Virtual Private Networking

A Virtual Private Network (VPN) is the creation of a secured, point-to-point connection across a private network or a public network such as the Internet. VPNs are used to establish secure communications channels over an existing dial-up or broadband connection. The data is encapsulated (data packets inserted into other data packets) before it is sent over the VPN connection. Because you send data on one end and it comes out the other end, it is often referred to as tunneling. In reality, a tunnel is logically defined where data is encrypted and sent embedded with data packets over a public network such as the Internet. Because the packets are encrypted, the data is unreadable by anyone who might get hold of the packets.

The VPN client authenticates to the remote access server, at which time they negotiate the tunneling and encryption technologies. Windows 7 supports the following VPN protocols:

▶ **Point-to-Point Tunneling Protocol (PPTP)**: Based on PPP, which uses the Internet as a connection medium. Uses Microsoft Point-to-Point Encryption (MPPE) for 40-, 56-, and 128-bit encryption. PPTP is considered to have weak encryption and authentication; therefore, IPsec is usually preferred.

▶ **Layer 2 Tunneling Protocol (L2TP) with IP security (IPsec)**: L2TP is the next-generation tunneling protocol based partially on PPTP. To provide encryption, L2TP uses IPsec. Because IPsec is considered a strong encryption, it is preferred over PPTP.

▶ **Secure Socket Tunneling Protocol (SSTP)**: A tunneling protocol that uses the HTTPS protocol over TCP port 443 to pass traffic through firewalls and Web proxies that might block PPTP and L2TP/IPsec traffic. SSTP provides a mechanism to encapsulate PPP traffic over the Secure Sockets Layer (SSL) channel of the HTTPS protocol. The use of PPP allows support for strong authentication methods, such as EAP-TLS. SSL provides transport-level security with enhanced key negotiation, encryption, and integrity checking.

▶ **Internet Key Exchange (IKEv2)**: IKEv2 is a tunneling protocol that uses the IPsec Tunnel Mode protocol over UDP port 500. An IKEv2 VPN provides resilience to the VPN client when the client moves from one wireless hotspot to another or when it switches from a wireless to a wired connection. The use of IKEv2 and IPsec allows support for strong authentication and encryption methods.

ExamAlert

If you don't want to open any additional ports on your firewall, you need to use SSTP.

When using VPNs, Windows 7 supports the following forms of authentication:

▶ **Password Authentication Protocol (PAP)**: Uses plain text (unencrypted passwords). PAP is the least secure authentication.

▶ **Challenge Handshake Authentication Protocol (CHAP)**: A challenge-response authentication that uses the industry standard MD5 hashing scheme to encrypt the response. CHAP was an industry standard for years and is still quite popular.

▶ **Microsoft CHAP version 2 (MS-CHAP v2)**: Provides two-way authentication (mutual authentication). MS-CHAP v2 provides stronger security than CHAP.

▶ **EAP-MS-CHAPv2**: Extensible Authentication Protocol (EAP) is a universal authentication framework frequently used in wireless networks and Point-to-Point connections that allows third-party vendors to develop custom authentication schemes, including retinal scans, voice recognition, finger point identifications, smart card, Kerberos, and digital certificates. EAP-MS-CHAPv2 is a mutual authentication method that supports password-based user or computer authentication.

244

When configuring a VPN, you need to know the IP address or fully qualified domain name (FQDN) of the remote access server to which you are connecting. The steps for creating the VPN connection from a Windows 7 computer to a Windows Server 2008 computer are as follows:

1. From Control Panel, select **Network and Internet** to access the Network and Sharing Center.

2. From the Network and Sharing Center, choose **Set up a new connection or network** Wizard.

3. In Set Up a Connection or Network, choose **Connect to a workplace**.

4. In the Connect to a Workplace page, choose to **Use my Internet connection (VPN)**.

5. At the next screen, choose your VPN connection or specify the Internet Address for the VPN Server and a Destination Name. You can also specify the options to use a smart card for authentication, Allow other people to use this connection, and Don't connect now, just set up so I can connect later.

Often, you need to do additional configuration of your VPN connection, such as specifying the type of protocol, the authentication protocol to use, and the type of encryption, as shown in Figure 6.12 and Figure 6.13.

FIGURE 6.12   **VPN Connection Properties: General tab.**

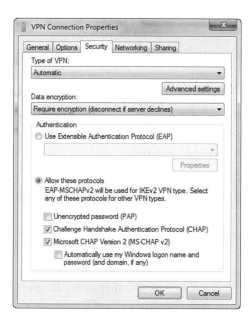

FIGURE 6.13   **VPN Connection Properties: Security tab.**

After the VPN connection is created and configured, to connect using the VPN, you just open the **Network and Sharing Center** and click **Change adapter settings**. Then right-click your VPN connection and click the **Connect** button.

Split Tunneling

By default, the Use Default Gateway on the Remote Network option is enabled. As a result, a new default route is created on the VPN client. Data that cannot be sent to the local network is forwarded to the VPN connection. In other words, if you connect from home to your corporate network, all network traffic, including surfing the Internet, is routed through the VPN connection when you are connected through the VPN unless you need to talk to another computer on your home network. Having this option enabled helps protect the corporate network because all traffic also goes through firewalls and proxy servers, which helps prevent a network from being infected or compromised. When you disable the Use Default Gateway on Remote Network option, you are using a split tunnel. With the split tunnel, only traffic that is meant for your corporate network is sent through the default gateway on the remote network. When you want to surf the Internet, you use your local connection instead of the corporate network.

To enable split-tunnel:

1. Right-click a VPN connection and click **Properties**.

2. Click the **Networking** tab.

3. Double-click the **Internet Protocol Version 4 (TCP/IPv4)** option.

4. Click the **Advanced** button.

5. Deselect **Use default gateway on remote network**.

DirectAccess

DirectAccess is a new feature in Windows 7 and Windows Server 2008 R2 that provides a secure, always-on connection that requires little or no user interaction using IPsec and IPv6. DirectAccess enables authorized users on Windows 7 computers to access corporate shares, view intranet websites, and work with intranet applications without going through a VPN. DirectAccess benefits IT professionals by enabling them to manage remote computers outside the office. Each time a remote computer connects to the Internet, before the user logs on, DirectAccess establishes a bi-directional connection that enables the client computer to remain current with company policies and to receive software updates.

Additional security and performance features of DirectAccess include the following:

▶ Support of multifactor authentication methods, such as a smart card for authentication.

▶ IPv6 to provide globally routable IP addresses for remote access clients.

▶ Encryption across the Internet using IPsec. Encryption methods include DES, which uses a 56-bit key, and 3DES, which uses three 56-bit keys.

▶ Integrates with Network Access Protection (NAP) to perform compliance checking on client computers before allowing them to connect to internal resources.

▶ Configures the DirectAccess server to restrict which servers, users, and individual applications are accessible.

ExamAlert

DirectAccess requires IPv6.

If your organization is not ready to fully deploy IPv6, IPv6 transition technologies such as ISATAP, 6to4, and Teredo enable clients to connect across the IPv4 Internet and to access IPv6 resources on the enterprise network.

DirectAccess helps reduce unnecessary traffic on the corporate network by sending traffic destined for the Internet through the DirectAccess server. DirectAccess clients can connect to internal resources by using one of the following methods:

- ▶ Selected server access
- ▶ Full enterprise network access

The connection method is configured using the DirectAccess console or it can be configured manually by using IPsec policies. For the highest security level, deploy IPv6 and IPsec throughout the organization, upgrade application servers to Windows Server 2008 R2, and enable selected server access. Alternatively, organizations can use full enterprise network access, where the IPsec session is established between the DirectAccess client and server.

DirectAccess clients use the following process to connect to intranet resources:

1. The DirectAccess client computer running Windows 7 detects that it is connected to a network.

2. The DirectAccess client computer attempts to connect to an intranet website that an administrator specified during DirectAccess configuration.

3. The DirectAccess client computer connects to the DirectAccess server using IPv6 and IPsec.

4. If a firewall or proxy server prevents the client computer using 6to4 or Teredo from connecting to the DirectAccess server, the client automatically attempts to connect using the IP-HTTPS protocol, which uses a Secure Sockets Layer (SSL) connection to ensure connectivity.

5. As part of establishing the IPsec session, the DirectAccess client and server authenticate each other using computer certificates for authentication.

6. By validating Active Directory group memberships, the DirectAccess server verifies that the computer and user are authorized to connect using DirectAccess.

7. If NAP is enabled and configured for health validation, the DirectAccess client obtains a health certificate from a Health Registration Authority (HRA) located on the Internet prior to connecting to the DirectAccess server.

8. The DirectAccess server begins forwarding traffic from the DirectAccess client to the intranet resources to which the user has been granted access.

To use DirectAccess, you need the following:

▶ One or more DirectAccess servers running Windows Server 2008 R2 with two network adapters

▶ At least one domain controller and DNS server running Windows Server 2008 or Windows Server 2008 R2

▶ A Public Key Infrastructure (PKI)

▶ IPsec policies

▶ IPv6 transition technologies available for use on the DirectAccess server

Review Questions

1. You have laptop with an 802.11a wireless network card. When you boot the Windows 7 machine and you double-check the SSID, you cannot connect to your company's wireless network. What is the problem?

   ○ **A.** Your company is most likely using an 802.11b or 802.11g wireless network, with which 802.11a is incompatible.

   ○ **B.** The 802.11a network card is too slow, which is preventing a connection.

   ○ **C.** You need to change the SSID because it expired.

   ○ **D.** You need to assign an IP address to the wireless card.

2. You work as the desktop support technician at Acme.com. Your company just purchased 20 new laptops with wireless adapters. You have to configure each computer to connect to the network wirelessly with the least amount of administrative effort. What should you do?

   ○ **A.** Manually configure each computer's wireless adapter

   ○ **B.** Save the wireless network settings to a USB device and apply it to each computer

   ○ **C.** Copy the wireless network settings to a shared folder and access the configuration from each laptop

   ○ **D.** Copy the wireless network settings to the hard disk of each of the new computers

3. You work as the network administrator at Acme.com. Your company just purchased 20 new laptop computers, which are going to connect to the new wireless network. You want the computers to connect to the network using TKIP without requiring the use of any security key or pass phrase. Which option would you select in the wireless network dialog box?

   ○ **A.** The WEP option

   ○ **B.** The WPA-Personal

   ○ **C.** The WPA2-Personal

   ○ **D.** WPA-Enterprise

   ○ **E.** WPA2-Enterprise

4. You are a desktop support technician for Acme.com. You are configuring several new laptops with Microsoft Windows 7 Enterprise. You need to configure a connection so that the users can connect to the Acme.com internal network while working from home. What steps do you need to do to set this up?

○ **A.** Open the Network and Sharing Center in Control Panel. Click Setup a new connection or network from the Task List. Choose Connect to a workplace under the Choose a connection option. Choose VPN under How do you want to connect. Enter the Internet address of the server to which you want to connect.

○ **B.** Click Manage Network connections from the Start menu. Click Setup connection or network from the Task List. Choose Connect to a workplace under the Choose a connection option. Choose Dial-up connection under How do you want to connect. Enter the Internet address of the server to which you want to connect.

○ **C.** Open the Network connections interface. Click Setup connection or network from the Task List. Choose Connect to a workplace under Choose a connection option. Enter the Internet address of the server to which you want to connect.

○ **D.** Open the Network and Sharing Center in Control Panel. Click Setup connection or network from the Task List. Choose Connect to a VPN under Choose a connection option. Choose Workplace under How do you want to connect. Enter the Internet address of the server to which you want to connect.

5. Your network administrator just installed a new wireless router to which you connect; however, you find out that you cannot discover other computers on the local wireless network. What should you do?

○ **A.** Configure the wired and wireless network adapters as a network bridge

○ **B.** Change the network category settings of the wireless connection to public

○ **C.** Change the network category settings of the wireless connection to private

○ **D.** Disable the Windows firewall

6. You have a wireless network to which you connect, but the SSID broadcasts have been disabled. What should you do to connect to the wireless network?

○ **A.** Click the Set up a connection or network link and select the Set up a wireless ad hoc network option

○ **B.** Click the Connect to network link and then right-click the appropriate network and select the Connect option

    ○ **C.** Click the View computers and devices link and then right-click the wireless access point (WAP) and select the Enable option

    ○ **D.** Click the Set up a connection or network link and select the Manually connect to a wireless network option

7. You have a computer with Windows 7. You create a VPN connection; however, you want to be able to connect to the VPN while making sure that Internet traffic does not go through the corporate network. What should you do?

    ○ **A.** Assign a static IP address and default gateway for the VPN connection

    ○ **B.** Configure the security settings of the VPN connection

    ○ **C.** Configure the Advanced TCP/IP settings of the VPN connection

    ○ **D.** Configure a static DNS server for the VPN connection

8. To protect a tunnel created with L2TP, what protocol should you use to provide encryption?

    ○ **A.** MPPE

    ○ **B.** IPsec

    ○ **C.** SSTP

    ○ **D.** CHAP

9. When using authentication, which of the following authentication methods is the least secure?

    ○ **A.** PAP

    ○ **B.** CHAP

    ○ **C.** MS-CHAPv2

    ○ **D.** EAP-MS-CHAPv2

10. DirectAccess requires which protocol to operate?

    ○ **A.** IPv4

    ○ **B.** IPv6

    ○ **C.** HTTPS

    ○ **D.** PPTP

Review Question Answers

1. Answer **A** is correct. In corporations today, most wireless networks use 802.11b, 802.11g, or 802.11n. Because 802.11a is not compatible with 802.11b/g, it is most likely the problem. Answer B is incorrect because the 802.11b and g can operate at lower speeds. Answer C is incorrect because although having the wrong SSID causes problems, the SSID does not expire. Answer D is incorrect because most networks have DHCP service to assign IP addresses.

2. Answer **B** is correct. You can save the information to a USB device and then use that device to copy the configuration to each computer. Answer A is incorrect because, although A works, it requires a lot more administrative effort. Answer C is incorrect because these computers do not have wired network cards to connect to a shared drive. Answer D is incorrect because copying the network settings also requires a lot more administrative effort because you need somehow get the setting to each hard drive.

3. Answer **D** is correct. WPA uses TKIP and WPA Enterprise does not require a security key or pass phrase. Instead a certificate or similar technology is used to provide the initial key. Answer A is incorrect because WEP does not use TKIP and requires a key to be supplied. Answer B is incorrect because Personal means that you have to enter a security key or pass phrase. Answers C and E are incorrect because they use AES instead of TKIP.

4. Answer **A** is correct. To connect to the office over the Internet you need to set up a VPN connection. The correct order to set up a VPN connection is the following:

   1. Open the **Network and Sharing Center** in Control Panel. This is the interface in Windows 7 that enables you to view, set up, and troubleshoot network connections as well as enable sharing on your computer.

   2. Click **Set up a connection or network** from the Tasks list. This is the option that enables you to create new connections, such as dial-up, wireless, or VPN connections.

   3. Under the **Choose a connection** option, choose **Connect to a workplace**. This is the section that enables you to set up VPN connections. The other options, such as Set up a dial-up connection, do not allow you to connect to an office over the Internet.

   4. Under **How do you want to connect**, choose **VPN**. A VPN connection enables you to tunnel over the Internet to a VPN server at the office.

   5. Enter the Internet address of the server to which you want to connect. To connect to a VPN server, you need to provide a name and IP address for the connection.

   Answer B is incorrect because you do not click Manage Network Connections from the Start menu. Answer C is incorrect because to set up a VPN, you do not open a network connections interface. Answer D is incorrect because you do not choose Connect to a VPN; instead, you first choose Connect to a workplace.

5. Answer **C** is correct. If the network category is set to public (Answer B), network discovery is disabled. Therefore, you need to change it from public to private. Answer A is incorrect because a bridge enables communications between a wired and wireless network through your computer. Answer D is incorrect because enabling or disabling the Windows firewall would not enable the network discovery feature.

6. Answer **D** is correct. If the wireless access point is configured not to broadcast, you need to configure your wireless connection manually. Answer A is incorrect because you use Ad hoc network options when you want to connect to fellow wireless hosts without using a wireless router. Answer B is incorrect because the network SSID is not broadcasted, so it does not show up on the list; therefore, you cannot right-click the connection. Answer C is incorrect because you are not be able see the wireless access point because the SSID broadcast is disabled, not the WAP itself.

7. Answer **C** is correct. By default, when connected through a VPN, all traffic goes through the default gateway on the remote network. If want to use your own local connection to surf the Internet, you need to enable split tunneling by configuring the Advanced TCP/IP settings and disabling the Use Default Gateway on the Remote Network option. Answer A is incorrect because assigning a static IP address and default gateway does not create a split tunnel. Answer B is incorrect because there is no security setting to create a split tunnel. Answer D is incorrect because using a static DNS server does not create a split tunnel.

8. Answer **B** is correct. To provide security for L2TP, you use IPsec. Answer A is incorrect because MPPE is the encryption used for PPTP. SSTP uses HTTPS protocol that uses SSL to encrypt data. Therefore, Answer C is incorrect. Answer D is incorrect because CHAP is an authentication protocol and is not used to encrypt the data.

9. Answer **A** is correct. PAP, short for Password Authentication Protocol, sends the password in plain text (unencrypted password). Answers B, C, and D use some form of encryption when dealing with passwords. Therefore, CHAP, MS-CHAPv2, and EAP-MS-CHAPv2 are all more secure than PAP.

10. Answer **B** is correct. DirectAccess is a new feature in Windows 7 and Windows Server 2008 R2 that provides a secure, always-on connection that requires little or no user interaction using IPsec and IPv6. Answers A, C, and D are incorrect because DirectAccess does not use IPv4, HTTPS, or PPTP.

CHAPTER 7

Configuring Windows Firewall and Windows Defender

This chapter covers the following 70-680 Objectives:

▶ Configuring Network Connectivity

▶ Configure Windows Firewall

In today's world, there is often a need for users to share data with other users. This chapter focuses on sharing files so those users can access files from a Windows 7 computer over the network and how to control such access so that it remains secure.

Spyware and Windows Defender

▶ **Configure Windows Firewall**

Cram**Saver**

1. What would you use to help protect against spyware when surfing the Internet?

   ○ **A.** CHKDSK

   ○ **B.** Scandisk

   ○ **C.** Windows Defender

   ○ **D.** IPsec

2. You work as the desktop support technician at Acme.com. You want to use the fastest scan that checks the most common locations where spyware is normally found. Which type of scan would you do?

   ○ **A.** Quick scan

   ○ **B.** Fast scan

   ○ **C.** Full scan

   ○ **D.** Custom scan

Answers

1. **C** is correct. To help protect against spyware, Microsoft includes two utilities. The first one specifically aimed at spyware is Windows Defender. The other utility is Windows Firewall. CHKDSK (Answer A) and Scandisk (Answer B) look for errors on the hard drive for older versions of Windows but do not protect against spyware. Scandisk has been replaced by Error-Checking. Answer D is incorrect because IPsec is a protocol used to secure packets sent between a source and a target.

2. **A** is correct. Quick scan checks all places that you normally find spyware, including those that execute during startup. Answer B is incorrect because a fast scan does not exist. Answer C is incorrect because full scans are much more thorough scans and take much longer. Answer D is incorrect because you need to manually specify where to search for spyware.

Spyware is a common threat to computers that can cause problems similar to a virus. Spyware (including adware) programs are malware that can be installed on computers, and they collect little bits of information at a time about a user without his or her knowledge. Some machines are infected with spyware when the spyware is bundled with other software, often without the user's knowledge. Sometimes spyware software might be added and the only notification the user gets is specified in the fine print of an End User License Agreement (EULA), which is usually a long document written with lots of legal jargon and is not read by most users. Spyware can also be picked up by simply visiting various websites because it is often hidden as ActiveX controls.

After it's installed, the spyware can monitor user activity on the Internet and transmit information such as email addresses, passwords, and credit card numbers without the user's knowledge. This information can be used for advertising or marketing purposes, to give the information to other parties, or to use the information for illegal purposes. Spyware can do the following:

▸ Generate annoying pop-ups

▸ Monitor keystrokes

▸ Scan files on the hard drive

▸ Snoop other applications such as chat programs or word processors

▸ Install other spyware programs

▸ Read cookies

▸ Change the default home page on a web browser to other links or default pages

▸ Open your computer to be accessed by others

> **ExamAlert**
>
> It is important that you know the symptoms of spyware so when you are presented with a troubleshooting question, you know the appropriate steps to mitigate spyware issues.

Spyware can also use network bandwidth and computer memory and can lead to system crashes or general system instability.

To reduce your chances of being affected by spyware, you should

▸ Use a good antivirus package such as Norton AntiVirus, McAfee VirusScan, or Microsoft Security Essentials.

▶ Use spyware detection and removal programs such as Windows Defender if the detection/removal capabilities are not included in the antivirus software.

▶ Be sure that your machine has all security patches and fixes loaded.

▶ Install software only from sources and websites you trust.

▶ Be careful what software you install on your system. Be sure to read the EULA for any piece of shareware or file sharing package you plan on installing.

▶ Keep your web browser security settings at medium or higher.

▶ Install or enable a personal firewall such as Windows Firewall that is included with Windows 7.

▶ Use pop-up blockers.

Windows Defender, included with Windows 7, helps users detect and remove known spyware and other potential unwanted software. Windows Defender protects your computer with automated and real-time scanning and software removal.

Because spyware and other potentially unwanted software can try to install itself on your computer any time you connect to the Internet or when you install programs, it is recommended that you have Windows Defender running whenever you are using your computer.

Windows Defender offers three ways to help keep spyware and other potentially unwanted software from infecting your computer:

▶ **Real-time protection**: When it runs in the background, Windows Defender alerts you when spyware or potentially unwanted software attempts to install itself or to run on your computer. It also alerts you when programs attempt to change important Windows settings.

▶ **Scanning options**: You can use Windows Defender to actively scan your disks for spyware and other potentially unwanted software that might be installed on your computer and to automatically remove any malicious software that is detected during a scan as demonstrated in Figure 7.1. You can set up Windows Defender to scan automatically according to a schedule, or you can run it manually.

▶ **SpyNet community**: The online Microsoft SpyNet community helps you see how other people respond to software that has not yet been classified for risks.

FIGURE 7.1 **Windows Defender.**

You can also use Windows Defender to constantly monitor your system, which offers your system real-time protection. The real-time protection uses nine security agents to monitor the critical areas of your computer that spyware might attack. When an agent detects potential spyware activity, it stops the activity and raises an alert. The agents include

▶ **Microsoft Internet Explorer Configuration**: Monitors browser security settings.

▶ **Internet Explorer Downloads**: Monitors applications that work with Internet Explorer, such as ActiveX controls and software installation applications.

▶ **Internet Explorer Add-ons (Browser Helper Objects)**: Monitors applications that automatically run when you start Internet Explorer.

▶ **Auto Start**: Monitors the list of applications that starts when Windows starts.

▶ **System Configuration**: Monitors security-related settings in Windows.

▶ **Services and Drivers**: Monitors services and drivers as they interact with Windows and applications.

▶ **Windows Add-ons**: Monitors software utilities that integrate with Windows.

▶ **Application Execution**: Monitors applications when they start and throughout their execution.

▶ **Application Registration (API Hooks)**: Monitors files and tools in the operating system where applications can insert themselves to run.

Windows Defender includes automatic scanning options to provide regular spyware scanning in addition to on-demand scanning options. The scan options include

▶ **Quick Scan**: A quick scan checks areas on a hard disk that spyware is most likely to infect.

▶ **Full Scan**: A full scan checks all critical areas, including all files, the registry, and all currently running applications.

▶ **Custom Scan**: A custom scan enables users to scan specific drives and folders.

> **Note**
>
> A quick scan checks locations where spyware is normally found.

When you perform a scan, you can configure what Windows Defender does when it identifies unwanted software, as shown in Figure 7.2. The actions include

▶ **Recommended action based on definition**: Windows Defender performs an action based on what is in the definition.

▶ **Quarantine**: Windows Defender places identified unwanted software in a quarantine or isolated holding folder. You can check the item before removing it from the system.

▶ **Remove**: Windows Defender removes the item from the system.

▶ **Allow**: Windows Defender does not take any action.

To prevent Windows Defender from automatically taking the recommended action, such as quarantining or removing software detected during a scan, you need to clear **Apply recommended actions** located at the bottom of the Options screen. As a result, Windows defender recommends an action to take for detected malicious software.

FIGURE 7.2   **Configuring Windows Defender options.**

Similar to antivirus software, Windows Defender uses a definition database that lists and details and characteristics of known spyware. Also similar to antivirus software, the definition database becomes out of date as new spyware is introduced. Therefore, you must update the database regularly for it to be effective.

To turn Windows Defender on or off, do the following:

1. Open **Windows Defender**, open a search box and type in **Windows Defender**, and press **Enter**.

2. Click **Tools** and then click **Options**.

3. Under Administrator options, select or clear the **Use this program** checkbox and then click **Save**. If you are prompted for an administrator password or confirmation, type the password or provide confirmation.

To turn Windows Defender real-time protection on or off, follow these steps:

1. Open **Windows Defender**.

2. Click **Tools** and then click **Options**.

3. Under Real-time protection options, as shown in Figure 7.3, select the **Use real-time protection (recommended)** checkbox.

4. Select the options you want. To help protect your privacy and your computer, you should select all real-time protection options.

5. Under Choose if Windows Defender should notify you about, select the options you want and then click **Save**. If you are prompted for an administrator password or confirmation, type the password or provide confirmation.

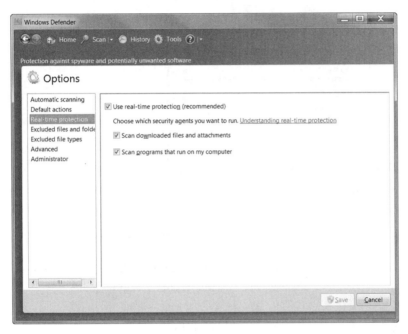

FIGURE 7.3   **Configuring Windows Defender real-time protection.**

If you trust software that Windows Defender has detected, you can stop Windows Defender from alerting you to risks that the software might pose to your privacy or your computer. To stop being alerted, you need to add the software to the Windows Defender allowed list. If you decide that you want to monitor the software again later, you can remove it from the Windows Defender allowed list at any time.

To add an item to the allowed list, the next time Windows Defender alerts you about the software, click **Always** Allow on the Action menu in the Alert dialog box. If you are prompted for an administrator password or confirmation, type the password or provide confirmation.

To remove an item from the allowed list, do the following:

1. Open **Windows Defender**.

2. Click **Tools** and then click **Allowed items**.

3. Select the item that you want to monitor again, and then click **Remove from List**. If you are prompted for an administrator password or confirmation, type the password or provide confirmation.

Cram Quiz

1. What do you call a type of malware that can monitor user activity on the Internet and transmit information such as email addresses, passwords, and credit card numbers without the user's knowledge?

   ○ **A.** Spyware

   ○ **B.** Worm

   ○ **C.** Cookies

   ○ **D.** EULA

2. When you find unwanted software, what do you call it when the unwanted software is placed in an isolated holding folder?

   ○ **A.** Quick scan

   ○ **B.** Quarantine

   ○ **C.** Recycle Bin

   ○ **D.** Cookie

Cram Quiz Answers

1. **A** is correct. Spyware is a common threat to computers that can cause problems similar to a virus. Some of the symptoms include generating annoying pop-ups, monitoring keystrokes, scanning files on hard drives, and transmitting confidential information. Answer B is incorrect because a worm is a form of malware that replicates and consumes valuable resources including bandwidth. Answer C is incorrect because a cookie is a text file used to remember settings when visiting a website. Answer D is incorrect because a EULA is the End User License Agreement.

2. **B** is correct. You can have Windows Defender place possible unwanted software into a quarantine folder so that it can be reviewed to determine if it is malware. Answer A is incorrect because a quick scan is a type of scan that is used by Windows Defender to verify key areas where spyware is most likely found. Answer C is incorrect because the Recycle Bin is a temporary holding area where deleted objects are stored. Answer D is incorrect because a cookie is a text file used to remember settings when visiting a website.

Windows Firewall

▶ **Configure Windows Firewall**

Cram**Saver**

1. Which network location used with Windows Firewall is more secure by disabling network discovery and homegroups?

   ○ **A.** Home network

   ○ **B.** Work network

   ○ **C.** Public network

   ○ **D.** Domain

2. Anytime you are having problems accessing a common network program or application and you cannot connect, what should you check?

   ○ **A.** Windows Defender

   ○ **B.** Your antivirus program

   ○ **C.** Windows Firewall

   ○ **D.** IPsec

Answers

1. **C** is correct. The public network location is designed to keep your computer from being visible to other computers around you and to help protect your computer from any malicious software on the Internet. A homegroup is not available on public networks, and network discovery is turned off. Answer A is incorrect because it is designed for home networks or when you know and trust the people and devices on the network. Network discovery is turned on for home networks. Answer B is incorrect because work network is for small office or other workplace networks. Network discovery is on by default, but you cannot create or join a homegroup when using the work network location. Answer D is incorrect because the domain network is used for domain networks found in corporations.

2. **C** is correct. Windows firewall is a packet filter and stateful host-based firewall that allows or blocks network traffic according to the configuration. You should check Windows Firewall to see if it is blocking you from accessing the network program or application. Answer A is incorrect because Windows Defender is used to protect a computer against spyware. Answer B is incorrect because although some antivirus programs have firewall capability, it is most likely the Windows Firewall that is blocking the program. Answer D is incorrect because IPsec is used to encrypt network traffic.

Because most computers are connected to the Internet through dialup, broadband (such as DSL or cable modems), or a local area network (LAN), computers are vulnerable to attack or unauthorized access. To help protect your system, you should have a firewall between you and the outside world. The firewall monitors all traffic coming in and going out to prevent unauthorized access.

Windows Firewall is a packet filter and stateful host-based firewall that allows or blocks network traffic according to the configuration. A packet filter protects the computer by using an access control list (ACL), which specifies which packets are allowed through the firewall based on IP address and protocol (specifically the port number). A stateful firewall monitors the state of active connections and uses the information gained to determine which network packets are allowed through the firewall. Typically, if the user starts communicating with an outside computer, it remembers the conversation and allows the appropriate packets back in. If an outside computer tries to start communicating with a computer protected by a stateful firewall, those packets are automatically dropped unless granted by the ACL.

ExamAlert

Remember that any program or service that needs to communicate on a network, including sharing files, must be opened in a firewall.

Note

Although Windows has a built-in software firewall, it is only one component used to protect your computer. If you have a home network, you should use a router that has a built-in firewall to help protect your network and your computers when the network is connected to the Internet. Organizations that have Internet connections should have a solution that includes one or more enterprise firewalls.

Firewall rules that can be defined include

- ▶ **Inbound rules**: These rules help protect your computer from other computers making unsolicited connections to it.

- ▶ **Outbound rules**: These rules help protect your computer by preventing your computer from making unsolicited connections to other computers.

- ▶ **Connection-specific rules**: These rules enable a computer's administrator to create and apply custom rules based on a specific connection.

Basic Configuration

Windows Firewall is on by default. When Windows Firewall is on, most programs are blocked from communicating through the firewall. If you want to unblock a program, you can add it to the Exceptions list (on the Exceptions tab). For example, you might not be able to send photos in an instant message until you add the instant messaging program to the Exceptions list.

To turn on or off Windows Firewall:

1. Open Windows Firewall by clicking the **Start** button, clicking **Control Panel**, clicking **System and Security**, and then clicking **Windows Firewall**.

2. In the left pane, click **Turn Windows Firewall on or off**, as shown in Figure 7.4. If you are prompted for an administrator password or confirmation, type the password or provide confirmation.

3. Below each network location type, click **Turn on Windows Firewall**, and then click **OK**. It is recommended that you turn on the firewall for all network location types.

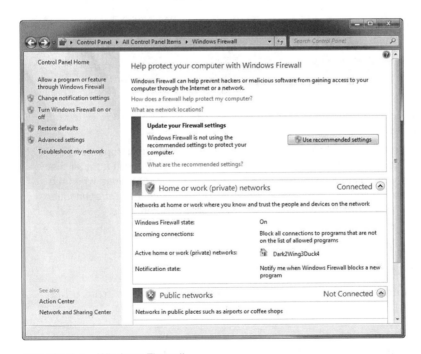

FIGURE 7.4 **Windows Firewall.**

Besides turning the firewall off and on for each profile, you also have the following options:

▶ **Block all incoming connections, including those in the list of allowed programs:** This setting blocks all unsolicited attempts to connect to your computer. Use this setting when you need maximum protection for your computer, such as when you connect to a public network in a hotel or airport, or when a known computer worm is spreading over the Internet. With this setting, you aren't notified when Windows Firewall blocks programs, and programs in the list of allowed programs are ignored. When you block all incoming connections, you can still view most web pages, send and receive email, and send and receive instant messages.

▶ **Notify me when Windows Firewall blocks a new program:** If you select this checkbox, Windows Firewall informs you when it blocks a new program and gives you the option of unblocking that program.

The first time you connect to a network, you must choose a network location (sometimes known as profiles). This automatically sets the appropriate firewall and security settings for the type of network that you connect to. If you connect to networks in different locations, such as work, home, or your favorite coffee shop or hotel, choosing a network location can help ensure that your computer is always set to the appropriate security level. See Figure 7.5.

ExamAlert

You need to know the various network locations and when to use them so that your computer is protected as much as possible while allowing the access that you need.

Traditionally with firewalls, you can open or close a protocol port so that you can allow or block communication through the firewall. With the Windows Firewall included with Windows 7, you specify which program or feature you want to communicate through the firewall. The most common options are available by clicking the **Allow a program or feature through Windows Firewall** option, as shown in Figure 7.6. If you need to open a port instead of specifying a program, you have to use the Windows Firewall with Advanced Security.

CHAPTER 7: Configuring Windows Firewall and Windows Defender

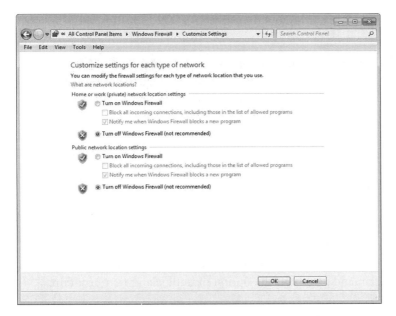

FIGURE 7.5   Setting Network Location in Windows Firewall.

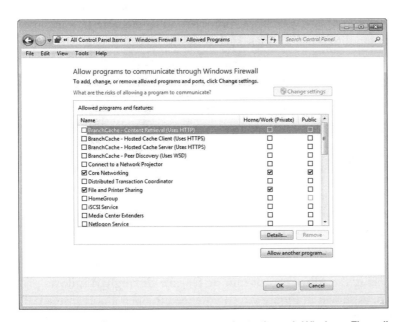

FIGURE 7.6   Allow programs to communicate through Windows Firewall.

ExamAlert

Remember if you want to use file and printer sharing, you need to allow File and Printer Sharing by using the Allow program to communicate through Windows Firewall option.

In addition to the notification setting available (configured by clicking Change notification settings) when you turn Windows Firewall on or off, you can display firewall notifications in the taskbar for three different behaviors:

▸ **Show icon and notifications**: The icon always remains visible on the taskbar in the notification area and notifications are displayed.

▸ **Hide icon and notifications**: The icon is hidden and notifications aren't displayed.

▸ **Only Show notifications**: The icon is hidden, but if a program needs to show a notification, it shows a notification balloon on the taskbar.

Notifications are also displayed in the Action Center in Control Panel.

Windows Firewall with Advanced Security

The new Windows Firewall with Advanced Security is a Microsoft Management Console (MMC) snap-in that provides more advanced options for IT professionals. With this firewall, you can set up and view detailed inbound and outbound rules and integrate with Internet Protocol Security (IPsec). To access the Windows Firewall with Advanced Security, follow these steps:

1. Open Administrative Tools by clicking the **Start** button, clicking **Control Panel**, clicking **System and Security**, and then clicking **Administrative Tools**.

2. Double-click **Windows Firewall with Advanced Security**, as shown in Figure 7.7. If you are prompted for an administrator password or confirmation, type the password or provide confirmation.

FIGURE 7.7   **Windows Firewall with Advanced Security console.**

You can also access the Windows Firewall with Advanced Security by clicking the **Advanced settings** option in the Windows Firewall screen. Of course, you must be a member of the Administrators group to use Windows Firewall with Advanced Security.

The Windows Firewall with Advanced Security management console enables you to configure the following:

▶ **Inbound rules**: Windows Firewall blocks all incoming traffic unless solicited or allowed by a rule, as shown in Figure 7.8.

▶ **Outbound rules**: Windows Firewall allows all outbound traffic unless blocked by a rule.

▶ **Connection security rules**: Windows Firewall uses a connection security rule to force two peer computers to authenticate before they can establish a connection and to secure information transmitted between the two computers. Connection security rules use IPsec to enforce security requirements.

▶ **Monitoring**: Windows Firewall uses the monitoring interface to display information about current firewall rules, connection security rules, and security associations.

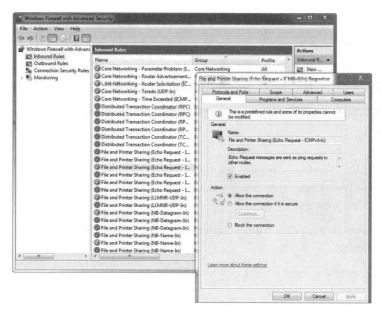

FIGURE 7.8   **Inbound rules.**

You create inbound rules to control access to your computer from the net-work. Inbound rules can prevent

▶ Unwanted software being copied to your computer.

▶ Unknown or unsolicited access to data on your computer.

▶ Unwanted configuration of your computer from remote locations.

To configure advanced properties for a rule using the Windows Firewall with Advanced Security, do the following:

1. Right-click the name of the inbound rule and then click **Properties**.

2. From the properties dialog box for an inbound rule, configure settings on the following tabs:

   ▶ **General**: The rule's name, the program to which the rule applies, and the rule's action (allow all connections, allow only secure con-nections, or block).

   ▶ **Programs and Services**: The programs or services to which the rule applies.

   ▶ **Computers**: The computers that can communicate through the firewall.

- **Users**: The users that can communicate through the firewall.

- **Protocols and Ports**: The rule's IP protocol, source and destination TCP or UDP ports, and ICMP or ICMPv6 settings.

- **Scope**: The rule's source and destination addresses.

- **Advanced**: The profiles or types of interfaces to which the rule applies.

You can also use the Windows Firewall with Advanced Security to create outbound rules to control access to network resources from your computer. Outbound rules can prevent

- Utilities on your computer from accessing network resources without your knowledge.

- Utilities on your computer from downloading software without your knowledge.

- Users of your computer from downloading software without your knowledge.

Computer Connection Security Rules

Because the Internet is inherently insecure, businesses need to preserve the privacy of data as it travels over the network. Internet Protocol Security (IPsec) creates a standard platform to develop secure networks and electronic tunnels between two machines. The two machines are known as endpoints. After the tunnel has been defined and both endpoints agree on the same parameters, the data is encrypted on one end, encapsulated in a packet, and sent to the other endpoint where the data is decrypted.

In Windows XP and Windows Server 2003, you configure the Windows Firewall and IPsec separately. Unfortunately, because both can block or allow incoming traffic, it is possible that the Firewall and IPsec rules can conflict with each other. In Windows 7, Windows Firewall with Advanced Security provides a single, simplified interface for managing both firewall filters and IPsec rules.

Windows Firewall with Advanced Security uses authentication rules to define IPsec policies. No authentication rules are defined by default. To create a new authentication rule, follow these steps:

1. In Windows Firewall with Advanced Security, select the **Computer Connection Security Rules** node.

2. Right-click the **Computer Connection Security Rules** node in the console tree and then click **New Rule** to start the New Connection Security Rule Wizard.

3. From the Rule Type page of the New Authentication Rule Wizard (as shown in Figure 7.9), you can select the following:

   ▶ **Isolation**: Used to specify that computers are isolated from other computers based on membership in a common Active Directory domain or current health status. You must specify when you want authentication to occur (for example, for incoming or outgoing traffic and whether you want to require or only request protection), the authentication method for protected traffic, and a name for the rule.

   ▶ **Authentication exemption**: Used to specify computers that do not have to authenticate or protect traffic by their IP addresses.

   ▶ **Server to server**: Used to specify traffic protection between specific computers, typically servers. You must specify the set of endpoints that exchange protected traffic by IP address, when you want authentication to occur, the authentication method for protected traffic, and a name for the rule.

   ▶ **Tunnel**: Used to specify traffic protection that is tunneled, typically used when sending packets across the Internet between two security gateway computers. You must specify the tunnel endpoints by IP address, the authentication method, and a name for the rule.

   ▶ **Custom**: Used to create a rule that does not specify a protection behavior. You would select this option when you want to manually configure a rule, perhaps based on advanced properties that cannot be configured through the pages of the New Authentication Rule Wizard. You must specify a name for the rule.

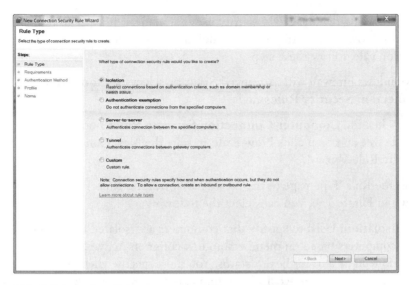

FIGURE 7.9   **Specifying a new connection security rule.**

To configure advanced properties for the rule, do the following:

1. Right-click the name of the rule and then click **Properties**.

2. From the properties dialog box for a rule, you can configure settings on the following tabs:

   ▸ **General**: The rule's name and description and whether the rule is enabled.

   ▸ **Computers**: The set of computers, by IP address, for which traffic is protected.

   ▸ **Authentication**: When you want authentication for traffic protection to occur (for example, for incoming or outgoing traffic and whether you want to require or only request protection) and the authentication method for protected traffic.

   ▸ **Advanced**: The profiles and types of interfaces to which the rule applies and IPsec tunneling behavior.

Cram Quiz

1. Which Windows Firewall profile includes access to homegroups?

   - ○ **A.** Home network
   - ○ **B.** Work network
   - ○ **C.** Public network
   - ○ **D.** Internet network

2. If you need to configure IPsec, what program would you use in Windows 7?

   - ○ **A.** IPsec Management console
   - ○ **B.** Computer Management console
   - ○ **C.** Windows Firewall with IPsec
   - ○ **D.** Windows Firewall with Advanced Security

Cram Quiz Answers

1. **A** is correct. The Home network location or profile is for home networks or when you know and trust the people and devices on the network. Network discovery is turned on for home networks, which enables you to see other computers and devices on the network. Answers B and C are incorrect because they have access to homegroups disabled. Answer D is incorrect because the Internet network is not a valid network location or profile.

2. **D** is correct. The Windows Firewall with Advanced Security enables you to fine-tune the Windows Firewall and configure IPsec. Answer B is incorrect because you cannot configure IPsec with the Computer Management console. Answers A and C are incorrect because these consoles do not exist.

Review Questions

1. Which of the following does spyware not do?

   ○ **A.** Monitors keystrokes in an attempt to retrieve passwords and other private information

   ○ **B.** Changes the default home page to another site

   ○ **C.** Causes pop-up windows to appear frequently

   ○ **D.** Changes the polarity of your monitor, causing physical damage

   ○ **E.** Slows down your machine

2. You work as a desktop technician at Acme.com. You have configured Windows Defender on all Microsoft Windows 7 machines on your domain. One user has an accounting application (which comes from a reputable company) that interacts with Microsoft Excel. When the application runs, an alert window opens up with a medium-level warning stating that the software might be spyware. You are sure that the application is not spyware. What do you need to do to stop these warnings from appearing? (Select the best answer.)

   ○ **A.** Open Windows Defender. Click Tools, click Options, and configure Windows Defender to ignore Medium alert items.

   ○ **B.** Configure Parental Controls to allow this application to run.

   ○ **C.** Open Windows Defender. Click Tools and click Options. Then under the Advanced options, click Add in the Do not scan these files or locations option. Then browse to the application executable. Click OK.

   ○ **D.** When the warning appears again, click Always Allow.

3. When running Windows Defender, you are constantly alerted about specific software. What can you do so that you stop getting alerts for that software?

   ○ **A.** Run Windows full scan

   ○ **B.** Run Windows quick scan

   ○ **C.** Add the application to the allowed list

   ○ **D.** Add the item to the quarantine list

4. You work as part of the IT support staff at Acme.com. You have a payroll application (PAY.EXE) that requires you to send data to the check printing company using TCP port 8787. What do you need to do to make this application able to function?

   ○ **A.** Open Windows Firewall and ensure that it is enabled. Add PAY.EXE to the exceptions list on the exceptions tab.

   ○ **B.** Open Windows Firewall and ensure that it is enabled. Add port 8787 to the exceptions list on the exceptions tab.

    ○ **C.** Open Windows Defender. Add PAY.EXE to the exceptions tab.

    ○ **D.** Open Windows Defender. In Software Explorer, click the disable button for PAY.EXE.

5. Your corporation has several FTP servers. You need to make sure that a Windows 7 computer can only connect to the FTP servers when connected to the private network. What should you do?

    ○ **A.** Change the application control policies from the local policy

    ○ **B.** Change the Advanced Sharing setting from the Network and Sharing Center Policy

    ○ **C.** Change the Allowed Programs and Features list from the Windows Firewall Policy

    ○ **D.** Create a new rule from the Windows Firewall with Advanced Security Policy

6. You create a shared folder called Docs on your computer running Windows 7. However, remote users cannot access the shared folder. What do you need to do to allow users to access the shared folder while keeping the system as secure as possible?

    ○ **A.** Disable Windows Defender

    ○ **B.** Enable the File and Printer Sharing exception in the firewall setting

    ○ **C.** Turn off the Windows Firewall

    ○ **D.** Enable all incoming connections in the Windows Firewall

7. What should you do to prevent all inbound traffic to your computer running Windows 7 without the end user being notified?

    ○ **A.** Set the network location to Public

    ○ **B.** Set the network location to Private

    ○ **C.** Set the network location to domain

    ○ **D.** Enable the Windows Firewall and select the Block all incoming connections checkbox

8. What do you call a firewall that monitors the state of active connections and uses the information gained to determine which network packets are allowed through the firewall?

    ○ **A.** Packet filter

    ○ **B.** Stateful

    ○ **C.** Stateless

    ○ **D.** Packet analyzer

9. Which of the following statements is true?

    ○ **A.** Windows Firewall is off by default.

    ○ **B.** Windows Firewall is on by default.

    ○ **C.** Windows Firewall is on by default if you install Windows Defender.

    ○ **D.** Windows Firewall is only on if auditing is turned on.

10. What protocol enables you to create a standard platform to develop secure networks and electronic tunnels between two machines?

    ○ **A.** Windows Firewall with Advanced Security

    ○ **B.** Windows Defender

    ○ **C.** Windows auditing

    ○ **D.** Windows Tunnel Maker

CHAPTER 8

User Management

This chapter covers the following 70-680 Objectives:

▶ Configure user account control (UAC)

▶ Configure authentication and authorization

▶ Configure remote connections

To keep a system secure, you need to use user accounts, which provide accountability and the ability to give rights and permissions to individuals. If your computer has many users, you can then use groups to simplify the granting of rights and permissions by assigning users to groups and then assigning the rights and permissions to those groups. To make your system secure, Windows 7 includes *User Account Control* to help protect against malware that might attack your system at any time by expanding what a standard user can do on a system without becoming an administrator.

Authentication and Authorization

▶ **Configure authentication and authorization**

Cram**Saver**

1. What is the process used to confirm a user's identity?

- ○ **A.** Authentication
- ○ **B.** Authorization
- ○ **C.** Auditing
- ○ **D.** Certificate

2. Which local user accounts are automatically created when you install a fresh copy of Windows 7 and are also disabled by default? (Choose all that apply.)

- ○ **A.** Administrator
- ○ **B.** Administrators
- ○ **C.** RemoteIdentity
- ○ **D.** Guest

Answers

1. **A** is correct. Authentication is the process used to confirm a user's identity, when he or she accesses a computer system or additional system resources. Answer B is incorrect because authorization occurs after authentication, which allows access to a network resource. Answer C is incorrect because auditing is the recording of activity to be used to track user actions. Answer D is incorrect because a digital certificate is a form of authentication.

2. **A** and **D** are correct. The built-in administrator account provides complete access to files, directories, and services. The Guest account is designed for users who need one-time or occasional access. The Administrator and Guest accounts are disabled by default. Answer B is incorrect because Administrators is a group, not an account. Answer C is incorrect because there is no user account called RemoteIdentity.

Authentication is the process used to confirm a user's identity when he or she accesses a computer system or an additional system resource. The most common authentication method is using a username and password. When working with transactions over the Internet that deal with money, credit cards, or personal information, username/password authentication has an inherent weakness given its susceptibility to passwords that can be stolen, accidentally revealed, or hacked.

Because of this weakness, these transactions usually employ digital certificates to prove the identity of users or companies and also contain an encryption key, which is used to encrypt data sent over the Internet.

Users must be authenticated to verify their identity when accessing files or other network resources over the network. The Windows 7 operating system includes the following authentication methods for network logons:

▶ **Kerberos version 5 protocol**: The main logon authentication method used by clients and servers running Microsoft Windows operating systems. It is used to authenticate both user accounts and computer accounts.

▶ **Windows NT LAN Manager (NTLM)**: Used for backward compatibility with pre-Windows 2000 operating systems and some applications. It is less flexible, efficient, and secure than the Kerberos version 5 protocol.

▶ **Certificate mapping**: Typically used in conjunction with smart cards for logon authentication. The certificate stored on a smart card (about the size of a credit card) is linked to a user account for authentication. A smart card reader is used to read the smart card and authenticate the user.

After you have authentication proving who or what an identity is, you can then use authorization, which allows a system to determine whether an authenticated user can access a resource and how they can access the resource.

A right authorizes a user to perform certain actions on a computer, such as logging on to a system interactively/locally to the computer, backing up files and directories, performing a system shutdown, or adding/removing a device driver. Administrators can assign specific rights to individual user accounts or group accounts. Rights are managed with the User Rights policy. For Windows Server 2008, you can find user rights by opening the group policy via the Group Policy Management console, opening Computer Configuration, opening Windows Settings, opening Security Settings, opening Local Policies, and opening User Rights Assignment.

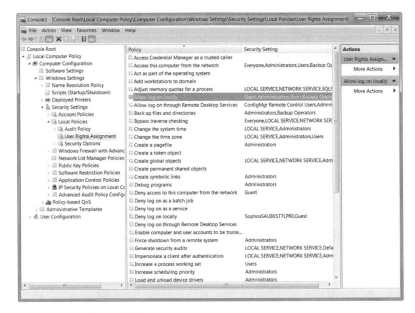

FIGURE 8.1   **User rights.**

A permission defines the type of access granted to an object or object attribute. The permissions available for an object depend on the type of object. For example, a user has different permissions than a printer, which has different permissions than a file or folder on an NTFS volume. When a user or service tries to access an object, its access is granted or denied by an Object Manager. File and Folder permissions as well as Shared permissions are handled by Windows Explorer.

User Accounts and Groups

Microsoft Windows 7 workstations can be configured as a member of a workgroup or member of a domain. When a workstation is configured as a member of a workgroup, user access and security are configured on the workstation itself. Each computer maintains its own security database, which includes its own local user accounts and groups. If a user on one computer needs to access resources on other computers, a user account has to be created on each computer. The user and group information is not shared with other computers.

A *domain* is a logical unit of computers and network that define a security boundary. A domain uses one database known as Active Directory, which is stored on one or more domain controllers. It gives the capability to share its common security and user and group account information for all computers within the domain. When a user logs onto the domain, he or she can access resources throughout the domain with the same logon (single sign-on). The domain allows for centralized network administration of all users, groups, and resources on the network.

A user account enables a user to log on to a computer or domain with an identity that can be authenticated and authorized for access to the resources of the computer or domain. Because the user account is meant to be assigned to one and only one user, it enables you to assign rights and permissions to a single user and gives you the ability to track what users are doing (accountability).

> **Note**
>
> It is highly recommended that all users who log on to the network should have their own unique user account and password.

Two general types of user accounts are defined in Windows 7:

- **Local user accounts**: User accounts defined on a local computer, which have access to the local computer only. You add or remove local user accounts with Control Panel's User Accounts options or the Local Users and Groups utility. Local Users and Groups is accessible through the Computer Management console, a Microsoft Management Console (MMC) tool that is found in Administrative tools.

- **Domain user accounts**: User accounts are defined in the Active Directory. Through single sign-on, these accounts can access resources throughout a domain/forest. When a computer is a member of an Active Directory domain, you can create domain user accounts using Active Directory Users and Computers. This MMC tool is available on the Administrative Tools menu when you install the Microsoft Remote Server Administration Tools (RSAT) for Windows 7 on your Windows 7 computer. RSAT can be found at http://www.microsoft.com/downloads/en/details.aspx?FamilyID=7d2f6ad7-656b-4313-a005-4e344e43997d.

A local user account allows users to log on at and gain access to resources on only the computer where they create the account. The user account tells Windows what files and folders the user can access, what changes you can make to the computer, and your personal preferences, such as your desktop background or color theme. User accounts enable you to share a computer with several people, but still have your own files and settings. Each person accesses his or her user account with a user name and password.

Default User Accounts

Every Windows 7 computer has local computer accounts, regardless of whether the computer is a member of a workgroup or a domain. When you install Windows 7, the operating system installs default user accounts, which are managed using the User Accounts applet. The key accounts you see are as follows:

- **Administrator**: Administrator is a predefined account that provides complete access to files, directories, services, and other facilities on the computer. You can't delete this account.

- **Guest**: Guest is designed for users who need one-time or occasional access. Although guests have only limited system privileges, you should be very careful about using this account because it opens the system to potential security problems. The risk is so great that the account is initially disabled when you install Windows 7.

The built-in administrator account is disabled by default in Windows 7 on new installations. If Windows 7 determines during an upgrade from Windows Vista that the built-in administrator is the only active local administrator account, Windows 7 leaves the account enabled and places the account in Admin Approval Mode. The built-in administrator account, by default, cannot log on to the computer in safe mode.

Windows 7 also provides groups, which you use to grant permissions to similar types of users and to simplify account administration. If a user is a member of a group that can access a resource, that particular user can access the same resource. Thus, you can give a user access to various work-related resources just by making the user a member of the correct group.

Windows 7 Local Accounts

When you create additional accounts in Windows 7 using the Control Panel, you choose between two different kinds of accounts:

- Standard user
- Administrator

Each account type gives the user a different level of control over the computer.

The standard user account is the account to use for everyday computing. A standard user account lets a person use most of the capabilities of the computer, but permission from an administrator is required if you want to make changes that affect other users or the security of the computer. You can use most programs that are installed on the computer, but you can't install or uninstall software and hardware, delete files that are required for the computer to work, or change settings on the computer that affect other users. If you're using a standard user account, some programs might require you to provide an administrator password before you can perform certain tasks.

The administrator account provides the most control over the computer, and should be used only when necessary. The administrator account lets you make changes that affect other users. Administrators can change security settings, install software and hardware, and access all files on the computer. Administrators can also make changes to other local user accounts.

> **Note**
>
> When you create an administrator user, it adds the user to the Administrator group. When you create a standard user, it adds the user to the Users group.

When you set up Windows, you are required to create a user account. This account is an administrator account that allows you to set up your computer and install any programs that you want to use. After you have finished setting up your computer, recommended practice dictates that you use a standard user account for your day-to-day computing.

> **Exam Alert**
>
> Because the administrator account has access to all network resources on the computer, it is always more secure to use a standard user account instead of an administrator account to do normal day-to-day tasks.

The guest account is primarily for people who need temporary access to the computer. The guest account is for users who don't have a permanent account on your computer or domain. It allows people to use your computer without having access to your personal files. People using the guest account can't install software or hardware, change settings, or create a password.

> **Note**
>
> By default, the guest account is disabled. Therefore, you have to enable the guest account before it can be used.

All user accounts are identified with a logon name. In Windows 7, this logon name has two parts: the user name and the user's computer name or domain in which the user account exists. If you have a computer called PC1 and the username is called User1, the full logon name for Windows 7 is PC1\User1. Of course, User1 could log on to his or her local workstation and access local resources but would not be able to access domain resources.

When working with domains, the full logon name can be expressed in two different ways:

▶ The user account name and the full domain name separated by the at sign (@). For example, the full logon name for User1 in the Acme.com domain would be User1@Acme.com.

▶ The user account name and the domain separated by the backslash symbol (\). For example, the full logon name for User1 in the Acme domain would be Acme\User1.

Although Windows 7 represents a user account with a user name, the accounts key identifier is the security identifier (SID). SIDs are unique identifiers that are automatically generated when a user account is created. They consist of a computer or domain security ID prefix combined with a unique relative ID for the user. Having a unique identifier enables you to change user names. It also enables you to delete accounts without worrying that someone might gain access to resources simply by re-creating an account.

To provide security, user accounts can have passwords. Passwords are authentication strings for an account that consist of upper- and lowercase characters, digits, and special characters.

ExamAlert

It is recommended that all local computer accounts have passwords. If an account is created without a password, anyone can log on to the account, and there is no protection for the account. However, a local account without a password cannot be used to remotely access a computer.

> **Note**
>
> It is always recommended that you use a strong password or a complex password. Microsoft defines a complex password used in group policies as
>
> - ▶ Passwords cannot contain the user's account name or parts of the user's full name that exceed two consecutive characters.
>
> - ▶ Passwords must be at least six characters in length or the number of characters specified in the Minimum password length policy setting.
>
> - ▶ Passwords must contain characters from at least three of the following four categories:
>
>   - ▶ English uppercase alphabet characters (A–Z)
>   - ▶ English lowercase alphabet characters (a–z)
>   - ▶ Base 10 digits (0–9)
>   - ▶ Non-alphanumeric characters (for example, !$#,%)
>
> Group policies can be used to enforce using complex passwords.

Managing Local Logon Accounts

The User Accounts console accessed through the Control Panel, as shown in Figure 8.2, provides an easy way to manage the user accounts. If you want more advanced control, you use the Users and Groups console (which is also part of the Computer Management console).

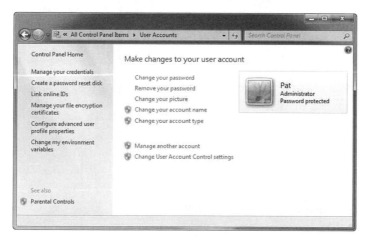

FIGURE 8.2 **User Accounts console.**

For a computer that is a member of a workgroup, you can create a local user account on a computer by following these steps:

1. In the Control Panel, click **Add or Remove User Accounts** under the User Accounts heading. This displays the Manage Accounts page, as shown in Figure 8.3. The Manage Accounts page lists all configurable user accounts on the local computer by account type with configuration details. If an account has a password, it is listed as being password protected. If an account is disabled, it is listed as being off.

2. Click **Create a new account**. This displays the Create New Account page.

3. Type the name of the local account. This name is displayed on the Welcome screen and Start menu.

4. Set the type of account as either Standard User or Administrator from the screen shown in Figure 8.4. To give the user full permissions on the local computer, select **Administrator**.

FIGURE 8.3 **Manage accounts.**

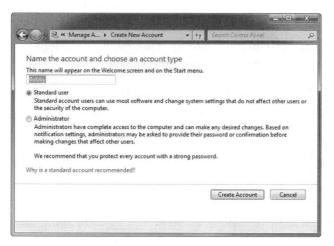

FIGURE 8.4   **Selecting the account type.**

If a user needs to be able to log on locally to a computer and has an existing domain account, you can grant the user permission to log on locally by completing the following steps:

1. In Control Panel, click User Accounts. On the User Accounts page, click the **Give other users access to this computer** link. This displays the User Accounts dialog box, as shown in Figure 8.5. The User Accounts dialog box lists all configurable user accounts on the local computer by account type with group membership details.

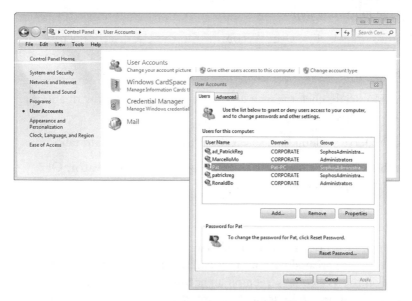

FIGURE 8.5   **User Accounts dialog box.**

2. Click **Add**. This starts the Add New User Wizard.

3. You are creating a local computer account for a user with an existing domain account. Type the user's domain account name and domain in the fields provided.

4. Using the options provided, select the type of user account, administrator, standard user or Other account. An Other account is created as a member of the specific group you choose. To give the user the permissions of a specific group, select **Other** and then select the desired group.

5. Click **Finish**.

You can change the account type for a local computer user by completing the following steps:

1. In Control Panel, click **Add or Remove User Accounts** under the User Accounts heading. This displays the Manage Accounts page.

2. Click the account you want to change and then click **Change the Account Type**.

3. On the Change the Account Type page, set the level of access for the user as either Standard User or Administrator and then click **Change the Account Type**.

In a domain, you can change the account type for a local computer user by completing the following steps:

1. In Control Panel, click **User Accounts**. On the User Accounts page, click the **Change account type** link. This displays the User Accounts dialog box.

2. On the Users tab, click the user account you want to work with and then click **Properties**.

3. In the Properties dialog box, select the **Group Membership** tab.

4. Select the type of account as **Standard User** or **Administrator**. Or select **Other** and then select the desired other group.

5. Click **OK** twice.

When the computer is not part of a domain (workgroup configuration), by default, local users are created without passwords. Therefore, if you click the account name on the Welcome screen on an account that does not have a password, you are automatically logged in.

You can create a password for a local user account by completing the following steps:

1. Log on as the user whose password you want to create. In Control Panel, click **Add or Remove User Accounts** under the User Accounts heading. This displays the Manage Accounts page.

2. All user accounts available on the machine are shown, and you need to click the account you want to work with. To prevent possible data loss, this should be the same as the account under which you are currently logged on. Any account that has a current password is listed as Password Protected. Any account without this label doesn't have a password.

3. Click **Create a Password**. Type a password and then confirm it. Afterward, type a unique password hint. The password hint is a word or phrase that can be used to obtain the password if it is lost. This hint is visible to anyone who uses the computer.

4. Click **Create Password**.

In a workgroup, you can remove a user's local account and effectively deny logon by completing these steps:

1. Log on as a user with local administrator privileges. In Control Panel, click **Add or Remove User Accounts** under the User Accounts heading. This displays the Manage Accounts page.

2. Click the account you want to remove.

3. Click **Delete the Account**.

4. Before deleting the account, you have the opportunity save the contents of the user's desktop and Documents folder to a folder on the current user's desktop. To save the user's documents, click **Keep Files**. To delete the files, click **Delete Files**.

5. Confirm the account deletion by clicking **Delete Account**. Keep in mind that in a domain, unless there are further restrictions with regard to logon workstations, a user might still be able to gain access to the workstation by logging on with a domain account.

To access the Users and Groups in the Computer Management console, do the following:

1. Click the **Start** button.

2. Click **Control Panel**.

3. Click **System and Maintenance**.

4. Click **Administrative Tools**.

5. Click **Computer Management**.

6. Double-click **Local Users and Groups**.

7. Select either **Users** (shown in Figure 8.6) or **Groups** (shown in Figure 8.7).

To create a user or group, just right-click **Users or Groups** and select **New User** or **New Group**. To modify a user or group, double-click on the identity.

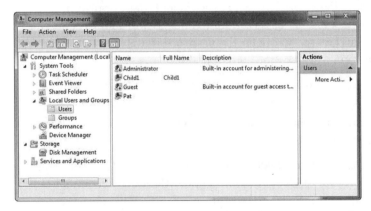

FIGURE 8.6   Managing Users with Computer Management console.

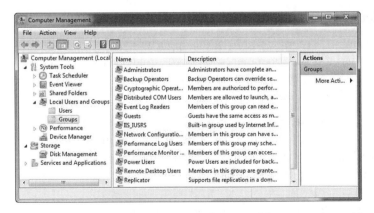

FIGURE 8.7   Managing Groups with Computer Management console.

Credential Manager

Credential Manager enables you to store credentials, such as user names and passwords, so that the next time you or an application that you are using accesses a website or network resource, the credentials are automatically applied so that you can access the website or network resource automatically. Credentials are saved in special folders on your computer called vaults.

To add a password to your Windows vault:

1. Open **User Accounts** in the Control Panel.

2. In the left pane, click **Manage your credentials**. You see the screen shown in Figure 8.8.

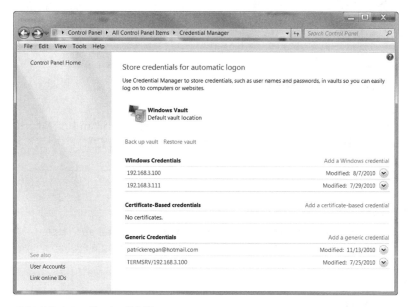

FIGURE 8.8   **Credential Manager.**

3. Click **Add a Windows credential**.

4. In the Internet or network address box, type the name of the computer on the network that you want to access, as shown in Figure 8.9.

FIGURE 8.9   **Adding a Windows credential.**

5. In the User name and Password boxes, type the user name and password that you use for the computer or websites and then click **OK**.

Cram Quiz

1. What authorizes a user to perform certain actions on a computer such as logging on to a system interactively, backing up files, or performing a system shutdown?

    ○   **A.** A right

    ○   **B.** A permission

    ○   **C.** A digital certificate

    ○   **D.** Auditing ability

2. Where do you locate the User Accounts console?

    ○   **A.** Accessories

    ○   **B.** Maintenance

    ○   **C.** Control Panel

    ○   **D.** System Properties

Cram Quiz Answers

1. **A** is correct. A right authorizes a user to perform certain actions on the computer. Answer B is incorrect because a permission defines the type of access granted to an object or object attribute. Answer C is incorrect because a digital certificate is used for authentication. Answer D is incorrect because auditing is used to track user actions and activities.

2. **C** is correct. To create and manage users in Windows 7, you usually use the User Accounts console from the Control Panel. You will not find any tools to manage users in Accessories, Maintenance, or System Properties. Therefore, the other answers are incorrect.

User Account Control

▶ **Configure authentication and authorization**

Cram**Saver**

1. What feature prevents a program from making unauthorized changes to your computer running Windows 7?

   ○ **A.** UAC

   ○ **B.** USB

   ○ **C.** GMT

   ○ **D.** ActiveX

2. Which UAC slider option dims the desktop causing other programs not to run when the UAC dialog box appears? (Choose all that apply.)

   ○ **A.** Always notify

   ○ **B.** Notify me only when programs try to make changes to my computer

   ○ **C.** Notify me only when programs try to make changes to my computer (do not dim my desktop)

   ○ **D.** Never notify

Answers

1. **A** is correct. User Account Control (UAC) is a feature in Windows that can help prevent unauthorized changes to your computer. If you are logged in as an administrator, UAC asks you for permission, and if you are logged in as a standard user, UAC asks you for an administrator password before performing actions that could potentially affect your computer's operation or that change settings that affect other users. Answer B is incorrect because USB is short for Universal Serial Bus, which is used to connect devices to the computer. Answer C is incorrect because Greenwich Mean Time (GMT) is used with time zones. Answer D is incorrect because ActiveX is a framework for defining reusable components known as controls.

2. **A** is correct. The only option that dims the screen when a UAC prompt appears is Always notify; therefore, all other answers are incorrect.

Need-to-know is a basic security concept that says information should be limited to only those individuals who require it, and they should be given only enough access to carry out their specific job functions. When planning for how you assign the rights and permissions to the network resources, follow these two main rules:

▶ Give the rights and permissions for the user to do his or her job.

▶ Don't give any additional rights and permissions that a user does not need.

Although you want to keep resources secure, you want to make sure that the users can easily get what they need. For example, give users access to the necessary files, and give them only the permissions they need. If they need to read a document but don't need to make changes to it, they need to have only the read permission. Giving a person or group only the required amount of access and nothing more is known as the rule or principle of least privilege.

When you ran earlier versions of Windows, including Windows XP, and you logged in with an administrative account, every task that you execute and every process that ran in the account's session ran as an as administrator with elevated privileges. Because the elevated privileges provided access to everything, it opened the possibility of human error, which could cause problems in Windows functionality or data loss, and it allowed malicious software to access any part of the computer. Unfortunately, most legacy applications and even new applications were or are not designed to work without full administrator privileges.

User Account Control (UAC) is a feature in Windows that can help prevent unauthorized changes to your computer. If you are logged in as an administrator, UAC asks you for permission, and if you are logged in as a standard user, UAC asks you for an administrator password before performing actions that could potentially affect your computer's operation or that change settings that affect other users. When you see a UAC message, read it carefully and then make sure the name of the action or program that's about to start is one that you intended to start.

The Application Information Service (AIS) is a system service that facilitates UAC and launching applications that require one or more elevated privileges or user rights to run, such as Administrative Tasks, as well as applications that require higher integrity levels. If you disable AIS, when you try to run applications that require administrative access, you get an Access Denied error.

To keep track of a user's access, when a standard user logs in to Windows 7, a token is created that contains only the most basic privileges assigned. When an administrator logs in, two separate tokens are assigned. The first token contains all privileges typically awarded to an administrator, and the second is a restricted token similar to what a standard user receives. User applications, including the Windows Shell, are then started with the restricted token resulting in a reduced privilege environment even under an Administrator account.

When an application requests elevation or is run as administrator, UAC prompts for confirmation and, if consent is given, starts the process using the unrestricted token.

The default UAC setting allows a standard user to perform the following tasks without receiving a UAC prompt:

▶ Install updates from Windows Update

▶ Install drivers from Windows Update or those that are included with the operating system

▶ View Windows settings

▶ Pair Bluetooth devices with the computer

▶ Reset the network adapter and perform other network diagnostic and repair tasks

Administrative users automatically have:

▶ Read/Write/Execute permissions to all resources

▶ All Windows privileges

When your permission or password is needed to complete a task, UAC alerts you with one of the following messages:

▶ **A setting or feature that is part of Windows needs your permission to start**: A Windows function or program that can affect other users of this computer needs your permission to start. Check the name of the action to ensure that it's a function or program you want to run.

▶ **A program that is not part of Windows needs to your permission to start**: A program that's not part of Windows needs your permission to start. It has a valid digital signature indicating its name and its publisher, which helps to ensure that the program is what it claims to be. Make sure that this is a program that you intended to run.

▶ **A program with an unknown publisher) needs your permission to start** (see Figure 8.10): An unidentified program is one that doesn't have a valid digital signature from its publisher to ensure that the program is what it claims to be. This doesn't necessarily indicate danger, as many older, legitimate programs lack signatures. However, you should use extra caution and only allow this program to run if you obtained it from a trusted source, such as the original CD/DVD or a publisher's website.

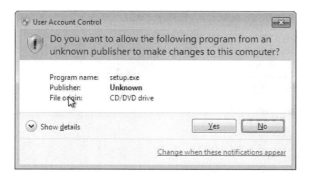

FIGURE 8.10   **User Account Control alert.**

▶ **You have been blocked by your system administrator from running this program**: This is a program that your administrator has specifically blocked from running on your computer. To run this program, you must contact your administrator and ask to have the program unblocked. Of course, it is recommended that you log on to your computer with a standard user account most of the time. With a standard user account, you can run standard business applications such as a word processor or spreadsheet, surf the Internet, or send email. When you want to perform an administrative task, such as installing a new program or changing a setting that affects other users, you don't have to switch to an administrator account. Windows prompts you for permission or an administrator password before performing the task.

To help protect your computer, you can create standard user accounts for all the users who share the computer. When someone who has a standard account tries to install software, Windows asks for an administrator account's password so that software can't be installed without the user's knowledge and permission.

UAC can be enabled or disabled for any individual user account. If you disable UAC for a user account, you lose the additional security protections UAC offers and put the computer at risk. To enable or disable UAC for a particular user account, follow these steps:

1. In Control Panel, click **User Accounts**.

2. On the User Accounts page, click **User Accounts**.

3. Click **Change User Account Control settings**.

4. Move the slider to the appropriate options, as shown in Figure 8.11 and Table 8.1.

5. When prompted to restart the computer, click **Restart Now** or **Restart Later** as appropriate for the changes to take effect.

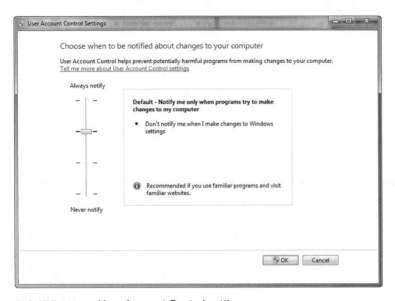

FIGURE 8.11 **User Account Control settings.**

TABLE 8.1 **UAC Settings**

Setting	Description	Security Impact
Always notify	You are notified before programs make changes to your computer or to Windows settings that require the permissions of an administrator.	This is the most secure setting. When you are notified, you should carefully read the contents of each dialog box before allowing changes to be made to your computer.
	When you're notified, your desktop is dimmed, and you must either approve or deny the request in the UAC dialog box before you can do anything else on your computer. The dimming of your desktop is referred to as the *secure desktop* because other programs can't run while it's dimmed.	

TABLE 8.1 **Continued**

Setting	Description	Security Impact
Notify me only when programs try to make changes to my computer	You are notified before programs make changes to your computer that require the permissions of an administrator. You are not notified if you try to make changes to Windows settings that require the permissions of an administrator. You are notified if a program outside of Windows tries to make changes to a Windows setting.	It's usually safe to allow changes to be made to Windows settings without you being notified. However, certain programs that come with Windows can have commands or data passed to them, and malicious software can take advantage of this by using these programs to install files or change settings on your computer. You should always be careful about which programs you allow to run on your computer.
Notify me only when programs try to make changes to my computer (do not dim my desktop)	You are notified before programs make changes to your computer that require the permissions of an administrator. You are not notified if you try to make changes to Windows settings that require the permissions of an administrator. You are notified if a program outside of Windows tries to make changes to a Windows setting.	This setting is the same as to make changes to my computer, but you are not notified on the secure desktop. Because the UAC dialog box isn't on the secure desktop with this setting, other programs might be able to interfere with the dialog's visual appearance. This is a small security risk if you already have a malicious program running on your computer.

TABLE 8.1 **Continued**

Setting	Description	Security Impact
Never notify	You are not notified before any changes are made to your computer. If you are logged on as an administrator, programs can make changes to your computer without you knowing about it. If you are logged on as a standard user, any changes that require the permissions of an administrator are automatically denied. If you select this setting, you need to restart the computer to complete the process of turning off UAC. After UAC is off, people who log on as administrator always have the permissions of an administrator.	This is the least secure setting. When you set UAC to never notify, you open your computer to potential security risks. If you set UAC to Never notify, you should be careful about which programs you run, because they have the same access to the computer as you do. This includes reading and making changes to protected system areas, your personal data, saved files, and anything else stored on the computer. Programs are also able to communicate and transfer information to and from anything your computer connects with, including the Internet.

Note

UAC can prevent you from saving files to the root directory of your hard drive.

Besides enabling or disabling UAC, you control the behavior of the UAC by using local or group policies. Local policies are managed from each local computer while group policies are managed as part of Active Directory. Table 8.2 defines the settings found in local and group policies.

TABLE 8.2 **UAC Policy Settings Available in the Policy Editor Snap In**

Policy	Security Settings
Admin Approval Mode for the Built-in Administrator account	Enabled
	Disabled (Default)
Behavior of the elevation prompt for administrators in Admin Approval Mode	Elevate without prompting
	Prompt for credentials
	Prompt for consent (Default)

TABLE 8.2 **Continued**

Policy	Security Settings
Behavior of the elevation prompt for standard users	Automatically deny elevation requests
	Prompt for credentials (Default)
Detect application installations and prompt for elevation	*Enabled (Default)*
	Disabled
Only elevate executables that are signed and validated	Enabled
	Disabled (Default)
Only elevate UIAccess applications that are installed in secure applications	*Enabled (Default)*
	Disabled
Run all administrators in Admin Approval Mode	*Enabled (Default)*
	Disabled
Switch to the secure desktop when prompting for elevation	*Enabled (Default)*
	Disabled
Virtualize file and registry write failures to per-user locations	*Enabled (Default)*

To change the behavior of the User Account Control message for administrators in Admin Approval Mode:

1. Click **Start**, type **secpol.msc** in the Search programs and files box, and press **Enter**.

2. If UAC is currently configured in Admin Approval Mode, the User Account Control message displays. Click **Continue**.

3. From the Local Security Policy tree, click **Local Policies** and then double-click **Security Options**.

4. Scroll down to and double-click **User Account Control: Behavior of the elevation prompt for administrators in Admin Approval Mode**.

5. From the drop-down menu, select one of the following settings:

   ▶ **Elevate without prompting**: In this case, applications that have been marked as administrator applications, as well as applications detected as setup applications, automatically run with the full administrator access token. All other applications automatically run with the standard user token.

▶ **Prompt for credentials**: In this case, in order to give consent for an application to run with the full administrator access token, the user must enter administrator credentials. This setting supports compliance with Common Criteria or corporate policies.

▶ **Prompt for consent**: This is the default setting.

6. Click **Apply**.

Use the following procedure to change the User Account Control message behavior for standard users:

1. Click **Start**, type `secpol.msc` in the Search programs and files box, and press **Enter**.

2. If UAC is currently configured to prompt for administrator credentials, the User Account Control message displays. Click **Continue**.

3. From the Local Security Policy tree, click **Local Policies** and then double-click **Security Options**, as shown in Figure 8.12.

4. Scroll down and double-click **User Account Control: Behavior of the elevation prompt for standard users**.

5. From the drop-down menu, select one of the following settings:

▶ **Automatically deny elevation requests**: In this case, administrator applications are not able to run. The user should see an error message from the application that indicates a policy has prevented the application from running.

▶ **Prompt for credentials**: This is the default setting. In this case, for an application to run with the full administrator access token, the user must enter administrator credentials.

6. Click **Apply**.

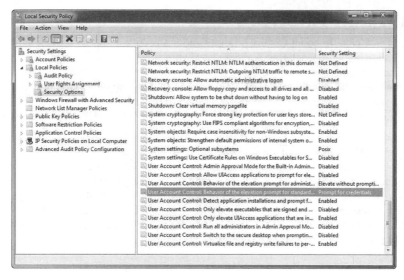

FIGURE 8.12   **Controlling UAC with Group Policies.**

Cram Quiz

1. You download a software package from the Internet and decide to install it. What would you use to ensure that the software package does not make changes that you are not aware of?

   ○ **A.** Windows Defender

   ○ **B.** Windows Firewall

   ○ **C.** User Account Control

   ○ **D.** System Configuration

2. You are logged in as a local administrator. You are trying to save a file to C:\ but you are denied. What could be the cause?

   ○ **A.** Windows Defender

   ○ **B.** Windows Firewall

   ○ **C.** User Account Control

   ○ **D.** Software Explorer

Cram Exam Answers

1. **C** is correct. User Account Control prompts you if a program tries to make a sys-tem change, including installing additional software. Answer A is incorrect because Windows Defender is used to protect against spyware. Answer B is incorrect because Windows Firewall blocks traffic that should not go through the firewall. Answer D is incorrect because it is used to manage which programs start during boot.

2. **C** is correct. User Account Control is used to make sure software does not make any system changes without your knowledge or administrative permission. It can also prevent you from saving files to the C drive root directory. Answer A is incorrect because Windows Defender is used to protect against spyware. Answer B is incorrect because Windows Firewall blocks traffic that should not go through the firewall. Answer D is incorrect because Software Explorer was part of Windows Defender that came with Windows Vista but was discontinued with Windows 7.

Security Auditing

▶ **Configure remote connections**

Cram**Saver**

1. What feature tracks and records various security-related events so that you can detect intruders and attempts to compromise the system?

    ○ **A.** Auditing

    ○ **B.** ACL

    ○ **C.** Permissions

    ○ **D.** Rights

2. You want to enable auditing of a folder called Reports. What is the first step you need to do?

    ○ **A.** Enable user auditing

    ○ **B.** Enable file auditing

    ○ **C.** Enable object auditing

    ○ **D.** Enable ACL auditing

Answers

1. **A** is correct. If you enable auditing, you can track and record various security-related events, such as when someone logs on to the computer or when a file or folder is accessed. Answer B is incorrect because the access control list (ACL) is used to specify who can access an object and what permissions they have for that object. Answer C is incorrect because permissions are assigned to an object and recorded in the ACL. Answer D is incorrect because rights are used to determine what actions a user can perform on a computer running Windows.

2. **C** is correct. The first step in enabling auditing for a printer, file, or folder is that you must first enable object auditing. Printers, files, and folders are examples of objects. User auditing and ACL auditing are not specifically used in Windows audit policies and, therefore, Answers A and D are incorrect. Answer B is incorrect because configuring file auditing would be the second step after you enable object auditing.

Auditing is a feature of Windows 7 that tracks and records various security-related events so that you can detect intruders and attempts to compromise data on the system. Therefore, you want to set up an audit policy for a computer to

▶ Minimize the risk of unauthorized use of resources.

▶ Maintain a record of user and administrator activity.

Examples of auditing including tracking the success and failures of events, such as attempts to log on, attempts by a particular user to read a specific file, changes to user accounts, or changes to security settings.

Some events that you can monitor are access to an object such as a folder or file, management of user and group accounts, and logging on and off a system. The security events are provided in the Event Viewer, specifically the security logs, which contain the following information:

▶ The action that was performed

▶ The user who performed the action

▶ The success or failure of the event and when the event occurred

▶ Additional information, such as the computer where the event occurred

Therefore, auditing is one way to find security holes in your network and to ensure accountability for people's actions.

Not all events are audited by default. If you have Administrator permissions, you can specify what types of system events to audit using group policies or the local security policy (Security Settings\Local Policies\Audit Policy). In addition, Windows 7 also offers Advanced Audit Policy configuration, which allows more granular control, as shown in Figure 8.13. The amount of auditing that needs to be done depends on the needs of the organization. A minimum-security network might only audit failed logon attempts so that brute-force attacks can be detected. A high security network most likely audits both successful and failed logons to track who successfully gained access to the network.

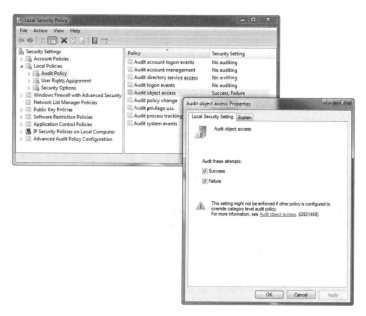

FIGURE 8.13   **Auditing policy.**

Auditing can be configured on any Windows computer, including workstations and servers. Because a user working on a workstation often accesses
remote network resources, it makes sense that you have to configure auditing
on those Windows servers so that you monitor how those resources are being
accessed. In addition, because many organizations are using Active Directory
domains, you need to enable auditing at the domain level so that you can
monitor when a user logs in to the domain, no matter what computer they are
logging from.

The first step in implementing an audit policy is to select the types of events
that you want Windows 7 to audit. Table 8.3 describes the events that
Windows 7 can audit.

TABLE 8.3   **Audit Events**

Event	Example
Account Logon	When a user logs on to the local computer, the computer records the Account Logon event. When a user logs on to a domain, the authenticating domain controller records the Account Logon event.
Account Management	An administrator creates, changes, or deletes a user account or group; a user account is renamed, disabled, or enabled; or a password is set or changed.

TABLE 8.3   **Continued**

Event	Example
Directory Service Access	A user accesses an Active Directory object. Note: You must then configure specific Active Directory objects for auditing.
Logon	A user logs on or off a local computer or a user makes or cancels a network connection to the computer; the event is recorded on the computer that the user accesses, regardless of whether a local account or a domain account is used.
Object Access	A user accesses a file, folder, or printer. Note: You must then configure specific files, folders, or printers to be audited, the users or groups that are being audited, and the actions that they are audited for.
Policy Change	A change is made to the user security options (for example, password options or account logon settings), user rights, or audit policies.
Privilege Use	A user exercises a user right (not related to logging on or off), such as changing the system time or taking ownership of a file.
Process Tracking	An application performs an action. This is generally used only for programmers and can be very intensive.
System	A user restarts or shuts down the computer, or an event occurs that affects Windows security or the security log.

With file and folder auditing, you can audit only those volumes that are formatted with NTFS. In addition, you must first enable Object Access auditing using group policies. After the group policy has been applied, you can set, view, or change auditing a file or folder by doing the following:

1. Using a group or local policy, enable object access auditing.

2. Open Windows Explorer and locate the file or folder that you want to audit.

3. Right-click the file or folder and select the **Properties** option.

4. Click the Security tab, click the **Advanced** button, and click the **Auditing** tab:

   ▶ To set up auditing for a new group or user, click **Add**, specify the name of the user you want, and click the **OK** button to open the Auditing Entry box.

   ▶ To view or change auditing for an existing group or user, click the name and then the **View/Edit** button.

   ▶ To remove auditing for an existing group or user, click the name and then the **Remove** button.

Because the security log is limited in size, select only those objects that you need to audit and consider the amount of disk space that the security log needs. The maximum size of the security log is defined in Event Viewer by right-clicking **Security Log** and selecting the **Properties** option.

Cram Quiz

1. Where do you look to see the events you audited?

   - ○ **A.** System Configuration
   - ○ **B.** Registry Editor
   - ○ **C.** Logs folder
   - ○ **D.** Event Viewer

2. How do you enable auditing in Windows?

   - ○ **A.** Modify the boot.ini
   - ○ **B.** Right-click Computer applet and select properties
   - ○ **C.** Use group policies
   - ○ **D.** System Configuration

Cram Exam Answers

1. **D** is correct. If auditing is enabled, the security logs in the Event Viewer contain events. If not, the security logs are empty. Therefore, the other answers are incorrect.

2. **C** is correct. You would enable auditing in Windows using group policies including local policies. Therefore, the other answers are incorrect.

Review Questions

1. What allows a system to determine whether an authenticated user can access a resource and how they can access the resource?

    ○ **A.** Authentication

    ○ **B.** Authorization

    ○ **C.** Auditing

    ○ **D.** Certificate

2. Which protocol is the main logon authentication method used when logging onto a computer running Windows Server 2008 that is part of an Active Directory domain?

    ○ **A.** Kerberos

    ○ **B.** Windows NT LAN Manager

    ○ **C.** Certificate mappings

    ○ **D.** Password Authentication Protocol

3. Which of the following does UAC prompt for permission or administrative credentials? (Choose two answers.)

    ○ **A.** Change time zone

    ○ **B.** Change power management settings

    ○ **C.** Install fonts

    ○ **D.** Install a device driver

    ○ **E.** Install an application

4. Which of the following is used to prevent unauthorized changes to your computer?

    ○ **A.** Computer Management Console

    ○ **B.** User Account Control (UAC)

    ○ **C.** Windows Firewall

    ○ **D.** Event Viewer

5. You receive a message asking for your permission to continue a certain action. What would usually generate this warning?

    ○ **A.** Windows Firewall

    ○ **B.** NTFS permissions

    ○ **C.** User Account Control (UAC)

    ○ **D.** Internet Sharing Console

6. You work as the desktop support technician at Acme.com. You have many computers running Windows 7 that are part of a Windows domain. Your company decides to allow only applications that have been approved by the IT department. You have a handful of users who need to make configuration changes to these applications. However, when they try to make the appropriate changes, they always receive the following error message:

You need to ensure that <username> is able to make configuration changes to <computer name>.

After verifying that these users have administrative access to their computer, what do you need to do to make sure that they no longer receive these messages?

○ **A.** Add all users to the Power Users group

○ **B.** Add all users to the Users group

○ **C.** Turn off the Windows Firewall

○ **D.** Change the Elevation prompt for administrators in User Account Control (UAC) Admin Approval Mode

7. You work as the desktop support technician at Acme.com. You need to assign a handful of users to install applications without giving administrative permissions. What do you do?

○ **A.** Make these users part of the local administrator group

○ **B.** Turn User Account Control off in the User Accounts Control Panel tool

○ **C.** Configure Parental Controls to block each user from the ability to download unapproved software

○ **D.** Configure the User Account Control not to prompt during software installation in the Security Options section of the Local Security Policy.

8. What program do you need to download and install so that you can manage Active Directory resources from your computer running Windows 7?

○ **A.** ADManager

○ **B.** WFW

○ **C.** UAC

○ **D.** RSAT

9. To create local user accounts, you use which of the following? (Choose two answers.)

○ **A.** User Accounts in the Control Panel

○ **B.** Computer Management Console

○ **C.** Active Directory Users and Computers

○ **D.** Users and Groups Administrator console

10. Which auditing do you need to enable if you want to see if someone is deleting a user account from a computer running Windows 7?

○ **A.** Account logon

○ **B.** Account management

○ **C.** Object access

○ **D.** Policy change

Review Question Answers

1. Answer **B** is correct. Authorization occurs after authentication, which allows access to a network resource. Answer A is incorrect because authentication is the process to confirm a user's identity when he or she accesses a computer system or additional system resources. Answer C is incorrect because auditing is the recording of activity to be used to track user actions. Answer D is incorrect because a digital certificate is a form of authentication.

2. Answer **A** is correct. Kerberos is the main logon authentication method used by clients and servers running Microsoft Windows operating systems to authenticate both user accounts and computer accounts. Answer B is incorrect because Windows NT LAN Manager (NTLM) is an authentication protocol used for backward compatibility with pre-Windows 2000 operating systems and applications. Answer C is incorrect because certificate mappings are used with smart cards (which contain a digital certificate) for logon authentication. Answer D is incorrect because Password Authentication Protocol (PAP) is used as a remote access authentication protocol that sends username and password in clear text (unencrypted).

3. Answers **D** and **E** are correct. Installing device drivers and installing applications require administrative permission. Therefore, UAC prompts you to make sure it is something that you want done. Answers A, B, and C are incorrect because standard users can perform these actions.

4. Answer **B** is correct. User Account Control is used to prevent unauthorized changes to the computer. Answer A is incorrect because the computer management console is used to manage the computer including managing volumes, using the Event Viewer and managing local users and groups. Answer C is incorrect because the Windows firewall helps block unwanted packets from getting to your computer. Answer D is incorrect because the Event Viewer is used to look at warning and error messages and the security logs.

5. Answer **C** is correct. User Account Control asks for permission to continue when you are performing tasks that require you to be an administrator to make sure that they are tasks that you really want to complete. Answer A is incorrect because Windows Firewall prevents unwanted packets from the outside. Answer B is incorrect because NTFS permissions help protect the files on an NTFS volume. Answer D is incorrect because there is no such thing as an Internet Sharing Console.

6. Answer **D** is correct. The message is generated by User Account Control, which you can configure by using local or group policies. Answer A is incorrect because the Power Users group is left behind from Windows 2000 and XP for backward compatibility. Answer B is incorrect because all standard user accounts should already be members of the Users group. Answer C is incorrect because turning off the firewall would not get rid of the message.

7. Answer **D** is correct. You need to edit the Local Security Policy to not prompt during installs by disabling the Detect application installations and prompt for elevation setting. This allows applications to be installed without prompting for the administrative credentials. Answer A is incorrect because you don't want to give administrative permission. Answer B is incorrect because turning off User Account Control stops protecting the system. Answer C is also incorrect because Parental Controls cannot be used when a computer is connected to a domain.

8. Answer **D** is correct. Active Directory consoles including Active Directory Users and Computers console and Group Policy Management console. To install these consoles, you need to install the Microsoft Remote Server Administration Tools (RSAT) for Windows 7. Answer A is incorrect because ADManager does not exist in Windows. Answer B is incorrect because WFW is short for Windows Firewall, which is used to protect a computer from unauthorized access. Answer C is incorrect because UAC is short for User Access Control, which helps protect a computer from unauthorized changes.

9. Answer **A** and **B** are correct. The Control Panel User Accounts and the Computer Management Console, specifically under Users and Groups, are used to add and manage user accounts. Answer C is incorrect because Active Directory Users and Computers console is used to manage domain user accounts. Answer D is incorrect because the Users and Groups Administrator console does not exist.

10. Answer **B** is correct. When you enable auditing of account management, events are recorded when someone creates, changes, or deletes a user account or group; a user account is renamed, disabled, or enabled; or a password is set or changed. Answer A is incorrect because account logon auditing records when a user logs on to the local computer. Answer C is incorrect because object access auditing is the first step in monitoring access to objects, including printers, folders, and files. Answer D is incorrect because policy change audits change in local policies.

CHAPTER 9

Managing Files and Folders

This chapter covers the following 70-680 Objectives:

▶ Configure file and folder access

▶ Configure BitLocker and BitLocker To Go

The disk structure does not describe how a hard drive or floppy disk physically works, but how it stores files on the disk. In other words, it describes the formatting of the disk (file system, partitions, the root directory, and the directories). A file system is the overall structure in which files are named, stored, and organized. File systems used in Windows 7 include FAT, FAT32, and NTFS. Although FAT and FAT32 were primarily used in older operating systems, NTFS is the preferred file system in Windows 7.

NTFS

▶ **Configure file and folder access**

CramSaver

1. Which of the following file systems is the most secure and the most reliable used by Windows 7?

   ○ **A.** FAT

   ○ **B.** FAT32

   ○ **C.** NTFS

   ○ **D.** VFAT

   ○ **E.** NFS

2. You work as the desktop support technician at Acme.com. Pat is a member of the manager group. There is a shared folder called DATA on an NTFS partition on a remote Windows 7 computer. Pat is given the Write NTFS permission, the Manager group is giving the Read & Execute NTFS permissions, and the Everyone group has the Read NTFS permission to the DATA folder. In addition, Pat, Manager, and Everyone are assigned the shared Contributor permission to the DATA folder. When Pat logs on to the Windows 7 computer that has the DATA folder and accesses the DATA folder directly, what would be Pat's permissions? (Choose all that apply.)

   ○ **A.** Read the files in that folder

   ○ **B.** Write to the files in the folder

   ○ **C.** Execute the files in the folder

   ○ **D.** Delete the files in the folder

   ○ **E.** Have no access to the files in the folder

Answers

1. **C** is correct. NTFS is the only one that provides security features such as encryption and NTFS permissions and the ability to use transaction tracking to keep the file system reliable. Answers A and B are incorrect because they do not offer the features just mentioned for NTFS. Answer D is incorrect because this was the name given to the FAT file system that supported long file names. NFS is a file system used in UNIX/Linux machines and is not supported by Windows 7 as a file system.

2. **A, B, C,** and **D** are correct. When you combine the NTFS permissions assigned to Pat and to the Manager group that Pat is a member of, Pat can read, write, execute, and delete the files in the folder. When you access a folder directly on a local computer, Share permissions do not apply.

As mentioned earlier in the book, NTFS is the preferred file system for Windows 7. It allows support for larger hard drives, has better security, including permissions and encryption, and offers disk compression and disk quotas. It is also more fault tolerant because it is a journaling file system.

NTFS Permissions

A primary advantage of NTFS over FAT and FAT32 is that NTFS volumes have the capability to apply NTFS permissions to secure folders and files. By setting the permissions, you specify the level of access for groups and users for accessing files or directories. For example, to one user or group of users, you can specify that they can only read the file; another user or group of users can read and write to the file; and others have no access. No matter if you are logged on locally at the computer or accessing a computer through a network, NTFS permissions always apply.

The NTFS permissions that are granted are stored in an access control list (ACL) with every file or folder on an NTFS volume. The ACL contains an access control entry (ACE) for each user account and group that has been granted access for the file or folder as well as the permissions granted to each user and group. To simplify the task of administration, the NTFS permissions have been logically grouped into the standard folder and file NTFS permissions, as shown in Table 9.1. If you need finer control, you need to use special permissions. Table 9.2 shows the special permissions.

> ### Note
> Remember that to manage your folders and files and when you open up a drive or folder, you are using Windows Explorer.

> ### ExamAlert
> Be sure that you understand the various NTFS permissions and how they are explicitly assigned and how those permissions flow down (inherited).

TABLE 9.1 **Standard NTFS Folder and File Permissions**

Permission Level	Description
Full Control	Users can read files and folders; execute files; write, modify and delete files; change attributes of files and folders; change permissions; and take ownership of files.
Modify	Users can read files and folders, execute files, write and modify files, delete files and folders, and change attributes of files and folders.
List Folder Contents	Users can view the names of folders and subfolders in the folder. This permission is only available at the folder level and is not available at the file level.
Read & Execute	Users can see the contents of existing files and folders and can run programs in a folder.
Read	Users can see the contents of a folder and open files and folders.
Write	Users can create new files and folders and make changes to existing files and folders. Users cannot create new files or folders.

TABLE 9.2 **NTFS Folder Special Permissions**

Special Permissions	Full Control	Modify	Read & Execute	List Folder Contents	Read	Write
Traverse Folder/ Execute File	✔	✔	✔	✔		
List Folder/ Read Data	✔	✔	✔	✔	✔	
Read Attributes	✔	✔	✔	✔	✔	
Read Extended Attributes	✔	✔	✔	✔	✔	
Create Files/ Write Data	✔	✔				✔
Create Folders/ Append Data	✔	✔				✔
Write Attributes	✔	✔				✔
Write Extended Attributes	✔	✔				✔
Delete Subfolders and Files	✔					
Delete	✔	✔				
Read Permissions	✔	✔	✔	✔	✔	✔
Change Permissions	✔					
Take Ownership	✔					
Synchronize	✔	✔	✔	✔	✔	✔

> **Note**
>
> Although List Folder Contents and Read & Execute appear to have the same per-
> missions, these permissions are inherited differently. List Folder Contents is inherit-
> ed by folders but not files, and it should only appear when you view folder permis-
> sions. Read & Execute is inherited by both files and folders and is always present
> when you view file or folder permissions.

To set, view, change, or remove permissions on files and folders:

1. Right-click the file or folder for which you want to set permissions and
   click **Properties**.

2. Click the **Security** tab, as shown in Figure 9.1.

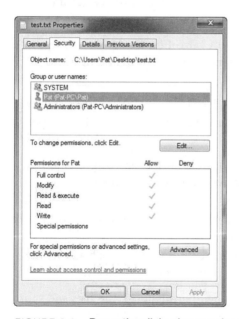

FIGURE 9.1   Properties dialog box can be used to configure NTFS permissions.

3. Click **Edit** to open the Permissions for <name of file or folder> dialog
   box and then do one of the following:

   ▶ To set permissions for a group or user that does not appear in the
   Group or user names box, click **Add**. Type the name of the group
   or user you want to set permissions for and then click **OK**.

> ▶ To change or remove permissions from an existing group or user,
> click the name of the group or user. To allow or deny a permission,
> in the Permissions for <User or Group> box, select the **Allow** or
> **Deny** checkbox. To remove the group or user from the Group or
> user names box, click **Remove**.

4. To view the special permissions, click the **Advanced** button.

5. To change the special permissions, click the **Edit** button.

When you are managing NTFS permissions, remember the following:

▶ You can set file and folder permissions only on drives formatted to use
NTFS.

▶ To change permissions, you must be the owner or have been granted
permission to do so by the owner.

▶ Groups or users that are granted Full Control for a folder can delete
files and subfolders within that folder, regardless of the permissions that
protect the files and subfolders.

▶ If the checkboxes under Permissions for <User or Group> are shaded or
if the Remove button is unavailable, the file or folder has inherited permissions from the parent folder.

▶ When adding a new user or group, by default this user or group has
Read & Execute, List Folder Contents, and Read permissions.

Permissions are given to a folder or file as either explicit permissions or inherited permissions. Explicit permissions are those granted directly to the folder
or file. Some of these permissions are granted automatically, such as when a
file or folder is created, while others have to be assigned manually.

When you set permissions to a folder (explicit permissions), the files and subfolders that exist in the folder inherit these permissions (called inherited permissions). In other words, the permissions flow down from the folder into the
subfolders and files, indirectly giving permissions to a user or group. Inherited
permissions ease the task of managing permissions and ensure consistency of
permissions among the subfolders and files within the folder.

When viewing the permissions, the permissions will be checked, cleared
(unchecked), or shaded. If the permission is checked, the permission was
explicitly assigned to the folder or file. If the permission is clear, the user or

group does not have that permission explicitly granted to the folder or file. Note that a user may still obtain permission through a group permission or a group may still obtain permission through another group. If the checkbox is shaded, the permission was granted through inheritance from a parent folder.

Windows offers the ability to deny individual permissions. The Deny permission always overrides the permissions that have been granted, including when a user or group has been giving full control. For example, if the group has been granted read and write, yet a person has been denied the Write permission, the user's effective rights would be the Read permission.

Similar to permissions granted at a lower level, NTFS file permissions override folder permissions. Therefore, if a user has access to a file, the user is still able to gain access to a file even if he or she does not have access to the folder containing the file. Of course, because the user doesn't have access to the folder, the user cannot navigate or browse through the folder to get to the file. Therefore, a user has to use the universal naming convention (UNC) or local path to open the file.

When assigning permissions to a folder, by default, the permissions apply to the folder being assigned and the subfolders and files of the folder. If you show the permission entries, you can specify how the permissions are applied to the folder, subfolder, and files.

To stop permission from being inherited, you can select the **Replace all existing inheritable permissions on all descendants with inheritable permissions from this object** option in the Advanced Security Settings dialog box. It then asks you if you are sure. You can also clear the **Allow inheritable permissions from parent to propagate to this object** checkbox. When the checkbox is clear, Windows responds with a Security dialog box. When you click on the **Copy** button, the explicit permission is copied from the parent folder to the subfolder or file. You can then change the subfolder's or file's explicit permissions. If you click on the **Remove** button, it removes the inherited permission altogether.

Because users can be members of several groups, it is possible for them to have several sets of explicit permissions to a folder or file. When this occurs, the permissions are combined to form the effective permissions, which are the actual permissions when logging in and accessing a file or folder. They consist of explicit permissions plus any inherited permissions.

Copying and Moving Files

When you copy and move files and folders from one location to another, you need to understand how the NTFS folder and file permissions are affected. If you copy a file or folder, the new folder and file automatically acquire the permissions of the drive or folder that the folder and file is being copied to.

If the folder or file is moved within the same volume, the folder or file retains the same permissions that were already assigned. When the folder or file is moved from one volume to another volume, the folder or file automatically acquires the permissions of the drive or folder that the file is being copied to. An easy way to remember the difference is this: When you move a folder or file from within the same volume, the folder and file are not physically moved but the Master File Table is adjusted to indicate a different folder. When you move a folder or file from one volume to another, it copies the folder or file to the new location and then deletes the old location. Therefore, the moved folder and files are new to the volume and acquire the new permissions.

> **ExamAlert**
>
> When you copy a file or folder or move a file or folder to a new volume, the file or folder automatically acquires the permission and attributes (compressions and encryption) of the drive or folder that the folder and file is being copied to. If you move the file or folder to the same volume, it keeps the same permissions and attributes that it already has.

Windows Vista, Windows 7, and Windows Server 2008 also include robocopy or "Robust File Copy" to copy files and folders from one place to another (even including between computers) while keeping their NTFS permissions, attributes, and properties. Robocopy includes many parameters. For more information about these parameters, visit the following website:

http://technet.microsoft.com/en-us/library/cc733145(WS.10).aspx

Folder and File Owners

Every folder and file has an owner, a person who controls how permissions are set on a folder or file and who grants permissions to others. When a folder or file is created, the user that creates the folder automatically becomes the owner. To be able to take ownership of a folder or file, the user has to be granted Take Ownership permission or be the administrator. After logging in, the user can take ownership by doing the following:

1. Right-click the folder or file and select the **Properties** option.

2. Click the **Security** tab and then the **Advanced** button.

3. Click the **Owner** tab.

4. Click the **Edit** button.

5. Click the user or group who is taking ownership. If the user to which you want to give ownership is not listed, you can click the **Other users or groups** button. When the user is selected, click the **OK** button.

6. When the Windows Security dialog box appears, click **OK**.

7. Click on the **OK** button to close the Advanced Properties dialog box.

8. Click **OK** to close the Properties dialog box.

Controlling Who Can Access a USB Flash Device

By using Group Policies with Windows 7, you can block automatic installation of USB storage devices on computers, specifically by enabling the Computer Configuration\Policies\Administrative Templates\System\Devices Installation\Device Installation Restrictions\Prevent Installation of Removable Devices policy. This prevents someone from connecting a USB drive and copying sensitive data to it, assuming that the device has not already been installed prior to the group policy being applied.

Cram Exam

1. You work as the desktop support technician at Acme.com. Pat is a member of the manager group. There is a shared folder called MANAGEMENT on an NTFS partition on a remote Windows 7 computer. Pat is given the Allow Write NTFS permission, the Manager group is giving the Read & Execute NTFS permissions, and the Everyone group has the Allow Read NTFS permission to the DATA folder. In addition, Pat, Manager, and Everyone are assigned the shared Contributor permission to the MANAGEMENT folder. When Pat logs on his client computer and accesses the MANAGEMENT folder, what would be Pat's permissions? (Choose all that apply.)

   ○ **A.** Read the files in that folder

   ○ **B.** Write to the files in the folder

   ○ **C.** Execute the files in the folder

   ○ **D.** Delete the files in the folder

   ○ **E.** Have no access to the files in the folder

2. You have a file, c:\data\reports.doc, on an NTFS volume. You move the file to the d:\reports folder, also on an NTFS volume. What permissions does the reports.doc receive?

 ○ **A.** It retains the same permissions that it had before.

 ○ **B.** It inherits the same permissions of the c:\data\reports folder.

 ○ **C.** It inherits the same permissions of the d:\reports folder.

 ○ **D.** All permissions are removed and you as the owner are set to full control.

Cram Exam Answers

1. **A, B**, and **C** are correct because NTFS permissions includes Write permission combined with Read and Execute. The Contributor share permission gives the ability to read, write, execute, and delete. When you combine the two, you take the least permissions, so that would be read, write, and execute. Answer D is incorrect because there was no delete NTFS permission assigned. Because they have permissions, Answer E is incorrect.

2. **C** is correct. If you move a file from the one NTFS volume to another NTFS volume, the file receives the same permissions as the target folder; therefore, the other answers are incorrect.

Windows 7 File Structure

▶ **Configure file and folder access**

Cram**Saver**

1. You have a user called Jsmith. What is the location of JSmith's Desktop folder on the C drive?

   ○ **A.** C:\Desktop

   ○ **B.** C:\Windows\JSmith\Desktop

   ○ **C.** C:\Users\JSmith\Desktop

   ○ **D.** C:\Documents and Settings\JSmith\Desktop

2. Which of the following describes a view that enables you to aggregate information or folders from different locations?

   ○ **A.** Library

   ○ **B.** Search connector

   ○ **C.** Federation

   ○ **D.** Local index

Answers

1. **C** is correct. The user's profile that contains the Desktop and My Documents folder is located in the C:\Users folder; therefore, the other answers are incorrect.

2. **A** is correct. A library is a new view that enables you to aggregate information from different locations. It consists of library locations. Answer B is incorrect because a search connector is an XML-based file used to search remote data stores. Answer C is incorrect because a federation provides the ability to search a remote data store, such as SharePoint. Answer D is incorrect because a local index is a component that enables a user to search his computer's content.

As you maintain and manage Windows, you need to understand how the folders and files are organized in Windows. Table 9.3 shows the most common referred folders when managing Windows. Of course, Windows is installed in the C:\Windows folder and the other programs are installed in the C:\Program Files and C:\Program Files (x86) folders.

TABLE 9.3   **Windows 7 Popular Folders**

Folder	Description
C:\Windows	The Default folder that holds the Windows operating system.
C:\Windows\System32	The C:\Windows\System32 is a folder that has many of the Windows system programs.
C:\Windows\CSC	Windows 7 store offline files in the C:\Windows\CSC folder.
C:\Windows\Fonts	The Fonts folder for Windows XP and Windows Vista. If you need to add fonts, you typically use an install program or you use the Fonts applet in the Control Panel.
C:\Windows\Logs	A place where many logs are placed.
C:\Windows\Winsxs	A folder that stores all versions of components, including DLLs, so that the system, upgrades, and rollbacks are more reliable. Over time as you install more updates (Windows and other components), this folder grows quite large. Therefore, you should make sure you leave significant free space on your C drive to avoid problems in the future.
C:\Windows\Syswow64	WoW64 stands for Windows on 64-bit Windows. It contains the 32-bit binary files required for compatibility on 64-bit Windows.
C:\Users	The Users folder has individual folders for each user who has logged into the computer. Underneath these folders, you find a Desktop, My Documents, and Start Menu folder that is mapped for each user as they logged, and these folders are combined with the Desktop, My Documents, and Start Menu of the All Users folder.
C:\Program Files	The default program to contain programs that are not part of Windows. If it is a 64-bit Windows, it contains the 64-bit programs.
C:\Program Files (x86)	The default program for x86 programs loaded on 64-bit Windows.
C:\Windows\Temp	By default, Windows uses the C:\Windows\Temp folder to store temporary files. You can sometimes manually clear this out (although some of the files might be in use) or use the disk cleanup utility.

When a user first logs onto a Windows 7 system, a profile is created under the C:\users folder. The Profile contains several folders for the user, including the Desktop folder, My Documents folder, and the Start Menu. As demonstrated in Figure 9.2, if you save a file to your desktop, it is stored in the C:\Users\<username>\Desktop. If a file is placed in the C:\Users\All Users\Desktop folder, it appears for all users who log on to the system.

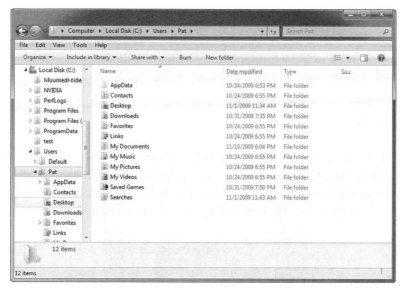

FIGURE 9.2 **Profile folder structure.**

Libraries

Libraries help you view, organize, manage, and find files that are stored in different folders, on different disk drives, and on other PCs in the network. All of these locations can be combined in a library and then searched as if they are in one location. The library consists of the following components:

- ▶ **Library**: A new view that enables you to aggregate information from different locations. It consists of library locations.

- ▶ **Library location**: A component of a library that contains content—for example, a file folder, a Microsoft Office Outlook store, or a search connector.

- ▶ **Search connector**: An XML-based file used to search remote data stores.

- ▶ **Autosuggestions suggestions**: Used in a library's search box that enables building complex queries.

- ▶ **Top views**: A component that enables users to visualize the content of a library in different ways—for example, sorted by author or grouped by date.

> ▶ **Federation**: Provides the ability to search a remote data store, such as SharePoint.

> ▶ **Local search**: Search the local index, including the file system, Microsoft Office Outlook, and Microsoft Office OneNote.

> ▶ **Local index**: The component that enables users to search their computer's content.

Windows 7 includes several libraries, as shown in Figure 9.3. Of course, others can be created. The Documents library includes the My Documents folder and the Public Documents folder. The Music library includes My Music and Public Music. There is also a Pictures library and a Videos library.

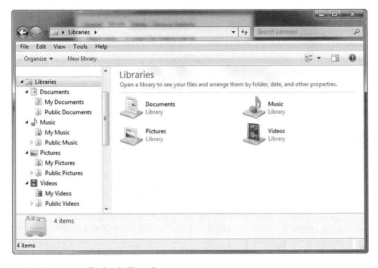

FIGURE 9.3   **Default libraries.**

There are two types of libraries: search-only and browse:

> ▶ **Search-only libraries**: You cannot browse them, and you must type in the search box to view any content from the library.

> ▶ **Browse libraries**: You must navigate to them to view their contents.

To make libraries faster for viewing and searching, libraries are automatically indexed. In addition, Windows 7 automatically creates libraries such as Documents, Music, Pictures, and Videos. Each library has specific top views and autosuggestions. After a suggestion is selected, a list of all the choices (derived from the available data) appears. Users add their favorite local and remote file stores to a library in Windows 7 and one query searches across all these stores.

There are two ways to create a new library in Windows Explorer:

▶ Click **Libraries** in the left pane and then click **New library** on the taskbar.

▶ Right-click **Libraries** in the left pane, click **New**, and then click **Library**.

To share a library with another user

▶ Right-click the library and then click **Share with**.

▶ Select the library and then click **Share with** from the taskbar.

To modify an existing library, right-click the library and then click **Properties** to generate the Library properties window shown in Figure 9.4.

FIGURE 9.4   **Library options.**

Folder Options

You can change the way files and folders function and how items are displayed on your computer by using the Folder Options in Control Panel. The Folder Options contains three tabs: General, View, and Search.

The General tab enables you to specify if each time you open a folder, it opens in the same window or in its own window. It also enables you to define how to click certain items and how to configure the navigation pane, as shown in Figure 9.5.

FIGURE 9.5   **Folder Options General tab.**

The View tab has the many advanced settings. Some of these include the following:

- ▶ Display hidden files, folders, and drives
- ▶ Hide extensions for known file types
- ▶ Hide protected operating system files
- ▶ Launch folder windows in a separate process
- ▶ Show encrypted or compressed NTFS files in color
- ▶ Use the Sharing Wizard

To restore the original settings on the View tab, click **Restore Defaults**, and then click **OK**, as shown in Figure 9.6.

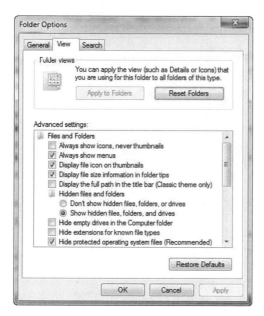

FIGURE 9.6   **Folder Options View tab.**

While browsing folders in the Computer folder, you can apply the current view setting to all folders on your computer that are optimized for the same content as the folder you have open. For instance, the My Pictures folder is optimized for picture files. If you open this folder and change the view to Large Icons, you can apply the Large Icons view to every folder that's optimized for pictures. (This setting does not apply when viewing files and folders using libraries.)

On the Search tab, you can configure how searches occur and what items are included in the search, including subfolders, system directories, and compressed files, as shown in Figure 9.7. You can also specify if it finds partial matches or not.

FIGURE 9.7   **Folder Options Search tab.**

Searching in Windows

With larger hard drives and sometimes complicated network environments, it is more difficult to find the necessary files when you need them. Windows 7 includes the following search improvements:

- ▶ Cleaner navigation

- ▶ Arrangement views

- ▶ Instant search

- ▶ Straightforward previews

- ▶ Rich metadata

- ▶ Libraries

- ▶ Federated Search

Navigation is intuitive and optimized around storage with less overall clutter. You can now collapse nodes in the navigation pane and make it look cleaner, as demonstrated in Figure 9.8. This lack of clutter simplifies navigation in your personal files, drives, network shares, and so on.

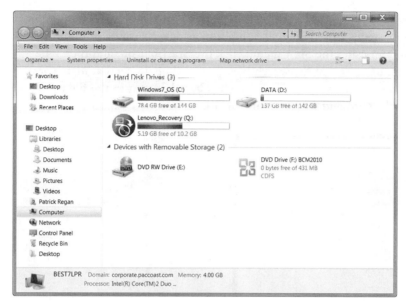

FIGURE 9.8   **Windows Explorer.**

At the top of a Windows Explorer window, you can configure what view you want, such as icon (Small, Medium, Large, and Extra Large), List, Tiles, and Content. You can also create folders and burn files to an optical disk.

One handy tool to help you navigate your disks and network folders is in the left pane of an open Windows Explorer window. From there, you see short-cuts to your Desktop, Downloads, Recent Places, Libraries, and Homegroup. If you scroll down a little further, you can navigate each drive using a tree structure and Network to help you navigate computers on your local network.

In addition, searching is simpler based on improved relevance, search builder, and previews. By incorporating these enhancements into Windows Explorer, libraries and Federated Search offer incredible power to search across the enterprise without learning a new user interface.

Windows Search Tools

Windows provides several ways to find files and folders. There isn't one best way to search—you can use different methods for different situations. They include the following:

- ▶ Search box on the Start menu
- ▶ Search box located at the top of the open window
- ▶ Search box at the top of a library

You can use the Search box on the Start menu to find files, folders, programs, and email messages stored on your computer, as demonstrated in Figure 9.9. To find an item using the Start menu, click the Start button, and then type a word or part of a word in the search box. As you type, items that match your text appear on the Start menu. The search is based on text in the file name, text in the file, tags, and other file properties.

FIGURE 9.9   **Search box on the Start menu.**

When searching from the Start menu, only files that have been indexed appear in search results. Most files on your computer are indexed automatically. For example, anything you include in a library is automatically indexed.

You're often likely to be looking for a file that you know is in a particular folder or library, such as Documents or Pictures. Browsing for the file might mean looking through hundreds of files and subfolders. To save time and effort, use the search box at the top of the open window, as shown in Figure 9.10.

The search box is located at the top of every library. It filters the current view based on text that you type. The search looks for text in the file name and contents, and in the file properties, such as in tags. In a library, the search includes all folders included in the library as well as subfolders within those folders.

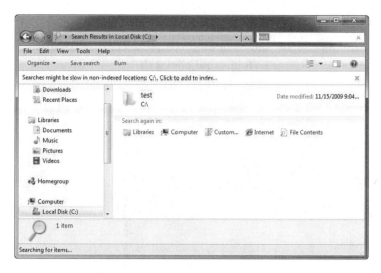

FIGURE 9.10   **Search box at top of open window.**

If you're searching for a file based on one or more of its properties (such as a tag or the date the file was last modified), you can use search filters to specify the property in your search.

In a library or folder, click in the search box, and then click the appropriate search filter below the search box. For example, to search the Music library for songs by a particular artist, click the Artists search filter.

Depending on which search filter you click, choose a value. For example, if you click the Artists search filter, click an artist from the list. You can repeat these steps to build complex searches on multiple properties. Each time that you click a search filter or value, terms are automatically added to the search box. If you can't find what you're looking for in a specific library or folder, you can expand the search to include different locations.

Improving Searches Using the Index

To improve search performance, Windows uses indexes to catalog your files. By default, the commonly used files are indexed, including your libraries, email, and offline folders. Program and system files are not indexed.

If you need to add or remove index locations:

1. Click the Start menu and search for Indexing Options using the Search Programs and Files text box. Then double-click the **Indexing Options.** The Indexing options dialog box displays.

2. Click **Modify**.

3. From the resulting window shown in Figure 9.11, select to add a drive or folder or deselect a drive or folder and click **OK**.

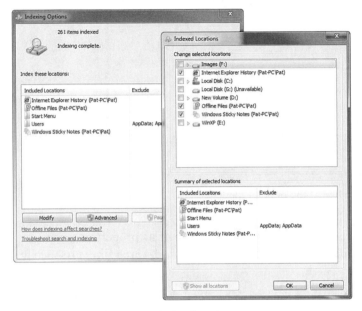

FIGURE 9.11 **Changing indexing location.**

If you don't see all locations on your computer in the list, click **Show all locations**. If all locations are listed, Show all locations won't be available. If you are prompted for an administrator password or confirmation, type the password or provide confirmation.

If you click the **Advanced Options**, you can rebuild your index, specify to index encrypted files, and specify where to keep the index folder and which files you want to include or not based on filename extension.

Cram Exam

1. Which of the following is not a Windows 7 Search tool?

○ **A.** Search box on the Start menu

○ **B.** Search box located at the top of an open window

○ **C.** Indexer Search tool

○ **D.** Search box at the top of the library

2. Which folder would you find the 32-bit applications on a 64-bit version of Windows?

   ○ **A.** C:\Program Files

   ○ **B.** C:\Program Files (x86)

   ○ **C.** C:\Windows

   ○ **D.** C:\Windows\System32

Cram Exam Answers

1. Answer **C** is correct. The Search box on the Start menu, search box located at the top of an open window, and the search box at the top of the library are all search tools available in Windows 7. The Indexer Search tool is not. Therefore, the other answers are incorrect.

2. Answer **B** is correct. On a 64-bit version of Windows, 32-bit applications are loaded to the C:\Program Files (x86) folder by default. Therefore, the other answers are incorrect.

Encryption

▶ **Configure file and folder access**

▶ **Configure BitLocker and BitLocker To Go**

Cram**Saver**

1. Which of the following is not a valid requirement for BitLocker?

   ○ **A.** A computer with a TPM

   ○ **B.** A computer with only one large NTFS volume

   ○ **C.** A computer that has a compatible BIOS with TPM

   ○ **D.** A USB flash drive if your system does not have TPM

2. What would you use to encrypt individual files on your system?

   ○ **A.** NTFS

   ○ **B.** Compression

   ○ **C.** EFS

   ○ **D.** BitLocker

Answers

1. **B** is correct. You need to have two NTFS volumes, not one. Answers A, C, and D are incorrect because they are requirements for BitLocker.

2. **C** is correct because EFS, which is short for Encrypted File System, is used to encrypt individual files. Answer A is incorrect because NTFS is the secure file system used in Windows that supports both compression and EFS. Answer B is incorrect because compression is used to compress files, not encrypt them. Answer D is incorrect because BitLocker is used to encrypt entire disk volumes.

If someone has administrative privilege on a Windows 7 computer or has unauthorized physical access to the device, including if the computer and/or hard drive was stolen, he or she can take ownership of files and folder, change permissions of a file, and access the file. Data can be secured against these risks by using encryption.

Encryption is the process of converting data into a format that cannot be read by another user. After a user has encrypted a file, it automatically remains encrypted when the file is stored on disk. *Decryption* is the process of converting data from encrypted format back to its original format. After a user has decrypted a file, the file remains decrypted when stored on disk.

Windows 7 offers two file encrypting technologies:

- **Encrypting File System (EFS)**: EFS is used to help protect individual files on any drive on a per-user basis.

- **BitLocker Drive Encryption**: BitLocker is designed to help protect all the personal and systems files on the drive Windows is installed on if your computer is stolen or if unauthorized users try to access the computer. You can use BitLocker Drive Encryption and EFS together to get the protection offered by both features.

Table 9.3 provides a comparison of the main differences between BitLocker Drive Encryption and EFS.

TABLE 9.3 **Comparison Between Encrypting File System (EFS) and BitLocker Drive Encryption**

Encrypting File System (EFS)	BitLocker Drive Encryption
Encrypts individual files on any drive.	Encrypts all personal and system files on the drive where Windows is installed.
Encrypts files based on the user account associated with it. If a computer has multiple users or groups, each can encrypt their own files independently.	Does not depend on the individual user accounts associated with files. BitLocker is either on or off, for all users or groups.
Does not require or use any special hardware.	Uses the Trusted Platform Module (TPM), a special microchip in some newer computers that supports advanced security features.
You do not have to be an administrator to use EFS.	You must be an administrator to turn BitLocker encryption on or off after it's enabled.

Encryption File System

Windows 7 includes the encrypting file system (EFS), which allows a user to encrypt and decrypt files that are stored on an NTFS volume. By using EFS, folders and files are kept secure against those intruders who might gain unauthorized physical access to the device, for example, as by stealing a notebook computer or a removable drive.

EFS is used to encrypt data in files and folders with a key. This key is stored in protected storage as part of your user profile, and it provides transparent access to the encrypted data.

Smart cards are supported for storing user EFS keys in addition to administrative recovery keys. If you use smart cards for logon, EFS can operate as a single sign-on service that gives transparent access to your encrypted files. The System Page file can also be protected by EFS when you configure it by using group policy.

When you are using encrypted files on a network, client-side cached copies of network files can also be encrypted, providing security for these files even if the portable computer is lost or stolen. When you use Windows in conjunction with a supported server platform, encrypted files can be transmitted over the network, and the receiving Windows client decrypts them.

> ### Exam**Alert**
>
> EFS is only available in the Windows 7 Professional, Enterprise, and Ultimate versions. EFS is not fully supported on Windows 7 Starter, Windows 7 Home Basic, and Windows 7 Home Premium.

To encrypt a folder or file, do the following:

1. Right-click the folder or file you want to encrypt and then click **Properties**.

2. Click the **General** tab and then click **Advanced** to generate the Advanced Attributes box, as shown in Figure 9.12.

3. Select the **Encrypt contents to secure data** checkbox and then click **OK**.

After you encrypt the file, encrypted files are colored green in Windows Explorer.

> ### Exam**Alert**
>
> You cannot encrypt files or folders that are compressed.

FIGURE 9.12 **Encrypting a folder.**

To decrypt a folder or file, use the following steps:

1. Right-click the folder or file you want to decrypt and then click **Properties**.

2. Click the **General** tab and then click **Advanced**.

3. Clear the **Encrypt contents to secure data** checkbox and then click **OK**.

Encryption Certificates

The first time you encrypt a folder or file, you should back up your encryption certificate. If your certificate and key are lost or damaged and you do not have a backup, you won't be able to use the files that you have encrypted. To back up your EFS certificate, do the following:

1. Open Certificate Manager by clicking the Start button, typing `certmgr.msc` into the Search box, and then pressing **Enter**.

2. Click the arrow next to the Personal folder to expand it.

3. Click **Certificates**.

4. Click the certificate that lists Encrypting File System under Intended Purposes. (You might need to scroll to the right to see this.) If there is more than one EFS certificate, you should back up all of them.

5. Click the **Action** menu, point to **All Tasks**, and then click **Export**.

6. In the Export Wizard, click **Next**, click **Yes**, export the private key, and then click **Next**.

7. Click **Personal Information Exchange** and then click **Next**.

8. Type the password you want to use, confirm it, and then click **Next**. The export process creates a file to store the certificate.

9. Enter a name for the file and the location (include the whole path) or click Browse and navigate to the location, and then enter the file name.

10. Click **Finish**.

11. Store the backup copy of your EFS certificate in a safe place.

If the encrypted file needs to be shared with another user on the same computer, you then need to do the following:

1. Export the EFS certificate.

2. Import the EFS certificate.

3. Add the EFS certificate to the shared file.

The person with whom you want to share files needs to export her EFS certificate and give it to you by doing the following:

1. Open Certificate Manager by clicking the **Start** button, typing `certmgr.msc` into the Search box, and then pressing **Enter**.

2. Click the arrow next to the Personal folder to expand it and then click the EFS certificate that you want to export.

3. Click the **Action** menu, point to **All Tasks**, and then click **Export**.

4. In the Certificate Export Wizard, click **Next**.

5. Click **No**, do not export the private key, and then click **Next**.

6. On the Export File Format page, click **Next** to accept the default format.

7. The export process creates a file to store the certificate in. Type a name for the file and the location (include the whole path), or click **Browse**, navigate to the location, and then type the file name.

8. Click **Finish**.

After you get the EFS certificate from the person you want to share the file with, you need to import the certificate:

1. Open Certificate Manager by clicking the **Start** button, typing `certmgr.msc` into the Search box, and then pressing **Enter**.

2. Select the Personal folder.

3. Click the **Action** menu, point to **All Tasks**, and click **Import**.

4. In the Certificate Import Wizard, click **Next**.

5. Type the location of the file that contains the certificate, or click **Browse**, navigate to the file's location, and then click **Next**.

6. Click **Place all certificates in the following store**, click **Browse**, click **Trusted People**, and then click **Next**.

7. Click Finish.

To add the EFS certificate to the shared file, use the following steps:

1. Right-click the file you want to share and then click **Properties**.

2. Click the **General** tab and then click **Advanced**.

3. In the Advanced Attributes dialog box, click **Details**.

4. In the dialog box that appears, click **Add**.

5. In the Select User dialog box, click the certificate and then click **OK**.

EFS Recovery Agent

To recover encrypted files with lost or damaged keys, you use a special EFS certificate. To use this special certificate, you have to create the recovery certificate, install it, and then update other EFS certificates with the recovery certificate.

To create a recovery certificate, do the following:

1. Open a command prompt.

2. Insert the removable media (a disk or USB flash drive) that you're using to store your certificate.

3. Navigate to the directory on the removable media drive where you want to store the recovery certificate by typing **drive letter** (where drive letter is the letter of the removable media) and then pressing **Enter**.

4. Type **cipher /r:** *filename* (where *filename* is the name that you
   want to give to the recovery certificate) and then press **Enter**. If you're
   prompted for an administrator password or confirmation, type the password or provide confirmation.

Windows stores the certificate in the directory shown at the command prompt.

To install the recovery certificate, use the following steps:

1. Insert the removable media that contains your recovery certificate.

2. Click the **Start** button. In the search box, type **secpol.msc**, and then
   press **Enter**. If you're prompted for an administrator password or confirmation, type the password or provide confirmation.

3. In the left pane, double-click **Public Key Policies**, right-click **Encrypting
   File System**, and then click **Add Data Recovery Agent**. This opens the
   Add Recovery Agent Wizard.

4. Click **Next** and then navigate to your recovery certificate.

5. Click the certificate and then click **Open**.

6. When you are asked if you want to install the certificate, click **Yes**, click
   Next, and then click **Finish**.

7. Click to open Command Prompt.

8. At the command prompt, type **gpupdate** and then press **Enter**.

To update previously encrypted files with the new recovery certificate, do the
following:

1. Log on to the account you were using when you first encrypted the files.

2. Click to open Command Prompt.

3. At the command prompt, type **cipher /u** and then press **Enter**.

If you choose not to update encrypted files with the new recovery certificate at
this time, the files are automatically updated the next time you open them.

BitLocker Drive Encryption

A new feature that was added to Windows Vista was BitLocker Drive
Encryption, which is designed to protect computers from attackers who have
physical access to a computer. Without BitLocker Drive Encryption, an attacker

could start the computer with a boot disk and then reset the administrator password to gain full control of the computer. Or the attacker could access the computer's hard disk directly by using a different operating system to bypass file permissions.

BitLocker Drive Encryption is the feature in Windows 7 that makes use of a computer's Trusted Platform Module (TPM), which is a microchip that is built into a computer. It is used to store cryptographic information, such as encryption keys. Information stored on the TPM can be more secure from external software attacks and physical theft then have the information stored on a USB flash drive. BitLocker Drive Encryption can use a TPM to validate the integrity of a computer's boot manager and boot files at startup, and to guarantee that a computer's hard disk has not been tampered with while the operating system was offline. BitLocker Drive Encryption also stores measurements of core operating system files in the TPM.

If a computer has a functional TPM, the encryption keys can be stored in the TPM. If someone removes the hard drive from the system, the information on the hard drive cannot be accessed because it must be decrypted with the keys stored on the TPM.

In addition, the TPM performs a hash on a snapshot of the important operating system configuration files. When the system boots, TPM performs another hash on the same system configuration files and compares the two hash values. The TPM releases the key to unlock the encrypted volume. If the values do not match, BitLocker determines that the system has been compromised, locks the drive, and goes into recovery mode. To unlock the system that is in recovery mode, you have to enter a 48-decimal-digit key. Of course, you must make sure that you create the recovery password when you turn on BitLocker for the first time. If you don't, you could permanently lose access to your files. Recovery mode is also used if a disk drive is transferred to another system.

BitLocker can be used in three ways:

▶ **TPM-only**: This is transparent to the user, and the user logon experience is unchanged. If the TPM is missing or changed, or if the TPM detects changes to critical operating system startup files, BitLocker enters its recovery mode, and you need a recovery password to regain access to the data.

▶ **TPM with startup key**: In addition to the protection provided by the TPM, a part of the encryption key is stored on a USB flash drive. This is referred to as a *startup key*. Data on the encrypted volume cannot be accessed without the startup key.

▸ **TPM with PIN**: In addition to the protection provided by the TPM, BitLocker requires a PIN to be entered by the user. Data on the encrypted volume cannot be accessed without entering the PIN.

By default, the BitLocker Setup Wizard is configured to work seamlessly with the TPM. An administrator can use Group Policy or a script to enable additional features and options.

On computers without a compatible TPM, BitLocker can provide encryption, but not the added security of locking keys with the TPM. In this case, the user is required to create a startup key that is stored on a USB flash drive.

On computers with a compatible TPM, BitLocker Drive Encryption can use one of two TPM modes:

▸ **TPM-only**: In this mode, only the TPM is used for validation. When the computer starts up, the TPM is used to validate the boot files, the operating system files, and any encrypted volumes. Because the user doesn't need to provide an additional startup key, this mode is transparent to the user and the user logon experience is unchanged. However, if the TPM is missing or the integrity of files or volumes has changed, BitLocker enters recovery mode and requires a recovery key or password to regain access to the boot volume.

▸ **Startup key**: In this mode, both the TPM and a startup key are used for validation. When the computer starts up, the TPM is used to validate the boot files, the operating system files, and any encrypted volumes. The user must have a startup key to log on to the computer. A startup key can be either physical, such as a USB flash drive with a machine-readable key written to it, or personal, such as a personal identification number (PIN) set by the user. If the user doesn't have the startup key or is unable to provide the correct startup key, BitLocker enters recovery mode. As before, BitLocker also enters recovery mode if the TPM is missing or the integrity of boot files or encrypted volumes has changed.

The system requirements of BitLocker are as follows:

▸ Because BitLocker stores its own encryption and decryption key in a hardware device that is separate from your hard disk, you must have one of the following:

▸ A computer with TPM. If your computer was manufactured with TPM version 1.2 or higher, BitLocker stores its key in the TPM.

- ▶ A removable USB memory device, such as a USB flash drive. If your computer doesn't have TPM version 1.2 or higher, BitLocker stores its key on the flash drive.

- ▶ Your computer must have at least two partitions. One partition must include the drive Windows is installed on. This is the drive that BitLocker encrypts. The other partition is the active partition, which must remain unencrypted so that the computer can be started. Partitions must be formatted with the NTFS file system.

- ▶ Your computer must have a BIOS that is compatible with TPM and supports USB devices during computer startup. If this is not the case, you need to update the BIOS before using BitLocker.

To find out if your computer has TPM security hardware, do the following:

1. Open BitLocker Drive Encryption by clicking the **Start** button, clicking **Control Panel**, clicking **Security**, and then clicking **BitLocker Drive Encryption**. If you are prompted for an administrator password or confirmation, type the password or provide confirmation.

2. If the TPM administration link appears in the left pane, your computer has the TPM security hardware. If this link is not present, you need a removable USB memory device to turn on BitLocker and store the BitLocker startup key that you need whenever you restart your computer.

To turn on BitLocker, follow these steps:

1. Open BitLocker Drive Encryption by clicking the **Start** button, clicking **Control Panel**, clicking **System and Security**, and then clicking **BitLocker Drive Encryption**. If you are prompted for an administrator password or confirmation, type the password or provide confirmation.

2. Click **Turn On BitLocker**. This opens the BitLocker Setup Wizard.

3. Choose how to store the recovery key:

    - ▶ Save the recovery key to a USB flash drive.

    - ▶ Save the recovery key to a file.

    - ▶ Print the recovery key.

    Follow the wizard to set the location for saving or printing the recovery key. Then click **Next**.

4. When it asks if you are ready to encrypt the drive, make sure the Run BitLocker system checkbox is selected and click **Continue**.

5. When you are ready to restart the system, click the **Restart now** button.

6. While the drive is being encrypted, the Encrypting status bar is displayed, showing the progress of the drive encryption. When the drive is encrypted, a message is displayed.

To turn off or temporarily disable BitLocker, do the following:

1. Open Bitlocker Drive Encryption by clicking the **Start** button, clicking **Control Panel**, clicking **System and Security**, and then clicking **BitLocker Drive Encryption**. If you are prompted for an administrator password or confirmation, type the password or provide confirmation.

2. Click **Turn Off BitLocker**. This opens the BitLocker Drive Encryption dialog box.

3. To decrypt the drive, click **Decrypt the volume**. To temporarily disable BitLocker, click **Disable BitLocker Drive Encryption**.

The BitLocker control panel applet enables you to recover the encryption key and recovery password at will. You should consider carefully how to store this information, because it allows access to the encrypted data. A domain administrator can also use group policies to automatically generate recovery passwords and back them up to Active Directory.

BitLocker To Go

BitLocker To Go extends the BitLocker protection to removable data drives to ensure that critical data is protected when a USB drive is misplaced. You can enable BitLocker protection on a removable device by right-clicking the drive in Windows Explorer. You can also use new Group Policy settings to configure removable drives as Read-Only unless they are encrypted with BitLocker To Go.

ExamAlert

You can use group policies to force all files copied to a removable drive to be encrypted.

When you turn on BitLocker To Go, the ensuing wizard requires that you specify how you want to unlock the drive. Select one of the following methods:

▶ A recovery password or passphrase

▶ A smart card

▶ Always auto-unlock this device on this PC

After the device is configured to use BitLocker, the user saves documents to the external drive. When the user inserts the USB flash drive on a different PC, the computer detects that the portable device is BitLocker protected; the user is prompted to specify the passphrase.

At this time, the user can specify to unlock this volume automatically on the second PC. It is not required that the second PC be encrypted with BitLocker. If a user forgets the passphrase, there is an option from the BitLocker Unlock Wizard—I forgot my passphrase—to assist. Clicking this option displays a recovery Password ID that can be supplied to an administrator. The administrator uses the Password ID to obtain the recovery password for the device. This Recovery Password can be stored in Active Directory and recovered with the BitLocker Recovery Password tool.

Cram Quiz

1. Which technology would you use to encrypt all data on a USB flash drive?

   ○ **A.** BitLocker

   ○ **B.** BitLocker To Go

   ○ **C.** Compressed (Zipped) Folder

   ○ **D.** EFS

2. You right-click a file to encrypt it. You later decide to right-click the file and compress it. A few days later, you notice that the file is no longer encrypted. What is the problem?

   ○ **A.** The file is only encrypted for 72 hours.

   ○ **B.** The file was resaved in unencrypted format.

   ○ **C.** You do not have permission to encrypt the file.

   ○ **D.** You cannot have a file compressed and encrypted using NTFS at the same time.

Cram Quiz Answers

1. **B** is correct. BitLocker To Go extends the BitLocker protection to removable data drives to ensure that critical data is protected when a USB flash drive is misplaced. Answer A is incorrect because BitLocker is designed for hard drives. Answer C is incorrect because compression does not encrypt a drive. Answer D is incorrect because EFS could be used; however, it is designed just to encrypt individual folders and files.

2. **D** is correct. Because you compressed the file using NTFS, the file was automatically decrypted; therefore, the other answers are incorrect.

Compression

▶ **Configure file and folder access**

Windows 7 supports two types of data compression:

▶ Compressed (Zipped) Folders

▶ NTFS compression

Compressed (Zipped) Folders

Files and folders compressed using the Compressed (Zipped) Folders feature remain compressed under all three supported file systems: NTFS, FAT, and FAT32. Compressing any system folders, such as the \Windows folder or the \Program Files folder, is not recommended and should be avoided. Compressed (Zipped) Folders are identified by a zipper symbol that is part of the folder's icon.

To create a Compressed (Zipped) Folder, right-click a folder, point to Send To, and click Compressed (Zipped) Folder. This action actually creates a Zip file that Windows 7 recognizes as a Compressed (Zipped) Folder that contains the folder you selected to be compressed along with all of that folder's contents.

You can also use any popular third-party utility, such as WinZip or PKZip, to read, write, add to, or remove files from any Compressed (Zipped) Folder. Unless you install such a third-party zip utility, Windows 7 displays standard zip files as Compressed (Zipped) Folders.

NTFS Compression

NTFS compression is the ability to selectively compress the contents of individual files, entire directories, or entire drives on an NTFS volume. NTFS compression uses file compression that works by substitution. It starts by locating repetitive data with another pattern, which is shorter. Windows tracks which files and folders are compressed via a file attribute. As far as the user is concerned, the compressed drive, folder, or file is simply another drive, folder, or file that works like any other. Although you expand the amount of space for volume, the performance of the PC is slower because it has to process the compression and decompression of files. Therefore, do not use compression unless you are compressing files that are rarely used or when disk space is critical. If disk space is critical, use this as a temporary solution until you can delete or move files from the drive or can extend the volume.

To compress a file or folder on an NTFS drive, do the following:

1. Open Windows Explorer.

2. Right-click the file or folder that you want to compress and select the **Properties** option.

3. Select the **Advanced** button.

4. Select the **Compress contents to save disk space** checkbox.

5. Click on the **OK** or **Apply** button.

6. If you select to compress a drive or folder, select **Apply changes to this folder only** or **Apply changes to the folder, subfolder, and files** and click on the **OK** button.

To compress an NTFS drive, do the following:

1. Click the **Start** button entire and click **Computer**.

2. Right-click the drive that you want to compress.

3. Select the **Compress this drive to save disk space** checkbox.

4. Click the **OK** or **Apply** button.

To uncompress a drive, folder, or file, uncheck the **Compress this drive to save disk space** or **Compress drive to save disk space** box.

ExamAlert

You cannot compress files or folders using NTFS compression that are encrypted with EFS.

Cram Quiz

1. What program do you use to manage Compressed (Zipped) or NTFS compressed files?

   ○ **A.** Internet Explorer

   ○ **B.** WinZip

   ○ **C.** Windows Explorer

   ○ **D.** zip.exe

Cram Quiz Answer

1. **C** is correct. Windows Explorer is used to manage both compressed and NTFS compressed files. Answer A is incorrect because Internet Explorer is your web browser. Answer B is incorrect because WinZip is a third-party application that can only access the Compressed (Zipped) format. Answer D is incorrect because zip.exe does not come with Windows.

Review Questions

1. You want to control the permissions of files and directories on an NTFS drive on the network. Which application must you use?

   ○ **A.** Windows Explorer

   ○ **B.** Active Directory Users and Computers console

   ○ **C.** Computer Management console

   ○ **D.** Disk Administrator console

2. Which is the minimum standard NTFS permissions needed for users to read files and folders, execute files, write and modify files, delete files and folders, and change attributes of files and folders?

   ○ **A.** Full Control

   ○ **B.** Modify

   ○ **C.** Read and Execute

   ○ **D.** Write

3. You want to modify permissions for a folder for the Everyone group; however, the permission options are grayed out. What does this mean?

   ○ **A.** You do not have sufficient permissions to change permissions.

   ○ **B.** You do not the current owner of the file.

   ○ **C.** Permissions are inherited from above.

   ○ **D.** You do not have the Take Ownership right.

4. What is the best way to prevent users from adding a USB flash drive to a Windows 7 computer?

   ○ **A.** Disable USB ports in the Device Manager

   ○ **B.** Physically disconnect the USB ports

   ○ **C.** Disable the USB ports in the BIOS

   ○ **D.** Use group policies

5. You work as the desktop support technician at Acme.com. You have configured BitLocker Drive Encryption on a computer, which has TPM installed. Unfortunately when Windows 7 starts a TPM error is displayed and the user cannot access the data on her computer because it is encrypted. What should you do?

   ○ **A.** Restart the computer and enter the recovery password at the BitLocker Driver Encryption Recovery console

   ○ **B.** Restart the computer and login as the local administrator

   ○ **C.** Disable the TPM component in the BIOS and reboot the computer

   ○ **D.** Open the TPM management console

6. You have several computers running Windows 7 connected to an Active Directory domain. You want to set up your computer with the ability to recover all EFS encrypted files on your partner's computers running Windows 7. What do you need to do?

    ◯ **A.** Back up the %systemroot%\DigitalLocker.

    ◯ **B.** Run Secedit.exe /export on your partner's computer and run secedit.exe /import on your computer.

    ◯ **C.** Run the cipher.exe /removeuser on your partner's computer. Then run cipher /adduser on your computer.

    ◯ **D.** Export the data recovery agent certificate on your partner's computer and import the data recovery agent certificate on your computer.

7. You work as the desktop support technician at Acme.com. Your boss wants to protect the laptops if they get stolen. What would you do? (Choose the best answer.)

    ◯ **A.** Make sure that all volumes are using NTFS file system

    ◯ **B.** Implement BitLocker

    ◯ **C.** Implement IP Security (IPsec) for all network communications

    ◯ **D.** Implement Encrypted File System (EFS) on key data files

8. What can you use to ensure that all files are encrypted if they are copied to a removable drive?

    ◯ **A.** Enable BitLocker To Go Drive encryption using group policies

    ◯ **B.** Initialize TPM from the TPM snap-in

    ◯ **C.** Enable BitLocker Drive Encryption in the Control Panel

    ◯ **D.** Enable EFS on the D drive

9. What folders does the Documents library include? (Choose all that apply.)

    ◯ **A.** All Documents folder

    ◯ **B.** My Documents

    ◯ **C.** Public Documents

    ◯ **D.** Favorites

10. What is used for quick searches on your hard drives?

    ◯ **A.** XML search file

    ◯ **B.** Index

    ◯ **C.** Search cache

    ◯ **D.** Hash of all files

Review Question Answers

1. Answer **A** is correct. Folders and files and their NTFS permissions are managed by the Windows Explorer. Answer B is incorrect because Active Directory Users and Computers console is used to manage the user and computer accounts within Active Directory, not NTFS permissions. Answer C is incorrect because the Computer Management console, which includes the disk administrator console, can be used to look at the event viewer, status of the disks, and manage the file system volumes but nothing with NTFS permissions. Answer D is incorrect because the disk administrator has nothing to do with NTFS permissions.

2. Answer **B** is correct. The Modify permission allows users to read files and folders, execute files, write and modify files, delete files and folders, and change attributes of files and folders. Answer A is incorrect because Full Control also gives the ability to change permissions and take ownership. Answer C is incorrect because read and Execute only allows the user to see the contents of existing files and folders and run programs. Answer D is incorrect because the write command only allows the user to create new files and folders and make changes to existing files and folders.

3. Answer **C** is correct. If the checkboxes under Permissions for <User or Group> are shaded or if the Remove button is unavailable, the file or folder has inherited permissions from the parent folder. Therefore, the other answers are incorrect.

4. Answer **D** is correct. The best way is to use group policy to prevent users access to USB flash drives, specifically the Prevent Installation of Removable Devices policy. Answers A, B, and C are incorrect because you do not want to totally disable USB, which causes other USB devices, such as mice and keyboards, to fail.

5. Answer **A** is correct. When you get a TPM error, you need to restart the computer and enter the recovery password in the recovery console. Answer B is incorrect because you cannot log in as any user because of the TPM error. Answer C is incorrect because disabling the feature in BIOS does not decrypt the disk. Answer D is incorrect because it is not able to open the TPM management console.

6. Answer **D** is correct. If you want to be able to recover files from another computer that are encrypted with EFS, you should export the data recovery agent certificate on the source computer and import the certificate to the target computer. Therefore, the other answers are incorrect.

7. Answer **B** is correct. Because BitLocker encrypts the entire drive, BitLocker is the best solution. Answer A is incorrect because you can connect a stolen hard drive to another system that has another operating system and bypass much of the security on the drive including those set by NTFS permissions. Answer C is incorrect because IPsec is used to encrypt data being transmitted over the network. Answer D is incorrect because EFS is made only to encrypt data files, not system files.

8. Answer **A** is correct. To enforce encryption, you need to enable BitLocker To Go using group policies. Answer C is incorrect. You cannot use the Control Panel because users can override the settings if they choose. Answer D is incorrect because enabling EFS does not enforce it on all removable drives. Answer B is incorrect because using the TPM snap-in does not enforce the settings.

9. Answers **B** and **C** are correct. The Documents library includes the My Documents folder and the Public Documents folder. Therefore, the other answers are incorrect.

10. Answer **B** is correct. Windows uses the index to perform very fast searches of the most common files on your computer. By default, all of the most common files on your computer are indexed. Answers A and C are incorrect because they do not exist as part of the Windows 7 operating system. Answer D is incorrect because a hash value (mathematical computation of a file) is not used for searching.

CHAPTER 10

Sharing Files and Folders

This chapter covers the following 70-680 Objectives:

▶ Configuring Access to Resources:

   ▶ Configure shared resources

   ▶ Configure file and folder access

   ▶ Configure BranchCache

Although many people think that Windows 7 is a workstation that requests services from other computers, typically servers, it can also act as a server to provide services. One of the traditional services that Windows 7 computers can use and provide is file sharing.

Sharing Files and Folders

▶ **Configure shared resources**

▶ **Configure file and folder access**

Cram**Saver**

1. You work as the desktop support technician at Acme.com. A Windows 7 computer contains a shared folder on an NTFS partition. Which one of the following statements concerning access to the folder is correct?

   ○ **A.** A user who is accessing the folder remotely has the same or more restrictive access permissions than if she accesses the folder locally.

   ○ **B.** A user who is accessing the folder remotely has less restrictive access permissions than if she accesses the folder locally.

   ○ **C.** A user who is accessing the folder remotely has the same access permissions than if she accesses the folder locally.

   ○ **D.** A user who is accessing the folder remotely has more restrictive access permissions than if she accesses the folder locally.

2. You work as the desktop support technician at Acme.com. You have two users who share a computer running Windows 7 Professional Edition. Both users are working on a major report, but you don't want one user to access the other user's data files. What should you do?

   ○ **A.** Give the appropriate NTFS permissions to both users' My Documents folders

   ○ **B.** Have the users log in with the same account

   ○ **C.** Instruct these users to store the report in the public folder

   ○ **D.** Instruct these users to log out as themselves and log in as the other user to access the report

3. What technology was released with Windows 7 to make it easier for home users to share files and printers?

   ○ **A.** EasyShares

   ○ **B.** Homegroup

   ○ **C.** UserShares

   ○ **D.** PrivateShare

Answers

1. **A** is correct. When you access a computer remotely through the share, you include the share permissions and the NTFS permissions, which can both restrict access. When you access the local folder directly, only the NTFS permissions apply. Therefore, they could have the same or more restrictive access if both are applied. Answers B and C are incorrect because if the user is accessing it remotely, the share permissions might further restrict. Answer D is incorrect because the share and NTFS permissions combined might also give the same access rather than just be more restrictive.

2. **C** is correct. One place to store the report is in the public folder where they both can have access to it. Answers A, B, and D are not the best answers because they do not provide a secure environment where one user cannot look at the data files of another user.

3. **B** is correct. A homegroup, new to Windows 7, makes it easier to share files and printers on a home network. You can share pictures, music, videos, documents, and printers with other people in your homegroup. EasyShares, UserShares, and PrivateShares do not exist in Windows 7. Therefore, the other answers are incorrect.

A shared folder on a computer makes the folder available for others to use on the network. A shared drive on a computer makes the entire drive available for others to use on the network. Shared drives and folders can be used on FAT, FAT32, and NTFS volumes. If used on an NTFS volume, the user still needs NTFS permissions before accessing the share.

When you share a folder with Microsoft Windows, file sharing is based on the network basic input/output system (NetBIOS) protocol and server message block (SMB). NetBIOS, which runs on top of TCP/IP, was created for IBM for its early PC networks, but it was adopted by Microsoft and has since become a de facto industry standard. It is responsible for establishing logical names (computer names) on the network, establishing a logical connection between the two computers, and supporting reliable data transfer between computers that established a session.

After a logical connection is established, computers can exchange data in the form of a NetBIOS request or in the form of a server message block. The SMB protocol, which was jointly developed by Microsoft, Intel, and IBM, allows shared access to files, printers, serial ports, and miscellaneous communications between nodes on a network.

SMB 2.0 was introduced with Windows Vista and was used in Windows Server 2008 and Windows 7, which provided the capability to compound multiple actions into a single request, significantly reducing the number of round-trips the client needs to make to the server and improving performance as a result. Larger buffer sizes are supported, which also increases performance with large file transfers. In addition, durable file handles were introduced, which allow a connection to an SMB server to survive brief network outages, such as with a wireless network, without having to construct a new session.

When using the SMB protocol to share a directory or drive, these resources are accessed using the Universal Naming Convention (UNC):

\\servername\sharedname

The *servername* could be a NetBIOS name (computer name) or an IP address.

Network Discovery and Browsing

With earlier versions of Windows, you could use Network Neighborhood to browse network resources such as shared folders and printers; however, this system was inefficient because it relied on network broadcasts to gather such information.

To fix this problem, Windows Vista introduced Link Layer Topology Discovery (LLTD), which queries each device that supports Plug and Play Extensions (PnP-X) or web services for devices to determine its capabilities and to determine the topology of the network. LLTD also uses version control to keep the information current. It also describes the Quality of Service (QoS) Extensions that enable stream prioritization and quality media streaming experiences, even on networks with limited bandwidth.

The information that is gathered to create the network map and which information the computer gives out to other Windows Vista, Windows 7, and Windows Server 2008 computers depends on which network services that you have enabled or configured using the Network and Sharing Center.

To enable network discovery, you need to do the following:

1. Open the **Network and Sharing Center**.

2. Click **Change advanced sharing settings**.

3. Select **Turn on network discovery**, as shown in Figure 10.1.

4. Click the **Save changes** button.

FIGURE 10.1   **Managing Network Services with the Network and Sharing Center.**

The network services configurable under Advanced sharing settings are as follows:

▶ **Network discovery**: Allows this computer to see other network computers and devices and is visible to other network computers.

▶ **File and printer sharing**: Files and printers that you have shared from this computer can be accessed by people on the network.

▶ **Public folder sharing**: People on the network can access files in the public folder.

▶ **Media streaming**: People and devices on the network can access pictures, music, and videos on the computer. In addition, the computer can find media on the network.

▶ **File-sharing connections**: Windows 7 uses 128-bit encryption to help protect file-sharing connections. Some devices don't support 128-bit encryption and must use 40- or 56-bit encryption.

▶ **Password protected sharing**: Only people who have a user account and password on the computer can access shared files, printers attached to the computer, and the public folders. To give other people access, you must turn off password protected sharing.

▶ **Homegroup connections**: If you have the same user accounts and passwords on all of your computers, you can choose to allow Windows to manage homegroup connections when you connect to another computer in the same homegroup. Or you can use the user account and password to connect to other computers.

Similar to Windows firewall, the network services use separate network profiles based on Home/Work and Public profiles.

To view the topology or to view the network resources, you open a network folder or the Network and Sharing Center, as shown in Figure 10.2. However, a Windows 7 computer is not visible on the network map, and it is not able to map other hardware devices on the network until you enable Network Discovery service. To see the full map, you click the View full map link in the Network and Sharing Center.

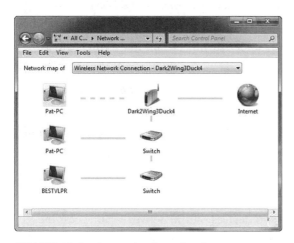

FIGURE 10.2 **A sample of a network map.**

ExamAlert

LLTD is installed by default, but it only functions if you enable Network Discovery.

Sharing Folders

In Windows 7, there are three types of sharing:

- ▶ Public sharing

- ▶ Basic sharing

- ▶ Advanced sharing

Of these three models, basic file/advanced sharing is preferred because it is more secure than public file sharing. However, public folder sharing is designed to enable users to share files and folders from a single location quickly and easily.

Public Folders

The Public folders are handy if you want to temporarily share a document or other file with several people. It's also a handy way to keep track of what you're sharing with others; if it's in the folder, it's shared. Unfortunately, you can't restrict people to seeing just some files in the Public folder. It's all or nothing. Also, you can't fine-tune permissions. But if these aren't important considerations, then Public folders offer a convenient, alternative way to share.

Windows 7 supports the use of only one Public folder for each computer. You can copy or move any files that you want to make available publicly to an appropriate folder inside the Public folder. The Public folder is located at C:\Users\Public and contains the following subfolders, as shown in Figure 10.3:

- ▶ Public Documents

- ▶ Public Downloads

- ▶ Public Music

- ▶ Public Pictures

- ▶ Public Recorded TV

- ▶ Public Videos

FIGURE 10.3 **Public folders.**

Another folder worth mentioning is the Public Desktop folder, which is used for shared desktop items. Any files and program shortcuts placed in the Public Desktop folder appear on the desktop of all users who log on to the computer (and to all network users if network access has been granted to the Public folder).

For Windows 7, public folder sharing is disabled by default. By default, files stored in the Public folder hierarchy are available to all users who have an account on this computer and can log on to it locally. You cannot access the Public folder from the network. To enable and configure public folder sharing, you need to enable the public folder sharing service using Network and Sharing Center.

Public folder sharing is turned off by default, except on a homegroup (homegroups are discussed later in this chapter). To access public folders using Windows Explorer, access the Documents library, Music library, Picture library, or Video library. You can also access the public user folders at c:\users\public.

Public folder sharing settings are set on a per-computer basis. If you want to share a file, you just need to copy or move the file into the C:\Users\Public folder. When the file is copied or moved to the Public folder, access permissions are changed to match that of the Public folder so that all users who log on to the computer and all network users that has been granted access to the Public folder can access the file.

Basic Sharing

Creating and managing a shared folder is a little bit more of a manual process than the public sharing model, but it enables you to share any folder on the Windows 7 computer, and it gives you more fine-tuned control over sharing the folders.

Basic file sharing enables you to use a standard set of permissions to allow or deny initial access to files and folders over the network. Basic file-sharing settings are enabled or disabled on a per-computer basis. To enable File Sharing, you have to do the following:

1. Open the **Network and Sharing Center**.

2. Click the **Change advanced sharing settings**.

3. To enable file sharing, select **Turn on file and printer sharing**. To disable file sharing, select **Turn off file and printer sharing**.

4. Click **Save changes**.

There are two ways to share a folder. The first (and quickest) way is to right-click the folder you want to share and click **Share with**, as shown in Figure 10.4. You can also click the **Share with** button at the top of the Windows Explorer window. Then, select who you want to share the folder with. Your choices are Nobody, Homegroup (Read), Homegroup (Read/Write), and Specific people. If you select Specific people, you can give Read access or Read/Write access, as shown in Figure 10.5.

FIGURE 10.4 **Share with options.**

FIGURE 10.5   **Specifying people to access a share and their permissions levels.**

You can also right-click a folder and select Properties to display the window shown in Figure 10.6. If you click the **Share** button, you can share a folder similar to selecting specific people using a wizard.

FIGURE 10.6   **Folder Properties Sharing tab.**

Advanced Sharing

If you click **Advanced Sharing**, you can specify the name of the shared folder. A shared folder can be shared several times with different share names and permissions. To configure the permissions for the Shared folder, click the **Permissions** button (see Figure 10.7).

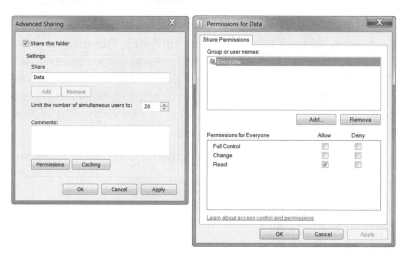

FIGURE 10.7   **Advanced Sharing.**

When a user accesses a file or folder in a Share over the network, the two levels of permissions are user: share permissions and NTFS permissions (if it is on an NTFS volume). The three share permissions are as follows:

- ▶ **Full Control**: Users allowed this permission have Read and Change permissions, as well as the additional capabilities to change file and folder permissions and take ownership of files and folders. If you have Owner/Co-owner permissions on a shared resource, you have full access to the shared resource.

- ▶ **Change**: Users allowed this permission have Read permissions and the additional capability to create files and subfolders, modify files, change attributes on files and subfolders, and delete files and subfolders. If you have Change permissions on a shared resource, the most you can do is perform read operations and change operations.

- ▶ **Read**: Users with this permission can view file and subfolder names, access the subfolders of the share, read file data and attributes, and run program files. If you have Read permissions on a shared resource, the most you can do is perform read operations.

> **ExamAlert**
>
> If the user accesses the computer directly where the share folder is located and accesses the folder directly without going through the share, share permissions do not apply.

Because a user can be a member of several groups, it is possible for the user to have several sets of permissions to a shared drive or folder. The effective permissions are the combination of all user and group permissions. For example, if a user has the Change permissions to the user and a Read permission to the group, of which the user is a member, the effective permissions are the Change permissions. Like NTFS permissions, Deny permissions override the granted permission.

To create a shared folder using the shared folder model is a multipart process:

1. Share the folder so that it can be accessed.

2. Set the share permissions.

3. Check and modify the NTFS file system permissions.

When accessing a shared folder on an NTFS volume, the effective permissions that a person can have in the share folder are calculated by combining the shared folder permissions with the NTFS permissions. When combining the two, first determine the cumulative NTFS permissions and the cumulative shared permissions and apply the more restrictive permissions—the one that gives the least permission.

> **ExamAlert**
>
> When figuring out the overall access a person has, combine the NTFS permissions and determine the cumulative NTFS permissions. Then determine the cumulative shared permissions and apply the more restrictive permissions between the NTFS and shared permission. Don't forget that deny permissions supersede all others.

Special and Administrative Shares

In Windows 7, there are several special shared folders that are automatically created by Windows for administrative and system use, as described in Table 10.1. Different from regular shares, these shares do not show when a user browses the computer resources using My Network Places, Network, or similar software. In most cases, special shared folders should not be deleted or modified. For Windows 7 computers, only members of the Administrators, Backup Operators, and Server Operators group can connect to these shares.

Table 10.1   Special Shares

Special Share	Description
Drive letter$	A shared folder that allows administrative personnel to connect to the root directory of a drive, also known as an administrative share. It is shown as A$, B$, C$, D$, and so on. For example, C$ is a shared folder name by which drive C might be accessed by an administrator over the network.
ADMIN$	A resource used by the system during remote administration of a computer. The path of this resource is always the path to the Windows system root (the directory in which Windows is installed: for example, C:\Windows).
IPC$	A resource sharing the named pipes that are essential for communication between programs. It is used during remote administration of a computer and when viewing a computer's shared resources.
PRINT$	A resource used during remote administration of printers.
FAX$	A shared folder on a server used by fax clients in the process of sending a fax. The shared folder is used to temporarily cache files and access cover pages stored on the server.

An administrative share is a shared folder typically used for administrative purposes. To make a shared folder or drive into an administrative share, the share name must have a $ at the end of it. Because you cannot see the share folder or drive during browsing, you have to use a UNC name, which includes the share name (including the $). Instead, you have to access it by using the **Start** button, selecting the **Run** option, and typing the UNC name and clicking the **OK** button. By default, all volumes with drive letters automatically have administrative shares (C$, D$, E$, and so on). You can create other administrative shares as needed for individual folders.

Homegroup

A homegroup, new to Windows 7, makes it easier to share files and printers on a home network. You can share pictures, music, videos, documents, and printers with other people in your homegroup. Other people can't change the files that you share, unless you give them permission to do so. When you set up a computer with Windows 7, a homegroup is created automatically if one doesn't already exist on your home network. If a homegroup already exists, you can join it. After you create or join a homegroup, you can select the libraries that you want to share. You can prevent specific files or folders from being shared, and you can share additional libraries later. You can help protect your homegroup with a password, which you can change at any time.

> **ExamAlert**
>
> Homegroups are only available with Windows 7. You can join a homegroup in any edition of Windows 7, but you can only create one in Home Premium, Professional, or Ultimate.

To join a homegroup, your computer's network location must be set to Home. To change a network location, do the following:

1. Open the **Network and Sharing Center**.

2. Click **Work network, Home network**, or **Public network** to open the Set Network Location dialog box, as shown in Figure 10.8, and then click the network location you want: **Home network, Work network**, or **Public network**.

Computers that belong to a domain can join a homegroup, but they can't share files with the homegroup. They can only access files shared by others.

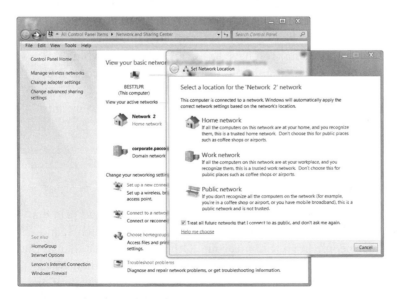

FIGURE 10.8   Selecting a network location.

After someone on your network creates a homegroup, the next step is to join it. You need the homegroup password, which you can get from the person who created the homegroup. When you join a homegroup, all user accounts on your computer become members of the homegroup. To join a homegroup, follow these steps on the computer that you want to add to the homegroup:

1. Click to open Homegroup.

2. Click **Join now** and then complete the wizard.

If you don't see the Join now button, there might not be a homegroup available. Make sure that someone has created a homegroup first. Or you can choose to create a homegroup yourself.

To create a homegroup, follow these steps:

1. Open the Control Panel and click **Choose homegroup and sharing options**.

2. On the Share with other home computers running Windows 7 page, click a homegroup to start the wizard.

To remove a computer from a homegroup, follow these steps on the computer you want to remove:

1. Open the Control Panel and click **Choose homegroup and sharing options**.

2. Click **Leave the homegroup**.

3. Click **Leave the homegroup**, and then click **Finish**.

If everyone leaves the homegroup, it no longer exists.

If your computer is part of a homegroup, you can change settings by following these steps:

1. Open the Control Panel and click **Choose homegroup and sharing options**.

2. Select the settings you want (see Table 10.2) and then click **Save changes**.

TABLE 10.2 **Homegroup Options**

Option	Description
Share libraries and printers	Select the libraries and printers you want to share in their entirety with your homegroup.
Share media with devices	Use this setting to share media with all devices on your network. For example, you can share pictures with an electronic picture frame, or share music with a network media player. Unfortunately, shared media is not secure. Anyone connected to your network can receive your shared media.
View or print the homegroup password	View or print the password for your homegroup.
Change the password	Change the password for your homegroup.
Leave the homegroup	Leave your homegroup.
Change advanced sharing settings	Change settings for network discovery, file sharing, public folder sharing, password-protected sharing, homegroup connections, and file-sharing connections.
Start the Homegroup troubleshooter	Troubleshoot homegroup problems.

To prevent a library from being shared (*while* creating or joining a homegroup), follow these steps:

1. Open the **Network and Sharing Center**.

2. Click **Choose homegroup and sharing options**.

3. Do one of the following:

   ▶ To create a new homegroup, click **Create a homegroup**.

   ▶ To join an existing homegroup, click **Join now**.

4. On the next screen of the wizard, clear the checkbox for each library you don't want shared. The Create a Homegroup dialog box appears.

5. Click **Next**, and then click **Finish**.

To prevent a library from being shared (*after* creating or joining a homegroup), do the following:

1. Click to open Homegroup.

2. Clear the checkbox for each library you don't want shared and then click **Save changes**.

To prevent specific files or folders from being shared (after creating or joining a homegroup), follow these steps:

1. Click the **Start** button and then click your user name.

2. Navigate to the file or folder you want to exclude from sharing and then select it.

3. Do one of the following:

   ▶ To prevent the file or folder from being shared with anyone, in the toolbar, click **Share with**, and then click **Nobody**.

   ▶ To share the file or folder with some people but not others, in the toolbar, click **Share with**, click **Specific people**, select each person you want to share with, and then click **Add**. Click **Share** when you are finished.

   ▶ To change the level of access to a file or folder, in the toolbar, click **Share with** and then select either **Homegroup (Read)** or **Homegroup (Read/Write)**.

Managing Shares

By using the Shared Folders snap-in (included in the Computer Management Console), you can manage the server's shared folders. With the Shared Folder snap-in, you can do the following:

▶ Create, view, and set permissions for shares, including shares on Windows 2000, Windows XP, Windows Vista, Windows 7, Windows Server 2003, and Windows Server 2008

▶ View a list of all users who are connected to the computer over a network and disconnect one or all of them

▶ View a list of files opened by remote users and close one or all of the open files

Connecting to a Shared Folder

After you share a file or folder, users can connect to it as a network resource or map to it by using a drive letter on their machines. After a network drive is mapped, users can access it just as they would a local drive on their computer.

You can map a network drive to a shared file or folder by completing the following steps:

1. Click **Start** and then click **Computer**.

2. In Windows Explorer, click the **Map Network Drive** button on the toolbar. This displays the Map Network Drive dialog box, as shown in Figure 10.9.

3. Use the Drive field to select a free drive letter to use and then click the Browse button to the right of the Folder field.

4. In the Browse for Folder dialog box, expand the Network folders until you can select the name of the workgroup or the domain with which you want to work. When you expand the name of a computer in a workgroup or a domain, you see a list of shared folders. Select the shared folder you want to work with and then click **OK**.

5. Select **Reconnect at logon** if you want Windows 7 to connect to the shared folder automatically at the start of each session.

6. If your current logon doesn't have appropriate access permissions for the share, click the **Different User Name** link. You can then enter the user name and password of the account with which you want to connect to the shared folder. Typically, this feature is used by administrators who log on to their computers with a limited account and also have an administrator account for managing the network.

7. Click **Finish**.

Figure 10.9   The Map Network Drive dialog box.

If you later decide you don't want to map the network drive, click **Start** and then click **Computer**. In Windows Explorer, under Computer in the right pane, right-click the network drive icon and choose **Disconnect**.

You can also type in a UNC in the Search program and files box, a Run box, or the address bar in Windows Explorer. To display the Run box quickly, use the Windows logo key + R shortcut. If you don't have a Windows logo key or if you prefer to use the mouse, you can add the Run option to the Start menu in Windows 7:

1. Right-click the Start button and choose **Properties**.

2. On the Start Menu tab, click the **Customize** button to the right of the Start Menu option.

3. In the Customize Start Menu dialog box, scroll down and place a check-mark next to the **Run** command.

4. Click **OK** to save your changes.

Cram Quiz

1. What type of share is not displayed when browsed using Network?

    ○ **A.** Public share

    ○ **B.** Hidden share

    ○ **C.** Administrative shares

    ○ **D.** NTFS share

2. Which editions of Windows 7 allow you to create a homegroup? (Choose all that apply.)

    ○ **A.** Home Basic

    ○ **B.** Home Premium

    ○ **C.** Professional

    ○ **D.** Ultimate

3. You have shared a couple of folders on your Windows 7 computer. Unfortunately, they are not visible on anyone's network map so that users can find the shares easily. What is most likely the problem?

   ○ **A.** You need to enable the Network Discovery service.

   ○ **B.** You did not give the appropriate share permissions to the Everyone group.

   ○ **C.** You did not give the appropriate NTFS permission to the Everyone group.

   ○ **D.** You need to make sure there is a DNS entry in the DNS server for the Windows 7 computer.

Cram Quiz Answers

1. **C** is correct. Different from regular shares, these shares do not show when a user browses the computer resources using Network, My Network Place, or similar software. The public share, hidden share, and NTFS are not types of shares. Therefore, the other answers are incorrect.

2. **B, C,** and **D** are correct. You can join a homegroup in any edition of Windows 7, but you can only create one in Home Premium, Professional, or Ultimate; therefore, Answer A (Home Basic) is incorrect.

3. **A** is correct. To view the computer using the network map, you need to have the Link Layer Topology Discovery (LLTD) operational. Therefore, you need to enable the Network Discovery service. Answers B and C are incorrect because Share and NTFS permissions have nothing to do with a computer showing on the network map. Answer D is incorrect because there is no indication that there is a name resolution problem.

BranchCache

▶ **Configure BranchCache**

Cram**Saver**

1. What technology is designed to reduce traffic (including web and file sharing traffic) between two remote sites, specifically between the central site and a smaller remote site?

   ○ **A.** Distributed File System

   ○ **B.** ProxyServer

   ○ **C.** IIS

   ○ **D.** BranchCache

Answer

1. Answer **D** is correct. BranchCache caches files on a remote site after it communicates with the central office so that in the future, it can use the cache to provide files without always going to the central office. As a result, BranchCache reduces traffic. Answer A is incorrect because Distributed File System (DFS) is used to group shares together or to create redundancy among shared folders. Answer B is incorrect because the Proxy Server is used to cache web pages. Answer C is incorrect because IIS, short for Internet Information Service, is used to provide web services.

Branch offices are often connected to enterprises with a low-bandwidth link. Therefore, accessing corporate data located in the enterprise is slow. BranchCache helps to resolve these challenges by caching content from remote file and web servers so that users in branch offices can access corporate information more quickly. The cache can be hosted centrally on a server (such as a Windows Server 2008 R2) in the branch location, or it can be distributed across user computers.

If the cache is distributed, the branch users' computer automatically checks the cache pool to determine if the data has already been cached. If the cache is hosted on a server, the branch users' computer checks the branch server to access data. Each time a user tries to access a file, his or her access rights are authenticated against the server in the data center to ensure that the user has access to the file and is accessing the latest version.

In the distributed caching mode, cache is distributed across client computers in the branch. Using this type of peer-to-peer architecture, content is cached on Windows 7 clients after it is retrieved from a Windows Server 2008 R2. Then it is sent directly to other Windows 7 clients as they need it.

When you use the hosted caching mode, cache resides on a Windows Server 2008 R2 computer that is deployed in the branch office. Using this type of client/server architecture, Windows 7 clients copy content to a local computer (Hosted Cache) running Windows Server 2008 R2 that has BranchCache enabled.

Compared to Distributed Cache, Hosted Cache increases cache availability because content is available even when the client that originally requested the data is offline. A computer must obtain the identifier that describes a piece of content to decrypt that content after downloading. The identifiers, provided by the server, include a digest of the content. After downloading from the cache, the client computer verifies that the content matches the digest in the identifier. If a client downloads an identifier from the server but cannot find the data cached on any computers in the branch, the client returns to the server for a full download.

BranchCache caches content for the most common protocols including HTTP, HTTPS, and SMB, and it supports network security protocols SSL and IPsec. On Windows 7 clients, BranchCache is off by default. Client configurations can be performed through Group Policy or it can be done manually.

BranchCache is disabled by default on client computers. Take the following steps to enable BranchCache on client computers:

1. Turn on BranchCache.

2. Enable either Distributed Cache mode or Hosted Cache mode.

3. Configure the client firewall to enable BranchCache protocols.

Most of these steps are done with Windows Server 2008 R2 domain controllers and group policies. You then need to configure the Windows 7 computers using group policies and make sure that the BranchCache service is started.

Cram Quiz

1. Which mode of BranchCache has the cached data reside on local clients at a remote site?

   ○ **A.** Distributed Cache

   ○ **B.** Hosted Cache

   ○ **C.** Proxy Cache

   ○ **D.** Link Cache

Cram Quiz Answers

1. **A** is correct because Distributed Cache is distributed across Windows 7 client computers in the branch. Answer B is incorrect because when you use the hosted caching mode, cache resides on a Windows Server 2008 R2 computer that is deployed in the branch office. Answers C and D are incorrect because they are not types of cache used in the BranchCache.

Review Questions

1. What is the minimum share permission that allows you to read and execute files, create files and subfolders, modify files, and change attributes?

   - ○ **A.** Full Control
   - ○ **B.** Change
   - ○ **C.** Write
   - ○ **D.** Read

2. You have a shared folder on an NTFS volume. What is the best way to share the folder and lock it down?

   - ○ **A.** Set Everyone to have full control share permission and lock it down with NTFS permission
   - ○ **B.** Set Everyone to have full control NTFS permissions and lock it down with share permissions
   - ○ **C.** Set Everyone to have full control NTFS and share permissions and lock it down with file attributes
   - ○ **D.** Lock it down with both share and NTFS permissions

3. You work as the desktop support technician at Acme.com. Pat is a member of the manager group. There is a shared folder called DATA on an NTFS partition on a remote Windows 7 computer. Pat is given the Write NTFS permission, the Manager group is giving the Read & Execute NTFS permissions, and the Everyone group has the Read NTFS permission to the DATA folder. In addition, Pat, Manager, and Everyone are assigned the shared Reader permission to the DATA folder. When Pat logs on his client computer and accesses the DATA folder, what would be Pat's permissions? (Choose all that apply.)

   - ○ **A.** Read the files in that folder
   - ○ **B.** Write to the files in the folder
   - ○ **C.** Execute the files in the folder
   - ○ **D.** Delete the files in the folder
   - ○ **E.** Have no access to the files in the folder.

4. You work as the desktop support technician at Acme.com. Pat is a member of the manager group. There is a shared folder called DATA on an NTFS partition on a remote Windows 7 computer. Pat is given the Write NTFS permission, the Manager group is giving the Deny All NTFS permissions and the Everyone group has the Read NTFS permission to the DATA folder. In addition, Pat, Manager, and Everyone are assigned the shared Contributor permission to the DATA folder. When Pat logs on his client computer and accesses the DATA folder, what would be Pat's permissions? (Choose all that apply.)

○ **A.** Read the files in that folder

○ **B.** Write to the files in the folder

○ **C.** Execute the files in the folder

○ **D.** Delete the files in the folder

○ **E.** Have no access to the files in the folder

5. Which type of sharing is designed to enable users to share files and folders from a single location quickly and easily?

○ **A.** Public sharing

○ **B.** Basic sharing

○ **C.** Advanced sharing

○ **D.** Password sharing

6. Where would you enable network discovery?

○ **A.** Network and Sharing Center

○ **B.** Services console

○ **C.** Shared console

○ **D.** Network console

7. You need to access the C:\Data folder on your partner's computer. Unfortunately, he did not share the folder. If you are an administrator on his computer, how can you access the Data folder remotely?

○ **A.** Open the C:\Data folder

○ **B.** Open the \\Computername\C\Data folder

○ **C.** Open the \\Computername\C$\Data folder

○ **D.** Open the \\Computername\C:\Data folder

8. Where does the Public shared folder reside?

○ **A.** C:\Public

○ **B.** C:\Users\Public

○ **C.** C:\Windows\Public

○ **D.** C:\Shares\Public

9. Which special or administrative share is used during remote administration of a computer and for viewing a computer's shared resources?

○ **A.** NetLogin

○ **B.** PRINT$

○ **C.** C$

○ **D.** IPC$

10. Which mode of BranchCache has the cached data reside on a Windows Server 2008 R2 server?

   ○ **A.** Distributed Cache

   ○ **B.** Hosted Cache

   ○ **C.** Proxy Cache

   ○ **D.** Link Cache

Review Question Answers

1. Answer **B** is correct. The Change permission allows you to read files, create files and subfolders, modify files, change attributes on files and subfolders, and delete files and subfolders. Answer A is incorrect because the Full Control permission also allows you to change permissions. Answer C is incorrect because the Write share permission does not exist. Answer D is incorrect because the Read permission does not give you write capability.

2. Answer **A** is correct. With Microsoft's best practices, you should grant full control to Everyone and use NTFS to lock it down. Answer B is incorrect because setting full control NTFS permissions to everyone does not control users who access the folder locally. Answer C is incorrect because you cannot secure files and folders with attributes. Answer D is incorrect because while you could lock down the folder with share and NTFS permissions, it is simpler to control through one mechanism instead of two.

3. Answers **A** and **C** are correct. When you combine the NTFS permissions assigned to Pat and to the Manager group that Pat is a member of, Pat can read, write, execute, and delete the files in the folder. However, because the Reader share permission only allows reading and executing the files, blocking writing, and deleting when going through the shared folder. Answers B and D are incorrect because the Reader permission blocks the Write and Delete permissions.

4. Answer **E** is correct. Pat is a member of the Managers group. Because Deny All NTFS permissions has been granted to the Managers group, it blocks all permissions for Pat. Answers A, B, C, and D are incorrect because no access permissions always wins.

5. Answer **A** is correct. Public folder sharing is designed to enable users to share files and folders from a single location quickly and easily. The Public folders are handy if you want to temporarily share a document or other file with several people. Answers B and C are incorrect because basic sharing (B) and advanced sharing (C) are preferred because these options are more secure than public file sharing; however, these sharing methods are not as easy to set up. Answer D is incorrect because password sharing is not one of the three methods of sharing.

6. Answer **A** is correct. Network discovery allows this computer to see other network computers and devices and is visible to other network computers. It is enabled or disabled in the Network and Sharing Center. Answer B is incorrect

because the Services console is used to manage your services. Answer C is incorrect because there is no Shared console, although there is a Shared Folder MMC, which is part of the Computer Management console. Answer D is incorrect because there is no Network console. However, there is Network, which allows you to browse network computers and their shared folders and printers.

7. Answer **C** is correct. To access the C: drive remotely, you can use the drive letter$ administrative share, which is available only to administrators. Therefore, the other answers are incorrect. Answer A is incorrect because C:\Data cannot be accessed remotely. Answers B and D are incorrect because there are no shared folders called C or C.

8. Answer **B** is correct. Windows 7 supports the use of only one Public folder for each computer. Any files that you want to make available publicly can be copied or moved to an appropriate folder inside the Public folder. The Public folder is located at C:\Users\Public. Answer A is incorrect because the Public folder is located at C:\Users\Public, not C:\Public. Answer C is incorrect because the shared folder is not C:\Windows\Public. Answer D is incorrect because the Shared Folder is not C:\Shares\Public.

9. Answer **D** is correct. The ADMIN$ and IPC$ are both used by the system during remote administration of the computer. Answer A is incorrect because the NetLogon folder is used by the Net Logon service. Answer B is incorrect because the PRINT$ share is used during remote administration of printers. Answer C is incorrect because the C$ is a shared folder to connect to the C drive root directory.

10. Answer **B** is correct. When you use the hosted caching mode, cache resides on a Windows Server 2008 R2 computer that is deployed in the branch office. Answer A is incorrect because Distributed Cache is distributed across client computers in the branch. Answers C and D are incorrect because they are types of cache used in the BranchCache.

CHAPTER 11

Managing and Sharing Printers

This chapter covers the following 70-680 Objectives:

▶ Configuring Access to Resources:

    ▶ Configure shared resources

▶ Configuring Network Connectivity

    ▶ Configure networking settings

Users in a home environment mostly print to a local printer directly attached to their home computer. In a business environment, client computers often print to a centralized print server that forwards the print jobs to a print device. Network printing or print sharing allows several people to send documents to a centrally located printer or similar device in an office so that you do not have to connect expensive printers to every single computer in the office. By using a print server, the network administrator can centrally manage all printers and print devices.

Printer in Windows

▶ **Configure shared resources**

▶ **Configure networking settings**

CramSaver

1. In Windows 7, the printer is considered which of the following?

   ○ **A.** The logical device that represents the printer device

   ○ **B.** The physical printer device

   ○ **C.** The network IP address located in DNS

   ○ **D.** The print driver

2. What permission do you have to give to a user to change the permissions assigned for a printer?

   ○ **A.** Manage Printers

   ○ **B.** Manage Documents

   ○ **C.** Full Control for Documents

   ○ **D.** Modify permission for Printers

3. Where do you find the logs of printer activity as well as printer errors?

   ○ **A.** The System log in the Event Viewer

   ○ **B.** The Application log in the Event Viewer

   ○ **C.** The C:\Windows\Spooler\Logs folder

   ○ **D.** The C:\Windows\System32\Logs folder

Answers

1. **A** is correct. The printer is the logical representation of the physical printer device. Answer B is incorrect because a physical printer device in Windows is known as the print device. Answer C is incorrect because the only time a printer is assigned to an IP address is when it is a network printer that is connected directly to the network. Answer D is incorrect because the print driver acts as a translator to translate your print jobs to a language that the printer can understand.

2. **A** is correct. To change the permissions, the user has to have the Manage Printers permission. Answer B is incorrect because if a user has the Manage Documents permissions, he or she can only manage documents sent to the print queue. Answers C and D are incorrect because there is neither a Full Control permission nor a Modify permission for printers.

3. **A** is correct. To look at spooler and printer activity, you can use the logs shown in the Event Viewer. The System log shown in the Event Viewer shows printer creation, deletion, and modification. You can also find entries for printer traffic, hard disk space, spooler errors, and other relevant maintenance issues. Answer B is incorrect because the application log shows log events for general applications. Answer C is incorrect because the C:\Windows\Spooler\Logs folder does not exist in Windows 7. Answer D is incorrect because the C:\Windows\System32\Logs folder does not exist in Windows 7. However, there is a C:\Windows\system32\LogFiles folder that holds logs for IIS web server, fax, firewall, MemDiag, WMI, and other items.

The Microsoft definitions of printer-related terms are as follows:

▶ **Print device (physical printer)**: The physical print device, such as a printer, copy machine, or plotter.

▶ **Printer (logical printer)**: The printer is the software interface between a print device and the print clients or applications. It is a logical representation of a printer device in Windows that has an assigned printer name and software that controls a printer device. When you print to the printer device, you print to the printer, which then prints to the printer device.

▶ **Spooler**: Often referred to as a *queue*, the spooler accepts each document being printed, stores it, and sends it to the printer device when the printer device is ready.

▶ **Print driver**: A program designed to enable other programs to work with a particular printer without concerning themselves with the specifics of the printer's hardware and internal language.

ExamAlert

Make sure you understand the difference between a printer and a print device when taking the exam. A printer is the logical representation and the printer device is the physical representation.

You can connect a print device (printer, plotter, copy machine, or similar device) directly to your Windows 7 computer usually using a Universal Serial Bus (USB) or wireless technology such as Bluetooth or indirectly through a network. You can then print to the printer when running applications on the

Windows 7 computer, or you can share the printer so that other users and network applications can print to the printer over the network.

Local Versus Network Printing

As an administrator, you can install two types of printers: a local or a network printer. Both types of printers must be created before sharing them for others to use. Table 11.1 lists the advantages and disadvantages of printing to a local printer or a network printer.

Table 11.1   Comparing Local and Network Printers

	Local Printer	Network Printer
Advantages	The print device is usually in close proximity to the user's computer.	Many users can access print devices.
	Plug and Play can detect local printers and automatically install drivers.	Network printers support distributing updated printer drivers to multiple clients.
		The print server manages the printer driver settings.
		A single print queue appears on every computer connected to the printer, enabling each user to see the status of all pending print jobs, including their own jobs.
		All users can see the state of the printer.
		Some processing is passed from the client computer to the print server.
		You can generate a single log for administrators who want to audit the printer events.
Disadvantages	A print device is needed for every computer.	The print device might not be physically close to the user.
	Drivers must be manually installed for every local printer.	Security is physically limited on the print device.
	A local printer takes more processing to print.	

> **Note**
>
> Whether you choose to print locally or on a network, make sure that your system has sufficient memory and free disk space to handle your print jobs.

When you print to a local or network printer, you must have a print driver that is compatible with the print device to which you are printing. The print driver is software used by computer programs to communicate with a specific printer or plotter, which translates the print jobs from a certain platform to information that the printer understands. The print driver also helps define the capabilities of the printer to the system.

As with any driver that you load on a Windows system, it is strongly recommended that you use only device drivers with the Designed for Microsoft Windows 7 or Designed for Microsoft Windows 2008 Server logos. Installing device drivers that are not digitally signed by Microsoft might disable or impair the operation of the computer or allow viruses on to your computer.

> **ExamAlert**
>
> Whenever possible, you should use digital signed device drivers. Having a digital signed device driver means that the driver has been tested, verified, and signed by Microsoft so that it is safe for your computer.

> **Note**
>
> A computer running Microsoft Windows 7 Professional can also function as a print server. However, it is limited to only 10 network connections.

Printing Process

When users print a document, most know only to click the print icon or select Print from the File menu and go grab their document from the printer. Of course, a lot happens in the background that gets the document out of the printer.

The following briefly describes the printer process:

1. If a printer is connected directly to its computer, you must load the appropriate driver so that it knows what commands to send to the printer. If a client computer connects to a printer, the print server downloads a print driver to the client computer automatically.

2. When a user prints from an application such as Microsoft Word, he selects the print option or button, and a print job is created. The application calls up the graphical device interface (GDI), which calls the printer driver associated with the target print device. The GDI renders the print job in the printer language of the print device, such as HP's Printer Control Language or Adobe's Postscript, to create an enhanced metafile (EMF). The application then calls the client side of the spooler (Winspool.drv).

3. After it has been formatted, the print job is sent to the local spooler, which provides background printing.

   ▶ If the print job is being sent to the local print device, it saves it to the local hard drive's spool file. When the printer is available, the print job prints on the local print device.

   ▶ If the local spooler determines that the job is for a network print device, it sends the job to the print server's spooler. If the local printer is being sent to a shared printer (\\server\printer), the print job goes to the server message block (SMB) redirector on the client. The print server's spooler saves the print job to the print server's hard drive spool file. When the network print device becomes available, the print job prints on the network print device.

The print spooler (spoolsv.exe) manages the printing process, which locates the correct print driver, loads the driver, spools (queues) the print job, and schedules the print job.

Installing a Printer on Windows 7

If you have the correct permissions to add a local printer or a remote shared printer, use the Add Printer Wizard. After the printer is installed, it then is listed in the Devices and Printers folder.

Installing Local Printer

To add a local printer to a Windows 7 system, perform the following steps, as illustrated in Figure 11.1:

1. Click the **Start** button and open the **Control Panel**.

2. Under Hardware and Sound, click **View Devices and Printers**.

3. To start the Add Printer Wizard, click **Add a printer**.

4. Select **Add a Local Printer**.

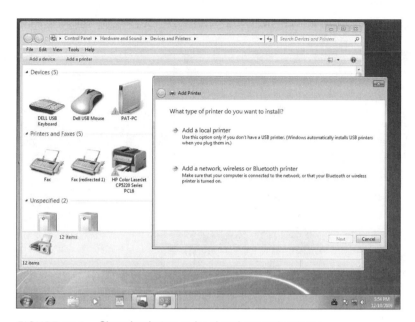

FIGURE 11.1   **Choosing between local and network printing.**

5. When the Choose a Printer dialog box displays, as shown in Figure 11.2, you specify the port to which the printer is connected. If the port already exists, such as an LPT1 or a network port specified by an IP address, select the port from the **Use an existing port** drop-down list. If the port does not exist, click **Create a new port**, select **Standard TCP/IP Port**, and click **Next** (see Figure 11.3). For the device type, you can select either auto detect, TCP/IP device, or web services device. Then specify the IP address or DNS name of the printer and the Port Name. If you type the address in the hostname or IP address box, it populates the IP address in the port name (see Figure 11.4). It then tries to communicate with the printer using the address you specified.

> **Note**
>
> The TCP/IP printer port uses host port 9100 to communicate.

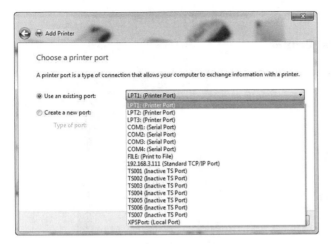

FIGURE 11.2   Choosing a printer port.

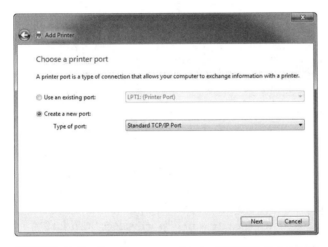

FIGURE 11.3   Creating a new standard TCP/IP device port.

6. If Plug and Play does not detect and install the correct printer automatically, you are asked to specify the printer driver (printer manufacturer and printer model), as shown in Figure 11.5. If the printer is not listed, you have to use the Have Disk option.

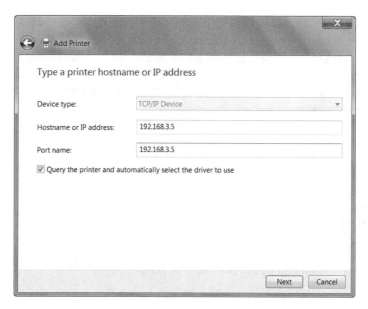

FIGURE 11.4 **Specifying the printer hostname or IP address.**

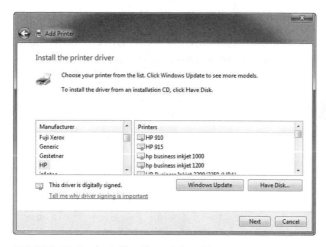

FIGURE 11.5 **Installing the printer driver.**

7. When the Type a Printer Name dialog box displays, specify the name of the printer. If you want this to be the default printer for the system on which you are installing the printer, select the **Set as the default printer** option. Click the **Next** button.

8. On the Printer Sharing dialog box, specify the share name. You can also specify the Location or Comments. Although Windows 7 supports long printer names and share names including spaces and special characters, it is best to keep names short, simple, and descriptive. The entire qualified name, including the server name (for example, \\Server1\HP4100N-1), should be 32 characters or fewer.

9. When the printer was successfully added, you can print the standard Windows test page by clicking the **Print a test page** button. Click the **Finish** button.

Install a Network Printer

To add a network printer to a Windows 7 system, perform the following steps:

1. Click the **Start** button and open the **Control Panel**.

2. Under Hardware and Sound, click **View Devices and Printers**.

3. To start the Add Printer Wizard, click **Add a printer**.

4. Select **Add a network, wireless or Bluetooth printer**.

5. If the printer is not automatically found, click **The Printer that I want isn't listed** option to generate the dialog box shown in Figure 11.6.

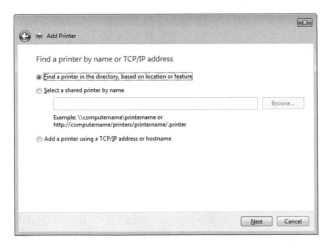

FIGURE 11.6   **Specifying the location of a network printer.**

6. If you have a printer published in Active Directory (assuming you are part of a domain), you choose **Find a printer in the directory, based on location or feature**. If you know the UNC, you select the **Select a shared printer by name**. If you know the TCP/IP address, choose the last option, **Add a printer using a TCP/IP address or hostname**. Click the **Next** button.

7. In the Type a printer name dialog box, specify the printer name. If you want this to be the default printer for the system you are installing, select **Set as the default printer** option. Click the **Next** button.

8. When the printer is successfully added, you can print the standard Windows test page by clicking the **Print a test page** button. Click the **Finish** button.

Printer Properties

After installing the logical printer, you can right-click the printer from the Devices and Printers folder and select **Printer Properties** to configure numerous settings. The following tabs enable you to configure the settings:

▶ The General tab, as shown in Figure 11.7, enables you to configure the printer name, location, comments, and to print a test page.

  If you click the **Preferences** button on the General tab, the default paper size, paper tray, print quality/resolution, pages per sheet, print order (such as front to back or back to front), and number of copies are available. The options that are available vary depending on your printer.

▶ The Sharing tab enables you to share a printer. You can also publish the printer in Active Directory if you choose the **List in the directory** option. Because the printer on a server can be used by other clients connected to the network, you can add additional drivers by clicking the **Additional Drivers** button. By default, Windows includes drivers for 32-bit clients (x86 drivers), 64-bit clients (x64), and Itanium PCs.

▶ The Ports tab, as shown in Figure 11.8, enables you to specify which port (physical or TCP/IP port) the printer uses as well as to create new TCP/IP ports.

▶ The Advanced tab enables you to configure the driver to be used with the printer, the priority of the printer, when the printer is available, and how print jobs are spooled.

▶ The Security tab enables you to specify the permissions for the printer.

▶ The Device Settings tab enables you to configure the trays, font substitution, and other hardware settings.

▶ The Color Management tab ensures that color content is rendered as accurately as possible on both the monitor and the printer.

▶ The About tab (not available on all printers) enables you to see the printer and drivers (and their versions) installed for the printer.

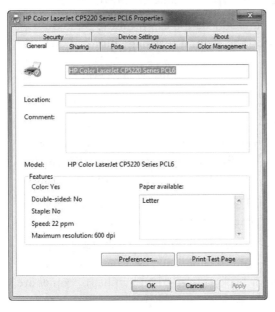

FIGURE 11.7   **Printer properties.**

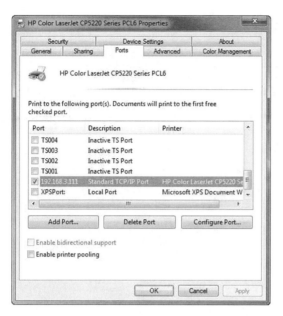

FIGURE 11.8   Configuring the printer ports.

Location-Aware Printing

If you have a mobile computer that you use in multiple locations, it is likely that you need to print in various locations. With Windows 7 Professional, Ultimate, and Enterprise editions, you define default printers for each network you use. Then instead of manually switching printers when you connect to a network, Windows 7 automatically prints to the local printer:

1. Click the Start menu and select **Devices and Printers**.

2. Select your local printer.

3. Click **Manage Default Printers** in the menu bar.

4. In the Manage Default Printers dialog box, shown in Figure 11.9, click **Change my default printer when I change networks**, specify which printer should be the default for each network, and then click **OK**.

5. From the Select network list, select a network. Then select a printer used in that location. Click the **Add** button.

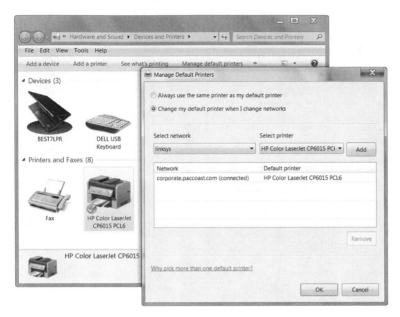

FIGURE 11.9   Configuring location-aware printers.

Printer Permissions

To control who can use the printer and who can administer the print jobs and printers, use the Security tab to specify printer permissions for those who are not otherwise administrators. Windows provides three basic levels of printer permissions, as shown in Figure 11.10:

▶ **Print**: Allows users to send documents to the printer

▶ **Manage this printer**: Allows users to modify printer settings and configuration, including the ACL itself

▶ **Manage documents**: Provides the ability to cancel, pause, resume, or restart a print job

There is a fourth level of printer permissions called special permissions, which enables you to choose more specific permissions, including

▶ Print

▶ Manage this printer

▶ Manage documents

- ▶ Read permissions

- ▶ Change permissions

- ▶ Take ownership

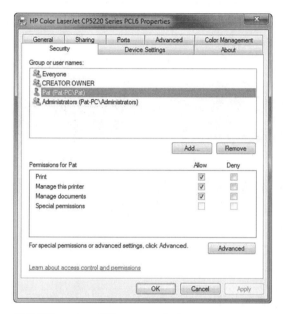

FIGURE 11.10   **Printer permissions.**

By default, the Print permission is assigned to the Everyone group. If you need to restrict who can print to the printer, you will need to remove the permission and assign the Print permission to other groups or individual users. Much like file permissions, you can deny Print permissions.

The Creator Owner group is granted the allow Manage documents permission. This means that when a user sends a print job to the printer, he can manage his own print job. Administrators, print operators, and server operators have the Manage documents and the Manage the printer permissions.

Managing the Print Spooler

The print spooler is an executable file that manages the printing process, which includes retrieving the location of the correct print driver, loading the driver, creating the individual print jobs, and scheduling the print jobs for printing.

Typically, the print spooler is loaded during startup and continues to run until the operating system shuts down. You can restart the print spooler by doing the following:

1. Open the **Services** console located in Administrative Tools.

2. Right-click **Print Spooler** and select **Restart**, as shown in Figure 11.11.

3. You can also stop and start the service.

> ### Exam**Alert**
>
> If the print spooler becomes unresponsive or you have print jobs that you cannot delete, you should try to restart the Print Spooler service.

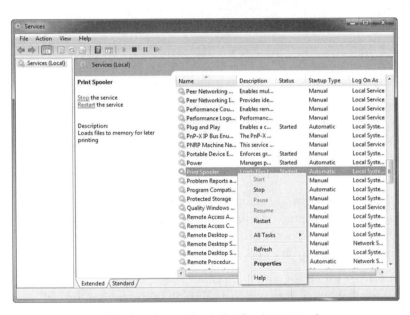

FIGURE 11.11   **Print Spooler service in the Services console.**

After the print jobs are created, they are stored as files on the hard drive. When the print device is available, the spooler retrieves the next print job and sends it to the print device. By default, the spool folder is located at

%SystemRoot%\System32\Spool\Printers. So, on most installations, this is the C:\Windows\System32\Spool\Printers folder. If the system drive becomes full, the performance of the computer might slow down dramatically, services and applications running on the computer might degrade or not function at all, and the system can become unstable. Because the print spooler is on the same volume that holds the Windows system files, the administrator must ensure that spooling print jobs do not accidentally fill up the system volume.

If your computer running Windows 7 acts as a printer server for multiple users or you are printing multiple large print jobs, you might choose to move the spool folder to another volume if your volume with the Windows folder is close to being full.

> **Note**
>
> When you print a Word document or a PDF file, the actual print job sent to the printer is many times larger than the original Word or PDF file itself. Therefore, you should make sure that you have sufficient disk space to hold the print jobs while printing.

Managing Print Jobs

As a user or an administrator, at times you might need to manage individual print jobs or documents. To view documents waiting to print, do the following:

1. Open the **Devices and Printers** folder.

2. Double-click the printer on which you want to view the print jobs waiting to print.

3. To view the print queue, select **See what's printing**. You can also click **Printer: Ready or # document(s) in queue** at the top of the screen where the # represents how many documents are in the queue, as shown in Figure 11.12.

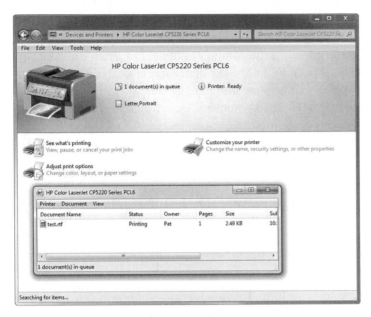

FIGURE 11.12   **Viewing documents in the print queue.**

The print queue shows information about a document such as print status, owner, and number of pages to be printed. From the print queue, you can cancel or pause the printing of a document that you have sent to the printer. You also can open the print queue for the printer on which you are printing by double-clicking the small printer icon in the Notification area on the taskbar.

To pause a document, open the print queue, right-click the document you want to pause, and select the **Pause** option. If you want to stop printing the document, right-click the document that you want to stop printing and select the **Cancel** option. You can cancel the printing of more than one document by holding down the **Ctrl** key and clicking each document that you want to cancel.

By default, all users can pause, resume, restart, and cancel their own documents. To manage documents that are printed by other users, however, you must have the Manage Documents permission.

Looking at the Logs

To look at spooler and printer activity, you can use the logs shown in the Event Viewer. By default, the Administrative Events or the System log shows printer creation, deletion, and modification. You can also find entries for printer traffic, hard disk space, spooler errors, and other relevant maintenance issues. See Figure 11.13.

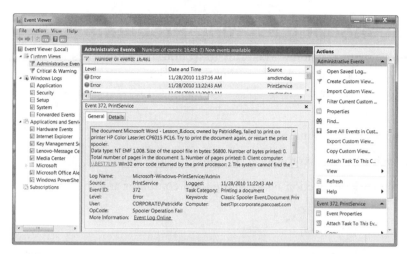

FIGURE 11.13 **Administrative Events showing printer activity.**

Auditing Printer Access

Similar to file and folder access, you can also audit printers. You can specify which users or groups and which actions to audit for a particular printer. Before you can do printer auditing, you need to enable an Audit Object Access policy, which is done using local or group policies (Computer Configuration\Windows Settings\Security Settings\Local Policies\Audit Policy). After the policy has taken effect, you would then do the following:

1. Open the **Devices and Printers** folder.

2. Right-click the printer you want to audit and select **Printer Properties**.

3. Choose the **Security** tab.

4. Select the **Advanced** button.

5. Choose the **Auditing** tab.

6. Select **Add** and then choose the groups or users you want to audit.

7. Check the boxes for auditing successful or failed events.

8. Click **OK** to close the Advanced Security Settings box.

9. Click **OK** to close the Printer Properties box.

You would then look in the Security logs in the Event Viewer for inappropriate or unauthorized printing.

Troubleshooting Printing Problems

When problems occur, you must be ready to troubleshoot those problems. Of course, when looking at what is causing the problem, you need to look at everything that can cause the problems. When it comes to printing, this includes

- The application attempting to print

- The logical printer on the local computer

- The network connection between the local computer and the print server

- The logical printer on the server

- The network connection between the print server and the print device

- The print device itself, including hardware, configuration, and status

The first step is to identify the scope of the failure; in other words, determine what is working and what is failing. For example, if a user can print from one application but not another on the same computer, the problem is most likely related to the application that is having problems printing. If the user can print to other printers with no problem, you should then try to print from another system in an attempt to duplicate the problem. If the problem occurs on multiple computers, you need to focus on the logical printer on the server or the print device. Of course, one place that might give you insight into some problems is the logs in the Event Viewer, specifically if the spooler has written any errors to the event logs.

You can confirm connectivity between the print client and the print server by opening the **Printers and Faxes** folder and double-clicking the printer to open the printer window. If the printer window opens and it shows documents in the print queue, the client is communicating with the print server. If you cannot open the printer window, the problem is with authentication, security permissions, or a network connectivity problem. You can test connectivity further by trying to ping the print server or by clicking the Start button, selecting Search, and typing in \\printservername. Also, make sure that the printer has not been disabled or offline within Windows.

If you suspect that the print server cannot connect to the printer, you should first check to see if the print device is in operation: Make sure that the printer is on and online; make sure that it is connected to the server or network; and make sure that the printer is not showing any errors. Next, from the print server, make sure that the print server can access the print device. You can also make sure that the IP address on the logical printer port matches the address of the print device. You could test network connectivity by pinging the address of the print device.

If you suspect a problem with the print server itself, you need to make sure that the Print service and the remote procedure call (RPC) service is running. You might also try to restart the print service and make sure that you have sufficient disk space on the drive where the spool folder is located.

If you have trouble connecting to a printer on a Windows 7 computer, you can check the Advanced sharing settings and make sure the following settings are on:

- ► Network discovery
- ► File and printer sharing
- ► Sharing in the Public folder sharing section

You can also make sure that the Server service is running on the computer that is hosting the printer and that the workstation service is running on the client. Both of these are on by default for all Windows computers. If pages are only partially printed, check that there is sufficient memory on the printer to print the document. If text is missing, verify whether the missing text uses a font that is valid and installed. Of course, another reason might be that you need to replace the printer's toner cartridge.

If your printed documents have garbled data or strange characters, you should verify that you have the correct print driver loaded for the printer. You might also consider reinstalling the drivers because they could be corrupt. Finally, check for bad cables or electromagnetic interference. See Table 11.2 for a list of common printing problems and how to fix them.

ExamAlert

Anytime you have garbled data or strange characters, you should always suspect that you have the wrong print driver installed.

TABLE 11.2 **Troubleshooting Common Printing Problems**

If You Encounter This Problem:	Do This:
Printer server cannot connect to the printer.	Make sure print device is operational (printer is on and online, printer is connected to the server or network, and printer is not showing any errors).
	Make sure IP address on the logical printer port matches the address of the print device.
	Try pinging the address of print device.
Print server is having problems.	Make sure that the printer services and remote procedure call (RPC) service is running.
	Restart the print service.
	Make sure you have sufficient disk space on the drive where the spool folder is located.
Pages are partially printed.	Check that there is sufficient memory on the printer.
	Check to see if the printer's toner or ink cartridge needs to be replaced.
Text is missing.	Verify whether the missing text uses a font that is valid and installed.
	Check to see if the printer's toner or ink cartridge needs to be replaced.
Documents have garbled data or strange characters.	Verify that the correct print driver is loaded on the printer.
	Reinstall the drivers because they could be corrupt.
	Check for bad cables.
	Check for electromagnetic interference.

Cram Quiz

1. What do you call the component that holds and forwards the print jobs that are sent to the physical printer?

   ○ **A.** The print driver

   ○ **B.** The spooler

   ○ **C.** The PrintTemp folder

   ○ **D.** The Processor area

2. What printer permission allows you to modify printer settings and configuration?

○ **A.** Print

○ **B.** Manage the printer

○ **C.** Manage documents

○ **D.** Full Control

3. Which permission is assigned to the Everyone group?

○ **A.** Print

○ **B.** Manage the printer

○ **C.** Manage documents

○ **D.** Full Control

Cram Quiz Answers

1. **B** is correct. The printer spooler is often referred to as a queue, which accepts each document being printed, stores it, and sends it to the printer device the printer device is ready. Answer A is incorrect because the print driver is a program designed to enable other programs to work with a particular printer without the other programs concerning themselves with the specifics of the printer's hardware and internal language. Answers C and D are incorrect because there is no PrintTemp folder or Processor area in Windows 7.

2. **B** is correct. Manage the printer allows users to modify printer settings and configuration, including the ACL itself. Answer A is incorrect because the Print permission allows users to send documents to the printer. Answer C is incorrect because the Manage documents permission provides the ability to cancel, pause, resume, or restart a print job. Answer D is incorrect because Full Control is not a Printer permission.

3. **A** is correct. The Print permission allows users to send documents to the printer. By default, the Print permission is assigned to Everyone. Answer B is incorrect because the Manage the printer permission allows users to modify printer settings and configuration, including the ACL itself. Answer C is incorrect because the Manage documents provides the ability to cancel, pause, resume, or restart a print job. Answer D is incorrect because Full Control is not a Printer permission.

Review Questions

1. You add a printer directly to the network using a built-in Ethernet card. What port would you use to connect to the printer?

   ○ **A.** TCP/IP port

   ○ **B.** USB port

   ○ **C.** UDP port

   ○ **D.** NetBIOS printer

2. What do you call a program designed to enable other programs to work with a particular printer without concerning themselves with the specifics of the printer's hardware and internal language?

   ○ **A.** Print device

   ○ **B.** Printer

   ○ **C.** Spooler

   ○ **D.** Print driver

3. You have a shared printer that is installed on a computer running Windows 7. Pat prints a large document several times by mistake. What do you have to do to enable Jane to delete the extra print jobs?

   ○ **A.** Configure the printer permissions for Jane to Allow Manage Printers permission

   ○ **B.** Configure the printer permission to assign the Allow Manage Documents permission

   ○ **C.** Create a new print queue that points to the same print device and assign full permission to Jane

   ○ **D.** Configure the Allow Manage queue permission

4. What is the default port if you configure a TCP/IP printer?

   ○ **A.** 25

   ○ **B.** 80

   ○ **C.** 443

   ○ **D.** 9100

5. You are the administrator for Acme.com. You have a shared printer called Printer1 connected to a computer running Windows 7 called Win7. You assign the Everyone group the Allow Print permission. When a user tries to print to the \\Win7\Printer1, the user is unable to print. You soon discover that a few other users also cannot print to the same printer. You log on to a computer that has been mapped to the shared printer and try to print several documents to the printer but none will print. You soon discover the following message when you try to access the print queue:

Printer1 on Win7 is unable to connect.

You are able to ping the Win7 computer. What do you need to do to ensure that the print jobs will print? (Choose the best answer.)

- ○ **A.** On a Windows server, create a share printer that points to \\Win7\Printer1.
- ○ **B.** From a command prompt, run `net print \\Win7\printer1`.
- ○ **C.** Restart the Print Spooler service on the local computer.
- ○ **D.** Restart the Print Spooler service on the print server.

6. What permission do you need for a user to print to a Windows printer?

- ○ **A.** Print
- ○ **B.** Write
- ○ **C.** Manage this printer
- ○ **D.** Manage documents

7. You have a print job that you cannot delete and it does not finish. What should you try?

- ○ **A.** Restart the printer
- ○ **B.** Restart the server service
- ○ **C.** Restart the print spooler
- ○ **D.** Make sure the printer is connected

8. Where is the print spooler kept on a computer running Windows 7?

- ○ **A.** C:\Windows\spool
- ○ **B.** C:\Spool
- ○ **C.** C:\Windows\System32\Spool\Printers
- ○ **D.** C:\Windows\Spool\Printers

9. You enable auditing in Windows 7 so you can keep track of who is using a printer connected to a computer running Windows 7. Where would you find the audit logs so that you can review them?

   ○ **A.** In the Application logs in the Event Viewer

   ○ **B.** In the C:\Logs folder

   ○ **C.** In the C:\Windows\System32\Logs folder

   ○ **D.** In the Security logs in the Event Viewer

10. You print a document, but all that you get is garbled text. What is the problem?

   ○ **A.** The print spooler became unresponsive.

   ○ **B.** The printer is not using the right ink cartridge.

   ○ **C.** The printer has not been calibrated.

   ○ **D.** You are using the incorrect driver.

Review Question Answers

1. Answer **A** is correct. When you have a printer that is connected directly to the network, you can connect to it through a TCP/IP port or through a printer that is shared on a Windows server or a Windows 7 workstation. Answer B is incorrect because a USB port is a local port, not a network port. Answer C is incorrect because UDP is one of the core protocols used in the TCP/IP suite. Answer D is incorrect because NetBIOS provides the mechanism to share files and printers.

2. Answer **D** is correct. A print driver is a program designed to enable other programs to work with a particular printer without concerning themselves with the specifics of the printer's hardware and internal language. In other words, the print driver acts as translator for the printer. Answer A is incorrect because a print device is the physical print device. Answer B is incorrect because a printer is the software interface between a printer device and the print clients or applications. Answer C is incorrect because the spooler accepts each document being printed, stores it, and sends it to the printer device when the printer device is ready.

3. Answer **B** is correct. By default, users can delete their own print jobs. To be able to delete any print job, the user needs to have the Manage documents permission for the printer. Therefore, the other answers are incorrect.

4. Answer **D** is correct. The TCP/IP printer port uses host port 9100 to communicate. Answer A is incorrect because port 25 is used by SMTP. Answer B is incorrect because port 80 is used by HTTP. Answer C is incorrect because port 443 is used by HTTPS.

5. Answer **D** is correct. If the print spooler stalls, you need to stop and restart the service. After deleting the queues, the users need to resubmit their print jobs. Of course, because this affects more than one user, the problem is with Windows 7 computer servicing more than one user and not the local computer. Therefore, Answer C is incorrect. Answer A is incorrect because creating a shared printer on a printer does not overcome the problem that the Win7 computer is having problems communicating with the printer. Answer B is incorrect because running a **net print** command does not fix any printer problems.

6. Answer **A** is correct. The Print permission allows a user to send documents to the printer. Answer B is incorrect because Write is an NTFS permission, not a printer permission. Answer C is incorrect because the Manage this printer permission allows users to modify printer settings and configuration, including the ACL itself. Answer D is incorrect because the Manage documents permission provides the ability to cancel, pause, resume, or restart a print job.

7. Answer **C** is correct. If the print spooler becomes unresponsive or you have print jobs that you cannot delete, you should try to restart the Print Spooler service. Answer A is incorrect because restarting the printer does not clear out the queue because the queue is kept on Windows and sends print jobs when the printer is available. Because you cannot delete print jobs, the printer is not the problem. Answer B is incorrect because the Server service enables your computer to act as a file server. Answer D is incorrect because if the printer is not connected, the print jobs might not be forwarded to the printer. However, the fact that you cannot delete print jobs tells you the problem is with the print queue.

8. Answer **C** is correct. By default, the spool folder is located at %SystemRoot% \System32\Spool\Printers. So, on most installations, this is the C:\Windows\ System32\Spool\Printers folder. If the system drive becomes full, the performance of the server might slow down dramatically, services and applications running on the server might degrade or not function at all, and the system can become unstable. Therefore, the other answers are incorrect.

9. Answer **D** is correct. You look in the Security logs in the Event Viewer for inappropriate or unauthorized printing, assuming auditing is turned on. To enable auditing, you have to use a group policy or a local policy to enable object auditing and then enable auditing on the printer. Therefore, the other answers are incorrect.

10. Answer **D** is correct. If you have the incorrect print driver, you get strange characters, garbled characters, or snippets of programming code. Answer A is incorrect because if the printer spooler becomes unresponsive, the print jobs stay in the print queue and you cannot delete them. Answer B is incorrect because if the printer is not using the right ink cartridge, you might have poor print quality or the colors might be off, but you won't encounter garbled characters. Answer C is incorrect because if the printer is not calibrated, usually something you have to do with some inkjet printers, the colors might be off.

CHAPTER 12

Working with Applications

This chapter covers the following 70-680 Objectives:

▶ Configuring Hardware and Applications:

  ▶ Configure application compatibility

  ▶ Configure application restrictions

So far, the preceding chapters have looked at installing and configuring Windows and how to enable some of the common services that Windows can provide; however, you have not yet looked at how to use Windows to run applications. This chapter looks at some of the common applications that come with Windows 7 and how to configure other applications to work with Windows 7.

Windows Live Essentials

Cram**Saver**

1. In Windows 7, where do you find the mail program similar to the one that was included with Windows Vista?

   ○ **A.** Under Accessories.

   ○ **B.** You need to load the Add-on pack included on the Windows 7 installation DVD.

   ○ **C.** You need to download and install Windows Live Essentials.

   ○ **D.** You need to run Windows Programs and Features and install Windows Mail.

Answer

1. **C** is correct. Several programs that were in Windows Vista are not included in Windows 7 but are part of Windows Live Essentials, including Windows Live Mail and Windows Live Movie Maker. Therefore, the other answers are incorrect.

Windows 7 includes a wide range of applications so that you can have basic functionality from the start. Some of these applications include WordPad as a basic word processor, Paint as a basic paint program, and Windows Media Player to play videos.

Windows 7 does not have a few productivity applications, such as Windows Mail and photo-editing applications, that were in Windows Vista. If you have a need for these applications, you can access them as part of the Windows Live Essentials suite.

Windows Live Essentials is a suite of freeware applications by Microsoft that aims to offer integrated and bundled email, instant messaging, photo-sharing, blog publishing, security services, and other Windows Live entities. Windows Live Essentials enables users to select and install the following Windows Live software applications:

▶ Windows Live Family Safety

▶ Windows Live Mail (which includes calendars)

▶ Windows Live Messenger

- ▶ Windows Live Movie Maker (Windows Vista and Windows 7 only)
- ▶ Windows Live Photo Gallery
- ▶ Windows Live Sync (integrated with Toolbar and Photo Gallery)
- ▶ Windows Live Toolbar
- ▶ Windows Live Writer
- ▶ Microsoft Office Outlook Connector
- ▶ Microsoft Office Live Add-in
- ▶ Microsoft Silverlight

You can install all the Windows Live Essentials applications except Windows Live Movie Maker on the following operating systems: Windows XP with Service Pack 2 (32-bit edition only), Windows Vista (32-bit or 64-bit editions), Windows 7 (32-bit or 64-bit editions), or Windows Server 2008. Windows Live Movie Maker, unlike the other Essentials programs, is not supported on Windows XP.

To download Windows Live Essentials 2011, visit the following website:

http://explore.live.com/windows-live-essentials?os=other

Cram Quiz

1. Which of the following programs is not included as part of the Windows Live Essentials?

- ○ **A.** Windows Live Mail
- ○ **B.** Microsoft Outlook
- ○ **C.** Windows Live Writer
- ○ **D.** Windows Live Messenger

Cram Quiz Answer

1. Answer **B** is correct. Microsoft Outlook is part of Microsoft Office and not Windows Live Essentials; therefore, the other answers are incorrect.

Application Compatibility

▶ **Configure application compatibility**

Cram**Saver**

1. What two methods can you use to run applications that are written for Windows XP that won't normally run under Windows 7?

   ○ **A.** Use the application compatibility option

   ○ **B.** Run the application as an administrator

   ○ **C.** Modify the NTFS permissions of the application

   ○ **D.** Use XP Mode

2. What do you call small fixes that may allow applications to run under Windows 7?

   ○ **A.** A permission package

   ○ **B.** A shim

   ○ **C.** A definition

   ○ **D.** A language pack

Answers

1. **A** and **D** are correct. When an application does not run under Windows 7, you can first try to run the application using the application compatibility option where you specify that Windows should emulate an older operating system. If that does not work, you can also run the application under XP Mode, which allows you to run the program using a virtual computer running Windows XP that runs inside Windows 7. Answers B and C are incorrect because running the application as an administrator or modifying the NTFS permissions of the application do not let the application run in Windows 7.

2. **B** is correct. In Windows 7, Microsoft includes numerous "shims" or minor fixes that are used to improve compatibility with existing non-Microsoft software. Answer A is incorrect because there is no such thing as a permission package. Answer C is incorrect because a definition is an update file used in antivirus software so that it knows of the newest virus. Answer D is incorrect because a language pack is used with certain applications to support languages such as French or Spanish.

Because the Windows 7 architecture is not significantly different from that of Windows Vista, most applications that are written for Windows Vista work in Windows 7. Unfortunately, there are some programs that are written for Windows XP or older versions of Windows that run poorly or not all. When this occurs, you can change the compatibility settings for the application.

If changing the compatibility settings doesn't fix the problem, go to the program manufacturer's website to see if there is an update for the program.

> **Note**
>
> Do not use the Program Compatibility troubleshooter on older antivirus programs, disk utilities, or other system programs because it might cause data loss or create a security risk.

To change compatibility settings using the Program Compatibility Troubleshooter, perform the following steps:

1. Right-click the executable file and select **Troubleshoot Compatibility**.

2. You can first try the recommended settings. If this does not work, select **Troubleshoot program**.

3. When it asks what problems you noticed, select one or more of the following and click the **Next** button:

   ▸ The program worked in earlier versions of Windows but won't install or run now.

   ▸ The program opens but doesn't display correctly.

   ▸ The program requires additional permissions.

   ▸ I don't see my problem listed.

4. If you selected **The program worked in earlier versions of Windows but won't install or run now**, the wizard asks what version of Windows the program worked on before. Select the appropriate version of Windows and click the **Next** button.

5. If you selected **The program opens but doesn't display correctly**, select one or more of the following options and click the **Next** button:

   ▸ Error message saying the program needs to run in 256 colors.

   ▸ Program starts up in a small window (640 × 480 pixel) and won't switch to full screen.

▶ Window transparency isn't displayed properly.

▶ Program does not display properly when large scale font settings are selected.

▶ Windows controls appear cut off, or the program changes visual themes when started.

▶ I don't see my problems listed.

6. If you selected **The program requires additional permission**, the wizard tests the application when running with UAC. Click the **Start the program** button. Then click the **Next** button.

To change compatibility settings manually for a program, right-click the program icon, click **Properties**, and then click the **Compatibility** tab, as shown in Figure 12.1. Table 12.1 describes the options available under the Compatibility tab.

FIGURE 12.1   Application compatibility options.

TABLE 12.1 **Application Compatibility Options**

Option	Description
Compatibility mode	Runs the program using settings from a previous version of Windows. Try this setting if you know the program is designed for (or worked in) a specific previous version of Windows.
Run in 256 colors	Uses a limited set of colors in the program. Some older programs are designed to use fewer colors.
Run in 640 × 480 screen resolution	Runs the program in a smaller-sized window. Try this setting if the graphical user interface appears jagged or is rendered improperly.
Disable visual themes	Disables themes on the program. Try this setting if you notice problems with the menus or buttons on the title bar of the program.
Disable desktop composition	Turns off transparency and other advanced display features. Choose this setting if window movement appears erratic or you notice other display problems.
Disable display scaling on high DPI settings	Turns off automatic resizing of programs if large-scale font size is in use. Try this setting if large-scale fonts are interfering with the appearance of the program. For more information, see Make the text on your screen larger or smaller.
Privilege level	Runs the program as an administrator. Some programs require administrator privileges to run properly. If you are not currently logged on as an administrator, this option is not available.
Change settings for all users	Enables you to choose settings that apply to all users on this computer.

Microsoft Application Compatibility Toolkit (ACT) and Shims

Besides Windows 7 being a new version of Windows, there are several new technologies that might cause applications to fail. Some of these include the following:

▶ **User Account Control (UAC):** Technology that limits administrator level access to a computer running Windows 7.

▶ **Windows Resource Protection (WRP):** A mechanism that prevents writing to protected system files or registry locations.

▶ **Internet Explorer Protected Mode:** A mechanism used in Internet Explorer that prevents a web page from accessing local computer resources other than the temporary Internet files.

To assist in dealing with compatibility issues, Microsoft created the Application Compatibility Toolkit (ACT), which is a collection of programs that enables administrators to gather information about incompatibilities between specific applications and Windows 7 and deploy fixes to overcome these incompatibilities. Included in ACT, you find the following:

▶ Compatibility Administrator

▶ Application Compatibility Manager

▶ Internet Explorer Compatibility Test Tool

▶ Setup Analysis Tool

▶ Standard User Analyzer

You can download ACT 5.6 from http://www.microsoft.com/downloads/en/ details.aspx?FamilyId=24DA89E9-B581-47B0-B45E-492DD6DA2971& displaylang=en. However, to use ACT, you need a SQL server to store the data gathered by ACT. For the SQL server, you can use the full version of SQL or you can use the free versions, SQL Server Express.

Compatibility Administrator is a central database of known compatibility problems for hundreds of Windows 7 applications. In new versions of Windows, Microsoft includes numerous "shims" or minor fixes that are used to improve compatibility with existing non-Microsoft software. Microsoft analyzed the application and provided an application compatibility shim. These shims are applied on a per-application basis. Shims can be used to fool Windows when a specific application is running. For example, if an application checks to see what version of Windows is running, a shim can tell Windows to report an different version of Windows instead of Windows 7. Another example would that if the application is looking for a file or registry setting that is different between Windows 7 and older versions of Windows, the shim will tell Widnows to redirect the application to the correct location

Of course, although shims are useful tools, they are only temporary bandages for the application until the application can be properly updated to work with the newer version of Windows. In addition, because of revised Windows architecture, shims don't work for all applications and shims must be created for the application you are trying to get working under Windows 7.

To help ensure application compatibility, the Application Compatibility Manager (ACM) is a tool provided by Microsoft that enables you to analyze and collect information on running applications before you upgrade to or deploy Windows 7. You can collect information, analyze the data, and test and mitigate your applications.

For more information about ACM, visit the following website:

http://technet.microsoft.com/en-us/library/cc766464(WS.10).aspx

The Internet Explorer Compatibility Test Tool collects compatibility information for web pages and web-based applications in real-time. When completed, it can identify compatibility problems with web applications and pages for Internet Explorer 8.

The Setup Analysis Tool is designed to analyze application setup programs for potential issues, including the installation of kernel mode drivers, installation of 16-bit components, installation of graphical identification, and authentication (GINA) DLLs and changes to system files and registry keys that are protected with the Windows Resource Protection (WRP).

UAC limits what an application can do, even if logged in as administrator. As a result, the Standard User Analyzer analyzes an application while it's running to determine if an application is compatible with UAC and give you a set of recommended compatibility fixes. After you review the fixes, you can click **Apply** to test the fixes to see if they worked.

XP Mode

Although most applications written for Windows XP also run on Windows 7, there are still quite a few applications that do not. If a shim is not available, you can use Windows XP Mode to run older applications on your Windows 7 desktop. Windows XP Mode was primarily designed to help businesses move from Windows XP to Windows 7. It isn't optimized for graphic-intensive programs such as 3D games, nor is it suited for programs with hardware requirements such as TV tuners.

Windows XP Mode enables you to run a virtual Windows XP machine in its own window. Much like a physical machine running Windows XP, you can still access the computer resources including drives and other hardware devices. In addition, when you install an application in Windows XP Mode, it appears within the Windows XP window and the Windows 7 application list.

To run Windows XP Mode, you need to be running Windows 7 Professional, Enterprise, or Ultimate edition. You are also recommended to have 2 GB of memory and an additional 15 GB of hard disk space per virtual Windows environment.

When Windows 7 was introduced, Windows XP Mode required a computer that is capable of hardware virtualization (Intel-VT or AMD-V virtualization) and a BIOS that supports hardware virtualization. Virtualization must also be enabled in the BIOS Setup program. Since then, the Windows XP Mode components have been upgraded to allow Windows XP Mode to run without these requirements.

To use Windows XP Mode, you should first download and install Windows Virtual PC, which is the program that runs virtual operating systems on your computer. Then, you can download and install Windows XP Mode, which is a fully licensed version of Windows XP with Service Pack 3.

To download and install Windows Virtual PC, do the following:

1. Go to the Windows XP Mode and Windows Virtual PC website.

2. In the Windows 7 system type drop-down list, click **32-bit** or **64-bit** depending on what version of Windows 7 you're currently running. In the Windows XP Mode language drop-down list, click the language you want to use for Windows XP Mode and then click **Download Windows Virtual PC**. To find out whether you have a 32-bit or 64-bit version of Windows 7, click the **Start** button, right-click **Computer**, and then click **Properties**. The information appears under System, next to System type.

3. Click **Open** to install the program immediately, or click **Save** to save the installation file to your computer and then double-click the file.

4. Click **Yes** to install Update for Windows (KB958559).

5. If you accept the license terms, click **I Accept**.

6. After installation is complete, click **Restart Now** to restart your computer.

After your computer restarts, you should see Windows Virtual PC and Windows XP Mode listed in your list of programs. If you haven't installed Windows XP Mode yet, you can click it to install the program.

To download and install Windows XP Mode:

1. Click the **Start** button, click **All Programs**, click **Windows Virtual PC**, and then click **Windows XP Mode**.

2. In the Windows XP Mode dialog box, click **Download** to go back to the Windows XP Mode and Windows Virtual PC webpage.

3. In the Windows 7 system type drop-down list, click **32-bit** or **64-bit** depending on what version of Windows 7 you're currently running. In the Windows XP Mode language drop-down list, click the language you want to use and then click **Download Windows XP Mode**.

4. Click **Open** to install the program immediately; or click **Save** to save the installation file to your computer and then double-click the file. For best practice, you should click **Save** and keep the file on your computer in case you ever need to reinstall Windows XP Mode.

5. In the Welcome to Setup for Windows XP Mode dialog box, click **Next**.

6. Choose the location for the virtual hard disk file that Windows XP Mode uses or accept the default location and then click **Next**.

7. On the Setup Completed screen, select the **Launch Windows XP Mode** checkbox and then click **Finish**.

8. If you accept the license terms, click **I accept the license terms**, and then click **Next**.

9. On the Installation folder and credentials page, accept the default location where Windows XP Mode files are stored or enter a new location.

10. Enter a password, enter it again to confirm it, and then click **Next**.

11. On the Help protect your computer screen, choose whether you want to protect your computer by turning on automatic updates and then click **Start Setup**.

After setup is complete, Windows XP Mode opens in a separate window.

When you install a program in Windows XP Mode, the program becomes available for use in both Windows XP Mode and Windows 7.

To install and use a program in Windows XP Mode, follow these steps:

1. In Windows 7, click the **Start** button, click **All Programs**, click **Windows Virtual PC**, and then click **Windows XP Mode**.

2. In Windows XP Mode, insert the program's installation disc into your computer's CD/DVD drive; or browse to the program's installation file, open the file, and follow the instructions to install the program.

3. Click the **Close** button at the top of the Windows XP Mode window.

4. In Windows 7, click the **Start** button, click **Windows Virtual PC**, click **Windows XP Mode Applications**, and then click the program you want to open.

For more information about XP Mode, visit the following website:

http://windows.microsoft.com/en-US/windows7/install-and-use-windows-xp-mode-in-windows-7

Cram Quiz

1. You have a customized accounting application that was written for Windows XP. Unfortunately, it does not run under Windows 7. What should you do?

   - ○ **A.** Run the application under XP Mode
   - ○ **B.** Modify the privilege level for the application to run as a standard user
   - ○ **C.** Run the MST transform on the application
   - ○ **D.** Run the application under 256 colors

2. What do you call a package of multiple shims bundled together by Microsoft?

   - ○ **A.** A MSI package
   - ○ **B.** XP package
   - ○ **C.** Microsoft Application Compatibility Toolkit
   - ○ **D.** Microsoft Application Reconfig Kit

Cram Quiz Answers

1. **A** is correct. You need to run the application under Windows XP Mode because the enhanced security in Windows 7 does not allow the application to run. Modifying the privilege level or running the program under 256 colors does not allow the program to run under Windows 7. Therefore, Answers B and D are incorrect. Answer C is incorrect because MST transforms are used to install executables that are not available as an MSI file using group policies.

2. **C** is correct. In new versions of Windows, Microsoft includes numerous "shims" or minor fixes that are used to improve compatibility with existing non-Microsoft software. Microsoft analyzed the application and provided an application compatibility shim. These shims are bundled together with the Microsoft ACT are applied on a per-application basis. They are not bundled in an MSI package or an XP package. Therefore, Answers A and B are incorrect. Answer D is incorrect because there is no such thing as a Microsoft Application Reconfig Kit.

Software Restrictions

▶ **Configure application restrictions**

Cram**Saver**

1. What are the two tools used to restrict what applications a user can run on Windows 7? (Select all that apply.)

   ○ **A.** AppLocker in group policies

   ○ **B.** System Configuration tool

   ○ **C.** Software restriction policy in group policies

   ○ **D.** Application Compatibility Toolkit

2. Which of the following is NOT a rule you can create with software restrictions?

   ○ **A.** Hash

   ○ **B.** Path

   ○ **C.** Certificate

   ○ **D.** Location

Answers

1. **A** and **C** are correct. You can use group policies to restrict which software, specifically software restriction policies and AppLocker. Answer B is incorrect because the System Configuration tool is a valuable tool used to troubleshoot boot problems, particular with programs that start during boot or services. Answer D is incorrect because the Application Compatibility Toolkit is used to load band aids or shims for non-Microsoft applications to function under Windows 7.

2. **D** is correct. The four types of rules used with software restrictions include hash, certificate, path, and zone. Location is not a method for software restrictions. Answers A, B, and C are incorrect because they are valid rules that you can create with software restrictions.

They can be assigned to a site, domain, or organizational unit in Active Directory. Many of these settings can also be set locally on a workstation, which are known as local policies.

To increase security, you can also use local policies and group policies to restrict which software can run a computer. Software restriction policies can be used to:

- ▸ Fight viruses and other forms of malware

- ▸ Regulate which ActiveX controls can be downloaded

- ▸ Run only digitally signed scripts

- ▸ Ensure that only approved software is installed on system computers

- ▸ Lock down the computer

To restrict software, you must first create a software restriction policy that consists of security levels, rules, and settings. A policy consists of a default rule about whether programs are allowed to run (unrestricted) and exceptions to that rule (disallowed). The default rule can be set to Unrestricted or Disallowed. When you use the unrestricted rule as the default, you then specify which programs are not allowed to run as exceptions. When you use the restricted rule as the default, you then specify which programs are allowed to run as exceptions.

To identify which software can run or not run, you create rules based on the following criteria (in order of precedence):

- ▸ **Hash**: A cryptographic fingerprint based on a mathematical calculation of the file that uniquely identifies a file regardless where it is accessed or what it is named, as shown in Figure 12.2

- ▸ **Certificate**: A software publisher certificate used to digitally sign a file

- ▸ **Path**: The local or universal naming convention (UNC) path and name of where the file is stored

- ▸ **Zone**: Internet Explorer security zone

You can also use group policies to install software; specifically, you can install Windows Installer packages (.MSI files), Transform Files (.MST files), and patch files (.MSP files).

ExamAlert

If you suspect a conflict rules, remember that the order of precedence is hash rules, certificate rules, path rules, zone rules, and default rules.

FIGURE 12.2   **Software restrictions.**

A new feature added to Windows 7 Ultimate and Enterprise is AppLocker, which enables IT professionals to specify exactly what is allowed to run on user desktops. It enables users to run the applications, installation programs, and scripts they need to be productive while still providing the security, operational, and compliance benefits of application standardization.

If AppLocker and the software restriction policy are configured for the same Group Policy Object (GPO), only the AppLocker settings are enforced on computers running Windows 7. Because earlier versions of Windows do not support AppLocker, they still receive the software restriction settings and not the AppLocker settings. Although AppLocker is an additional Group Policy mechanism, it includes the following new enhancements:

▶ The ability to define rules based on attributes derived from a file's digital signature, including the publisher, product name, file name, and file version.

▶ A more intuitive enforcement model—only a file that is specified in an AppLocker rule is allowed to run.

▶ A user interface accessed through an extension to the Local Policy snap-in and Group Policy Management snap-in.

▶ An audit-only enforcement mode that enables administrators to determine which files are prevented from running if the policy were in effect.

▶ Besides setting policies for .exe files, you can also set policies for .msi files, scripts, and DLLs.

Creating rules based on the digital signature of an application helps make it possible to build rules that don't need to be updated when a new version of the application is released. When testing AppLocker, carefully consider how you will organize rules between linked Group Policy Objects (GPOs). If a GPO does not contain the default rules, either add the rules directly to the GPO or add them to a GPO that links to it. Figure 12.3 shows the Getting Started Window for using AppLocker.

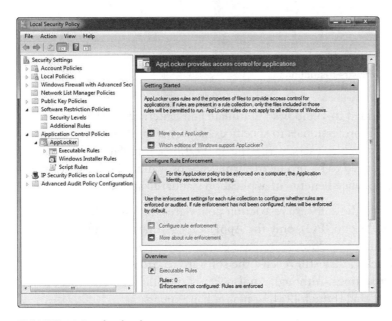

FIGURE 12.3   **AppLocker.**

Specifically, the default rules enable the following:

▶ All users to run files in the default Program Files directory

▶ All users to run all files signed by the Windows operating system

▶ Members of the built-in Administrators group to run all files

By creating these three rules, you automatically prevent all non-administrator users from being able to run programs that are installed in their user profile directories. You can re-create these rules at any time.

If you want to lock down a user computer, which protects the user and your network, you can use AppLocker to use signatures so that you can identify genuine applications. However, you need to ensure that all of the files that you want your users to run are digitally signed. Unfortunately, this is beyond the scope of the book. If any applications are not signed, consider implementing an internal signing process to sign unsigned applications with an internal signing key.

To allow only signed applications to run, do the following:

1. Open the Local Security Policy MMC snap-in by typing **secpol.msc** in the Search programs and files box.

2. Double-click **Application Control Policies** and then double-click **AppLocker** in the console tree.

3. Right-click **Executable Rules** and then click **Create New Rule**.

4. When the Before You Begin page appears, click **Next**.

5. When the Permissions page appears (see Figure 12.4), click **Next** to accept the default settings.

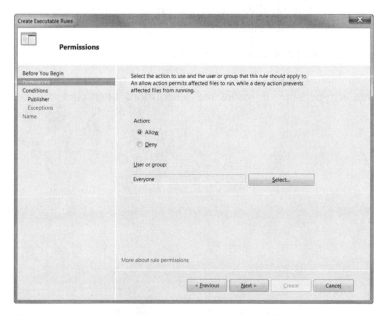

FIGURE 12.4   **Configuring permissions for AppLocker rules.**

6. When the Conditions page appears (see Figure 12.5), click **Next**.

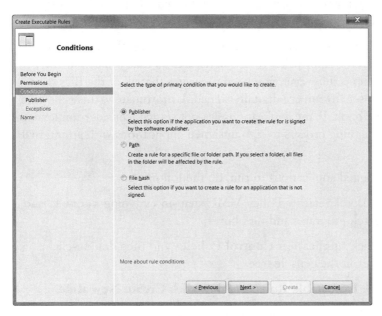

FIGURE 12.5   **Configuring conditions for AppLocker rules.**

7. When the Publisher page appears, select any executable file using the Browse button. Then move the slider to the top to Any publisher, as shown in Figure 12.6. Then click **Next**.

8. When the Exceptions page appears, click **Next**.

9. When the Name and Description page appears, you can accept the default name or type a custom name and description. Then click **Create**.

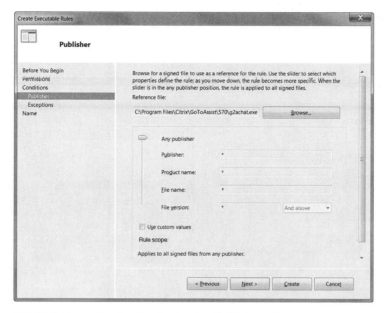

For this work, you must also define a default rule that prevents standard users from running Per-user Applications. The default rule is created by doing the following:

1. Open the Local Security Policy MMC snap-in by entering `secpol.msc` in the Search programs and files box.

2. Double-click Application Control Policies and then double-click **AppLocker** in the console tree.

3. Right-click **Executable Rules** and in the resulting drop-down menu shown in Figure 12.7, click **Create Default Rules**.

FIGURE 12.7   Create default rules in AppLocker.

Cram Quiz

1. You are trying to use a software restriction policy to block a new game called GV.EXE. So, you make a policy based on the path. However, you soon find out that some users just renamed the GV.EXE to a different name to get around the policy. What can you do to overcome this?

   ○ **A.** Use a certificate rule

   ○ **B.** Use a Hash rule

   ○ **C.** Use a Path rule

   ○ **D.** Use a Zone rule

2. When using AppLocker, what are your rules based on?

   ○ **A.** File passwords

   ○ **B.** NTFS permissions of file

   ○ **C.** Size of the file

   ○ **D.** File's digital signature

Cram Quiz Answers

1. **B** is correct. If you use a Hash rule, you can block the software regardless of where the file is accessed or what it is named. Answer A is incorrect because a certificate uses a digital certificate assigned to a file. Answer C is incorrect because the path did not work in the past and setting a new path can only be circumvented again. Answer D is incorrect because the zone is based on the Internet Explorer security zone.

2. **D** is correct. Creating rules based on the digital signature of an application helps make it possible to build rules that don't need to be updated when a new version of the application is released. Therefore, the other answers are incorrect.

Review Questions

1. Which application can be used to test compatibility issues with UAC?
   - ○ **A.** Compatibility Administrator
   - ○ **B.** Application Compatibility Manager
   - ○ **C.** Setup Analyzer Tool
   - ○ **D.** Standard User Analyzer

2. Which application is used to test web applications and web pages for compatibility problems with Internet Explorer 8?
   - ○ **A.** Compatibility Administrator
   - ○ **B.** Application Compatibility Manager
   - ○ **C.** Internet Explorer Compatibility Test Tool
   - ○ **D.** Standard User Analyzer

3. How do you enable and configure AppLocker?
   - ○ **A.** The Registry
   - ○ **B.** Group Policies
   - ○ **C.** Control Panel
   - ○ **D.** Computer Management console

4. Which of the following will AppLocker not support?
   - ○ **A.** .exe file
   - ○ **B.** .dll file
   - ○ **C.** .msi file
   - ○ **D.** Office document files

5. You upgraded your computer running Windows XP with SP2 to Windows 7 Professional. When you run the widget.exe program, you receive the following error message:

   This application is only designed to run on Windows XP or later.

   What should you do?
   - ○ **A.** You should run the application with elevated privileges.
   - ○ **B.** You should run the application in VGA mode.
   - ○ **C.** You should install Windows XP Mode and run the application under Windows XP mode.
   - ○ **D.** You should make sure your machine has all of the Windows updates.

6. You are having problems running a non-Microsoft application. Where can you get help in overcoming this problem? (Choose three answers.)

   ○ **A.** Check to see if the software vendor has an update

   ○ **B.** Look in the Microsoft Application Compatibility Toolkit

   ○ **C.** Load the application in XP Mode

   ○ **D.** Recompile the program

7. For you to run Windows XP Mode, which of the following are not requirements? (Choose two answers.)

   ○ **A.** 2 GB of memory

   ○ **B.** A video card with 512 MB of memory

   ○ **C.** Processor and motherboard that supports hardware virtualization

   ○ **D.** 15 GB of additional free disk space.

8. Which editions of Windows 7 can Windows XP Mode be used on? (Choose all that apply.)

   ○ **A.** Windows 7 Professional

   ○ **B.** Windows 7 Enterprise

   ○ **C.** Windows 7 Home Premium

   ○ **D.** Windows 7 Ultimate

9. Which type of rule would you use when creating a software restriction policy that blocks an application based on an exact location and name of the executable file?

   ○ **A.** Hash

   ○ **B.** Certificate

   ○ **C.** Path

   ○ **D.** Zone

10. Where do you configure an individual application to run as an administrator?

   ○ **A.** Under a local security policy

   ○ **B.** Use System Configuration Tool

   ○ **C.** Computer Management Tool

   ○ **D.** Application Compatibility Options under the application properties

Review Question Answers

1. Answer **D** is correct. UAC limits what an application can run, even if logged in as administrator. As a result, the Standard User Analyzer analyzes an application to identify compatibility problems with Windows 7 User Account Control. Answer A is incorrect because the Compatibility Administrator is a central database of known compatibility problems for hundreds of Windows 7 applications. Answer B is incorrect because the Application Compatibility Manager (ACM) is a tool provided by Microsoft that enables you to analyze and collect information on running applications before you upgrade to or deploy Windows 7. Answer C is incorrect because the Setup Analyzer Tool is designed to analyze application setup programs for potential issues, including the installation of kernel mode drivers, installation of 16-bit components, installation of graphical identification, and authentication (GINA) DLLs and changes to system files and registry keys that are protected with the Windows Resource Protection (WRP).

2. Answer **C** is correct. The Internet Explorer Compatibility Test Tool collects compatibility information for web pages and web-based applications in real-time. When completed, it can identify compatibility problems with web applications and pages for Internet Explorer 8. Answer A is incorrect because the Compatibility Administrator is a central database of known compatibility problems for hundreds of Windows 7 applications. Answer B is incorrect because the Application Compatibility Manager (ACM) is a tool provided by Microsoft that enables you to analyze and collect information on running applications before you upgrade to or deploy Windows 7. Answer D is incorrect because the Standard User Analyzer analyzes an application to identify compatibility problems with Windows 7 User Account Control.

3. Answer **B** is correct. Software Restrictions and AppLocker are used to allow or disallow applications from running on a Windows 7 computer. Both software restrictions and AppLocker are configured through Group Policies including the computer's local policy. Answer A is incorrect because the Registry is a centralized database that contains configuration information for Windows, applications, and hardware devices. Answer C is incorrect because although the Control Panel is the primary configuration tool for Windows 7, the Control Panel is not used to configure software restrictions. Answer D is incorrect because the Computer Management console is used to perform most administrative tasks for Windows.

4. Answer **D** is correct. AppLocker is used to allow or disallow .exe files, .msi files, scripts, and DLLs. AppLocker does not allow or disallow data files, including office document files. Therefore, the other answers are incorrect.

5. Answer **C** is correct. When an application does not run under Windows 7 that was written for an older version of Windows, you should try compatibility mode or run the application under Windows XP Mode. Because the application needs to run under Windows XP Mode, running under elevated privileges or in VGA mode does not work. Therefore, Answers A and B are incorrect. Answer D is incorrect because Windows updates do not allow the application to run under Windows 7.

6. Answers **A**, **B**, and **C** are correct. You should always look to see if the vendor has an update. You can also look in the Microsoft Application Compatibility Toolkit. If that does not work, you can always try to load the application in XP Mode. Answer D is incorrect as you typically cannot recompile the program because you do not typically have the source code and recompiling the program requires special skills and software.

7. Answers **B** and **C** are correct. To run Windows XP mode, you need a minimum of 2 GB of memory (Answer A) and an additional 15 GB of free disk space (Answer D). When Windows 7 was first released, you needed a computer that was capable of hardware virtualization (Intel-VT or AMD-V virtualization) and a BIOS that supports hardware virtualization (Answer C). You do not need additional memory on the video card (Answer B) to run Windows XP Mode.

8. Answers **A**, **B**, and **D** are correct. To run Windows XP Mode, you need to be running Windows 7 Professional, Enterprise, or Ultimate edition. Answer C is incorrect because Windows 7 Home Premium does not run in Windows XP Mode.

9. Answer **C** is correct. The path criteria specify the local or universal naming convention (UNC) path and name of where the file is stored. Answer A is incorrect because the hash criteria is based on a cryptographic fingerprint based on a mathematical calculation of the file that uniquely identifies a file regardless of where it is accessed or what it is named. Answer B is incorrect because the certificate criteria are based on a software publisher certificate used to digitally sign a file. Answer D is incorrect because the zone criteria is based on the Internet Explorer security zone.

10. Answer **D** is correct. If you right-click the executable and select properties, you can select the Compatibility tab to configure what OS to run under, 256 colors, 640 × 480 resolution, and privilege level. Answer A is incorrect because local policies can only be used to restrict an application, not to elevate an application when it runs. Answer B is incorrect because the System Configuration Tool is used to troubleshoot startup problems. Answer C is incorrect because although it includes many tools within a single console, none of them are used for configuring individual applications.

CHAPTER 13

Working with Internet Explorer 8.0

This chapter covers the following 70-680 Objectives:

▶ Configuring Hardware and Applications:

   ▶ Configure application compatibility

   ▶ Configure Internet Explorer

A web browser is the client program or software that you run on your local machine to gain access to a web server. It receives commands, interprets the commands, and displays the results. It is strictly a user-interface/document presentation tool. It knows nothing about the application to which it is attached and only knows how to take the information from the server and present it to the user. It also able to capture data entry made into a form and gets the information back to the server for processing. Because these browsers are used to search and access webpages on the Internet and can be used by an organization's website or provide interface to a program, you need to understand how to configure, customize, and troubleshoot browser issues.

Microsoft Internet Explorer (IE) is the most common browser available because it comes with every version of Windows. Windows 7 includes Internet Explorer 8.0, which has new functionality while reducing online risks.

Features of Internet Explorer 8.0

▶ **Configure application compatibility**

▶ **Configure Internet Explorer**

CramSaver

1. You have a user who is accessing a website located on your company's local intranet. When the user accesses the website, he is prompted for a username and password. How can you make the authentication occur automatically?

   - ○ **A.** Change the authentication for the website to anonymous
   - ○ **B.** Add the website's URL to the Local Intranet zone
   - ○ **C.** Add the website's URL to Trusted Sites zone
   - ○ **D.** Change the credentials in the Credential Manager

2. What can you use to prevent Internet Explorer from saving any data while browsing the Internet?

   - ○ **A.** Use BranchCache
   - ○ **B.** Use InPrivate Browsing
   - ○ **C.** Turn on the use of cookies
   - ○ **D.** Disable the save data option in the Internet zone

3. What can you use to easily invoke an online service by using only the mouse?

   - ○ **A.** Cookies
   - ○ **B.** ActiveX
   - ○ **C.** Accelerators
   - ○ **D.** SmartScreen Filter

Answers

1. **B** is correct. When you add the website to the Local Intranet zone, Internet Explorer automatically tries to use your Windows username and password. Answer A is incorrect because if you choose anonymous for the website, the website is not secure. Answer C is incorrect because adding a website to the Trusted Sites zone does not automatically use your Windows username and password. Answer D is incorrect because using Credential Manager does not automatically use your Windows username and password.

2. **B** is correct. InPrivate Browsing (new to IE 8) enables you to surf the Web without leaving a trail in Internet Explorer. This helps prevent anyone else who might be using your computer from seeing what sites you visited and what you looked at on the Web. Answer A is incorrect because BranchCache is used to cache data at a local site so that it does not always have to download the data over a slower WAN link. Answer C is incorrect because cookies are necessary for some sites, and they usually store information so that a website can automatically identify you and your settings on a particular website. Answer D is incorrect because there is no disable the save data option in the zones.

3. **C** is correct. An accelerator is a form of selection-based search that enables a user to invoke an online service from any other page using only the mouse. Answer A is incorrect because a cookie is a message given to a web browser by a web server, which is typically stored in a text file on the PC's hard drive to identify users for websites and possibly prepare customized webpages for them. Answer B is incorrect because ActiveX is a set of controls used to make a webpage more functional. Answer D is incorrect because a SmartScreen Filter includes protection from socially engineered malware that helps identify sites that have been labeled as an imposter or harmful (in other words, phishing).

Compared to Internet Explorer 6 and older version, the most obvious difference in Internet Explorer 8.0 is its redesigned streamlined interface, which is simpler and less cluttered. As a result, IE 8.0 maximizes the space available for display of webpages. In addition to a simpler interface, Internet Explorer 8.0 introduced tabs that enable you to open multiple webpages in a single browser window. If you have a lot of tabs, you can use Quick Tabs to easily switch between open tabs.

Other features in Internet Explorer 8.0 include the following:

▶ The Instant Search box lets you search the Web from the Address bar. You can also search using different search providers to get better results.

▶ Internet Explorer lets you delete your temporary files, cookies, webpage history, saved passwords, and form information from one place. Delete selected categories or everything at once.

▶ Click the Favorites Center button to open the Favorites Center to manage favorites, feeds, and history in one place.

▶ Printing now scales webpages to fit the paper you're using. Print Preview gives more control when printing, with manual scaling and an accurate view of what you're about to print.

▶ By subscribing to a feed, you can get updated content, such as breaking news or your favorite blog, without having to visit the website.

▶ The Zoom feature lets you enlarge or reduce text, images, and some controls.

▶ Suggested sites suggest websites when you do not input a valid website address.

▶ A new security mode, called InPrivate, helps protect privacy by preventing one's browsing history, temporary Internet files, from data, cookies, usernames, and passwords from being retained by the browser.

▶ Accelerators are a form of selection-based search that allows a user to invoke an online service from any other page using only the mouse.

▶ Web slices are snippets of an entire page to which a user can subscribe. Web slices are kept updated by the browser automatically and can be viewed directly from the Favorites bar.

▶ SmartScreen Filter includes protection from socially engineered malware, which helps identify sites that have been labeled as an imposter or harmful (in other words, phishing).

▶ Full-page zoom now reflows the text to remove the appearance of horizontal scrollbars on zooming.

▶ If a website or add-on causes a tab to crash in Internet Explorer 8, only that tab is affected, leaving the other tabs unaffected.

For more information about Internet Explorer, visit the following website:

http://www.microsoft.com/windows/products/winfamily/ie/default.mspx

Internet Explorer Zoom

Internet Explorer Zoom lets you enlarge or reduce the view of a webpage. Unlike changing font size, zoom enlarges or reduces everything on the page, including text and images. You can zoom from 10% to 1000%.

To zoom a webpage, do the following:

1. On the bottom right of the Internet Explorer screen, click the arrow to the right of the Change Zoom Level button.

2. Do one of the following:

▶ To go to a predefined zoom level, click the percentage of enlargement or reduction you want.

▶ To specify a custom level, click **Custom**. In the Percentage zoom box, type a zoom value and then click **OK**.

If you have a mouse with a wheel, hold down the Ctrl key and then scroll the wheel to zoom in or out. If you click the Change Zoom Level button, it cycles through 100%, 125%, and 150%, giving you a quick enlargement of the webpage. From the keyboard, you can increase or decrease the zoom value in 10% increments. To zoom in, press Ctrl + plus sign. To zoom out, press Ctrl + minus sign. To restore the zoom to 100%, press Ctrl + 0.

Common Internet Explorer Settings

Most of the configuration options for Internet Explorer are accessed by starting Internet Explorer, clicking the **Tools** button and selecting **Internet Options**. You can also access them from the Internet Options applet in the Control Panel. The Internet Options dialog box has several tabs, including General, Security, Privacy, Content, Connections, Programs, and Advanced, as shown in Figure 13.1.

FIGURE 13.1   Internet Explorer Options dialog box.

At the top of the General tab, you can configure the home page or the default page that is loaded when you start Internet Explorer. This enables you to have your favorite search engine, news, website, portal, or an organization's internal website load automatically when you start Internet Explorer. By going to a webpage and then clicking the **Use Current** button, you make the page that is currently being displayed your home page. You can also configure it to show a blank page. Of course, to make the change take effect, you have to click the **Apply** or **OK** button.

Some organizations might configure the organization's home page as the default home page so that users cannot make changes to Internet Explorer using group policies. Other times, if you are experiencing an unexpected change in the home page, it was most likely caused by visiting a particular website (usually you have to click on **Yes** to change the website, but that is not always the case), installing a program that changes the Internet Explorer home page, or being infected by a virus or spyware.

Below the home page, you find the section to configure browsing history including how Internet Explorer uses temporary Internet files, which is used as a disk cache for Internet browsing. When you visit a website, parts of the webpage (such as pictures, sound, and video files) are copied on the system as a temporary Internet file so that on future visits to that site, it loads faster. If you click on the **Settings** button, you can configure the browser to check for newer versions of the saved page on every visit, every time you start Internet Explorer, automatically, or never. If you need to force Internet Explorer to reload a fresh webpage, you can hold down the Shift key while you click **Refresh**, or press **Shift+F5**. You can also click the **View Files** button to view the temporary Internet files.

You can determine how much disk space you want to use as a cache and where the folder is located that stores the temporary files. If you click on **View Files**, you open the folder that stores the temporary files so that you can inspect them directly.

History specifies the number of days that Internet Explorer should keep track of your viewed pages in the History list. IE creates shortcuts to pages you viewed in this and previous browsing sessions. If you are low on disk space, you might want to decrease the number. You can also clear your history from here.

The AutoComplete feature remembers previous entries that you made for web addresses, forms, and passwords. When you type information in one of these fields, AutoComplete suggests possible matches. These matches can include folder and program names you type into the Address bar, as well as search queries, stock quotes, or other information that you type in forms on webpages.

To use AutoComplete, start typing the information in the Address bar, in a field on a webpage, or in a box for a user name or password. If you have typed a similar entry before, AutoComplete lists possible matches as you type. If a suggestion in the list matches what you want to enter in that field, click the suggestion. If no suggestion matches what you are typing, continue typing.

To select AutoComplete settings in Internet Explorer, click **Tools** and then click **Internet Options**. On the Content tab, click **Settings** in the AutoComplete section. You can specify whether you want to use AutoComplete for web addresses, forms, user names, and passwords. You can also clear the history of previous AutoComplete entries. When typing information in web forms, and when typing passwords, you can remove an item from the list of suggestions by clicking the item and then pressing the Delete key.

As shown in Figure 13.2, if you click the **Advanced** tab, you can configure a wide range of configuration options, including disabling script debugging, enabling folder view for FTP sites, enabling a personalized favorites menu, enabling notification when downloads are complete, enabling automatic image resizing, and playing sounds and videos in webpages. It also has several security features, such as emptying temporary Internet Files when the browser is closed, enabling Profile Assisting, using SSL 2.0 or 3.0 (needed to connect to secure webpages as indicated by https://), warning about invalid site certificates, and warning if a form is being redirected.

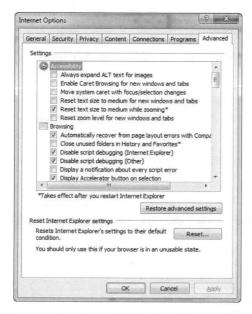

FIGURE 13.2 **Advanced settings in Internet Explorer.**

Plug-Ins/Add-Ons and Scripting Languages

To make Internet Explorer more powerful and more flexible and by adding additional functionality, Internet Explorer has the capability to use add-ons and scripting languages. The four basic add-ons supported by IE are

- ▶ Toolbars and extensions

- ▶ Search providers

- ▶ Accelerators

- ▶ InPrivate filtering

An add-in (also known as plug-in) is a software module that adds a specific feature or service to the browser to display or play different types of audio or video messages. Common plug-ins are Shockwave, RealMedia (RealAudio and Real Video), and Adobe Reader (used to read Portal Document Format (PDF).

In an effort to make browsing more functional, web developers created and enable active content. Active content, which is based on various add-ins, is done by using small executable or script code that is executed and shown within the client's web browser. Unfortunately, this feature is an added security risk where some scripts could be used to perform harmful actions on a client machine. Some of the most popular types of active content are VBScript, JavaScript, and ActiveX components.

To view current Add-ons, click the **Tools** button, click **Manage Add-ons**, and then click **Enable or Disable Add-ons**. In the Show box, select one of the following options:

- ▶ To display a complete list of the add-ons that reside on your computer, click **All Add-ons**.

- ▶ To display only those add-ons that were needed for the current webpage or a recently viewed webpage, click **Currently loaded Add-ons**.

- ▶ To display add-ons that were pre-approved by Microsoft, your computer manufacturer, or a service provider, click **Add-ons that run without permission**.

- ▶ To display only 32-bit ActiveX controls, click **Downloaded Controls**.

When you run an add-on for the first time, Internet Explorer asks permission, which should notify you if a website is secretly trying to run malicious code.

Internet Explorer has a list of pre-approved add-ons that have been checked and digitally signed. The add-on list can come from Microsoft, your computer manufacturer, your Internet Service provider (if you are using a private branded version of Internet Explorer), or your corporation's network administrator. The add-ons in this list are run without displaying the permissions dialog.

Add-ons are typically fine to use, but sometimes they force Internet Explorer to shut down unexpectedly. This can happen if the add-on was created for an earlier version of Internet Explorer or has a programming error. When you encounter a problematic add-on, you can disable it and/or report it to Microsoft. If disabling add-ons doesn't solve the problem, try resetting Internet Explorer to its default settings.

To permanently disable an add-on, do the following:

1. Click the **Tools** button and then click **Manage Add-ons**.

2. In the Show list, click **All add-ons**.

3. Click the add-on you want to disable (as shown in Figure 13.3) and then click **Disable**.

4. When you are finished, click the **Close** button.

To re-enable an add-on, you click the **Enable** button.

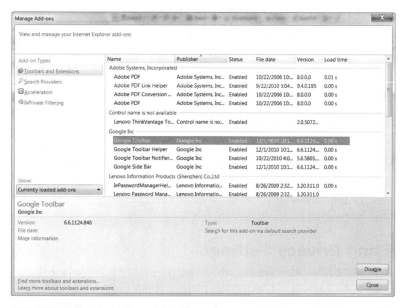

FIGURE 13.3 **Managing add-ons.**

To temporarily disable all add-ons, follow these steps:

1. Click the **Start** button and click **All Programs**.

2. Click **Accessories**.

3. Click **System Tools**.

4. Click **Internet Explorer (No Add-ons)**.

You can only delete ActiveX controls that you have downloaded and installed. You cannot delete ActiveX controls that were pre-installed or add-ons of any kind, but you can disable them. To delete an ActiveX control that you have installed, use Programs and Features in Windows Control Panel.

Internet Explorer Security Features

Internet Explorer offers a number of features to help protect your security and privacy when you browse the Web. They include

- ▶ **Phishing Filter**: Helps protect you from online phishing attacks, fraud, and spoofed websites

- ▶ **Protected Mode**: Helps protect you from websites that try to save files or install programs on your computer

- ▶ **Pop-up Blocker**: Helps block most pop-up windows

- ▶ **Add-on Manager**: Enables you to disable or allow web browser add-ons and delete unwanted ActiveX controls

- ▶ **Notification**: Notifies you when a website is trying to download files or software to your computer

- ▶ **Digital signatures**: Tells you who published a file and whether it has been altered since it was digitally signed

- ▶ **128-bit secure (SSL) connection for using secure websites**: Helps Internet Explorer create an encrypted connection with websites such as banks and online stores

Cookies and Privacy Settings

As spyware has become more common, the need to protect your personal information, including browser history, has grown. A cookie is a message given to a web browser by a web server, which is typically stored in a text file on the PC's hard drive. The message is then sent back to the server each time the browser requests a page from the server. The main purpose of cookies is to identify users and possibly prepare customized webpages for them. When you enter a website using cookies, you might be asked to fill out a form providing some information, such as your name and interests. This information is packaged into a cookie and sent to your web browser, which stores it for later use. The next time you go the same website, your browser sends the cookie to the web server. The server can use this information to present you with custom webpages. So, for example, instead of seeing just a generic welcome page you might see a welcome page with your name on it. Some uses of cookies include keeping track of what a person buys, using online ordering systems, personalizing a website, storing a person's profile, storing user IDs, and providing support to older web browsers that do not support host header names. A cookie cannot be used to get data from your hard drive, get your email addresses, or steal sensitive information about you.

From the General tab, you can delete the cookies that are stored on your hard drive. By clicking the Privacy tab, you can adjust the tab slider on the privacy scale to determine how much of your personal information can be accessed by websites and whether a website can save cookies on your computer.

To view privacy settings, select the Privacy tab from the Internet Options dialog box. To adjust your privacy settings, adjust the tab slider to a new position on the privacy scale. A description of the privacy settings that you select displays on the right side of the tab slider. The default level is Medium; it is recommended that you configure Medium or higher. You can also override the default for cookies in each security zone. In addition, you can override certain settings (automatic cookie handling and session cookies) by clicking the **Advanced** button, or you can allow or block cookies from individual websites by clicking the **Edit** button.

Many websites provide privacy statements that you view. A site's privacy policy tells you what kind of information the site collects and stores and what it does with the information. Information that you should be mostly concerned with is how the websites use personally identifiable information such as your name, email addresses, address, and telephone number. Websites also might provide a Platform for Privacy Preferences (P3P) privacy policy, which can be used by browsers to filter cookie transactions on the basis of a cookie's content and purpose. To view the Privacy Report, open the View menu and click **Privacy Report**. To view a site's privacy statement, select the website and click on the **Summary** button.

Content Zones

Typically when you are surfing the Internet, there are certain sites that you visit often and there are other sites which you visit for the first time. Typically, you tend to trust those sites that you visit often and you are less trusting of new sites, especially sites that are not popular. To help manage Internet Explorer security when visiting sites, Internet Explorer divides the network connection into four content types, which are as follows:

▶ **Internet Zone**: Anything that is not assigned to any other zone and anything that is not on your computer, or your organization's network (intranet). The default security level of the Internet zone is Medium.

▶ **Local Intranet Zone**: Computers that are part of the organization's network (intranet) that do not require a proxy server, as defined by the system administrator. These include sites specified on the Connections tab, network paths such as \\computername\foldername, and local intranet sites such as http://internal. You can add sites to this zone. The default security level for the Local internet zone is Medium=Low, which means Internet Explorer allows all cookies from websites in this zone to be saved on your computer and be read by the website that created them. Lastly, if the website requires NTLM or integrated authentication, it automatically uses your username and password.

▶ **Trusted Sites Zone**: Contains trusted sites that from which you believe you can download or run files without damaging your computer or data or that you consider are not security risks. You can assign sites to this zone. The default security level for the Trusted sites zone is Low, which means Internet Explorer allows all cookies from websites in this zone to be saved on your computer and be read by the website that created them.

▶ **Restricted Sites Zone**: Contains sites that you do not trust from which downloading or running files might damage your computer or data or that are considered a security risk. You can assign sites to this zone. The default security level for the Restricted sites zone is High, which means Internet Explorer blocks all cookies from websites in this zone.

For each of the web content zones, there is a default security level. The security levels available in Internet Explorer are

▶ **High**: Excludes any content that can damage your computer.

▶ **Medium**: Warns you before running potentially damaging content.

▶ **Low**: Does not warn you before running potentially damaging content.

► **Custom**: A security setting of your own design. Use this level to customize the behavior of Active Data Objects (AD) and Remote Data Services (RDS) objects in a specific zone.

Whenever you access a website, Internet Explorer checks the security settings for the zone of the website. To tell which zones the current webpage falls into, you look at the right side of the Internet Explorer status bar. Besides adjusting the zones or assigning the zones or assigning a website to a zone, you can also customize settings for a zone by importing a privacy settings file from a certificate authority.

To modify the security level for a web content zone, do the following:

1. Click the **Tools** button and then click **Internet Options**.

2. In the Internet Options dialog box, on the Security tab, click the zone on which you want to set the security level.

3. Drag the slider to set the security level to **High**, **Medium**, or **Low**. Internet Explorer describes each option to help you decide which level to choose, as shown in Figure 13.4. You are prompted to confirm any reduction in security level. You can also choose the **Custom level** button for more detailed control.

4. Click **OK** to close the Internet Options dialog box.

FIGURE 13.4   **Security options within Internet Explorer.**

Software publisher certificates (third-party digital certificates) are used to validate software code such as Java or ActiveX controls or plug-ins. Depending on the security settings for a zone, when software code is accessed from a website you automatically download the software code, disable the software code, or prompt to download the software code via a security warning. If you open the Tools menu and select **Internet Options**, select the **Security** tab, and click the **Custom Level** button, you can select **enable**, **disable**, or **prompt** to download ActiveX controls (signed and unsigned) and scripting of Java applets.

To view the certificates for Internet Explorer, open the Internet Options dialog box, click the **Content** tab and click on the **Certificates** button. To see list of certificates, click the appropriate certificates. From here, you can also import and export individual certificates.

Dynamic Security and Protected Mode

Because threats can come from any place at any time, Internet Explorer has added several features to protect your system. Dynamic Security options for Internet Explorer 8.0 offer multiple security features to defend your computer against malware and data theft. The Security Status Bar keeps you notified of the website security and privacy settings by using color-coded notifications next to the address bar. Some of these features include

▶ Address Bar turns green to indicate website bearing new High Assurance certificates, indicating the site owner has completed extensive identity verification checks.

▶ Phishing Filter notifications, certificate names, and the gold padlock icon are now also adjacent to the address bar for better visibility.

▶ Certificate and privacy detail information can easily be displayed with a single click on the Security Status Bar.

▶ The Address Bar is displayed to the user for every window, whether it's a pop-up or standard window, which helps to block malicious sites from emulating trusted sites.

▶ To help protect you against phishing sites, Internet Explorer warns you when visiting potential or known fraudulent sites and blocks the site if appropriate. The opt-in filter is updated several times per hour with the latest security information from Microsoft and several industry partners.

▶ International Domain Name Anti-Spoofing notifies you when visually similar characters in the URL are not expressed in the same language.

To protect your system even further, Internet Explorer includes the following features:

- ▶ ActiveX Opt-in disables nearly all pre-installed ActiveX controls to prevent potentially vulnerable controls from being exposed to attack. You can easily enable or disable ActiveX controls as needed through the Information Bar and the Add-on Manager.

- ▶ Cross-Domain Barriers limits scripts on webpages from interacting with content from other domains or windows. This enhanced safeguard helps to protect against malicious software by limiting the potential for malicious websites to manipulate flaws in other websites or cause you to download undesired content or software.

If Internet Explorer is still using its original settings, you see the Information bar in the following circumstances:

- ▶ If a website tries to install an ActiveX control on your computer or run an ActiveX control in an unsafe manner.

- ▶ If a website tries to open a pop-up window.

- ▶ If a website tries to download a file to your computer.

- ▶ If a website tries to run active content on your computer.

- ▶ If your security settings are below recommended levels.

- ▶ If you access an intranet webpage, but have not turned on intranet address checking.

- ▶ If you started Internet Explorer with add-ons disabled.

- ▶ If you need to install an updated ActiveX control or add-on program.

- ▶ The webpage address can be displayed with native language letters or symbols, but you don't have the language installed.

When you see a message in the Information bar, click the message to see more information or to take action.

To stop the information bar from blocking file and software downloads, do the following:

1. Click to open **Internet Explorer**.

2. Click the **Tools** button and then click **Internet Options**.

3. Click the **Security** tab and then click **Custom level**.

4. Do one or both of the following:

▶ To turn off the Information bar for file downloads, scroll to the Downloads section of the list and then, under Automatic prompting for file downloads, click **Enable**.

▶ To turn off the Information bar for ActiveX controls, scroll to the ActiveX controls and plug-ins section of the list and then, under Automatic prompting for ActiveX controls, click **Enable**.

5. Click **OK**, click **Yes** to confirm that you want to make the change, and then click **OK** again.

Table 13.1 lists some of the more common messages that might appear in the Information bar, along with a description of what each message means.

TABLE 13.1 **Common Messages Found in Internet Explorer 8.0**

Message	What It Means
To help protect your security, Internet Explorer stopped this site from installing an ActiveX control on your computer. Click here for options.	The webpage tried to install an Active X control and Internet Explorer blocked it. If you want to install the ActiveX control and you trust the publisher of the ActiveX control, right-click the information and select Install Software.
Pop-up blocked. To see this pop-up or additional options, click here.	Pop-up Blocker has blocked a pop-up window. You can turn Pop-up Blocker off or allow pop-ups temporarily by clicking the Information bar.
This website is using a scripted window to ask you for information. If you trust this website, click here to allow scripted windows.	Internet Explorer has blocked a website that tried to display a separate window such as a login screen in an attempt to gather confidential information. If you trust the website, click the Information bar and click select Temporarily Allow Scripted Windows or Allow websites to prompt for information using scripted windows customer security setting.
To help protect your security, Internet Explorer blocked this site from downloading files to your computer. Click here for options.	A webpage tried to download a file that you might not have requested. If you want to download the file, click the Information bar and then click Download File.
Your security settings do not allow websites to use ActiveX controls installed on your computer. This page may not display correctly. Click here for options.	The website tried to install an ActiveX control but your security settings did not allow it. This is caused when a website is listed in the Restricted Site list. If you trust the site, remove the site from the Restricted site. If the problem still exists, try adding the site to the Trusted sites list.

TABLE 13.1　**Continued**

Message	What It Means
Internet Explorer has blocked this site from using an ActiveX control in an unsafe manner. As a result, this page may not display correctly.	A website tried to access an ActiveX control on your computer without your permission.

Internet Explorer's protected mode is a feature that makes it more difficult for malicious software to be installed on your computer. In addition, it enables users to install wanted software when they are logged in as a standard user instead of an administrator. Protected mode is turned on by default and an icon appears on the status bar to let you know that it's running. When you try to install software, protected mode warns you when webpages try to install software or if a software program runs outside of protected mode. If you trust the program and want to allow it to run on any website, select the **Always allow websites to use this program to open web content** checkbox.

ExamAlert

Protected mode makes it more difficult for malicious software to be installed on your machine.

If you suspect problems caused by Protected Mode, you can try the following:

- ▶ Move the site to the Trusted Sites zone
- ▶ Disable protected mode in IE
- ▶ Modify the application

InPrivate Browsing

InPrivate Browsing (new to IE 8) enables you to surf the Web without leaving a trail in Internet Explorer. This helps prevent anyone else who might be using your computer from seeing what sites you visited and what you looked at on the Web. You can start InPrivate Browsing from the New Tab page, as shown in Figure 13.5, or the Safety button.

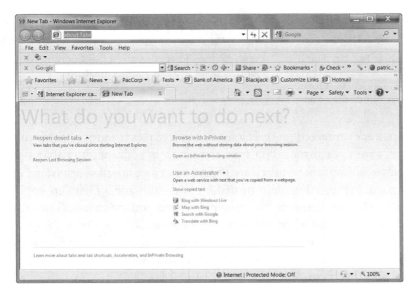

FIGURE 13.5   **The New Tab page.**

When you start InPrivate Browsing, Internet Explorer opens a new browser window. The protection that InPrivate Browsing provides is in effect only during the time that you use that window. You can open as many tabs as you want in that window, and they are all protected by InPrivate Browsing. However, if you open another browser window, that window is not protected by InPrivate Browsing. To end your InPrivate Browsing session, close the browser window.

While you are surfing the Web using InPrivate Browsing, Internet Explorer stores some information (such as cookies and temporary Internet files) so the webpages you visit work correctly. However, at the end of your InPrivate Browsing session, this information is discarded. The following table describes which information InPrivate Browsing discards when you close the browser and how it is affected during your browsing session:

▸ **Cookies**: Kept in memory so pages work correctly, but cleared when you close the browser.

▸ **Temporary Internet files**: Stored on disk so pages work correctly, but deleted when you close the browser.

▸ **Webpage history**: This information is not stored.

▸ **Form data and passwords**: This information is not stored.

▶ **Anti-phishing cache**: Temporary information is encrypted and stored so pages work correctly.

▶ **Address bar and search AutoComplete**: This information is not stored.

▶ **Automatic Crash Restore (ACR)**: ACR can restore a tab when it crashes in a session, but if the whole window crashes, data is deleted and the window cannot be restored.

▶ **Document Object Model (DOM) storage**: The DOM storage is a kind of "super cookie" web developers can use to retain information. Like regular cookies, they are not kept after the window is closed.

InPrivate doesn't clear any history or information about toolbars or browser extensions that is stored on your computer. To help protect your privacy, Internet Explorer disables all toolbars and extensions by default in an InPrivate Browsing window. If you would prefer to enable specific toolbars and extensions during a browsing session, you can do the following:

1. In Internet Explorer, click **Tools** and then click **Manage Add-ons**.

2. Click **Toolbars and extensions**, click the toolbar or extension you want to use, and then click **Enable**.

3. Click **Close**.

Parental Controls

If you have children who use your computer, you can take extra steps to make sure that they are protected when using Internet Explorer. As mentioned in Chapter 3, Windows 7 offers Parental Controls that enable parents to control browsing behavior in order to help keep children safer online. A child's browsing session can even be examined by a parent afterward, and it cannot be removed without the parent's permission. You can configure Parental Controls from the User Accounts and Family Safety section of Control Panel.

Certificates for Secure Websites

When you visit a website that begins with https, you are visiting a secure website. Hypertext Transfer Protocol Secure (HTTPS) is a combination of the Hypertext Transfer Protocol with the SSL/TLS protocol to provide encryption and secure identification of the server. Secure Sockets Layer (SSL) is a protocol for transmitting private documents via the Internet. SSL uses a cryptographic system that uses two keys to encrypt data—a public key known to everyone and a private or secret key known only to the recipient of the message. Internet Explorer supports SSL and many websites use the protocol to obtain confidential user information, such as credit card numbers.

Certificates provide website identification and encryption for secure connections, as shown in Figure 13.6. If you open Internet Options and click the Content tab, you can remove personal security information that is stored when you use a smart card or public computer kiosk by clicking the **Clear SSL state** button. You can also view or manage the certificates that are installed on your computer by clicking the **Certificates and Publishers** button.

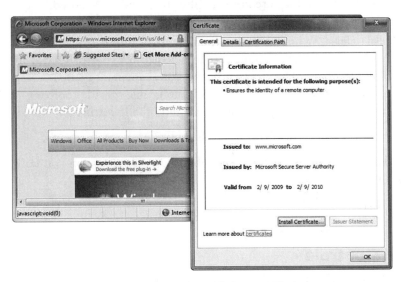

FIGURE 13.6   **Digital certificate viewed in Internet Explorer.**

Using Offline Mode and Saving Webpages

You can configure Internet Explorer to view webpages while you are not connected to the network or web server. To enable a website to be offline, you just add your website to your favorites while selecting the Make available offline option.

You can also save a webpage as a file so that you can access at a later time. To save a webpage, do the following:

1. Go to the webpage you want to save.

2. Click the **Page** button and then click **Save As**.

3. Navigate to the folder where you want to save the webpage.

4. Type a new name in the File name box if you want to change the name.

5. In the Save as type box, do one of the following:

   ▶ To save all the files associated with the page, including graphics, frames, and style sheets in their original format, click **Webpage, complete**.

   ▶ To save all information as a single file, click **Web Archive, single file (*.mht)**.

   ▶ To save just the current HTML page, without graphics, sounds, or other files, click **Webpage, HTML only**.

   ▶ To save just the text from the current webpage, click **Text File**.

6. Click **Save**.

Lastly, you can also highlight most webpages or content on a webpage, right-click the highlighted area, and copy the content to the clipboard. You can then paste it into Microsoft Word, WordPad, or some other program.

RSS Feeds

RSS, short for RDF Site Summary or Rich Site Summary, is an XML format for syndicating web content. A website that wants to allow other sites to publish some of its content creates an RSS document and registers the document with an RSS publisher. A user who can read RSS-distributed content can use the content on a different site. Syndicated content includes such data as news feeds, events listings, news stories, headlines, project updates, excerpts from discussion forums, or even corporate information.

A feed can have the same content as a webpage, but it's often formatted differently. When you subscribe, Internet Explorer automatically checks the website and downloads new content so you can see what is new since you last visited the feed.

To see if a webpage has a feed, the Feeds button changes color, letting you know that feeds are available on the webpage. To subscribe to a feed, do the following:

1. Open **Internet Explorer**.

2. Go to the website that has the feed you want to subscribe to.

3. Click the **Feeds** button to discover feeds on the webpage.

4. Click a feed (if more than one is available). If only one feed is available, you go directly to that page.

5. Click the **Subscribe to this Feed** button and then click **Subscribe to this Feed**.

6. Type a name for the feed and select the folder to create the feed in.

7. Click **Subscribe**.

To view feeds, go to the Feed tab in the Favorites Center. To view your feeds, click the **Favorites Center** button and then click **Feeds**. You can also use other programs, such as email clients like Microsoft Outlook and Windows Sidebar, to read the feeds set up with Internet Explorer. To configure how often feeds are updated or if a sound is played when a feed is found, open Internet Options, select the **Content** tab, and click the **Settings** button.

Reset Internet Explorer to Default Settings

To reset Internet Explorer settings and to help troubleshoot problems, you can remove all changes that have been made to Internet Explorer since it was installed without deleting your favorites or feeds. To reset Internet Explorer, do the following:

1. Close all Internet Explorer or Windows Explorer windows.

2. Click to open **Internet Explorer**.

3. Click the **Tools** button and then click **Internet Options**.

4. Click the **Advanced** tab and then click **Reset**.

5. Click **Reset**.

6. When you are done, click **Close** and then click **OK**.

7. Close Internet Explorer and reopen it for the changes to take effect.

You can also restore the options in the Advanced tab of the Internet Options dialog box by clicking the **Restore Advanced Settings** button on the Advanced tab.

Exam Alert

To reset Windows Explorer, click on the **Reset** button within the Advanced tab. If you only want to reset the Advanced options, click the **Restore Advanced Settings** button.

Compatibility View Mode

Websites designed for earlier versions of Internet Explorer might not display correctly in the current version. Often, you can improve how a website looks in Internet Explorer by using Compatibility View.

When you turn on Compatibility View, the webpage you're viewing (and other webpages within the website's domain) are displayed as if you were using an earlier version of Internet Explorer.

If Internet Explorer recognizes a webpage that isn't compatible, you see the Compatibility View button on the Address bar. To turn Compatibility View on or off, click the **Compatibility View** button, or follow these steps:

1. Click to open Internet Explorer.

2. Click the **Tools** button and then click **Compatibility View**.

The website is displayed in Compatibility View until you turn it off or the website is updated to display correctly in the current version of Internet Explorer.

Using Accelerators

You can use accelerators with text that you select on a webpage to perform such tasks as opening a street address in a mapping website or looking up the dictionary definition for a word. You can also choose the web services or websites that accelerators use to handle different types of tasks. Internet Explorer comes with a selection of accelerators included by default, but you can add or remove them as you like.

When you first start Internet Explorer, you can accept a selection of default accelerators, or you can choose your own from an online list of accelerators.

The list of new accelerators is frequently updated, so be sure to check back from time to time.

To use an accelerator, follow these steps:

1. Click to open **Internet Explorer**.

2. Go to the webpage that contains the text that you want to use with an Accelerator and select the text.

3. Click the **Accelerator** button to display a list of Accelerators.

If you rest your mouse pointer over each accelerator, you see a preview of the information or content. In many cases, the preview tells you what you want to know, such as a word definition or translation. If not, click the accelerator and Internet Explorer opens the web service using the text you've highlighted.

You can also use an accelerator from the new tab page with text you've copied to the Clipboard, such as from an email message or word-processing document. For example, if you receive a street address in an email that you want to get directions for, you can copy the address to the Clipboard, open Internet Explorer, and open a new tab. On the new tab page, under Use an accelerator, click **Show copied text** if you want to check the text you copied and then click the accelerator you've chosen for mapping.

Although Internet Explorer comes with a selection of accelerators to get you started, you might want to take a look at some of the other accelerators that are available. To find new accelerators, follow these steps:

1. Click to open **Internet Explorer**.

2. Click the **Tools** button and then click **Manage Add-ons**.

3. In Manage Add-ons, under Add-on Types, click **Accelerators** to display a list of your current Accelerators.

4. At the bottom of the screen, click **Find More Accelerators**.

5. On the Internet Explorer Gallery webpage, click the accelerator you want to install and then click **Install Accelerator**.

6. In the Add Accelerator dialog box, do one of the following:

   ▶ If you're adding a new accelerator, click **Add**. When you add an accelerator, you can also select the **Make this my default provider for this Accelerator Category** checkbox.

> ▶ If you're replacing an existing Accelerator, click **Replace**.

> ▶ If you're not sure you trust the website listed in the From field, click **Cancel**.

Search Providers

By default, the Instant Search box found in Internet Explorer enables users to perform searches using Microsoft's Bing engine. However, you can add other search engines such as Google and Webopedia to quickly use these services to find what you are looking for.

To add search providers to the Instant Search List, do the following:

1. Open **Internet Explorer**.

2. Click the down arrow on the right side of the Instant Search box and then, from the context menu, select **Find More Providers**.

3. Click the **Add to Internet Explorer** button for one of the Web Search or Topic Search providers.

4. If you want the selected provider to replace Bing as the IE default, select the **Make this my default search provider** checkbox. If you want the provider to provide suggestions as you type searches, select the **Use search suggestions from this provider** checkbox. Then click **Add** to add the selected provider to the Instant Search list.

5. To add a search provider that does not appear on the page, click the **Create your own search provider** link at the bottom of the page to open the Create your own search provider page.

Cram Exam

1. How can you configure IE to automatically delete temporary Internet files when you close Internet Explorer?

   ○ **A.** Modify the properties of the Recycle Bin

   ○ **B.** Modify the security level of the Internet zone

   ○ **C.** Create a script and execute it with Task Scheduler

   ○ **D.** Modify the advanced settings from the Internet Options

2. You have a website that appears not to display properly. What can you do for the website to display properly?

   ○ **A.** Enable an accelerator

   ○ **B.** Enable a SmartScreen Filter

   ○ **C.** Enable Compatibility View

   ○ **D.** Enable a RSS feed

3. What do you use that helps prevent applications from being installed when visiting a website?

   ○ **A.** InPrivate Browsing

   ○ **B.** Protected mode

   ○ **C.** Enable Parental Control

   ○ **D.** Enable Compatibility View

Cram Exam Answers

1. **D** is correct. If you go into Advanced settings from Internet Options, you can configure IE to automatically delete their temporary files. Answer A is incorrect because the Recycle Bin is a temporary place to hold delete files. It does not actually delete files. Answer B is incorrect because configure zones do not delete temporary files. Answer C is incorrect because you cannot configure the Task Scheduler to delete temporary files when you close Internet Explorer.

2. **C** is correct. Websites designed for earlier versions of Internet Explorer might not display correctly in the current version. Often, you can improve how a website looks in Internet Explorer by using Compatibility View. Answer A is incorrect because an accelerator is a form of selection-based search that enables a user to invoke an online service from any other page using only the mouse. Answer B is incorrect because a SmartScreen Filter includes protection from socially engineered malware, which helps identify sites that have been labeled as an imposter or harmful (in other words, phishing). Answer D is incorrect because RSS enables a user to read RSS-distributed content on a different site using IE.

3. **B** is correct. Internet Explorer's protected mode is a feature that makes it more difficult for malicious software to be installed on your computer. In addition, it enables users to install wanted software when they are logged in as a standard user instead of an administrator. Answer A is incorrect because the InPrivate Browsing enables you to surf the Web without leaving a trail in Internet Explorer. Answer C is incorrect because parental control is used to help keep children safer online, including restricting websites inappropriate for children. Answer D is incorrect because Compatibility View is used to allow websites that do not display correctly in Internet Explorer 8.

Review Questions

1. You work as the desktop support technician at Acme.com. How do you reset Internet Explorer to its original settings?

   ○ **A.** Reinstall Internet Explorer 8.0

   ○ **B.** Navigate to the Security tab in Internet Options and click Reset all zones to default level

   ○ **C.** Navigate to the Advanced tab in Internet Options and click Restore advanced settings

   ○ **D.** Navigate to the Advanced tab and click **Reset**

2. You work as the desktop support technician at Acme.com. How do you remove the stored passwords from a computer?

   ○ **A.** On the Security tab in Internet Options, set the Internet zone security to High.

   ○ **B.** On the Privacy tab in Internet Options, set the level to Medium.

   ○ **C.** On the Privacy tab in Internet Options, set the level to High.

   ○ **D.** Navigate to the Advanced tab in Internet Options and click Restore advanced settings.

   ○ **E.** Click Tools in the Internet Explorer and then click Delete Browsing History. Click Delete passwords.

3. How do you prevent passwords from being stored locally when visiting websites that require usernames and passwords?

   ○ **A.** On the Security tab in Internet Options, set the Internet zone security to High.

   ○ **B.** On the Privacy tab in Internet Options, set the level to Medium

   ○ **C.** On the Privacy tab in Internet Options, set the level to High.

   ○ **D.** On the Content tab in Internet Options, click the AutoComplete Settings button and clear the Usernames and passwords on forms checkbox.

   ○ **E.** Click Tools in the Internet Explorer and then click Delete Browsing History. Click Delete passwords.

4. You have a user who is complaining that the images shown in Internet Explorer are too small. What do you need to do?

   ○ **A.** You need to decrease the screen resolution.

   ○ **B.** You need to increase the screen resolution.

   ○ **C.** You need to decrease the zoom level for the tab.

   ○ **D.** You need to increase the zoom level for the tab.

5. You work as part of the IT support staff at Acme.com. You have a user that saves files that she downloads from various websites. You want to make sure that when she visits these websites that those websites don't modify those files that she saved previously. What do you need to do?

   ○ **A.** Disable all ActiveX controls that are currently loaded

   ○ **B.** Enable the Phishing Filter

   ○ **C.** Change the security level for the Internet zone to High

   ○ **D.** Enable Protected Mode option

6. You work as the desktop support technician at Acme.com. When a user clicks a link in a website, nothing happens. What do you think the problem is?

   ○ **A.** You need to enable an Add-on that the link points to.

   ○ **B.** You need to open the Internet Options dialog box. On the Security tab, add the URL to the Trusted sites list.

   ○ **C.** You need to open the Pop-up Blocker Settings dialog box. Add the URL to the Allowed sites list.

   ○ **D.** You need to open the Internet Options dialog box. On the Privacy tab, add the URL to the Allowed sites list.

   ○ **E.** You need to open the Internet Options dialog box. On the Advanced tab, choose the Disable Phishing Filter option.

7. What technology in Internet Explorer is used to protect you from spoofed sites that might try to trick you into divulging confidential information?

   ○ **A.** Protected mode

   ○ **B.** Phishing filter

   ○ **C.** Junk mail filter

   ○ **D.** Fake Site filter

8. What can be done to notify you when a website has changed?

   ○ **A.** Configure autoupdate within IIS.

   ○ **B.** Configure dynamic update with IIS.

   ○ **C.** If a website supports RSS, configure an RSS feed.

   ○ **D.** Close Internet Explorer and restart it.

9. You want to delete your cookies and temporary files used by Internet Explorer. You open up Internet options. Which tab enables you to accomplish this?

   ○ **A.** General tab

   ○ **B.** Security tab

   ○ **C.** Privacy tab

   ○ **D.** Connections tab

10. Which of the following does InPrivate Browsing do? (Choose all that apply.)

- **A.** Clear out all cookies
- **B.** Delete temporary files
- **C.** Prevent the storage of form data and passwords
- **D.** Enable anti-phishing technology

Review Question Answers

1. Answer **D** is correct. To reset Internet Explorer to its original settings, navigate to the Advanced tab and click Reset. Answer A is incorrect because reinstalling Internet Explorer does not generally overwrite the settings that are already configured. Answer B is incorrect because resetting zones only affects information specified in the security zones. Answer C is incorrect because this only resets the Advanced options.

2. Answer **E** is correct. To delete saved passwords in Internet Explorer, you must delete the browsing history. Answers A, B, and C are incorrect because these do not affect any saved passwords. Answer D is incorrect because passwords are not stored with the Advanced settings.

3. Answer **D** is correct. To prevent passwords from being stored, you have to configure AutoComplete. Answers A, B, and C do not affect AutoComplete and passwords. Answer E is used to delete saved passwords.

4. Answer **D** is correct. When you have trouble seeing an image, you can use the zoom feature. Answers A and B are incorrect because they affect all programs. Answer C is incorrect because decreasing the zoom makes the image smaller.

5. Answer **D** is correct. Protected mode helps protect you from websites that try to save files or install programs on your computer. Answer A is incorrect because disabling all ActiveX components might disable functionality that you might use for other websites. Answer B is incorrect because the phishing filter is used to stop users from being tricked into fake sites that emulate corporate sites in an attempt to steal confidential information. Answer C might or might not affect the control, but it is never stated what level the website is.

6. Answer **B** is correct. When you click some links, the links open separate windows. If you have a pop-up blocker set up, the site might be blocked. Answer A is incorrect because add-ons are designed to run within a website, not as a standalone application. Adding a URL to a trusted site might have some effect on functionality, but it does not allow or disallow the entire window for opening. Answers C and D are incorrect because neither of these affect whether a website opens.

7. Answer **B** is correct. Some sites are created to look as other sites and are used to lure people to divulge confidential information. Because these sites are "fishing" for information, these sites are referred to as *phishing*. Answer A is incorrect because protected mode tries to secure the Internet Explorer by securing other files. Answer C is incorrect because a junk mail filter is used in email. Answer D is incorrect because there is no such thing as a fake site filter.

8. Answer **C** is correct. RSS feeds are used to get automatic updates and notifications when a website posts something new. Answer B is incorrect because dynamic updates are a set of technology to help protect your system when using Internet Explorer. Answer A is incorrect because configuring autoupdate within IIS is used to automatically update Windows security patches and fixes. Answer D is incorrect because closing Internet Explorer and restarting opens up the home page again. It does not notify when other websites get updated.

9. Answer **A** is correct. The General tab is where you can delete temporary files, history, cookies, saved passwords and web form information. Answer B is incorrect because the Security tab is where you configure the security zones. Answer C is incorrect because the Privacy tab is used to configure the use of cookies and to enable or disable the pop-up blocker. Answer D is incorrect because the Connections tab is used to configure IE to use a proxy server or an Internet connection.

10. Answers **A**, **B**, and **C** are correct. InPrivate Browsing (new to IE 8) enables you to surf the Web without leaving a trail in Internet Explorer. This includes clearing out cookies, deleting temporary files, preventing the storage of form data and passwords, and not storing webpage history. Answer D is incorrect because although InPrivate Browsing encrypts and stores the anti-phishing cache, it does not enable or disable anti-phishing technology.

CHAPTER 14

Mobile Computers and Remote Management

This chapter covers the following 70-680 Objectives:

▶ Configuring Network Connectivity:

  ▶ Configure remote management

▶ Configuring Mobile Computing:

  ▶ Configure remote connections

  ▶ Configure mobility options

Mobile computers are computers that are meant to be mobile. Just like desktop computers, mobile computers (including laptops, notebook computers, tablet PCs, and Ultra-Mobile computers) can come in various sizes and configurations. Mobile computers have an inherent set of challenges as they are not always connected to the Internet or corporate offices where they can be managed and they are designed to be portable, to conserve power for a longer battery life, and to run cooler, which usually affect performance.

A mobile device is a computing device that has been optimized for specific mobile computing tasks. Mobile device types include the following:

▶ PDAs

▶ Windows Mobile devices

▶ Portable media players

▶ Mobile phones

Mobile devices offer their own challenges because they are often configured to synchronize with a desktop or mobile computer to obtain data.

While you are using mobile computers as well as desktops, you might have a need to remotely connect to and control another computer or server. Windows 7 offers several tools that enable you to do that, including Remote Desktop, Remote Assistant, and PowerShell.

Control Panel and Windows Mobility Center

▶ **Configure mobility options**

▶ **Configure performance settings**

Cram**Saver**

1. Which of the following do you find in the Mobility Center? (Choose all that apply.)

   ○ **A.** Volume

   ○ **B.** Presentation Settings

   ○ **C.** Display Settings

   ○ **D.** External Display

2. What command would you use to turn off the hibernate function and to remove the hiberfil.sys file?

   ○ **A.** Run the `powercfg -hibernate off` command

   ○ **B.** Open a command prompt and delete the hiberfil.sys file

   ○ **C.** Open the Power settings within the Control Panel and uncheck Enable Hibernate option

   ○ **D.** Run the `Hibernate On` command

3. What application do you use to manage your offline folders?

   ○ **A.** System Configuration tool

   ○ **B.** Offline folder console

   ○ **C.** Sync Center

   ○ **D.** Mobility Share tool

Answers

1. **A**, **B**, and **D** are correct. The Mobility Center includes Volume, Battery Status, Wireless Network, External Display, Sync Center, Presentation Settings, and Screen Rotation. Because the Display Settings are not listed, Answer C is incorrect as you cannot modify your display settings from the Mobility Center.

2. **A** is correct. The `powercfg` command is a command-line tool that enables you to control the power settings on a system. To disable hibernate and remove the hiberfil.sys file, you use the `powercfg -hibernate` command. Answer B is incorrect because deleting the hiberfil.sys command does not disable hibernate. Answer C is incorrect because there is no Enable Hibernate option. Answer D is incorrect because there is no `Hibernate On` command.

3. **C** is correct. When you set up the synchronization, you may set up a one-way or two-way synchronization. To configure Offline Files, click Open the Sync Center and then click Manage offline files. Answer A is incorrect because the System Configuration tool is a tool to troubleshoot startup problems. Answers B and D are incorrect because there is neither an Offline folder console nor a Mobility Share tool.

All mobile and power settings are configured within the Control Panel. To make finding these settings quick and easy, Windows 7 includes the Windows Mobility Center, which provides a single location that enables you to quickly adjust mobile PC settings, as shown in Figure 14.1. Depending on your system, the Mobility Center window has some, but perhaps not all, of the following tiles:

▶ **Volume**: Move the slider to adjust the speaker volume of your mobile PC or select the Mute check box

▶ **Battery Status**: View how much charge remains on your battery or select a power plan from the list

▶ **Wireless Network**: View the status of your wireless network connection or turn your wireless adapter on or off

▶ **External Display**: Connect an additional monitor to your mobile PC or customize the display settings

▶ **Sync Center**: View the status of an in-progress file sync, start a new sync or set up a sync partnership, and adjust your settings in Sync Center

▶ **Presentation Settings**: Adjust settings, such as the speaker volume and the desktop background image, for giving a presentation

▶ **Screen Rotation**: Change the orientation of your Tablet PC screen, from portrait to landscape, or vice versa

If a tile doesn't appear, it might be because the required hardware, such as a wireless network adapter, or drivers are missing.

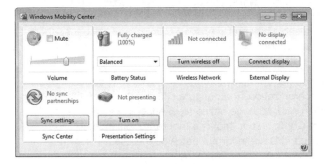

FIGURE 14.1   **Windows Mobility Center.**

If you need to make additional adjustments to your mobile PC settings that require you to access Control Panel, click the icon on a tile to open Control Panel for that setting. For example, you can select an existing power plan from the Battery Status tile, or you can click the icon on the tile to open Power Options in Control Panel to create a power plan.

The Mobility Center can be opened using any one of the following methods:

▶ Click the **Start** button, click **Control Panel**, click **Mobile PC**, and then click **Windows Mobility Center**.

▶ Click the battery meter icon in the notification area in the Windows taskbar, and then click **Windows Mobility Center**.

▶ Press the **Windows logo key + X**.

Configuring Presentation Settings for Mobile PCs

Presentation settings are options on your mobile PC that you can apply when giving a presentation. If you've ever had your display screen turn black during a presentation, you'll appreciate that you can automatically turn off your screen saver every time that you give a presentation.

When presentation settings are turned on, your mobile PC stays awake and system notifications are turned off. You can also choose to turn off the screen saver, adjust the speaker volume, and change your desktop background image. Your settings are automatically saved and applied every time that you give a presentation, unless you manually turn them off.

You can turn on presentation settings by using one of the following methods:

1. Open the Windows Mobility Center by clicking the **Start** button, clicking **Control Panel**, clicking **Mobile PC**, and then clicking **Windows Mobility Center**.

2. On the Presentation Settings tile, click **Turn on**.

3. Click **OK**.

To turn presentation settings on or off for the current monitor or projector that the mobile PC is connected to, follow these steps:

1. Open Windows Mobility Center by clicking the **Start** button, clicking **Control Panel**, clicking **Mobile PC**, and then clicking **Windows Mobility Center**.

2. On the Presentation Settings tile, click the **Change Presentation Settings** icon to generate the window in Figure 14.2.

3. In the Presentation Settings dialog box, click **Connected displays**.

4. In the Current Displays dialog box, select or clear the **I always give a presentation when I use this display configuration** checkbox, and then click **OK**.

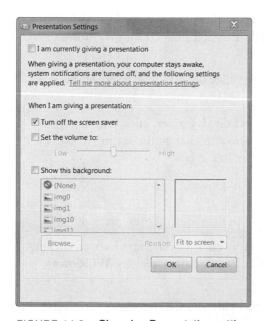

FIGURE 14.2   **Changing Presentation settings.**

Presentation settings automatically turn off when you disconnect your mobile PC from a network projector or additional monitor, and when you shut down or log off from your mobile PC. Or, you can manually turn off presentation settings:

1. Open Windows Mobility Center by clicking the **Start** button, clicking **Control Panel**, clicking **Mobile PC**, and then clicking **Windows Mobility Center**.

2. On the Presentation Settings tile, click **Turn off**.

To customize presentation settings:

1. Open Windows Mobility Center by clicking the **Start** button, clicking **Control Panel**, clicking **Mobile PC**, and then clicking **Windows Mobility Center**.

2. On the Presentation Settings tile, click the **Change Presentation Settings** icon.

3. In the Presentation Settings dialog box, adjust settings for giving a presentation and then click **OK**.

To keep the display on during presentations:

1. Open Windows Mobility Center by clicking the **Start** button, clicking **Control Panel**, clicking **Mobile PC**, and then clicking **Windows Mobility Center**.

2. On the Presentation Settings tile, click the **Change Presentation Settings** icon.

3. Expand **Display**, expand **Turn off display after**, click **On battery** or **Plugged in,** and then click the arrow to change the setting to **Never**. You can also type the word **Never** in the box.

4. Click **OK** and then click **Save changes**.

To prevent the mobile PC from going to sleep during presentations:

1. Open Windows Mobility Center by clicking the **Start** button, clicking **Control Panel**, clicking **Mobile PC**, and then clicking **Windows Mobility Center**.

2. On the Presentation Settings tile, click the **Change Presentation Settings** icon.

3. Expand **Sleep**, expand **Sleep after**, click **On battery** or **Plugged in**, and then click the arrow to change the setting to **Never**. You can also type the word `Never` in the box.

4. Click **OK** and then click **Save changes**.

Power Management

One of the goals of mobile computers is to run off the battery for as long as possible. Therefore, the mobile computers use components that typically use less power than components that you would find in a desktop computer. For example:

▶ Mobile computers use processors that run on a lower voltage and consume less power.

▶ Mobile processors, including Intel SpeedStep and AMD PowerNow, have the capability to adjust voltage and the capability to throttle (temporarily run at a slower clock speed) to use even less power when running off the battery.

▶ LCD monitor can be dimmed so that it consumes less power.

▶ Mechanical Hard drives can be spun down when not in use.

> **Note**
>
> Although Solid State Drives (SSD) are based on a relatively new technology, SSDs are starting to replace traditional mechanical devices. Because Solid State Drives do not contain mechanical parts, they consume less power, allowing for a longer battery life.

Power Plans

A power plan (formerly known as a power scheme in earlier versions of Windows) is a collection of hardware and system settings that manages how your computer uses and conserves power. You can use power plans to save energy, maximize system performance, or balance energy conservation with performance.

Windows 7 includes three default power plans, as shown in Figure 14.3:

▶ **Balanced**: Offers full performance when you need it and saves power during periods of inactivity.

▶ **Power saver**: Saves power by reducing system performance. This plan can help mobile PC users get the most from a single battery charge.

▶ **High performance**: Maximizes system performance and responsiveness. Mobile PC users might notice that their battery doesn't last as long when using this plan.

If a default plan doesn't meet your needs (even if you change some settings), you can create your own plan by using a default plan as a starting point.

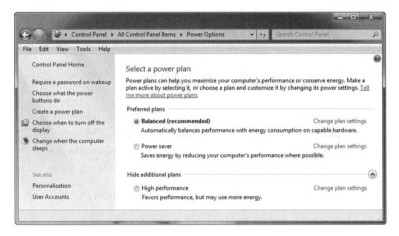

FIGURE 14.3   Configuring power plans using the Control Panel.

To change an existing plan, do the following:

1. Open Power Options by clicking the **Start** button, clicking **Control Panel**, clicking **System and Security**, and then clicking **Power Options**.

2. On the Select a power plan page, click **Change plan settings** under the plan that you want to change.

3. On the Change settings for the plan page, choose the display and sleep settings that you want to use when your computer is running on battery and when it's plugged in.

4. If you don't want to change any more settings, click **Save changes**. To change additional power settings, click **Change advanced power settings**.

5. On the Advanced settings tab, expand the category that you want to customize, expand each setting that you want to change, and then choose the values that you want to use when your computer is running on battery and when it's plugged in.

6. Click **OK** to save the changes and then click the **Close** button on the Change settings for the plan page.

To create your own plan, use the following steps:

1. Open Power Options by clicking the **Start** button, clicking **Control Panel**, clicking **System and Security**, and then clicking **Power Options**.

2. On the Select a power plan page, in the task pane, click **Create a plan**.

3. On the Create a power plan page, select the plan that's closest to the type of plan that you want to create.

4. In the Plan name box, type a name for the plan and then click **Next**.

5. On the Change settings for the plan page, as shown in Figure 14.4, choose the display and sleep settings that you want to use when your computer is running on battery and when it's plugged in and then click **Create**.

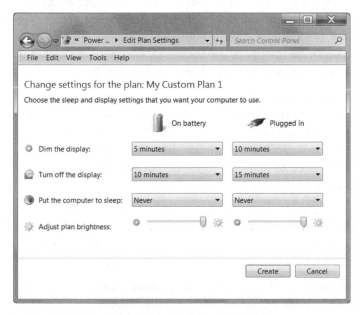

FIGURE 14.4 **Changing settings for a power plan.**

If you created power plans that you no longer use or need, you can delete them. To delete a plan, do the following:

1. Open Power Options by clicking the **Start** button, clicking **Control Panel**, clicking **System and Security**, and then clicking **Power Options**.

2. If the active plan is the one that you want to delete, make a different plan the active plan.

3. On the Select a power plan page, click **Change plan settings** under the plan that you want to delete.

4. On the Change settings for the plan page, click **Delete this plan**.

5. When prompted, click **OK**.

> **Note**
>
> You can't delete any of the three default power plans (Balanced, Power saver, or High performance).

Shut Down Options

When you shut down your computer, all open files are saved to the hard disk, the contents of the memory are saved to the hard disk or discarded as appropriate, the page file is cleared, and all open applications are closed. The active user is then logged out of Windows and the computer is turned off. Of course, this might take a minute or two, depending on the computer and the applications that the computer was running at the time of shutdown.

Windows 7 offers two other modes besides shutdown. When you hibernate your computer, the system state, along with the contents of the system memory, is saved to a file (hiberfil.sys) on the hard disk and the computer is shut down. The hiberfil.sys file is same size as the amount of physical memory (RAM). No power is required to maintain this state because the data is stored on the hard disk. You can then continue where you left off within a short time.

Sleep is a power-saving state that saves work and open programs to memory. To maintain the contents of memory while the computer is in sleep mode, the system still consumes a small amount of power. The advantage of Sleep mode is that you can continue where you left off, typically within a few seconds.

Hybrid sleep, a combination of sleep and hibernate, saves your work to your hard disk and puts your mobile PC into a power-saving state. If you suffer a power failure on a computer when it is in a hybrid sleep state, your data is not lost. Hybrid sleep is turned off by default on mobile PCs.

When you click the power button on the Start menu, Windows 7 automatically goes into Sleep mode. If your battery power is low, Windows 7 hibernates the computer.

In addition to power plans, you can configure what the computer does when you press the power button or when you close the lid (on a laptop computer), as shown in Figure 14.5. You can also tell Windows 7 whether to prompt for a user password when returning to its power-on state. You can also control button actions depending on whether the computer is plugged in or running on battery power.

FIGURE 14.5 System settings for power, sleep buttons, and lid settings.

By default, hibernate is enabled. If you want to disable hibernate and remove the hiberfil.sys file on the C drive, you use the following command:

```
powercfg -hibernate off
```

Battery Meter

Displayed in the notification area of the Windows taskbar, the battery meter helps you manage your computer's power consumption by indicating how much charge is remaining on your battery and which power plan your computer is using.

Windows continuously monitors the power level of your battery and warns you when the battery power reaches low and critical levels. When your battery charge gets low, the battery icon on the Windows taskbar indicates a low-battery power level. Make sure that you have sufficient time to install a fully charged battery, find an AC power outlet, or save your work and turn off the mobile PC. When your battery is almost out of power, the battery icon changes to indicate a critical-battery level.

To choose low and critical power levels, do the following:

1. Open Power Options by clicking the **Start** button, clicking **Control Panel**, clicking **System and Security**, and then clicking **Power Options**.

2. On the Select a power plan page, click **Change plan settings** under the selected plan.

3. On the Change settings for the plan page, click **Change advanced power settings**.

4. On the Advanced settings tab, expand **Battery**, expand **Low battery level** and **Critical battery level**, and then choose the percentage that you want for each level.

5. Click **OK** to save the changes and then click the **Close** button on the Change settings for the plan page.

File and Data Synchronization

While using mobile computers, sometimes you are connected to a corporate network and other times you are not. Sometimes you might want to work on the files stored on a network server even when you are not connected to the network that holds the network server. You might also want to connect mobile devices such as phones and PDAs to your mobile computer or desktop computer so that information can be copied back and forth.

The Windows 7 Sync Center provides a single easy-to-use interface to manage data synchronization between multiple computers including network servers and with mobile devices you connect to your computer. To start the Sync Center, click the **Start** button, click **All Programs**, click **Accessories**, and then click **Sync Center** to generate the screen shown in Figure 14.6.

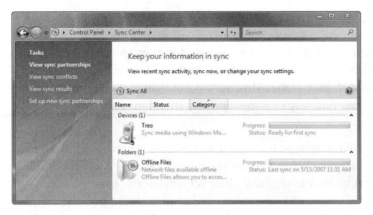

FIGURE 14.6 **Sync Center.**

To set up synchronization between two computers, you create a sync partner-ship between two or more sync locations, which specifies what files and fold-ers to sync, where to sync them, and when. You can schedule an automatic sync on a daily, weekly, or monthly basis, or when a specific event occurs, such as every time you log on to your computer. You can also perform a manual sync at any time, such as when you are getting ready to disconnect a mobile PC from the network and want to make sure you have the latest copies of files on a network server.

> **Note**
>
> The ability to sync with network folders is not included in Windows 7 Starter, Windows 7 Home Basic, or Windows 7 Home Premium.

Every time you sync files between two locations (such as between a computer and a mobile device), Sync Center compares the files in both locations to see if they still match or if any have changed. It determines if any files need to be updated in order to stay in sync.

If the files differ, Sync Center determines which version of each file to keep and copies that version to the other location, overwriting the other version there. It selects the most recent version to keep, unless you have set up the sync partnership to sync differently. Sometimes, Sync Center prompts you to choose which version of a file to keep. This usually occurs when a file has changed in both locations since the last sync. When this happens, Sync Center notifies you of a sync conflict, which you must resolve before it can sync the items in conflict.

When you set up the synchronization, you may set up a one-way or two-way synchronization. In one-way sync, files are copied from a primary location to a secondary location, but no files are ever copied back to the primary location. In two-way sync, Sync Center copies files in both directions, keeping the two locations in sync with each other. Most sync partnerships are automatically set up to perform either one-way or two-way sync, although some sync partnerships let you choose.

You might set up two-way sync between a network folder and your computer, where you instruct Sync Center to copy the newest version of any file it finds to the other location, overwriting any older versions of the same file. This is a good way to sync if you work with the same files on both the network folder and your computer, and you want to make sure you always have the most recent version of every file you've worked on.

You might set up one-way sync for a portable music player, for example, where you instruct Sync Center to copy every new music file from your computer to the mobile device but never to copy music files in the other direction (from the device to your computer).

Offline Folders

Because many users use portable computers many users have a need to access files in a shared folder while not being connected to the network where the shared folder is. To overcome this problem, you can use offline files.

To configure Offline Files, click **Open the Sync Center** and then click **Manage offline files**. From the General tab in the Offline Files dialog box, you can enable or disable offline files by clicking the top button. You can also use the General tab to open Sync Center and to view your offline files, as shown in Figure 14.7.

The Disk Usage tab enables you to see how much disk space is currently being used by offline files and enables you to change the limits of storage that offline uses. The Encryption tab enables you to encrypt or decrypt your offline files.

The Network tab enables you to choose to automatically work on any locally cached offline files when your connection to the network is slow. You can also choose how often to check for a slow network connection.

In addition, you can encrypt your offline files to help secure private information using the Sync Manager. Of course, when you encrypt offline files, only your user account can access the cached data.

FIGURE 14.7   **Offline Files options.**

After a folder is shared, you can control if a folder is available as an offline folder and how remote users access files inside each of your shares. The Caching settings for shared folders are configured by clicking the **Advanced Sharing**, on the Sharing tab of the folder's property sheet and clicking the **Caching** button to generate the resulting window in Figure 14.8. The options are as follows:

▶ **Only the files and programs that users specify will be available offline**: This setting is the default and enables any files or programs in the share to be available offline to users but users must make the decision.

▶ **No files or programs from the shared folder are available offline**: This setting disables caching from the share.

▶ **All files and programs that users open from the share will be automatically available offline**: This setting ensures that any files a user accesses from this share while online are available offline.

▶ **Optimized for performance**: This checkbox enables the caching to take place in the background, therefore helping to optimize network performance.

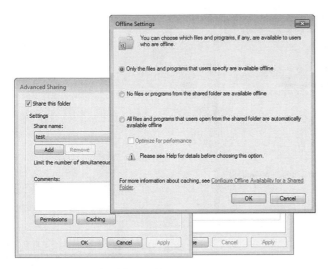

FIGURE 14.8   **Caching options.**

To make files or folders available offline, do the following:

1. While connected to the network, locate the network file or folder that you want to make available offline.

2. Right-click the file or folder and then click **Always available offline**.

Windows automatically creates a copy of that file or folder on your computer. Anytime you reconnect to that network folder, Windows syncs the files between your computer and the network folder. You can also sync them manually at any time.

If you work with offline files in different folders, you might want to view all of them without opening each folder individually. To enable this functionality, do the following:

1. Open the **Sync Center**.

2. Click the **Manage offline files** option.

3. On the General tab, click **View your offline files**.

If you want to sync your offline files right away to be sure you have the latest versions of files stored on the network, do the following:

1. Click to open **Sync Center**.

2. Click the **Offline Files** folder. Then, on the toolbar, click **Sync** to sync all your offline files.

If you want to sync only one file or folder, or a selection of files, you don't need to open Sync Center. Simply right-click the item, point to Sync, and then click **Sync selected offline files**.

Connecting Mobile Devices

Many mobile devices can connect to your Windows 7 computer and synchronize data and files between the two. Typically, you connect your device to your computer either using a USB cable or cradle or through a wireless signal (infrared, Bluetooth, or Wi-Fi). Most devices ship with a USB cable or cradle, and most modern computers are equipped with infrared or Bluetooth.

If you are connecting a mobile device using Bluetooth technology, you need to configure that the device is discoverable. You also need to set up the passkey to associate the device with the Bluetooth signal. This ensures that each device is connected to the device to which it is intended to connect.

> **ExamAlert**
>
> You can use the Windows Mobility Device Center to disable USB connections and Bluetooth connections. You can access Mobility Device Center by opening the Control Panel, clicking Mobile PC, and selecting Mobility Device Center.

Before you can synchronize information with devices, you must set up sync partnerships. To create a sync partnership with a portable media player, you just need to do the following:

1. Connect your device to a computer running Windows 7 and open Sync Center. Windows 7 includes drivers for many common devices, but you can also obtain drivers from the CD that came with your device or from Windows Update.

2. Set up a sync partnership. Clicking **Set up for a media device sync partnership** opens Windows Media Player 11.

3. Select some media files or a playlist to synchronize to the device. To select media, simply drag it onto the sync dialog box on the right side of Windows Media Player.

4. Click **Start Sync**. When your chosen media has transferred to the device, you can disconnect it from your computer and close Windows Media Player.

You can sync your contacts with some mobile devices, enabling you to take your contacts with you wherever you go. To sync contacts with a mobile device, the device must be able to read the contact file that Windows creates for each individual contact. The device must also be compatible with Sync Center, which Windows uses to sync files between a computer and a mobile device.

If you have Exchange Server 2003 or later deployed in your organization, take advantage of its integration with Windows Mobile, which provides direct push email using ActiveSync technology, Global Address List lookup, and numerous security features.

Windows SideShow

Windows SideShow is a new technology in Windows 7 that supports a secondary screen on your mobile PC. With this additional display, you can view important information such as running Windows Media Player or check email whether your laptop is on, off, or in sleep mode. Windows SideShow is available in Windows 7 Home Premium, Windows 7 Professional, Windows 7 Enterprise, and Windows 7 Ultimate.

Windows SideShow uses gadgets, convenient mini programs, to extend information from your computer to other devices. Gadgets can run on a Windows SideShow–compatible device and update that device with information from your computer. Using a gadget, you can view information from your computer regardless of whether your mobile PC is on, off, or in the sleep power state, which can save you both time and battery life.

To configure Windows SideShow, you have to search Windows Help and Support for "Turn on Windows SideShow." After clicking the **Turn a Windows SideShow gadget on or off**, click the **Click to open Windows SideShow** link to generate the window shown in Figure 14.9. You can then turn gadgets on or off for each of your devices (assuming you have SideShow gadgets). From Control Panel, you can also set your computer to wake periodically (such as every hour) so that all gadgets that are turned on can update your devices with the latest information.

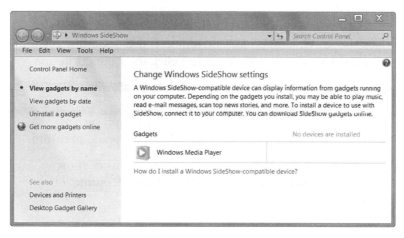

FIGURE 14.9   **Windows SideShow.**

Windows SideShow–compatible devices can take many forms. Hardware manufacturers are already including secondary displays in their designs for mobile PCs and devices such as keyboards, mobile phones, and remote controls.

Remote Projector

A network projector is a video projector that's connected to a wireless or wired local area network (LAN). What sets the network projector apart from other presentation methods is that you can connect to, and operate the projector remotely over, a network connection. If your computer can connect to the projector, you can deliver a presentation from any location that has network access, whether it's your private office or a conference room where the projector is located. Those who want to view your presentation must be in the same room as the projector; they can't view the presentation over the network from a different location.

To start, connect to the projector by using one of the following methods:

1. Open the Connect to a Network Projector Wizard by clicking the **Start** button, clicking **All Programs**, clicking **Accessories**, and then clicking **Connect to a Network Projector**.

2. Then do one of the following:

   a. Click the search for a projector (recommended option). Click the projector you want to connect to and click the Connect button.

   b. Click **Enter the projector network address** and enter the address as a URL (a web address, such as http://server/projectors/projector_1) or as a UNC path (a path on a server, such as \\server\projectors\projector_1) and the appropriate password.

3. After you're connected, you can control your presentation in the Network Presentation dialog box by clicking **Pause**, **Resume**, or **Disconnect**.

> **Note**
>
> Network projectors are designed to transmit and display still images, such as photographs and Microsoft Office PowerPoint slides—not high-bandwidth transmissions, such as video streams. The projector can transmit video, but the playback quality is often poor.

Cram Quiz

1. You have a folder that you want to make available offline. What do you need to do?

   ○ **A.** Share a folder and ensure that the Allow caching of files in this shared folder checkbox is selected

   ○ **B.** Map a network drive to the folder and select the cached option

   ○ **C.** Use the `cache` command

   ○ **D.** Grant the cache permission to the user

2. You are ready to give a presentation using your computer, running Microsoft PowerPoint. What should you do to prepare your system for the presentation? (Choose the best answer.)

   ○ **A.** Create a second hardware profile, reboot the computer and load the second hardware profile

   ○ **B.** Shut off your email and messengers, change your volume, change your screen, and disable screen savers and sleep features

   ○ **C.** Create a second user profile, configure the profile for presentations, and log in as that user to give the presentation

   ○ **D.** Configure your Presentation Settings and enable Presentation Settings On

3. Which of the following shutdown option enables you to save the contents of RAM into a file, shut down the system, quickly boot the system, and continue working with the same applications that you had open when you shut down the system?

- ○ **A.** Sleep
- ○ **B.** Hibernate
- ○ **C.** Reduced Power mode
- ○ **D.** Deep Sleep mode

Cram Quiz Answers

1. **A** is correct. After you share a folder, make sure that you ensure that the Allow caching of files in this shared folder check box is selected. Answer B is incorrect because when you map a network drive, there is no cached option. Answer C is incorrect because there is no cache command. Answer D is incorrect because there is no cache permission.

2. **D** is correct. The best way to give presentations is to configure Presentation Settings with the Mobility Center and turn the Presentation Settings to On when you are to give a presentation. You could create profiles (user or hardware) but this is requires more work and it is not as efficient as using Presentation mode. Therefore, Answers A and C are incorrect. Answer B is incorrect because by changing your settings each time you give a presentation is time consuming and not efficient.

3. **B** is incorrect. When you hibernate your computer, the system state, along with the contents of the system memory, is saved to a file (Hiberfil.sys) on the hard disk and the computer is shut down. The hiberfil.sys file is the same size as the amount of physical memory (RAM). No power is required to maintain this state because the data is stored on the hard disk. You can then continue where you left off within a short time. Answer A is incorrect because Sleep mode is similar to hibernate but uses a small amount of memory to keep the contents of memory active instead of saving to a file. Answers C and D are incorrect because there is neither a Reduced Power mode nor a Deep Sleep mode.

Remote Desktop and Remote Assistance

▶ **Configure remote management**

▶ **Configure remote connections**

Cram**Saver**

1. Which tool would you use to view the desktop of remote user so that you can see the problem as she tries to open a program?

   ○ **A.** Remote Assistance

   ○ **B.** Remote Desktop

   ○ **C.** Computer Management console

   ○ **D.** System Information console

2. You want to view someone's Event Viewer without logging directly onto his computer. What option should you use?

   ○ **A.** System Information

   ○ **B.** Computer Management console

   ○ **C.** System Configuration tool

   ○ **D.** Remote Management console

Answers

1. **A** is correct. Remote Assistance enables you to view and interact a user's session on a computer running Windows 7 so that you can work with the user to troubleshoot and fix the problem. Answer B is incorrect because Remote Desktop only enables you to log in to a remote computer but not enable you to connect to another user's session. Answer C is incorrect because the Computer Management console enables you to run several Administrative tools from a single console but it does not enable you to view a user's desktop. Answer D is incorrect because the System Information program (not console) enables you to view system information so that you can provide it easily to people troubleshooting problems.

2. **B** is correct. By using Computer Management console, you can connect to remote computers to manage including viewing the Event Viewer. Answer A is incorrect because the System Information is used to view a systems configuration. Answer C is incorrect because the System Configuration tool is used to troubleshoot boot problems. Answer D is incorrect because there is no Remote Management console.

Starting with Windows XP, Microsoft introduced Remote Desktop and Remote Assistance. Similar to Terminal Services used in Windows 2000 servers, you can have access to a Windows session that is running on your computer when you are at another computer. This means, for example, that you can connect your work computer from home and have access to all of your applications, files, and network resources as though you were in front of your computer at work. You can leave programs running at work and when you get home, you can have your desktop at work displayed on your home computer, with the same programs running. Another example of using Remote Desktop and Remote Assistance is to remotely troubleshoot or administer a computer that is not nearby.

While using Remote Desktop and Remote Assistance, you can use your keyboard and mouse just like you are connected to the computer. You can click the **Start** button and click **Windows Security**, you can access the Security Window so that you can log off, reboot the computer, access the Task Manager, or change the password. If for some reason the Explorer taskbar is not available, you can also press the **Ctrl+Alt+End** keys to open the same window.

To use Remote Desktop and Remote Assistance, you have to use TCP port 3389. Therefore, it needs to be opened using the Windows Firewall and any other firewalls between your computer and the remote host.

Remote Desktop and Remote Desktop Connections

You use Remote Desktop to access one computer from another remotely. With Remote Desktop Connection, you can access a computer running Windows from another computer running Windows that is connected to the same network or to the Internet. For example, you can use all your work computer's programs, files, and network resources from your home computer, and it's just like you're sitting in front of your computer at work.

ExamAlert

You cannot use Remote Desktop Connection to connect to computers running Windows 7 Starter, Windows 7 Home Basic, Windows 7 Home Premium, and you can only create outgoing connections from those editions of Windows 7. Only Windows 7 Professional, Ultimate, and Enterprise editions support Remote Desktop Hosting.

> **Note**
>
> You cannot use Remote Desktop Connection to connect to computers running Windows XP Home Edition.

To connect to a remote computer, it must meet the following criteria:

- ▶ The remote computer must be turned on.

- ▶ The remote computer must have a network connection.

- ▶ Remote Desktop must be enabled.

- ▶ You must have network access to the remote computer (this could be through the Internet).

- ▶ You must have permission to connect (a member of the administrators group or the Remote Desktop Users group. For permission to connect, you must be on the list of users.

> **ExamAlert**
>
> To use Remote Desktop, the computer that you are trying to connect to must be on, Remote Desktop must be enabled, and you must have the proper rights.

> **Note**
>
> Remote Desktop uses port 3389.

To allow remote connections on the computer you want to connect to, do the following:

1. Click the **Start** button. Right-click **Computer** and select **Properties**.

2. Click **Remote Settings** and then select one of the three options under Remote Desktop, as shown in Figure 14.10. If you are prompted for an administrator password or confirmation, type the password or provide confirmation.

3. Click **Select Users**. If you are enabling Remote Desktop for your current user account, your name is automatically added to this list of remote users, and you can skip the next two steps.

4. In the Remote Desktop Users dialog box, click **Add**. This adds users to the Remote Desktop Users group.

5. In the Select Users dialog box, do the following:

   ▶ To specify the search location, click **Locations** and then select the location you want to search.

   ▶ In Enter the object names to select, type the name of the user that you want to add and then click **OK**.

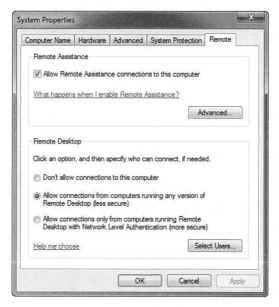

FIGURE 14.10 **Remote Assistant and Remote Desktop settings.**

The name is displayed in the list of users in the Remote Desktop Users dialog box, as shown in Figure 14.11.

FIGURE 14.11   **Adding remote desktop users.**

To start Remote Desktop on the computer you want to work from, do the following:

1. Open Remote Desktop Connection by clicking the **Start** button, select **Accessories**, and select **Remote Desktop Connection**.

2. From the screen shown in Figure 14.12, in the Computer field, type the name of the computer that you want to connect to and then click **Connect**. (You can also type the IP address instead of the computer name if you want.)

For more advanced options before the connection, click the **Options** button.

FIGURE 14.12   **Using Remote Desktop Connection.**

Using Remote Assistance

Remote Assistance is used to give or receive assistance remotely. For example, a friend or a technical support person can access your computer to help you with a computer problem or show you how to do something. You can help someone else the same way. In either case, both you and the other person see the same computer screen. If you decide to share control of your computer with your helper, you are both able to control the mouse pointer.

To use Remote Assistance, first you invite a person to help you, using email or an instant message, as shown in Figure 14.13. You can also reuse an invitation that you have sent before. After the person accepts the invitation, Windows Remote Assistance creates an encrypted connection between the two computers over the Internet or the network that both computers are connected to. You give the other person a password so that he or she can connect. You can also offer assistance to someone else, and when that person accepts your offer, Windows Remote Assistance creates an encrypted connection between the two computers. To start a Remote Assistance session and to create invitations, click **All Programs**, select **Maintenance**, and select **Windows Remote Assistance**.

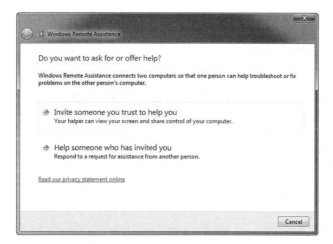

FIGURE 14.13 **Remote Assistance invitation.**

ExamAlert

To allow a user to remotely access a Windows 7 computer, you need to enable Remote Desktop or Remote Assistance through the firewall.

To enable Remote Assistance from the GUI, do the following:

1. Click **Start**, click **All Programs**, click **Maintenance**, and then click **Windows Remote Assistance**. This launches the Windows Remote Assistance screen, as shown in Figure 14.13. You can also click **Start** and type `assist` in the Start menu search box.

2. To get help, click **Invite someone you trust to help you**.

3. Select one of the following options:

   ▸ **Save This Invitation to a File**: Selecting this option enables you to save your Remote Assistance invitation file to a folder. This folder can be a location on your computer or an available network Share.

   ▸ **Use E-mail to Send an Invitation**: Selecting this option launches your default email client. A message is then created with an attached invitation file.

   ▸ **Use Easy Connect**: Selecting this option creates and publishes your Remote Assistance invitation file using a 12-character password that you must communicate to whoever is helping you.

If you need to help someone, open Windows Remote Assistance and select **Help someone who has invited you**.

Using Administrative Tools for Remote Hosts

Many of the Administrative Tools on a Windows 7 computer can be used to remotely manage a computer including those tools that are based on the Microsoft Management Console (MMC). To manage a computer using an MMC snap-in, follow these steps:

1. Log on to a remote computer.

2. Start an MMC snap-in, such as Computer Management, as shown in Figure 14.14.

3. In the left pane, right-click the top of the tree and click **Connect to another computer**. For example, in the Computer Management Console, you would right-click **Computer Management (Local)**.

4. In Another computer, type the computer name or IP address and click **OK**.

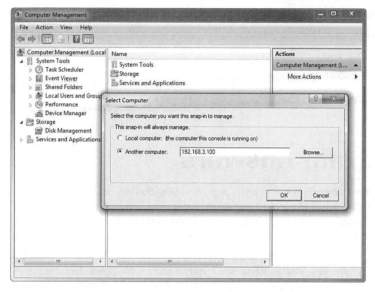

FIGURE 14.14   **Connecting to another computer using MMC.**

5. You can now use the MMC snap-in to manage the computer as you would any other computer running a Windows operating system.

You can also connect to a user's registry by opening the Registry Editor, opening the File menu, and selecting the **Connect Network Registry** option. For you to do this, the Remote Registry service must be running and you must have administrative permissions to the computer you want to connect to.

Cram Quiz

1. What are the three ways that you can use to send an invitation to a user to connect using Remote Assistance? (Choose three answers.)

   ○ **A.** Save the invitation to a file

   ○ **B.** Use email to send an invitation

   ○ **C.** Use the Publish in Active Directory Invitation

   ○ **D.** Use Easy Connect

2. Which version of Windows 7 does NOT support Remote Desktop Hosting?

- ○ **A.** Windows 7 Home Premium
- ○ **B.** Windows 7 Professional
- ○ **C.** Windows 7 Ultimate
- ○ **D.** Windows 7 Enterprise

Cram Exam Answers

1. **A, B**, and **D** are correct. You can invite someone you trust by saving the invitation to file, using email to send an invitation, and using Easy Connect. You cannot send an invitation using Active Directory. Therefore, Answer C is incorrect because it is an option that does not exist.

2. **A** is correct. You cannot use Remote Desktop Connection to connect to computers running Windows 7 Starter, Windows 7 Home Basic, Windows 7 Home Premium, and you can only create outgoing connections from those editions of Windows 7. Only Windows 7 Professional, Ultimate, and Enterprise editions support "Remote Desktop Hosting."

PowerShell

▶ **Configure remote management**

1. What task-based command-line shell and scripting language is provided with Windows 7 that enables you to control local and remote computers and their Microsoft network services?

- ○ **A.** ActiveX
- ○ **B.** PowerShell
- ○ **C.** GPO
- ○ **D.** BackScript

2. What PowerShell command would you use to establish a connection with a remote computer running Windows 7?

- ○ **A.** Set-Location
- ○ **B.** EstablishPS
- ○ **C.** PSEstablishSession
- ○ **D.** New-PsSession

Answers

1. **B** is correct. Windows PowerShell is a task-based command-line shell and scripting language to help IT professionals and users control and automate the administration of the Windows operating system and the applications that run on Windows. Answer A is incorrect because ActiveX is a control set used with web pages. Answer C is incorrect because GPO (short for Group Policy Object) is used to configure network environments. Answer D is incorrect because there is no such thing as BackScript.

2. **D** is correct. To establish a new session with a remote computer, you use the New-PsSession command. You can use PowerShell to execute commands remotely. Answer A is incorrect because the Set-Location command is used to change directories. Answers B and C are incorrect because these commands are invalid in PowerShell.

Windows PowerShell is a task-based command-line shell and scripting language to help IT professionals and users control and automate the administration of the Windows operating system and the applications that run on Windows. Windows PowerShell requires the Microsoft .NET Framework 2.0, while the Windows PowerShell ISE requires the Microsoft .NET Framework 3.5 with Service Pack 1.

The Built-in Windows PowerShell commands are called cmdlets and enable you to manage client computers and servers, edit the registry and file system, perform WMI calls, and connect to the .NET Framework development environment. The Windows PowerShell commands can also be used to manage other Windows technologies, such as

▶ Active Directory Domain Services

▶ Windows BitLocker Drive Encryption

▶ DHCP Server service

▶ Group Policy

▶ Remote Desktop Services

▶ Windows Server Backup

Figure 14.15 shows the Windows PowerShell console.

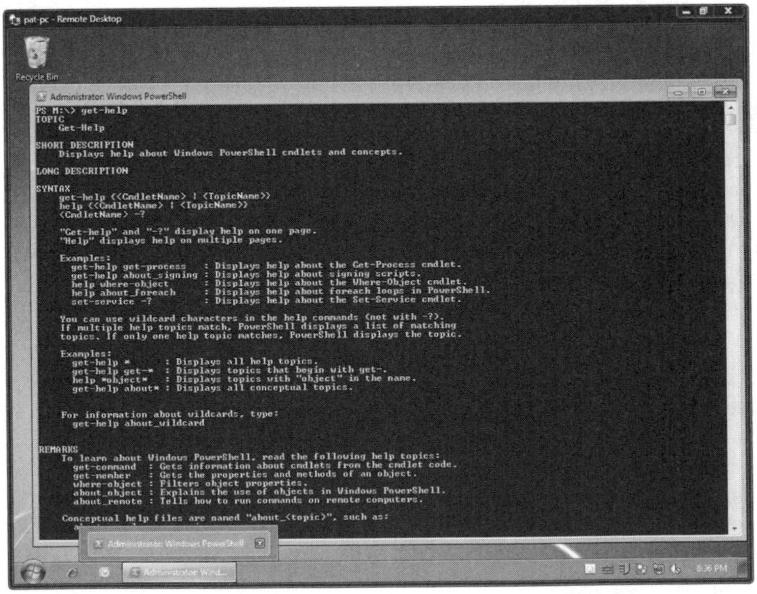

FIGURE 14.15   **PowerShell console.**

Although PowerShell was introduced with Windows Server 2007, the Windows PowerShell included with Windows 7 is PowerShell 2.0. PowerShell 2.0 includes the following improvements of PowerShell 1.0:

- ▶ Hundreds of new cmdlets including Get-Hotfix, Send-MailMessage, Get-ComputerRestorePoint, New-WebServiceProxy, Debug-Process, Add-Computer, Rename-Computer, Reset-ComputerMachinePassword, and Get-Random.

- ▶ Remote management as commands can be run on one or multiple computers by establishing an interactive session from a single computer. Additionally, you can establish a session that receives remote commands from multiple computers.

- ▶ Windows PowerShell Integrated Scripting Environment (ISE), which is a graphical user interface where you can run commands and write, edit, run, test, and debug scripts in the same window. It includes a built-in debugger, multiline editing, selective execution, syntax colors, line and column numbers, and context-sensitive Help.

- ▶ Background jobs that run commands asynchronously and in the background while continuing to work in your session. You can run background jobs on a local or remote computer and store the results locally or remotely.

- ▶ The Windows PowerShell debugger helps debug functions and scripts. You can set and remove breakpoints, step through code, check the values of variables, and display a call-stack trace.

- ▶ Use Windows PowerShell modules to organize your Windows PowerShell scripts and functions into independent, self-contained units and package them to be distributed to other users. Modules can include audio files, images, Help files, and icons, and they run in a separate session to avoid name conflicts.

- ▶ The new event infrastructure helps you create events, subscribe to system and application events, and then listen, forward, and act on events synchronously and asynchronously.

Some popular PowerShell commands are as follows:

- ▶ **Clear-Host**: Clear the screen

- ▶ **Copy-Item**: Copy files or a directory

- ▶ **Get-ChildItem**: List all files or directories in the current directory

▶ **Get-Location**: Show the current directory

▶ **Move-Item**: Move a file or directory

▶ **Remove-Item**: Delete a file or directory

▶ **Rename-Item**: Rename a file or directory

▶ **Set-Location**: Change the current directory

▶ **Write-Output**: Print a string or variable onto the screen

One use for Windows 7 PowerShell is to execute a command on a target computer just as if you were sitting at the computer. To accomplish this, you perform these three steps:

1. Establish a session.

2. Execute any command, script, or cmdlet using the session.

3. Delete the session.

To establish a session, click the **Start** button, select **All Programs**, select **Accessories**, select **Windows PowerShell**, and select **Windows PowerShell**.

To create a session with a computer name called RemotePCName, use the following:

```
New-PsSession -ComputerName myremotepc
```

If you want to log in with a different username than you are currently logged in as, you execute the following command:

```
New-PsSession -ComputerName RemotePCName -credential $prompt
```

To run a command, such as the `ipconfig` command at a remote computer, perform the following commands:

```
$mysession = New-PSSession -ComputerName RemotePCName
Invoke-Command { ipconfig } -Session $mysession
```

When you are done, it is always recommended to delete the session. To end the session, execute the following command:

```
Remove-PsSession -session $mysession
```

Cram Quiz

1. What provides you a graphical user interface that enables you to run commands and write, edit, run, test, and debug scripts?

   ○ **A.** ISE

   ○ **B.** GPO

   ○ **C.** PSDebug

   ○ **D.** PS-Run

2. What PowerShell command is used to copy files?

   ○ **A.** Copy-Item

   ○ **B.** Set-Location

   ○ **C.** Write Output

   ○ **D.** Move-Item

Cram Quiz Answers

1. **A** is correct. Windows PowerShell Integrated Scripting Environment (ISE) is a graphical user interface where you can run commands and write, edit, run, test, and debug scripts in the same window. Answer B is incorrect because GPO, short for Group Policy Object, enables you to configure network environments. Answers C and D are incorrect because the PSDebug or PS-Run programs don't exist.

2. **A** is correct. To copy files or a directory using PowerShell, you use the Copy-Item command. Answer B is incorrect because the Set-Location command is used to change directories. Answer C is incorrect because the Write-Output command is used to print a string or variable onto the screen. Answer D is incorrect because the Move-Item command is used to move a file or directory.

Review Questions

1. You work as the desktop support technician at Acme.com. You need to give a presentation using your mobile computer. So, you take the computer to the conference room and connect the projector to the computer with an S-Video cable. You want the desktop and Start menu to be displayed on the projector. What should you do in Windows 7?

   ○ **A.** Open Screen Resolution. Select the Projector from the Display options. Then select the Make this my main display option.

   ○ **B.** Open Personalization Settings. Select the icon that represents the laptop display. Then clear the Extend the desktop onto this monitor option.

   ○ **C.** Clear the Lock the taskbar option of the taskbar's context menu. Drag the taskbar as far to the right as possible.

   ○ **D.** Clear the Lock the taskbar option of the taskbar's context menu. Drag the taskbar as far to the left as possible.

2. You work as the desktop support technician at Acme.com. You have a laptop in a conference room connected to a large TV monitor. Because you forgot the power connector for the mobile computer, you want the battery to last as long as possible. What should you do to conserve the most power during the presentation?

   ○ **A.** Reduce the brightness settings in the Windows Mobility Center to the lowest setting

   ○ **B.** Select External display only in the New Display Detected dialog box

   ○ **C.** Select Extended in the New Display Detected dialog box

   ○ **D.** Turn on Presentation Mode in the Windows Mobility Center

3. You work as the desktop support specialist at Acme.com. You want to add a Bluetooth-enabled handheld device to your personal area networks (PAN). What do you need to do?

   ○ **A.** Configure the passkey and ensure that the device is discoverable

   ○ **B.** Configure the appropriate wireless security method and ensure that the device is discoverable

   ○ **C.** Turn on the Network Discovery and configure the passkey

   ○ **D.** Configure the passkey and ensure that the mobile device is Wi-Fi enabled

4. You work as the desktop support technician at Acme.com. You are planning to give a presentation on a tablet PC workstation. During the presentation, you need to temporarily block notifications and disable your screen saver. What should you do?

   ○ **A.** You should set the screen saver to none in the Display Settings.

   ○ **B.** You should select Extended in the New Display Detected dialog box.

   ○ **C.** You should turn on and configure Presentation Mode in the Windows Mobility Center.

   ○ **D.** You should click Connect External Display in the Windows Mobility Center.

5. You work as the desktop support technician at Acme.com. You are in the office and get an emergency call to visit a client. You must be able to stop your work and resume as quickly as possible when you get to the client site. They also want to be protected from data loss if there is a power problem. What do you suggest?

   ○ **A.** Ensure that the laptop workstations have Centrino hardware. You should configure hybrid sleep on the laptop workstations.

   ○ **B.** Ensure that the users are administrators. You should configure hybrid sleep on the laptop workstations.

   ○ **C.** Ensure that there is available disk space equivalent to the amount of RAM. Configure sleep on the laptop workstations.

   ○ **D.** Ensure that there is available disk space equivalent to the amount of RAM. You should configure hybrid sleep on the laptop workstations.

   ○ **E.** Ensure that there is available disk space equivalent to the amount of RAM. Configure hibernation on the laptop workstations.

6. You work as the desktop support technician at Acme.com. A user shuts down her PC by clicking the Power button icon on the Start menu; however, when she starts up her computer again, the same programs that were open when she tried to shut down are still open. What do you need to do so that her machine does a complete shutdown?

   ○ **A.** Open Power Options, click the Choose what power buttons do link, and choose the option to shut the computer down when the power button is pressed.

   ○ **B.** Open Power Options, click the Change when computer sleeps link, and choose the option to never put the computer to sleep when it is running on battery.

   ○ **C.** Open Advanced Settings for the current power plan in Power Options. Change the Start menu power button setting to Shut down.

   ○ **D.** Change the On battery setting in the Sleep after category to Never.

7. You work as the desktop support technician at Acme.com. When you close the lid on your Windows 7 computer, you want to start working as soon as you restart the computer. You also don't want to use any battery power while the computer is shut down. What should you do?

○ **A.** Configure the computer to hibernate when lid is closed

○ **B.** Configure the computer to sleep when lid is closed

○ **C.** Configure the computer to shut down when lid is closed

○ **D.** Configure the computer to go into standby when lid is closed

8. You work as the desktop support technician at Acme.com. You want to disable the Windows Media Player through the Windows SideShow. What should you do?

○ **A.** Open the Windows SideShow and then turn off the Windows Media Player gadget

○ **B.** Open the Sync Center and remove the appropriate Sync partnership

○ **C.** Open the Windows Sidebar and turn off the Windows Media Player gadget

○ **D.** Open the Windows Media Player and then remove the appropriate plug-in

9. To use Windows Remote Desktop, a user must be added to one of two groups. What are the two groups? (Choose two.)

○ **A.** Administrator

○ **B.** Power Users

○ **C.** Remote Desktop Administrators group

○ **D.** Remote Desktop Users group

10. What program is used to connect to a network project directly?

○ **A.** Remote Desktop

○ **B.** Remote Assistance

○ **C.** Network Projector

○ **D.** Remote SideShow

Review Question Answers

1. Answer **A** is correct. If you want to use the project as the main monitor, right-click the desktop and select Screen Resolution. Then select the Projector from the Display option and select Make this my main display. Answer B is incorrect because if you extend the desktop onto this monitor, the monitor and the project act together as if they were sitting side-by-side. Answers C and D are incorrect because the taskbar has nothing to do with the monitor configuration.

2. Answer **B** is correct. The LCD panel is one of the components on a laptop computer that uses the most power, so disabling the LCD panel conserves power. Therefore, you should select External display only in the New Display Detected dialog box. Answer A helps with power consumption but not as much as shutting off the LCD panel. Answers C and D do not reduce power consumption.

3. Answer **A** is correct. When you configure a Bluetooth-enabled handheld device, you need to enable Bluetooth and assign a passkey. Answers B, C, and D are incorrect because they are used to configure a wireless network connection, not Bluetooth.

4. Answer **C** is correct. When you turn on Presentation mode, your mobile PC stays awake and system notifications are turned off. You can also choose to turn off the screen saver, adjust the speaker volume, and change your desktop background image. Answer A is not the best answer because this only affects the screen saver and does not turn off system notifications and does not adjust speaker volume. Answers B and D affect only display settings.

5. Answer **C** is correct. When you perform hybrid sleep, it keeps the memory alive so that you can do a quick restart to where you left off. It also writes to the hard drive in case power is interrupted. Answer A is incorrect because you don't have to be an administrator. Answer B does not protect against power interruption. Answer D is incorrect because it is not the fastest to restart.

6. Answer **C** is correct. When the shutdown button is clicked, the system goes into either sleep mode or hibernate mode. Answer A is incorrect because you have to go into the Advanced options. Answer B is incorrect because you have to go into the Advanced options and there is not an option to never put to sleep mode. Answer D is incorrect because there is no such option.

7. Answer **A** is correct. You should configure the computer to hibernate when the lid is closed. Answer B is incorrect because hibernate is faster than setting the computer to sleep. Answer C is incorrect because shutdown is the slowest option from which to bring the computer back on. Answer D is incorrect because there is no standby mode in Windows 7.

8. Answer **A** is correct. Media Player can be accessed through SideShow. Therefore, you need to disable using the Control Panel. Answer B is incorrect because Sync is for data files, not Windows Media Player. Answer C is incorrect because, although both reference using gadgets, the Windows Media Player gadget is handled in the SideShow, not Sidebar. Answer D is not correct because the Windows Media Player is an application, not a plug-in.

9. Answers **A** and **D** are correct. All administrators are automatically given the necessary permission to use Windows Remote Desktop. For other users, you must add them to the Remote Desktop Users group. Answer B is incorrect because Power Users is mostly used for backward compatibility. Answer C is incorrect because there is no Remote Desktop Administrators group.

10. Answer **C** is correct. A network projector is a video projector that's connected to a wireless or wired local area network (LAN). What sets the network projector apart from other presentation methods is that you can connect to and operate the projector remotely over a network connection. If your computer can connect to the projector, you can deliver a presentation from any location that has network access, whether it's your private office or a conference room where the projector is located. Remote Desktop and Remote Assistance enables you to connect to a Windows computer. Answer D is incorrect because Windows SideShow uses gadgets, convenient mini programs, to extend information from your computer to other devices.

CHAPTER 15

Optimizing Windows 7 Systems

This chapter covers the following 70-680 Objectives:

▶ Monitoring and Maintaining Systems that Run Windows 7:

▶ Monitor systems

▶ Configure performance settings

Performance is the overall effectiveness of how data moves through the system. To be able to improve performance, you must determine the part of the system that is slowing down the throughput; it could be the speed of the processor, the amount of RAM on the machine, the speed of the disk system, the speed of the network adapter card, or some other factor. This limiting factor is referred to as the bottleneck of the system.

Windows Performance Monitoring Tools

▶ **Monitor systems**

▶ **Configure performance settings**

CramSaver

1. What tool gives you quick access to processor and memory utilization and which programs are using the processor and memory?

   ○ **A.** Task Manager

   ○ **B.** Performance Monitor

   ○ **C.** Windows Experience Index

   ○ **D.** Event Viewer

2. Which technology is used to improve performance of computers using a USB flash drive?

   ○ **A.** ReadyBoost

   ○ **B.** ReadyCache

   ○ **C.** ReadyDrive

   ○ **D.** ReadyUp

3. What measurement indicates that your processor is working too hard?

   ○ **A.** Consistently greater than 25%

   ○ **B.** Consistently greater than 50%

   ○ **C.** Consistently greater than 80%

   ○ **D.** Occasionally greater than 95%

Answers

1. **A** is correct. A common tool used to quickly view system performance is the Windows Task Manager. Answer B is incorrect because the Performance Monitor provides a visual display of built-in Windows performance counters, either in real time or as a way to review historical data. Although the Performance Monitor is more powerful, it is not a quick-use tool. Answer C is incorrect because the Windows Experience Index measures the capability of your computer's hardware and software configuration and expresses this measurement as a number called a base score. Answer D is incorrect because the Event Viewer is used to view the Windows logs.

2. **A** is correct. Windows ReadyBoost boosts system performance by using USB flash devices as additional sources for caching. Answer C is incorrect because ReadyDrive boosts system performance on mobile computers equipped with hybrid drives. Answers B and D are incorrect because ReadyCache and ReadyUp do not exist in Windows 7.

3. **C** is correct. If the processor is at 80% all the time, you should upgrade the processor (using a faster processor, or adding additional processors) or move some the services or programs to other systems. Therefore, the other answers are incorrect.

Several tools that you can use to measure and monitor performance are as follows:

▶ Task Manager

▶ Windows Reliability and Performance Monitor

▶ Windows Experience Index

Task Manager

A common tool used to quickly view system performance is the Windows Task Manager. As shown in Figure 15.1, the Performance tab includes four graphs. The top two graphs show how much CPU is being used at the moment and for the past few minutes. (If the CPU Usage History graph appears split, your computer either has multiple CPUs, a single dual-core CPU, or both.) A high percentage means that programs or processes are requiring a lot of CPU resources, which can slow your computer. If the percentage appears frozen at or near 100%, a program might not be responding.

The bottom two graphs display how much RAM, or physical memory, is being used in megabytes (MB), both at the current moment and for the past few minutes. The percentage of memory being used is listed at the bottom of the Task Manager window. If memory use seems consistently high or slows your computer's performance noticeably, try reducing the number of programs you have open at one time or installing more RAM.

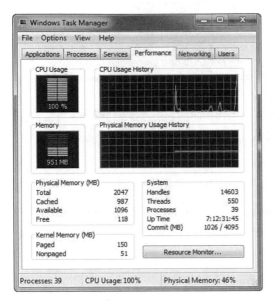

FIGURE 15.1   Window Task Manager showing the Performance tab.

To get a list of all individual processes or programs running in memory and how much processor utilization and memory usage each application is using, click the Processes tab to display the screen shown in Figure 15.2. You can also manually end any process here, which comes in handy when a process stops responding.

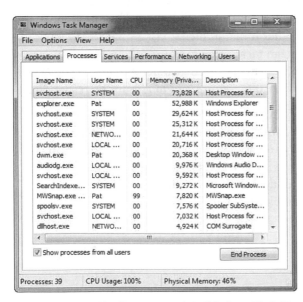

FIGURE 15.2   The Processes tab in Windows Task Manager.

Resource Monitor

Resource Monitor is a powerful tool that takes the Task Manager Processes tab one more step. Instead of just showing you the amount of processor and memory utilized for a process, it can also show you which applications are using files.

Windows Resource Monitor is a powerful tool for understanding how your system resources are used by processes and services. In addition to monitoring resource usage in real time, Resource Monitor can help you analyze unresponsive processes, identify which processes are accessing the disk, and which processes are utilizing the network.

To start Resource Monitor, click the **Start** button, click in the **Search programs and files** box, type **resmon.exe**, and then press **Enter**. You can also click the **Resource Monitor** button on the Performance tab within Task Manager.

Resource Monitor includes five tabs: Overview, CPU, Memory, Disk, and Network. The Overview tab displays basic system resource usage information; the other tabs display information about each specific resource.

By default, Resource Monitor displays real-time information about all of the processes running on your system. However, if you want to focus on a specific process or processes, you can filter data by doing the following:

1. Start **Resource Monitor** (see Figure 15.3).

2. Within any of the key tables, select the checkbox next to the name of each process you want to monitor in the Image column. Selected processes are moved to the top of the column.

To stop filtering for a single process or service, clear its checkbox. To stop filtering altogether, in the key table, clear the checkbox next to Image.

FIGURE 15.3   **Resource Monitor.**

Performance Monitor

Performance Monitor provides a visual display of built-in Windows performance counters, either in real time or as a way to review historical data. You can add performance counters to Performance Monitor by dragging and dropping or by creating custom Data Collector Sets (DCS). Performance Monitor features multiple graph views that enable you to visually review performance log data. You can create custom views in Performance Monitor that can be exported as DCSs for use with performance and logging features. DCSs are explained shortly.

To be able to use Performance Monitor, the user must be an administrator or be a member of either the Performance Monitor Users group or the Performance Log Users group. Members of the Performance Monitor Users and Performance Log Users groups can view real-time performance data in Performance Monitor and can change the Performance Monitor display properties while viewing real-time data. The Performance Log Users group can also create or modify Data Collector Sets.

The four primary sub-systems that affect performance the most are processors, RAM, disk, and network performance. For example, the computer is centered around the processor. Therefore, the performance of the computer is greatly affected by the performance of the processor. The Processor:%Processor Time measures how busy the processor is. Although the processor might jump to 100% processor usage, the overall average is still important. If the processor is at 80% all the time, you should upgrade the processor (using a faster processor, or adding additional processors) or move some the services or programs to other systems.

> **ExamAlert**
>
> For the exam, be sure you know the multiple tools that can show you processor utilization, including the Task Manager and Performance Monitor. The processor utilization should not be consistently greater 80%.

RAM is another important factor in server performance. You can use the Performance Monitor to view how much available memory you have or how much paging is being done. *Paging* is when the disk space is used like RAM (virtual memory) so that it can allow Windows to load more programs and data. If the Performance Monitor shows no or little available memory or has a high pages/sec (20 or higher) or the paging file usage is high, you should increase the memory.

> **ExamAlert**
>
> Your pages/sec should not be 20 or higher and your paging file usage should not be greater than 1.5 times the RAM.

The Performance Monitor can also benefit you because if the server has a high processor utilization or high memory usage, you can determine which application is using most of the processor utilization or memory. Lastly, you can use Performance Monitor to set a baseline so that you know what is normal for the system. Then when you suspect poor performance, you can use the Performance Monitor to compare to the baseline so that you can quickly determine where the system is slowing down (bottleneck).

An important feature in Performance Monitor is the DCS, which groups data collectors into reusable elements. After a DCS is defined, you can schedule the collection of data using the DCS or see it in real time.

You can create a custom DCS containing performance counters and configure alert activities based on the performance counters exceeding or dropping below limits you define. After creating the DCS, you must configure the actions the system takes when the alert criteria are met.

> **ExamAlert**
>
> A DCS can be used to define performance counters and how they are to be used, which can be saved and reused.

You can add performance counters to Performance Monitor by dragging and dropping or by creating custom DCSs. Performance Monitor features multiple graph views that enable you to visually review performance log data. You can create custom views in Performance Monitor that can be exported as DCSs for use with performance and logging features, as shown in Figure 15.4.

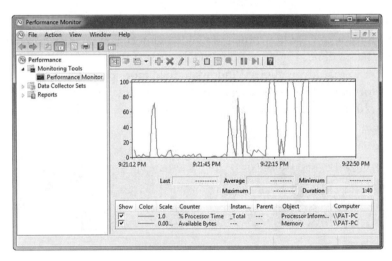

FIGURE 15.4   **Performance Monitor.**

Windows Experience Index

The Windows Experience Index (WEI) measures the capability of your computer's hardware and software configuration and expresses this measurement as a number called a base score. A higher base score generally means that your computer performs better and faster than a computer with a lower base score, especially when performing more advanced and resource-intensive tasks.

To access the WEI, right-click **Computer** and select **Properties**. Then click **Windows Experience Index** to result in the screen shown in Figure 15.5.

If you recently upgraded your hardware, including changing drivers, and want to find out if your score has changed, click **Re-run the assessment**.

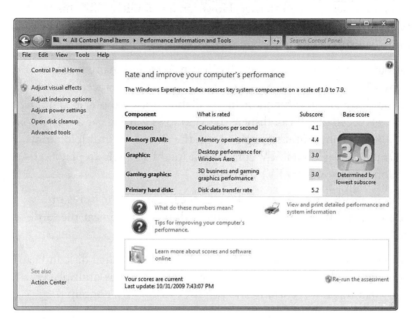

FIGURE 15.5 **Windows Experience Index.**

When looking at WEI, you see a base score, which is the lowest of all of the subscores. The subscores include processor, memory (RAM), graphics, gaming graphics, and primary hard disk. If you have processor, memory (RAM), graphics, and primary hard disk at 5.5 and the gaming graphics at 3.2, the base score is 3.2. Each score ranges from 1.0 to 7.9. Keep in mind that as hardware becomes faster, higher scores are achieved. When you purchase programs, keep in mind that some programs require a minimum WEI score.

The base score represents the minimum performance of your system based on the capabilities of different parts of your computer, including RAM, CPU, hard disk, general graphics performance on the desktop, and 3-D graphics capability.

Here are general descriptions of the experience you can expect from a computer that receives the following base scores:

▶ A computer with a base score of 1.0 or 2.0 usually has sufficient performance to do general computing tasks, such as run office productivity programs and search the Internet. However, a computer with this base score is generally not powerful enough to run Aero or the advanced multimedia experiences that are available with Windows 7.

▶ A computer with a base score of 3.0 can run Aero and many features of Windows 7 at a basic level. Some of the Windows 7 advanced features might not have all their functionality available. For example, a computer with a base score of 3.0 can display the Windows 7 theme at a resolution of 1280 × 1024 but might struggle to run the theme on multiple monitors. Or it can play digital TV content but might struggle to play high-definition television (HDTV) content.

▶ A computer with a base score of 4.0 or 5.0 can run new features of Windows 7, and it can support running multiple programs at the same time.

▶ A computer with a base score of 6.0 or 7.0 has a faster hard disk and can support high-end, graphics-intensive experiences, such as multiplayer and 3-D gaming and recording and playback of HDTV content.

Memory Usage and the Paging File

When your computer does not have enough memory to perform all of its functions, Windows and your programs can stop working. To help prevent data loss, Windows notifies you when your computer is low on memory. Other signs of low memory include poor performance and screen problems. You can also check the Event Viewer and the Windows Reliability and Performance Monitor.

Your computer has two types of memory: random access memory (RAM), also known as physical memory, and virtual memory, also known as a paging file. All programs use RAM, but when there is not enough RAM for the program you're trying to run, Windows temporarily moves information that is normally stored in RAM to the virtual memory.

Virtual memory is disk space that acts like RAM, which enables the operating system to load more programs and data. Parts of all the programs and data to be accessed are constantly swapped back and forth between RAM and disk so the virtual memory looks and acts like regular RAM. This is beneficial to the user because disk memory is far cheaper than RAM.

The RAM and virtual memory are broken down into chunks called pages, which are monitored by the operating system. When the RAM becomes full, the virtual memory system copies the least recently used programs and data to the virtual memory. Because this frees part of the RAM, it then has room to copy something else from virtual memory, load another program, or load more data. Windows 7 calls its virtual memory a paging file.

If you have low memory, you should consider the following:

- Installing more memory

- Increasing the size of the paging file

- Determining if a program overuses memory

To determine how much RAM you have, you can use the Welcome Center, Task Manager, or System Information. To open System Information:

1. Click the **Start** button and select **All Programs**.

2. Select **Accessories**, followed by selecting **System Tools**.

3. Select **System Information**.

4. The total amount of RAM is listed under total physical memory.

Windows 7 does a much better job in managing virtual memory than older versions of Windows. Windows 7 sets the minimum size of the paging file at the amount of RAM installed on your computer plus 300 MB and the maximum size at three times the amount of RAM installed on your computer. For most systems, if your paging file usage exceeds 1.5 times your RAM, your system experiences performance problems as it is paging to a slower disk more than it should.

If you want to manually manage virtual memory, you use a fixed virtual memory size in most cases. To do this, set the initial size and the maximum size to the same value. This ensures that the paging file is consistent and can be written to a single contiguous file (if possible, given the amount of space on the volume).

ExamAlert

A high value for pages/sec counter in performance monitor most likely means that you are low on physical memory because pages/sec shows how often it has to access the paging file.

Manually configure virtual memory by completing the following steps:

1. Click **Start** and then click **Control Panel**.

2. In Control Panel, click the **System and Security** category heading link.

3. Click **System**.

4. Click **Advanced System Settings** in the left pane.

5. Click **Settings** in the Performance section to display the Performance Options dialog box.

6. Click the **Advanced** tab and then click **Change** to display the Virtual Memory dialog box, as shown in Figure 15.6.

7. Clear the **Automatically manage paging file size for all drives** checkbox.

8. Under Drive [Volume Label], click the drive that contains the paging file you want to change.

9. Click **Custom size**, type a new size in megabytes in the Initial size (MB) or Maximum size (MB) box, click **Set**, and then click **OK**.

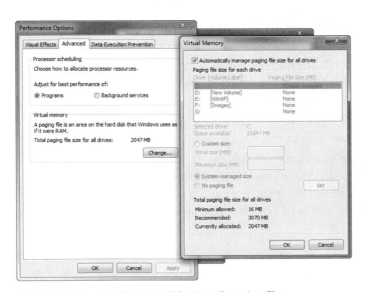

FIGURE 15.6   **Modifying the Windows 7 paging file.**

Increases in size usually do not require a restart, but if you decrease the size, you need to restart your computer for the changes to take effect. You should not disable or delete the paging file.

Processor Scheduling

Computers running Windows 7 are usually used actively by users. Typically, these users want the programs that they are currently using to be given a higher priority than programs running in the background. However, if you have a Windows 7 workstation that is dedicated to a specific task, such as monitoring an assembly line or acting as a print server, you can have Windows share processor resources equally between background and foreground programs. To change the processor scheduling, you do the following:

1. Click the **Start** button, right-click **Computer**, and select **Properties**.

2. Click the **Advanced system settings**.

3. Click the **Advanced** tab.

4. Under Performance click **Settings**.

5. Click the **Advanced** tab.

6. Under Processor scheduling, choose one of the following:

   ▸ Click **Programs** to assign more processor resources to the foreground programs.

   ▸ Click **Background** services to assign equal amounts of processor resources to all running services.

7. Click **OK** to apply the changes and then click **OK** to close the System Properties dialog box.

SuperFetch

SuperFetch is the caching technology used in Windows Vista and 7 that preloads commonly used applications into memory to reduce their load times. Besides caching recent applications (figuring that recent applications are more prone to be used again), it also keeps track of what time an application is being used so that it can load scheduled applications as necessary. To function more intelligently, SuperFetch can also ignore backups and virus scanners as normal caching technology that would also cache this information, although it is not necessary.

ReadyBoost and ReadyDrive

Windows 7 has several features that affect how disks are used. These include the following:

▶ Windows ReadyBoost boosts system performance by using USB flash devices as additional sources for caching.

▶ Windows ReadyDrive boosts system performance on mobile computers equipped with hybrid drives.

With Windows ReadyBoost, USB flash devices with sufficiently fast memory (flash devices can be read up to 10 times faster than physical disk drives) are used to extend the disk caching capabilities of the computer's main memory. Using flash devices for caching enables Windows 7 to make random reads faster by caching data on the USB flash device instead of a disk drive. Because this caching is applied to all disk content, not just the page file or system dynamic-link libraries (DLLs), the computer's overall performance is boosted.

USB flash devices you can use with Windows ReadyBoost include USB 2.0 flash drives, Secure Digital (SD) cards, and CompactFlash cards. These devices must have sufficiently fast flash memory and be at least 256 MB or larger in size. Windows 7 can use up to eight devices totaling up to 256 GB.

When you insert a USB flash device into a USB 2.0 or higher port, Windows 7 analyzes the speed of the flash memory on the device. When you click **Speed Up My System Using Windows ReadyBoost**, Windows 7 extends the computer's physical memory to the device. The default configuration enables Windows ReadyBoost to reserve all available space on the device for boosting system speed.

To use Windows ReadyBoost with a USB flash device that you either already inserted or that you previously declined to use with Windows ReadyBoost, follow these steps:

1. Click **Start** and then click **Computer**.

2. Right-click the USB flash device in the **Devices with Removable Storage** list and then choose **Properties**.

3. On the **ReadyBoost** tab, select **Use This Device** and then click **OK**.

4. For USB flash devices that do not support ReadyBoost, you cannot enable the device. The only option you have is to stop retesting the device when you plug it in. The **Stop Retesting This Device When I Plug It In** option is selected by default.

If the USB flash drive has both slow and fast flash memory, you are not able to use the slow flash memory portion of the USB storage device to speed the computer performance. As a result, you might not see all of the memory of the USB device when it is added to your physical memory.

Windows ReadyDrive improves performance on mobile computers equipped with hybrid drives. A hybrid drive is a drive that uses both flash RAM and a physical drive for storage. Because flash RAM is much faster than a physical disk, mobile computers running Windows 7 write data and changes to data to the flash memory first and periodically sync these writes and changes to the physical disk. This approach reduces the spinning of the physical drive and thus saves battery power.

The flash RAM on hybrid drives can be used to provide faster startup and resume from sleep or hibernation. In this case, the information needed for starting or resuming the operating system is written to the flash RAM prior to shutting down, entering sleep, or going into hibernation. When you start or wake the computer, this information is read from the flash RAM.

You do not need to enable ReadyDrive as it is automatically enabled on mobile computers with hybrid drives.

Cram Quiz

1. You have a computer running Windows 7. You need to frequently view perform-ance data that encompasses processor usage, memory usage, disk usage, and network traffic over several days. What should you do?

   - ○ **A.** Use the Task Manager
   - ○ **B.** Add counters to the Performance Monitor
   - ○ **C.** Use User Defined Data Collector Set
   - ○ **D.** Use the Reliability Monitor

2. What measurement tool does Windows 7 offer to help determine if your system can run certain applications or perform certain functions of Windows 7?

   - ○ **A.** WEI
   - ○ **B.** CPUIndex
   - ○ **C.** PagingGuide
   - ○ **D.** PerfMon

3. How large does your USB drive have to be to make use of ReadyBoost?

- ○ **A.** 256 MB
- ○ **B.** 512 MB
- ○ **C.** 1 GB
- ○ **D.** 2 GB

Cram Quiz Answers

1. **C** is correct. An important feature in Performance Monitor is the Data Collector Set (DCS), which groups data collectors into reusable elements. After a Data Collector Set is defined, you can schedule the collection of data using the DCS or see it in real time. Answer A is incorrect because Task Manager only shows in real time and is not useful when you need to view overall performance over time. Answer B is incorrect because adding counters to the Performance Monitor only helps you view performance real time. Answer D is incorrect because the Reliability Monitor shows you potential problems with a system, not performance data.

2. **A** is correct. The Windows Experience Index (WEI) measures the capability of your computer's hardware and software configuration and expresses this measurement as a number called a base score. A higher base score generally means that your computer performs better and faster than a computer with a lower base score, especially when performing more advanced and resource-intensive tasks. Answer D is incorrect because PerfMon is short for Performance Monitor, which is used to view performance indicators. It is mostly used to identify bottlenecks. It cannot determine if your system can run certain applications or perform certain functions. Answers B and C are incorrect because these terms do not exist in Windows 7.

3. **A** is correct. USB flash devices that can be used with Windows ReadyBoost include USB 2.0 flash drives, Secure Digital (SD) cards, and CompactFlash cards. These devices must have sufficiently fast flash memory and be at least 256 MB or larger in size. Therefore, the other answers are incorrect.

Review Questions

1. You work as the desktop support technician at Acme.com. You have a computer with 1 GB of memory running Windows 7 Ultimate. You want to add a fast removable flash drive to improve performance. What should you use?

   ○ **A.** Windows SuperFetch

   ○ **B.** Windows ReadyBoost

   ○ **C.** Windows ReadyDrive

   ○ **D.** Windows Memory Diagnostic tool

2. By default, what is the default configuration for processor scheduling on a computer running Windows 7?

   ○ **A.** Programs

   ○ **B.** Background

   ○ **C.** Balanced

   ○ **D.** Alternating

3. You insert a flash drive and discover that you cannot make use of all the memory on the USB flash device when configuring ReadyBoost. What do you think the problem is?

   ○ **A.** The USB flash drive has slow flash memory.

   ○ **B.** The USB flash drive has fast flash memory.

   ○ **C.** The USB flash drive has both slow and fast flash memory.

   ○ **D.** The USB flash drive does not meet the minimum requirement to configure ReadyBoost.

4. You work as the desktop support technician at Acme.com. You suspect an application is not releasing memory. You would like a user who is using the Windows 7 machine to run Performance Monitor. What do you need to do in order for the user to have access to Performance Monitor?

   ○ **A.** Add the user to the Power Users group

   ○ **B.** Add the user to the Performance Log Users group

   ○ **C.** Add the user to the Performance Monitor Users group

   ○ **D.** Add the user to the Administrator group

5. If you want to see if you are running out of physical memory, which counter should you use?

   ○ **A.** CPU utilization

   ○ **B.** Pages\sec

   ○ **C.** Network utilization

   ○ **D.** interrupts\sec

6. What tool can help you quickly determine what processes are writing to disk and how much each is writing?

   ○ **A.** System Information

   ○ **B.** System Configuration

   ○ **C.** Resource Monitor

   ○ **D.** Windows Experience Index

7. What should be the maximum memory page rate used for Windows 7?

   ○ **A.** Less than 5

   ○ **B.** Less than 10

   ○ **C.** Less than 20

   ○ **D.** Less than 50

8. You have a system with 2 GB of memory. You notice that the processor utilization is around 65%, the paging file is around 4 GB, and the network traffic is around 5%. Your system seems sluggish. What do you think the problem is?

   ○ **A.** Your processor is too slow.

   ○ **B.** You do not have enough memory.

   ○ **C.** Your network card is overtaxed.

   ○ **D.** Your disk system cannot keep up.

9. What can you use to quickly capture performance data of multiple performance counters and configure alert activities based on the performance counters?

   ○ **A.** Alert Counter

   ○ **B.** Task Parameter

   ○ **C.** Data Collector Set

   ○ **D.** Windows Experience Index

10. What should the minimum WEI be if you want to support multiplayer or 3-D gaming and recording and playback of HDTV?

   ○ **A.** 1.0

   ○ **B.** 2.0

   ○ **C.** 3.0

   ○ **D.** 4.0

   ○ **E.** 6.0

Answers to Review Questions

1. Answer **B** is correct. Windows ReadyBoost boosts system performance by using USB flash devices as additional sources for caching. Answer A is incorrect because SuperFetch utilizes machine learning techniques to analyze usage patterns in order to enable Windows 7 to make intelligent decisions about what content should be present in system memory at any given time. Answer C is incorrect because ReadyDrive boosts system performance on mobile computers equipped with hybrid drives. Answer D is incorrect because the Windows Memory Diagnostic tool is used to test memory and not to increase performance.

2. Answer **A** is correct. By default, processor scheduling is set to Programs, which assigns more processor resources to the foreground programs. Answer B is incorrect because when Background services is selected, equal amounts of processor resources go to all running services. Answers C and D are incorrect because Balanced and Alternating do not exist in processor scheduling.

3. Answer **C** is correct. To get the benefit of ReadyBoost, your USB device needs to use fast flash memory. Therefore, if you insert a USB flash device that consists of slow and fast flash memory, ReadyBoost only uses the fast flash memory. Answers A and B are incorrect. Because ReadyBoost recognizes some of the memory, you can assume that the USB flash device meets the minimum requirements, so Answer D is incorrect.

4. Answers **B** and **C** are correct. For standard users to run the performance monitor, you must add them to the Performance Monitor Users group or Performance Log Users group, or you can make them administrators. Because there is no need to make them administrators, it is best to add them only to the Performance Monitor group or the Performance Log Users group. The difference between the two groups is that the Performance Log Users group can also create and modify Data Collector Sets but the Performance Monitor group cannot. Therefore, Answer D is incorrect. Answer A is incorrect because Power Users groups are only there for backward compatibility for older applications created for older versions of Windows.

5. Answer **B** is correct. To see how much paging takes place between physical RAM and the paging file (disk space acting as RAM), you refer to the pages\sec measurement. A high value indicates that you are utilizing the paging often, which means you are running out of physical memory. Answer A is incorrect because CPU utilization shows how hard the processor is working. Answer C is incorrect because network utilization indicates how much bandwidth is being used on the network. Answer D is incorrect because a high value for Interrupts\sec might indicate a faulty device or device driver.

6. Answer **C** is correct. Resource Monitor shows you the amount of processor and memory utilized for a process in addition to indicating which applications are using files. Windows Resource Monitor is a powerful tool for understanding how your system resources are used by processes and services. Answer A is incorrect because System Information shows the hardware and software running on a computer. Answer B is incorrect because the System Configuration is a troubleshooting tool to help you isolate problematic startup programs. Answer D is incorrect because the Windows Experience Index is used to gauge the performance of a system.

7. Answer **C** is correct. If the Performance Monitor shows no or little available memory or has a high pages/sec (20 or higher) or the paging file usage is high, you should increase the memory. Therefore, the other answers are incorrect.

8. Answer **B** is incorrect. Most likely your paging file is too large, which causes excessive paging because the paging file (disk) is much slower than RAM. Therefore, you should add more memory. Answer A is incorrect because if the processor was too busy, it would consistently be greater than 80%. Answer C is incorrect because the network traffic is low. Answer D is incorrect because the paging file has grown beyond 1.5 times memory. If you have a bottleneck for disk, you have to look at additional performance counters such as the length of the disk queue.

9. Answer **C** is correct. An important feature in Performance Monitor is the Data Collector Set (DCS), which groups data collectors into reusable elements. After a DCS is defined, you can schedule the collection of data using the DCS or see it in real time. Answer D is incorrect because the Windows Experience Index measures the capability of your computer's hardware and software configuration and expresses this measurement as a number called a base score. Answers A and B are incorrect because alert counter and task parameters are not part of performance monitoring or do not exist.

10. Answer **E** is correct. A computer with a base score of 6.0 or 7.0 has a faster hard disk and can support high-end, graphics-intensive experiences, such as multiplayer and 3-D gaming and recording and playback of HDTV content. Therefore, the other answers are incorrect.

CHAPTER 16

Backups and System Recovery

This chapter covers the following 70-680 Objectives:

▶ Monitoring and Maintaining Systems That Run Windows 7:

  ▶ Monitor systems

▶ Configuring Backup and Recovery Options:

  ▶ Configure backup

  ▶ Configure file recovery options

  ▶ Configure system recovery options

Reliability is the ability of a computer to perform and maintain its functions in routine circumstances. When problems (application crashes, service freezes and restarts, driver initialization failures, and operating system failures) occur, reliability is affected because the computer cannot perform and maintain its functions.

Windows 7 architecture has the capability to detect and correct some problems. Windows 7 also provides multiple diagnostic programs to guide you through troubleshooting a wide range of problems. Of course, with the more complicated problems, you need to use basic troubleshooting methodology while using the wide range of troubleshooting tools available. Don't forget that performing backups on a regularly basis is invaluable when all else fails.

Looking at Events

▶ **Monitor systems**

▶ **Configure system recovery options**

CramSaver

1. In Windows 7, what can be used to quickly view if your antivirus is up to date and if Windows is patched?

   ○ **A.** Event Viewer

   ○ **B.** Action Center

   ○ **C.** Reliability Monitor

   ○ **D.** System Information

2. What key do you need to press to enter Safe mode?

   ○ **A.** F1

   ○ **B.** F4

   ○ **C.** F8

   ○ **D.** F10

3. What tool do you use to disable several programs that automatically start up during boot up?

   ○ **A.** System Configuration

   ○ **B.** System Information

   ○ **C.** Action Center

   ○ **D.** BCDBoot

Answers

1. **B** is correct. Action Center is a central place to view alerts and take actions that can help keep Windows running smoothly. Action Center notifies you when items need your attention and lists important messages about security and maintenance settings that need your attention. Answer A is incorrect because the Event Viewer enables you to look at the Windows logs. Answer C is incorrect because the Reliability Monitor gives you an overview of the system stability and enables you to view individual events that effect overall stability. Answer D is incorrect because the System Information gives you an overview of the system, including the recognized hardware and software.

2. **C** is correct. By pressing the F8 key, you can enter the Advanced Startup menu and select Safe Mode. Answer A is incorrect because the F1 key is usually used for help. It could also be used to access the ROM BIOS program on some computers. Answer B is incorrect because the F4 key was used to load disk drivers during the installation of Windows XP, not Windows 7. Answer D is incorrect because the F10 key can be used to access the ROM BIOS program on some computers.

3. **A** is correct. System Configuration is an advanced tool that can help identify problems that might prevent Windows from starting correctly. You can start Windows with common services and startup programs turned off and then turn them back on, one at a time. Answer B is incorrect because the System Information is used to view a system's configuration. Answer C is incorrect because the Action Center is a central place to view alerts and take actions that can help keep Windows running smoothly. Answer D is incorrect because the BCDBoot is used to configure which operating system to boot if you have more than one copy of Windows installed.

When trying to troubleshoot problems, you usually need to gather as much information as possible to provide insight on the actual problem or help you to identify potential problems. Windows 7 has several tools to help you take a look at the system and its health.

Event Viewer

Event Viewer, as shown in Figure 16.1, is a utility that is used to view and manage logs of system, application, and security events on a computer. Event Viewer gathers information about hardware and software problems and monitors Windows security events. Event Viewer can be executed by opening Administrative Tools and clicking **Event Viewer**, or by adding it to the Microsoft Management Console (MMC). It is also part of the Computer Management Console. You can also open it by executing `eventvwr.msc` at a command prompt or using the **Run** option.

ExamAlert

Most Windows and application errors are displayed in the Event Viewer, which you can access by itself or as part of the Computer Management Console.

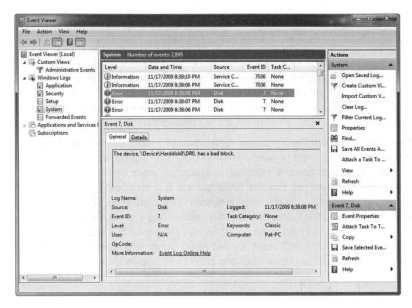

FIGURE 16.1   **Event Viewer.**

The newer version of Event Viewer available with Windows 7 is divided into Custom Views, Windows Logs, Applications and Services, and Subscriptions. Traditional logs that have been included with Windows XP and Windows Vista are found in the Windows Logs group. They include the following:

▶ **Application**: The application log contains events logged by programs. For example, a database program might record a file error in the programs log. Program developers decide which events to monitor. The application log can be viewed by all users.

▶ **Security**: The security logs contains valid and invalid logon attempts as well as events related to resource use such as creating, opening, or deleting files or other objects. For example, if you have enabled logon and logoff auditing, attempts to log on to the system are recorded in the security log. By default, security logging is turned off. To enable security logging, use Group Policies to set the audit policy or change the registry. To audit files and folders, you must be logged on as a member of the Administrators group or have been granted the Manage auditing and security log right in Group Policies. Security logs can only be viewed by administrators.

▶ **System**: The system log contains events that are logged by the Windows system components. For example, the failure of a driver or other system component to load during start-up is recorded in the system log. The event types logged by system components are predetermined by Windows. The system log can be viewed by all users.

There are five levels of events:

▶ **Error**: A significant problem occurs, such as loss of data or loss of functionality (for example, when a service fails during start-up).

▶ **Warning**: An event that is not necessarily significant, but might indicate a possible future problem. For example, when disk space is low, a warning is logged.

▶ **Information**: An event that describes the successful operation of an application, driver, or service. For example, when a network driver loads successfully, an information event is logged.

▶ **Success Audit**: An audited security access attempt that succeeds. For example, a user's successful attempt to log on to the system is logged as a success audit event.

▶ **Failure Audit**: An audited security access attempt that fails. For example, if a user tries to access a network drive and fails, the attempt is logged as a failure audit event.

When you double-click an event, the Event Properties window appears. The Event Properties can be divided into two parts, event header and event description. The event header information includes:

▶ **Date**: The date the event occurred.

▶ **Time**: Local time the event occurred.

▶ **User**: User name on whose behalf the event occurred.

▶ **Computer**: Name of the computer where the event occurred. The computer name is usually the local computer unless you are viewing an event log on another Windows computer.

▶ **Event ID**: Number identifying the particular event type.

▶ **Source**: Software that logged the event, which can be either a program name, such as SQL Server, or a component of the system or of a large program, such as a driver name.

▶ **Type**: Classification of the event severity: error, information, or warning in the system and application logs; and success audit and failure audit in the security log.

▶ **Category**: Classification of the event by the event source.

Filtering Events

When you go through an Event Viewer, you see that some of these logs have hundreds, even thousands, of entries. When you are looking for something specific, it can be a daunting task to find it. To help you cut down on the log entries to review, the Event Viewer enables you to filter the current logs by opening the Action menu and selecting Filter Current Log, as shown in Figure 16.2. From here, you can specify the event level, ID, keywords, users, and/or computers.

FIGURE 16.2 **Filtering the Event Viewer logs.**

Event Subscriptions

If you need to review the events of multiple computers, you have to log on to each computer to access the Event Viewer or open multiple event viewer views, one for each computer that you need to review. Starting with Windows Vista, Windows has the capability to collect copies of events from multiple remote computers and store them locally. To specify which events to collect, you create an event subscription.

To configure computers in a domain to forward and collect events:

1. Log on to each source computer with an account that has administrative privileges.

2. Execute the following command:

```
winrm quickconfig
```

3. Add the computer account to which you want the logs to be sent to the local Administrators group.

4. On the collector computer, execute the following command:

```
wecutil qc
```

The events appear in the Forwarded Events logs.

Reliability Monitor

Besides combing through the Event Viewer, you can use the Reliability Monitor to give you an overview of the system stability and to view individual events that effect overall stability, as shown in Figure 16.3. Some of the events shown are software installation, operating system updates, and hardware failures.

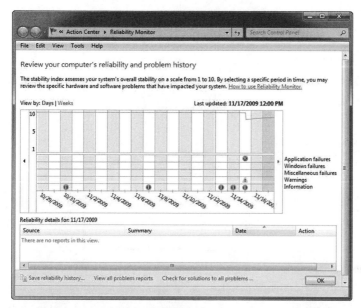

FIGURE 16.3 **Reliability Monitor.**

Reliability Monitor calculates a System Stability Index that reflects whether unexpected problems reduced the reliability of the system. A graph of the Stability Index over time quickly identifies dates when problems began to occur. The accompanying System Stability Report provides details to help troubleshoot the root cause of reduced reliability. By viewing changes to the system (installation or removal of applications, updates to the operating system, or addition or modification of drivers) side-by-side with failures (application failures, operating system crashes, or hardware failures), you can quickly develop a strategy for addressing the issues.

Action Center

Action Center is a central place to view alerts and take actions that can help keep Windows running smoothly, as illustrated in Figure 16.4. Action Center notifies you when items need your attention and lists important messages about security and maintenance settings that need your attention. Red items in Action Center are labeled Important and indicate significant issues that should be addressed soon, such as an outdated antivirus program that needs updating. Yellow items are suggested tasks that you should consider addressing, such as recommended maintenance tasks.

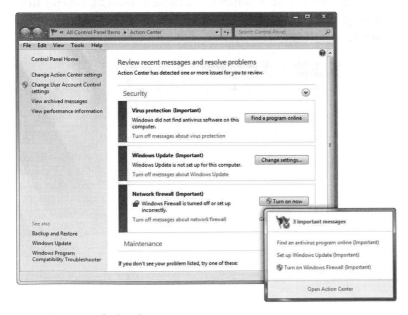

FIGURE 16.4   **Action Center.**

To view details about either the Security or Maintenance section, click the heading or the arrow next to the heading to expand or collapse the section. If you don't want to see certain types of messages, you can choose to hide them from view.

You can quickly see whether there are any new messages in Action Center by placing your mouse over the Action Center icon in the notification area on the taskbar. Click the icon to view more detail, and click a message to address the issue. Or open Action Center to view the message in its entirety.

System Information

System Information (also known as msinfo32.exe) shows details about your computer's hardware configuration, computer components, and software, including drivers, as shown in Figure 16.5. Microsoft created System Information so that support personnel can quickly identify the Windows configuration.

System Information lists categories in the left pane and details about each category in the right pane. The categories include the following:

- ▶ **System Summary**: Displays general information about your computer and the operating system, such as the computer name and manufacturer, the type of basic input/output system (BIOS) your computer uses, and the amount of memory that's installed

- ▶ **Hardware Resources**: Displays advanced details about your computer's hardware and is intended for IT professionals

- ▶ **Components**: Displays information about disk drives, sound devices, modems, and other components installed on your computer

- ▶ **Software Environment**: Displays information about drivers, network connections, and other program-related details

To find a specific detail in System Information, type the information you're looking for in the **Find what** box at the bottom of the window. For example, to find your computer's Internet protocol (IP) address, type `ip address` in the Find what box and then click **Find**.

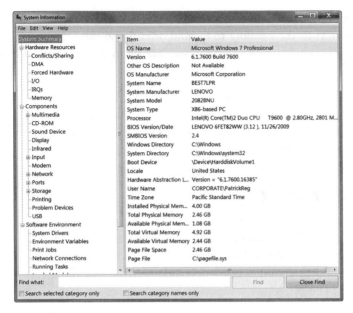

FIGURE 16.5   **System Information.**

Diagnostic Tools

Windows 7 has multiple tools for diagnosing and resolving problems. To proactively and automatically identify potential problems, Windows 7 includes built-in diagnostics that can automatically detect and diagnose common support problems. The Windows 7 built-in diagnostics can automatically identify and help users resolve the following problems:

- ▶ Hardware error conditions

- ▶ Failing disks

- ▶ Degraded performance

- ▶ Failure to shut down properly

- ▶ Memory problems

- ▶ Problems related to installing drivers and applications

- ▶ Problems related to using drivers and applications

In most cases, the built-in diagnostics prompt users to make them aware of any problems as they occur and then help to guide users through resolving the problem.

Memory Diagnostic Tool

Bad memory can cause a wide assortment of problems with your system including causing Windows not to be reliable. The Memory Diagnostic tool is used to diagnose physical memory problems, including memory leaks and failing memory. The tool also works with the Microsoft Online Crash Analysis tool to detect system crashes possibly caused by failing memory, which then prompts the user to schedule a memory test the next time the computer is restarted.

If you suspect that a computer has a memory problem that is not being automatically detected, you can run Windows Memory Diagnostics manually by completing the following steps:

1. Click **Start**, point to **All Programs**, and then click **Accessories**.

2. Right-click **Command Prompt** and then select **Run As Administrator**.

3. At the command prompt, type `mdsched.exe`.

4. You can choose to restart the computer and run the tool immediately or schedule the tool to run at the next restart.

You can also manually run the Windows Memory Diagnostics tool from Administrative Tools in Control Panel or from the boot menu before Windows loads.

If you choose to run the tool at the next restart, Windows Memory Diagnostics runs automatically after the computer restarts, enabling you to choose the type of testing to perform. When the computer restarts and the memory is tested, you are provided with an easy-to-understand report detailing the problem. Information is also written to the event log for future analysis.

While the test is running, you can press **F1** to access advanced diagnostic options. The advanced options include the following:

▶ **Test mix**: Choose what type of test you want to run

▶ **Cache**: Choose the cache setting you want for each test

▶ **Pass Count**: Type the number of times you want to repeat the tests

Press the **Tab** key to move between the different advanced options. When you have selected your options, press **F10** to start the test.

Network Diagnostic Tool

The Windows Network Diagnostic tool was discussed in Chapter 5, "Configuring Windows Networking," to help resolve network-related issues. When a user is unable to connect to a network resource, the user is presented with a repair option, which runs the Windows Network Diagnostic tool. You can also choose to run the tool manually by using the Diagnose option on the Local Area Connections Status property sheet.

Boot Tools

When dealing with Windows, you eventually deal with boot problems. Either the computer does not boot completely or you get errors during boot up. Windows 7 offers several tools in troubleshooting these types of problems, as described in the sections that follow.

Advanced Startup Options

The Advanced Boot Options menu lets you start Windows in advanced troubleshooting modes. To access the advanced startup options, do the following:

▶ If your computer has a single operating system installed, repeatedly press the **F8** key as your computer restarts. You need to press **F8** before the Windows logo appears. If the Windows logo appears, you need to try again.

▶ If your computer has more than one operating system, use the arrow keys to highlight the operating system you want to start in Safe Mode and then press **F8**.

On the Advanced Boot Options screen shown in Figure 16.6, use the arrow keys to highlight the Safe Mode option you want and then press **Enter**. Log on to your computer with a user account that has administrator rights. When your computer is in Safe Mode, you see the words Safe Mode in the corners of the display. To exit Safe Mode, restart your computer and let Windows start normally.

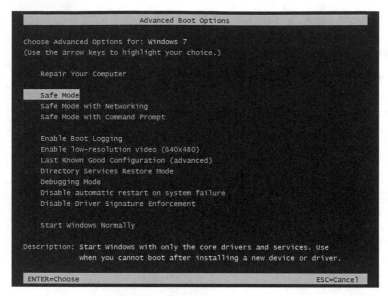

FIGURE 16.6   **Advanced Boot Options.**

Some options, such as Safe Mode, start Windows in a limited state, where only the bare essentials are started. If a problem does not reappear when you start in Safe Mode, you can eliminate the default settings and basic device drivers as possible causes. Other options start Windows with advanced features intended for use by system administrators and IT professionals.

The available options are as follows:

▶ **Repair Your Computer**: Shows a list of system recovery tools (Startup Repair Tool) you can use to repair startup problems, run diagnostics, or restore your system. This option is available only if you install the tools onto the computer. If they are not installed, the system recovery tools are located on the Windows installation disc.

▶ **Safe Mode**: Starts Windows with a minimal set of drivers and services. While in Safe Mode, shown in Figure 16.7, you can access the Control Panel, Device Manager, Event Viewer, System Information, Command Prompt, and Registry Editor.

▶ **Safe Mode with Networking**: Starts Windows in Safe Mode but also enables networking.

▶ **Safe Mode with Command Prompt**: Starts Windows in Safe Mode with a command prompt window instead of the Windows graphical user interface (GUI). This option is intended for IT professionals and administrators.

▶ **Enable Boot Logging**: Lists all of the drivers that are installed during startup in the ntbtlog.txt file. The ntbtlog.txt file can be used to determine which driver failed if Windows cannot start properly.

▶ **Enable low-resolution video (640 × 480)**: Boots to the Windows GUI in minimal VGA mode using the standard VGA drivers (640 × 480 resolution and 16 colors).

▶ **Last Known Good Configuration (advanced)**: Starts Windows with the last registry and driver configuration that worked when the last user logged on successfully.

▶ **Directory Services Restore Mode**: Starts Windows in Directory Services Restore Mode so that you can restore or repair Active Directory.

▶ **Debugging Mode**: Shows driver names as the drivers are loaded during the boot process.

▶ **Disable automatic restart on system failure**: Prevents Windows from automatically restarting if an error occurs during bootup. Use this option if Windows constantly fails and reboots.

▶ **Disable Driver Signature Enforcement**: Allows drivers containing improper signatures to be installed.

▶ **Start Windows normally**: Starts Windows in its normal mode.

FIGURE 16.7 **Safe Mode.**

System Configuration

System Configuration is an advanced tool that can help identify problems that might prevent Windows from starting correctly. You can start Windows with common services and startup programs turned off and then turn them back on, one at a time. If a problem does not occur when a service is turned off but does occur when turned on, then the service could be the cause of the problem. System Configuration is intended to find and isolate problems, but it is not meant as a startup management program.

The System Configuration tool can be loaded from the Administrative Tools. The tabs found in System Configuration tool are shown in Table 16.1.

TABLE 16.1 **System Configuration Tool Tabs**

Tab	Description
General	Lists choices for startup configuration modes:
	Normal startup: Starts Windows in its normal mode.
	Diagnostic startup: Starts Windows with basic services and drivers only. If Diagnostic startup starts without a problem, it verifies that the problem is not the basic Windows files.
	Selective startup: Starts Windows with basic services and drivers and enables you to select individual services and startup programs. Select startup is used to isolate problematic services and startup programs.
Boot	Shows configuration options for the operating system and advanced debugging settings, including:
	Safe boot-Minimal: Boots Windows into Safe Mode with GUI interface, which runs only essential system services. Networking is disabled.
	Safe boot-Alternate shell: Boots to the Safe Mode (command prompt). Networking and the graphical user interface are disabled.
	Safe boot-Active Directory repair: Starts Windows in Directory Services Restore Mode so that you can restore or repair Active Directory.
	Safe boot-Network: Boots Windows into Safe Mode, which runs only essential system services but also enables networking.
	Boot log: Lists all of the drivers that are installed during startup in the ntbtlog.txt file. The ntbtlog.txt file can be used to determine which driver failed if Windows cannot start properly.
	Base video: Boots to the Windows graphical user interface in minimal VGA mode using the standard VGA drivers (640 × 480 resolution and 16 colors).
	OS boot information: Shows driver names as the drivers are loaded during the boot process.
	Make all settings permanent: Does not track changes made in System Configuration. Options can be changed later using System Configuration, but must be changed manually. When this option is selected, you cannot roll back your changes by selecting Normal startup on the General tab.

TABLE 16.1 **Continued**

Tab	Description
Services	Lists all services that are registered with Windows and displays their current status (running or stopped). You can use the Services tab to enable or disable individual services so that you can isolate a problematic service that loads during boot up. You can select Hide all Microsoft services to show only third-party applications in the services list.
Startup	Lists applications that start when the computer boots, including the name of their publishers, the paths to the executable files, and the locations of the registry keys or shortcuts that cause the applications to run, as shown in Figure 16.8. This option is used to isolate problematic programs that load during boot up.
Tools	Provides a list of diagnostic tools, as shown in Figure 16.9.

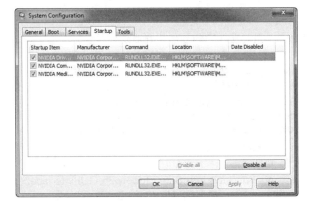

FIGURE 16.8 **System Configuration Startup tab.**

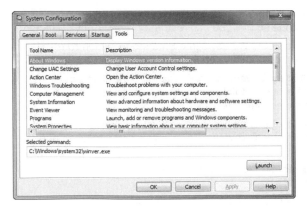

FIGURE 16.9 **System Configuration Tools tab.**

A new component that has been added to Windows 7 System Configuration is the ability to increase Windows 7 boot speed. If you select the Boot options and click the **Advanced Options**, you can increase the number of processors used during boot up, assuming you have multiple processors. As a result, you have a quicker boot time.

System Recovery Disc

The System Recovery Options menu contains several tools, such as Startup Repair, that can help you recover Windows from a serious error. This set of tools is on your computer's hard disk and on the Windows installation disc.

To open the System Recovery Options menu on your computer, do the following:

1. Remove all floppy disks, CDs, and DVDs from your computer and then restart your computer using the computer's power button.

2. Do one of the following:

   ▸ If your computer has a single operating system installed, press and hold the **F8** key as your computer restarts. You need to press **F8** before the Windows logo appears. If the Windows logo appears, you need to try again by waiting until the Windows logon prompt appears and then shutting down and restarting your computer.

   ▸ If your computer has more than one operating system, use the arrow keys to highlight the operating system you want to repair and then press and hold **F8**.

3. On the Advanced Boot Options screen, use the arrow keys to highlight Repair your computer and then press **Enter**. (If Repair your computer isn't listed as an option, your computer doesn't include preinstalled recovery options, or your network administrator has turned them off.)

4. Select a keyboard layout and then click **Next**.

5. On the System Recovery Options menu, click a tool to open it, as shown in Figure 16.10.

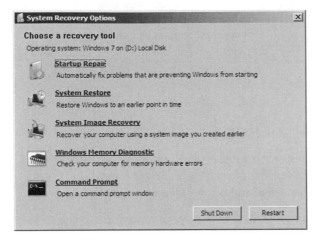

FIGURE 16.10   **System Recovery Options.**

If your computer's system is severely damaged and you cannot access the System Recovery Options menu on your computer, you can access it using the Windows 7 installation disc or a system repair disc you created earlier. To use this method, you need to restart (boot) your computer using the disc.

1. Insert the repair disc.

2. Restart your computer using the computer's power button and boot the repair disc. You might need to press a key to boot from the disc and might have to configure your BIOS to boot from the disc.

3. Choose your language settings and then click **Next**.

4. If you are using the Windows installation disc, click **Repair your computer**.

5. Select the Windows installation you want to repair and then click **Next**.

6. On the System Recovery Options menu, click a tool to open it.

A System recovery disc is used to boot your computer if you must recover Windows from a serious error or to restore your computer.

To create a system repair disc in Windows 7, do the following:

1. Click **Start, All Programs, Maintenance, Create a System Repair Disc**.

2. Insert a CD/DVD into the drive and click **Create disc**.

The options in the system repair include

▸ **Startup Repair**: Fixes certain problems, such as missing or damaged system files that might prevent Windows from starting correctly.

▸ **System Restore**: Restores your computer's system files to an earlier point in time without affecting your files, such as email, documents, or photos. If you use System Restore from the System Recovery Options menu, you cannot undo the restore operation. However, you can run System Restore again and choose a different restore point, if one exists.

▸ **System Image Recovery**: You need to have created a system image beforehand to use this option. A system image is a personalized backup of the partition that contains Windows and includes programs and user data, such as documents, pictures, and music.

▸ **Windows Memory Diagnostic Tool**: Scans your computer's memory for errors.

▸ **Command Prompt**: Advanced users can use Command Prompt to perform recovery-related operations and also run other command-line tools for diagnosing and troubleshooting problems.

Windows PE Disk

As mentioned earlier in the book, the Windows Preinstallation Environment (Windows PE) 3.0 is a minimal Win32 operating system with limited services that is built on the Windows 7 kernel. It is used to prepare a computer for Windows installation, to copy disk images from a network file server, and to initiate Windows Setup. Besides being used to deploy operating systems, it is an integral component in recovery technology with Windows Recovery Environment (Windows RE). Some of the tools included in the Windows PE disk include

▸ **BCDBoot**: A tool used to quickly set up a system partition or to repair the boot environment located on the system partition.

▸ **BCDEdit**: A command-line tool for managing the BCD Store, which describes the boot application and boot application settings, such as the boot menu.

▸ **BootSect**: Used to restore the boot sector on your computer.

▸ **Deployment Image Servicing and Management (DISM)**: Used to service Windows images offline before deployment.

- ▸ **DiskPart**: Text-mode command interpreter to manage disks, partitions, and volumes.

- ▸ **DrvLoad**: Adds out-of-box drivers.

- ▸ **OscdImg**: A command-line tool for creating an image file (.iso) of a customized 32-bit or 64-bit version of Windows PE.

- ▸ **Winpeshl**: Controls whether a customized shell is loaded in Windows PE or default command prompt window. To load a customized shell, create a file named Winpeshl.ini and place it in %SYSTEMROOT%\ System32 of your customized Windows PE image.

- ▸ **WpeInit**: A command-line tool that initializes Windows PE each time that Windows PE boots. It installs Plug and Play devices, processes Unattend.xml settings, and loads network resources.

- ▸ **WpeUtil**: A command-line tool that enables you to run various commands in a Windows PE session.

For more information about Windows PE and its tools, visit the following websites:

http://technet.microsoft.com/en-us/library/cc749538(WS.10).aspx

http://technet.microsoft.com/en-us/library/cc749055(WS.10).aspx

http://download.microsoft.com/download/5/b/5/5b5bec17-ea71-4653-9539-204a672f11cf/WindowsPE_tech.doc

Problem Steps Recorder

You can use Problem Steps Recorder to automatically capture the steps you take on a computer, including a text description of where you clicked and a picture of the screen during each click (called a screen shot). After you capture these steps, you can save them to a file that can be used by a support professional or someone else helping you with a computer problem.

When you record steps on your computer, anything you type is not recorded. If what you type is an important part of re-creating the problem you're trying to solve, use the comment feature described later in the chapter to highlight where the problem is occurring.

To record and save steps on your computer, do the following:

1. Click the **Start** button and search for `problem steps recorder` in the Search Programs and Files text box. When it finds record steps to reproduce a problem, select the link under Control Panel.

2. Click **Start Record**, as shown in Figure 16.11.

3. On your computer, go through the steps on your computer to reproduce the problem. You can pause the recording at any time and then resume it later.

4. Click **Stop Record**.

5. In the Save As dialog box, type a name for the file and then click **Save** (the file is saved with the .zip filename extension).

6. To view the record of the steps you recorded, open the .zip file you just saved and then double-click the file. The document opens in your browser.

FIGURE 16.11   **Problem Steps Recorder.**

After recording and saving a .zip file, click the help down arrow and then click **Send to E-mail recipient**. This opens an email message in your default email program with the last recorded file attached to it. Note: You won't be able to click the Send to E-mail recipient option until you've recorded and saved a file.

When you want to add a comment, click **Add Comment**. Use your mouse to highlight the part of the screen that you want to comment on, type your text in the Highlight Problem and Comment box, and then click **OK**.

If you select the down arrow, you can configure the recorder settings. If you don't want to capture the screen shots along with each click that you performed, select **No**. This might be a consideration if you are taking screen shots of a program that contains personal information, such as bank statements, and you are sharing the screen shots with someone else.

The default is 25 screens, but you can increase or decrease the number of screen shots. Problem Steps Recorder only records the default number of screen shots. For example, if you took 30 screen shots during a recording but only had 25 screen shots as the default, the first five screen shots would be missing. In this case, you would want to increase the number of default screen shots.

Cram Quiz

1. Which tool can you use to increase the number of processors used during boot?
   - ○ **A.** Computer Management Console
   - ○ **B.** System Information
   - ○ **C.** System Configuration
   - ○ **D.** IIS

2. Windows fails to start. What can you use to load the minimal set of Windows drivers and services so that you can troubleshoot the problem?
   - ○ **A.** Safe Mode
   - ○ **B.** WinPE
   - ○ **C.** Windows Backup
   - ○ **D.** System Information

3. What tool can be used to thoroughly test memory?
   - ○ **A.** Computer Management Console
   - ○ **B.** System Information
   - ○ **C.** Memory Diagnostic tool
   - ○ **D.** Safe Mode

Cram Quiz Answers

1. **C** is correct. To increase the performance during bootup, you can select Windows to use multiple processors (assuming your system has multiple processors) by starting System Configuration, clicking the **Boot** tab, and clicking the **Advanced Options** button. Answer A is incorrect because the Computer Management Console includes multiple Microsoft Management Consoles but none that allows you to modify the number of processors used during boot. Answer B is incorrect because System Information is used view the configuration of Windows. Answer D is incorrect because IIS, short for Internet Information Services, is Microsoft's web server.

2. **A** is correct. Safe Mode starts Windows with a minimal set of drivers and services. While in Safe Mode, you can access the Control Panel, Device Manager, Event Viewer, System Information, Command Prompt, and Registry Editor. Answer B is incorrect because although WinPE is a very useful troubleshooting tool, it does not load the Windows minimal set of drivers and services. Answer C is incorrect because Windows Backup is used to back up and restore data, not to specify what is loaded during bootup. Answer D is incorrect because System Information is a tool used to view a system's configuration.

3. **C** is correct. Windows 7 has multiple diagnostic tools, including a Memory Diagnostic tool and Network Diagnostic tool. The Memory Diagnostic tool can diagnose physical memory, including memory leaks and failing memory. Answer A is incorrect because the Computer Management Console has multiple MMC add-ins that help you manage your computer. Answer B is incorrect because the System Information gives you a single place to look to see what computer hardware and software a computer has. Answer D is incorrect because Safe Mode is a bootup option that loads minimum drivers and services, primarily used for troubleshooting and fixing boot problems.

Backups and System Recovery

▶ **Configure backup**

▶ **Configure file recovery options**

▶ **Configure system recovery options**

CramSaver

1. What technology is used with NTFS volumes to automatically make extra copies of data files?

    ○ **A.** Shadow Copy

    ○ **B.** IIS

    ○ **C.** Windows Backup

    ○ **D.** Msconfig

2. What program do you use to quickly restore your computer's system files to an earlier point in time without affecting your data?

    ○ **A.** System Restore

    ○ **B.** Shadow Copy

    ○ **C.** System Image Backup

    ○ **D.** Safe Mode

Answers

1. **A** is correct. Shadow copies (introduced in Windows Server 2003), when configured, automatically create backup copies of the data stored in data folders on specific drive volumes at scheduled times. The drive volume must be formatted as NTFS. Windows 7 utilizes Shadow copies to provide previous versions of files even if they have never been backed up. Answer B is incorrect because IIS, short for Internet Information Services, is Microsoft's web server. Answer C is incorrect because Windows Backup must be manually executed or scheduled. Answer D is incorrect because System Configuration (MSConfig) is used to troubleshoot boot problems.

2. **A** is correct. System Restore helps you restore your computer's system files to an earlier point in time. It's a way to undo system changes to your computer without affecting your personal files, such as email, documents, or photos. Answer B is incorrect because Shadow Copy is used to provide previous versions of data files. Answer C is incorrect because the System Image Backup is a copy of the system drives required for Windows to run. Answer D is incorrect because Safe Mode is used to load only the minimum drivers and services for Windows 7 to run.

If you have been working with computers long enough, you know that no matter what you do, computers eventually fail, which causes a loss or corruption of data. Therefore, you need to take additional steps to recover your data. You should also know that the best method for data recovery is backup, backup, backup. By using Windows Backup, you can perform backups, and when it is necessary, perform restores to recover damaged or lost files, or repair corrupted system settings.

Backup Overview

Data is the raw facts, numbers, letters, or symbols that the computer processes into meaningful information. Examples of data include a letter to a company or a client, a report for your boss, a budget proposal of a large project, or an address book of your friends and business associates. Whatever the data is, you can save it (or write it to disk) so that you can retrieve it at any time, you can print it on paper, or you can send it to someone else over the telephone lines.

Data stored on a computer or stored on the network is vital to the users and probably the organization. The data represents hours of work and is sometimes irreplaceable. Data loss can be caused by many things, including hardware failure, viruses, user error, and malicious users. When disaster occurs, the best method to recover data is backup, backup, backup. When disaster has occurred and the system does not have a backup of its important files, it is often too late to recover the files.

A backup of a system is to have an extra copy of data and/or programs. As a technician, consultant, or support person, you need to emphasize at every moment to back up on servers and client systems. In addition, it is recommended that the clients save their data files to a server so that you have a single, central location to back up. This might go as far as selecting and installing the equipment, doing the backup, or training other people in doing the backup. When doing all of this, be sure to select the equipment and method that assures that the backup is completed on a regular basis. Remember that if you have the best equipment and software but no one completes the backup, the equipment and software is wasted.

THE BEST METHOD FOR DATA PROTECTION AND RECOVERY IS BACKUP, BACKUP, BACKUP.

When developing for a backup, three steps should be followed. They are as follows:

1. Develop a backup plan.

2. Stick to the backup plan.

3. Test the backup.

When developing a backup plan, you must consider the following:

- What equipment will be used?
- How much data needs to be backed up?
- How long will it take to do the backup?
- How often must the data be backed up?
- When will the backup take place?
- Who will do that backup?

Whatever equipment, person, or method is chosen, you must make sure that the backup will be done. If you choose the best equipment, the best software, and the brightest person, and the backup is not done for whatever reason, you wasted your resources and you put your data at risk.

How often the backup is done depends on the importance of the data. If you have many customers loaded into a database, which is constantly changed, or your files represent the livelihood of your business, you should back them up everyday. If there are a few letters that get sent throughout the week with nothing vitally important, you can back up once a week.

Types of Backups

All types of backups can be broken into the following categories:

- **Normal/Full**: The full backup backs up all files selected and shuts off the archive file attribute, indicating the file has been backed up.

- **Incremental**: An incremental backup backs up the files selected if the archive file attribute is on (files since the last full or incremental backup). After the file has been backed up, it shuts off the file attribute to indicate that the file has been backed up. Note: You should not mix incremental and differential backups.

- **Differential**: A differential backup backs up the files selected if the archive file attribute is on (files since the last full backup). Different from the incremental backup, it does not shut off the archive attribute. Note: You should not mix incremental and differential backups.

▶ **Copy backup**: A copy backup is like a normal backup, but it does not shut off the archive attribute. This is typically used to back up the system before you make a major change to the system. The archive attribute is not shut off so that your normal backup procedures are not affected.

You decide to back up the entire hard drive once a week on Friday. You decide to use the full backup method. Therefore, you perform a full backup every Friday. If the hard drive goes bad, you use the last backup to restore the hard drive.

You decide to back up the entire hard drive once a week on Friday. You decide to use the incremental method. Therefore, you perform a full backup on week 1. This shuts off all of the archive attributes, indicating that all of the files have been backed up. On week 2, week 3, and week 4, you perform incremental backups using different tapes or disks. Because the incremental backup turns the archive attribute, it backs up only new files and changed files. Therefore, all four backups make up the entire backup. It is much quicker to back up a drive using an incremental backup than a full backup. Of course, if the hard drive fails, you must restore backup #1, backup #2, backup #3, and backup # 4 to restore the entire hard drive.

After the backups are complete, you should check to see if the backups actually worked. You can do this by picking a nonessential file and restoring it to the hard drive. This helps discover if the backups are empty or a backup/restore device is faulty.

You should keep more than one backup. Tapes and disks do fail. One technique is to rotate through three sets of backups. If you perform a full backup once a week, you would then use three sets of backup tapes or disks. During week 1, you use tape/disk #1. During week 2, you use tape/disk #2, and during week 3, you use tape/disk #3. On week 4, you start over and use tape/disk #1. If you have to restore a hard drive and the tape or disk fails, you can always go to the tape or disk from the week before. In addition, you should perform monthly backups and store then elsewhere. You might be surprised how many times a person loses a file but does not realize it for several weeks. If the data is important enough, you might consider keeping a backup set in a fireproof safe offsite. Lastly, when a system is initially installed and when you make any major changes to the system's configuration, it is always recommended to make two backups before proceeding. This way, if anything goes wrong, you have the ability to restore everything to the way it was before the changes. The reason for the two backups is that tapes have been known to go bad on occasion.

Some places use the Grandfather, Father, Son (GFS) backup rotation, which requires 21 tapes based on a five-day rotation. Each month, you create a grandfather backup, which is stored permanently offsite, never to be reused. Each week, you create a full weekly backup (father), and each day you create a differential or incremental backup (son).

After completing a backup, you should properly label the tape or disk before removing it and then store the tape and disk to a secure, safe place. In addition, you should keep a log of what backups have been done The log keeps track of what was backed up and when it was backed up, which is especially useful if you need to rebuild the server. It also lets you know if someone is forgetting to do the backup.

Backup and Restore Center

To back up your drives and files, you can use the Backup and Restore Center. To access the Backup and Restore Center, do the following:

1. Click the **Start** button, click **All Programs**, click **Maintenance**, and click **Backup and Restore**.

2. To set a backup, click the **Set up backup** link.

3. Specify where you want to store your backups. You can specify a secondary drive or the network and click **Next**.

4. You can let Windows choose your files or you can choose your files.

5. If you choose what to back up, you can include what drives and folders you want to back up. The System drives are automatically chosen, as shown in Figure 16.12.

6. Review your settings and click the **Save settings and run backup** button.

You can make a backup at any time by clicking the **Back up now** button. You can also schedule a backup, including configuring a recurring backup that backs up on a regular basis. You can then use the options at the bottom of the window to restore user files, system settings, or all files, as shown in Figure 16.13.

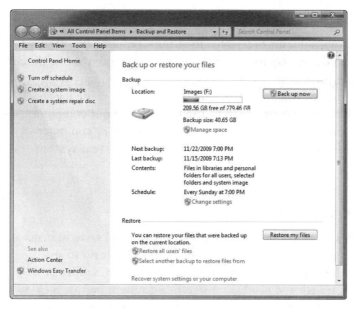

FIGURE 16.12 **Choosing what to back up.**

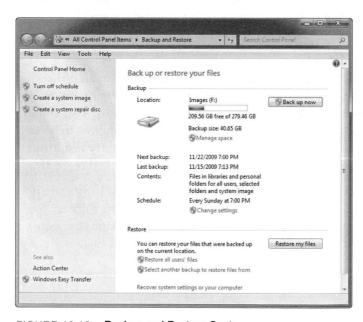

FIGURE 16.13 **Backup and Restore Center.**

System Image Backup

A System Image Backup, sometimes referred to as the Complete PC Backup, is a copy of the system drives required for Windows to run, and it is one of the fastest ways to restore your hard disk. It can also include additional drives. It is an exact copy of the disk or volume at the time the image was made (cluster by cluster). Because it is an exact copy, it can be used to restore your computer, including all configuration settings and files, if your hard disk or computer stops working. You can create a system image by clicking **Create a system image** in the Backup and Restore Center.

System Protection

System protection is a set of features that regularly creates and saves information about your computer's system files and settings (System Restore) and saves previous versions of files that you've modified. It saves these files in restore points, which are created just before significant system events, such as the installation of a program or device driver. They're also created automatically once every seven days if no other restore points were created in the previous seven days, but you can create restore points manually at any time.

System Restore

System Restore helps you restore your computer's system files to an earlier point in time. It's a way to undo system changes to your computer without affecting your personal files, such as email, documents, or photos. This comes in handy when you install a program or a drive that causes Windows to behave unpredictably. If uninstalling does not fix the problem, you can try restoring your computer's system to an earlier date when everything worked correctly.

Restore points are created automatically every day and also just before significant system events, such as the installation of a program or device driver. You can also create a restore point manually. The System restore points back up the following settings:

- Registry
- DLLcache folder
- User profile
- COM+ and WMI information
- IIS metabase
- Certain monitored system files

System restore points are different from data backup. It is not intended for backing up personal files. Therefore, it cannot help you recover a personal file that is deleted or damaged. You should regularly back up your personal files and important data using a backup program.

If you know you are going to make significant changes to your machine including loading drivers or programs, you should create a restore point.

When a problem occurs, you can also choose from a list of restore points. Try using restore points created just before the date and time you started noticing problems.

To configure which volumes are protected with System Restore, do the following:

1. Right-click **Computer** and choose **Properties**.

2. Click **System protection**.

If you click the drive you want to configure and click the **Configure** button, you can specify to enable or disable restore system settings or previous versions of files (explained in the next section), as shown in Figure 16.14. You can also specify how much disk space you want to allocate toward system protection and delete any restore points if you are low on disk space. You can also manually create a restore point by clicking the Create button.

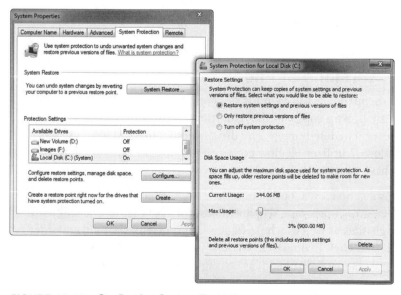

FIGURE 16.14   **Configuring System Protection.**

To access the System Restore utility, do the following:

1. Click the **Start** button and select **All Programs**.

2. Select **Accessories**.

3. Select **System Tools**.

4. Select **System Restore** to see the screen shown in Figure 16.15.

5. If you are prompted for an administrator password or confirmation, type the password or provide confirmation.

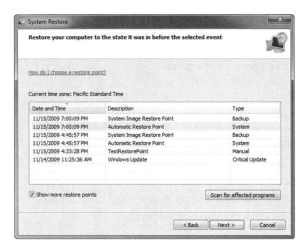

FIGURE 16.15   **System Restore.**

Previous Versions of Files

Shadow copies, introduced in Windows Server 2003, when configured, automatically create backup copies of the data stored in data folders on specific drive volumes at scheduled times. The drive volume must be formatted as NTFS. Windows 7 utilizes Shadow copies to provide previous versions of files even if they have never been backed up.

With Windows 7, Shadow Copy is automatically turned on as part of System Restore and creates copies on a scheduled basis of files that have changed. It works on single files as well as whole folders. If you right-click a data folder or individual file and click **Properties**, you can then click the **Previous Versions** tab to view and restore individual files, as shown in Figure 16.16.

Note

Because this only backs up periodically, it does not keep individual documents if you change the document several times in a short period of time.

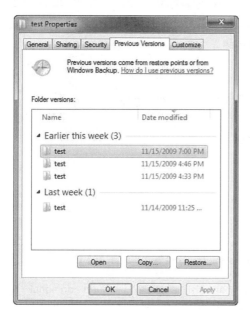

FIGURE 16.16   **Previous versions of a folder or file.**

Removing Restore Points and Previous Versions of Files

The Disk Cleanup utility was introduced in Chapter 4, " Disk Management." It removes temporary files, empties the Recycle Bin, and removes a variety of system files and other items that you no longer need. After you scan your disk using the Disk Cleanup utility, you can click the **More Options** tab and click the **Clean up** button in the System Restore and Shadow Copies section to delete all but the most recent restore point on the disk, including previous versions of files.

Cram Quiz

1. You are going to upgrade a couple of applications and you want to back up all system and data files. What should you use?

    ○ **A.** Create a System Image Backup

    ○ **B.** Use System Restore

    ○ **C.** Use Previous Versions of Files

    ○ **D.** Use System Configuration

2. Which of the following does System Restore NOT back up?

    ○ **A.** Registry

    ○ **B.** COM+ and WMI information

    ○ **C.** IIS metabase

    ○ **D.** Data files created by a user

Cram Quiz Answers

1. **A** is correct. A System Image Backup, sometimes referred to as the Complete PC Backup, is a copy of the system drives required for Windows to run and is one of the fastest ways to restore your hard disk. It can also include additional drives. Answer B is incorrect because System Restore only backs up System files, not data files. Answer C is incorrect because the Previous Versions of Files only backs up data files, not system files. Answer D is incorrect because System Configuration is a troubleshooting tool for boot problems, not a backup tool.

2. **D** is correct. System Restore backs up the registry, DLL cache folder, user profiles, COM+ and WMI information, IIS metabase, and certain monitored files. It does not back up data files.

Review Questions

1. You work as the desktop support technician at Acme.com. You have a user that loaded a driver but now Windows does not boot properly. You want to display the driver names while they are being loaded during startup. What should you do?

   - A. Start System configuration. On the Boot tab, select the Base video checkbox.

   - B. Start System configuration. On the Boot tab, you should select the Boot log checkbox.

   - C. Start System configuration. On the Boot tab, you should select the No GUI boot checkbox.

   - D. Start System configuration. On the Boot tab, select the OS boot information checkbox.

2. You work as the desktop support technician at Acme.com. You have a user who reports experiencing slowness problems over the last few weeks. You need to identify the cause of the failures. Therefore, you want to look at the historical view of workstation performance and see when the failures first started. What should you do?

   - A. Make use of Performance Monitor

   - B. Make use of the Reliability Monitor

   - C. Make use of a System Diagnostics Data Collector Set

   - D. Make use of the Resource Overview tool

3. You work as the Help Desk technician at Acme.com. You have a user who is getting a Stop error when the computer is started in Normal mode or Safe Mode. What should you do to troubleshoot this problem further?

   - A. Uninstall Windows 7 and reinstall the previous version of Windows

   - B. Reboot the computer using the Windows 7 installation DVD and run the Startup Repair tool

   - C. Run Software Explorer

   - D. Disable startup items by running Msconfig.exe

4. You make changes to the video refresh rate on your computer and now the display does not work properly. What should you do?

   - A. Run the SYSEDIT tool

   - B. Reinstall Windows

   - C. Reboot the system with the emergency repair disk

   - D. Press **F8** during the boot sequence and select Last Known Good Configuration

5. Your machine does not boot properly. You suspect a faulty driver that you just installed. Unfortunately, you cannot access the Device Manager because the system does not complete the boot process. What should you do next?

   ○ **A.** Restart the computer with another version of Windows

   ○ **B.** Insert a DOS bootable disk into the drive and boot the system

   ○ **C.** Reboot the computer in Safe Mode

   ○ **D.** Start the System Configuration tool

6. What tool would you use to temporarily disable a service that starts during the boot process?

   ○ **A.** Device Manager

   ○ **B.** System Configuration

   ○ **C.** Boot.ini tool

   ○ **D.** Last Known Configuration option

7. You just loaded a new application. Now your computer has gotten slow and sometimes causes Stop errors. Even after reinstalling the application, you still have the same problems. What can you try next?

   ○ **A.** Roll back the latest driver using Device Manager

   ○ **B.** Reboot the computer in Safe Mode

   ○ **C.** Press **F8** during the boot sequence and select Last Known Good Configuration

   ○ **D.** Use the System Restore to restore to a known good working restore point

8. Which type of backup can you perform using the Windows 7 Backup and Restore program if you only want to back up files that have their archive bits set and you want the backup job to clear each file's archive bit after each file has been backed up?

   ○ **A.** Incremental

   ○ **B.** Differential

   ○ **C.** Normal

   ○ **D.** Copy

9. You have a computer running Windows 7 with a C and D drives. Both hard drives are formatted with the NTFS file system. What do you need to disable the previous versions on the D drive?

○ **A.** Modify the Quota settings

○ **B.** Modify the Sharing settings

○ **C.** Use the Disk Management snap-in

○ **D.** Modify the System Protection settings from System Properties

10. What can you use to delete all System Protection snapshots on a computer running Windows 7?

○ **A.** Run Disk Defrag

○ **B.** Run Disk Cleanup for System Restore and Shadow copies

○ **C.** Restore files from Previous Versions

○ **D.** Restore files using System Restore

Review Question Answers

1. Answer **D** is correct. If you open System Configuration, select the Boot tab, and select OS boot information, it shows you the driver names that are loaded during startup. Answers A, B, and C are incorrect because those options do not provide that information. Base video starts the monitor with a 640 × 480 resolution. The Boot log generates a log that could be accessed after it boots. The No GUI boot checkbox starts in with a command prompt.

2. Answer **B** is correct. The two places to look for a history of problems are the Event Viewer and the Reliability Monitor. Answer A is incorrect because Performance Monitor is used to measure performance. Answer C is incorrect because the Data Collector Set is used to group counters together so that you can call them up as needed or schedule them to be measured. Answer D is incorrect because the Resource Overview tool shows the performance of the major subcomponents, including CPU, memory, network, and disk.

3. Answer **B** is correct. Because you cannot start the computer, there might be a problem with the startup files. Therefore, you need to run the Startup Repair tool. Answer A is incorrect because you don't want to go back to an old operating system. Answers C and D are incorrect because you cannot start Windows to get to the Software Explorer or msconfig.exe (System Configuration tool).

4. Answer **D** is correct. If you load a driver and your machine does not boot proper-ly, you can access the advanced boot menu and try Last Known Good Configuration. Answer A is incorrect because you cannot access Windows to use SYSEDIT. Answer B is incorrect because reinstalling Windows takes a lot of effort and might not correct the problem. Answer C is incorrect because there is no emergency repair disk to use with Windows 7; everything is included with the Windows 7 installation disk.

5. Answer **C** is correct. If you cannot boot the computer, the next logical step is to boot Windows in Safe Mode. In Safe Mode, minimum drivers are loaded. Answer A is not a viable option because most systems do not have another hard drive with another version of Windows. This solution can also become very messy. Answer B is incorrect because you cannot use DOS to correct most Windows problems. Answer D is incorrect because you need to first load Windows before you can use the System Configuration tool.

6. Answer **B** is correct. The system configuration tool is a diagnostic tool that can help you isolate startup programs and services that prevent Windows from boot-ing. Answer A is incorrect because Device Manager manages devices, not serv-ices. Answer C is incorrect because there is no such thing as the boot.ini tool or file in Windows 7. Answer D is used to revert back when you load a driver, serv-ice, or program that prevents Windows from loading. It does not disable a service.

7. Answer **D** is correct. System Restore can reconfigure Windows to its original set-tings before the problem occurred. Answer A is incorrect because this is not a device problem. Answer B is incorrect because you can load Windows, so you don't need to use Safe Mode. Answer C is incorrect because if you log in to Windows successfully, you overwrite the Last Known Good Configuration.

8. Answer **A** is correct. When you complete an incremental backup, you are back-ing up all new and changed files since the last backup. Answer B is incorrect because differential backups do not shut off the archive attribute. Answer C is incorrect because the normal or full backup copies all files regardless of the archive attribute. Answer D is incorrect because the Copy command backs up all files but does not shut off the archive attribute.

9. Answer **D** is correct. To enable or disable what is affected by System Restore and Previous Versions, you must use the System Protection settings from System Properties. Answer A is incorrect because the Quota settings are used to limit how much space a user can use on a system. Answers B and C are incor-rect because you cannot use System Protection from the Sharing properties or Disk Management snap-in.

10. Answer **B** is correct. Disk Cleanup enables you to remove old copies of System Restore and Shadow copies. Answer A is incorrect because the Disk Defrag is used to optimize a disk by putting files back together on a disk, allowing for quicker access time. Answer C is incorrect because restoring files or reverting to an earlier snapshot does not remove old copies of the System Restore or Shadow copies.

Practice Exam

This element consists of 50 questions that are representative of what you should expect on the actual exam. The questions here are multiple choice, however, and not simulations because of the limitations of paper testing. Still, this exam should help you determine how prepared you are for the real exam and provide a good base for what you still need to review. As you take this exam, treat it as you would the real exam: Time yourself (about 90 minutes), and answer each question carefully, marking the ones you want to go back to and double check. The answers and their explanations are at the end of the exam.

1. Which of the following describes Windows Aero?

   ○ **A.** A new hardware-based graphical user interface intended to be cleaner and more aesthetically pleasing than those of previous versions of Windows

   ○ **B.** A special theme that is based on the aerospace industry

   ○ **C.** A background theme that shows the blue skyline

   ○ **D.** A search-oriented desktop interface

2. You work as a desktop support technician at Acme.com. Because you need to connect to the domain, you need to install Windows 7 Professional Edition on a computer for the graphics department. The computer has the following specifications:

   ▶ 1.5 GHz AMD processor

   ▶ 2 GB of RAM

   ▶ Drive C (system drive) has 15 GB of free disk space

   ▶ Drive D (program drive) has 60 GB of free disk space

   ▶ Integrated sound card

   ▶ Intel 10/100 network adapter

   Which hardware does not meet the minimum requirements to install Windows 7?

   ○ **A.** You should add a faster processor to the computer.

   ○ **B.** You should add more memory to the computer.

   ○ **C.** You need to free up space on drive C.

   ○ **D.** You should install Windows 7 on drive D.

3. You are the network administrator for Acme.com. You have ordered some new computers and the new computers only have one partition with Windows 7 Home Basic. Unfortunately, each computer must be running Windows 7 Professional Edition so that they can connect to the Windows domain. When you upgrade Windows 7, which directory holds the old operating system files and directories in case you need to access to the Documents and Settings folders and Program Files folder?

   ○ **A.** Windows\panther folder

   ○ **B.** Windows folder

   ○ **C.** Windows.OLD folder

   ○ **D.** Files and Settings folder

   ○ **E.** Explorer folder

4. If you want to migrate user settings from a Windows Vista computer, which parameter should you use with the ScanState.exe command?

   ○ **A.** `/vista`

   ○ **B.** `/target:vista`

   ○ **C.** `/targetvista`

   ○ **D.** No options are required.

5. You have an offline Windows 7 image of a reference computer. What program can you use to perform an offline installation of language packs specified in an answer file?

   ○ **A.** The `imagex` command-line utility

   ○ **B.** The `pkgmgr.exe` utility

   ○ **C.** The Windows SIM

   ○ **D.** The DISM tool

6. How many primary partitions without an extended partition can reside on a basic MBR disk under Windows 7?

   ○ **A.** 3

   ○ **B.** 4

   ○ **C.** 1

   ○ **D.** 128

7. You want to assign an address to a computer that will be available on the Internet, and it will have the same address for both IPv4 and IPv6. What kind of address is this?

   ○ **A.** A unique private address

   ○ **B.** A multicast local address

○ **C.** A site-local address

○ **D.** A global unicast address

8. Which authentication protocol is used for backward compatibility with pre-Windows 2000 operating systems?

○ **A.** Kerberos

○ **B.** Windows NT LAN Manager

○ **C.** Certificate mappings

○ **D.** Password Authentication Protocol

9. You work as part of the IT support staff at Acme.com. You have upgraded several computers from Windows XP Professional to Windows Vista Enterprise to Windows 7 Enterprise. You had an accounting application that worked fine in Windows XP but does not run fine on Windows 7. After further research, you find when the user tries to run the application, it asks for a login. When the user uses a standard user account, the application fails, but when you use an administrator user account and password, the application works. What is the best solution to fix this problem?

○ **A.** Add the user accounts to the local administrator group.

○ **B.** Add the user accounts to the domain administrator group.

○ **C.** Use Parental Control for the users to access the applications.

○ **D.** Right-click the executable and select Properties. Use the application's Properties dialog box to run this program as an administrator.

10. What is used to help you identify fake websites that are made to look like legitimate websites?

○ **A.** Protected Mode

○ **B.** Phishing filter

○ **C.** Add-on Manager

○ **D.** Digital signature

11. You have purchased some devices that have been sitting on the shelf at a store for several months and are about ready to be discontinued. You installed the drivers for those devices and now your system has some sporadic errors. What should you do?

○ **A.** Look on the Windows DVD for more up to date drivers

○ **B.** Check with the manufacturer's website and the Windows update website for more up-to-date drivers

○ **C.** Upgrade Windows 7 to the Ultimate edition so that it can make proper use of the drivers

○ **D.** Disable the prompting of unsigned driver warnings

12. You have a new computer with Windows 7 on it. When you visit certain websites using Internet Explorer, you click on the links and nothing happens. What is the problem?

- ○ **A.** You have been denied access to the website by the network administrator.
- ○ **B.** The website has been taken offline.
- ○ **C.** The links generate pop-up windows, which are blocked by default.
- ○ **D.** The website is not on your trusted list.

13. You have Windows 7 loaded on a computer with one primary volume that holds Windows, your applications, and your data files. What happens if the C drive starts to run out of disk space? (Choose all that apply.)

- ○ **A.** Your computer runs slower.
- ○ **B.** Your machine is less reliable.
- ○ **C.** If you attempt to move files from one location to another drive, such as a USB drive, Windows might say that you are out of disk space.
- ○ **D.** Windows shifts into compression mode to save disk space.

14. You have a user that made some changes to the advanced options in Internet Explorer. Unfortunately, the user cannot access certain websites. What can you do to reset those options?

- ○ **A.** Reinstall Internet Explorer
- ○ **B.** Navigate to the Advanced tab in Internet Options and click Restore advanced settings
- ○ **C.** Navigate to the Advanced tab in Internet Options and click Reset
- ○ **D.** Navigate to the Security tab in Internet Options and click Reset all zones to default level

15. How do you turn off the prompts generated by User Account Control? (Choose two answers.)

- ○ **A.** Use local or group policies
- ○ **B.** Click the Turn User Account Control Off link under User Accounts
- ○ **C.** Use the Computer Management console
- ○ **D.** Open the System properties of the computer and click the Turn Off button under the UAC

16. You have more than 50 laptop computers that are running Windows 7 Enterprise Edition that you need to connect to your corporate wireless network. What is the easiest way to do that?

- ○ **A.** Log in to each computer and manually configure the wireless settings

    ○ **B.** Copy the wireless settings to a shared folder and then copy the wireless settings to each computer

    ○ **C.** Save the wireless network settings to a USB flash drive and use that flash drive on each computer to copy the configuration

    ○ **D.** Use the Autodetect feature of Windows 7 to detect the wireless settings

    ○ **E.** Use group policies to automatically configure the wireless settings

17. You think some of your boot files have gotten corrupted, resulting in improper loading of Windows 7. What can you do to fix the problem?

    ○ **A.** Start safe mode and run further diagnostics to figure out which file is causing the problem.

    ○ **B.** Insert the Windows 7 installation disc using the Startup Repair Tool to fix the problem.

    ○ **C.** Insert the Windows 7 installation disc and start Windows in safe mode.

    ○ **D.** Insert the Windows 7 installation disc and start Windows from the DVD. Then run further diagnostics to figure out which file is causing the problem.

18. A user from your office has reported some strange errors. Where can you look at the logs to see if they report some of the errors?

    ○ **A.** Log Trace in Administrative Tools

    ○ **B.** Event Viewer in the Computer Management console

    ○ **C.** Logging in the Control Panel

    ○ **D.** Debugging Logs in Administrative Tools

19. Which of the following are not TCP/IP private addresses?

    ○ **A.** 10.1.2.50

    ○ **B.** 172.16.23.42

    ○ **C.** 172.32.34.202

    ○ **D.** 192.168.4.5

20. You have several laptops that you are trying to make as secure as possible in the event that they are stolen. What should you implement to protect their entire volumes?

    ○ **A.** NTFS

    ○ **B.** Share permissions

    ○ **C.** BitLocker

    ○ **D.** EFS

21. You suspect that a program that you started is using too much memory. How can you verify this?

- ○ **A.** Use the Event Viewer
- ○ **B.** Use the Task Manager
- ○ **C.** Use the Computer Management console
- ○ **D.** Use the Windows Defender

22. Which utility would you use to prepare an installed system so that its image could be copied to multiple computers?

- ○ **A.** imagex
- ○ **B.** setup
- ○ **C.** diskpart
- ○ **D.** sysprep

23. You are looking at the Device Manager. You see a device that has a down arrow on it. What is the problem?

- ○ **A.** The device is having a problem.
- ○ **B.** The device is disabled.
- ○ **C.** The device is sleeping.
- ○ **D.** The device is not connected.

24. What command can be used to show network connectivity to a computer?

- ○ **A.** ipconfig
- ○ **B.** arp
- ○ **C.** ping
- ○ **D.** nslookup

25. Which of the following will you not find in the Windows Mobility Center?

- ○ **A.** Brightness
- ○ **B.** Battery Status
- ○ **C.** Pointer Devices
- ○ **D.** Presentation Settings

26. What do you call an XML file that scripts the answers for a series of GUI dialog boxes and other configuration settings used to install Windows?

- ○ **A.** Answer file
- ○ **B.** Installation script
- ○ **C.** Windows image
- ○ **D.** Catalog

27. Which utility would you use to migrate the files and settings to removable media or to a network share and later restore the files and settings to the target computer?

- ○ **A.** Windows Easy Transfer
- ○ **B.** User State Migration Tool
- ○ **C.** Windows PE
- ○ **D.** Sysprep

28. You are a desktop technician for Acme.com. You have 20 different computers used by your company. You want to quickly check to see if they support a Windows 7 installation. What utility can you use to easily determine their capability to run Windows 7?

- ○ **A.** Run the Windows 7 Upgrade Advisor
- ○ **B.** Run the System Checker program
- ○ **C.** Run the System Information program
- ○ **D.** Run the Computer Management console

29. Which utility would you use to manage the volumes on your system?

- ○ **A.** Disk management applet in the Control Panel
- ○ **B.** Computer Management console found in administrative tools
- ○ **C.** Disk administrator found on the desktop
- ○ **D.** Disk runner found in My Computer

30. When you run a new application, you get a warning saying User Account Control stops unauthorized changes to your computer and that your computer needs your permission to continue. What should you do when you get this warning?

- ○ **A.** You need to determine if the application comes from a reliable source. If it does, click the Continue button.
- ○ **B.** You need to verify the NTFS permissions for the application.
- ○ **C.** You need to run the application as an administrator.
- ○ **D.** You need to log out and log in as an administrator and retry the application again.

31. Besides allowing and blocking programs from communicating over the Internet and blocking ports to communicate, what else would you use the Windows Firewall with Advanced Security console for?

- ○ **A.** To monitor network traffic
- ○ **B.** To configure IPsec
- ○ **C.** To view network attacks
- ○ **D.** To manage your anti-virus program
- ○ **E.** To manage your anti-spyware program

32. What does Protected Mode in Internet Explorer do?

- ○ **A.** Prevents Component Object Model (COM) objects, such as ActiveX controls, from automatically modifying files and settings
- ○ **B.** Helps stop phishing websites
- ○ **C.** Helps stop viruses from infecting your computer
- ○ **D.** Helps prevent packet sniffing on the network

33. What would you use to check for but not fix errors on Drive D?

- ○ **A.** Run the `chkdsk D:` command at the command prompt
- ○ **B.** Run the `chkdsk D: /f` command at the command prompt
- ○ **C.** Run the `scandisk D:` command at the command prompt
- ○ **D.** Run the `scandisk D: /F` command at the command prompt
- ○ **E.** Right-click the D drive and select Error-Checking

34. ReadyBoost and ReadyDrive increase performance on your machine. What is the difference between the two? (Choose two answers.)

- ○ **A.** Windows ReadyBoost uses USB flash devices as additional sources for caching.
- ○ **B.** Windows ReadyDrive uses hybrid drives on laptop computers.
- ○ **C.** Windows ReadyBoost uses hybrid drives on laptop computers.
- ○ **D.** Windows ReadyDrive uses USB flash devices as additional sources for caching.

35. You loaded a new video card driver, which now causes your machine to not boot properly. What can you do to correct this problem?

- ○ **A.** Boot to VGA mode (Base Video) and roll back the old driver
- ○ **B.** Boot to the command prompt and roll back the old driver
- ○ **C.** Boot with the Window 7 DVD and run the repair
- ○ **D.** Connect to the Windows Update website to get the correct driver

36. You have a few programs that are causing some strange errors to appear when Windows starts. You want to isolate which program is generating the errors. What can you do? (Select the best answer.)

- ○ **A.** Use Parental Control to disable each program
- ○ **B.** Use Windows Defender to temporarily disable programs
- ○ **C.** Edit the Registry to disable each program
- ○ **D.** Use `msconfig` and temporarily disable programs

37. Which of the following statements are true when discussing wireless technology used with Windows 7? (Choose two answers.)

- ○ **A.** Personal mode provides authentication via a preshared key or password.
- ○ **B.** Enterprise mode provides authentication using IEEE 802.1X and EAP.
- ○ **C.** Enterprise mode provides authentication via a preshared key or password.
- ○ **D.** Personal mode provides authentication using IEEE 802.1X and EAP.

38. Your browser cannot find a website that you are trying to access. You eventually correct an error on the DNS server, which now knows the correct address to the website. What do you need to do to now access the website?

- ○ **A.** You need to run the `ipconfig /registerdns` command.
- ○ **B.** You need to run the `ipconfig /flushdns` command.
- ○ **C.** You need to shut down your machine and restart it.
- ○ **D.** You need to change the IP address of your DNS server.

39. You have a Windows 7 computer used in the office through shared folders. You also want users to be able to remotely access the computer to run programs from that computer from their own computers by using Remote Desktop. What do you need for them to access the computer?

- ○ **A.** You need to add the users to the administrator's group.
- ○ **B.** You need to add users to the Power Users group.
- ○ **C.** You need to add the users to the Remote Desktop Users group.
- ○ **D.** You need to add users to the Telnet group.

40. You have BitLocker Drive Encryption on a computer that is running Microsoft Windows 7 Enterprise Edition, which has the Trusted Platform Mobile (TPM) installed. When you set up the computer, you printed out the recovery password, which you keep in your files. What do you need to recover the system if a TPM error occurs and the user cannot access the data on the computer?

- ○ **A.** Start the computer and enter the recovery password.
- ○ **B.** Start the computer with the USB flash drive.
- ○ **C.** Start the computer and enter the TPM management console.
- ○ **D.** Boot the computer with the Windows 7 installation disc. Enter the recovery password when you need to log in.

41. What command do you use to check what IP address is resolved for a host name?

- ○ **A.** `ipconfig /dns`
- ○ **B.** `nslookup`

○ **C.** NBTStat

○ **D.** resolve

42. You work as the desktop support technician at Acme.com. Pat is a member of the manager group. There is a shared folder called MANAGEMENT on an NTFS partition on a remote Windows 7 computer. Pat is given the Write NTFS permission, the Manager group is given the Read & Execute NTFS permissions and the Everyone group has the Read NTFS permission to the DATA folder. In addition, Pat, Manager, and Everyone are assigned the shared Contributor permission to the MANAGEMENT folder. When Pat logs on his client computer and accesses the MANAGEMENT folder, what are his permissions? (Choose all that apply.)

○ **A.** Read the files in that folder

○ **B.** Write to the files in the folder

○ **C.** Execute the files in the folder

○ **D.** Delete the files in the folder

○ **E.** Have no access to the files in the folder

43. What do you call a bootable tool that replaced MS-DOS as the pre-installation environment?

○ **A.** Windows PE

○ **B.** Installation script

○ **C.** Windows image

○ **D.** Catalog

44. What is the name of the answer file used on removable media when you install Windows 7?

○ **A.** Answer.txt

○ **B.** Answer.xml

○ **C.** autoattend.xml

○ **D.** Install.xml

45. When discussing content zones used in Internet Explorer, what defines the Local Intranet Zone?

○ **A.** Anything that is not assigned to any other zone and anything that is not on your computer or your organization's network

○ **B.** Computers that are part of the organization's network that do not require a proxy server, as defined by the system administrator

○ **C.** Contains trusted sites from which you believe you can download or run files without damaging your computer or data or that you consider is not a security risk

○ **D.** Contains sites that you do not trust from which downloading or running files might damage your computer or data or that are considered a security risk

46. When you visit several websites using Internet Explorer, additional windows appear. At times, you try to close these windows, but more windows are appearing faster then you can close then. What should you make sure you have enabled?

○ **A.** Phishing protection

○ **B.** Dynamic protection

○ **C.** Pop-up blocker

○ **D.** Windows Defender

47. What is a special microchip in some newer computers that supports advanced security features, including BitLocker encryption?

○ **A.** ActiveX controls

○ **B.** Trusted Platform Module

○ **C.** Dynamic Protection

○ **D.** NTFS

48. What do you use to encrypt individual files on your system?

○ **A.** NTFS

○ **B.** Compression

○ **C.** EFS

○ **D.** BitLocker

49. When your machine goes into hibernate, what is the name of the file to which it saves the contents of the system memory?

○ **A.** page.sys

○ **B.** pagefile.sys

○ **C.** hiberfil.sys

○ **D.** power.sys

50. You want to have events from the Event Viewer from computer1 sent to computer2. What command do you execute on computer1?

○ **A.** `winrm quickconfig`

○ **B.** `wecutil qc`

○ **C.** `tether computer2`

○ **D.** `subscribe computer2`

Answers to Exam Questions

1. Answer **A** is correct. Windows Aero is a new hardware-based graphical user interface intended to be cleaner and more aesthetically pleasing than those of previous Windows. Answers B, C, and D have nothing or little to do with the Windows Aero theme.

2. Answer **C** is correct. The system requirements specify 16 GB free hard disk space. The system in question only has 15 GB of free disk space. Of course, it is recommended that you have a much larger hard drive. Because the system requirements specify 1 GHz processor and 1 GB of RAM, Answers A and B are incorrect. Because it has been specified that Windows goes on drive C and programs go on drive D, Answer D is incorrect.

3. Answer **C** is correct. When you perform a clean installation of Windows 7 on a hard disk partition that contains an existing Windows installation (assuming you did not reformat the hard disk), the previous operating system, user data, and program files are saved to a Windows.OLD folder. Answer A is incorrect because the Windows\panther folder is used for installation logs. Answer B is incorrect because the Windows folder is where the Windows files reside. Answers D and E do not exist in a normal Windows 7 installation.

4. Answer **C** is correct. When you want to migrate from a Windows Vista computer, you should use the `/targetvista` option. Answers A and B are incorrect because `/vista` and `/target:vista` are invalid options. Therefore, the other answers are incorrect.

5. Answer **D** is correct. Deployment Image Servicing and Management (DISM) is a command-line tool that is used to service and manage Windows images. You can use it to install, uninstall, configure, and update Windows features, packages, drivers, and international settings. Answer A is incorrect because `imagex` is used to create and manage a WIM file. Answer B is incorrect because `pkgmgr.exe` (short for Package Manager) installs, uninstalls, configures, and updates features and packages for Windows. Answer C is incorrect because Windows SIM is used to create or validate answer files.

6. Answer **B** is correct. You can create up to four primary partitions on a basic disk without an extended partition. Answer A is incorrect because you are limited to three primary partitions only if there is an extended partition on the disk. Answer C is incorrect because you can have more than one primary partition on a basic disk. Answer D is incorrect because you are limited to a maximum of four primary partitions on a basic MBR disk; a basic GPT disk can host up to 128 partitions.

7. Answer **D** is correct. If you want an address to be available from the Internet and be the same address for both IPv4 and IPv6, it must have a global address that can be seen on the Internet. Answer A is incorrect because private addresses cannot be used on the public network such as the Internet. Answer B is incorrect because it has to be a single address assigned to a single computer, not a multicast local address, which is used to broadcast to multiple addresses at the same time. Answer C is incorrect because a local address cannot be seen on the outside.

8. Answer **B** is correct. Windows NT LAN Manager (NTLM) is an authentication protocol used for backward compatibility with pre-Windows 2000 operating systems and some applications. Answer A is incorrect because Kerberos is the main logon authentication method used by clients and servers running Microsoft Windows operating systems to authenticate both user accounts and computer accounts. Answer C is incorrect because certificate mappings are used with smart cards (which contain a digital certificate) for logon authentication. Answer D is incorrect because Password Authentication Protocol (PAP) is used as a remote access authentication protocol that sends the username and password in clear text (unencrypted).

9. Answer **D** is correct. To configure legacy applications to run under Windows 7, you can right-click an executable and open the Properties dialog box. From there, you can specify what environment to run under and, if necessary, specify if the application can run under an administrator account. Answer A is incorrect because adding an account to the Administrators group opens your system up as a security risk when running other applications. Answer B is incorrect because adding an account to the domain administrator group opens your system as a security risk when running other applications. Answer C is incorrect because Parental Controls are not available on domains.

10. Answer **B** is correct. The Phishing filter helps protect you from online phishing attacks, fraud, and spoofed websites. Answer A is incorrect because the Protected Mode helps protect you from websites that try to save files or install programs on your computer. Answer C is incorrect because the Add-on Manager lets you disable or allow web browser add-ons and delete unwanted ActiveX controls. Answer D is incorrect because the digital signature tells you who published a file and whether it has been altered since it was digitally signed.

11. Answer **B** is correct because it is obvious that these drivers are not the newest. Therefore, you should check the Windows update website and manufacturer websites for newer drivers. Answer A is not the best answer because it might not have the newest drivers either. Answer C is incorrect because the edition has no effect on how a driver is loaded. Answer D is incorrect because it is always recommended to load only signed drivers whenever possible.

12. Answer **C** is correct because, by default, Internet Explorer blocks most pop-up windows. To allow these sites to work properly, you need to open the Pop-up Blocker Settings dialog box and add the URL of the website to the Allowed sites list to allow pop-ups to be displayed from a specific website. Answer A is incorrect because if the site has been blocked by the network administrator, you usually get a message saying that is the case. Answer B is incorrect because you get a message similar to site not found or site not available. Answer D is incorrect because when a site is not on your trusted list, it typically stops certain programs, such as ActiveX, from running.

13. Answers **A**, **B**, and **C** are correct. As you run out of disk space, your computer cannot swap information using the paging file and cannot create temporary files such as those that are needed when you move files from one drive to another. Your machine also becomes less reliable. Answer D is incorrect because although NTFS supports compression, it does not automatically start compressing files because it is low on disk space.

14. Answer **B** is correct because the Restore advanced settings button on the Advanced tab of the Internet Options dialog box does not affect the other security and privacy setting used by Internet Explorer. Answer A does not change settings if you reinstall Internet Explorer, and this is not an option because Internet Explorer is not part of the OS. Answer C is incorrect because there is no need to use the Reset button on the Advanced tab of the Internet Options dialog box because it results in all of the Internet Explorer settings being reset. Answer D is incorrect because there is no need to reset the zone settings on the Security tab; doing so affects the security level in Internet Explorer, which is not the problem.

15. Answers **A** and **B** are correct because you can shut off the prompts for an individual user account or by using group policies. Answers C and D are incorrect because prompts generated by User Account Control cannot be controlled using the Computer Management console or by using the System Properties.

16. Answer **C** is the correct answer because it is the easiest to implement. Answer A is a possible answer, but it takes much more work to perform. Answer B is not correct because although you could copy wireless settings to the shared folder, the laptop computers would not be able to access them until the wireless network is configured on each laptop. Answer D is incorrect because there is no Autodetect feature that detects a wireless network found on most corporations because of security settings. Answer E is incorrect because there is no group policy that configures wireless settings and the laptops have to be connected to the network to get those settings.

17. Answer **B** is correct. When the boot files become corrupted, you can boot with the Windows 7 installation disk and run the Startup Repair Tool. Answer A is incorrect because Safe mode is used to isolate a bad or corrupt driver or service by loading only the minimum drivers and services for Windows to function. Answer C is incorrect because Safe mode is not started from the Windows 7 installation disc. Answer D is incorrect because you already know that the boot files are corrupted. Therefore, you can repair them by running the Startup Repair Tool.

18. Answer **B** is correct because the Event Viewer shows the logs. Answers A, C, and D are incorrect because none of these utilities exist.

19. Answer **C** is correct because it does not fall in the range of private addresses. Answers A, B, and D are incorrect because they are private addresses. The private addresses are 10.x.x.x, 172.16.x.x to 172.31.x.x, and 192.168.0.x and 192.168.255.x.

20. Answer **C** is correct because BitLocker is the only choice that protects the entire volume. Answers A, B, and D are incorrect because they do not protect everything on the volume.

21. Answer **B** is correct because Task Manager shows processor and memory utilization of all processes. Answer A is incorrect because the Event Viewer shows you the logs. Answer C is incorrect because the Computer Management console is for configuring the system. Answer D is incorrect because the Windows Defender is used to protect against spyware.

22. Answer **D** is correct because `sysprep` removes the SID from the image and cleans up various user and machine settings and log files. Answer A is incorrect because `imagex` is a command-line tool that captures, modifies, and applies installation images for deployment in a manufacturing or corporate environment. Answer B is incorrect because Windows Setup (`setup.exe`) installs the Windows 7 operating system. Answer C is incorrect because `diskpart` is a command-line hard disk configuration utility.

23. Answer **B** is correct because a down arrow means that the device is disabled. Answer A is incorrect because the exclamation point indicates a device that is having a problem. Answers C and D are not indicated in the Device Manager.

24. Answer **C** is correct because the `ping` command is used to test network connectivity. Answer A is incorrect because `ipconfig` is used to show IP addresses of a system. Answer B is incorrect because the `arp` command is used to show the ARP cache. Answer D is incorrect because the `nslookup` command is used to look at and resolve DNS problems.

25. Answer **C** is correct because you will not find Pointer Devices in the Windows Mobility Center. Answers A, B, and D are incorrect because you will find Brightness, Battery Status, and Presentation Settings in the Windows Mobility Center.

26. Answer **A** is correct because an answer file is an XML file that scripts the answers for a series of GUI dialog boxes and other configuration settings used to install Windows. Answer C is incorrect because a Windows image is a copy of a disk volume saved as file. Answer D is incorrect because a catalog is a binary file (.clg) that contains the state of the settings and packages in a Windows image. Answer B is incorrect because it is a made-up answer.

27. Answer **B** is the correct answer because the User State Migration Tool (USMT) is used to migrate the files and settings to a removable media or to a network share and later restore the files and settings to the target computer. Answer A is incorrect because the Windows Easy Transfer (WET) does not use removable media or work over the network; use WET to perform a side-by-side migration to migrate the settings to a new computer that is already running Windows 7. Answer C is incorrect because Windows PE is a bootable tool that replaces MS-DOS as the pre-installation environment. Answer D is incorrect because Sysprep is a utility that facilitates image creation for deployment to multiple destination computers.

28. Answer **A** is correct because the Windows 7 Upgrade Advisor is a utility that enables one to access an easy-to-understand report after scanning your computer. This report specifies whether the currently installed hardware works with Windows 7. Answer B is incorrect because there is no Microsoft utility called System Checker for Windows 7. Answer C is incorrect because System Information gives you a quick view of what components and software your computer has; it does not specify which components do not meet Windows 7 minimum requirements. Answer D is incorrect because the Computer Management console is used to manage the computer.

29. Answer **B** is correct because volumes are managed using the Computer Management console, which is found in administrative tools. Answers A, C, and D are incorrect because these do not exist.

30. Answer **A** is correct because this warning is generated by User Account Control to protect you from an application that might be performing functions that it should not be performing. Answer B is incorrect because this problem has nothing to do with NTFS permissions. Answers C and D are incorrect because this application is asking you to continue, which means you are already running the application as administrator.

31. Answer **B** is correct because Windows Firewall with Advanced Security is used to manage your IPsec configuration because the firewall rules and IPsec settings might conflict with each other. Answers A, C, D, and E are incorrect because the console does none of these.

32. Answer **A** is correct because the Protected Mode prevents COM objects, such as ActiveX controls, from automatically modifying files and settings. With Protected Mode enabled, only users can initiate these types of requests. Answers B, C, and D are incorrect because Protected Mode does not do any of these.

33. Answer **A** is correct because `chkdsk` is used in Windows 7. Answer B is incorrect because the `/F` parameter fixes those errors. Answers C and D are incorrect because `scandisk` was used by the Windows 9X versions of Windows. Answer E is incorrect because it is not Error-Checking, which is accessed from the disk properties.

34. Answers **A** and **B** are correct because Windows ReadyBoost boosts system performance by using USB flash devices as additional sources for caching and Windows ReadyDrive boosts system performance on mobile computers equipped with hybrid drives. Answers C and D state the opposite, so they are incorrect.

35. Answer **A** is the correct answer because if you load the basic VGA driver instead of the new driver, you can then roll back to the previous driver. Answer B is incorrect because you cannot roll back the driver using the command prompt. Answer C is not correct because you cannot roll back the driver, and you don't want to reinstall Windows. Answer D is incorrect because you cannot connect to the update site until you can boot to Windows.

36. Answer **D** is correct because `msconfig` enables you to temporarily disable each program one by one to see which one is causing the problem. Answer A is only available when the computer is not part of the domain and is a clumsy way of performing the same tasks. Answers B and C are incorrect because they are clumsy ways to do it as well.

37. Answers **A** and **B** are correct because Personal mode provides authentication via a preshared key or password and Enterprise mode provides authentication using IEEE 802.1X and EAP. Answers C and D are incorrect because they state the opposite.

38. Answer **B** is correct because you need to flush the DNS cache so that it can get the new address from the DNS server. Answer A is incorrect because it only registers your computer's IP address with the DNS server. Answer C clears the cache, but it is not the most efficient way. Answer D does not correct the problem because the address is still cached.

39. Answer **C** is correct. For a user to access a Windows 7 machine using Remote Desktop, he must be added to the Remote Desktop Users group. Users must also have passwords. Answer A does work but would most likely be a security problem. Answer B is incorrect because the power users group is for backward compatibility. Answer D is incorrect because there is no Telnet group that comes with Windows.

40. Answer **A** is correct because you start the computer and enter the recovery password in the BitLocker Driver Encryption Recovery console. Answer B is incorrect because you did not save the password to disc. Answer C is incorrect because you cannot enter the TPM management console. Answer D is incorrect because you cannot access the BitLocker Driver Encryption Recovery console using the Windows 7 installation disc.

41. Answer **B** is correct because `nslookup` is used to diagnose your DNS infra-structure. Answer A is incorrect because there is no `/dns` option with the `ipconfig` command. Answer C is incorrect because `NBTStat` is used trou-bleshoot NetBIOS name resolution problems. Answer D is incorrect because there is no `resolve` command that comes with Windows.

42. Answers **A**, **B**, and **C** are correct because NTFS permissions include Write per-mission combined with Read and Execute. The Contributor share permission gives the ability read, write, execute, and delete. When you combine the two, you take the least, so that would be read, write, and execute. Answer D is incor-rect because there was no delete NTFS permission given. Because Pat has per-missions, Answer E is incorrect.

43. Answer **A** is correct because Windows PE is short for Microsoft Windows Pre-installation Environment. It is a bootable tool that replaces MS-DOS as the pre-installation environment. Windows PE is not a general purpose operating system. Instead it is used to provide operating system features for installation, trou-bleshooting, and recovery. Answer C is incorrect because a Windows image is a copy of a disk volume saved as file. Answer D is incorrect because a catalog is a binary file (.clg) that contains the state of the settings and packages in a Windows image. Answer B is incorrect because it is a fictional answer.

44. Answer **C** is correct because the name of the answer file is autoattend.xml. Answers A, B, and D are incorrect because they are fictional answers.

45. Answer **B** is correct because an intranet is defined as part of the organization's network that does not require a proxy server. Answer A is incorrect because it defines this as the Internet zone. Answer C is incorrect because this describes the trusted zone. Answer D is incorrect because this defines the restricted zone.

46. Answer **C** is correct because you need to have a pop-up blocker to stop the windows from opening. Answers A and B are incorrect because they do not stop the pop-up windows. Answer D is incorrect because Windows Defender is designed to primarily protect against spyware; however, Windows Defender helps a little against some pop-ups that are generated by spyware programs.

47. Answer **B** is correct because the Trusted Platform Module (TPM) is a special microchip that supports advanced security features. Answer A is incorrect because ActiveX includes special controls used in Internet Explorer plug-ins. Answer C is incorrect because Dynamic Protection is used to make sure web applications cannot access files on the computer. Answer D is incorrect because NTFS is a file system.

48. Answer **C** is correct because EFS, which is short for Encrypted File System, is used to encrypt individual files. Answer A is incorrect because NTFS is the secure file system used in Windows 7 that support both compression and EFS. Answer B is incorrect because compression is used to compress files, not encrypt them. Answer D is incorrect because BitLocker is used to encrypt entire disk volumes.

49. Answer **C** is correct because the file the memory content is saved during hibernation is hiberfil.sys. Answer A is a fictional file. Answer B is the name of the paging file used in Windows XP, Vista, and 7. Answer D is incorrect because power.sys is a system file used in Windows to help manage power settings.

50. Answer **A** is correct. When you want to configure event subscriptions, you run the `winrm quickconfig` command on all source computers and run the `wecutil qc` command (Answer B) on the target computer. You must also add the computer account of the target computer to the local Administrators group of the source computer. Answers C and D are incorrect because there is no `tether` or `subscribe` command available.

Index

Numerics

A

S

LAWYERS AS COUNSELORS

A Client–Centered Approach

David A. Binder

Paul Bergman

Susan C. Price

LAWYERS AS COUNSELORS:

A CLIENT–CENTERED APPROACH

By

David A. Binder
Professor of Law, University of California, Los Angeles

Paul Bergman
Professor of Law, University of California, Los Angeles

Susan C. Price Ph.D.
Associate Clinical Professor of Psychology,
University of California, Los Angeles

AMERICAN CASEBOOK SERIES®

WEST GROUP

A THOMSON COMPANY

ST. PAUL, MINN., 1991

COPYRIGHT © 1991 By WEST PUBLISHING CO.
     610 Opperman Drive
     P.O. Box 64526
     St. Paul, MN 55164–0526
     1–800–328–9352

Library of Congress Cataloging-in-Publication Data

Binder, David A.
  Lawyers as counselors : a client centered approach / by David A.
Binder, Paul Bergman, and Susan C. Price.
    p. cm. — (American casebook)
  Includes index.
  ISBN 0–314–77002–X

  1. Interviewing in law practice—United States. 2. Attorney and
client—United States. 3. Counseling—United States. I. Bergman,
Paul, 1943– . II. Price, Susan C. III. Title. IV. Series:
American casebook series.
KF311.B52 1990
340'.023'73—dc90   90–43832
               CIP

ISBN 0–314–77002–X

 *TEXT IS PRINTED ON 10% POST CONSUMER RECYCLED PAPER*

7th Reprint — 2001

Preface

Like the earlier *Legal Interviewing and Counseling: A Client-Centered Approach*, this book also adopts a client-centered approach. More than a set of techniques, the client-centered approach is an attitude of looking at problems from clients' perspectives, of seeing problems' diverse natures, and of making clients true partners in the resolution of their problems.

Clients often complain that, "My lawyer doesn't listen to me." Behind this complaint lies the reality that clients' problems typically embrace both legal and nonlegal aspects—e.g., economic, social and psychological aspects. But lawyers, trained to focus on problems' legal aspects, tend to pigeonhole problems along substantive law lines such as a "medical malpractice case" or a "real property subdivision matter." As a result, lawyers tend to miss much of what clients are trying to explain and accomplish. Our hope is that the client-centered approach can help produce decisions that take account of all aspects of clients' problems and thereby make the world a bit better for both you and your clients.

While retaining many of the earlier work's client-centered themes, we have tried in this book to move beyond it in several ways.

First, we have tried to be more explicit about the principles that constitute a client-centered approach. Set forth in Chapter 2, these principles underlie many of the book's concepts and techniques.

Second, we examine interviewing (information-gathering) not as a separate task, but as an integral part of the counseling process. Because we see lawyers' principal role as helping clients solve problems, we approach interviewing as an opportunity to learn about problems from clients' perspectives as well as to gather legally salient data.

Third, in an effort to write a book that will be useful in nearly all attorney-client relationships, we examine counseling principles and techniques in both litigation and transactional contexts. Thus, some chapters focus primarily on litigation matters (e.g., Chapters 8, 9, 10 and 21); others on proposed business deals (e.g., Chapters 11, 12 and 22); while the remaining chapters illustrate concepts and techniques with examples drawn from both litigation and transactional matters.

Fourth, we set forth and explore an explicit counseling standard. Most notably, the standard (described in Chapter 15) is process-based rather than content-based. That is, we do not attempt to define how much "actual awareness" of relevant factors a client should have before making a decision. Rather, our standard encourages lawyers to engage clients in counseling dialogues during which clients' decisions are

preceded by joint examination of objectives, options and likely consequences. Since the state of clients' "actual awareness" is unknowable,
and the extent of counseling typically varies according to each client's
unique circumstances, we think that our process standard is best suited
to helping clients become active and knowledgeable participants in the
resolution of their problems.

Finally, we recognize that in some circumstances, it is both proper
and desirable for lawyers to give advice about what clients ought to do.
Moreover, lawyers may even intervene in decisions when clients mispredict their likely outcomes or when decisions are likely to have
"immoral" consequences. The earlier book, perhaps in over-reaction to
the tendency of many lawyers to tell their clients what to do, gave little
comfort to those who thought that clients often expected and benefitted
from their lawyers' opinions. Taking what we now believe is a more
realistic approach to advice-giving enables us to discuss how to give
advice in a way that preserves client autonomy.

DAVID A. BINDER
PAUL BERGMAN
SUSAN C. PRICE

Los Angeles, California
April, 1990

Acknowledgments

Through four years of arduous effort, no one has given us more help than our research assistants. Amy Klein, Birgit Huber and Diana Wollman spent hours first finding, and then doing research at UCLA libraries generally populated entirely by people with either stethoscopes or psychiatric couches. In addition, they were always at our computers editing text and footnotes. For their dedication and friendship, we are extremely grateful.

Many colleagues here at UCLA carried on the law school's tradition of collegiality by reading and commenting on drafts of various chapters. To Alison Anderson, Susan Gillig, Bill Klein, Carrie Menkel-Meadow, Albert Moore, Sam Thompson and Pamela Woods, thank you for not only carrying on the tradition, but also suppressing your laughter until we were out of earshot.

Thanks also to Kate Bartlett of Duke University School of Law who, while a Visiting Professor at UCLA, provided us with valuable feedback.

Jerry Lopez of Stanford Law School and Avrom Sherr of Warwick School of Law read and commented extensively on the first draft of Chapter 1. But for their advice and encouragement, the remaining 22 chapters might never have been written. Therefore, those looking to assign blame might want to start with Jerry and Avrom.

We benefitted greatly from Peter Klika's extensive knowledge and experience as a practicing lawyer. His own professional skills bear testimony to the fact that client-centered principles and representation of sophisticated corporate clients are eminently compatible.

Special thanks to Bill Rutter, President of The Rutter Group, a leading organization in continuing legal education. On more than one occasion, Bill provided us with insightful and detailed written critiques.

Judith Wilson provided substantial editorial assistance.

Melinda Binder provided numerous helpful comments and relentlessly attended to commas, semicolons; and colons: we are, extremely grateful.

We must not overlook Andrea Sossin-Bergman, who but for this reference would have gone unmentioned.

Thanks also to the UCLA Academic Senate for its financial support.

Finally we owe Chapter 24 almost entirely to Kenney Hegland.

*

Summary of Contents

*

Table of Contents

PART FOUR. DECISION–MAKING

*

LAWYERS AS COUNSELORS:

A CLIENT-CENTERED APPROACH

Part One

INTRODUCTION TO CLIENT-CENTERED COUNSELING

Part One (Chapters 1 through 3) explores the general nature of clients' problems, and a client-centered counseling approach for resolving them.

Chapter 1

THE LEGAL AND NONLEGAL DIMENSIONS OF A CLIENT'S PROBLEM

* * *

John Crampton of Mid–Marine Insurance enthusiastically describes Mid–Marine's potential acquisition of Enterprises Inc., a small aluminum manufacturer. Gary Swartz of the Crestwood Home Owners Association frantically wants to enjoin a Crestwood property owner who, despite deed restrictions, wants to split his lot. Alex Combs sadly wonders how his arrest for burglary will affect his job and children. Louise Harris, manager of Blake County Water District, discusses the District's need to raise capital through a new bond issue. Marlene Fox excitedly describes a new record deal that Columbia wants her to sign. Phil Bondchefski, the CEO of Apex Steel, is furious that Apex has been sued for price fixing. Arlene Wagner, executive director of the local NAACP chapter, is concerned about renewing the chapter's lease. Helen Reston angrily relates that she was fired for reporting the company's practice of overcharging on government contracts and wants to sue her former employer for compensatory and punitive damages. Charles Winnegar quietly states that he wants to make a will leaving nothing to his son. Grace Parker dispassionately expresses her desire to sell her $750,000 lakeside vacation house without capital gains liability.

* * *

1. INTRODUCTION

Clients come to lawyers seeking help in solving problems. And as the opening examples suggest, the range of people and problems that lawyers encounter is enormous. The array embraces differences in size, complexity, emotional content and legal status.[1] Some problems

---

1. By size, lawyers typically mean the amount at stake. Cf. M. Galanter, "Mega–Law & Mega–Lawyering in the Contemporary United States," in *The Sociology of the Professions*, 156–57 (1983). Complexi-

ty, on the other hand, usually has no single meaning. Cases are seen as factually, procedurally and/or legally complex. Factual complexity typically refers to the amount of investigation involved. See J. Freund,

involve disputes over past events and others focus on planning for the future.

But no matter who the client, what the substantive legal issues or whether the situation involves litigation or planning, your principal role as lawyer will almost always be the same—to help clients achieve effective solutions to their problems. The process by which you facilitate the resolution of client problems—that is, the process of counseling—is the subject of this book.

Although law school perhaps gives a contrary impression, identifying and helping clients resolve problems requires more than knowledge of relevant legal principles.[2] You also need to know about clients' individual circumstances if you are to help them shape satisfactory solutions.[3] Thus, two clients may have the same "legal" problem, but a solution that satisfies one may be unthinkable to the other. Accordingly, effective counseling demands understanding of how each client's unique goals and needs intertwine with legal issues.

Achieving this understanding requires that you acquire knowledge in at least two broad areas not directly linked with legal principles. Skilled lawyers' knowledge in each of these areas helps demonstrate why the practice of law requires much more than knowledge of the law.

The first area concerns the context(s) in which clients' problems are embedded. Helping fashion solutions to problems involving surgical malpractice requires knowing something about medical diagnostic techniques, surgical procedures, and hospital practices. Similarly, if a client's proposed business venture concerns marketing a new software program, you probably need some knowledge of software products, marketing practices and venture capital. This first "extralegal" area,

"Handling Clients," 6 Legal Econ. 32, 34 (Oct. 1980). Procedural complexity typically refers to the necessity to comply with a host of rules. When terming a case legally complex, lawyers use different criteria. Sometimes legal complexity encompasses the notion that the subject matter is intellectually demanding. (For a discussion of the substantive subject areas lawyers in the Chicago, Illinois area perceive as intellectually demanding, see E. Laumann & J. Heinz, "Specialization and Prestige in the Legal Profession: The Structure of Deference," 1977 Am.B.Found.Res.J. 155, 166–68). Or, the term may mean that the matter involves legal issues for which the substantive law is unclear or in a state of continual flux, (see Id.) or needs to be modified or perhaps even reversed in order to protect the client. Or, legal complexity may mean that the substantive law involves a number of rules that are unfamiliar to all but those who are specialists in the particular substantive area. For example, even lawyers who have some expe-

rience in areas such as securities fraud, anti-trust or murder prosecutions, might well describe such areas as complex because of the number of rules with which one must be familiar in order to handle such cases.

2. Arguably, the typical law school casebook substantially contributes to the erroneous impression that solving clients' problems begins and ends with an ability to apply a proper legal rule. The usual appellate case begins with a short summary of facts, and then immediately launches into a statement such as, "The first issue we must decide is • • •" Such statements may accurately describe a problem as it appears to appellate courts; law students and new attorneys can therefore be excused for characterizing clients' problems in the same manner.

3. See C. Peck, "A New Tort Liability For Lack of Informed Consent in Legal Matters," 44 La.L.Rev. 1289, 1301 (1984).

then, is principally content-based; its focus is "industry knowledge" that you either have or will need to acquire.[4]

This book does not purport to define the "industry knowledge" that you will need in every situation, or indeed even in "typical" situations. However, by using examples that cover a broad range of legal and factual settings, in the contexts of both litigation and planning, the book does attempt to illustrate how contextual knowledge typically bears on the counseling process. "Industry" data, as you will see, both identifies subjects requiring investigation, and helps you create and explore potential solutions tailored to each client's individual needs and objectives.

The second extralegal area focuses more on process than content. Clients come to you with differing degrees of knowledge, emotion and sophistication. Some you will know personally; others will be strangers. Some will readily make decisions; others will be in a continuous quandary. Accordingly, for legal principle and contextual knowledge to lead to effective solutions, you need understanding and skills in a variety of interpersonal spheres including interviewing, counseling and negotiation.

This book focuses on this second extralegal area—the personal interaction between lawyer and client. It primarily explores the processes of interviewing and counseling. The book attempts to provide a general approach to interviewing and counseling and an array of skills that you can employ when talking to clients.

Effective interviewing and counseling is broadly seen as having two components: understanding and action.[5] The first component involves being receptive and responsive to clients by listening to their problems and concerns with sensitivity, warmth and understanding. The second component complements this responsiveness with action-oriented activities, such as identifying problems, gathering information and structuring the decision-making process. While these two components may seem quite independent of each other, they become fused and highly interrelated when counselor and client successfully interact.

In earlier times, the nearly universal view was that good interviewers and counselors were "born and not made."[6] However, substantial evidence now indicates that communication skills can be learned, and that even those thought of as "born interviewers" benefit from various opportunities to observe, practice and receive corrective feedback.[7] Of course, like recipes for Thousand Island salad dressing, no two clients or problems are precisely alike. Moreover, lawyers are no less unique than clients in behavior, idiosyncrasies and attitudes. Nevertheless,

4. For discussion of using "industry knowledge," see Chapter 9, sec. 5; Chapter 18, sec. 2.

5. See R. Carkhuff, *Helping and Human Relations* 35 (1969).

6. L. Cormier, W. Cormier & R. Weisser, *Interviewing and Helping Skills for Health Professionals* 3 (1984).

7. See G. Goodman, *The Talk Book* 303 (1988).

general skills and techniques exist which you can employ in counseling clients who are very different from each other.

With practice, the principles and skills explored in this book should enable you to establish professional attorney-client relationships; to motivate clients to reveal salient legal and nonlegal information; to help clients feel personally comfortable; and to encourage them to make choices among alternatives that best achieve their individual needs.

2. CLIENTS' TYPICAL NONLEGAL CONCERNS

As suggested above, lawyers' principal societal role is to help clients resolve problems, not merely to identify and apply legal rules. Nonetheless, too often lawyers conceive of clients' problems as though legal issues are at the problems' center, much as Ptolemy viewed the Solar System as though the Earth were at the center of the universe.[8] But legal issues may be no more the essence of a client's problem than, perhaps, religion might be its essence if a troubled client chose to talk to a minister rather than to you, a lawyer. Whatever the legal aspects of a problem, nonlegal aspects frequently are at the heart of a client's concerns. Effective counseling inevitably requires that you elicit information about these nonlegal aspects and factor them into a problem's resolution.

Because legal writing's proclivity to see problems through courts' eyes overlooks problems' nonlegal dimensions,[9] we illustrate the ubiquitousness of nonlegal concerns through three short hypotheticals. As you read through them, please think about the types of nonlegal concerns that clients are likely to have; why those concerns are inevitably present; and why the nonlegal aspects of problems so frequently create difficulty for clients. Also, please consider how awareness of the nonlegal aspects of problems might alter your analysis of what a client's problem consists of and how you might assist the client to resolve it.

* * *

When Phil Kretsky got off the elevator, he was immediately struck by the stereotypical law firm look. Large bronze letters on the wood paneled wall spelled out the firm name. The reception area was large, expensively furnished, nicely pictured and virtually unpeopled. Only the receptionist in her tailored dark blue suit prevented the space from being completely uninhabited. Kretsky gave his name and was told, as was common, that someone would be out in a moment to take him to Mr. Kamp's office.

8. For a reminder of Ptolemy's views see O. Neugebauer, *A History of Ancient Mathematical Astronomy* (1975); R. Newton, *The Origins of Ptolemy's Astronomical Parameters* (1982).

9. For a refreshing exception see J. Collins, "Improving the Relationship Between Lawyers and Business Clients," 20 Am.Bus. L.J. 525, 530 (1983).

As soon as Kretsky entered, Kamp rose to greet him. "Mr. Kretsky; Bob Kamp. Pleased to meet you; why don't we sit over here. I find the formality of a desk often interferes." Kamp beckoned to what might best be described as a small living room set-up near the south wall. Kretsky took the club chair and Kamp opted for the sofa at Kretsky's right.

There was then some chitchat about the weather and some inquiry into the difficulty of finding parking. When this concluded, Kamp began: "Maybe the easiest way to start is for you to explain how I can help you." What Kretsky thought and said were quite different. *In his mind,* the response was quite straightforward:

"You can help by drawing and negotiating a lease which sticks to the basic terms we've already worked out with Midland. You can help by letting me worry about the economics of the deal and not insisting that every conceivable contingency known to the legal mind be covered in the lease. You can get this done quickly so we can start moving our upholstery operation into the building by the end of next month and so I can report to next month's Board meeting that the deal has been concluded. By the way, make sure that Midland does deliver possession by that date; the old tenant isn't out yet. Finally, you can help by keeping the fees reasonable so that the Board does not complain about my using outside counsel."

In words, however, the reply was much less direct: "I'd like you to help us with a lease deal for some new factory space."

* * *

For three quarters of an hour, Joyce Cappetta sat in the reception area. Normally, the wait would have angered her considerably. As a litigator with 10 years' experience and a partner, she was not used to such treatment. However, if Weldon Frazer wanted her to wait, she'd wait. Yesterday afternoon she had received a telephone call from Frazer's secretary. Frazer was president of West Coast Timber; the secretary had asked if Cappetta could meet with Frazer at his office sharply at 3:00 p.m. today. Of course, the answer was yes; West Coast had paid the firm almost $400,000 in fees last year, and if Frazer wanted a meeting at 3:00, Cappetta could certainly rearrange her calendar.

As she waited, Cappetta kept speculating about why Frazer had asked for her personally. There were two partners in the corporate department who dealt directly with Frazer and each was senior to her. Moreover, the work she did for West Coast was but glorified collection work that took place under the rubric of construction industry litigation. Cappetta received her cases from Dave Moore, the credit manager, and she had never had any contact with Frazer or any other corporate officer.

When she was finally ushered into Frazer's office, Frazer began immediately. "Ms. Cappetta, nice to see you; I've heard a lot of good things about your work for us. Won't you have a seat?" The chair to which Frazer motioned was one of two upholstered arm chairs that sat directly in front of the almost barren rosewood table which Frazer apparently used as a desk. Frazer's back was to the window and the glare from the window made it hard to see his face.

Before she had time to respond, take in her surroundings, or express any thoughts, Frazer got to what Cappetta presumed was the point. "I understand you're handling a couple of lien claims against Holly Building Supplies where Regency Homes is the general?" When Cappetta nodded her affirmance, Frazer continued: "From what Dave Moore tells me, the real problem is Regency. Building suppliers beside Holly are now falling substantially behind on six other Regency projects, and potentially we could be talking about losses in excess of $750,000. What I'd like your thoughts on is whether law suits and liens on these six other projects make sense or whether we should be talking about some other approach. Also, I'd like your frank opinion on how carefully you think Moore is monitoring the accounts. As you probably know, our sales people are always complaining that Moore is too tight on his credit limits, but I'd like your views. We've got to keep selling; without sales we're not going anywhere. On the other hand, we've got to maintain some control over the amount of credit we let these suppliers have. You've worked on the Holly matters and several others, so your thoughts about how closely Moore monitors our accounts is important to me. I want to know whether, in your judgment, Moore is becoming too solicitous toward the sales department and has become too liberal in giving credit. Also I need your ideas about whether litigation is the best course at this time on each of the Regency matters."

* * *

Mrs. Howard arrived on time, gave her name to the receptionist and took a seat in the waiting room. Before she had done much more than pick up a magazine, she heard her name, and Ms. Spriggs was introducing herself: "Mrs. Howard, I'm Elizabeth Spriggs; won't you come in?"

As the women entered the twelfth floor office, Ms. Spriggs suggested that the older woman would be comfortable in the rather straight-backed chair that stood in front of a large oak desk. Ms. Spriggs then moved to the high back leather swivel-chair that clearly belonged to the desk's proprietor. Seated and secure, Ms. Spriggs began. "Mrs. Howard, how might I help you?"

Although she was expecting a question of this sort, the older woman hesitated as she thought:

"How can I be helped? What help is there for a 47–year–old woman whose husband has announced that after 19 years of marriage he is leaving to share an apartment with his 28–year–old lover? Sure there is the question of my legal rights. Certainly I need to know what kind of financial and child support I am entitled to. But will rights restore Harry's love? Will rights take away the pain, the hurt, the humiliation? Will they help me find my way as a single person? How can this lawyer help? "

*   *   *

Many lawyers (perhaps Ptolemeians) would tend to say that Kretsky, Frazer and Howard, have a lease problem, a collection problem and a dissolution problem respectively.[10] However, as each story suggests, the unsettled matters people bring to lawyers raise many questions in addition to pristine legal ones. Business people such as Kretsky are not worried merely about what provisions must be included in a lease to make it "legal". Kretsky's overriding concern is to conclude the deal in a way that allows the company's upholstery operations to go forward in a timely manner. As a result, he appears willing to forgo some legal protections in order to make the deal. He wants to keep down costs and conclude the lease so that he can move on to other affairs of the business.

Nonlegal concerns are as prevalent in litigation as they are in planning matters such as Kretsky's. Corporate officers such as Frazer are not concerned merely with the corporation's rights in potential lawsuits. Frazer, like many potential litigants, wonders whether it makes sense to sue. This arguably legal concern is enmeshed with broader business worries. Frazer is also uneasy about West Coast's credit practices and the adequacy of the company's credit manager. Individual clients as well face a host of nonlegal concerns. Think back to Mrs. Howard. What nonlegal concerns is she likely to have?

As the three hypotheticals illustrate, nonlegal ramifications typically are economic, social and psychological in nature. Often there also will be moral, religious and/or political consequences. Consider, therefore, what each of these varying consequences entails.

Economic Consequences: Economic ramifications are the monetary effects of a course of action. Almost every action will produce some economic ramifications. Legal fees, damages and time spent preparing to testify are typical economic ramifications of litigation. In planning matters, typical economic consequences include time spent in preparing for negotiation, legal fees and implementing the selected course of action. For example, Kretsky's company surely will be economically affected by the amount of rent, taxes, and maintenance costs the lease requires it to pay.

Social Consequences: Social ramifications are those that affect a client's relations with others. The situations of Kretsky, Frazer and Howard all demonstrate this kind of consequence. Kretsky's actions will influence his company's future relationships with the prospective landlord and Kretsky's future relationship with the board of directors.[11]

---

10. Lawyers, whether litigators or planners, tend to think of themselves as handling matters that fall into various substantive law categories. For lists of the common substantive subject areas that lawyers use in describing their work, see

Laumann & Heinz, *supra* note 1; J. Carlin, *Lawyers On Their Own* 41–122 (1962).

11. An attorney representing a corporation is likely to find the situation fraught with conflicts of interest. EC 5–18 of the Model Code states that corporate counsel

Frazer's action, too, will impact on numerous relationships including Moore, West Coast's board of directors and people in the sales department. Finally, Mrs. Howard's choice will influence her future relations with her spouse, her children and her friends.

Psychological Consequences: Psychological ramifications are the internal personal feelings that clients experience as the result of the choices they make. For example, some litigation clients feel cowardly and cheated when they give up certain claims as part of a settlement. Other clients feel anxious as long as a case remains unresolved. Similarly, some business clients are elated if their economic power produces a final deal in which the price is better than the market price. Others are happiest when a final agreement benefits both parties economically.[12]

Moral, Political and Religious Consequences: [13] Actions may create results or reactions that implicate clients' moral, political and/or religious values. That is, choices often arouse feelings based on clients' underlying personal values. For example a landlord's decision not to evict a tenant during December may emanate from the landlord's belief that people should not be made homeless during the holiday season.

Moral, political and/or religious values are often intertwined with one or more other nonlegal concerns. It is probably rare that a client makes a moral, political and/or religious decision that is devoid of economic, social and/or psychological overtones. For example, if a client is considering whether to leave the bulk of his estate to a son who has repeatedly squandered money, economic considerations might lead the client to disinherit the son. However, if the client's moral value is that blood ties outweigh all other considerations, the client may feel morally obligated to leave his estate to his son.

"owes his allegiance to the entity and not to a stockholder, director, officer, employee, representative, or other person connected with the entity." However, several authorities have come to different conclusions. Some assert that the corporation is composed of its stockholders and they are therefore the client. E. Sloter & A. Sorenson, "Corporate Legal Ethics—An Empirical Study: The Model Rules, the Code of Professional Responsibility and Counsel's Continuing Struggle Between Theory and Practice," 8 J. of Corp.Law 601, 632 (1983), relying on *Garner v. Wolfinbarger,* 430 F.2d 1093 (5th Cir.1970) and *SEC v. National Student Marketing Corp.,* 457 F.Supp. 682 (D.D.C.1978). Others suggest that the client is the board of directors. S. Lorne, "The Corporate and Securities Advisor, the Public Interest, and Professional Ethics," 76 Mich.L.Rev. 425, 436 (1978). Still others feel that management is the client. M. Riger, "The Lawyer–Director—'A Vexing Problem,'" 33

Bus.Law 2381, 2384 (1978); *accord City of Philadelphia v. Westinghouse Elec. Corp.,* 210 F.Supp. 483, 485 (E.D.Pa.1962). A study by Sloter and Sorenson found that 41% of the attorneys surveyed felt that management was the real client of the attorney. Sloter & Sorenson, *supra,* at 712. For an excellent review of the conflicts of interest that arise when representing corporate clients, see W. Sogg & M. Solomon, "The Changing Role of the Attorney with Respect to the Corporation," 35 Cleve.St.L.Rev. 147, 154 (1986–87).

12. The categories of economic, social and psychological are certainly not water tight. If a client believes that a decision will cause a relative to think poorly of him or her, is the ramification social, psychological or both?

13. Special thanks to Carrie Menkel-Meadow, who has continually stressed the importance of including these factors in the analysis of clients' problems.

3. ALL SOLUTIONS PRODUCE NONLEGAL CONSEQUENCES

Had Sir Isaac Newton gone to law school, his Third Law might have been, "For every solution, there are both legal and nonlegal consequences." Thus, you must help clients craft solutions that respond to both types of consequences.[14] At worst, failure to do so may leave a client worse off than before she or he sought your advice. At best, your oversight will leave a problem only partially resolved.

For example, assume that in West Coast Timber's matter, Cappetta devises a brilliant legal theory which gives West Coast claims against the other building suppliers who have fallen behind on the Regency projects. Based on this theory, Cappetta advises Frazer to sue each of these suppliers. West Coast ultimately prevails, but (a) can only partially recover its losses; (b) incurs substantial legal fees; (c) alienates other building suppliers who are West Coast customers; and (d) incurs "opportunity costs" because West Coast employees devoted significant time and energy to the lawsuit instead of to other business affairs. Cappetta's advice may have been "legally sound," but it has arguably left West Coast in a worse position than when it started. Had Cappetta and Frazer thought through the potential nonlegal ramifications before West Coast instituted suit, West Coast might have avoided at least some of these adverse consequences.

4. THE PROMINENCE OF NONLEGAL DIMENSIONS

Your intuitive sense may lead you to readily agree that problems have nonlegal dimensions. What may surprise you, however, is the notion that nonlegal concerns often outweigh legal ones in a client's calculus of what solution to adopt. For example, Frazer might choose to forgo litigation in order for West Coast to maintain good relations with its other building supply customers. Similarly, Mrs. Howard's decision to press all possible property claims might grow primarily out of her desire to punish a husband who she thinks has treated her and the children unfairly. Finally, Kretsky might forgo negotiating for provisions such as an option to renew the lease in order to conclude the deal quickly.

In the next subsections, examine the reasons that nonlegal concerns often predominate in clients' thinking.

---

14. Sometimes, legal and nonlegal consequences are virtually indistinguishable. For example, you might view the possibility of a client's recovering damages either as a legal or nonlegal economic consequence of filing suit.

A. EVEN DESIRED SOLUTIONS TYPICALLY ENTAIL NEGATIVE NONLEGAL CONSEQUENCES

One factor that accounts for the prominence of nonlegal concerns is that typically, in legal matters as in everyday life, achieving any benefit usually entails costs. Thus, the legal and nonlegal benefits that any solution may create are typically accompanied by nonlegal costs. If a client is not already aware that the silverest of linings has a cloud, having to make a decision typically causes a client to realize that every option has potential nonlegal downsides. As a result, clients often spend a good deal of time and energy weighing nonlegal consequences.

For instance, a lawsuit may provide Mr. Frazer with the positive satisfaction of putting pressure on Regency to pay West Coast the money it is owed. On the other hand, he may be frustrated by realizing that filing a lawsuit will also result in substantial legal costs and employee time devoted to the litigation. Similarly, a dissolution decree may provide Mrs. Howard with a degree of financial independence and the psychological satisfaction of taking control of her own life. However, obtaining the decree may be at the expense of her moral value that marriages should not be dissolved when children are still in the home. Because each solution will produce negative nonlegal consequences, both clients are likely to focus on these consequences as they think through whether a solution is satisfactory.

B. CHOOSING ONE SOLUTION MAY CUT OFF POSITIVE NONLEGAL CONSEQUENCES OF ALTERNATIVE SOLUTIONS

A second factor accounting for the prominence of nonlegal concerns is that by opting for the positive nonlegal consequences of one choice, a client necessarily forgoes the positive nonlegal consequences of others. When clients realize they must forgo one set of positive consequences in order to achieve another, they again typically feel conflicted. When clients feel the conflict, they tend to focus on it.

To see this point more clearly, imagine that an American is planning a vacation to Europe. During initial planning, she has a variety of choices, all of which have attractions she desires to see. ("I can go to Rome, or maybe to Scandinavia, or maybe to the cave area of France.") However, assuming finite resources and time, she cannot do all of these things; choosing the attractions of Rome, for example, may mean she cannot enjoy those of Scandinavia and France. Hence, our would-be traveler is likely to experience conflict and to dwell on it when deciding which attractions she must forgo.

Unlike our would-be world traveler who might take solace in choosing Rome in the thought that next year she might be in Scandinavia, in legal matters one choice frequently permanently forecloses all other choices. By way of example, return to Mr. Kretsky's situation. Assume that Mr. Kretsky wants to finalize a lease arrangement expeditiously so that he can turn his attention to other matters, but he also wants certain protections included in the lease so that he can enhance his standing before the board of directors. Either choice carries beneficial nonlegal ramifications, but making one choice (say, expeditiousness) may permanently foreclose the other. The resultant conflict will probably cause nonlegal concerns to figure prominently in Kretsky's choice.

C. CHOOSING A SOLUTION OFTEN REQUIRES A CLIENT TO TRADE ONE SET OF NEGATIVE CONSEQUENCES FOR ANOTHER

If clients find it difficult to choose between the positive nonlegal consequences of alternative solutions, they typically find it even more difficult to do so when alternative solutions each produce negative nonlegal consequences.

Consider again Mrs. Howard, for whom one legal option is dissolution. Assume that Mrs. Howard considers dissolution undesirable because she believes in the inviolability of marriage and because she is still in love with her husband. Another legal option is a legal separation, which she considers undesirable because it is ambiguous and because it hampers her need for financial independence. Like Kretsky, Howard will experience conflicts that cause her to focus on the nonlegal aspects of her situation.

D. NONLEGAL CONSEQUENCES ARE OFTEN DIFFICULT TO PREDICT

Uncertainty is another factor that commonly puts nonlegal consequences in the forefront of client concerns. Nonlegal consequences are not prescribed by statutes or Supreme Court decisions. Economic, social and psychological consequences vary considerably according to individual personalities, general social and economic conditions, and the like. Accordingly, when choosing between (or among) possible solutions, clients and lawyers need to predict the nonlegal consequences that are likely to flow from each. As the predictions are likely to be uncertain, clients often focus considerable time and energy on them.

Consider some routine examples of how predictions of nonlegal consequences are likely to be uncertain. When sued, some defendants feel pressure to settle, but others become more intransigent. How will Regency respond if West Coast sues? For that matter, how will Frazer react if Regency responds with intransigency and hostility? How accurately can West Coast predict its legal fees based on Regency's initial response, be it intransigence or accommodation? Similarly, will Kretsky's requiring a ten-year option to renew his company's lease cause the prospective landlord to delay or cancel the deal? Certainly you and your clients will sometimes be able to predict nonlegal ramifications with some degree of confidence. But often choices must be made in the face of some uncertainty. And for most clients, uncertainty produces concern.[15]

E. LEGAL CONSEQUENCES ARE OFTEN SECONDARY

Thus far, the argument has shown why nonlegal ramifications invariably figure prominently in decision-making. The perhaps surprising flip side of this argument is that often a decision's probable legal consequences are not a client's primary concern. The reason is that in many (though certainly not all) situations, each potential course of action a client might pursue is legally proper. In such situations, therefore, nonlegal factors, and not legal ones, primarily influence client choices.

For example, a will planning client may have a choice among an inter vivos trust, a testamentary trust, or a will with no trust provisions. Each of these options is legally proper. Thus, the client's choice is likely to be influenced by such nonlegal concerns as the options' relative costs, and which option the client feels best meets the family's needs. Similarly, in litigation, doctrine frequently does not declare any remedy a client desires to pursue as legally out of bounds.[16] For instance, if Mrs. Howard wanted to obtain spousal support, prevent her husband from obtaining joint custody, and/or obtain an order allowing her to remain in the family residence after the dissolution, each such remedy would probably be legally allowable in most jurisdictions.[17] Again, nonlegal factors such as likely relative costs and levels of aggravation will probably weigh heavily in Mrs. Howard's choice.

Second, the legal consequences of pursuing a particular option are often relatively predictable. Both in litigation and transactional contexts, you will frequently be able to predict likely legal results. For example, some litigation clients seek assistance in matters in which the adversary will have virtually no legal or factual defense. For instance, clients may consult you with regard to collecting a debt in situations in which the debtors have no valid defense. In such situations, the clients' concerns are often focused on such nonlegal concerns as whether suing a relative on a debt will destroy a family relationship or suing a customer will jeopardize goodwill in a closely knit business community.

---

15. See G. Bellow & B. Moulton, *The Lawyering Process* 1062–63 (1978); for a discussion of how people attempt to reduce uncertainty, see R. Abelson & A. Levi, "Decision Making & Decision Theory," in 1 *The Handbook of Social Psychology*, 269–77 (3d ed. 1985).

16. Note that often in litigation a client may obtain through settlement a result that a court could not award. Nonetheless, the result would be legal. For example, assume that a mandatory injunction is not available to a plaintiff in a particular civil action. However, the plaintiff and defendant may lawfully agree that the defendant will perform some act that the plaintiff will accept in full settlement. For a discussion of the importance in settlement negotiations of thinking creatively beyond the remedies courts can award, see C. Menkel–Meadow, "Toward Another View of Legal Negotiation: The Structure of Problem Solving," 31 UCLA L.Rev. 754, 795–801 (1984).

17. Of course, if Mrs. Howard wanted to prevent a divorce, the law in most jurisdictions would deny her that remedy.

Even in contested matters, you may be able to predict important aspects of legal outcomes. For example, in Mrs. Howard's situation, you may be able to predict accurately which spouse will be awarded custody of minor children, even if you are less certain of whether spousal support will be awarded and, if so, in what amount.[18]

Predictability of outcome often exists also in planning matters. In the estate planning example above, you could probably advise the client with a high degree of accuracy as to the tax consequences attached to the different options. Even in circumstances where the legal outcome depends largely upon the decision of some outside person or agency, accurate prediction is often possible. For example, when a business deal hinges on a party acquiring a license to engage in certain conduct, the facts are often so clear that you can state with substantial certainty whether the appropriate authority will approve the proposed course of action. For instance, after being apprised of the facts, you might know with substantial certainty that the Alcoholic Beverage Control Board will issue a liquor license or that the Commissioner of Corporations will approve the issuance of stock.

Finally, the plain fact is that in many situations nonlegal concerns are more important to clients than legal ones. For example, you may personally feel at ease reassuring a client threatened with a lawsuit that legally she is in the right. But the client can be excused for remaining uneasy. For most people, apart from the question of winning and losing, the prospect of litigation is unnerving and foreshadows costs in time, money and emotional distress. Likewise, nonlegal concerns tend to predominate in planning matters. Most businesspeople are far more concerned about the economic consequences of various provisions of a deal than they are with, say, the enforceability of various clauses in the event of default.

5. PROMINENCE OF NONLEGAL CONCERNS: COUNSELING IMPLICATIONS

The prominence of nonlegal aspects of client problems affects our entire view of counseling, from initial interview through problem resolution. To help clients effectively resolve their problems, you must continually take account of, and help clients think through, nonlegal as well as legal dimensions. When interviewing clients, gather information about all of their concerns, not merely evidence that might prove or disprove a legal claim or that may incline you to include a certain provision in an agreement. When developing potential resolutions to problems, take care that your suggestions respond to nonlegal as well

18. Of course, this degree of predictability may not be available in complex matters in which the verdict is in doubt and damages are highly speculative. However, in many situations, a lawyer may ultimately, and after full investigation, be able to predict accurately a legal outcome. In such situations, it is fair to say that during the pendency of the matter clients will have concerns about legal as well as nonlegal matters.

as legal concerns.   And when helping clients choose a course of action, discuss with them the possible nonlegal and legal impacts of available options.

In short, problem resolution is not guided by a "closed set" in which all that matters is statutes, regulations and court opinions. People's economic, social, psychological and moral concerns are as much a part of their problems as any worries about legal doctrine.   The more you understand this reality, the better lawyer you will be.

Chapter 2

A CLIENT–CENTERED
APPROACH

* * *

From our hour together, Ms. Woods, I think I have an idea of what Sontex is trying to accomplish by combining with Universal so that both companies can make a joint bid on the Lockheed satellite project. You've done an excellent job of filling me in on how the proposed deal would work and how it might affect Sontex's current operations. I think I also understand what terms you and Universal have worked out thus far. At this point, your major concern, apart from your economic requirements, is to structure the deal in a way that keeps members of your engineering department, especially the team leaders, happy. Balanced against this need is the necessity to make the people at Universal feel they are participating in this deal as a full partner with Sontex. Have I stated the problems correctly?

You've got it.

Good. Now let's start talking about possible solutions. What we've got to do is to think through the various ways we can structure this deal to meet as many of the needs of both Sontex and Universal as possible. I've got a couple of ideas and I want to hear yours. When we've got some options on the table, we can then begin to flesh them out. Sound okay?

* * *

1. CLIENT–CENTERED VS. TRADITIONAL CONCEPTIONS OF CLIENTS AND PROBLEMS

This chapter describes a framework for helping clients resolve problems.[1] The framework consists of a counseling approach which we term "client-centered." The approach permeates this book and pro-

1. Helping clients solve problems is one of a lawyer's primary roles. This is not to suggest that lawyers do not also owe obligations to third persons, to society as a whole, and to themselves as human beings. For a discussion of lawyers' obligations to persons other than the client see J.L. Maute, "Allocation of Decision-making Authority Under The Model Rules of Professional Conduct." 17 U.C.Davis L.Rev. 1049, 1070–80 (1984).

16

vides the foundation for exploring interviewing and counseling techniques.

The client-centered approach encompasses conceptions of both problems and clients. Insofar as problems are concerned, the approach is anchored on the reality stressed in Chapter 1 that problems have both legal and nonlegal dimensions.

Contrast the client-centered conception of problems with a more traditional view. Under the traditional conception, lawyers view client problems primarily in terms of existing doctrinal categories such as contracts, torts, or securities.[2] Information is important principally to the extent the data affects the doctrinal pigeonhole into which the lawyer places the problem.[3] Moreover, in the traditional view, lawyers primarily seek the best "legal" solutions to problems without fully exploring how those solutions meet clients' nonlegal as well as legal concerns.[4]

Next, compare client-centered and traditional conceptions of clients. A client-centered conception assumes that most clients are capable of thinking through the complexities of their problems. In particular, it posits that clients are usually more expert than lawyers when it comes to the economic, social and psychological dimensions of problems. The client-centered conception also assumes that, because any solution to a problem involves a balancing of legal and nonlegal concerns, clients usually are better able than lawyers to choose satisfactory solutions. Moreover, the approach recognizes that clients' emotions are an inevitable and natural part of problems and must be factored into the counseling process. Finally, the approach begins with the assumption that most clients seek to attain legally legitimate ends through lawful means.[5]

Clients are less well regarded in the traditional conception. Lawyers adhering to the traditional view have often muttered, "The practice of law would be wonderful if it weren't for clients."[6]. Such lawyers tend to regard themselves as experts who can and should determine, in a detached and rational manner, and with minimal client input, what

2. See E.H. Steele and R.T. Nimmer, "Lawyers, Clients, and Professional Regulation," 3 Am Bar Found.Res.J. 917, 950–51 (1976); Maute, *supra* note 1, at 1058–59; D.E. Rosenthal, *Lawyer and Client: Who's In Charge* 7–8 (1974). See also, Audiotape One, "Trying a Wrongful Employment Termination Case," (Cal. CEB 1986).

3. For a discussion of the kind of client frustrations produced by interviewing confined to this sort of pigeonholing, see V.H. Appel & R.E. Van Atta, "The Attorney–Client Dyad: An Outsider's View," 22 Okla.L.Rev. 243, 245–246 (1971).

4. See, e.g., M.H. McCormack, *The Terrible Truth About Lawyers* 39 (1987).

5. This assumption does not suggest, of course, that all or even most clients are legally correct. That about fifty percent of the clients whose names appear in the case reporters were "legally wrong" does not mean that they were seeking illegitimate ends or employing unlawful means.

6. This is of course an old canard. See "Solicitor/Client Relationship," a videotape produced by the Law Society (England; April, 1984); cf. T.L. Shaffer and J.R. Elkins, *Legal Interviewing and Counseling in a Nutshell* 14 (2d ed. 1987): "The instrumental theory regards the client as a necessary nuisance."

solution is best.[7] Three common attributes that lawyers who hold a traditional view tend to ascribe to clients are: (1) Clients lack sophistication; (2) Clients are too emotionally wrapped up in their problems; and (3) Clients do not adequately consider the potential long-term effects (risks) of decisions.[8]

As you might imagine, despite these differing conceptions, client-centered and traditional conceptions of lawyering have much in common. Both, for example, recognize the critical importance of legal analysis and have as their ultimate goal maximum client satisfaction. Moreover, most lawyers do not follow one conception to the complete exclusion of the other. However, the client-centered conception "fills in" the traditional approach by stressing that problems have nonlegal as well as legal aspects, and by emphasizing the importance of clients' expertise, thoughts and feelings in resolving problems. In a client-centered world, your role involves having clients actively participate in identifying their problems, formulating potential solutions, and making decisions.[9] Thus, client-centered lawyering emanates from a belief in the autonomy, intelligence, dignity and basic morality of the individual client.[10]

Client-centered lawyering does not, however, place you at the mercy of every client caprice and demand. Admittedly, the approach may from time to time require you to support client values and decisions with which you disagree.[11] But when clients seek to go

7. See, e.g. S.S. Clawar, *You & Your Clients: A Guide to a More Successful Law Practice Through Behavior Management,* (Section of General Practice, ABA 1988) at 83, suggesting that frequent client complaints include, " 'He didn't hear my side.' Clients often feel that they are not being understood in terms of their specific problems or needs." The propriety of traditional lawyer behavior would seem to be in conflict with a number of ethical considerations. See, e.g., J.C. Freund, *Lawyering: A Realistic Approach to Legal Practice* 277–9 (1979) (discussing the impropriety of the lawyer presenting his personal judgment in the guise of objective facts and thereby preventing the client from making the decision independently. Freund rejects the common rationalization that this kind of "subtle coercion" is permissible since the lawyer's position is "right".) See also Rosenthal, note 2 *supra* 13–22.

8. Cf. McCormack, *supra* note 4, at 111.

9. See Clawar, *supra* note 7, at 86 (Discussion of research showing that clients are more satisfied with legal services when lawyers treat them like people and provide understanding in addition to legal services.)

10. We recognize that not all clients will fully possess these capabilities. However, our experience suggests that the percentage of relatively sophisticated and knowledgeable people who seek legal assistance, whether rich or poor, is quite high. For suggestions on how to interact with clients when these assumptions appear incorrect, see Chapter 14; Chapter 15, sec. 5.

11. Troublesome problems may arise when a client's values do not conflict with fundamental societal values or rules but do conflict with your personal values. For example, assume you believe that spousal support should always be awarded to a wife who is awarded custody of minor children. Assume further that you represent a husband who is adamant that his wife, who will receive custody of the parties' two minor children, receive no spousal support. The husband points out that the wife has always been employed full time as a software engineer. Though the husband's position may not be illegal or immoral, some would assert that you should be free to decline to represent the husband. See W.H. Simon, "Ethical Discretion in Lawyering," 101 Harv.L.Rev. 1083 (1988) (lawyers should have discretion to refuse to pursue legally permissible courses of action which they believe conflict with their ethical responsibility to the legal profession and the overall pursuit of justice); ABA

beyond the bounds of what is legal or just, a client-centered approach does not dictate that you disregard fundamental legal concepts and moral values.[12] Nor does it suggest that you close your eyes and mouth to a client's desire to adopt a course of action fraught with the likelihood of disaster.[13] Finally, when a client's values conflict with fundamental moral precepts and positive legal rules, the approach does not require that you become a blind instrumentalist.[14]

2. ATTRIBUTES OF A CLIENT–CENTERED APPROACH

The complexity of human interaction makes a precise definition of client-centered lawyering impossible. However, a client-centered approach has at least the following attributes.

A. THE LAWYER HELPS IDENTIFY PROBLEMS FROM A CLIENT'S PERSPECTIVE

Central to the client-centered approach is the idea that you are most helpful to clients if from the outset you try to understand a problem from a client's point of view. Clients vary enormously in regard to such matters as their cultural-religious-ethnic characteristics; socio-economic status; financial needs; prior experience with lawyers and the legal system; willingness to take risks; desire to win; desire to establish harmonious working relationships; desire to prove a point, get revenge, or avoid conflict altogether; level of anxiety, anger or depression; and willingness to consider long-range as well as short-term consequences.[15] Such factors almost inevitably influence a client's perception of what the problem is and what solutions are possible and worth pursuing.

Moreover, the context (environment) in which problems arise will be no less unique than the clients themselves. For example, a problem

---

Model Rules of Professional Responsibility, Rule 1.16(b)(3): "[A] lawyer may withdraw from representing a client if withdrawal can be accomplished without material adverse effect on the interests of the client, or if . . . the client insists upon pursuing an objective that the lawyer considers repugnant or imprudent."

12. For suggestions on counseling clients who seek to achieve immoral or illegal ends, see Chapter 15, sec. 5(B); Chapter 20, sec. 4(B).

13. For suggestions on counseling clients who mispredict an option's likely consequences, see Chapter 15, sec. 5(A); Chapter 20, sec. 4(A).

14. A client-centered approach does not neatly allow you to draw a clear line on the one hand between those values which contravene your personal values and on the other those which conflict with fundamental moral precepts and positive legal rules. However, the approach can help you begin to differentiate between these different circumstances. As discussed in Chapter 20, sec. 4, the approach may help you distinguish between cases where clients mispredict the likely results of their choices and cases where clients adopt values with which you disagree.

15. This uniqueness pertains whether the client is an individual or an entity such as a corporation. Apart from the reality that the problems of organizations are the problems of the people who comprise it, corporations, like people, vary according to financial needs, willingness to take risks, etc. See "A Businessman's View of Lawyers," 33 Bus.Lawyer 817 (1978).

that arises at a time when inflation is low and social concern about "runaway jury verdicts" nonexistent will be different from one that arises at a time when inflation is higher and many people think jurors are awarding large windfalls to undeserving litigants. And, even at the same point in time, the facially similar problems (e.g., two manufacturing companies preparing dealership contracts) of two personally similar clients will very likely be quite unique. If one client is in the computer business in a small town and the other is in the furniture business in a big city, the different contexts will inevitably affect the nature and scope of their problems. Geographic areas and industries vary according to such factors as growth potential, custom and trade practices, standard operating procedures, composition of the labor force, capital needs, and the like.[16] Hence, two problems which might in the traditional conception be housed in the same legal pigeonhole will, because of differing environments, often be viewed differently by individual clients.

B. THE LAWYER ACTIVELY INVOLVES A CLIENT IN THE PROCESS OF EXPLORING POTENTIAL SOLUTIONS

This aspect of client centeredness involves two features. First, since there is rarely only one obvious solution to a client's problem, you try to make sure that the client considers the broadest range of options. You both suggest potential solutions and encourage a client to develop additional ones. Second, you encourage a client to identify the potential nonlegal consequences of each potential solution so that ultimately a solution is fashioned which takes into account the client's unique needs and goals.

C. THE LAWYER ENCOURAGES A CLIENT TO MAKE THOSE DECISIONS WHICH ARE LIKELY TO HAVE A SUBSTANTIAL LEGAL OR NONLEGAL IMPACT

The client-centered approach emphasizes the value and importance of clients' taking the role of primary decision maker.[17] It adopts this emphasis for two reasons. First, decisions having significant impact on a client are best based on an evaluation of which potential solution is most likely to satisfy the client. Second, because each client generally

---

16. Of course such variations will also be found among different clients (companies) within the same industry.

17. Of course, in instances where a client has not reached majority, suffers from mental incapacity, etc. the approach cannot be used. See for example, P.R. Tremblay, "On Persuasion and Paternalism: Lawyer Decision Making and the Questionably Competent Client," 1987 Utah L.Rev. 515 (discussing ways to identify problems of client competence and investigating various courses of action open to a lawyer); ABA Model Rules of Professional Conduct (hereafter "Model Rules") Rule 1.14 ("Cli-

ent Under a Disability"), Subsection (a): "When a client's ability to make adequately considered decisions in connection with representation is impaired, whether because of minority, mental disability or for some other reason, the lawyer shall, as far as reasonably possible, maintain a normal lawyer-client relationship with the client." The Comment to Rule 1.14 stresses the obligation to allow a client to make decisions whenever possible and, in all cases, to keep a client informed. If a legal representative is appointed for a client, the lawyer should follow the decisions of that representative.

has unique values and goals, a client is typically in a better position than you to choose which potential solution is best.

For example, clients are generally in the better position to know how willing they are to spend money and how big a risk they are willing to take to achieve a particular goal. Assume that a client who has been fired is considering whether to file suit for wrongful termination, and if so, whether to seek reinstatement. The decision will rest on such factors as how willing the client is to incur attorney's fees, to relive his or her employment history in open court, and to bear the discomfort that may attach to returning to work in a possibly unfriendly environment. Since any one client is likely to weigh these factors differently, this pivotal decision is best left to the client.[18]

Of course, you need not remain silent during the decision-making process. You must provide clients with an assessment of the likely legal (and sometimes nonlegal) consequences of following potential courses of action. Indeed, as the next section suggests, at times you may even recommend what course of action a client should adopt. Nonetheless, the basic point remains. Usually only a client can decide how willing he or she is to run the risks and bear the potential costs of adopting a particular course of action. Therefore, a client should make critical choices whenever possible and practical.[19]

D. THE LAWYER PROVIDES ADVICE BASED ON A CLIENT'S VALUES

No amount of wishing for a world filled with fully autonomous clients—clients who make decisions on their own—can eliminate the reality that many clients will not feel comfortable making a decision until they hear your advice. Hence, while clients usually are best off making their own decisions, a client-centered conception recognizes that you may provide advice in many instances. However, your advice should generally be based on your understanding of the client's values. Giving advice based on the consequences you personally think important would impose your values on a client and would be antithetical to client-centeredness.

E. THE LAWYER ACKNOWLEDGES A CLIENT'S FEELINGS AND RECOGNIZES THEIR IMPORTANCE

Client-centered counseling also requires that you understand and respond to clients' feelings. Legal problems do not exist in an emotion-

---

18. In addition, many commentors have suggested that clients can best live and are more motivated to follow through with a decision if they feel the decision is one that they have made for themselves. See for example, Rosenthal, *supra* note 2, at 20. Cf. G. Egan, *The Skilled Helper* 264 (1986). In addition, a client who is actively involved in decisions may be less anxious and more cooperative. See Clawar, *supra* note 7, at 20. Contrast the traditional view, according to which clients do not feel satisfied unless their lawyers tell them what to do. See Rosenthal, at 19.

19. Of course, there will be instances when, for practical reasons, you will make a decision which otherwise would be one for a client to make. See Tremblay, *supra* note 17.

less vacuum.[20] Clients' emotional reactions to situations are as significant an aspect of problems as are the facts which generate the problems. Recall from Chapter 1 that feelings are an inherent part of legal problems. Worries and concerns form the heart of problems and motivate clients to seek help in the first place.[21] It is not surprising, then, that clients *want* and *need* to talk about their feelings. Thus, by focusing on both feelings as well as facts, you can build rapport, elicit detailed and accurate information, and help fashion solutions that best meet clients' needs.

F. THE LAWYER REPEATEDLY CONVEYS A DESIRE TO HELP

Another aspect of a client-centered approach consists of an amazingly simple step. Convey, explicitly, that you want to help a client. For example, you might say, "I really want to help you decide whether incorporating the business makes sense." Perhaps this suggestion seems fatuous. After all, won't a client assume that you are there to provide help? Maybe. But a formal attorney-client relationship does not always assure a client that you are personally committed to providing help. Asserting your desire to help is an explicit form of reassurance that clients often find comforting and motivating.[22]

3. THE ADVANTAGES OF A CLIENT-CENTERED APPROACH

Through the foregoing attributes, the client-centered approach encourages clients to participate actively in the description and resolution of their problems. As the discussion of the attributes suggests, the advantages of active client participation are substantial. Active client participation enhances the likelihood of producing satisfactory resolutions. It does so by (1) embracing both the legal and nonlegal dimensions of a client's problem; (2) employing the combined expertise of lawyer and client in identifying and evaluating potential solutions; and

20. In their excellent work on legal interviewing and counseling, Shaffer and Elkins make the point that in a law office, "Feelings are facts." See Shaffer and Elkins, *supra* note 6 at 9–10.

21. See, Egan, *supra* note 18, at 32 (psychological context); Clawar, *supra,* note 7, at 3–6. Cf. V.A. Church, "People Come to Lawyers Wanting a Good Parent, Magical Bodyguard, and Political Ally with Muscle," Student Lawyer (Dec. 1973), at 10: "The fact that a client first seeks you, an attorney, rather than a minister, marriage counselor, psychologist, therapist, or doctor, may have little to do with the nature of his underlying problem (or even with the best means of effectively resolving it)."

22. We recognize that some readers may regard this as a minor point and question the wisdom of including it as an essential client-centered attribute. But our experience is that explicit, and sometimes repeated, affirmations of a desire to help is enormously reassuring to many clients. This is especially true for new clients, who have had little opportunity to assess your personal commitment, or for clients who have had previous negative experiences with other lawyers. The psychological literature supports this notion. See Egan, *supra* note 18, at 61 (discussing importance of communicating interest and commitment to helping client through "attentive physical presence" as contrasted to communicating lack of interest and commitment through "poor physical presence".); Cf. Id. at 74–79.

(3) encouraging decisions to be made by clients, who are generally better able than lawyers to assess whether solutions are likely to be satisfactory.

Moreover, active client participation respects the autonomy of the person who "owns" the problem. A client does not lose the right to make decisions which are likely to have a substantial impact on his or her life for having sought legal assistance.

4. OTHER ESSENTIAL ATTRIBUTES OF A PROFESSIONAL ATTORNEY–CLIENT RELATIONSHIP

This section briefly examines three additional attributes of a professional attorney-client relationship. We discuss these additional attributes separately from those described above not to demean them, but because they are consistent both with client-centered and traditional views of counseling.

A. THE LAWYER ESTABLISHES A CLEAR FEE ARRANGEMENT

Attorneys' fees are a major source of client misunderstanding and dissatisfaction.[23] Perhaps in the belief that fees are always "bad news" to clients, or perhaps because of a vestigial sense that fees are inconsistent with the practice of a learned profession, many lawyers avoid discussing fees for as long as possible.[24] Some lawyers even cloak their reluctance to talk about fees in client-centered dress, arguing that delay makes clients more comfortable.[25]

Absent exceptional circumstances, you are obligated to make fee arrangements clear at the outset. The fee discussion should include at least three topics: (1) the method of computing the fee—e.g. $100 per hour; 30% contingent fee; (2) when the fees are payable; and (3) the consequences of non-timely payment. In addition, when the nature and duration of your services are uncertain, you will need to explore estimated fees.

23. See Steele and Nimmer, *supra* note 2, at 952–54. The dissatisfaction may be particularly acute with new or "one-shot" clients. See *Avoiding Client Grievances: Professional Responsibility and the Lawyer* (ABA Center for Professional Responsibility 1988) 1: "Many fee complaints are made by clients with little knowledge of the legal system, its processes, and the factors determining the amount of the fee to be charged." Cf. Clawar, *supra* note 7, at 10–11 (clients turn fear of their problems into mistrust of the lawyer, particularly the lawyer's fees).

24. See H.M. Kritzer, "The Dimensions of Lawyer–Client Relations: Notes Toward a Theory and a Field Study," 1984 Am.Bar Found.Res.J. 409, 418.

25. See Id. Cf. D.N. Stern and J. Martin, "Mitigating The Risk of Being Sued By Your Former Client," 51 Okla.Bar J. 459, 463 (1980) (some lawyers avoid reducing fee agreements to writing on the ground that clients will view a fee document as a sign of distrust.).

B. THE LAWYER KEEPS A CLIENT INFORMED

Clients also commonly complain that lawyers fail to keep them informed.[26] From your point of view, a client's problem may seem rather routine: "No big deal; just another . . . ." However, the client views the problem as new, unexpected, critical and/or unmanageable. Therefore, regular reports regarding a matter's progress are usually essential. Indeed, even reporting that there is nothing to report is often reassuring. Without periodic reports, clients may feel cast adrift.[27]

C. THE LAWYER RESPONDS PROMPTLY TO CLIENTS' INQUIRIES

Perhaps nothing frustrates clients more than unreturned phone calls.[28] Obviously, you cannot respond immediately to every phone call. In accordance with an old bromide, return every call on the day it is received; if you cannot do so, have someone else inform a client as to when you will respond.[29]

26. See R.E. Mallen and V.B. Levit, *Legal Malpractice* (2nd ed. 1981) 46–47. Subjects that clients complain that they are not informed about include sufficient information for client to make an independent decision about how to proceed; current status of the matter (*Avoiding Client Grievances, supra* note 23, at 7); explanation of fees (Clawar *supra* note 7 at 83); progress of the matter (Id. at 83). See also, McCormack, *supra* note 4, at 82.

27. How and how often you need to communicate with clients will vary from client to client and matter to matter. See Model Code, Rule 1.4. A common suggestion for keeping clients informed is to send the client copies of all documents you prepare and receive. See for example, Mallen and Levit, supra note 26, at 49–50; J.W. McElhaney, "Keep the Client Happy," 10 Litigation 43, 44 (1984). Query: Is this suggestion workable in an era when many attorneys charge clients for every page that is copied? Obviously, in certain matters this procedure will result in overkill and overcharge.

28. See Steele and Nimmer, *supra* note 2, at 967–68.

29. Similar considerations apply to written inquiries.

Chapter 3

AN OVERVIEW OF THE COUNSELING PROCESS

Chapters 1 and 2 have explained how a client-centered approach responds both to the legal and the nonlegal aspects of clients' problems. The remainder of the book explores methods and techniques of client-centered interviewing and counseling. To avoid your overlooking the "forest" of client-centeredness in the "trees" of numerous methods and techniques, this chapter briefly describes the overall process of understanding a problem from a client's perspective, gathering pertinent information, and involving a client actively in a problem's resolution.[1]

1. PRELIMINARILY IDENTIFYING A CLIENT'S PROBLEM

* * *

How might I help you, Ms. Santiago?

They say they're going to sell our house; I don't know what it's all about. We've always made the payments on time, except once. They say they're going to hold the sale next Tuesday. We don't know what to do. Can you help us?

* * *

Mr. Marshall, please tell me what I can do for you.

Well, I own a fancy grocery business and I want to merge my business with this other guy, Patrick Moore, who owns a similar operation. Together we would then open up a third store. But I'm really not sure how we should go about it. Also, if things don't work out, I want to get out of the arrangement quickly and preserve my assets without any hassles.

* * *

Typically, you direct initial counseling efforts toward attempting to preliminarily identify why a client has come to you. That is, you attempt to learn what a client thinks is her or his problem. Some-

---

1. You are likely to utilize the overall process to its fullest extent only when you handle a relatively complex new matter for new clients.

times, of course, a problem turns out to be very different from a client's initial description. Or, a "presenting" problem may in the end be accompanied by several others. Nevertheless, a client's preliminary description of a problem often provides clues to such significant matters as what a client is seeking to accomplish, what aspect of a problem a client considers to be most important, a client's emotional investment in a problem, and the range of solutions a client might ultimately be willing to consider. Hence, "Preliminary Problem Identification" is the essential starting place of a client-centered approach.[2]

2. INITIAL DATA–GATHERING

* * *

Ms. Santiago, I think I have a fairly good idea of your concerns. You're worried foremost about saving your house. In addition, the matter of legal fees is of concern, as is the time you and your husband will have to spend fighting this matter. Before I can begin to advise you about what might be done in your case and what the fees might be, I need to get some more information from you. What I'd like to do is have you start from the beginning and tell me step by step everything that has happened in connection with this attempt to sell your house. Can you do that?

I guess the first time I heard anything about it was when Mr. Baldwin phoned up about the late payment.

Okay, tell me about that.

* * *

Mr. Marshall, you've given me a good description of your principal concerns. You want to go ahead with this deal as quickly as possible and at the same time you want an escape hatch if things don't work out. You want the new operation to continue the name "Marshall Foods." Finally, you want to have a veto over all expenditures in excess of $2,000. Before I can talk with you in depth about what type of business arrangement would be best for you and Mr. Moore, I'm going to need some more information. Why don't you start out by telling me about what arrangements, if any, you and Mr. Moore have already worked out.

Sure. We haven't gotten into too much detail. We've agreed . . . ..

* * *

After preliminarily identifying a client's problem, you typically turn a dialogue to the data you need before you and a client can begin to construct and evaluate possible solutions.

In litigation, that data almost always concerns the history of whatever problem caused the client to seek legal assistance. Note that in the Santiago matter, you ask her to "start from the beginning." Proving what happened in the past is usually necessary if you are to

---

2. How much of an initial meeting you devote to preliminarily identifying a client's problem usually varies according to such factors as a matter's complexity, the extent of a client's concerns, and the level of rapport between client and you.

establish a client's legal rights.[3] In turn, a client's legal rights typically greatly influence which option a client ultimately chooses. For example, Ms. Santiago probably could not realistically consider what option is likely to most satisfy her until you could provide her with some understanding of how she might fare in an action to enjoin the threatened sale of her house. Hence, in litigation, initial data-gathering almost always focuses on the historical events underlying a client's problem.[4]

Transactional matters typically are not as heavily dependent as litigation matters on past happenings. For example, history usually does not control the terms that parties to a proposed deal may agree upon. Thus, Marshall's and Moore's prior business practices, though probably germane to the final deal's shape, do not prevent them from agreeing to whatever terms they choose. In transactional matters, then, initial data-gathering usually focuses on topics related to the kind of transaction that a client contemplates. For instance, in Marshall's matter, you would focus on topics related to mergers of small businesses, such as each company's method of operation and current financial position.

In both litigation and transactional matters, you will often be unable to complete initial data-gathering at a single sitting. In litigation matters, you need to develop a chronology of events giving rise to a client's problem, and then to probe those events in the light of relevant legal and factual theories. That probing typically involves eliciting numerous details. Moreover, stories that wind up as litigated disputes tend to be emotion laden. Also, several theories potentially apply to most stories. Finally, often you may need to do research to familiarize yourself with such theories before you can complete initial data-gathering. For all of these reasons, and perhaps others, initial data-gathering in litigation matters is often quite time consuming.

The time consuming aspect of initial data-gathering in transactional matters usually grows out of the complex nature of the typical transaction. You often need to prepare a number of documents covering a wide range of subjects. Here too you typically need to do research and make a variety of inquiries to insure that your documentation covers the various subjects it needs to address. Thus, even in transactional settings initial data-gathering may well require more than one meeting.

3. FORMULATING AND EVALUATING POTENTIAL SOLUTIONS

* * *

Ms. Santiago, now that we've discussed the events leading up to the threatened sale of your house next Tuesday, we can begin to think

---

3. See Frank, *supra* note 2, at 37–40.

4. Regardless of the substantive legal principles underlying a dispute, the focus on historical events remains the same.

about what might be done. I really want to help you in this matter, and I think we have several choices available. What I'd like to do is tell you what options I see. Then we can go through the pros and cons of these options as well as any others you can think of.

Do you think I can keep my house?

Yes, and there are a few ways we might accomplish this. One option is to file a lawsuit to stop the sale. If you do that, there is a very good chance that the court will rule in your favor. But you have a couple of other options, and I want to talk with you about those too. All right?

* * *

Mr. Marshall, you've given me a very nice picture of your business, what you're trying to accomplish and the preliminary understanding you have with Mr. Moore. I can see why you are anxious to join forces with Moore. I see a couple of different options for structuring the deal. What I think we should do is go over them, and any others you have been thinking about, and think through the pros and cons of each. Do you think there is anything else I should know before we get started?

No. I think we've covered most everything I had in mind. I would like to talk about incorporating, since a number of people have told me that having a corporation is the way to go.

Well, incorporating is certainly one option, and we can talk about that one first. But I think we should also discuss the simpler possibility of forming a partnership. Given your need for some additional capital, perhaps it also makes sense to talk about a limited partnership. Now why don't we begin by . . . ..

* * *

After gathering preliminary data, your attention shifts to potential solutions for resolving a client's problem. Together, you and a client identify alternative solutions and explore the likely legal and nonlegal consequences of each. For example, among the possible solutions you would likely ask Ms. Santiago to consider are "seek injunctive relief" and "arrange a settlement meeting with the mortgagee." Following this discussion, and perhaps with the benefit of your advice, a client chooses a course of action.

4. THE NON–LINEAR PATH FROM IDENTIFYING TO RESOLVING PROBLEMS

The overall counseling process described in sections 1 through 3 may strike you as a linear one. You begin by identifying a client's problem; then you gather data; then, together with a client, you formulate and evaluate options. Completing these steps helps a client decide which option is most likely to resolve the problem satisfactorily. All that remains is to implement the client's choice: "sue the jerks;" "form a partnership."

A linear conception of the overall counseling process is not entirely baseless. For example, some data-gathering almost always precedes exploration of potential solutions.[5] However, a number of factors typically cause the road from problem identification to problem resolution to be anything but smooth and straight. For one thing, evaluating the likely consequences of various options often makes you and a client realize the need for additional data. By way of example, assume that you and Mr. Marshall are discussing the option, "form a partnership with Moore." You point out that a consequence of this option is that Moore's creditors, if any, will be able to reach the partnership assets. As a result, before finally evaluating the option, you may ask Mr. Marshall to gather data about Moore's financial condition.

Second, while "choosing a course of action" may sound like the end of the counseling process, often it is not. In the course of implementing a decision, factors such as changed circumstances, a client's change of heart, or unforeseen hurdles may result in the decision's revision or abandonment. That, in turn, may require additional data-gathering as part of a search for a new solution. For example, assume that Marshall's and Moore's decision was to form a limited partnership in order to attract outside investors. Before you could fully implement this decision, interest rates fell. As a result, the pair decide to borrow the necessary capital instead of taking in additional partners. This decision results in more meetings with Marshall, in which you engage in further data-gathering in pursuit of other options such as incorporation.

Similarly, assume that Ms. Santiago's initial decision was to sue to enjoin the sale, and to pursue the suit aggressively. Shortly thereafter, she tells you that she and her husband are moving out of state, and that she does not want to put a lot of money or effort into the suit. This information will lead you both to revisit and perhaps revise Ms. Santiago's initial decision.

Finally, counseling tends to be non-linear because typically, a client must make more than one decision. During Preliminary Problem Identification, a client typically describes a central problem: "I found out that the house I bought has a cracked foundation, and that it'll cost me about $47,000 to repair it. What can I do?" "I'm here to see about avoiding probate. What can you suggest?" And, almost always, a client ultimately decides which option best resolves the central problem: "I'd like to sue the seller;" "I'll establish a revocable living trust."

But inevitably, intertwined with central problems are auxiliary issues concerning which clients also need to make decisions. For example, after deciding to sue the seller, the buyer of the defective house may have to make decisions about whether to hire an expert and

---

5. For example, in litigation, you typically do need to elicit rule-specific evidence before beginning to assess a client's legal rights. See J. Frank, *Courts On Trial* 14–16 (1949); D. Binder & P. Bergman, *Fact Investigation* 58 (1984). See also Fed.R. Civ.P. 11, which concerns requirements that plaintiffs must satisfy before filing suit. By contrast, in the initial phases of transactional matters, you are rarely concerned with identifying evidence before discussing potential alternatives. See Chapter 11.

how many depositions to take. Similarly, the client who chose the living trust may have to decide who to name as successor trustee and whether family members should be told of the trust's terms. In turn, each of these decisions may require you to repeat the processes of gathering data and identifying and evaluating options.

Part Two

FUNDAMENTAL
COUNSELING SKILLS

Part Two (Chapters 4 through 6) explores skills which underlie the client-centered counseling approach. You employ the listening and questioning techniques described here throughout the entire counseling process.

Chapter 4

MOTIVATION

1. INTRODUCTION

In a client-centered counseling approach you serve clients best by encouraging clients to be active participants in the description and resolution of their problems. Left to themselves, however, clients may not participate as fully as they might. Hence, it behooves you to understand what factors tend to obstruct active client participation, and how you might overcome them.

This chapter begins with a brief general explanation of the concept of motivation and then examines that concept in the interviewing and counseling context. The explanation does not rely on any particular theory of psychology or motivation. Rather, it explores a few well accepted, broad-based ideas about human behavior. Though these ideas may be elementary, they should help you understand and apply the specific motivational techniques explored in ensuing chapters.

2. A GENERAL DESCRIPTION OF MOTIVATION

A. THE NATURE OF HUMAN NEED

Human beings have a variety of needs. These needs have been variously described, and there exists no precise agreement about their exact nature or number.[1] In general, needs can be divided into two broad categories: (1) physical needs and (2) psychosocial needs. Physical needs are often called primary and include the need for food, shelter, sex, and the like. These needs are inborn and common to all people, although the particular ways in which they are satisfied are learned and consequently show tremendous variation.

1. For a description of some of the various theories regarding the nature of human needs see: R. Evans, *Carl Rogers: The Man and His Ideas*, 3–8 (1975); R. Bolles, *Theory of Motivation* 117–20 (1975); H. Murray, "Types of Human Needs," in *Studies in Motivation* 63–70 (D. McClelland ed. 1955).

Psychosocial needs are often referred to as secondary. These needs are learned through an individual's association or affiliation with a particular society and culture. Included among these secondary needs are the desire for love, status, recognition, and so on. Attempts to enumerate all psychosocial needs and to arrange them in a hierarchy of importance have produced little consensus. Secondary needs vary greatly from one society to another. In addition, they find unique organization and expression within each individual.

Although there is little agreement as to the precise nature of psychosocial needs, there tends to be universal agreement that these needs, in combination with the primary ones, profoundly influence patterns of thought, attitude, and behavior. In general, a person acts (or refrains from acting) primarily to fulfill one or more primary or secondary needs. Thus, motivation to act exists principally when people perceive (either at a conscious or intuitive level) that their conduct will satisfy one or more of their needs.

Though these needs serve to energize and direct (motivate) human behavior, the individual is rarely aware of their presence or the influence they exert. The needs are usually experienced in the form of feelings. Typically, the feelings involve some sort of discomfort [2] accompanied by a desire to find relief.[3]

B. CONFLICT AMONG CLIENT NEEDS

Needs exist contemporaneously and are often in conflict. For example, assume that a client named John Bridgeport has consulted you regarding a potential divorce and bankruptcy. He is an aerospace engineer who has been unable to find employment for the past six months. His house and car are about to be foreclosed, and his wife is threatening to leave him because of their impoverished state. The local high school district has offered him a janitorial job on the swing shift. The job pays fairly well, but Mr. Bridgeport is in doubt as to whether or not to accept it. Though the income may indeed be sufficient to save his material possessions and his marriage, his needs for self-respect and esteem may not enable him to accept working as a "janitor".

When needs are in conflict, motivation to act likely exists only when an individual feels that a course of action will satisfy one or more needs without unduly interfering with others. Thus, only when an individual perceives overall gain in terms of need satisfaction will there be sufficient motivation to act.

The hypothetical concerning Mr. Bridgeport points to another aspect of needs which bears explicit mention. As frequently noted,

2. The discomfort can appear in any number of forms—e.g., fear, dissatisfaction, anxiety, etc; the intensity will vary from minimal to extreme.

3. There are theories of motivation which postulate that not all behavior is

motivated by a desire for relief from discomfort. See A. Maslow, *Motivation and Personality* 97–104 (2d ed. 1970).

some of the strongest needs which an individual experiences have to do with feelings of self-esteem and self-regard.[4] Consequently, in many situations an individual will choose a course of action which produces little material satisfaction over one that is materially beneficial. An individual's need for self-respect is often of greater importance than whatever needs material gain might satisfy.

3.   MOTIVATION IN LAWYER–CLIENT DIALOGUES

If people generally act (or refrain from acting) in order to satisfy their needs, what might motivate clients to participate in, or withdraw from, the interviewing and counseling process?   Clients are usually motivated to participate in an interview.   After all, a client presumably seeks you out because the client believes that you can help resolve her or his problem.[5]   However, even though a client may be generally motivated to talk with you, the interviewing and counseling process is typically fraught with motivational difficulties.   Frequently, full participation is contrary to certain client needs.   From a psychological perspective, a client often has needs which disclosure of relevant information will undermine.   For example, a client's need for self-esteem may motivate a client to withhold information that he or she was "at the scene of the crime" because it would mean disclosing that the client was having an extramarital affair.   Similarly, a perception that information is irrelevant may prevent a client from fully searching his or her memory to try to recollect additional data.

Hence, it makes sense to examine the common psychological factors that often affect clients in their dialogues with attorneys.   These factors fall into one of two groups.   "Interfering" or "inhibiting" factors tend to prevent clients from fully participating in dialogues.   "Positive" or "facilitating" factors tend to facilitate full client participation.[6]   If you want clients to participate actively in describing and resolving their problems, you must be skilled both at minimizing the factors that tend to inhibit clients, and at maximizing the factors that tend to motivate them.

The suggestion that you incorporate elementary psychological principles in your conversations with clients is not a mandate to develop complex profiles of each client's unique configuration of needs.   Your professional task is to help clients resolve their legal problems, not to provide psychological counseling.   Unless you are a trained psycholo-

---

4.   R. Kahn & C. Cannell, *The Dynamics of Interviewing* 40 (1957).

5.   This is not always the case, however. A client who comes to see a lawyer about a will may be doing so simply to please a spouse.   A businessperson about to enter into an agreement may want nothing more than for the lawyer simply to document terms the parties have already agreed up-

on rather than to provide any counsel.   In each of these situations, the client may well not be particularly motivated to participate in a full and thorough discussion.

6.   These factors have been described in different ways.   See R.L. Gorden, *Interviewing: Strategy, Techniques, and Tactics* 70–95 (1969); Kahn & Cannell, *supra* note 4, at 45–53.

gist, you cannot expect to identify and remove the deep psychological needs blocking a client's full participation. The process of uncovering unmet needs and conflicts is most appropriately undertaken by a trained mental health specialist.[7] The following example illustrates the distinction between a lawyer's and a trained psychologist's level of psychological understanding. As a lawyer, you may recognize that a client is reluctant to file a lawsuit because a client is highly risk-averse. However, only a trained psychologist is capable of delving into the reasons why a client is so highly risk-averse, and to help a client become more willing to take risks.

4. INHIBITORS

The seven inhibitors described below are common in lawyer-client dialogues. While other phenomena may also inhibit active client participation, these seven operate across a wide range of client personality types. Though the discussion treats each inhibitor as a separate phenomenon, in practice each often intertwines with others.

Of the seven inhibitors, the first two—ego threat and case threat— probably play the most pervasive role in blocking full communication.

A. EGO THREAT

Clients tend to withhold information which they perceive as threatening to their self-esteem. The requested information may relate either to past or anticipated behavior, and the feelings that a question may arouse can range from mild embarrassment to a strong sense of guilt or shame. If a client believes that a truthful response will lead you to evaluate the client negatively, such a response threatens the client's self-esteem; the response is "ego threatening." Rather than risk your negative evaluation, the client may answer falsely, or become reluctant to participate in the conversation.

Consider two examples of how "ego threat" may arise during an interview. First, assume you are consulted by Al, a businessperson of relatively high regard in the community. Al claims that he was fraudulently induced to invest in a large real estate venture. Though quite experienced in business matters, Al had neglected to make even a cursory investigation of the venture before parting with his money. He had simply relied upon the smooth talk of the person who presented him with "the deal." When you inquire about Al's knowledge of the venture at the time the investment was made, Al is reluctant to admit that he knew nothing. He believes that he was stupid and naive. Additionally, he is afraid that you will think him stupid and a poor businessperson if he admits to knowing nothing about the venture

---

7. Certainly, this book's brief discussion does not provide you with the training to uncover and resolve an individual's deep psychological needs and conflicts. However, some authors believe lawyers can be trained to engage in a fair degree of psychosocial analysis. See A. Watson, *The Lawyer in the Interviewing and Counselling Process* 153–54 (1976).

before investing. The "ego threat" posed by your inquiry thereby inhibits Al's full and open participation in the interview.

Next, assume that you have asked your client Barbara about what she sees as the advantages of proceeding to trial. Barbara may be reluctant to reveal that in her mind a major advantage of proceeding to trial is that it will cause the adversary great financial and emotional discomfort. Barbara is ashamed to admit that revenge is a principal motive. She believes that revealing her true motive will lead you to view her as an unconscionable person.

Ego threat may at times arise not because a client fears your personal negative evaluation but because a client fears that certain information may become public. In other words, a client may fear that disclosing information may lead friends, relatives or others to think ill of the client. In such a situation, a client may admit damaging information as long as the client believes that you will keep the information confidential.

B. CASE THREAT

A second major factor tending to inhibit client communication is "case threat." A client may believe that revealing information will "hurt my case." For example, an innocent criminal defendant may not want to reveal to you that she was near the scene of a crime because she fears that if the judge and jurors find it out she will lose. Alternatively, the client may fear that revealing the information will cause you to believe that the case is a loser and to fail to pursue it zealously.[8] In either event, "case threat" is present. Similarly, assume that in a civil matter you ask a client about the whereabouts of a business document. If the client fears that information on the document contains damaging information, case threat may lead the client not to reveal its whereabouts.

"Case threat" may also inhibit clients who have transactional matters. Assume that Jean consults you in connection with a proposal to lease space in an office building. During a conversation about negotiation strategy, you inquire about the maximum length lease that Jean will accept. Jean is willing to accept a ten year lease, but she hopes the owner will agree to a five-year term. Jean may be unwilling to reveal her willingness to accept a ten year deal, feeling that once you know her "bottom line," you will not press as hard as you otherwise might for a shorter lease term.

C. ROLE EXPECTATIONS

Role expectations often affect communication between lawyers and clients. Most of us have sets of beliefs about what kind of behavior is

---

8. In such situations, ego threat may be present as well. If the client believes that revealing that she was at the scene of the crime will cause the lawyer to disbelieve her claim of innocence, the potential loss of self-esteem may well inhibit a truthful response.

appropriate within the confines of particular relationships. For example, most people think there are certain ways that one should (or should not) behave when interacting with parents. Similarly, most people have beliefs about how employers should relate to employees. We may each have different sets of beliefs, but most of us do approach many relationships with preset expectations.[9]

Beliefs about what constitutes proper behavior are "expectations." Since the expectations under discussion here pertain to what a person believes constitutes proper behavior in a particular relationship, the entire phenomenon may be labeled "role expectations." The effect of role expectations is that when a person interacts with another about whom the person has preset role expectations, those beliefs may (if only unconsciously) come into play and cause the person to modify his or her behavior to conform with the beliefs.

Role expectations develop from a variety of sources, from both actual and vicarious experiences. Family, friends, associates, news media, institutions and the like constantly deliver messages about what constitutes appropriate behavior when one assumes a particular position. In short, role expectations are learned and shaped by life experiences.

In most relationships, one person assumes a position of authority or leadership over the other. Therefore, when people initially enter into a particular relationship, they often expect to be in either a dominant or subordinate position. If one is a parent one expects to dominate; if one is a child, one expects to be dominated. Teachers often see their students as occupying subordinate roles. Again, these beliefs develop unconsciously from years of cultural infusion. Undoubtedly, people might be better off if they saw more relationships as involving shared responsibility, but the fact is that frequently they do not. Rather, they see relationships in terms of dominant and subordinate positions.

What does this phenomenon have to do with lawyers and clients? Clients will frequently enter your office with a set of expectations about what constitutes appropriate "client behavior." The expectations will vary from client to client; not all clients will have acquired their expectations from the same learning sources. In many instances, however, clients think of their lawyers as occupying positions of authority. Such clients may be somewhat reluctant to communicate fully in the belief that you know what subjects are deserving of inquiry. Thus, if you fail to broach a topic which a client feels is important, the client may assume (again, either consciously or intuitively) that the topic is not a significant one.

Interestingly, many clients have an opposite set of beliefs. This second group of clients tends to believe that a lawyer's role is limited to carrying out their wishes and that it is their privilege to speak their

9. R. Nisbett & L. Ross, *Human Inference: Strategies and Shortcomings of Social Judgment* 7 (1980); R. Verderber & K. Verderber, *Inter-act: Using Interpersonal Communication Skills* 34 (2d ed. 1980).

minds about any and all topics. In short, these clients see themselves in a dominant position vis a vis their counsel, and they are often not interested in fully responding to inquiries they perceive as unimportant.

The closer a client's expectations come to either extreme of the dominant-subordinate spectrum, the more difficulties you may expect to encounter in developing full information. The subordinate client must be motivated to talk much more freely; after all, not even the most brilliant lawyer will be able to think of everything relevant to the best possible resolution for a client's problem. On the other hand, you must provide a "dominating" client with the impetus to speak about topics you deem important.

D. ETIQUETTE BARRIER

A fourth inhibitor is the "etiquette barrier." [10] Often, an individual has information that he or she will freely provide to some persons but not to others. For example, there are things that women tell women but not men; that blacks tell blacks, but not whites; that students tell students, but not teachers; that doctors tell doctors, but not patients. Information is perceived to be appropriate for peers but not for those in other groups or roles. The etiquette barrier arises from people's desires not to shock, embarrass, offend or discomfort. It reflects a person's thinking about the effect of information on a listener, not a person's thinking about how the listener will view him or her. Hence, loss of self-esteem is not a component of the etiquette barrier.

For example, assume that you represent a juvenile charged with murder. The client insists that a member of a rival gang was the actual culprit and that the client had heard this other person swearing and making threats toward the victim. But when you ask your client what swear words the actual killer uttered, the client becomes reluctant to talk. The etiquette barrier may be at the heart of this reluctance. The client would probably have little difficulty uttering or repeating profanity to his peers, but may feel that profanity is improper in a conversation with a lawyer.

When you sense that a client feels that a topic is "taboo," you need to convey the idea that the topic is open for discussion. If you do not take the initiative in granting permission, a client affected by the "etiquette barrier" will usually continue to withhold the data.

E. TRAUMA

This phenomenon occurs when you ask a client to recall an experience which evokes unpleasant feelings. Many events cause people to experience such negative feelings as fear, anger, humiliation, and sadness. When you ask clients to recall such events, they may re-

---

10. The term is borrowed from Raymond L. Gorden. See Gorden, *supra* note 6, at 76–78.

experience the negative feelings. Consequently, a client may be motivated to avoid thinking and talking about unpleasant past events. For example, a parent asked about a severe injury to the parent's child may be reluctant to talk about the incident; the parent may want to avoid re-experiencing the anger, frustration, and sadness which the incident caused. Likewise, an estate planning client who is considering disinheriting a close relative may for similar reasons be reluctant to talk about the reasons he or she wants to disinherit the person.

F. PERCEIVED IRRELEVANCY

This inhibitor is often more difficult to recognize, as it does not involve any feelings of discomfort or threat. The feeling involved here is one of "no reason to provide that data." A client feels that nothing will be gained by providing the information you request and so is reluctant to provide it.

An interview of a parent accused of child abuse provides an illustration. Those who have worked in the area of child abuse have observed that battering parents tend to be individuals who have very few and infrequent social contacts.[11] If you represent a parent accused of child abuse, therefore, you may wish to uncover information about the nature and extent of the client's social contacts. However, to a parent accused of child abuse, questions about the general nature of the parent's social activities are quite likely to seem irrelevant, if not frivolous. The questions are not concerned with the relationship between the parent and the child. They seemingly have nothing to do with the case. As a consequence, the client may feel little motivation to provide a detailed response.

"Perceived irrelevancy" is just as likely to arise in a transactional context. Assume you represent a partnership which has asked you to negotiate the purchase of a building. You may ask the partners for information about why the owner wants to sell, so that in problem-solving fashion you can structure the deal in such a way that it meets both your clients' and the seller's needs.[12] But the clients, perhaps seeing little importance in exploring the seller's needs, may provide only perfunctory information.

G. GREATER NEED

The last inhibitor is "greater need." This situation is characterized by a client's need or desire to talk about a subject other than that which is of immediate interest to you.[13] As a consequence, the client

11. C. Schneider, R. Helfer & C. Pollock, "The Predictive Questionnaire: A Preliminary Report," in *Helping the Battered Child and His Family* 272, 275 (1972).

12. For a discussion of the importance of needs analysis particularly when using a problem solving approach to negotiation, see C. Menkel-Meadow, "Toward Another View of Legal Negotiation: The Structure of Problem Solving," 31 UCLA L.Rev. 754, 794–829 (1984).

13. Sometimes the phenomenon is present in the form of the interviewee wishing to do anything other than talk. A potential witness busy with his or her work is an obvious example. For a discussion of competing time demands, see Gorden, *supra* note 6, at 117–18.

cannot concentrate on your question, and full and accurate information is not forthcoming. For example, an incarcerated defendant concerned primarily with bail or O.R. release will often be unable to turn full attention to questions relating to the underlying charge. Similarly, a tenant threatened with eviction may be more concerned with when and where he can move than with inquiries related to a potential "habitability defense."

In such situations, your questions are not perceived as irrelevant or threatening. Rather, the client is simply concerned with a subject which, while perhaps secondary to you, is primary to the client.

5. FACILITATORS

The five facilitators described below encourage clients to participate fully in counseling dialogues. This chapter describes the facilitators but does not explore techniques for employing them. However, please note that you typically may employ facilitators without waiting for client reluctance to rear its annoying head. That is, you routinely incorporate the facilitators into all dialogues, whether the clients are enthusiastic or reluctant participants.

A. EMPATHIC UNDERSTANDING

Empathic understanding typically gives clients feelings of trust and confidence in an attorney-client relationship and thereby motivates clients to participate fully in conversations. Despite the motivational power of empathic understanding, lawyers commonly fail to utilize it when talking with clients.

Empathy probably cannot be defined or precisely described.[14] Perhaps the following comments by Carl Rogers give some sense of what empathy involves:

> Empathy in its most fundamental sense . . . involves understanding the experiences, behaviors, and feelings of others as they experience them. It means that [lawyers] must, to the best of their abilities, put aside their own biases, prejudices, and points of view in order to understand as clearly as possible the points of view of their clients. It means entering into the experience of clients in order to develop a feeling for their inner world and how they view both this inner world and the world of people and [events] around them.[15]

People have limited opportunities in our society to express their thoughts and feelings to someone who is willing to (1) listen, (2) understand, and (3) at the same time, not judge. People on the receiving end of a communication are often too busy to really listen, and too interested in their own ideas to avoid responses that include the listener's "two cents." The "two cents" appears in a variety of forms, including:

14. See G. Goodman, *The Talk Book* 41 (1988).

15. See G. Egan, *The Skilled Helper* 87 (3d ed. 1986).

(a) Advice on how to handle the situation: "Don't worry. You'll feel less angry as time goes on."

(b) Analysis of why the feelings have arisen: "You probably feel angry because you feel you should have seen through that smoke screen."

Providing advice or analysis, even if done with a genuine desire to be of help, ironically tends to give an individual little impetus to delve further into a subject. There is little point in expressing your ideas and feelings if all you get in return is lay psychoanalysis or advice on how to change or ignore your feelings.

However, in the presence of someone who exhibits non-judgmental understanding—a listener who provides empathic responses—most people are strongly motivated to continue communicating. Almost without realizing it, people will tend to provide an ever-increasing amount of information. Precisely why non-judgmental understanding results in increased inducement to communicate is not known.[16] However, many experts in the field of psychology have stressed the fact that it does have this self-propelling effect.[17]

The opportunities for you to utilize empathic understanding are endless. Clients almost always are emotionally involved in their problems, and thus repeatedly express feelings about what has occurred or is likely to occur. Their recitals of information are likely to be accompanied by and intertwined with feelings about such diverse matters as: (1) how they felt at the time an event occurred; (2) how they feel about people or institutions involved in their problem; (3) why events have unfolded, and why people have behaved as they have; (4) how they feel about an event at present; and (5) how they feel about what is likely to happen in the future. Consider these examples:

(a) "When the policeman told me she was dead, I was stunned. The week before, she told me she had made out a new will, but I didn't attach any significance to it. And now those vicious people want to contest the will; they are the ones that must be crazy."

(b) "Now I have to decide whether to accept the $3,500. If I don't accept it, I may regret my decision for a long time. On the other hand, if I don't go to trial I may always wonder if I could have gotten a lot more."

(c) "My partner and I couldn't believe it when we heard the building was for sale. We had been looking for a site in that area for years."

You can provide empathic understanding by acknowledging the feelings attached to factual descriptions such as these. So doing will enable you to receive information that clients might not otherwise

16. Cf. Goodman, *supra* note 14, at 51: "When it comes to professionals . . . There's some debate about how reflections help healing or when they heal, and how often to employ them, but it's unusual to find a practitioner who doesn't use them at all."

17. C. Rogers, *Counseling and Psychotherapy*, 131–51 (1942).

disclose, develop clients' trust, and encourage clients to participate actively in the solutions to their problems.

B. FULFILLING EXPECTATIONS

"One of the important forces in social interaction is the tendency for one person to communicate, verbally and nonverbally, his expectations to another person. The second person then tends to respond, consciously or unconsciously, to those expectations. This may be viewed as one manifestation of the more general human tendency to conform to the group of peers and to the suggestion of higher status persons in the society."[18]

The phenomenon of "fulfilling expectations" refers to people's tendencies to want to satisfy the perceived expectations of those with whom they interact. Your simply communicating, verbally or nonverbally, your expectations will often be the catalyst that motivates a client to undertake a particular discussion.

This facilitator is especially useful when you sense that certain inhibitors are making a client reluctant to provide information. On sensing the reluctance, you can verbally convey a strong expectation that the sought data should be revealed. The client's need to conform to your expectations may well be stronger than whatever needs have given rise to the reluctance to respond. In such situations, the inhibitors will be overcome and the information revealed.

Note two additional points about fulfilling expectations. First, the phenomenon can be useful in overcoming memory difficulties as well as inhibitors. Second, the phenomenon can be inadvertently employed to create an expectation that the sought data need not be revealed. The following example will help you consider both points.

Assume that a client has indicated that she cannot remember much of what occurred at a meeting held two years earlier. You may convey your expectation that by probing her memory further, the client will be able to recollect more information:

"I understand how hard it is to recall; I've often had that difficulty myself. Often I find, however, that if I concentrate for a while things start to come back. Why don't you think about it a little more?"

This statement employs two facilitators. First, you empathize; you articulate your understanding of the difficulty. Additionally, you convey your expectation that with more effort, the client will be able to provide more information. Your message is, "though the task may be difficult, I expect that you will attempt it.

Unfortunately, you may inadvertently convey an expectation that a client need make no further effort to recall information. For example, assume that in the example above you had said:

"I understand that it is difficult to remember the details of an event that happened so long ago."

18. Gorden, *supra* note 6, at 84.

This statement does nothing more than empathize with the client's difficulty, and standing alone it may be counterproductive. While you convey understanding of the client's dilemma, you also convey the idea that you do not expect an answer.

C. RECOGNITION

Human beings often need attention and recognition from people outside their close circle of family and friends. They enjoy feeling important and seek the attention and esteem of outsiders. Thus, giving an interviewee "recognition" motivates the interviewee to be more cooperative and open.[19]

Assuming you are not a client's close friend or relative, you may supply "recognition" simply by sincerely praising a client's cooperation or help: "Your giving me that information is very helpful." "That was very important information you just gave me." "You're really doing a good job of setting out the consequences of not demanding an option to renew at this time."

D. ALTRUISTIC APPEALS

People often need to identify with a high value or cause that is beyond their immediate self-interest. This need may be a form of identification with the objectives of a large social group. A person's performance of altruistic deeds usually increases the person's self-esteem. Thus, clients are often motivated to participate fully when doing so makes them feel altruistic.[20]

In counseling clients, you will have many opportunities to appeal to clients' desires to perform altruistic deeds. The following examples are illustrative:

"I know that the planning board's insistence on a density rollback in the project detracts from the initial profit projections. But you mentioned earlier your environmental concerns, and going along with the rollback allows you to dedicate some park space to the community."

"Before you reject the idea of filing suit out of hand, maybe we can spend a few moments discussing that option. I realize it is unfair for you individually to bear the time and expense of a suit to establish a right that the legislature provided in this consumer legislation. But if you were to win, others who come along later and who maybe can't afford a lawyer may be able to collect damages without having to go through what you have. In view of that, would you like to talk some more about the possibility of filing suit?"[21]

---

19. Gorden, *supra* note 6, at 86–87.

20. Altruism is distinct from recognition, since a person may feel altruistic even if his or her actions never become public knowledge. See Gorden, *supra* note 6, at 87–88.

21. For a discussion of giving clients a reasonable opportunity to consider options that they have precipitously rejected, see Chapter 18, sec. 6.

E. EXTRINSIC REWARD

Realizing that certain behavior is in their self-interest usually motivates people to engage in that behavior. Thus, a person with the mind set, "what's in it for me?" at times is reluctant to provide information. Hence, you may facilitate disclosure of information that a client seems reluctant to discuss by pointing out why the sought data may aid in resolving the client's problem. You thereby indicate that providing the information is in the client's best interest.

As the term "extrinsic" may suggest, this facilitator differs in an important way from those previously discussed. The earlier phenomena drew their motivational strength from satisfying clients' psychological needs within the counseling interaction itself. Use of extrinsic reward, on the other hand, achieves motivational force from a client's realizing how participation in the interview will satisfy needs external to the interview—i.e., a favorable resolution of a client's matter. A client's reward comes from outside the interview: "Mr. Edwards, if you will tell me a bit more about your investments, I'll be able to draft the trust in a way that minimizes taxes."

6. SUMMARY

As the common inhibitors and facilitators are referred to frequently throughout the remainder of this book, we list them all together:

INHIBITORS	FACILITATORS
Ego Threat	Empathic Understanding
Case Threat	Fulfilling Expectations
Role Expectations	Recognition
Etiquette Barrier	Altruistic Appeals
Trauma	Extrinsic Reward
Perceived Irrelevancy	
Greater Need	

7. PERSONALITY CONFLICTS

Though this chapter has described a number of psychological phenomena, you have perhaps noted that it has not mentioned one factor that all would recognize as important to the interaction of any two people—their personalities. All of us are more comfortable with some people than with others. Thus, lawyer-client communications are often inhibited by some degree of personality conflict. If a client, for one reason or another, perceives you as someone with whom he or she is not comfortable, or someone who is too aggressive or too passive to handle a matter effectively, the client may feel reluctant to participate fully. By the same token, you may, for one reason or another, perceive a client as too aggressive, passive, unscrupulous, or disorganized; and such perceptions may inhibit your interaction with the client.

There is no ideal type of lawyer personality—what is pleasing to one client can be abrasive to another. With self-examination and specialized training, lawyers might learn how certain aspects of their personalities come across to most clients. Self-examination and training, therefore, may help some lawyers interact more effectively with clients. However, intensive training is not readily available to most law students and lawyers.[22] Moreover, no amount of personality restructuring or self-awareness will enable you or any other lawyer to work effectively with every client.

Nevertheless, even in the absence of specialized training, you can interact more successfully with most clients by learning to relate to them in an open and supportive manner. Whatever your individual personality, you can undoubtedly employ the elementary facilitators described above. By combining these facilitators with the skills described in subsequent chapters, you can develop the sensitivity and ability necessary to maintain satisfactory rapport with most clients.

22. There are some authors who believe that intensive training in personality analysis should be the cornerstone of any beginning course in legal interviewing and counseling. See Watson, *supra* note 7, at 75–93.

Chapter 5

ACTIVE LISTENING

1. INTRODUCTION

Listening is a skill of paramount importance, and one which few lawyers employ successfully.[2] Most lawyers are too busy asking questions and giving advice to take the time to listen. However, if you are to see problems from clients' perspectives, develop full information and involve clients fully in the decision-making process, you must become a good listener.

Just what is it a good listener will hear? Of course, a good listener will hear factual content. But a good listener will also hear the feelings that accompany that content. When recalling an event, a client often describes not only what occurred, but also the feelings that the event aroused in the client.[3] Moreover, a client's very act of recall may trigger still further emotional reactions: "At the time I was

1. Reprinted by permission: Tribune Media Services.

2. Lawyers, however, are not alone. The psychologist Goodman notes that this "most effective talk tool that exists for demonstrating understanding" is not known by 98% of the population. G. Goodman, *The Talk Book* 38 (1988). Doctors also seem to be part of this 98%. See R. Winslow, "Sometimes, Talk Is the Best Medicine," Wall St.J., B1 (Oct. 5, 1989).

3. Indeed, it has been suggested that human beings are incapable of viewing facts without emotion. For a discussion, see P. Rhinelander, *Is Man Incomprehensible to Man?* 48–50 (1973).

somewhat upset, but now just talking about it makes me really mad." Finally, proposed solutions almost inevitably generate emotional reactions for clients. For example, a client may say, "I'm nervous about leaving the terms of the payout provision so uncertain." Accordingly, good listeners hear both content and current and past feelings.

Your reaction may be that good listening is a very simple and easily accomplished task: "I just have to sit back and pay attention." In reality, listening requires enormous concentration and positive action. Far from being an intuitively simple task, listening is a skill. Like other skills, its mastery requires awareness and practice of specialized techniques.

Chapter 4 stressed the importance of empathic understanding as a communication facilitator. It noted that providing clients with the feeling that they have been heard, understood, and not judged often motivates clients' full participation. Active listening is the technique through which you may most readily communicate empathic understanding and is the principal technique described in this chapter. Listening actively is important not simply to insure that you hear and understand a client, but also to motivate a client's full participation.

2. IDENTIFYING CONTENT AND FEELINGS

"Content" is the data that determines clients' legal rights or is relevant to their proposed transactions. "Feelings" are the labels that clients use to describe their emotional reactions to events or to contemplated transactions. Words typically used to describe feelings include happy, amused, excited, sad, angry, anxious, disappointed, frightened, irritated, and confused.

From a legal point of view, you may be primarily interested in content. However, you can usually provide empathic understanding only if you also identify and respond to a client's feelings.[4] To develop your skill in recognizing both content and feelings, consider the following examples.

Client 1:

"My husband and I sat down years ago and wrote a will together, but I guess I never really thought we'd use it. Then they called to say my husband had had a heart attack at work. He died two days later. When he died, I felt overwhelmed. Lately, I've been worrying about our finances. It's hard to think of money at a time like this, but I feel like I should. I can't sleep at night, and I just sit around depressed all day. Other times, when I think about him, I start crying and it seems like it will never stop. On top of all this, the children are saying they are going to contest the will. They've already hired a lawyer. I'm really surprised, I never expected this."

4. Recall from Chapter 2 that recognizing and responding to clients' feelings is an   essential attribute of a client-centered approach.

What is the content of the client's situation?

What are the client's past and current feelings?

Client 2:

"The chance to be part owner of a restaurant is really the dream of a lifetime. Over the last few years I've gotten increasingly disenchanted with being an aerospace engineer—you're always dependent on government contracts, and having to meet deadlines. When Mike called and said he had found a third investor and a great neighborhood restaurant for sale, it was like a huge weight came off my shoulders. My wife said, 'Do it—it's what you've always wanted.' She's been great. I'm sure it'll work out. The cash flow could be a little tight in the beginning, but according to the books the restaurant has always made money."

What is the content of the client's situation?

What are the client's past and current feelings?

Client 3:

"I think that filing a lawsuit is the best thing to do at this point. I know that the doctor should not have prescribed that medication for me given that I have a history of asthma. He just never took much time with me and by suing I will recover what I can and maybe I can protect other patients. I'll never be the same as I was before—I guess you can't get my health back for me. But at least I'll show the bastard."

What is the content of the client's situation?

What are the client's past and current feelings?

Here is how you might have conceptualized these three matters:

Client 1:

Content: Husband died unexpectedly and wife must assume responsibility for family finances. Children plan to contest the will and have already hired a lawyer.

Feelings: Sad, overwhelmed, depressed, worried, surprised.

Client 2:

Content: Client, an aerospace engineer, has an opportunity to purchase an interest in and operate a restaurant. Two other people will be involved in the venture, and his spouse is supportive.

Feelings: Disenchanted, happy, relieved, optimistic, somewhat anxious.

Client 3:

Content: Client suffered ailments after a doctor who spent little time with her prescribed the wrong medication.

Feelings: Satisfied, angry, sad, frustrated, revengeful.

3. OBSTACLES TO GOOD LISTENING

Effective listening requires a number of skills. Of these, perhaps the hardest to master is clearing your mind of various common distractors. We all are easily distracted by our own feelings and needs, and therefore may only "half listen" to what clients are saying. Consider the following factors that can easily distract you from fully attending to your clients:

1. Performance distractors: You are so eager to display how competent you are that you focus on what YOU are going to say next, rather than on what your client is saying now. Or, in contrast, you are so worried you will not know what to say next you can barely focus on the client's concerns.

2. Personal distractors: You are preoccupied with your own personal worries, such as a case that is not going well, a deadline you forgot, or an argument with your spouse, and therefore less attentive to the client.

3. Client distractors: This category involves your reactions to any of a number of client characteristics. Perhaps a client's personality is such that you are more focused on the sort of person a client is than on what the client is saying. Or, you may be so concerned about whether a client's goals are consistent with your personal values that you become distracted. Perhaps you find a client either very attractive or very unattractive, and you pay more attention to your feelings about the client's appearance than to what the client is saying.

4. Time and money distractors: Rather than focusing on a client, you are busy mentally calculating how much time a client's matter will require and whether your client can afford to have you continue with the matter.

Keeping your mind clear of these common distractors requires considerable concentration and effort. Even if at the outset of a discussion you wipe your mind clear of distractors, they commonly creep back. A conscious effort to identify a distractor when it arises may help you push it aside more effectively.[5]

4. PASSIVE LISTENING TECHNIQUES

Passive listening techniques are those that keep clients talking with relatively little activity or encouragement on your part. Often, a client is describing useful information, and you simply want the client

---

5. Though this discussion focuses on obstacles to hearing clients' feelings, obviously such obstacles can block your reception of content as well.

to continue doing so. Yet, you want the client to know that you are hearing and understanding what is being said *without interrupting the client's train of thought.* Passive listening techniques are ideal for this common situation.

A. SILENCE

The technique of "silence" involves your consciously creating a brief but definite pause in a conversation.[6] By remaining silent for a short period of time when a client pauses, and allowing a client to continue on without interruption, you further your goal of full client participation.

Unfortunately, many lawyers feel uncomfortable allowing a period of silence. They seem to feel that a good interview must have a constant flow of words and that clients will take silence as a sign of incompetence, a sign that the lawyer does not know the right thing to say. To cope with their discomfort, lawyers often meet every client pause with a series of questions. Rather than moving an interview efficiently toward a full picture of a client's situation, such questions can distract clients and confuse their trains of thought.

When a client makes a statement and then pauses, this technique requires that you remain silent. At the same time, keep your attention on the client and give other non-verbal cues (such as leaning forward, maintaining eye contact, or nodding your head) to indicate your expectation that the client will continue speaking. Commonly, a client will pick up again within two to five seconds. If a longer period of time goes by, you may consider continuing to remain silent or using other passive or active listening techniques.[7]

"Silence" utilizes the facilitator, "fulfilling expectations." Your silence, combined with your non-verbal bearing and apparent interest in what a client is saying, convey your expectation that the client will continue on.

B. MINIMAL PROMPTS

Silence, particularly if lengthy or repeated, sometimes has an inhibiting effect on clients. In the absence of an audible response that reassures them that you have heard what they have said, some clients may feel anxious and on the spot, and as a result "clam up." To assure clients that you are listening and taking in what they are saying, you

---

6. Goodman refers to this technique as the "power of positive waiting", and notes that "some lawyers . . . understand the utility of giving people long silence responses." Goodman, *supra* note 2, at 166.

7. What you think of as a long pause in a conversation may in reality be a very short one. Goodman notes that most people are uncomfortable with "conversation-al allowing" because the typical amount of time between when one person in a conversation stops talking and the other person starts is nine-tenths of a second. Goodman, *supra* note 2, at 147–48. He gives an example of a conversation between Carl Rogers, a master of client-centered therapy, and a patient in which Rogers allowed pauses of up to 17 minutes. Id. at 167–68.

can respond with brief expressions termed "minimal prompts." [8] These include such brief comments as:

"Oh"

"I see"

"Mm-hmm"

"Interesting"

"Really"

"No fooling"

"You did, eh"

Here is an example of this technique in an interview:

Client: I can see a lot of problems with this contract.

Lawyer: Mm-hmm

Client: It really locks me in for five years and I'm not sure I want to do that.

Lawyer: I see.

Minimal prompts can be *nonverbal* as well. Consider this example:

Client: My partner is very stubborn. He resists every suggestion to computerize our operations. (Pause)

Lawyer: [Nods her head.]

Client: Maybe it's not so much stubbornness as fear. He's afraid we'll dramatically, and perhaps needlessly, increase our overhead and end up in bankruptcy.

Lawyer: Mm-hmm

Minimal prompts are non-committal; they give no indication of how you are evaluating a message. Yet, they can be quite effective. Noncommittal responses tend not to interrupt a client's train of thought. They tend to serve as reinforcers that encourage further elaboration. As with silence, it is important to accompany prompts with body language that communicates your interest and involvement with what the client is saying.

C. OPEN-ENDED QUESTIONS

An open question is one which asks a client to discuss a subject in a broad manner.[9] An open question may simply indicate that the client should continue to talk about the subject under discussion. Thus, an open question, like a minimal prompt, allows you to indicate that a

---

8. This term is borrowed from G. Egan, *The Skilled Helper* 114–15 (3d ed. 1986). This technique is also sometimes referred to as "minimal verbal activity," H. Hackney & L. Cormier, *Counseling Strategies and Objectives* 68 (2d ed. 1979), and "brief assertions of understanding and interest," R.L. Kahn & C.F. Cannell, *The Dynamics of Interviewing* 205–210 (1957).

9. For a more detailed discussion of open questions, see Chapter 6.

client is on the right track with little risk of interrupting the client's train of thought. Examples of open questions are:

"What else happened?"

"What other reasons are there?"

"Can you tell me some more about that?" [10]

"Please continue."

These techniques—silence, minimal prompts, and open-ended questions—are basically passive. They function primarily to give a client space in an interview to freely communicate his or her thoughts and feelings. At the same time, these techniques involve little activity on your part. However, they do not communicate empathic understanding. To accomplish that goal, you must employ the active listening technique.

5. ACTIVE LISTENING

A. GENERALLY

Active listening is the "most effective talk tool that exists for demonstrating understanding and reducing misunderstanding." [11] It is the process of picking up a client's message and sending it back in a reflective statement which mirrors what you have heard.

Client: "When I asked him for the money, he had the nerve to tell me not to be uptight."

Lawyer: "Rather than offering to pay you back, he suggested that you were somehow wrong for asking. You were angry."

Your reply is a classic active listening response. It demonstrates that you understand the content of the client's remark. Also, the reply reflects back to the client your understanding of the client's feelings that accompanied the incident. Further, the statement only mirrors the client's statement; it does not in any way "judge" it.[12] And, though your statement reflects the client's feelings, you do not ask the client to explore those feelings in greater detail. Rather, the statement simply indicates your awareness that the client was angered.

Note that you do not simply repeat, or "parrot," what the client said. Rather, your reply reflects the *essence* of the content of the client's remark, as well as your perception, based both on the statement and on the client's non-verbal cues, of the client's feelings. You distill the information and emotion from the client's statement, and then

---

10. Often, open-ended questions are used interchangeably with directive probes such as "Tell me more about that" and "Please continue." Clients will generally perceive a directive request in the same way as an open-ended question. In this book, the two are treated as synonymous. See Chapter 6, sec. 2(B).

11. Goodman, *supra* note 2, at 38.

12. For an excellent discussion of active listening which contains illustrative samples drawn from actual recorded dialogues, see Goodman, *supra* note 2, at 38–70. (Goodman uses the term "reflection" instead of "active listening.")

convey back what you have heard and understood—hence the term, "active listening".

Active and passive listening responses share some similarities. Neither type of response is likely to disrupt a client's train of thought, or switch a client from one topic to another. The primary difference is that a reflective response explicitly communicates to a client that you have actually heard and understood what the client has said; it explicitly demonstrates your comprehension. By contrast, passive responses, such as "Mm-hmm" or "Tell me some more about that," can only imply that you have heard and understood. An active listening response demonstrates empathy and understanding, but it does so in a way that allows a client to continue speaking on whatever subject the client desires.

Moreover, active listening responses probably fulfill the empathic ideal of "non-judgmental acceptance" more effectively than passive ones. Reflective statements generally imply a greater degree of non-judgmental acceptance than do passive remarks. Again, it is the explicit mirroring of a client's remarks that suggests a non-judgmental attitude.

While an active listening response may mirror both **content** and **feelings,** we primarily emphasize techniques for using active listening responses to reflect feelings. We do so for two reasons:

1. As a general rule, lawyers pay far too little attention to the feelings of their clients. Lawyers all too often see themselves as rational fact-gatherers and decision-makers. At either a conscious or intuitive level, lawyers perceive feelings as either irrelevant, or as unwelcome impediments to what should ideally be a completely rational process. This attitude towards the importance of feelings in the attorney-client relationship is wrong on at least two grounds. First, empathy is the real mortar of an attorney-client (indeed, *any* [13]) relationship. To be empathic you need to hear, understand and accept a client's feelings, and to find a way to convey this empathic understanding to your clients. Second, as stressed in Chapters 1 and 2, clients' problems do not come in nice, neat, rational packages devoid of emotional content. Problems evoke feelings, and feelings in turn shape problems. Lawyers can neither communicate fully with their clients nor help fashion satisfactory solutions if they ignore feelings.

2. Everyday life and years of schooling have given most of us the skill to understand and respond to content. For example, what do we study more in secondary education—the strategic importance of Civil War battles, or the feelings of the participants? We really have little formal training in listening for and articulating the human feelings that accompany events and future plans. And many of us do not intuitively discuss feelings with people with whom we are not close.

13. See Goodman, *supra* note 2, at 40.

Therefore, you are likely to need to devote more effort to learning to reflect feelings than to learning to reflect content.

Feelings, however, often do not come tightly packaged, ready to be reflected on. How a client expresses feelings influences how you reflect them. Hence, the next sections examine the different ways that clients are likely to express feelings, and the manner in which you may respond reflectively.

B. RESPONDING TO VAGUELY EXPRESSED FEELINGS

Clients often express feelings in poorly articulated, rather vague terms. In such situations, you can be empathic by giving a reflective response that puts a precise label on the feelings. By specifically labeling feelings, you can help a client understand her or his own emotions. The labeling helps bring the feelings out into the open, so that the feelings are explicitly included in the counseling process. Examine a few examples of client statements which articulate feelings in a vague, abstract, or general way, and responses which attempt to identify and label the feelings:

Client: "I felt **bummed out** when I found out she was having an affair with him. I thought our marriage meant something. I **guess I was wrong.**"

Lawyer: "You felt **hurt** and **disappointed** when you learned about the affair."

Client: "**I've felt out of it** ever since I moved to Los Angeles. I **don't have friends** here or even neighbors to talk to."

Lawyer: "**You've felt lonely** and **isolated** since you came to Los Angeles."

Client: "With Marcia in the business **I know we can make it.** She **knows more** about accounting in the fashion industry than anyone."

Lawyer: "You feel **happy** and **confident** with Marcia as a partner."

In each example, the lawyer attempts to restate in more specific terms the feelings each client expressed only vaguely. Note that reflective responses may begin with phrases such as, "That must have made you very . . ."; or, "It sounds like you felt . . .." However, the simple and direct responses illustrated in the three examples above are just as effective.

Try your own hand at active listening. As the lawyer in the examples below, what precisely-labeled feelings might you reflect back to the client?

Client: "When I told him I was going to a lawyer for a divorce, he just looked at me. He looked for a long time and then he left. It was strange."

Client: "After she told me the loan for the dental equipment had been approved, tears almost came to my eyes. My parents had worked so hard to put me through school, and I wish they could have been there with me."

C. RESPONDING TO UNSTATED FEELINGS

Frequently, without explicitly expressing emotion, clients discuss situations which your everyday experience suggests are emotion-laden. In such situations, your tendency may be to focus only on content; the absence of expressed emotions causes you to overlook a client's real but unstated feelings.

For example, assume that you represent a parent whose young child was injured at a day-care center. The parent is describing what happened after the parent was notified of the child's injury:

Client: It took them about an hour to find me at work to get the message to me that something had happened to Jan. After about 15 minutes Ms. Wyden, the day care director, told me that Jan wasn't hurt too badly, and she told me which emergency room Jan had been taken to. When I got to the emergency room, the nurse in the reception area couldn't give me any details on how Jan was or where Jan was. I had to wait for about 45 minutes for the doctor to come out.

Lawyer: Then what happened?

Here, the client's statement is devoid of expressed emotion. And, perhaps focused only on content, your response was, "Then what happened?"

However, the client has described a situation which, for most people, would be extremely stressful. Therefore, an active listening response would certainly have been apropos. You might have reflected the emotions that the client did not put into words, but which the client undoubtedly felt: "Despite the director's assurance, you must have been anxious about Jan and upset that you had to wait so long for information."

Providing empathic responses to a client who neither directly nor indirectly asserts any emotions is a two step process. Once you recognize that a situation was probably emotion-laden, the first step is to identify and label the feelings. The second step is to mirror the feelings with a reflective response.[14]

---

14. For Goodman, three rather than two steps are involved; his steps are: (1) "Active waiting"—focus on the other person's message, not your reply; (2) Empathizing—quickly search your mind for analogous experiences you have had; and (3) Finding the Words—reflect the essence of the other person's message, with an emphasis on feelings. Goodman, *supra* note 2, at 227–34.

To carry out the first step of identifying and labeling a client's unstated feelings, place yourself "in a client's shoes." [15] If you had been in the client's situation, what emotions would you probably have felt? Even if you have never experienced a client's precise situation, you can almost always hazard an educated guess about how the client felt. Through vicarious (films, books, friends' stories) and analogous experiences, you generally have a reasonably good idea of the emotions a client was feeling. Then, in the second step, you incorporate the feelings in a reflective response.

The examples below provide practice in this two-step process. The clients' statements do not overtly state feelings. Formulate an active listening response which you might make in response to each statement.

> Client: "When he failed to pay, I sent him two letters. I got no response. I called three times. He was never in. The secretary said he would return the calls; he never did."

> Client: "The bank has been dealing with these builders for over 40 years. We've always provided all their construction financing, and often gone out on a limb to make loans when times were hard. Now they say that if we don't refinance on more favorable terms they will take their business elsewhere."

> Client: "We've known each other for over 50 years. I know that people usually appoint their children as executors, but Pat is so familiar with everything and such a trusted friend that I really want Pat to be my executor."

Sometimes, you may be confident that a situation was an emotional one, but less confident about precisely what emotion was aroused. If so, you may doubt whether the feeling you identify in a reflective response will be completely accurate. As a result, you may shy away from verbalizing feelings when a client has not done so first.

However, a reflective response need not be "spot on" to provide empathy. For example, assume that in the second situation above, your reflective response was, "You sound pretty aggravated." If you are correct, your client may well validate the accuracy of your statement: "Yeah, I really am; given how we have helped these people for all this time, I can't believe they are doing this." But even if you are somewhat off the mark, a client may at most clarify the inaccuracy— "Well, I'm not aggravated yet, but I certainly am puzzled. What do you think they're up to?" [16] Thus, even if your statement is somewhat

---

15. Researchers have discovered that metaphorically placing oneself in the shoes of another is an important step in making empathic responses. Goodman, *supra* note 2, at 43.

16. Goodman agrees that some distortion in labeling another's feelings is una-

voidable. However, Goodman believes that it is uncommon for an interviewee to identify and amend an understated or overstated reflection. Goodman, *supra* note 2, at 70.

inaccurate, in all likelihood it will facilitate communication. The reflective response indicates your desire to understand, and may even elicit further clarifying information.

D.　RESPONDING TO NON–VERBAL EXPRESSIONS OF FEEL-INGS

Your everyday knowledge of how people are likely to react to situations is one basis for identifying unstated feelings. A second is a client's non-verbal cues. Non-verbal cues are generally of two types—auditory and visual.[17] Auditory cues include such things as voice intonation, pitch, rate of speech, and pauses in conversation. Visual cues include posture; gestures; facial expressions; body movements such as fidgeting fingers and constantly shifting positions; and auto-nomic physiological responses such as sweating and blushing. When non-verbal cues indicate the presence of a particular emotion, an active listening response is often appropriate.

Though non-verbal behavior is extremely difficult to illustrate in a book, an attempt may be helpful. Assume that a client's voice cracks and that the client talks rapidly while describing the tentative terms of a proposed partnership deal. The deal is not of the sort that strikes you as laden with emotion. However, the non-verbal cues suggest that this particular client is extremely anxious to conclude the deal. Hence, an active listening response would be appropriate: "You seem anxious to have this deal concluded as quickly as possible."

You may feel somewhat hesitant to identify and respond to feelings evidenced by non-verbal cues, perhaps out of fear that you will make an inaccurate interpretation. After all, both individual and cultural varia-tions in the way people express themselves may leave you uncertain about what inference to draw from non-verbal behavior. For example, is a smile a client's way of showing happiness or anxiety, or is it simply the client's typical facial expression? Do a client's tears signify sad-ness, relief, or your having left an onion on the floor? Unless you are confident that you are reading a client's non-verbal behavior correctly, you should be understandably reticent to make a reflective response based on that behavior.

Developing a "baseline picture" of a client's non-verbal behavior is one technique for evaluating the meaning of possibly ambiguous non-verbal behavior. Over the course of representing a client, you may recognize that certain non-verbal behavior is "standard," and thus does not signify significant emotion. But a change of standard behavior may be an emotional clue.

For example, if a client habitually wrings his hands, wringing hands is probably not a sign that a particular topic is producing a significant emotional reaction. However, if a client who does not

---

17. For a more detailed discussion of the interpretation of non-verbal behavior, see P. Ekman & W. Friesen, "Nonverbal Leakage and Clues to Deception," 32 Psy-chiatry 88 (1969).

normally wring his hands suddenly begins to do so when you mention a particular topic, you may be able to infer that the client's emotions have been aroused.

Non-verbal cues tend to appear spontaneously; they are much less subject to conscious control than verbal expressions. Thus, they tend to "leak" information about a person's inner life. Sometimes, clients try very hard to "maintain composure" by masking non-verbal cues. However, unless they have won an "Oscar" for "Best Actor," most clients are unable to repress all non-verbal expression. For example, an anxious client may avoid facial expressions, but be unable to hide body movements such as drumming fingers or rapid changes in position. Hence, if you are observant, you may detect those feelings that a client tries to conceal, and respond empathically.

However, a more difficult question is whether you *ought* to make an active listening response when you sense that a client is *consciously* attempting to leave feelings unstated, perhaps by speaking and behaving in a very guarded and restrictive manner.[18] If a client does not want to face the emotional dimensions of a problem, should you attempt to pressure the client to do so?

From the standpoint of technique, the question is probably irrelevant. As you recall, an active listening response does not direct a client to talk about his or her feelings. Rather, it is a method for keeping a client on track in an empathic manner. After an active listening response, clients typically respond by continuing to talk about whatever aspect of a situation they feel comfortable discussing.

However, a client who is consciously attempting to mask feelings may *perceive* an active listening remark as an attempt to probe feelings. For example, noting a client's clenched fists, you say, "This subject seems to worry you." If the client has been attempting to conceal that emotion from you, the client may interpret your active listening comment as an attempt to probe her or his feelings.

If a client is likely to perceive an active listening response as an intrusive probe into feelings, client-centeredness suggests that sometimes you should respect the client's wishes and avoid injecting feelings into a discussion. For one thing, for some clients, the assumption that a solution should be chosen after all facets of a problem have been examined may be incorrect. For example, a client may be paralyzed and unable to choose an effective solution if too many issues are on the table. Thus, a client's masking of feelings may be an attempt to simplify a problem and keep it manageable. In such a situation, client-centeredness may suggest that you accede to a client's implicit wish.

Second, as autonomous individuals, clients are entitled to privacy and should be allowed to decide how much of their emotions and private thoughts to convey to you. Some clients may value their

---

18. Please understand that we are not discussing or attempting to deal with sub- conscious or unconscious repression of feelings.

privacy more than they do a solution which is reached only after consideration of all possible dimensions of a problem. Again, client-centeredness may lead you to respect a client's wishes.

More specifically, then, the question is how to identify those situations in which you are likely to help a client by bringing forth consciously-masked feelings. In the abstract, no answer may be possible. You cannot take refuge in the bromide of "informed consent." A client cannot give informed consent until the client is aware of the extent to which disclosure of emotions and private thoughts will increase the chances of finding a satisfactory solution. But the very process of making the client fully aware of whether disclosure will provide increased chances for success requires an extensive foray into a client's privacy! Hence, a conundrum exists. Informed consent about whether to disclose feelings is possible only after an invasion of that which the client may want to keep quiet.[19] In the end, then, you must exercise professional judgment about whether to reflect an emotion which a client seems anxious to avoid.

E. RESPONDING TO CLEARLY–ARTICULATED FEELINGS

The discussion thus far may give you the impression that clients characteristically fail to express emotions. In fact, many clients articulate their feelings in no uncertain terms. Your task then is to provide empathic responses without simply "parroting", or repeating, a client's words.

As you recall, an active listening response mirrors the essence of a statement. When a client clearly states his or her feelings, reflecting back those same feelings is likely to affect the client negatively. For example, assume a client describes a situation, and mentions that she was disappointed in the reaction of her partner. You mirror the remark by saying, "You were disappointed." The client's internal reaction may well be something like, "Yes, that's what I said, you dummy; I was disappointed." The client's verbal reply, however, will hopefully be more polite: "Yes, I really was." But in terms of the self-generating force usually associated with empathic understanding, parroting responses are minimally effective. A client usually will do little more than confirm that he or she was heard correctly.

However, when clients do clearly articulate their feelings, you may still provide empathic responses. Sometimes, a client will describe a situation that is so common that the client will readily believe that you have been in the same or similar situation. When a situation is of this type, you can empathize by directly expressing your understanding of the client's reaction:

Client: I was so angry and frustrated when he again refused to go through with the deal.

19. For further discussion of issues related to informed consent, please see Chapter 15, sec. 4.

Lawyer: I can understand how upset you'd be after he did it again.

Verbalizing your understanding often avoids the irritating aspect of "parroting" and is fully empathic at the same time.

Be hesitant, however, to make such a response when a client is likely to realize that his or her situation is probably quite foreign to you. If you assert your direct understanding of a situation that is obviously outside your world of experience, a client is likely to think you insincere or patronizing. For instance, assume that a client who is unemployed and homeless states, "I really feel humiliated when I have to talk with the welfare worker about finding a place to stay." The client is unlikely to feel empathy from your response, "I know just how humiliating that is." In such a situation, a passive listening response may be more facilitative. Or, if you have had ongoing contact with the client and believe you know the client well, you might say something like, "I know how much you hate situations like this." This response conveys understanding but does not imply that you have been in the same situation.

F. NON–EMPATHIC (JUDGMENTAL) RESPONSES

Often, lawyers do respond to statements on an emotional level without providing the empathy of active listening responses. Typically, the lack of empathy is a product of a lawyer's wanting to provide immediate advice or to judge the appropriateness of a client's conduct. Examine, for example, these responses:

Client: When the promotion list came out, I was not on it. And I know I had been on the preliminary list. To see such blatant discrimination made me realize it was finally time to do something about it.

Lawyer:

No. 1: I don't blame you.

No. 2: But I guess after a while you calmed down.

No. 3: You finally acknowledged what you probably knew all along. You as well as many others were victims of discrimination, and would probably continue to be.

Lawyer No. 1 has judged the appropriateness of the reaction. Lawyer No. 2 has treated the feeling as irrelevant and shifted the discussion to another time frame. Lawyer No. 3 has played amateur psychologist, by attempting to analyze the reason for the reaction. None has simply mirrored back the client's likely emotions—"You were really furious," or "You feel wronged and want to take action."

To reflect feelings in a non-judgmental manner requires that you practice reflections and receive constructive feedback. Most of us are far more used to giving advice and searching for underlying causes of emotions than we are to simply reflecting another's feelings.[20]   And, generally, we do so out of a genuine desire to be of help.   However, judgmental responses may actually reflect our own discomfort in dealing with feelings.   None of the lawyers above encourage the client to continue talking about his or her feelings; if anything, the replies divert the client's attention away from the feelings.   For these reasons, judgmental replies are not empathic.

Consider the following examples, and analyze the lawyers' responses.

Case # 1

Client: We had only been married for three years.   She was only 32 and now she is gone.   I can't believe it; she had so much to give.   I feel like I'm not in this world.

Lawyer:

No. 1:   Don't worry; most people feel that way at first.   The feeling will pass with time.

No. 2:   It's probably because her death was so unexpected; you had no time to prepare.

No. 3:   It's perfectly proper for you to feel that way.   Under the circumstances, no one could expect anything else.

Case # 2

Client: We've been working on landing this account for over 2 years.   Our competitors were sure they were going to get it.   I've got so many ideas for positioning the whole product line; I can't wait to finalize the contract and get going.

Lawyer:

No. 1:   You have every right to gloat after pulling off a deal like this.

No. 2:   That's great but you have to take your time and go over the contract carefully.   If you don't you may regret it.

No. 3:   You're probably happy because you feel you are achieving a potential you always knew you had.

6. DIFFICULTIES IN MASTERING ACTIVE LISTENING

Without doubt, many lawyers and law students find it difficult to become immediately comfortable with, and proficient in the use of, active listening.   You may be tempted to use this initial discomfort as an excuse to abandon your efforts to improve your listening skills.   However, most people have little difficulty mastering active listening, especially when they realize that feelings of initial discomfort are

20.   See Goodman, *supra* note 2, at 227.

common. Therefore, if your initial reaction to active listening is one of discomfort, persevere. Your clients will be much better off for your patience and willingness to learn an unfamiliar technique.

To put your potential personal reactions into perspective, consider the following objections to learning active listening that some lawyers have advanced to active listening, and responses to those objections.

A. "FEELINGS ARE FOR 'SHRINKS,' NOT LAWYERS"

1. "I'm afraid we'll get so involved in feelings, I won't properly deal with the legal issues."

2. "Cases are decided on the basis of facts. Lawyers deal in facts; psychiatrists, psychologists, and social workers deal with feelings."

Expressions such as these reflect assumptions that feelings are irrelevant, and have no legitimate place in the rational process of legal analysis. But as the book has attempted to make abundantly clear, how people react emotionally to situations and to proposed solutions strongly influences the nature and amount of information they provide and the decisions they make.

A belief that feelings are largely irrelevant to a legal interview may come from a number of sources. For some, the word "feelings" connotes irrationality and triggers the idea that feelings must be avoided so that lawyers can function as they should, i.e., in a rational and objective manner. Others may simply lack experience with the role that feelings actually play in human affairs generally, and in attorney-client dialogues specifically. Finally, the views of some may be colored by denial and rationalization. Thinking about feelings may generate discomfort. The easiest way to avoid the discomfort is to deny the existence and importance of feelings. If the rationalization is successful, the discomfort can be put to rest.

Remember, however, that as a lawyer your role is not to analyze feelings, but to acknowledge a problem's emotional aspect when a client raises it. Active listening is simply a useful technique for carrying out this role. As one scholar has noted,

> A reflection doesn't try to understand the other person's thoughts or feelings better than he does. It doesn't try to solve the other's problems. It doesn't try to add new meaning or to analyze the message. Reflections simply show that meaning has been registered. They reveal an act of empathy. They tell the listener that he or she has been *heard*.[21]

B. "I FEEL EMPATHIC, BUT I JUST CAN'T FIND THE RIGHT WORDS"

1. "Reflecting feelings make me feel awkward."

2. "It feels so mechanical, reflecting back what they feel."

21. Goodman, *supra* note 2, at 38.

3. "When I listen to myself, it sounds so hollow and forced. I'm sure the client will feel that way, too."

Acquiring a new skill can require time and effort, and reactions such as those expressed above are normal. Initially, active listening techniques may seem awkward and forced. Your uncertainty about when and how to engage in active listening may produce statements which suggest, by their content or tone, that perhaps you are not empathic. However, with practice, uncertainty generally disappears and reflective statements flow smoothly and naturally. To increase your level of comfort you may want to practice reflecting content and feelings in your conversations with family and friends, or under your breath while you watch television. It is much easier to practice new skills and cope with feelings of embarrassment and self-consciousness in low risk situations such as these.[22] In time, you will no longer be "consciously employing a technique" and instead will be able to comfortably reflect feelings.

Also, your comfort with active listening may be enhanced if you recognize that there is no one way to phrase an active listening response. Empathy results from a reflection of feelings, not from a magic combination of words. For example, assume a client says, "I had always trusted my broker, but then she went and bought shares over-the-counter without any authorization from me at all." Assume further that the emotion you believe that the client is expressing is "disappointment." Any of these reflections, and undoubtedly more that you can think of, would be appropriate:

"You must have been disappointed."

"You felt disappointed."

"You were disappointed."

"It was very disappointing."

"Your broker really disappointed you."

"That must have been disappointing."

"I imagine you were disappointed."

"I can understand how much that must have disappointed you."

Moreover, recall that reflections do not need to be absolutely correct to be useful. If a client feels that your reflection does not quite "fit," the client may clarify and thereby gain additional insight into his or her feelings. For example, had the client above felt that "disappointment" did not accurately capture her or his feelings, the client might have responded, "It's not just disappointment. I'm pretty angry."

Finally, note that if you find that reflecting feelings is extremely uncomfortable, you might start the learning process by reflecting only

22. Goodman notes that many people feel initially awkward when employing reflections. Goodman, *supra* note 2, at 223–

24. He describes a number of exercises which can help you learn to make empathic responses. Id. at 234–44.

the content of a client's statements. Once you feel comfortable making reflective statements about content, reflections of feelings will come more easily to you.

C. "THERE'S NO WAY I CAN EMPATHIZE WITH THAT CLIENT"

1. "Look, I just feel phony. There is no way I could say, 'So you felt like you just couldn't stop yourself.' I can't say that; people can control themselves."

2. "Even if I try to be empathic, I'm sure my voice will give away the fact that I don't really mean it."

3. "Acknowledging those feelings makes me feel like I'm condoning that behavior."

4. "The guy seems so slick that it makes me feel if I respond to his feelings, he'll think I'm weak or just plain foolish."

5. "She's so aggressive, I feel that if I respond to her feelings, she'll see me as saying it's OK to act out of spite."

You are bound to encounter many individuals who tax your willingness to be empathic and non-judgmental. Many of us are reluctant to help people who have engaged in certain behavior or who have certain kinds of personalities. For example, some people may find that they have little desire to help welfare recipients, bankrupts, tax evaders, child molesters, con artists, or rapists. Others find they are reluctant to assist people who have personalities which are, say, extremely passive, dependent, aggressive or manipulative.

When a client is a person who, by dint of personality or situation, you are reluctant to help, you may experience a reaction similar to those above. If you pursue your own feelings further, you may understand that on some occasions you cannot empathize with any of a client's feelings, while on others, you cannot empathize with particular feelings. For example, you may be unable to empathize with the passions that consumed a child molester, but able to empathize with the abused childhood that helped produce those passions.

Unless you totally lack empathy for a client, you probably will be able to make some active listening responses to the emotional aspects of a client's problem. On the other hand, if you feel no empathy at all for a client, you may consider withdrawing or referring the client to another lawyer.[23]

D. "USING ACTIVE LISTENING WILL MAKE A CLIENT TOO EMOTIONAL"

1. "I really feel uncomfortable when the client starts crying."

23. Ethical rules may, however, constrain your ability to withdraw in certain circumstances. See Model Rules of Professional Responsibility EC 2–32 & DR 2–110 (1980); Model Rules of Professional Conduct Rule 1.16 (1983).

2. "I 'active-listened' to his anger and he just seemed to keep on going; I didn't know what to do."

3. "I think it might be a good idea, but I'm afraid the client will get so upset he'll fall apart. What'll I do then?"

Responding to feelings often results in an outpouring of even more intense emotions. If you are a beginner, experiencing such intense feelings may make you uncomfortable and lead you to back away from the use of active listening. You may feel that you are unable to stop the outpouring of emotion; that you inadvertently made the client feel worse; or that you are wrong to elicit all the emotion since there is little that you can do to resolve the feelings.

Your concerns about eliciting an excessive amount of emotion can usually be overcome if you recognize two propositions. First, although a client may express solely negative feelings, the client's overall reaction may be quite positive. The client has had the opportunity to get "feelings off his or her chest," along with the satisfaction of being heard and understood. Usually this experience will result in a feeling that a discussion was, as a whole, quite beneficial.

Second, often the best way to alleviate a client's distress is to let an outpouring of emotion continue. Continued empathy usually causes an emotional tide to recede. If you can struggle through the initial discomfort, admittedly a difficult task, you will generally find that a client regains composure. Thus, if you can, on a couple of occasions, continue to be empathic despite your discomfort, you will usually experience the success that comes from allowing a client the opportunity to ride out the emotion. With this success, you will likely experience less anxiety about eliciting and empathizing with intense emotions the next time they arise.

E. "TALKING ABOUT FEELINGS MAKES IT DIFFICULT FOR ME TO GET BACK ON TRACK"

1. "After talking about how angry she was with the Board's decision, and how it had double-crossed the employees, I felt uncomfortable having to return to questions about the specific terms of the deal."

2. "After he poured out his heart about how hurt he was when his wife left, I felt terrible having to start talking about what property they had and how title was held."

Once active listening has put a client's feelings on the table, you may find it difficult to shift gears to matters of content. It seems awkward when clients "pour their hearts out" to suddenly ask questions as if nothing of emotional importance had happened.

To smooth the transition, you may find it helpful first to summarize a client's situation, including the emotional reactions, and then to ask if the client feels ready to move to other topics. Consider this example:

Lawyer: You invested your lump sum retirement in various real estate projects with your friend Bill, whom you've known on and off since high school. He didn't follow through on his promises, and as far as you can tell you've lost most of your investment. You're extremely upset, and to make matters worse his family is calling at all hours of the night begging you to help find a way to stop him from squandering even more money. You find it hard to be sympathetic and helpful because you're so angry at Bill. And to top it off, your doctor just told you that you're headed for a heart attack, which isn't surprising given all that you've been through.

Client: That's right. Sometimes I wish I were dead and didn't have to face this mess. It's hard to live with myself, I feel so stupid for ever getting mixed up with him.

Lawyer: I can see how upset and aggravated you are, and I want to start helping as quickly as possible. If you feel ready, I'd like to ask some questions about the deal you had with Bill.

Client: I think I'm ready to get on with this, but I get furious talking about what happened.

Lawyer: That's fine, feel free to express your anger as we go along.

Note that here, in addition to summarizing the client's situation and feelings, you explicitly state your desire to help.

F. "THE CLIENT IS SO CONFUSED THAT I DON'T KNOW WHICH FEELINGS TO REFLECT"

"He says he's eager to go ahead with the deal, yet in the same breath says he's afraid of committing himself."

Sometimes clients express confused and contradictory feelings. You may feel stymied—should you focus on all the feelings, or just on one?

Recognize that contradictory feelings are the norm, not the exception. For example, when buying their first home, people typically have a variety of contradictory feelings such as wanting to put down roots vs. being afraid of feeling trapped; wanting to save money vs. being worried about taking on a big debt. Here, a young woman describes her feelings about buying a house alone:

"I want to put an offer on this house. I've been looking for months and I know this one will be a good investment. Best of all, I like this house. But the mortgage payments scare me and I'll be living there alone and it feels so disappointing. But my accountant says I'd be crazy to go on paying so much rent and taxes . . . .."

When clients have contradictory feelings, your professional role is not to try to decipher and resolve the conflicts. Your most helpful response is to try to reflect the contradictory feelings:

1. "It seems like you feel very torn about buying this house all alone."

2. "Right now you seem to have very mixed feelings. On the one hand it seems like a good investment, but on the other hand living there alone feels very empty."

G. "ACTIVE LISTENING IS MANIPULATIVE"

1. "Maybe she's not stating her feelings because she doesn't want to talk about her feelings. I don't think I should do things to try to make her talk about feelings."

2. "I don't think lawyers should manipulate people to expose their feelings. It's an invasion of their privacy."

3. "Look, I can go through the right motions to make the person believe I feel understanding and supportive, but I'm really just doing it to get information."

The use of active listening skills is in part the use of a technique to gain information. However, you do not employ active listening simply out of a voyeuristic interest in a client's private feelings. Rather, active listening is one among many techniques you employ in order to assist a client in finding an adequate solution to a problem. If any technique which produces information that a client might not otherwise reveal is to be denounced as "manipulative", then perhaps such standard practices as putting clients at ease with a bit of chit-chat and a cup of coffee, eliciting information in chronological fashion, probing for details with closed rather than open questions, and showing clients documents to refresh their recollection are all unfairly "manipulative."

For us, the answer to the claim that active listening is unfairly "manipulative" is this: Clients come to you for assistance and advice, and a client's full participation is necessary if you are to help a client find a solution that addresses all dimensions of a problem. Active listening, which provides non-judgmental understanding, is an essential technique for gaining full client participation.[24]

24. As suggested in section 5(C) above, you may sometimes limit your use of active listening when you sense that a client is consciously avoiding a discussion of feelings. In the absence of client reluctance to discuss feelings, you need not routinely tell clients what active listening is, and secure permission to use it. Such routine requests are likely to drive a wedge into an attorney-client relationship, as clients do not normally come to attorneys for enlightenment as to lawyer techniques, whether it be active listening, forms of questions, sequencing of questions, or the inclusion or omission of particular topics. Moreover, seeking client permission to employ active listening, or any other "technique", would almost certainly lead to the informed consent dilemma discussed in section 5(C). Finally, if one could not use any information-gathering technique without warning a client in advance that a response may in some way hurt the client's cause, it would seem that attorneys would have to preface all remarks with warnings. Others may disagree with this view. See S. Ellmann, "Lawyers and Clients," 34 UCLA L.Rev. 717 (1987). But see J. Morris, "Power and Responsibility Among Lawyers and Clients: Comment on Ellmann's 'Lawyers and

7. HOW MUCH ACTIVE LISTENING?

Clients typically reveal emotions repeatedly as you gather information about their problems and seek to resolve them. Given this continual emotional presence, how often should you reflect feelings?

There is no single, right, or easy answer to this question.[25] You might think that some kinds of legal matters (say, marriage dissolution and wrongful termination) are inherently more prone to emotion than others (say, antitrust litigation or a simple lease deal), and thus give rise to more active listening. Or, your reaction may be that the extent to which you use active listening typically depends on how open, reticent or emotional a client is. However, none of these categories are a sure guide to how much active listening is appropriate with any individual client.

For example, if a client is talking fully and openly, you may make a number of active listening responses simply to be empathic. But if a client is not participating fully in a discussion, you may make a like number of active listening responses in an effort to encourage the client to "open up." Similarly, of two clients involved in antitrust litigation, one may be an eager participant in a discussion, while the other may be the opposite. Hence, despite the subject matter similarity, you may use active listening in the latter matter more than in the former. Finally, whatever a client's general personality, the same client may be quite open in one matter, and rather reticent in another. Hence, in any individual matter, you must ultimately rely upon your judgment when deciding how frequently to reflect a client's feelings.

Clients'," 34 UCLA L.Rev. 781 (1987); Ellmann, "Manipulation By Client and Context: A Response to Professor Morris," 34 UCLA L.Rev. 1003 (1987).

25. Psychologists have praised helping conversations in which the helper's remarks consisted almost entirely of reflections. See Goodman, *supra* note 2, at 53. In lawyer-client dialogues, you probably will not active listen to this extent.

Chapter 6

Questioning

---

1. INTRODUCTION

Most of us pay scant attention to the types of questions used in everyday conversation. But a moment's reflection will demonstrate that you probably react differently according to the kind of question you are asked. For example, assume that at a restaurant, a friend asks you either: (1) "What kind of food are you in the mood for?" or (2) "Are you going to have the chicken breast with Dijon mustard sauce?" Or, that during one of your favorite law school classes, an instructor asks you either: (1) "Please tell us about *Palsgraf*." or (2) "In *Palsgraf,* what did the trainman do to bring about the plaintiff's injuries?"

In the restaurant example, would you be likely to respond more expansively to one question than the other? Does one question indicate more interest in your underlying feelings and attitudes than the other? In the law school example, do you have a preference for one question rather than the other? Would one put you more "on the spot" than the other? If your friend or your law school instructor is interested in specific information, which question is more likely to elicit it?

Perhaps not everybody would answer our questions in the same way. But most people would probably, for instance, state that the first restaurant question indicates more interest in them as a person than the second. Moreover, apart from the issue of whether everyone would react in an identical manner, undoubtedly most people would answer *differently* depending on which question in each pair was asked of them.

What is true in everyday life is true in lawyer-client conversations. The information you get from clients, their motivation to speak and their attitudes towards you are all influenced to some degree by the kinds of questions that you ask. Of course, human behavior is too complex to conclude that a particular form of question will always generate the same type of client response. Nonetheless, research and experience demonstrate that different forms of questions are likely to alter the amount, nature and quality of information that you receive.

69

By understanding the forms of questions, and the typical consequences each is likely to produce, you can make explicit questioning choices tailored to your goals, the type of information you are seeking and the particular client with whom you are dealing.[1]

2. FORMS OF QUESTIONS

A. GENERALLY

Questions come in a variety of forms, ranging from open to leading. No hard and fast line separates one form from another. But the principal touchstone that distinguishes forms of questions is the degree of freedom a question allows in a response. For example, consider the following questions:

1. "Tell me about the car."

2. "Tell me about the color of the car."

3. "Tell me whether the car was red."

On the surface, each question seems pretty much like the others; each begins with "Tell me" and asks about a car. But further analysis demonstrates that the questions differ in the freedom of response they allow. The first question allows a client to discuss any or all characteristics about the car that the client wishes. The second question restricts the client's discussion to characteristics pertaining to the car's color. The third question allows no description at all; it restricts the client to verifying whether the car was red.

The freer a client is to choose the scope of a response, the more "open" a question is. And the more a question restricts a response, the more "closed" it is. Neither form of question is necessarily more effective than the other. Given how clients typically react to open and closed questions, each has its purposes.

B. OPEN QUESTIONS

Open questions allow clients substantial latitude to select the content and wording of a response. Open questions indicate your expectation that a client respond at some length and allow a client to respond in his or her own words. At their broadest, open questions even allow a client to choose the subject matter of a response.

---

1. This chapter proceeds for the most part on the assumption that clients are generally able to recall and report their observations, experiences, and feelings. In reality, of course, clients are not perfect recording devices. The accuracy with which clients perceive, recall, and report data is subject to a variety of influences. These influences include factors within a client personally (e.g., how much attention a client was paying to an event; whether a client was under stress); and factors within the environment (e.g., light or dark when a client saw something.) For the most part, such factors potentially affect credibility, and are the subject of an extensive literature. See, e.g., J. Lipton, "On the Psychology of Eyewitness Testimony," 62 J. Applied Psychology 90 (1977). The chapter also proceeds on a second assumption—that clients for the most part are capable of tailoring their responses to your questions. Sometimes this is not the case; see Chapter 14 for further discussion of this point.

Examine the following questions:

1. "Tell me what brought you in here." [2]

2. "Tell me about your family."

3. "What happened after the meeting?"

4. "What took place during the conversation."

5. "How will your employees react if you move the business to a new location?"

Each question is open. Each invites a lengthy response, on a variety of potential topics, and in words of the clients' own choosing.

Even within the open question category, you find distinctions. No. 1 imposes no subject matter restriction at all. Granted, a client will probably talk about a legal problem, rather than, say, an insight into the poetry of Byron. But the question allows the client to describe the problem in any way he or she sees fit, and to delve into whatever aspects seem most important to the client.

No. 2 imposes some subject matter limitation—the client is limited to a discussion of "family." But its openness allows the client to talk about family heritage; occupations of family members; statistical data such as names, addresses and ages; personality traits of family members, and the like. Also, the client can decide whether the term "family" means "immediate family" or includes cousins, nieces and nephews.

No. 3 imposes a chronological limitation—the client is limited to talking about what took place "after the meeting." But which post-meeting events to discuss are entirely up to the client.[3]

No. 4 imposes a different sort of limitation—the client's response is limited to a single conversation. Yet, this question too is open. The client may talk about the parties to the conversation, what they said, and/or what activities took place during the conversation.

Lastly, No. 5 asks the client to discuss possible consequences of a proposed decision on a group of employees. Its openness allows the client to discuss a variety of possible consequences, to differentiate among different groups of employees, and perhaps to talk about the client's long-range business goals.

---

2. Note that an inquiry in the assertive form can be the equivalent of a question. Psychologists sometimes refer to such inquiries as probes since the comment is in the form of a statement rather than a question. See B. Okun, *Effective Helping: Interviewing and Counseling Techniques* 76 (3d ed. 1987).

3. At trial, when open questions ask a witness to describe events that unfolded over a period of time, an attorney will often object to them on the ground that they "call for a narrative response." The basis of the objection, and the reason that the objection is sometimes sustained, is that the question leaves the witness to talk about a series of events in whatever words the witness chooses, and some portions of the response might be inadmissible. See P. Bergman, *Trial Advocacy in a Nutshell* 90–96 (2d ed. 1989); T. Mauet, *Fundamentals of Trial Techniques* 347–48 (2d ed. 1988); see also Fed.R.Evid. 611(a). Other forms of open questions, which do limit a witness to a particular chronological point in time, are much less likely to be ruled improper.

C. CLOSED QUESTIONS

Closed (narrow) questions select the subject matter of a client's response and also limit the scope of a reply. Closed questions seek specific data. Examples of closed questions include:

1. "In which hand was she holding the gun?"

2. "How fast was the blue car going?"

3. "Just where did the chicken cross the road?"

4. "How many employees are likely to quit if you move the business to a new location?"

D. YES–NO QUESTIONS

"Yes–No" questions are a commonly employed form of closed question. Yes–No questions even more severely limit the scope of a client's response by including in the question all the information you seek and asking the client only to confirm or deny it. All closed questions can, of course, be restated in Yes–No form. Thus, the Yes–No versions of the closed questions above are:

1. "Was she holding the gun in her left hand?"

2. "Was the blue car exceeding the speed limit?"

3. "Did the chicken cross the road at the crosswalk?"

4. "Will some employees quit if you move the business to a new location?"

E. LEADING QUESTIONS

As you are no doubt aware, leading questions not only provide all the information that you seek but also suggest the desired answer. Leading questions are little more than outright assertions, accompanied either by a tone of voice or language clue that you desire a particular answer. They are closed questions in assertive form. For example, in leading form the closed questions from subsection (C) are as follows:

1. "She was holding the gun in her left hand?"

2. "The blue car was going over 65, correct?"

3. "The chicken crossed the road at the crosswalk, didn't it?"

4. "I take it you'll lose some employees if you move the business to a new location?"

The rather dramatic "Isn't it true * * *" phrase that cross-examiners tend to use during trial is certainly not a necessary characteristic of leading questions. Questions two and three have other and less dramatic verbal clues, while the first and fourth rely on voice intonation.

3. ADVANTAGES AND DISADVANTAGES OF THE DIFFERENT FORMS OF QUESTIONS

In addition to delineating the scope of a response, a question's form can also impact a client's ability and willingness to recall and provide information. This section examines this impact.

A. OPEN QUESTIONS

The typical advantages of open questions are as follows:

1. *Open Questions Often Motivate Full Client Participation*

a. Because they allow clients to decide what information is significant, open questions provide "recognition." You show confidence in their ability to know what information is significant. Both the recognition and the fact that they are talking about what they see as important tend to provide motivation.

b. Open questions typically avoid potential inhibitors. The primary inhibitors that open questions avoid are ego threat, case threat, and the etiquette barrier. Often clients are uncomfortable about certain aspects of their problems and are therefore reluctant to talk about those aspects. A closed question seeking information about an uncomfortable topic may therefore harm rapport by forcing a client either to talk about an uncomfortable topic or consciously avoid it. Open questions leave clients free to avoid talking about threatening subjects.[4]

As a lawyer, you often have to ask clients about sensitive subjects. When planning a client's estate, for example, you may raise the possibility that a client's child may predecease the client. Talking to a business client, you may ask about the integrity of the client's partner or office manager. As a criminal defense lawyer, you may ask about a client's mental state and past criminal record. Clients may be uncomfortable and reluctant to talk if, with a closed question, you directly seek such sensitive information. Open questions allow clients to discuss sensitive information in their own way and when they are ready to do so.

Similarly, open questions also tend to overcome the inhibitor of "greater need." Since open questions allow clients to talk about what to them seems most important, you avoid any reluctance that would be created were you to ask closed questions about topics that a client regarded as of secondary importance.

2. *Open Questions Often Facilitate Your Gaining Complete Data*

a. Because both problems and clients' experiences are unique, you almost never will be able to think of everything that might be impor-

---

4. Often, you cannot avoid discussion of uncomfortable topics entirely. But open questions may allow you to postpone discussion until your relationship with a client is solid.

tant to achieving a satisfactory solution. As one author has put it, "Qualitative answers—feelings, reasons, other experiences—can only come when the question is open-ended, not closed, and when the answer must be a paragraph, not a word." [5] For example, whether the issue is past events giving rise to a lawsuit, or potential consequences of a proposed resolution, you usually cannot think of all the factors that might bear on the issue. Thus, you cannot rely on closed questions to elicit all important data.

b. Open questions promote completeness by preserving clients' trains of thought. When clients are allowed to describe matters in their own words, their paths of association remain intact and they tend to recall data that they might not mention in response to closed questions.

c. Open questions also promote the accuracy of information. Psychological research has shown that answers to open questions are more accurate than answers to closed questions.[6]

d. Open questions tend to be more efficient in terms of time than closed questions.[7] Even if you could think of everything that might affect a client's matter, pursuing each and every detail with closed questions would consume an inordinate amount of time. An answer to a single open question will often cover the same ground as the answers to a series of closed questions.[8]

However, lest you be ready to award a Nobel Prize to open questions, be warned that a number of disadvantages are associated with them.

3. Open Questions Sometimes Inhibit Full Client Participation

Open questions put much of the burden for recalling and describing information on a client. Many people are not comfortable in the conversational limelight and will prefer you to carry the load. In such situations, open questions may elicit only short, minimal responses.

4. Open Questions Are Not Sufficient for Gaining Complete Data

a. Open questions do little to stimulate memory. As a noted psychologist suggests, "Compared to other forms of report, narrative reports . . . tend to be less complete . . .. [A] narrative produces much higher accuracy but much lower quantity." [9] As a result, events or other information known to a client typically remain undisclosed in

5. S. Hamlin, *What Makes Juries Listen* 63 (1985). See also G. Goodman, *The Talk Book* 127 (1988).

6. E. Loftus, *Eyewitness Testimony* 91–92 (1979).

7. See, e.g., D. Binder & P. Bergman, *Fact Investigation* 269–70 (1984).

8. Of course, in some situations you may need specific data very quickly. For example, if you are conducting a jailhouse interview of a recently arrested client, you may need bail data quickly. In such situations, you are likely to employ closed questions.

9. Loftus, *supra* note 6, at 91–92.

response to open questions. For example, the open question, "What happened next?" might unearth conversations A, B and C. But it may not uncover conversation D, nor details about A, B and C.

Thus, to get complete data you typically have to ask a combination of open and closed questions. Because of their ability to call specific data to a client's attention, closed questions are generally more successful than open ones at stimulating a client's recall.[10] For example, the closed question, "Did you talk about precise geographical limits during conversation A?" may remind the client of details that did not emerge in the answer to the open question. In short, in response to closed questions, clients often *recognize* data that they do not *recall* in response to open ones.[11]

b. Open questions may also fail to elicit information that clients do remember, but which they do not recognize as being legally salient. When a client is mistaken about or unaware of legal requirements, the client may well omit information from a narrative response in the belief that the information is without legal significance.

5. *Open Questions Are Sometimes Inefficient*

Open questions may not be effective with clients who ramble or are extremely verbose. Certain clients may regard a question such as, "What happened since our last meeting?" as an invitation to describe irrelevant events in great detail, and to vilify all with whom they disagree. Asking open questions of such clients may be the equivalent of pouring gasoline on a fire.

B. CLOSED QUESTIONS

The typical advantages of closed questions are as follow:

1. *Closed Questions Elicit Details*

Perhaps the most important advantage of closed questions is that they allow you to elicit details. For example, assume that a client is consulting you because of problems that have developed with his partner over how the partnership's business should be run. The client wants to know whether to dissolve the partnership. The following dialogue occurs:

Lawyer: And what occurred at the meeting?

Client: Well, Miyoko started off by noting that sales were down, especially in the sports apparel line, and asked us for

---

10. However, closed questions can be as suggestive as leading ones, and therefore produce inaccurate responses. S. Richardson, B. Snell Dohrenwend & D. Klein, *Interviewing: Its Form and Function* 173, 181 (1965). Because closed questions may pressure clients into believing that they *should* answer questions, Id. at 180, the risk of inaccurate replies in response to closed questions may be especially high in attorney-client interviews. See also sec. 3(B)(5), *infra*.

11. For a further discussion of the differences between recall and recollection, see J. Kagan & E. Haveman, *Psychology: An Introduction* 139 (4th ed. 1980); H. Ellis, T. Bennett, T. Daniel & E. Rickert, *Psychology of Learning and Memory* 299–301 (1979).

our ideas. There were a number of suggestions made, ranging from getting out of the line altogether to trying to get the line into bigger retail stores like Sears. Everyone had their own ideas—the meeting went on for almost an hour.

Lawyer: Anything else that you can recall?

Client: I know that Miyoko got really angry when we went over sales figures.

Lawyer: Anything else?

Client: Not that I can remember.

Here, you rely only on open questions. In response, the client quickly provides a picture of what took place at a meeting. But, as is often the case with responses to open questions, the picture is incomplete. It lacks many details that may well be significant. What specific sales figures did Miyoko report? What were the various suggestions that were presented at the meeting, and how did Miyoko respond to each? What exactly does the client mean by "really angry?" The answers to such questions are likely to be critical in helping the client to decide whether staying in business with Miyoko makes sense.

To elicit such details, you would probably need to ask closed questions. Such questions focus on specific topics, thereby stimulating memory and producing details that a client might otherwise omit or not remember.[12]

2. *Closed Questions Sometimes Motivate Clients*

Some clients may be uncertain of how to respond to an open question. For example, a question such as, "What consequences do you see if we reject the proposal?" may confuse some clients. Does the question call for every possible consequence, or only for the most significant ones? How much elaboration do you expect? Does the question somehow "test" the client to see how many consequences the client can identify? Clients for whom open questions create such thoughts will probably be reluctant to answer fully and openly. Such clients may find closed questions "easier" to answer: their topics are readily identifiable, their scope is readily apparent, and a client has only to produce a limited amount of information. Therefore, for such clients, closed questions may provide greater motivation to answer.

Closed questions may provide greater motivation than open questions in other contexts as well. Recall the suggestion that open questions often motivate clients by allowing them to postpone mention of sensitive topics until the client feels comfortable doing so. You may employ closed questions to delay discussion of sensitive matters as well. Closed questions allow you to "tippy toe" either into or around sensitive topics. When you know or strongly suspect that a client will be reluctant to discuss a particular topic, through closed questions you can

12. But see text at *supra* note 9.

pursue the topic a small bit at a time, and stop at the point that a client becomes obviously reluctant to proceed further.[13]

For instance, assume that in the partnership example above, the client has said things which lead you to believe that the client feels foolish for having started the partnership with Miyoko in the first place. Now, you want the client to examine the reasons for going into business with Miyoko initially. You might ask an open question: "Can you tell me how the partnership came about?" However, given the client's feelings, the client may be reluctant to respond fully to this question. Hence, to overcome reluctance, you may instead ask a series of closed questions, proceeding in tippy-toe fashion toward the sensitive topic:

When did you first meet Miyoko?

How many times did you meet before you formally entered into the partnership?

Who first suggested a formal partnership?

Did you talk about how long the partnership should continue?

You might continue this type of questioning into the reasons for the client entering the partnership, or you might stop questioning before arriving at that point. At least, closed questions may motivate some specific responses and provide you with some insight into how far to pursue the topic.

Alas, as you undoubtedly suspect, closed questions also have disadvantages:

3. Too Many Closed Questions May Harm Rapport

Over-reliance on closed questions may result in clients leaving meetings feeling that they never had a chance to say what was really on their minds. The more you ask questions which limit the scope of a response, the less likely are you to learn everything that a client thinks is important. In turn, a client is likely to be less engaged in identifying a problem and actively participating in its resolution.

4. Closed Questions Often Prevent You From Learning Important Information

Asking numerous closed questions is likely to cause you to miss both trees and the forest. You miss trees, because in any matter there are too many for you to find with closed questions. Moreover, clients tend not to volunteer information when faced with a plethora of closed questions, figuring that if a bit of data is important, surely you will seek it out.

---

13. This discussion assumes that a compelling reason to pursue a topic at once does not exist. In the absence of a compelling reason to pursue a sensitive matter at once, it often makes sense to postpone discussion until a client is comfortable.

At the same time, your focus on individual trees is likely to obscure your view of the forest. The immersion in bits of detail frustrates your learning a client's overall story.

Unfortunately, lawyers *tend to ask far too many closed questions.* Despite the advantages of open questions, lawyers traditionally favor closed questions. One reason may be the "filling" phenomenon. None of us approaches an event from a totally neutral perspective. We carry around "schema" which allow our past experiences to make sense of new ones.[14] We ordinarily apply these schema unconsciously, in order to make sense of daily life. Think how complicated life would be if each trip to a supermarket, say, were a completely new and unique experience. In turn, our schema often lead us to "fill in" the details of an event based on our expectations of how such events usually occur. To gain insight into your capacity to fill, think about the following situations:

1. Two cars collided in an intersection.

2. You are consulted by a thirty-five-year old father of two children whose wife has just left home.

Take a moment and try to conjure up a picture of each situation. In the first example, have you visualized, if only hazily, a particular intersection, makes of cars, the point of collision, and how the collision came about? In the second, do you have an image of the feelings, desires and concerns of the client whose spouse has left home?

Next, think of where such details came from. Not from the sentences themselves—they are far too brief. But your experiences furnish you with ample resources to formulate quite detailed pictures. You "filled in" gaps with details supplied by your own schemas.

Hence, as a client begins to describe past events, or to set forth her or his concerns, you may find yourself filling in the client's story with information drawn from your past experiences. For example, you may assume that one client who has been severely injured as a result of using a defective product will have the same financial objectives as most other clients; and you may assume that the reasons another client wants a long-term lease are the same reasons most other clients have had. This mind-set may lead you to believe, even before you have spoken with a client in any depth, that you are generally familiar with a client's specific situation. Perhaps subconsciously, then, open questions eliciting a general picture of a client's needs and concerns are therefore unnecessary. You need only a few details to clear up some fuzzy edges.

A total antidote to filling is neither available nor desirable. You cannot help but develop expectancies about clients and their problems. Mental pictures will form. The human mind works in this fashion;

14. See R. Nisbett & L. Ross, *Human Inference: Strategies and Shortcomings of Social Judgment,* 32–35 (1980).

nothing can be done to change that. However, you can make yourself aware of the tendency to fill, and try to prevent yourself from becoming a victim. Open questions and active listening are two techniques that may help you in that endeavor.[15]

The tendency of lawyers to ask too many closed questions may also be a product of "premature diagnosis." The traditional pigeonholes of legal analysis are powerful. When a client begins to discuss a matter, a lawyer may automatically begin to pigeonhole it as a "products liability" case, an "inter vivos trust" matter, or a "securities issuance" problem. The initial pigeonhole is often premature—your diagnosis may be inaccurate, or at least incomplete. But once you place a problem into a pigeonhole, you then turn to gathering data that fits the matter into that pigeonhole. From there, it is but a short step to using closed questions that elicit the specific data you need to process the matter.

As with filling, inoculating yourself against the tendency to engage in premature diagnosis may be impossible. Be aware of the tendency, but try not to let initial pigeonholes foreclose the way you think about ways a client's problem might be resolved. For example, the legal reality that a client may be entitled in a lawsuit only to monetary damages should not foreclose you from asking, "If you could write your own ticket, what result would you like to see?"

5. Closed Questions Can Create Inaccurate Responses

Closed questions tend to produce more erroneous information than open questions.[16] One potential reason may be a combination of the motivational factor, "fulfilling expectations," and the "filling" phenomenon. When you ask closed questions seeking details, clients usually try to fulfill your expectations by supplying such details. But because of the "filling" phenomenon, the answers may come not from clients' recollection of actual events, but from clients' past experiences. Therefore, clients who are asked for details may well respond with what their schemas tell them probably occurred, not what actually did occur.

Closed questions may distort responses in another way. Because closed questions define the topics for clients to a greater extent than do open questions, closed questions usually reflect a lawyer's choice of vocabulary, not a client's. For instance, compare the open question, "Describe his behavior" with the closed question, "Was he angry?" The closed question not only identifies a specific emotion, it also attaches a label to it. And closed questions' verbal labels often distort responses.

In one study, for example, changing a word in a question from "frequently" to "occasionally" produced markedly different results. In

15. For a discussion of filling in the context of eyewitness identification, see R. Buckhout, "Eyewitness Testimony," 231 Sci.Am. 23, 24–27 (1974).

16. See Loftus, *supra* note 6.

this study, which has been replicated often, one group of random respondents was asked, "Do you get headaches frequently and, if so, how often?" Another group was asked, "Do you get headaches occasionally, and, if so, how often?" The first group reported an average of 2.2 headaches per week; the second group only 0.7 headaches per week.[17] Changing even the word "a" to "the" in a question can affect results. It is not surprising that one researcher has concluded, "[I]n a variety of situations, the wording of a question about an event can influence the answer that is given." [18]

C. LEADING QUESTIONS

Although the term "leading question" is often accompanied by or greeted with sneers, such questions are sometimes proper and necessary for eliciting a full picture of a client's problem.

1. *Leading Questions Sometimes Overcome Potential Inhibitors*

Leading questions sometimes help you to overcome the inhibitors of ego threat, case threat and the etiquette barrier. These inhibitors sometimes make clients reluctant to disclose matters they perceive as sensitive. Hence, when a discussion may touch on a sensitive matter, use of leading questions suggests that you already know about the troublesome data, that the client need not fear letting the cat out of the bag, and that you are prepared to talk about it in a forthright manner.[19]

The classic example of this use of leading questions is provided by the Kinsey study of American sexual mores. Rather than asking individuals *if* they had engaged in such potentially embarrassing conduct as oral sex or homosexuality, Kinsey's researchers asked *when* or *how often* they had done so.[20] The leading form of the questions suggested to respondents that the interviewers expected that such activity had taken place, would not condemn the respondents for admitting it, and were prepared to discuss it openly. The examples below illustrate how leading questions may overcome embarrassment in two typical legal situations. Compare the following sets of questions:

A. 1. "Have you ever been arrested before?"

    2. "I guess you've had some problems with the police before?"

B. 1. "Do you see any problems in letting them look at your books?"

    2. "The acquiring company's examination of your books will bring to light things like allowing employees to use compa-

17. Loftus, *supra* note 6 at 94–95.

18. Id. at 97.

19. See R. Gorden, *Interviewing: Strategy, Techniques, and Tactics* 215 (1969).

20. Id. at 214.

ny cars for personal use. How should we talk to them about these matters?"

Assuming that you strongly suspect that the troublesome conduct has in fact occurred, the use of leading questions may overcome these clients' fear and embarrassment, and consequent reluctance to talk openly and honestly.

However, as the sneer that often accompanies or greets the term "leading" suggest, leading questions are not without their disadvantages.

2. *Leading Questions Sometimes Prevent You From Learning Important Data*

A leading question often reflects your ardent desire to have facts come out in a way favorable to a client. For example, if an appellate case or a statute uses a word, you might want a client to use precisely that word in recounting a past event. Hence, you incorporate that word in a leading question. Though that word may be an inaccurate label, the leading question may cause a client, consciously or unconsciously, to affirm it. You may thereby introduce inaccuracy into a discussion. When you later discover the inaccuracy (or have it pointed out to you by another party), it may be too late to seek solutions which you and a client might have pursued if the true data were known earlier.

3. *Leading Questions May Be Ethically Improper*

Use of leading questions in your office sometimes is even more improper than it may be at trial. Generally, you cannot ethically suggest "correct" answers to clients. For example, assume that a couple consults you about a new house that they purchased, based in part on their understanding that the roof on the house was brand new. When it later turns out that the roof is old and needs replacing, the clients seek advice about what they should do. Might you ask, "I take it that the seller actually told you that the roof was new?" The answer is clear—such a question does nothing except tell the clients what to say. Absent unusual circumstances, the question is improper.

4. *Conclusion*

As you can see, motivating clients to participate fully and gathering complete data usually requires you to employ each form of question. However, even employing the "correct" form of question at the "correct" time is no guarantee that motivation and complete, accurate data will result. Because no single client is typical in all respects, a question that motivates one client may inhibit another. Moreover, some clients will treat a yes-no question as little different than an open one, while others will respond quite literally. Lastly, any one client may respond to the same form of question differently at different times. Thus, you need to adapt the forms of questions to the dynamics of individual conversations.

*

Part Three

INFORMATION-GATHERING

Part Three (Chapters 7 through 14) examines a variety of subjects related to information-gathering. Chapter 7 explores approaches and techniques for beginning initial and follow-up meetings. Chapters 8 through 10 explore approaches and techniques for initial data-gathering in litigation matters. Chapters 11 and 12 explore these subjects in the context of proposed deals transactions. Chapter 13 concerns methods for concluding initial and follow-up conferences. Finally, Chapter 14 considers approaches and methods of conversing with problematic clients.

Chapter 7

BEGINNING CLIENT CONFERENCES

* * *

Nice to see you again, Ms. Thompson. How's that new plant that Trinomics built working out?

Very well. We've increased production by 50%, and we're still behind in our shipments. So things are going about as well as they can. Actually, having the new plant is the reason we're thinking about the deal I mentioned to you over the phone.

I'm delighted to hear that things are going so well. From what you said on the phone, this new deal sounds like a great opportunity for Trinomics. But before we get into any details, why don't you tell me what Trinomics is trying to accomplish by going into the deal.

* * *

1. INTRODUCTION

Daily life constantly reminds us of the importance of "first impressions." Whether evidenced by cliches such as "put your best foot forward", or by advice to trial lawyers to "win your case during voir dire",[1] everyone understands that relationships' beginnings often strongly influence their future course. Beginnings may even determine whether there *is* a future. Hence, you need to think carefully about how to begin client conferences.[2]

This chapter describes a client-centered approach to beginning initial and follow-up client conferences. Less a set of strict procedures

---

1. See. e.g., T.A. Mauet, *Fundamentals of Trial Techniques* 23 (2d ed. 1988); M.J. Berger, J.B. Mitchell & R.H. Clark, *Trial Advocacy—Planning, Analysis & Strategy* 164 (1989).

2. The importance of the beginning phase of interviews is illustrated by the fact that the subject is covered in nearly every work in an extensive interviewing literature for lawyers. See, e.g., T.L. Shaf-

fer & J.R. Elkins, *Legal Interviewing and Counseling in a Nutshell* 76 (2d ed 1987); A. Sherr, *Client Interviewing for Lawyers* 23–44 (1986); L. Cohn, "The Initial Client Interview—A Critical Point in the Relationship," Illinois Bar J. 178 (Nov.1979); S. Fey and S. Goldberg, "Legal Interviewing from a Psychological Perspective: An Attorney's Handbook" 14 Willamette L.J. 217, 221, 225–226 (1978).

to be slavishly copied and more a general guide to professional judgment, the approach is one you may use both in litigation and transactional matters, regardless of a matter's substantive law content. Moreover, the approach applies to every new matter, regardless of whether or not you have previously represented a client.[3]

2. GREETING CLIENTS

The first consideration (chronologically, if not in order of importance), is where to meet clients. You will probably have a choice between your office and a waiting/reception room. Most clients will prefer you to meet them in the waiting area and to escort them to your office. By meeting clients in a waiting area, you immediately demonstrate your personal concern. Also, as you walk to your office you can put clients at ease through casual conversation or by offering them a hot or cold drink. Moreover, you avoid awkward moments such as being on the phone at the moment a client enters your office or trying to shake hands while dodging the corner of your desk.

Generally, where you choose to greet clients remains the same whether a client is making an initial or follow-up visit. No matter how well you know a client, most clients appreciate the extra bit of attention you show them by coming to a waiting area to greet them.

Undoubtedly, many attorneys prefer to greet clients in the attorneys' offices. Either a receptionist or a lawyer's personal secretary usually escorts a client to the office.[4] Lawyers who follow this practice typically believe that it demonstrates that the lawyer is busy and competent, thereby stimulating client confidence. However, this practice lacks the special touch of a personal greeting. And, hopefully, how you represent a client will be a more meaningful demonstration of your competence than where the greeting occurs.

Whichever practice you follow, take care to follow ordinary social niceties. Greet a client by name and make sure that a new client knows your name. You may be surprised how often, even if you have spoken by phone to a client before an initial meeting, a new client will not be quite sure what your name is.[5] Have an area of your office

3. You will have to tailor the suggested techniques to circumstances so individually specific as to be beyond the scope of the book. For example, practicing law in rural areas or small towns is different from practicing law in a big city; sole practitioners do things a little differently from large-firm lawyers. While a client-centered approach is compatible with all types of legal practices, you may need to modify some of our specific suggestions.

4. In no case do we recommend that a client be given the mission of finding an attorney's office on his or her own, with such instructions as, "Turn left at the first corridor, then left again at the copy machine." Given the maze-like quality of many law offices, such clients may never be seen again.

5. For this reason, many attorneys hand clients a business card almost immediately upon meeting them. However, other attorneys view this practice as being too cold and wait for the conclusion of a meeting to hand out a card.

which is conducive to personal conversation rather than attempting to communicate across a large and often messy desk.[6] Smile.

3. ICEBREAKING

* * *

We can sit over here, Mr. Wilson. You can put your coffee right here.

Thanks; say, that's a nice view you have.

It is, and when things get crazy around here I like to stop and spend a few minutes just looking at the view; I find it's quite restful. Did you have any trouble parking?

None at all.

Good. The parking situation in this building can be quite horrid at times and I feel badly when clients get delayed by the inefficiency of our parking service. I normally warn new clients that parking may be a problem, and I realized I didn't say anything to you when you called. I'm glad things worked out well.

* * *

Lawyers almost always begin client meetings with a few moments of "chit-chat". As in many social situations that both parties know will eventually move to a "main topic," general conversation precedes the main topic. The preliminary conversation may, as above, involve that ubiquitous enemy, parking. Or, depending on such variables as where you live, how well you know a client, and what you and a client have in common, chit-chat may touch on local news or a sporting event, previous contacts, the person who referred the client to you, and the like.

However, attorneys are far less unanimous when the issue is *how much* chit-chat should proceed the substance of an interview. In one camp are those who favor considerable preliminary conversation. These campers emphasize the effectiveness of chit-chat for putting clients at ease and for demonstrating that the lawyer is a person with whom a client can easily talk.

Other lawyers, perhaps more of a "get down to business" lot, hold that clients tend to find extensive chit-chat annoying. They point out that clients seek solutions to anxiety-producing problems and believe that most clients appreciate the opportunity to talk about their problems quickly.

As you probably recognize, neither group of lawyers is universally correct. Too much chit-chat obviously wastes time and may decrease a client's confidence in you. Too little chit-chat may stamp you as cold and brusk and interested only in a legal problem, not in the "whole client." Unfortunately, what one client considers too much chit-chat may to another client be too little.

---

6. Substantial literature is devoted to how offices should be decorated and arranged in order to put clients at ease. See, e.g., P. Marcotte, "Was It Something I Said? Officer Decor Can Help Determine Whether You Keep Clients," A.B.A.J. 34 (Aug. 1987); Fey and Goldberg, *supra* note 2, at 221–224.

Ideally, then, you must tailor the amount of chit-chat to each individual client's needs and desires. But if you have had nothing more than a few moments with a new client, and perhaps a brief prior telephone conversation, how are you to decide how much chit-chat is right? Your decision can be based on your assessment of a client's *level of distress or well-being*. Because preliminary chit-chat is such a common social practice, even a few moments with a client will normally give you an adequate basis from which to make this assessment.

As you start to chat with a client, include a typical question such as, "How are you doing?", or, "Did you have any problems getting here?" Often the client's response will allow you to judge how ready a client is to get down to business. For example, a client may respond to a question regarding parking in a way that lets you know he or she is ready to get started:

> "No, no problems at all. In fact, I arrived early so I could go over my outline and be sure my documents were in order."

Comments such as this usually indicate that a client wants to focus on business, not the weather, parking or last night's TV. When a client does appear relaxed and comfortable, you can conclude chit-chat quickly. The icebreaking that is attendant to greeting a client and engaging in a bit of socially-common dialogue is sufficient for clients who are already at ease.

Some clients, however, may respond in ways that indicate that they are quite distressed:

> "Yes, it was a hassle getting here. I was stuck in bumper to bumper traffic for nearly an hour! I hate coming to this part of town."

> * * *

> "Yes, in fact I barely made it here today. I was up all night talking to my partner in New York; it was almost impossible to get back to sleep. I overslept and still don't feel totally awake."

Comments such as these signal that a client has arrived tense or tired. You therefore probably want to make a special effort to put the client at ease. You can do this by expressing concern and consideration for the client's distress:

> "I'm sorry you had such a difficult time getting here. Fortunately it's nice and cool here and I'd be happy to get you something cool to drink. In addition, I want you to know that once we start working together, I'm happy to do as much as possible over the phone. I know it's hard to get downtown at this time of day."

> * * *

> "I know what those late night calls are like. I always have trouble getting back to sleep when I get a late business call and I always feel lousy the next day. Would you like some coffee before we start?"

When clients evidence distress, you also can help by saying something like, "Would you like to take a few moments and catch your breath before we start?" If you receive an indication that the client would like more time, engaging in additional chit-chat may help.

However, the chit-chat should not be indiscriminate. One empathic approach is to share distressing experiences similar to those of the client:

> "You know, when you talk about being stuck in traffic it reminds me of the time . . .."

Such a statement reminds a client that though you are a lawyer, you are also a "real person."

Another approach is to personalize your chit-chat. Try to focus on something personal about the client. If you know the client's business or occupation, talk about that. If the client is wearing a Lion's Club pin, ask or comment about that. If the client's clothing indicates interest in a particular sport, comment or ask about that. Or, you might consider mentioning something about the person who referred the client: [7]

> "I'm really happy that Charlene referred you to me. She is such a fine person. I've known her for many years . . .."

Finally, what about the client whose distress grows out of the client's problem, not traffic woes or sleepless night? Should you forgo chit-chat and discuss the case immediately? Consider this example. In response to the question, "How are you?", the client states:

> "I'm furious. Take a look at these papers I was served with. I can't believe what those 'slimeballs' are trying to do."

While on the surface it appears that the client wants to talk about the case, the client may really just want to vent resentment and agitation. Hence, rather than moving into a structured exploration of the client's problem, you may simply sit back and let the client blow off steam. Ask the client to tell you more. Empathize with the client's feelings, and "park" your efforts at systematic data-gathering until the client begins to calm down.

To summarize, generally engage in a little chit-chat. When a client is distressed, attempt to learn the reason for the distress and tailor your chit-chat to that reason.

4. PRELIMINARY PROBLEM IDENTIFICATION

* * *

Mrs. Bishop, perhaps the easiest way to get started is for you to explain how I might be of help.

Well, I'm not exactly sure. My husband and I are having a second story put on our home and our neighbor, Mr. Young, has threatened to sue us if we don't stop.

---

7. When talking about the person who referred the client, be careful. Avoid making the client feel that the referring person disclosed confidences. Avoid making the client feel you "checked the client out" with the referral source. Also, consider whether you may be putting the client on "the spot" by asking how the client knows the referring person.

Understandably, you sound very concerned, and I certainly want to help you. Can you tell me a little bit more?

Well, Mr. Young, who lives next door, claims that deed restrictions prevent us from building a second story because it will block his view. But as far as we can tell, no such restrictions exist.

That's helpful; it gives me a sense of where this problem is coming from, and I have had some experience in these sorts of matters. However, before I get into the details, probably it would be useful for you to tell me if there are other concerns on your mind that you've not mentioned. Are there other things besides the threat that you would like to talk about this morning?

* * *

Mr. Falconi, why don't you start by telling me what's on your mind.

Sure. I've been talking to Bob Barton, the president of ABC Realty, a large real estate development company, about exchanging some property I own in Palm Beach for some stock in ABC. Economically, the deal makes sense if there are no taxes; I think ABC has a very good future. But what I want to know about are the likely tax consequences. I want the trade to be tax free if at all possible.

Tax free exchanges is an area I'm familiar with. To determine whether you can arrange such an exchange I'm going to need to get some details from you. However, before I get into those I want to make sure we get to go over everything that is on your mind. Besides the tax situation, are there other things that you'd like to review this afternoon?

* * *

A. CLIENTS' INITIAL AGENDAS

The client-centered approach emphasizes the need to see problems from clients' perspectives. In thinking about how to see a new problem from a client's perspective, begin by considering what is likely to be on a client's mind at the outset of an initial interview.

Clients typically enter your office wanting to talk about four general topics. Realizing what these topics are will help you understand why you should begin initial data-gathering with "preliminary problem identification," and how you can go about that task.

Consider a client with a litigation problem. The client's concerns will typically consist of the following: [8]

First, since litigation problems invariably have their genesis in disputes regarding past events, a client probably will want to describe something of the dispute's history.[9]

8. The agenda usually will be similar regardless of whether the client is new or ongoing, and regardless of the substantive law area involved.

9. A client's desire to describe past events will be present regardless of wheth-

er events have ripened into an actual dispute. For example, if a company's truck careens off a road and causes injuries, it may seek legal advice even before being contacted by a potential plaintiff.

Second, a client most likely will want to explain the outcome—the objectives or goals—he or she hopes to achieve. For example, Mrs. Bishop's comments suggest that her primary goal is to resolve the dispute with Mr. Young in such a way that she can continue her building project without interruption.[10]

Third, a client may have some ideas about how to achieve his or her objectives. That is, a client may have thought about what course of action—solution—will enable the client to achieve the client's goal. For instance, before talking to you, Mrs. Bishop might have thought about turning Mr. Young's threat over to the neighborhood architectural committee for resolution. Of course, if at the time of the initial interview the client does have solutions in mind, the client will probably want to explore them.[11]

Fourth, a client undoubtedly will want to discuss a number of legal and nonlegal concerns.[12] For example, Mrs. Bishop might be concerned not only about whether she will be able to build her second story, but also about such matters as attorney's fees, the possible delay in the project, and whether she should continue with the project before Young's threat is resolved.

Are clients with transactional matters likely to be interested in talking about the same four general topics? For the most part, the answer is "yes." Transactional matters are less dependent than litigation matters on "rights" created by prior events. But even in transactional matters, past events generally precipitate clients' seeking legal advice, and clients will want to discuss those past events. For example, if a client has partially worked out a proposed deal with another person, the client will want to talk about terms to which the parties have already agreed. Similarly, an estate-planning client will probably want to talk about how the past conduct of family members has affected her or his plans for dividing the property.

Second, as in litigation, most transactional clients will want to talk about the outcomes they hope to achieve. Some clients will have very specific ideas about their objectives: "To undertake the kind of capital improvements we plan, we need at least a 15–year lease." Others will have more vague goals: "The main thing is I don't want my husband to have to worry about a lot of financial details if something should happen to me." In the example above, Mr. Falconi clearly falls in the

---

10. In some instances, at this preliminary stage a client may not have fully though through his or her objectives. For example, in response to the question, "What do you hope to achieve?" a client may say only, "I want as much money as I can get" or, "I want whatever the law allows." As such vague objectives typically become more definite when you begin to explore potential solutions, you generally need not press clients to fully clarify their objectives during this preliminary dialogue.

11. Some clients will have little idea about how to resolve a problem at the time of an initial interview. At least, more clients will be aware of their objectives than of how to attain their objectives. For example, Mrs. Bishop may be totally at sea regarding how to respond to Young's threat.

12. The multiplicity of concerns will probably exist whether the client makes a claim or has one made against him or her.

former category: he wants to acquire ABC stock without paying taxes. However, on whatever level they have thought through their desired outcomes, clients will want to talk about them.

Third, transactional clients are just as likely as litigation clients to have in mind potential solutions for their problems. For example, many estate-planning clients wanting to avoid probate will have heard of (but not necessarily understood) "living trusts," and hence will want to discuss that planning device. And if Mr. Falconi is an experienced businessperson, he may want to talk about his own ideas for structuring the ABC deal.[13]

Lastly, transactional clients too generally want to talk about a variety of legal and nonlegal concerns. Mr. Falconi, for example, might want to talk not only about the tax free exchange but also about what kind of business relationship he should maintain with the seller once the deal is concluded. And attorney's fees and time lag between initial conference and final handshake are concerns that all clients share.

To summarize, a client who enters your office with a new matter, be it litigation or transaction based, usually wants to talk about at least the following four general topics:

    (1) The previous events that have generated the client's concerns.

    (2) The client's objectives.

    (3) The client's ideas for how to achieve the objectives.

    (4) A variety of legal and nonlegal concerns.

When you elicit information from a client in each of these categories, you indeed are engaging in "preliminary problem identification," and learning about a problem from the client's perspective.

As you might imagine, these four categories are not mutually exclusive. For example, a client who asks, "Can I sue them?" may be expressing a thought about a potential solution, as well as raising legal and nonlegal concerns. But the client may have other potential solutions in mind, as well as other concerns. Hence, viewing problems from clients' perspectives generally entails separate inquiry into each of the four general topics.

B. WHY BEGIN WITH PRELIMINARY PROBLEM INDENTIFICATION?

After chit-chat concludes, inquiry about a new matter often begins with your asking a client how you can be of help. In response, a client typically provides a brief description pertaining to two of the four general topics: (1) the events that prompted the client to seek assistance, and (2) the type of assistance the client desires. Thus, if you ask

---

13. Like their litigation counterparts, some transactional clients initially have no solutions in mind. For example, Mr. Falconi may want to unload a piece of property, but be unaware of the possibility of a tax free exchange.

a client, "How may I help you?", you may well receive responses such
as:

"I was injured in an automobile accident and I'd like to have the guy
who hit me pay."

* * *

"My wife died recently and I'd like to make out a new will."

* * *

"My sister-in-law and I are going to open up a travel agency and we'd
like to have a partnership agreement."

All too often, lawyers fail to respond to such initial problem
characterizations by (a) asking a client to elaborate on what the client
has already said, or (b) asking a client for information pertaining to
aspects of a problem a client does not initially mention. Rather than
attempting to obtain a picture of a problem as a client sees it, many
lawyers almost immediately begin to gather data which they believe to
be legally significant. For example, in response to the initial characterizations above, many lawyers might respond: "Tell me about the
accident;" "Why don't you start by giving me a list of relatives and
your property;" "What terms have you and your sister-in-law worked
out so far?" Starting so quickly down the trail of legal relevance is
almost always a *mistake*. Instead, begin data gathering with "preliminary problem identification."

Even conceding the importance of viewing problems from a client's
perspective, why is it important to gain that perspective so early in a
conference? Several reasons exist. First, fully understanding a client's
problem helps you decide what information to gather.[14] A client's
initial statement of objectives often is misleading. For example, a
client may use wrong terminology. The client above who asked for the
"will," for instance, may really be interested in an inter vivos trust, but
he might be unfamiliar with that term. Similarly, a client may
initially ask for the wrong type of relief. For example, the travel agent
client who asked for a "partnership agreement" might be better served
by doing business in the corporate form. Finally, if a client fails to
state an objective, you may impute a wrong one, thereby wasting time
and frustrating the client. For example, you may assume that the
client injured in the automobile accident wants to sue and immediately
pursue that option. However, if what the client really had in mind was
making a claim against the client's own carrier, most of the questions
would be largely irrelevant.

---

14. Data from the medical field shows
that doctors are continually misdiagnosing
their patients problems because they do
not allow them to *fully* explain their problem in the first instance. See F.W. Platt &
J.C. McMath, "Clinical Hypocompetence:
The Interview," 91 Ann.Intern.Med. 898,
900–01 (1979); H. Beckman & R. Frankel,
"The Effect of Physician Behavior on the
Collection of Data," 101 Ann.Intern.Med.
692, 694 (1984); V.M. Riccardi, & S.M.
Jurtz, *Communication and Counseling in
Health Care* 88–91 (1983).

Second, preliminary problem identification may help you avoid "premature diagnosis." [15] If you allow one or two scraps of data to control initial information-gathering, you may at best waste a good deal of time by trying to solve the wrong problem. Since during preliminary problem identification a client does most of the talking, you get a fuller picture of a client's problem and are less likely to rush to premature diagnosis.

A third reason for beginning with preliminary problem identification is that clients typically are more responsive to subsequent inquiries if they can first explain their problems. Think about your own experiences as a patient in a doctor's office. If a doctor asks numerous questions before you fully explain what is bothering you, you are more likely to be thinking about how to explain your problem than fully responding to the doctor's questions. Similarly, if you start to question Mrs. Bishop about Young's threat to stop construction before hearing that Mrs. Bishop is very concerned about attorney fees, Mrs. Bishop may be reluctant to provide information. Concerned about how much she may have to pay, and perhaps uncertain that she even wants to be represented by you or any other lawyer, she may not want to disclose details about her problem.

Fourth, from the outset you demonstrate empathy and build rapport when you encourage clients to describe their problems. Most people like and trust a helping professional who they believe understands their problem completely.[16] By establishing rapport, you motivate a client to provide information and to participate actively in the process of formulating and selecting solutions. Given that rapport is such an important element in an attorney-client relationship, it makes sense to begin to develop it as early as possible.

Lastly, preliminary problem identification can serve as a metaphorical string around your finger. Remember that a client comes to you not merely for technical legal advice, but for help in finding a solution that responds to the fullest extent to the client's unique legal and nonlegal concerns. Encouraging a client to describe, at the outset, both a problem and the client's concerns focuses you immediately on what is ultimately important and reminds you of the full range of a client's concerns throughout each attorney-client relationship.

15. See Chapter 6, sec. 3(B)(4).

16. See R.L. Kahn & C.F. Cannell, *The Dynamics of Interviewing* 46–48 (1957); J. Pietrofesa, A. Hoffman, H. Splete, D. Pinto, *Counseling: Theory, Research, and Practice* 195–96 (1978) [hereinafter Pietrofesa]; Cf. B.M. Korsch & V.F. Negrete, "Doctor-Patient Communication," 227 Sci.Am. 66 (Aug. 1972) (Using jargon and not fully heeding the patient's concerns leads to dissatisfaction for both patient and physician.); Cf. *Missouri Bar Prentice–Hall Survey 65–69 (1963).*

C. THE PROCESS OF PRELIMINARY PROBLEM IDENTIFICATION

The process of preliminary problem identification usually begins with an open-ended question calling for a narrative description of a client's problem. Questions such as the following are typical:

"How can I help you?"

"What brings you here today?"

"What can I do for you?"

Such open-ended questions allow a client to set forth a problem in any manner which feels comfortable and in as much detail as to the client seems appropriate. The open questions tend to facilitate rapport by permitting a client to avoid threatening topics and giving recognition that what the client has to say is important. Also, a client's narrative description of a problem allows you to interject passive or active listening responses, thereby building rapport and empathy.

The open form of question notwithstanding, clients often respond rather tersely. For example, a client may say, "I was injured in an automobile accident and I'd like to have the guy who hit me pay." Do not think to yourself, "My client has had a chance to narrate; now it's time to fire closed questions." Encourage narration by using additional open probes. For example, you might say, "Perhaps you can tell me a bit more." Or, you might interject an active listening response. Or, you might do both: "You still seem pretty upset about the accident. Can you tell me more about it?"

By themselves, open questions do not explicitly suggest your interest in obtaining a description of the four general topics which constitute the client's problem—triggering events, desired objectives, ideas for achieving the objectives, and concerns. Therefore, you might consider giving a client a brief *structural guide* to encourage a client to talk about each of these topics. Consider the following examples of structural guides:

"Can you give me a brief description of your problem, how it arose, and what solution you hope to find?"

* * *

"Please start by giving me a description of your problem, whatever concerns you have, and how you'd like things to come out."

* * *

"Tell me what your problem is, how it came about, and what you'd like to have done about it."

You can insert such a guide into a dialogue immediately after an initial open question and before a client's initial response. Or, you might wait until after a client's initial reply or two to open questions if the open questions alone are not eliciting fully descriptive responses.

The purpose of a structural guide is not to test a client's ability to remember each of the four topics. Thus, you might ask a separate question about each topic. For example, at one point during preliminary problem identification you might ask a client about objectives, and later ask about concerns. For example, these structural guides focus solely on a client's objectives:

"How would you like to see this situation turn out?"

* * *

"If you could write your own ticket about this situation, what would it look like?"

* * *

"What resolution would you like to see?"

You may be reluctant to inquire about desired objectives when an objective seems so obvious that you feel you would appear foolish by asking. For example, when a client has been sued in a civil action, the client's desired outcome seems quite apparent—dismissal of the case in the next 5 minutes without paying a nickel. Surely the client will question your sanity if you ask, "How would you like this to turn out?" But, as noted above, your assumption may be wrong. Not every defendant in a civil case wants complete vindication without paying for any injury the plaintiff may have suffered. Defendants sometimes feel partly responsible for harm to a plaintiff and will be willing to pay something. Similarly, not every client about to enter into a "deal" wants the best possible price. Business people, perhaps to preserve a long term relationship, save legal fees, or for other reasons, often will agree to terms that are less favorable than they might have insisted on. Hence, rather than overlooking entirely a client's desired outcome when it seems obvious, you might at least check out your assumption:

"I gather that in this case, you want the suit terminated without paying anything to the plaintiff. Am I correct?"

* * *

"I take it that you do not want the lease to include a rent escalation clause. Am I right?"

Usually, a client will agree with your assumption. Other times, you will be glad that you took a moment to check one out at the preliminary problem identification stage:

"No, I think we should go along with an escalation clause if they ask for one; the clause is so standard in this kind of lease that if we try to avoid it, I'm afraid they'll get the idea that we are going to be hard nosed at every turn. If they get that idea who knows what might happen; it's just not a risk I feel comfortable with." [17]

Better a brief bit of embarrassment than the icy silence which may follow your question near the end of a conference which begins, "What? You mean what you really want is . . .?"

Just as potential embarrassment may cause you to shy away from the topic of seemingly-obvious objectives, so too may it lead you to avoid

17. Of course, there is a third possibility: a client may indicate that your assumption is only partially correct. The lease client may state, for example, "I don't feel a rent escalation clause is warranted, but I'll agree to a minor one just to keep the negotiations going smoothly."

a discussion of seemingly-obvious concerns. For example, a shopowner whose landlord has refused to extend a shopping center lease obviously is worried about whether she will be able to stay in business. Similarly, a client who seeks a liquor license for his new restaurant obviously is concerned about adequate revenue. Again, check out your assumptions rather than avoid concerns that seem obvious. If your assumptions are wrong, better to find out during preliminary discussion of a problem than trying to solve the wrong problem. Also, a client's description of concerns typically allows you to make empathic responses, thereby building rapport.

To check assumptions about concerns, use the "verification" approach illustrated above: "It seems a major concern you have in wanting the liquor license is making sure the restaurant generates adequate income."

Somewhat different issues may arise when you attempt to elicit information about what course of action a client has in mind. Clients who know what outcomes they desire, and who can articulate their concerns, may yet have no idea about what steps might achieve their objectives. For example, if you ask, "Can you tell me what solutions, if any, you have in mind?", you may get a response such as, "I don't know what to do; that's why I'm coming to you." Such a statement conveys two thoughts: the client does not know how to solve a problem, and the client expects you to know how. Thus, asking a client what solutions he or she has in mind may embarrass a client and lead a client to wonder what you envision your job to be.

Do not, therefore, assume that a client will have thought about and can articulate possible solutions. Look first for clues that suggest that a client has ideas about possible solutions.[18] The absence of such clues does not mean you must abandon thoughts of asking a client for the client's ideas about how to solve a problem. Instead, consider prefacing your inquiry with an explanation that indicates that eventually you intend to suggest potential solutions, but that your experience is that clients often have good ideas of their own:

> "When I have gotten a fuller picture of what is involved here, I'll go over with you some options that might make the most sense in your situation. However, sometimes I find that clients have their own notions about how to best resolve a matter and I can be most helpful if I start out knowing them. Do you have some ideas about how we might best approach this situation?"

If your inquiry about solutions is greeted with a, "That's why I'm coming to you"–type response, empathize with the client's concern and, if you have not done so already, explain why you want to elicit information about solutions the client may have in mind. Also, empha-

---

18. Clues may include a client's general level of intelligence; the extent to which a client's responses indicate that the client has invested time thinking about a problem; a client's openness in answering questions; and the like.

size that you will discuss the matter of solutions when more information has been developed:

> "I can understand your desire for me to tell you what to do. But what might be best for one client might not be best for another. I asked the question because I find it very helpful to have your thoughts in mind while I am learning more about your situation. After I have more information, we will definitely talk in detail about how your situation might be resolved. So before I turn to the details, why don't you let me know any thoughts you have . . .."

In sum, throughout the process of preliminary problem identification, except when checking "obvious assumptions," use open-ended questions, active listening and structural guides to encourage a client to continue describing a problem until you feel you fully understand it from the client's perspective.

A useful way to conclude preliminary problem identification is with an active listening response summarizing a client's problem.[19] Your summary may briefly review what you have learned, and refer to each of the four general topics which together constitute the problem:

> "So, the situation is that your landlord wants you out, you'd like to remain, and you're concerned that the sheriff will take everything you have if you don't leave right away. And you feel that as we go through the facts we should keep in mind your idea of using the neighborhood mediation service as a possible method to resolve this matter."

> * * *

> "You want to acquire control of ABC Realty if you can do so through a tax free exchange. You're worried not only about the tax aspects but also about tying Mr. Zolton, ABC's president, to the company for at least a year." [20]

Brief summaries of this sort take early and maximum advantage of the facilitator of empathic understanding. A summary assures a client that you have heard and understood the principal aspects of a problem. The summary completes the groundwork for your more active role in the ensuing data-gathering stage of the relationship.

D. PRELIMINARY PROBLEM IDENTIFICATION PERMITS ONLY A TENTATIVE DIAGNOSIS

No matter how open and forthcoming a client is during preliminary problem identification, any diagnosis you may make of a problem is usually a tentative one. For one thing, problems are dynamic; they tend to shrink and expand. Hence, over the course of nearly every matter, a client's objectives and concerns change.

For example, assume that Martina Perez retains you to defend her in an action brought by Henry Dexter. Dexter's complaint seeks damages and an injunction on the ground that Perez's operation of an

---

19. Note that this active listening response will usually reflect the *content* of what the client has told you.

20. Remember that not every client in describing the problem will suggest possible solutions.

advertising business violated an anti-competition clause contained in a purchase agreement between Perez and Dexter. The agreement had been signed when Dexter bought out Perez's share of an advertising business in which the two had been partners. During preliminary problem identification, Perez's principal concern was to resolve the matter as quickly as possible, even if it meant paying Dexter off. Perez feared that if word of the lawsuit got out, her business reputation would be hurt and she would lose clients. A few days later, however, Perez calls you and states that she is no longer anxious to resolve Dexter's claim. According to Perez, many people already know about the lawsuit, and most have the opinion that Dexter is making a false claim to save his own failing business. In fact, Perez now wants to sue Dexter for abuse of process. Thus, as is so often the case, changes in the environment (people in the relevant industry becoming aware of the lawsuit and siding with Perez) affected the client's entire perspective on her problem, including her objectives, proposed solutions and concerns.

Never underestimate the frequency with which sudden and often unforeseen changes in clients' life situations alter problems. Otherwise, you may repeatedly become angry and frustrated when clients who start out with one set of objectives and concerns suddenly have an almost opposite set. A fact of life is that consistency is the exception, not the rule. Almost all of us change our perspectives on problems as our economic and social situations change.

A second reason that you should regard a diagnosis as tentative is that, as suggested in Chapter 4, clients (especially new ones) are often reluctant to reveal private and deep concerns at the inception of an initial meeting. Clients may not trust you with sensitive concerns until they feel genuine rapport with you, and that may not exist during the early days of a relationship. Third, quite apart from conscious withholding, many clients have rather narrow perspectives on their problems at the time of an initial conference. For example, a client may be so emotionally entangled in a dispute that the client is in a muddle about all four aspects of a problem, even including what events precipitated it and what outcome the client desires. Or, a problem may have surfaced so recently that a client has not had time to sort out her or his thoughts. For instance, assume that Syd, who owns a large and successful aluminum fabricating plant, receives an offer from a publicly held company to purchase his entire business two days before consulting with you. Under the circumstances, Syd may well not have had time to identify options and concerns.

Lastly, sometimes clients misperceive the source of their concerns. An automobile accident victim may identify the collision as the source of his or her continued medical worries, when the source in fact may have been medical malpractice by the physician who treated the client following the accident. Similarly, business clients who are in poor financial condition might view their customers' failures to make timely payments as the source of their money problems when in fact the source is monopolistic prices charged by their suppliers.

Because preliminary problem identification rarely permits more than a tentative diagnosis, you typically are not ready to discuss possible solutions during this stage of an initial meeting. However, you do generally emerge with a sense of how a client views a problem and the kind of information you need to gather in order to help a client explore possible solutions.

E. PRELIMINARY PROBLEM IDENTIFICATION FOLLOWING TELEPHONE CONVERSATIONS

Often, you first learn about a problem through a telephone call. When that happens, all or much of preliminary problem identification may take place during that phone call. For example, if you know a client well, or perhaps if you both own a "picturephone," initial information-gathering may be by phone even if you both contemplate a subsequent non-electronic meeting.

With a new client, trying to understand a client's perspective during an impersonal telephone call is usually not a good idea. In such instances, you are usually best off limiting an initial phone call to a few general questions like, "Tell me a bit about the problem," and "What do you have in mind?" You can thereby satisfy a client's immediate need to express concerns and your need to make sure a problem is one that you are competent to handle. Also, tell a new client during an initial phone call what documents or records to bring to a subsequent meeting.[21]

When you later meet a new client personally, apart from whatever brief references to the phone call are appropriate, you generally conduct an initial meeting as though you are talking to the client for the first time. Ask a client to restate whatever triggering events, concerns and potential solutions the client may have mentioned on the phone.[22] The client may have different thoughts and feelings in person than over the phone. And, whatever a client's perspective on a problem was on the phone, it may change in the days and sometimes weeks between phone call and initial meeting.

F. EXAMPLES FOR ANALYSIS

The three preliminary problem identification dialogues which follow will help you apply the principles set forth above to actual situations. In each dialogue, assume that "chit-chat" has concluded. As you read through each dialogue, think about what strikes you as

21. If a new client is extremely distressed, or will be unable to see you in person for some time, you may feel that it makes sense to conduct a lengthier preliminary problem identification dialogue over the phone. Of course, if a client seeks legal help elsewhere, or decides not to consult a lawyer at all, you may never get paid for your time.

22. These three topics may well come up during most initial telephone contacts. Less often, we think, are you likely to ask a client what course of action the client has thought about.

effective or ineffective. Our analysis follows the first two dialogues; analysis of the third is for you.

Case No. 1:

1. L: Mr. Cabello, why don't you start by simply telling me what is on your mind.

2. C: My mother died about four months ago. When she passed away she and my stepfather owed me some money, and now my stepfather won't pay me.

3. L: How much money does he owe you?

4. C: Oh, I guess about $15,000.

5. L: Has he signed a promissory note or anything in writing?

6. C: No.

7. L: How recently have you asked him for the money?

8. C: About a month ago.

9. L: What did he say?

10. C: He said he'd pay me when he could.

11. L: So you want to know if you're entitled to sue him to get the money back?

12. C: I guess so.

13. L: Besides the question of your right to get the money, are there other matters that are of concern to you?

14. C: Not really.

15. L: Are you sure?

16. C: Yes.

17. L: Are you worried about the possibility of a family squabble?

Analysis:

In No. 1 you encourage the client to talk generally. But you fail to employ a structural guide requesting a general description of the underlying transaction and the client's objectives and concerns.

In Nos. 3, 5, 7, and 9, you probe for specific details about the underlying transaction. Given that you will necessarily pursue these specific details later, these questions seem unnecessary at this preliminary stage. Moreover, these narrow questions may be distracting to the client, since they may not relate to the problem from his perspective. If you felt the need for more factual description, you could have employed a direct probe such as, "Tell me a little bit more about the situation."

In No. 11, you switch to the issues of objectives and solutions. However, instead of inquiring about what outcome the client desires, through a leading question you virtually decide that the client's aim is return of the money and that the best course of action is a lawsuit. Perhaps the client had other goals in mind or was thinking about another solution, such as renegotiating the loan and obtaining a security agreement. Not every potential plaintiff wants a lawsuit.

No. 13, however, is a useful open question which attempts to obtain a general description of the client's concerns. It recognizes that the client may have more than one worry. No. 17, on the other hand seems less appropriate. Rather than being an open inquiry into other concerns, No. 17 is a narrow question that fishes for a very specific concern. Especially during the early stages of a conference, before rapport is established, a client such as Mr. Cabello may be reluctant to talk about a potential family squabble even if that is one of his concerns.

Reviewing the dialogue as a whole, note that you do not treat the topics of concerns, objectives and solutions as distinct subjects. In No. 11, for example, which of these three topics do you have in mind? While there are no "magic words" to use to identify these topics, you should give a client a chance to address each topic separately if the client is to have a full opportunity to explain a problem as he or she sees it.

Case No. 2:

1. L: Now, Mr. Montgomery, how might I help you?

2. C: Well, I've been arrested, and I don't know what to do. Nothing like this has ever happened to me before.

3. L: I can tell you're quite concerned about the situation. I'd really like to help. Perhaps it would be best if you told me a little bit more about the situation—you know, how the arrest came about.

4. C: Well, they say I'm guilty of shoplifting over at Sears on 48th Street.

5. L: Can you tell me a little bit more about that?

6. C: Well, as I was near a store exit they stopped me and searched my jacket. They took out the calculator I was going to buy, and then they arrested me. I was going to pay for the calculator.

7. L: Okay, that gives me a good start on what happened. I'll get more details in a little while. I assume that if you could dictate how this would turn out, that you would have the charges against you dismissed as quickly as possible. Am I correct on this point?

8. C: Absolutely.

9. L: Are there other results you'd like to obtain besides a dismissal of the charges?

10. C: Could I get the people who arrested me to pay what it cost me to get out of jail?

11. L: That is certainly something we can try to accomplish, but I'll need more information before I can give you an answer. However, before I get to my questions, why don't you tell me about any concerns you have that I haven't discussed? Are there other things you are worried about that you'd like to talk about?

12. C: Well, sort of; I'm worried about my job.

13. L: I can understand how that would be a concern. Any other concerns I should have in mind?

14. C: Not really.

15. L: So the situation is that you've been arrested for shoplifting at Sears, and of course you want the charges dismissed. In addition, you would like to have Sears pay for your costs, and you're also concerned about how all of this may affect your job.

16. C: Yes, that's it; you've put it quite well.

17. L: As I said, I'm going to need a great deal more information from you before I can answer your questions. But before I turn to my questions, let me go into one other thing that's often worthwhile to talk about before we get into the details. I assume that you'd like me to work out how to proceed to best accomplish what you'd like. But sometimes I find clients have useful ideas about how to approach a case and I was wondering if you have any notions about how we should proceed so that we can get the charges dismissed and have Sears pay?

Analysis:

In No. 1, you begin appropriately with an open question. When it elicits only minimal information, you attempt in No. 3 to elicit further factual information. No. 3's active listening response demonstrates that you understand the client's feelings. Additionally, you attempt to reassure the client by expressing a willingness to help. You then provide a structural guide which asks for elaboration of the triggering events: "Perhaps it would be best if you told me a little more about the situation—you know, how the arrest came about." The request for elaboration does not press for details. Instead, it is quite open, giving the client leeway to describe in terms comfortable to the client what, in all probability, is an ego-threatening event. No. 5 is another appropriately open probe.

After Mr. Montgomery identifies the triggering transaction (No. 6), you turn to his likely objectives. In No. 7, you check out the correctness of your assumption that Mr. Montgomery's goal is to avoid a conviction. Then in No. 9, albeit through a narrow question, you recognize the possibility of other objectives and provide the client with an opportunity to state them.

In No. 11, after acknowledging the client's second goal of being recompensed, you use an open question to move to the separate subject of concerns. Both the open question and the separate discussion of objectives and concerns seem appropriate. However, before moving to the topic of concerns, you might have stayed a bit longer with the subject of objectives. Mr. Montgomery might have other objectives besides avoiding a conviction and being reimbursed for the expenses of getting out of jail.

Your treatment of Mr. Montgomery's potential concerns, however, is more thorough. Nos. 11 and 13 are both open questions seeking the client's concerns, and only after receiving the "not really" answer in No. 14 do you move to a new subject.

No. 13 bears further analysis. You state, "I can understand how that would be a concern. Are there any other concerns I should have in mind?" Though you perhaps have never faced a problem with a job because of an arrest, the client will probably accept the response as sincere and not patronizing. Apart from your actual experience, having a job affected by an arrest for a crime one feels he or she did not commit is a concern with which everyone would be familiar.

Note also in No. 13 that after empathizing with the client's plight, you ask about "other concerns." Yet, all you know is that the client is worried about "his job." Perhaps you assume that Mr. Montgomery is worried about losing his job. But quite possibly, his concern is losing a promotion or loss of face with co-workers. These concerns are quite different and knowledge of his actual concern undoubtedly would assist your ability to counsel your client. Hence, while preliminary problem identification is not the time to exhaust the topics a client raises, you might have asked in No. 13, instead of about "other concerns," "Tell me a little bit more about your concern with your job."

No. 15, an active listening summary of Mr. Montgomery's problem, informs him that you have heard and understood his problem.

Finally, No. 17 switches to the topic of solutions. Should you have raised that topic in this case? In any event, what do you think of the approach? Is this a situation where the client's likely reaction might be of the "That's what I'm coming to you for" genre? Is your explanation adequate to minimize the chances of such a reaction?

Case No. 3:

1. L: Ms. Rose, why don't you start by telling me what's on your mind?

2. C: Well, I have a small gold plating business. What I think I'd like to do is set up a pension plan of some type for my long-time employees.

3. L: You're considering providing retirement benefits for loyal employees. But it sounds as though you are not sure that's what you should do.

4. C: That's right.

5. L: How many employees are we talking about?

6. C: I have twenty employees but I'm only concerned about five or six.

7. L: How long have these people been with you?

8. C: They've all been with me for over six years.

9. L: How about the other employees; how long have they worked for you?

10. C: There's a real gap. Probably no one else has been there for more than three years.

11. L: Could you tell me why the notion of a pension plan is on your mind at this point? What prompted you to think about it now?

12. C: Well there have been a couple of things. First, it's time I started thinking about my retirement. Also, I recently lost a very good employee because we didn't have a plan; he went to work for a competitor who provided benefits. I don't want my other good employees to do the same thing.

13. L: Are there particular things that concern you in thinking about setting up a pension plan?

14. C: Nothing other than can I afford it.

15. L: So as I understand it what you'd like to do is set up a pension plan for your senior people provided you feel you could afford it. Have I stated the situation correctly?

Analysis:

Analyze for yourself the effectiveness of this preliminary problem identification dialogue. The following questions may aid your analysis:

1. Is No. 1 appropriately open, or is it perhaps too vague?

2. Assuming No. 2 was delivered in a tone of voice that indicated uncertainty, in what way, if any, would you alter No. 3?

3. Nos. 5, 7 and 9 are narrow questions. They ask for specific information rather than calling for an elaboration. Are these inquiries therefore inappropriate at this point?

4. Assuming that No. 11 represents the beginning of an attempt to identify the triggering transaction, how, if at all, could you have modified this inquiry?

5. How adequately did you cover the topic of the client's concerns?

6. What additional questions, if any, could you have asked regarding the client's objectives?

7. How accurate was your summary (No. 15)?

8. What additional topics, if any, would you have explored with the client during the problem identification stage?

5. BEGINNING FOLLOW-UP MEETINGS

Rarely is an attorney-client relationship confined to an initial conference. Over the phone and/or in person, you will usually review a matter with a client on a number of occasions. As you can undoubtedly imagine, the variety of circumstances giving rise to follow-up meetings makes a "standard" client-centered approach to their beginnings unrealistic.[23] Beginning most initial conferences with preliminary problem identification is sensible; no comparable standard goal for the beginnings of follow-up meetings exist. Nevertheless, the considerations set forth in this section may help you get follow-up meetings off on the right foot.

A. THE BACKDROP

To think about how to begin a follow-up meeting, consider first how a matter typically stands at the conclusion of an initial meeting. During a typical initial conference, you preliminarily identify a client's problem, probe for additional information, and chart at least a preliminary course of action.[24] At its conclusion, both you and a client usually have a number of tasks to perform. You may have to do some legal research, talk to witnesses or other third parties, and write letters. A client may have to gather and send documents to you, give you the names of additional people to contact and contact others personally. In addition, a problem may change between the time of an initial and a follow-up meeting. Your investigation may uncover information or legal doctrine which affects a problem. A client may learn new information which changes the nature of a problem. Also, in the interim, some of a client's initial concerns may vanish, and others may appear.

A portion of a typical follow-up interview, then, consists of (a) lawyer and client reporting on the tasks they were to perform; and (b) lawyer and client discussing in what way a problem has changed.[25] Often, these matters constitute the beginning of a typical follow-up discussion. They normally precede other aspects of follow-up discussions, such as your asking questions and counseling with respect to potential solutions. However, even this very general conception of the "beginning" and the "middle" of follow-up meetings is mushy. A potential solution, for example, may in a given case be so important that it demands immediate discussion. Similarly, a discussion may be preceded by a client's having sent you documents on a particular issue, and you may begin by discussing that issue.

23. Perhaps the only feature common to the beginning of perhaps every follow-up meeting is "chit-chat." At least, by the time of a follow-up meeting you have a more informed basis for deciding how much chit-chat a client will appreciate.

24. Chapter 13 examines approaches for concluding initial and subsequent client meetings.

25. Follow-up discussions may be in person or over the phone; in general, our comments regarding follow-up interviews apply equally to both.

Assume, as we must if we are to say anything sensible at all, that nothing extremely dramatic occurs between an initial and a follow-up meeting. The subsections below briefly examine the subjects that are typically explored at the beginning of follow-up meetings, and the age-old question, "Who goes first—lawyer or client?"

B. A CLIENT'S CHANGED CONCERNS AND OBJECTIVES

As you know, clients' concerns and objectives often change after an initial meeting. Changes in a client's economic or social situation may lead to new worries. Further reflection, or even the stray comment at a cocktail party, may bring to mind new concerns. Whatever the source, new concerns may replace those of earlier discussions or only supplement them. Therefore, for the same reasons you ask about concerns at the beginning of an initial interview, you may often inquire about new concerns at the beginning of a follow-up interview. For this purpose, you might ask,

"Have any new concerns or worries arisen since the last time we spoke?"

If a client does have new concerns, they may give rise to new or altered objectives. Hence, when a client does indicate that he or she has concerns that are substantially different from any voiced earlier, you may want to inquire whether the new concerns have altered the client's initial objectives. Again, a straightforward question may help a client sort through his or her thoughts:

"This is the first time you've mentioned anything about your need to conclude this matter quickly. In view of this concern, do you have any different thoughts about what we should try to accomplish?"

C. A CLIENT'S NEW INFORMATION

Frequently, a client acquires new data bearing on a problem. For instance, a client may learn of a new witness. Or, if you are negotiating a real estate purchase for a client, the client may learn that the seller is in desperate need of money because the seller has already agreed to purchase another property. New factual data may alter a client's legal rights in a litigation situation, the potential outcome in a transactional matter, and a client's concerns in all matters. Hence, inquiring about new information at the beginning of a follow-up interview prevents you from proceeding on the basis of incomplete information.

Again, a straightforward question is an appropriate means of inquiry:

"Have you learned anything new since the last time we met?"

Keep in mind that an inquiry about new information is distinct from one about new concerns. A client may have new information without having new concerns, and vice versa. Therefore, avoid a question such as, "Has anything new come up since we last met, or do you have any new concerns?" The question is confusingly compound and is no more desirable in the law office than in the courtroom. It is also vague; does "anything new" refer to information, concerns or both? Also, by inquiring about the two topics in the one question, you might signal that you are not terribly interested in the client's response. Hence, to encourage a client to think seriously about each topic separately, make each the subject of a separate question.

D. YOUR INTERIM ACTIVITY

Hosts of materials, ranging from Dickens' *Bleak House* to everyday newspaper and television stories, make people wary of legal matters that drag on seemingly endlessly. While the image of legal delay is perhaps most pronounced in litigation matters, the image affects transactional matters as well. Hence, you bolster a client's confidence by early on during a follow-up conference telling a client what actions you have undertaken and what you have accomplished. Clients usually perceive lawyers who actively work on cases as interested, concerned and competent.[26]

All well and good, you may say, but what if you have done nothing in the interim, or what you have done has produced little or no concrete gains? Generally, clients appreciate their lawyers keeping them informed.[27] Hence, if you have not taken any action since a prior meeting, say so and indicate when the client can expect a new development:

> "I haven't had a chance to get together with Graham's attorney yet; he's been tied up out of town, apparently. But we've scheduled a meeting for next Wednesday, and I'll call you Wednesday evening and let you know if we've ironed out the remaining disagreements."

Usually, the same policy of disclosure applies when the actions you have taken have gained little:

> "I did take the deposition of InterState's Vice-President, and as we figured, she claimed not to have seen the audit. But she did mention a couple of things that should prove useful; we can talk about those later. Meanwhile . . .."

For too long, lawyers have not been sufficiently cognizant of how deleterious an effect failing to keep a client up to date on what is happening can have on the entire attorney-client relationship.[28] You have an obligation to keep clients informed, and the beginning of a

---

26. See, e.g., *Missouri Bar Survey, supra* note 16, at 65–69.

27. See, *Missouri Bar Survey, supra* note 16, at 65–69; D.E. Rosenthal, *Lawyer and Client: Who's In Charge?* 20 & 51 (1974); R.E. Mallen & J.M. Smith, *Legal Malpractice* 185–87 (3d ed. 1989).

28. See, e.g., L.P. Peterson, "Keep the Customers Satisfied–Suggestions for Client Retention and Satisfaction," 7 The Bottom

Line 3 (Apr. 1985), as reprinted in *Establishing and Maintaining Effective Attorney–Client Relationships* (Cal.CEB 1985); W. Bailey, "The Attorney/Client Relationship—The Hidden Dimension of Advocacy," 8 Trial Dipl.J. 17 (Fall 1985); Annotations, "Failure to Communicate with Client as Basis for Disciplinary Action Against Attorney," 80 A.L.R.3d 1240 (1989).

follow-up conference is an excellent time to summarize what you have done since last speaking to a client.

E.   YOUR NEW INFORMATION [29]

A number of reasons support your telling a client during an early stage of a follow-up discussion about information you have learned since a prior discussion.   New information may alleviate one or more of the client's previously expressed concerns.   Also, the new information may bolster a client's confidence by demonstrating that you have been working on a problem.[30]   That confidence in turn typically encourages a client to work more closely with you to achieve a satisfying result.[31]   Finally, even if your news is bad, presenting that news early on seems important.   The new information may cause a client to reassess her or his objectives.[32]   Hence, good or bad, you should ordinarily disclose new information early in a follow-up interview.

To provide a client with new information, proceed in a very direct manner:

> "I've got some good news for you.   Since we last spoke, I talked with Ms. Hamilton at the bank.   She told me that the bank is prepared to go ahead with the takeout loan even if Interstate does file suit."

Sometimes you will not want to set forth new information at the beginning of a follow-up meeting.   For example, you may have gathered quite a bit of it, say through taking depositions or interviewing an expert, and you plan to organize the bulk of the conference around a discussion of the new information.   In such a situation, you may reassure a client at the outset that you do have new information and state that you will get to it after clearing away other beginning matters:

> "Ms. Daar, since our last meeting I've completed the depositions of the assistant manager and the cashier.   In a few moments I'd like to go over what they said in detail with you.   But before we get to that, have you come up with any new information since we last spoke?"

F.   ORDER OF DISCUSSION

Thus far, you have been advised to begin a follow-up conference by talking about a client's new information and concerns, and your new information and actions.   Either you and a client will have to talk very fast and loud, or you will have to choose with which beginning to begin.

29.   Often there will be overlap between the categories of "activity" and "information."   That is, activity often produces information.   But activity often has no informational aspect: it may consist, for example, of scheduling depositions.   And the contrary may also be true: you may garner information without engaging in activity.   For example, you may receive a report from an investigator or an accountant.

30.   See *Missouri Bar Survey, supra* note 16, at 119–20; Center for Professional Responsibility of the ABA, *Avoiding Client Grievances* 6–9 (1988).

31.   See Rosenthal, *supra* note 28, at 20 & 168–69.   See, generally, S.S. Clawar, *You & Your Clients* 19–29 (1988).

32.   For examination of how you might discuss bad news, see Chapter 13, sec. 3(D).

Obviously, your judgment about where to begin will depend on the dynamics of individual matters and the resulting priority of one of these topics over the others. All else being equal, however, you might wish to start by asking a client if the client has any new concerns, and then any new information, before you relate your new information to the client. Doing so allows a client to voice concerns at once. And, if a client is waiting anxiously to reveal a new concern, the client may pay less attention to what you are saying. Moreover, allowing clients to speak first often boosts their self-esteem and builds empathy.

6. PREPARATORY EXPLANATIONS

* * *

Mr. Jackson, am I correct in saying that what you'd like to do today is determine the best way for you and Mr. Richards to organize the insurance agency that the two of you contemplate opening?

That's right. Should we have a corporation or what? That's what I'd like to know.

Before I can fully answer your question, I'll first need to get some more information from you about your existing operation, Mr. Richard's existing business, and the proposed business the two of you intend to establish. I think we should be able to cover most of what I need to know this afternoon, although I may have to get back to you with some additional questions after we finish today. When we wrap up our conversation, which will probably be in another forty-five minutes or so, we can begin exploring the various options that would be available to you in setting up the new business.

* * *

The situation as I understand it, Ms. Gooden, is that you'd like to enjoin Xray Corp. from distributing these ABC software packages and put the issue of damages on the back burner. Is that right?

Exactly. We don't want to become involved in a lengthy trial about the amount of damages we may have suffered. What we want, as quickly as we can get it, is a permanent injunction.

Okay, let me start to get into the facts so that I'll have a basis for letting you know what I think your chances are of obtaining an injunction. The way I find it most helpful to approach the facts is for a client to first take me through the facts chronologically from the beginning right up to the present. When I've gotten the chronology, I'll then go back and ask some more detailed questions. Finally, since you were specifically concerned about fees, I'll try to give you a more accurate estimate of how much it is likely to cost to secure a permanent injunction. Do you have any questions?

* * *

OK, as you know from the letter that I sent you, the ones with the various charts attached to it, what we're going to do today is decide as much as we can what terms the inter vivos trust will have. We'll talk specifically about which of your children should be the first successor trustee, or whether it would make more sense to name them co-successor trustees. Then we'll have to think about whether you want to leave property free of encumbrances. The last major decision we have is which charity you want to be the ultimate beneficiary. As I promised you, I've set aside an hour for the discussion.

* * *

After a client describes a problem from his or her perspective, an initial conference typically takes on a decidedly more "legal" tone. Though a client may still do much of the talking, your legal knowledge and experience will largely determine the topics a client talks about. In the first example above, the client would be talking about his and his potential partner's business operations. In the second example, the client would be describing events in chronological order. And in the third example, a follow-up meeting, the client will make decisions concerning the terms of an inter vivos trust. Hence, each interview is about to focus on information that the lawyer thinks is particularly significant for solving the client's problem. How you might conduct this more "legal" aspect of meetings is the subject of most of Part III. This section briefly discusses "preparatory explanations," statements that explain to clients what will occur after the "preliminary" portion of a meeting concludes.

Preparatory explanations can preview both the length and content of a meeting, and prepare a client for the activities in which the lawyer and client will engage. Preparatory explanations serve several purposes. First, new and/or inexperienced clients are likely to be put at ease when they understand ahead of time what to expect in a conference.[33] Such clients are likely to be uncertain about such matters as how long a conference will last, when and if you will cover certain topics (e.g., legal fees, "what to tell my accountant", etc.); and whether information is confidential. For example, a client may think, "I can just tell my attorney a few details, get my answer, and get out of here." [34]

To the extent a client is uncertain about what will occur during a meeting, a client's attention will not be entirely on the subject at hand. By stating ahead of time what you intend to explore, and the way you will conduct a conference, you reduce discomfort and help a client concentrate on topics as they arise. And, if an explanation omits mention of a topic of concern to a client, the client can inquire about the omitted topic at once.[35]

Preparatory explanations may also help you avoid problems involving the inhibitor, "role expectations." For example, consider a client's

33. See Kahn & Cannell, *supra* note 16 at 81; A. Ivey & W. Matthews, "A Meta–Model for Structuring the Clinical Interview," 63 J. Counseling & Dev. 237, 238 (1984); Riccardi & Kurtz, *supra* note 14, at 72–75; Pietrofesa, *supra* note 16, at 222–27.

34. Such an attitude is not unrealistic. Certainly many students enter law school believing that they'll be learning cut-and-dried rules that they can select from much like a chef selects a seasoning for a particular dish.

35. Sometimes, to help the client focus fully on the topics one considers important, one will have to reorder one's proposed agenda and take up the client's desired agenda first.

perception of how active or passive the client should be in providing information. Is a client to tell you everything the client believes to be important? Or, should the client provide information only if you specifically request it? Can a client broach possible solutions, or is that your prerogative? Can a client expect you to explore solutions during an initial meeting, or must that discussion wait for another day? When a client's expectations are different from yours, rapport is likely to suffer. For example, if a client believes you will ask specific questions about any topic which is important, and you repeatedly ask open questions, the client may feel annoyed and perhaps even perceive you as incompetent. Preparatory explanations, by informing a client in advance what to expect, may help you prevent loss of rapport produced by divergent role expectations.

However, before you leap to the routine use of lengthy preparatory explanations, consider some drawbacks that may attach to their use. A client who knows what to expect during an interview may react negatively to a detailed explanation, viewing it as unnecessary and patronizing. Similarly, a client who feels that a matter is an emergency may become angry if you launch into a routine, perhaps somewhat lengthy preparatory explanation. Not only will you damage rapport in these circumstances, but the client may not pay close attention to an explanation anyway.

Apart from the brief examples above, model preparatory explanations are unlikely to help you. What you say during a preparatory explanation is largely determined by precise contexts. Some topics perhaps will be "standard." For example, you may always tell a new, unsophisticated client that what the client tells you is confidential. But usually, you will tailor what you say to a particular client, subject matter and case status. For example, if during preliminary problem identification a new client states concern over legal fees, you may tell the client in a preparatory explanation when you will talk about fees. But if a client does not initially mention fees as a concern, you may postpone mention of fees until the conclusion of an initial meeting.[36] Similarly, in the context of an initial interview you may be unable to state in your preparatory explanation precisely what topics you will discuss. In a follow-up meeting, such as in the third example above, you may have particular topics on your agenda, and you may mention them to your client in an explanation. Finally, an explanation that you give a litigation client is likely to differ from one you give to a client with a transactional matter.

Subsequent chapters include a variety of context-specific preparatory explanations. At this point, you need only be aware of reasons for using them, and their potential limitations.

36. For discussion of how you might talk about fees with clients, see Chapter 13, sec. 2(C).

Chapter 8

OBTAINING A TIME LINE

* * *

Mr. Hopkins, after Mr. Markey suggested that you contact Bollinger, what is the next thing that happened?

I called Bill Locklear and told him that Markey had suggested changing the records; I was scared and I wanted advice.

It must have been very upsetting. Markey is your boss and you didn't want to do anything to jeopardize your job. On the other hand, changing records to get rid of a federal inspection team is certainly not something you want to do.

It really was a nightmare.

What happened when you talked with Locklear?

He told me to sit tight and do nothing until he called me back.

What happened next?

Patricia Alvarez called me; she's one of the vice presidents. She said she had spoken to Locklear, and that I should make an appointment with her secretary. I did that and I planned to see her the next day. I think that would have been the tenth. But before I could see her, Bollinger called. He said he had talked with Markey and he was expecting me. I panicked.

That's very understandable. What happened then?

* * *

1. TWO STAGES OF INFORMATION-GATHERING

In litigation matters, without some understanding of how a case is likely to turn out in court, most clients find it difficult to choose which course of action is most satisfactory. Hence, your assessment of likely clients' legal rights typically controls a discussion of potential solutions.

As you recall, much of the information you gather to assess a client's legal rights pertains to past events. The reason is that any substantive legal rule is in effect a "conditional statement referring to

112

facts." [1] That is, rules provide, "If A and B are proved to have occurred, then legal consequence X follows." For instance, in a contract action one rule provides that if two parties enter into an agreement supported by consideration, a contract results. Pursuant to this rule, a plaintiff will produce evidence of past events in an effort to prove that the parties reached an agreement; a defendant will offer a competing version of past events to show that no agreement was reached.

Clients' versions of past events are stories. Stories at trial are in some respects just like those you read in nursery school or hear around the dinner table. They have starting and ending points, and typically consist of what people did, saw, and thought.

However, in other respects, stories at trial are very different from everyday stories. Stories at trial are shaped by such factors as legal principles, your need to combat an adversary's version of past events, and your desire to impress a trier of fact with your clients' credibility. Hence, learning a client's story for purposes of litigation requires much more than asking, "What happened?" It is a complex undertaking which typically is best carried out in two distinct phases: (1) Time Line; and (2) Theory Development and Verification. Consider briefly what each phase entails.

A. TIME LINE PHASE

During the time line phase, you seek a chronological, step-by-step (event by event) narrative of events giving rise to a client's problem. The chronology begins with whatever event a client believes first gave rise to a problem and continues to the time of the initial meeting. The events usually are those a client chooses to include, not ones for which you consciously search. By and large, a time line story is a client's unembellished narrative, refined only by your exhortations to relate the story in chronological fashion.

B. THEORY DEVELOPMENT AND VERIFICATION PHASE

A time line story typically suggests a number of potentially-applicable legal theories. During theory development, such theories prompt a rigorous and systematic search for additional data. The data typically consists of events that a client fails to mention during time line questioning and of details of events, including events that emerge during both time line and theory development questioning.

For example, assume a legal theory makes it important for you to prove on a client's behalf that the defendant was driving too fast immediately prior to colliding with the car driven by your client. During time line questioning, the client describes the collision itself, but says nothing about having spoken to bystanders following the collision. Hence, during theory development, you will probe for details

1. See J. Frank, *Courts on Trial* 14 (Ath. ed. 1971).

about the "collision" event. Additionally, "conversation with a by-stander" is a possibly-omitted event for which you might search. If that event occurred, you might then probe it for details—e.g., what the client and bystander said to each other, when and where the conversation took place, etc.

Sometimes, you proceed to theory development questioning as soon as you elicit a time line story. On other occasions, hours or even days may intervene between the two phases. Which course you follow is likely to depend on numerous factors, such as your familiarity with potentially applicable law, time pressures, and factual complexity. For example, sometimes a quick mental run-through of substantive law will be adequate to enable you to begin probing a time line story. But other times, you may need to engage in legal research before you can begin to probe a story rigorously and systematically.[2]

The time line phase is the subject of this chapter; theory development and verification is the subject of Chapters 9 and 10.

2. WHAT ARE TIME LINE STORIES?

Time line stories have three critical features:

1. They consist of discrete events.
2. The discrete events are chronologically ordered.
3. The discrete events are largely free of specific details.

Few clients, can, without aid, steer a conversational course that produces a story with these three attributes. For most clients, a question such as, "Why don't you start by giving me a time line of events" is unlikely to evoke more than unhappy memories of a high school world history course. Typically, rather than providing a sequential description of discrete events, a client is likely to provide a rather terse, partial description couched in conclusory terms.

Assume that your client is Mrs. West, and that during problem identification she indicates that her problem arose from purchasing a house which turned out to have a leaky roof. When you ask Mrs. West to tell you, step-by-step, everything that happened, starting from the beginning up to the present time, she tells this story:

> We went through the house a couple of times in August, and the sale concluded about September 15th. Then one rainy day, about the middle of November, I came home and found water running down the hall. I went into the second bedroom and saw that the ceiling had collapsed; there was water and plaster everywhere. I didn't know what to do so I called my friend Carol; she recommended a roofer. I called the roofer and got the roof fixed. With the damage to the inside, it cost me $15,000, and I had to get a loan from the bank. I think that the sellers knew about the leak; because when I was having the roof

2. For further discussion of adjourning information-gathering to consider poten-tially-applicable legal theories and develop potential evidence pursuant to those theories, see Chapter 9, sec. 6.

repaired, one of my neighbors, Mr. Harris, indicated that the prior owner had also done roof repairs. When I talked to the sellers, they said they never did anything to the roof.

This description provides a sense of events and chronology, but it is not a time line story. First, the sequence of events is far from clear. For example, when did Mrs. West talk to the sellers about the roof? Was it before, during, or after the roof repairs? Similarly, did Mrs. West arrange for the loan before she agreed to have the roof repaired? Such uncertainties prevent you from understanding the sequence of events.

Second, everyday experience suggests that the story probably omits a number of events. For example, what event or events led up to Mrs. West purchasing the house? How did she arrange for the roof repairs? Did she, as might be common, get several estimates? Also, if, as is often the case, the loan was not the result of a single visit to the bank, how did she arrange for it? Were there any problems with the roof between the time Mrs. West moved in to the house and the time she discovered the leak?

Finally, many seemingly discrete events in the story are "clumped events." [3] Consider Mrs. West's statement, "We went through the house a couple of times." Initially, you might regard "pre-purchase tours of house" as a single occurrence. But each tour probably took place over a period of time, and a variety of events may have occurred in the time period. For example, a conversation may have occurred while Mrs. West was in one room, and a physical examination of walls while she was in another. Without that more discrete focus, any picture you have of what happened on the tours is more likely the result of "filling in" on your part, not anything that Mrs. West actually said. [4]

Mrs. West has been kind enough to retell the first portion of her story in more ideal time line form. Here is her retold tale: [5]

One Sunday, during September, I saw an ad for the house in the Tribune. I telephoned the number listed in the ad and arranged to see the house that afternoon at 2:00 p.m. I left my house early and drove by the house; I wanted to get a sense of the neighborhood before I went inside. I also took some time to go up and down some other streets in the area. When I got to the front door, I met Mr. Rifter. He took me in and introduced me to Mrs. Rifter; he also gave me a little sheet that described the house and gave some information about it. Mr. Rifter then asked me if I would like to go through the house and I said I would. We left the living room, walked through the dining room, and went into the kitchen.

---

3. See D. Binder and P. Bergman, *Fact Investigation: From Hypothesis to Proof* 292 (1984).

4. See Chapter 6, sec. 3(B)(4).

5. Mrs. West's story appears here in uninterrupted narrative form, though in an actual conversation you are likely to interject active or passive listening responses, as well as ask open questions such as "What happened next" to keep the story on the chronological track.

As you can see, in this version of the story discrete events unfold in sequential order. For one thing, the order of the events seems clear. For instance, you understand that Mr. Rifter gave the client a sheet describing the house after he introduced the client to Mrs. Rifter, but before showing Mrs. West through the house.

Second, there are no obvious gaps in the story. For example, Mrs. West accounts for her time from leaving her house to speaking to Mrs. Rifter.

Also, the story consists of discrete as distinguished from "clumped" events. Mrs. West does not merely say, "I met the Rifters." Rather, she mentions meeting Mr. Rifter at the front door, then entering the house and meeting Mrs. Rifter. Similarly, the inspection of the house is dissected into a room by room tour, rather than merely being labeled as "a trip through the house." Yet, as you realistically might expect, the retold story does include some clumped events. Thus, Mrs. West states, "I also took some time to go up and down some other streets in the area." Given people's predilection to group incidents into larger conclusions, it is unlikely that any story of past occurrences will ever be told without the presence of some clumped events. In every day speech, a person will say, "I went to the store" rather than, "I entered the store, picked up a cart, went to the dairy section, then the meat section . . . ." At least the person will do so if he or she expects anyone to listen.

But conversation that might be unnatural in everyday social talk is a necessary part of legal counseling. In part, clients clump together events because they do not recognize the legal significance of discrete events. If you are to elicit a full picture of past events, and to extract evidentiary inferences from those events, you will need to encourage clients to break down clumped events into their component incidents.

Finally, note that Mrs. West's retold story is not overly detailed. She does mention that she went from one room to another, but she does not specify what occurred in each room. Similarly, she mentions that Mr. Rifter handed her a "listing sheet" but she does not proceed to itemize the contents of the sheet.

In sum, the retold time line story provides a chronological overview of discrete events that would allow you to select for further probing during theory development those events which seem particularly significant.

3. WHY BEGIN INFORMATION–GATHERING BY ELICITING A TIME LINE STORY?

"(C)hronological narrative is the spine and the blood stream that brings history closer to 'how it really was' and to a proper understanding of cause and effect."[6]

6. B.W. Tuchman, *Practicing History* 9
(1981).

After preliminarily identifying a client's problem, you might consider a variety of methods for gathering information. Without pursuing any particular legal theories, you might ask a client to tell you everything that the client believes to be important. Or, forming some tentative legal hypotheses, you might question a client searching for information that is relevant to those hypotheses.[7]

Both of these approaches, however, are seriously flawed. The "tell me everything" approach does place the client in the conversational limelight and thus has client-centered aspects. But the approach does not help a client organize a story in chronological or any other fashion, and it provides little memory stimulation. The "pursue legal theories" approach runs the risk of "premature diagnosis," [8] and may prevent you from learning about significant events that are not encompassed by initial theories.

A better approach is to follow preliminary problem identification by obtaining a time line. This recommendation flows from a number of considerations.

A. TIME LINE STORIES PROVIDE A COURTROOM PERSPECTIVE

Consider the following example of courtroom testimony that a plaintiff might give in a breach of contract action:

Q: When did you and the defendant first discuss surplus aluminum?

A: It was on the 12th of March, I believe.

Q: Where did the discussion take place?

A: At Universal's offices.

Q: Was anyone else present during this conversation?

A: No, just Johnson and myself.

Q: Please tell us what was said by each of you during this meeting of March 12.

A: Sure . . ..

Q: Now, when is the next time that you and Johnson discussed surplus aluminum?

A: About a week later. Johnson called me up.

Q: All right. Now, in that telephone conversation . . ..

As you can see, the witness is testifying to events in the order in which they occurred. When you elicit a time line story, therefore, you preview the form of story that may later be told in court.[9] That, in

7. You may, of course, come up with a combination or variation of these approaches.

8. See Chapter 6, sec. 3(B)(4).

9. See, e.g., Binder and Bergman, *supra* note 3, at 11; P. Bergman, *Trial Advocacy* *in a Nutshell* 75–80 (2d ed 1989); T. Mauet, *Fundamentals of Trial Techniques* 77 (1988). Of course, the *content* of testimony will usually vary greatly from a client's initial time line narrative. For instance, testimony is likely to include details that

turn, enables you to evaluate the story in much the same way that a judge, juror or opposing counsel might, and thus to begin to assess a client's legal rights.

B. TIME LINE QUESTIONING DRAWS UPON EVERYDAY CONVERSATIONAL STYLE

If the notion of time line stories seems familiar, perhaps it is because you listened to similar stories before you exchanged rattles for textbooks. Think back to a fairy tale like "Jack and the Beanstalk." The story tells us, chronologically, of Jack's pitiful social status, his trade of a cow for magic beans, his mother's anger and subsequent chucking of the beans out the window, the growth of the beanstalk, Jack's climb and confrontation with the giant, and Jack's eventual triumph.

In fact, chronological narratives are the typical medium of human communication.[10] Whether you are telling a fairy tale, relating a happening at a dinner party, or eliciting testimony in court, you are likely to do so through a chronological narrative. Such narratives hold our interest, allow us to relate discrete events to each other, and give us insight into how lives change over periods of time. Hence, clients will find it natural to tell, and you will find it natural to listen to, time line stories.

C. TIME LINE STORIES LEAD TO COMPLETE STORIES

If you begin information gathering by eliciting data in chronological sequence, without searching for details, you enhance the completeness of the stories you eventually obtain. A number of reasons account for this.

First, you promote clients' recall ability when you ask them to relate events chronologically and in their own words. Thinking through a problem sequentially often promotes recall.[11] Try an experiment. First, in a "gestalt" mode, try to remember everything you did yesterday. Next, try to remember everything you did yesterday by going through the day, step by step, starting from when you woke up and continuing until you went to sleep. If you are like most people who try this experiment, you will recall more of what occurred yesterday when you use the second approach.

you learn through theory development questioning, and may omit events that are not germane to a relevant legal theory. However, the *format* both of time lines and trial testimony is generally chronological.

10. W. Bennett and F. Feldman, *Reconstructing Reality in the Courtroom* 7 (1981).

11. See L.W. Barsalou, "The Content and Organization of Autobiographical Memories," in *Remembering Reconsidered:* *Ecological and Traditional Approaches to The Study of Memory* 213–214, 222–224 (1988). Where a person is asked only to recall only a single event a different order may be beneficial. See R.E. Geiselman and R.P. Fisher, "The Cognitive Interview Technique for Victims and Witnesses of Crime," 3–6 (1989) [Manuscript on file with authors.]

Time lines aid completeness in a second way. As you will see, your role in eliciting a time line story is largely confined to asking open questions such as, "What happened next? " Interruptions often disrupt people's trains of thought and cause them to forget the point they would have made next had the interruption not occurred. Haven't you often had the experience of being interrupted by a specific question in mid-narrative and having a point you were about to make driven from your mind forever?

Moreover, allowing a client to narrate a story with minimal interruption usually increases rapport and hence the client's willingness to talk. Your listening conveys the feeling that what the client has to say is important. This feeling usually motivates a client to provide still more information. Also, when telling a time line story a client enjoys substantial freedom to decide what information to include and exclude. Thus, a client can downplay or omit uncomfortable topics. By the time of theory development questioning, a client's rapport with you may be such that the client willingly discusses topics about which he or she would earlier have been reluctant to speak.[12]

Beginning information-gathering by seeking time lines also leads to complete stories by not relying on pre-conceived notions of relevancy either that a client may have or that you may form during preliminary problem identification. During the time line phase, you ask a client to relate events regardless of whether the client believes a given event is important. In response, clients often include matters that they might not mention if they were only asked to reveal events they thought significant.[13] A client's chronological narrative can thus serve as a check on how correctly a client identifies a problem during preliminary problem identification.

Probably more importantly, the time line phase does not depend on *your* sense of relevancy. You avoid "premature diagnosis" by holding the search for events and details in abeyance until theory development. Indeed, beginning with a time line inquiry can help you overcome two forms of premature diagnosis. In the first form, you identify a correct legal theory but make factual assumptions about how events probably occurred. Real world happenings are so diverse and complex that despite legal training and experience you cannot anticipate everything that may have occurred. Thus, if you allow clients to report data free of your sense of what might have happened, you will often elicit data to support a tentative legal theory about which you would not have thought to ask.[14]

12. See Chapter 6, sec. 3(A)(1).

13. Of course, in narrating the time line the client will do some filtering since the client will select only those events that he/she perceives as being somehow connected to the problem. However, since the client will not be limited to only those events the client believes are important, the client usually will include events that he or she might otherwise omit were a relevancy criteria imposed.

14. Perhaps as a theoretical matter, one could argue that lawyers' interruptions to ask about matters that they believe important need not preclude the client's sense of relevancy. After all, the client could simply provide his/her own ideas after a slight digression to discuss the law-

In the second form of premature diagnosis, a client's preliminary version of events causes you to fasten too quickly onto an erroneous or unsatisfactory legal theory and thus fail to consider others that may hold greater promise. Through a time line narrative, you may learn of events that suggest additional and more promising legal theories.

Finally, first eliciting a time line story usually enhances a client's ability and/or willingness to respond to your theory development questions. Time line events serve as a basis for theory development "topical searches." During theory development you frequently want to learn whether, in light of a given legal theory, certain things ever happened. For example, representing a plaintiff in a breach of contract action, you might want to learn whether a client ever took any steps to mitigate damages. To do so, you could of course simply ask questions such as, "Did you ever do anything to try to secure the goods at a lower cost?" But such "did you ever" questions, regardless of whether the answer is "yes" or "no," typically do not fully probe a client's recall. In the face of a "did you ever" question, a client is generally unable to think through every possible moment at which the client might have tried to secure the goods at lower cost:

> "The human mind is not yet like a computer. In response to a "Did you ever" type question, a (client) is unable to systematically search through all relevant time periods and spit out each instance in which the topic arose . . .. More likely, the (client) will consider the question in some quite unfocused way and respond affirmatively only if for some reason one or two such (instances) stick out in the (client's) mind." [15]

However, armed with a time line story, during theory development you need not rely solely on "did you ever" questions, and can make topical searches. Referring to time line events, you may ask a client whether a certain topic arose in connection with each event. For instance, in the breach of contract example, you might say, "Earlier you mentioned seeing another of your suppliers at a business luncheon. Did you talk about securing replacement goods during that luncheon?" Time line

yer's question. However true such assertion might be as a conceptual matter, it tends not to be true as an empirical matter. Our experience strongly suggests that once a lawyer's sense of relevancy is allowed to take over an interview, there is little likelihood that clients will be given a full opportunity to talk about what they know, unrestricted by a lawyer's sense of what is important. In short, once lawyers start to "get into the details," the client is virtually never allowed to return to his/her time line. Studies of interview techniques in the medical field show that physician-dominated interviews also result in the loss of valuable information. *See* H.B. Beckman, M.D. and R.M. Frankel, Ph.D.,

"The Effect of Physician Behavior on the Collection of Data," 101 Ann. of Intern. Med. 692 (1984); F.W. Platt, M.D. and J.C. McMath, M.D., "Clinical Hypocompetence: The Interview," 91 Ann. of Intern.Med. 898, 901 (1979); A.D. Poole and R.W. Sanson–Fisher, Understanding the Patient: A Neglected Aspect of Medical Education," 13A Soc.Sci. & Med. 37, 40–41 (1979); H.B. Beckman, M.D. and R.M. Frankel, Ph.D., "The Effect of Physician Behavior on the Collection of Data," 101(5) Ann. of Intern. Med. 692 (1984).

15. Binder and Bergman, *supra* note 3 at 294–295.

events can pinpoint a client's focus on discrete moments in time, often increasing a client's ability to recall information.

D. TIME LINES PROMOTE ACCURATE STORIES [16]

Beginning information-gathering with a time line story also tends to enhance the ultimate accuracy of a client's story. Research indicates that when people first relate a series of events in their own words and then are questioned in detail, they generally are more accurate than when they are asked for details before they can give a narrative account.[17]

Preceding a search for detail by asking for a narrative of events tends to promote accuracy in another way. As noted earlier, a client may withhold information the client considers damaging, at least until rapport has developed. Your asking pointed questions early on, therefore, may lead a client to color a story to avoid a harmful disclosure. Then, later, the client may stick to the untruthful story rather than suffer the loss of self-esteem that might accompany admission of an earlier misstatement. However, the open questions that you usually employ to elicit time line narratives allow clients to downplay or omit mention, for the moment, of troublesome events.

Moreover, because time line inquiries are typically open in form, a client may reveal information simply because there is less chance that the client will realize that the disclosure may be harmful. A common time line question such as, "What happened then?," obscures the purpose of your inquiry more than a specific question such as, "Did Mr. Rifter say anything about the condition of the roof?" Clearly a client can more easily assign a potential purpose to the roof condition question. Thus, if the client were inclined to slant or conceal information about what was said about the roof, the client would be more likely to do so in response to the roof question than to a general inquiry such as, "What happened next?"

E. TIME LINES CLARIFY INFERENCES

Beginning information-gathering with time lines also aids your own understanding of a client's story. Storytellers from Homer to Aesop to trial lawyers invariably relate events in chronological order. Especially in litigated matters, chronology is a critical part of giving a

---

16. The point here is only that a time line promotes a more accurate picture of what a client believes happened, not necessarily a more accurate picture of "what in fact happened." Given our limited powers of perception, memory and recall, the influence of lawyers' questions, and the circumstances of "legal relevance", query the extent to which litigation is capable of providing a picture of "what in fact happened."

17. E.F. Loftus, *Eyewitness Testimony* 90–94 (1979). See also Geiselman and Fisher, *supra* note 11 at 5.

trier of fact an accurate picture of events.[18] So great is our reliance on chronology that if you are told a series of events such as,

(a) Marsha and Jim shook hands;

(b) Marsha offered Jim $3000 for his car,

one of your first thoughts may be, "In what order did these events take place?" If a client did not specify an order of events, you would be likely, if only subconsciously, to "fill in" the picture yourself. Doing so might give you a false sense of what really happened. Chronology promotes comprehension, and time lines produce chronology.[19]

As you can see, chronology does more than provide a "big picture" of events. Chronology affects the particular evidentiary inferences that a factfinder is likely to draw when a client's story is told at trial. In the example above, evidence that Marsha and Jim shook hands *after* Marsha offered Jim $3000 for his car is some proof the pair had struck a bargain. But it is no proof whatsoever of a deal if they had shaken hands when their meeting began. Consider another example:

(a) Marty left his house, got in his car, drove down Forty–Second to Broadway, hit a power pole, went into a bar, and had two beers.

(b) Marty left his house, went into a bar, had two beers, drove down Forty–Second to Broadway and hit a power pole.

These stories contain the identical events. However, the inferences a factfinder might draw with respect to Marty's responsibility for hitting the power pole are clearly different because of the different order in which the events occurred. In (a), the two beers provide no basis for inferring that intoxication caused the accident; in (b), the two beers allow for the opposite inference.

Understanding how chronology affects inference-drawing may help you understand the importance of eliciting a story in the same format in which it might later be told at trial. You aid your comprehension by eliciting an overall picture of what happened, and you also can evaluate the inferences you might later ask the trier of fact to draw.

F. TIME LINES BROADEN YOUR EVIDENTIARY PERSPECTIVE

Litigated disputes typically center on happenings at discrete moments of substantive importance. For example, the dispute in a con-

---

18. See Bergman, *supra* note 9, at 75; J.A. Tanford, *The Trial Process* 346 (1983).

19. Arguably, you need not begin information gathering by seeking a time line. Why not simply make sure that before you adjourn an interview, you check your chronological understanding of a story? We have two responses. First, especially if a story is lengthy, a client may not be able to resurrect chronology if you have first engaged in detailed questioning without re-

gard to chronology. You may get a chronology, but it might not be the same one the client would have begun with. Second, our experience as teachers and practicing lawyers is that when lawyers do not pursue chronology at the outset, they rarely, if ever, go back and do so. Perhaps the frequent failure is due to the lawyers' unconscious "filling in" of a story for purposes of their own comprehension.

tract action may center upon whether A and B entered into an agreement for the sale and purchase of 15,000 bean bags on or about August 15th, and whether the defendant failed to deliver the promised bags by November 1st. In an automobile accident case, the central dispute might concern the physical condition of the defendant at 11:07 P.M. on June 22nd. In a securities fraud case, the core dispute might focus on whether, when the defendant issued its prospectus on October 30th, the defendant knew or should have known that the prospectus omitted mention of contingent liabilities amounting to $5,000,000.

When you talk to a client, then, you may instinctively focus on such "moments of substantive importance." You may question a client in great detail regarding substantively critical events and search for witnesses who can substantiate the client's version of those events. For instance, in the securities fraud matter, you may concentrate on what the officers and directors knew regarding the company's contingent liabilities at the time the prospectus was issued.

Of course, you need to be thorough in pursuit of events that substantive rules render critical. But you also need to develop information about what happened before and after these substantively critical events. Surrounding events are often important sources of inferences about how substantively critical events took place.[20] Moreover, awareness of surrounding events often expands the supply of witnesses. For example, in the securities fraud matter, a prior event leading to an inference that the board did not commit fraud might be a discussion in a board meeting one month before the meeting during which the prospectus was discussed. During this discussion, a financial adviser informed the board that the company was free of contingent liabilities. People who attended this prior board meeting might be witnesses you would not have known about had you focused only on the meeting in which the prospectus was discussed. With reference to "after" events, you may identify as potential witnesses close friends of board members, who say that after the prospectus was issued, they were urged by board members to buy stock in the company.

Almost by definition, a time line informs you, early on, about events occurring before and after the moments of critical importance. When a client talks about a problem from its inception, and follows it through to present time, a client talks about events leading up to and following the substantively critical ones. By beginning with a time line, then, you often discover at an early stage: (1) "before" and "after" incidents that are highly probative of what happened at the critical moment(s); and (2) the identity of witnesses who can substantiate a client's version of the substantively critical events.

---

20. Events occurring before and after the moment of critical importance furnish circumstantial evidence of what happened at that instant. And as any seasoned trial lawyer knows and as no jury is ever told, most evidence presented at trials is circumstantial. See Binder and Bergman, *supra* note 3 at 81–82.

G. TIME LINES OFTEN SUGGEST ADDITIONAL LEGAL THEORIES

As noted in section "C" above, failure to secure a time line may delay or prevent you from identifying legal theories that are more viable than those suggested by a client's preliminary problem description.

Assume, for example, that preliminary problem identification reveals that a client's problem concerns injuries sustained at work while the client was using a piece of machinery. Your legal diagnosis may be that the client's rights are probably governed by workers' compensation doctrine or products liability law. Armed with this diagnosis, you might be inclined to ask detailed questions pursuant to those theories. However, the client's time line story might indicate that before the accident the machine had been repaired, and also that the client's real difficulties arose after the client underwent surgery and began taking a particular medicine. Such information might alter your diagnosis considerably. Substantive rules pertaining to the liability of a repairer and medical malpractice might well supersede your initial, premature diagnosis.

H. TIME LINES PROMOTE EFFICIENCY

Lastly, time lines promote efficiency in at least three ways. First, a time line often prevents you from wasting time on the details of events which seem initially critical but which, in light of a whole story, seem insignificant.

Second, even if you could think of all the questions necessary to elicit a client's complete story through closed questions, asking the closed questions would undoubtedly take longer eliciting the story through narrative answers to open questions.

Third, both to understand a client's story and to prepare a case for trial, you need to organize a story chronologically. If you do not elicit a story that way initially, you will have to retrace much of the same territory when you later attempt to sort it out. You can avoid repetition and waste, then, by eliciting a time line at the outset.

4. TIME LINE PREPARATORY EXPLANATIONS

A preparatory explanation [21] following preliminary problem identification often aids time line development. As you recall, in ordinary social conversation, clients rarely speak the language of time lines. Too, many clients may expect only to answer specific questions. And others may be uncomfortable because they have no expectations whatsoever about how you want them to respond. A preparatory explanation may overcome such obstacles.

21. See Chapter 7, sec. 6.

Consider this sample preparatory explanation:

Lawyer: O.K., Mr. Aronow, what I have found most helpful in
this kind of situation is this: I'll start out by asking you
to go over your story from the beginning, and to go in
chronological order and event-by-event, telling me in
your own words everything that has happened right up
to today.   In telling me the story, it will be important
that you proceed step-by-step and give me some details.
Tell me about every event you can recall; don't worry
about whether or not you believe it is legally important.
I may have a few questions from time to time, but
basically I want you to do the talking.   I'm planning
about an hour for today.   When you finish going over
the story, I'll go back and ask you some questions which,
from a legal point of view, may be important.   From
what you've told me so far, I'm not sure we'll be able to
complete our initial discussion today; I may have to ask
you to come back in a day or two to finish up.   At that
point, I'll probably be pressing you for some detail so
that we can get at everything you can recall while your
memory is still fresh.   However, before you leave today,
I assure you that I will begin talking with you about
what approach might best resolve this matter.   Remember, everything you tell me is confidential; I cannot and
will not disclose it to anyone outside this office without
your permission.   Any questions?

Client: No.

Lawyer: Good.   Why don't you start your story from the beginning, going event-by-event.

This is a "generic" preparatory explanation that you might use
with all new and seemingly unsophisticated clients.   It gears a client to
a two-phased discussion, and warns that both may not be completed at
one sitting.   During the first phase, the client tells the story chronologically, event-by-event, and in the client's own words.   (Note that you
even repeat the "step-by-step" directive.)   Later, probably on a different
day, you will press for detail.   The explanation refers to confidentiality,
and mentions how long the interview is likely to take.   Lastly, the
explanation recognizes explicitly what is likely to be uppermost in the
client's mind—potential solutions.   In sum, it tells the client what to
expect during the initial conference.

You may be tempted to include other matters in a preparatory
explanation.   For example, some attorneys as a matter of routine
mention a client's need to be truthful; others feel that to do so
indicates mistrust.   Another component of a preparatory explanation
may be a "war story"—a tale about a different client with a similar
problem.   But be forewarned.   As you garner experience and encounter
the difficulties clients tend to have, you may want to head each off in

advance during the preparatory explanation. As a result, an explanation may become so lengthy that a client dozes off in mid-explanation.

But one matter not contained in the sample explanation that you may want to include concerns note-taking. You cannot convey empathy and interest in a client's story if your head is buried in a notepad. On the other hand, taking notes is necessary lest important data be lost and your theory development questioning be curtailed. Hence, you usually take notes as you listen to a time line narrative, and may want to explain your actions ahead of time in language such as:

> "As we go through the story, I'll be jotting down some notes on what you tell me so that I can go back to the point if it becomes important. The notes are simply to make sure I don't forget. If you have any question about what I'm writing down, feel free to ask me about it."

Clearly, in some situations you may choose not to give a preparatory explanation. A client may be one you have represented previously in a similar matter, legally sophisticated, or obviously anxious to relate a story at once. The first two types of clients may find a preparatory explanation condescending; a client particularly anxious to talk may find it frustrating.

In other situations, you may want to tailor the "generic" preparatory explanation to a specific client based on early information you have acquired. For example, if during initial discussion a client shows a marked tendency to excessive detail, you may want to include a remark along these lines:

> "Ms. Sossin, I understand you are anxious to tell me everything. But my experience is that we can proceed more quickly, and I can better advise you, if you can give me an overall picture of what happened before you go into all the details. I know you are trying to be helpful, and eventually I will want to hear all the details, but perhaps you can begin by giving me an overview through a step-by-step, event-by-event account of everything that occurred."

Of course, you need not routinely caution clients against excessive detail. The implied criticism is not the best method of fostering rapport. But this example indicates how you may tailor a preparatory explanation to an individual client.

Clients, often intent on their own problems, may not fully digest all of your explanatory comments. Hence, you may often find it useful to repeat part of a preparatory explanation as an interview proceeds. For example, if you notice that a client who initially was narrating freely is winding down, you may make a statement such as:

> "You've been doing a fine job so far of telling me your story. Remember, as I mentioned a while ago, it is important that you tell me as much as you can in the order that events took place. Now, we left off at _____. Why don't you pick it up from there, event-by-event, in your own words."

This statement praises the client while subtly repeating part of the preparatory explanation.

To further your understanding of preparatory explanations, and how you might tailor them to specific situations, consider the following three short hypotheticals.

Case No. 1:

Following preliminary problem identification, you regard this client as (a) not anxious to tell his story quickly, (b) legally unsophisticated, and (c) somewhat uncertain about what you expect of him. The dialogue picks up at the conclusion of preliminary problem identification:

1. L: So, Mr. Hamlin, the situation is that you've suffered a whiplash as the result of an automobile collision and you want to know whether it makes sense to make a claim against the other driver.

2. C: Right. Basically, is this the kind of case that I'll be able to collect on? I've been through a hell of a lot.

3. L: When we've had a chance to talk a bit more, I'll try to give you an answer. What I'm going to have to do first is to get your story, including a description of your injuries and how they've affected you. Start in, why don't you, by telling me everything that has happened; just use your own words.

Analysis:

This preparatory explanation seems shallow and lacking in adequate detail. Although the client was not anxious to tell his story at once and seemed unsure about what to expect, you do not tell him that the discussion will unfold in phases. That is, you do not tell the client that after he tells his story, you will probe for additional information. Also, you do not provide guidance as to how he should tell his story— e.g., by proceeding in chronological order. You hint at a discussion of solutions (No. 3), but do not estimate when this discussion might occur. Such omissions are likely to leave the client uncertain, or even with a false impression, of what will occur.

Case No. 2:

Your appraisal of the client is the same as in Case No. 1, with one exception. Here, you realize from the client's preliminary problem description that you need to brush up on potentially applicable legal doctrine before conducting theory development. Hence, you intend to ask the client to return for a second interview a few days after completing the time line phase. Again the dialogue picks up at the conclusion of preliminary problem identification:

1. L: As I understand it, your husband mortgaged the house to AA Credit Company without your knowledge, and now they are trying to foreclose. You want to know whether

anything can be done to stop the foreclosure, and you are concerned about how all this will affect your relationship with your husband.

2. C: That's it in a nutshell.

3. L: What I've found to be most helpful, Ms. Franklin, is that we start out by having you tell me in your own words just what happened. I want you to start at the beginning and go step-by-step, telling me in chronological order everything you can recall. Take your time and tell me as much detail as you can. When you've finished, I'll review the notes I'll be making and I'll probably have a number of specific questions for you. At first I won't interrupt too much, because many of my clients find it helps their memory to talk largely without interruption. Then I'll go through your story in detail with additional questions. Do you have a fairly good idea of what we'll do?

4. C: Yes, I think I understand.

5. L: Great. Just a couple of other points. In all probability, I'll ask you to return for a second interview after you tell me your story. This is an important matter, and I want to be sure you have a chance to tell your whole story. Also, that will give me a chance to do some legal checking before I finish my questioning. I'll try to give you today as good a legal judgment as I can based on your story, but it will have to be somewhat tentative. O.K.—shall we proceed?

6. C: Yes.

7. L: All right, please start at the beginning and tell me, event-by-event, everything that has occurred.

Analysis:

Given the client's uncertainty and lack of a sense of urgency, a preparatory explanation of some detail seems appropriate. Nos. 3 and 5 tell the client to expect a two-phased review of the facts. No. 3 also explains how the client is to proceed while telling the time line story, and prepares her for note-taking. No. 5 explains the likelihood that detailed questioning will take place another day and that a full legal judgment will not be made until after that time. You suggest openly your need to engage in legal research. Hopefully, you do so in such a way that the client does not fear that you lack legal competence. Finally, you end the explanation by reinforcing the client's duties during the time line phase.

This explanation would undoubtedly aid the client's understanding of what to expect, but it is by no means perfect. You do not tell the client how long the first meeting might take. No. 3 asks the client to "tell me as much detail as you can;" if the client adheres to that advice, you may end up seeing more leaves than trees. Lastly, No. 5 talks about making a "legal judgment." This statement is probably too obscure to assure the client that before the meeting ends, you will begin to respond to the client's legal and nonlegal concerns: preventing foreclosure, and protecting the husband-wife relationship.

Case No. 3:

Here, you again believe that the client is uncertain about what will take place during the interview, but you also believe that the client is extremely anxious to tell his story and get an immediate answer. After preliminary problem identification, the dialogue goes as follows:

1. L: The court awarded your wife custody of the children, but for the past two years you have been raising them. Your wife has now returned and is making noises about taking the kids. You want to prevent this, and to do so quickly without upsetting the children.

2. C: That's right. I want to stop her now, and I don't want the children involved.

3. L: O.K., let's get started. Have you ever been to a lawyer before?

4. C: Well, just in connection with the divorce.

5. L: All right, I think we can get at this fastest by having you tell me step-by-step everything that has happened. I need a good picture of the facts before I can get some idea of what we can do. Start in now and tell me, event-by-event, everything that has happened in relation to your wife since you've had the children. Keep going right up to today.

Analysis:

In reviewing this case please consider the following questions:

1. Was No. 3 appropriate?

2. Should No. 5 have omitted any explanation of why you needed the facts first?

3. Should No. 5 have included other instructions? If so, which ones?

5. "START AT THE BEGINNING"

Note that the sample preparatory explanations above do not instruct the clients just where to start their stories. For example, in Case No. 2, you do not tell the client to, say, "Start in from when you first realized that the bank might foreclose." Many of the same reasons that support the efficacy of time line stories underlie advising clients simply to "start at the beginning". Just as you might prematurely diagnose a client's problem, so too might you incorrectly guess where a story begins. If you tell a client to begin at a specific point in time, you may never learn of prior events that are important but which you did not anticipate. For instance, does an automobile mishap commence when a client starts out on a trip, with important personal news the client received the day before, or with a pre-existing medical condition? In the face of such uncertainty, you generally should not impose your sense of "beginning" on a client.

With this in mind, refer to No. 5 in Case 3 above. There, you tell the client to describe "everything that has happened in relation to your wife *since you've had the children*." Though you have just a bit of information, does this statement run a risk that the client will ignore prior events that may turn out to be important?

Of course, a client may be as uncertain about the "true" beginning as you are. How should you react if a client responds to your request to "start at the beginning" by asking, "Where should I start?" Perhaps your simplest rejoinder is to say something like, "Start wherever you feel the story begins." Such a statement permits the client to begin where the client feels comfortable.[22]

Often, when a client begins telling a story, you strongly suspect that the client has not begun his or her narrative at a problem's "true" beginning. Sometimes your suspicion will be based on information other people have given to you. Other times, intuition and your experience as a lawyer will suggest the likely possibility of earlier events.[23] For example, often events follow a "normal course"—banks take certain steps before they foreclose; doctors discuss certain matters with patients before they operate; police officers follow a prescribed "booking process," and the like. Finally, apart from any suspicions you may have, as a careful lawyer you may simply want to be sure that a client has not started a time line story somewhere in the middle.

In any of these situations, should you interrupt a client's narrative to inquire about possible earlier events? Generally, the answer is "no." So doing may convey a feeling that you doubt a client, and may deny a client the opportunity to delay mention of "troublesome" events. In either case, you may damage rapport. And, you have the ready alternative of postponing the inquiry for possible earlier events until theory development. Also, if you do wish to search for earlier events before beginning theory development, you might wait until a client has concluded a time line narrative, and then gently prod the client to reconsider the story's starting point with a statement such as:

> "Ms. Keely, you've really given me a great deal of helpful information. As I told you earlier, we'll meet again in a couple of days so I can check into some things before we get into more detail. Before we adjourn, let me ask you this. You started out by telling me about the foreclosure letter you got from the bank. Think carefully for a moment; are there any other events that took place before you got that letter that you think may be a part of what happened?"

---

22. If a client persists in asking you where to start a narrative, you may have no choice other than to select a topic. You do not facilitate rapport by forcing a truly puzzled client to guess at where to begin.

23. For example, our colleagues who are criminal defense attorneys tell us that their clients commonly start stories at the point of arrest, rather than with any of the events leading up to their arrest.

If you strongly suspect the occurrence of earlier events, and you think it likely that they are likely to be important, you may want to press a client even further. Thus, if in the example above Ms. Keely responded that she could not recall anything else, you might press her as follows:

"Please think back to the period before you got the letter, on occasions when you went into the bank. During that period, might you have had a conversation with someone from the bank in which the possibility of foreclosure was mentioned?"

Here, perhaps your experience with local banks' "normal course" for foreclosures suggested that Ms. Keely probably had a personal conversation with a bank officer before receiving the foreclosure letter. Since the open question did not elicit information about such earlier events, you pressed her with a "yes-no" question based on your sense of how events might "normally" have taken place. If the question does succeed in uncovering an additional event, you should then proceed to connect the new event to the already existing time line story: "How long before you got the foreclosure letter did this personal conversation take place?" Such a dialogue may prompt a client's recollection of still further events.

"Normal course" questions do of course run the risk of overlooking "abnormal" events that may have preceded a client's time line narrative. However, at least until theory development questioning, in the absence of a client's sudden recollection or divine intervention, abnormal events may not come to light.

6. EXPANDING "QUICKIE" TIME LINE STORIES

Sometimes, clients fail to understand what you want when you ask for a step-by-step chronological account. When this happens, you may repeat and amplify on a portion of the preparatory explanation. Consider the following example:

1. L: O.K., Mr. Thomas, please start from the beginning and tell me in your own words, step-by-step, everything that happened.

2. C: Sure. We were headed east on 43rd Street, when all of a sudden this car came out of a driveway. I tried to swerve, but he hit us. I was in the hospital about a week and off work for four. Now he's suing me.

This account is not a time line story. It may be chronological and shorn of detail, but it consists of conclusions, not a narration of discrete events. In such a situation, you might respond as follows:

3. L: You're quite angry, and I understand that. (Pause) What would help me, Mr. Thomas, is if you could start again and tell me, one step at a time, each and every thing that has happened. Go step by step; try not to leave out anything.

I need information about anything that happened before and after the collision that you feel is connected to your injuries. Take your time and go slowly through the story, one event at a time.

You might employ a second approach if, despite a repeat of your explanation, a client continues to talk in conclusory terms. The approach is to tell a client explicitly what you expect, and in what way what the client has said differs from what you expect. For example, you might say,

"Mr. Thomas, you've told me that after you changed lanes, he hit you. That's fine, it gives me some picture of what happened. But it really doesn't tell me step-by-step how the collision occurred. Can you go one step at a time, and tell me exactly what happened after you changed lanes?"

7. TIME LINE QUESTIONING TECHNIQUES

A. OPEN QUESTIONS

Time line questions are principally open. Open questions typically encourage clients to narrate events in their own words; keep a client's paths of association intact; free a client from any preconceived notions of relevancy you may have; allow a client to postpone discussion of troublesome events; and are generally empathic as they cast you primarily in the role of listener. Hence, open questions are ideally suited to the general time line goal of obtaining a chronological narrative free from excessive detail.

Three different forms of open questions typically serve to keep a client on a chronological track. As much as possible, limit time line questions to these three forms:

1. When a client mentions an event, you may want a client to move forward in time to the next event the client can recall. To accomplish this, ask open questions such as, "What happened next?" or "What occurred after that?"

2. When a client mentions an event, you may want the client to stay with that event and tell you a bit more about it. Thus, you may ask open questions such as, "Tell me more about that," or "Can you describe that for me in a little more detail?" Such questions move a client neither forward nor backward; the story figuratively idles in neutral.

3. When a client mentions an event, you may want to move the client back in time, to search for possibly-omitted events. For example, if a client has mentioned the event of the chicken crossing the road, you might ask, "Did anything happen before the chicken crossed the street?" When you do want a client to go back in time, you may aid a client's recall by repeating events the client has already mentioned which might "bookend" a possibly-omitted

event: "Between the time the chicken left the restaurant and the time the chicken crossed the road, what else happened?"

A brief example in the context of a "wrongful termination" matter demonstrates how you may orchestrate a time line relying principally on these three forms of open questions:

1. L: Ms. Kirkorian, after you complained to Ms. Epstein about the company's failure to inform its customers that it had switched to Grade 3 metal, what happened next?

2. C: The next day I got a note telling me to report to the sales office. When I got there, they told me I had no business complaining to Epstein about sales policies.

3. L: Can you tell me more about what went on in the sales office meeting?

4. C: (Response omitted)

5. L: What's the next thing that happened after the sales office meeting?

6. C: I received my annual employee evaluation. After that meeting, you can imagine what my supervisor wrote.

7. L: You must have been really upset—we'll talk more about that very soon. But think just for a moment. What happened between the time of the sales office meeting and your receiving the evaluation?

Nos. 1 and 5 move the client forward in time; No. 3 asks the client to stay with the just-mentioned event; No. 7 searches for possibly-omitted prior events.

B. CLOSED QUESTIONS

On some occasions, you will need to deviate from the pattern of open questions. Closed questions will sometimes be necessary to *clarify* a client's story. Though you try not to interrupt a time line narrative, you need to understand what a client is telling you. Thus, if some aspect of a client's story is ambiguous or uncertain, a closed question may help you quickly gain understanding. Consider the following dialogue with Mr. Kafka:

1. L: O.K., Mr. Kafka, what happened next?

2. C: Well, the seller and I were talking about the electrician. He told me that he would come the next day and see just what the problem was.

3. L: When you say "he" was to come the next day, who are you referring to?

4. C: Oh, sorry. The seller was going to come the next day.

5. L: All right, after the seller said he would come by the next day, what took place?

Inquiry no. 3 is a simple example of using a closed question to clarify a story. As you did not understand which of two people the client was referring to, you clarified the reference briefly and returned to the narrative.

Another typical ambiguity that you may want to clarify during time line questioning concerns the chronology of events. A closed question may help you clarify the order in which events happened, or the time gap between events. Consider this dialogue:

1. L: O.K., Ms. Handler, what happened next?

2. C: Well, my husband had been drinking lots of beer, and then he really beat our son, Jimmy.

3. L: That must have been awful for both you and Jimmy. But just so I am clear, do you recall which came first, the lickin' or the keg?

4. C: Oh, he got very drunk first. He never behaved this way unless he had been drinking.

In this instance, inquiry no. 3 is closed; it seeks to clarify confusion as to the *sequence* of events. Similarly, a closed question may clarify confusion about the length of a *gap* between events. The interview of Ms. Handler continues:

5. L: Please continue. What's the next thing you can recall?

6. C: After the big talk we had, when he promised to go to AA, he went ahead and got drunk again. He started yelling at Jimmy and I thought he was going to hit him again, but I was able to get Jimmy out of there before anything happened.

7. L: Just so I'm clear, how much time elapsed between the time your husband beat Jimmy and the time he got drunk again and you got Jimmy out of there?

8. C: It must have been about two weeks.

9. L: Thank you. OK, why don't you continue. I know this is hard, but you're doing a fine job of telling me what happened.

Inquiry no. 7 seeks information that potentially is very important. The length of time between the beating of Jimmy and Ms. Handler's decision to remove Jimmy from the home may reflect on her own culpability. Just as the order in which events occur can affect the inferences we draw, so too can variations in time gaps. Thus, your time lines should not only arrange events chronologically but they also should indicate the approximate intervals between events. Because clients typically fail to mention the interval between events in their stories, you will frequently need to ask closed questions to uncover this information.

Note that in all three examples, the closed questions are limited to clarifying what the clients said, and do not overly divert the clients' attention from the chronological narrative.

C. SUMMARY TECHNIQUE

Inquiry No. 5 in the Kafka example also merits a bit of comment. After the client clarifies his remark, you do not simply ask, "What happened next?" You first summarize where in the story the client was before the interruption: "All right, after the seller said he would come by the next day, what took place?" A brief summary often helps clients maintain their paths of association and stay on a chronological track. In the same vein, note how Nos. 3 and 9 in the Handler dialogue work motivational responses into the time line dialogue.

D. EVENTS VS. DETAILS

Throughout, this chapter has urged you to elicit time line stories primarily through open questions. At the same time, it has recognized that closed questions inevitably are necessary to clarify stories and to understand time intervals. Unfortunately, the "closed question" exception may swallow the "open question" rule. For some, permission to ask a closed time line question may be the equivalent of allowing an alcoholic one drink. Some lawyers tend to have an ever-increasing need to "clarify" a story. The result is a prevalence of closed questions and a plethora of detail that vitiates the benefits of event-focused time line stories. Since a rule such as, "ask only open questions," is unworkable, the decision as to how often to use closed questions to clarify a time line story becomes largely one for your judgment.

For example, assume that in a suit for workplace sexual harassment, a client refers to an incident in which her supervisor asked her for a drink after work. You ask, "Tell me more about his asking you for a drink." Does the question seek to clarify the event, or is it a quest for detail that can more properly await theory development? Your judgment, not a reference work, will have to supply the answer. Depending on the circumstances of each individual matter, sometimes you might consider such a question a necessary clarification, whereas other times you may hold off until theory development.

In general, however, when in doubt, hold off closed questions until theory development. As a litigator, your instinct when faced with a client's story may resemble that of a tiger faced with a hunk of raw meat: tear it apart! Aware of a number of potentially-applicable legal theories, you may find yourself champing at the bit to probe a story for details that might substantiate or vitiate those theories. And once you start down the road of detail pursuit, you will find it difficult to obtain a chronology of events. But do not despair. Even if you consciously restrain yourself largely to open questions, you will inevitably elicit a fair amount of detail. On their own, clients often describe some events in detail. When you ask an open question such as, "Can you please tell me more about . . . ?", a client will invariably provide some detail. Hence, time line stories should not and will not be totally free of detail. However, to gain the benefits of beginning information-gathering with complete time lines, you will need to reign in your lawyerly taste for clarification that may quickly descend to repeated probes for detail.[24]

8.   REFERRING CLIENTS TO DOCUMENTS

In many instances, a client will be unable to tell an adequate time line story employing only his or her present recollection. However, a client will usually not have to. Increasingly, roads to courthouses are cluttered with an array of documents. Letters, memos, reports, receipts and the like memorialize almost every human activity. Thus, if you have a chance to speak with a client prior to an interview, one request you should make as a matter of course is for the client to bring along any written documents pertaining to the matter the client wishes to discuss. And if during time line questioning you refer a client to such documents, you will usually enhance a client's recollection.

For example, assume that a client mentions that a lengthy meeting occurred but can recall almost nothing of what took place during the meeting. Asking the client to refer to a document may well refresh the client's recollection.[25] Consider this brief bit of dialogue from a matter involving an alleged wrongful termination:

Lawyer: What happened next?

Client: There was a big meeting, involving the head of Jones' department, Jones' immediate supervisor, the director of personnel, the union shop steward, and myself. It took most of the afternoon.

Lawyer: Can you tell me about the meeting? Perhaps you might want to look through your file to help refresh your recollection.

Note that here, you refer the client to documents before the client expresses any difficulty of recollection. Though you may often wait until a client does appear to need some help before suggesting that the client refer to documents, clients will often appreciate an earlier reference.

An important proviso pertains to the use of documents when developing a time line. Do not become so engrossed in the existence and contents of documents that you slip into theory development questioning. Documents, not subject to the whims and caprices of memory, are often quite rightfully of particular importance to a matter's outcome. Confronted with a variety of documents, then, you may want to focus your attention on them rather than on the client and the

---

24. For further discussion of the event/ detail distinction, see Chapter 10, sec. 2(B).

25. This discussion assumes that the client can identify and readily bring to an interview a relatively small number of documents that pertain to a matter. Where this is not the case, other considerations operate. See sec. 12, *infra.*

overall story. Hence, to keep on the time line, do refer a client to documents only if necessary to enable a client to tell a time line story. Leave detailed questioning about the documents and a thorough perusal of them for theory development.[26]

9. USING ACTIVE LISTENING

Active listening may be of particular value during time line questioning. Not only does it facilitate rapport, but also it provides questioning variety. After all, you cannot help but resemble a metronome if your questions consist of little more than variations on the theme, "What happened next."

Assume for example that you want a client to elaborate on a meeting which apparently angered the client. Instead of asking, "Tell me more about the meeting," you might empathically say, "I can see that meeting made you very angry." Statements such as this are gentler forms of probes than questions. They tend to convey that you are listening and trying to understand the client's thoughts and feelings, and they encourage clients to elaborate on the same topic.

10. TAKING PROBE NOTES

If a time line is to serve as a basis for theory development questioning, some note-taking is essential. Notes enable you both to reconstruct a fairly complete time line story after an interview is concluded, and to make intelligent choices about which events you need to probe further. But during a meeting you cannot take anything like verbatim notes and hope to maintain rapport. On the other hand, writing down only what immediately strikes you as important creates a real danger of omission. Matters which initially seem irrelevant, and which become meaningful only in the light of subsequent information, may be lost.

"Probe notes" are a helpful compromise. As a client mentions an event or topic, jot down a key word or two as a reminder. If possible, use a client's actual words. During theory development, using a client's own words helps you stimulate a client's recollection. Do not hoard yellow pads when taking probe notes. Leave space between entries, and fill in events and details from your memory after an interview has concluded.

Probe notes are generally sufficient for you to reconstruct a full account of a client's time line story shortly after you have elicited a time line story. Especially when you arrange the theory development phase for a later date, your fuller account, and not your probe notes, will serve as the basis of theory development questioning.

26. See A. Sherr, *Client Interviewing for Lawyers* 114 (1986).

The following example demonstrates how you may memorialize a time line story with probe notes. On the left is a time line dialogue with Jean, who is accused of being an accomplice in a liquor store robbery. The other suspects are Bill, Charlie and Ralph.

Interview	Notes
L: Tell me, from the beginning, what happened that night	
C: We were sitting around at Charlie's. I guess I got there around 6 P.M. Bill was already there. We had some beer and Charlie's wife made some dinner, and then we had a few more beers.	Charlie's, 6 P.M. Bill already there Charlie's wife Drinking beer
L: I see.	
C: Bill kept asking Charlie whether Ralph had called. Charlie kept saying no, it probably wouldn't be today. I didn't pay much attention—I hardly knew Ralph.	Bill asking about Call from Ralph "not today" Hardly knows Ralph
L: You're doing fine. Tell me more.	
C: We had the TV on, watching the fights. We were talking about playing poker. Charlie's wife came in and said there was a call for Bill. Bill came back and told Charlie that Ralph wanted to talk with him. Charlie came back and said he and Bill were going to pick up Ralph, buy some booze and come back. He said I should set up for poker.	TV Ralph calls—asks for Charlie C & B pick up Ralph & booze J set poker

While these notes may appear sparse, they are probably adequate for the time line phase. They preserve the essential chronology and story. Importantly, they retain remarks concerning possible witnesses (Charlie's wife) and a possible intoxication defense—beer.[27]

11. EXAMPLES AND ANALYSES OF TIME LINE STORIES

The three dialogues below explore many of the considerations addressed in this chapter. In each instance, assume that the preliminary problem identification has been completed, and you have already given a preparatory explanation.

Case No. 1:

1. L: Tell me now, step-by-step, everything that has occurred. Start at the beginning.

27. For discussion of considerations relating to mechanically recording interviews, see Chapter 10, sec. 13.

2.   C: Well, about four months ago I lost my job. At first I wasn't worried, but pretty soon my savings started to disappear. I tried to find another job, but I couldn't. Two months ago, in June, I missed the payment on my second mortgage.

3.   L: O.K., what happened next?

4.   C: I got a letter from the mortgage company. It said if I didn't pay, they would foreclose.

5.   L: Do you have the letter?

6.   C: Yes.

7.   L: Can I see it?

8.   C: Sure, here it is.

9.   L: Did you contact them after you got the letter?

10.   C: Yes, a while later.

11.   L: Tell me about that.

12.   C: I called up and told them I'd lost my job, and asked for more time to pay.

13.   L: Who did you talk to?

14.   C: I talked to a Ms. Howl. She said that under law I had time, and that I had no need to worry.

15.   L: That must have made you feel better.

16.   C: It did. But a few days ago I got this notice; it says they are foreclosing.

17.   L: When exactly did you get this notice?

18.   C: Last week.

19.   L: What happened when you received it?

Analysis:

This dialogue primarily illustrates how easily chronological gaps can creep into a time line story. Examine No. 9. It is likely to pull the client off a chronological track by moving from the point in time when the client received the letter (No. 4) to what you seemingly assumed was the next event—the client's contacting the company. Even if the client did eventually contact the company, the contact may not have been the next significant event to occur. Other significant events, such as the arrival of other letters, phone calls, or partial payments could have occurred before the client contacted the company. Hence, No. 9 should have been an open question, such as, "After you received this letter, what happened next"?

Examine next No. 16. Here the client may have created a chronological gap by overlooking events between the phone call with Howl and receipt of the notice. Hence, you might have asked in No. 17 a question such as, "Let's go back for a moment to your conversation with the mortgage company. What is the very next thing you can recall happening after this conversation?" Or, you might have asked, "Between the time you talked to Ms. Howl and you received the foreclosure notice, what else happened?"

The dialogue also illustrates how searching for details during the time line phase may draw you "off-side," or cause a client to be drawn off. Nos. 5, 7, and 13 exemplify unnecessary search for detail. While the questions may not call for excessive clarification or elaboration, they do divert the attention of both you and the client from the narrative. The information does not appear necessary for understanding the overall story, and could easily await theory development. By contrast, the detail sought in No. 17 is when an event occurred, and appropriately seeks to clarify the overall chronology.

Lastly, note that No. 15 is an active listening response reflecting the client's past feelings.

Case No. 2:

1. **L:** Start at the beginning and tell me, step-by-step, everything that has happened.

2. **C:** About 6 months before I got fired, this friend of mine, Monica, came to me and told me that she was being fired for insubordination.

3. **L:** Hmm. Please tell me a bit more about that.

4. **C:** She said she had gotten into an argument with the shift boss who had called her a "Mex." Monica told me the real reason she was being fired was that she reported the boss to the manager. Monica was real angry, and she asked me to help her.

5. **L:** I see.

6. **C:** Anyhow, I went to the shift boss and asked for an explanation.

7. **L:** Between the time Monica asked you to help her, and your going to the shift boss, what else occurred?

8. **C:** We formed a committee to help Monica, and I was elected representative to see the shift boss.

9. **L:** What you're telling me is very helpful. After you were elected, what happened?

10. **C:** I went to see him. He told me Monica was always demanding too much and not following orders. He said he was sorry for calling her a Mex, and that he had nothing against Mexicans. I told him we had a committee and that we were going to protect Monica. He said there was nothing he could do, so I went to see the personnel manager.

11. L: Just to make sure we don't miss anything, after you saw the shift boss but before you saw the personnel manager, did you do anything else?

12. C: No.

13. L: O.K., tell me about your conversation with the personnel manager.

14. C: We just talked a bit about the situation.

15. L: Tell me as much as you can remember.

16. C: All I really remember is she said she'd check with the shift boss and get back to me.

17. L: This conversation must have left you a bit frustrated.

18. C: It really did.

19. L: What happened next?

20. C: A meeting was set up to go over things.

21. L: Who was at the meeting?

22. C: Monica, me, the shift boss, Ms. Dawson from personnel, and Donald Furnish, another employee.

23. L: What happened?

24. C: Monica, me and Donald talked about the good job Monica always did, and that we thought her complaint was proper. The shift boss said he called her a "Mex" because he had heard Monica using that term herself when she referred to other Hispanics. That really made me angry; I called him a liar.

25. L: I can imagine you were very angry. By the way, has the shift boss ever used the term "Mex" when talking to you?

Analysis:

With a couple of exceptions, this is a competent time line approach. No. 7 demonstrates the use of known "bookend" events to try to fill a possible gap in chronology. Nos. 9 and 19 illustrate the use of open questions to move a story ahead in time. Nos. 3, 13 and 15 are open questions which keep the story in neutral; the client is asked to elaborate on already-mentioned events. No. 11, however, shows how you must be careful to use open questions even when seeking to fill in possible gaps. There, you ask whether the client *did* anything during the time period in question. You would have been safer to ask, "Did anything else occur during that time period?"

No. 21 is a closed question of the type that runs the risk of leaving the chronological track in favor of unnecessary detail. However, since it asks only for limited detail, and you have not to this point sought details, the digression seems to fall within allowable limits of reasonable judgment.

The beginning of No. 9 illustrates "recognition", and Nos. 17 and 25 are active listening responses. However, the follow-up question in No. 25 may take the client off the chronological track.

Case No. 3:

1. L: Go step-by-step from the beginning, Ms. Jong, and tell me everything that has happened.

2. C: Two police came to the door and asked if they could come in. I asked why, and they said they had a report of child neglect. I said I had done nothing wrong, and they could come in and look around.

3. L: Go ahead.

4. C: Well, they looked in all the rooms and asked if they could check the kitchen. I said sure. They went in and asked why there was so little food. I said I'd been sick, but that I was going to the market soon. They said they would have to take the baby and that my daughter Sylvia had already been detained at school.

5. L: You must have been stunned.

6. C: I really was. I was crying and shouting, almost hysterical I guess.

7. L: I can understand how you would be. Tell me, what else happened while the police were there?

8. C: Not much. They told me to come to court in two days.

9. L: O.K., then what happened?

10. C: I ran to my sister's house. We tried to find a lawyer but we couldn't. She took me home, and we found this telegram from the Welfare people.

11. L: Do you have the telegram?

12. C: It's home.

13. L: What did the telegram say?

14. C: I don't know, maybe who to call to find out where my kids were.

15. L: Did you call?

16. C: Sure, but they said I couldn't see them, just that I should be in court the next day.

17. L: What happened after this call?

Analysis:

Please evaluate this dialogue for yourself. For example, which of Nos. 3, 7, 9, 13, and 17 ask the client to continue with the narrative, and which seek detail? Do Nos. 5 and 7 reflect past or present feelings? Toward the end of the dialogue, how might you have caused a chronological gap?

12. SPECIAL TIME LINE ISSUES

A. THE TRAVELS OF ODYSSEUS

What might you do when a client's story, like Odysseus', is extremely lengthy? Your initial thought may be not to attempt a time line under such circumstances. However, the longer a story, the more necessary an overall chronology. In such circumstances, a narrative of events is particularly helpful for stimulating a client's memory and evaluating a story's inferential impact.

Hence, the usual upshot of a long story is simply a long time line, even if you need more than one meeting to complete it.

B. CO-AUTHORED TIME LINES

For the most part, this chapter has assumed that a time line story is within the grasp of a single person. However, especially in corporate litigation, a client's story may require the input of several contributors. Consider, for example, a products liability suit in which the client is a manufacturing company whose power saw was allegedly poorly designed. The client's full story probably includes how the saw was designed, tested and marketed. Hence, putting together a time line story may require that you talk to company executives, engineers and salespeople.

Documents may sometimes help you cut down on the number of people you have to contact to put together a time line story. If you can identify an individual as the "main contributor," and use documents to remind that individual of other events, talking to that individual may enable you to put together a fairly complete time line story.

Recognize that "co-authored" time lines often require you to make compromises with a pure time line approach. For example, it may be unrealistic to try to limit each of several contributors to "time lines only," and then after you have elicited a time line from each and put together a client's overall time line, go back to each for theory development. Instead, you may have to complete both phases with one person before moving on to the next.[28] Similarly, relying on documents to piece together a co-authored story may involve more immersion in documents than if a story were within a single person's grasp.

C. MULTIPLE TIME LINES

Think for a moment about the storyline of a typical hour-long television drama. It probably has two or three separate subplots. If you were asked for a time line of the show, you might find it easier to discuss each subplot separately. Because events pertaining to different subplots often occur concurrently, you might get confused trying to develop a chronology of all events. In like manner, when you can

---

28. Of course, you may not complete both phases during a single meeting.

identify separate strands in a client's story, you may help the client's recall by pursuing each strand separately. After you develop a chronology of one strand, you then pursue another, and so on until you have obtained the entire story.

For example, assume that the chief executive of our power saw manufacturer could, with the aid of documents, recall many events pertaining to the development, testing and marketing of the power saw. Assume further that many of the relevant events took place simultaneously. That is, even as research was in progress, marketing strategies were being planned; as models were tested, additional research took place. In this situation, you might try to obtain a time line of all events relating to research, another time line of events relating to testing, and yet another time line of events pertaining to marketing.

No rules can tell you when to break a story down into separate time lines. You will have to use your best judgment, taking into account such factors as a story's complexity, a client's memory ability, and perhaps considerations of time.[29]

29. Insofar as time is concerned, you may need, for example, to respond to an adversary's request for a preliminary injunction. You may not have time to pursue sub-stories separately.

Chapter 9

THEORY DEVELOPMENT: DEVELOPING POTENTIAL EVIDENCE

---

* * *

Bob, we've been at this for the better part of an hour. At this point, you've given me a quite clear picture of how this situation unfolded from the first day you met Ross right up to today. I've got a couple of ideas about what you can do now, and we can kick them around a bit. But what we'll really need to do is arrange for another meeting and get into a lot more detail than I've been able to get into today. Does that sound okay?

* * *

1. INTRODUCTION

With a time line in hand, you are probably anxious to ask a client a host of questions. Questions emanating from legal theories that might enable a client to prevail are well nigh irresistible.

Nonetheless, you often best serve a client by first evaluating a time line story in the light of potentially-applicable legal theories to identify possible evidence. This chapter explores how you might carry out that evaluation. As the evaluation typically requires a good deal of thought, it is often necessary to adjourn information-gathering temporarily at the conclusion of the time line phase, providing a client with tentative advice as appropriate.[1]

2. IDENTIFYING LEGAL THEORIES IN TIME LINE STORIES

The first step in the evaluation process is to discern all potentially-viable legal theories suggested by a client's time line story. Without legal theories, you cannot adequately conduct theory development ques-

---

1. For a discussion of giving tentative advice at the conclusion of an initial meeting, see Chapter 13, sec. 3.

tioning any more than a carpenter could build a fence without tools. Fortunately, even if you are a beginner, time line stories normally suggest some legal theories. Plaintiffs' stories suggest theories such as fraud, breach of contract and breach of warranty; defendant's stories suggest denial theories such as "no fraud" and "no breach," and affirmative theories such as laches and failure to mitigate damages.

Sometimes you may be uncertain about what legal theories to pursue during theory development. For instance, you may identify one or two potentially-viable theories, but sense that others are lurking. Or, your uncertainty may center on whether a theory is legally permissible.[2] Or, you may just draw a blank after listening to a story. Since a story does little to help resolve a client's problem unless it constitutes a legally cognizable claim or defense, you want to be sure that your questions seek information that pertain to all potentially-viable legal theories. Hence, your uncertainty may require a trip to the nearest law library or a phone call to the friendliest more experienced lawyer you know.

The remainder of the chapter assumes that you have identified one or more legal theories that, based on a time line story, you think applicable for resolving a client's problem.

3. FROM LEGAL THEORIES TO POTENTIAL EVIDENCE

The evaluation process which precedes theory development questioning normally centers on converting the applicable legal theories into specific items of evidence to pursue during theory development. The conversion involves a three step mental journey:

    1. Parsing each legal theory into its constituent elements;

    2. Converting legal elements into factual propositions;

    3. Identifying potential evidence tending to prove each factual proposition.

The remainder of this chapter examines each step of this journey.

4. CONVERTING LEGAL THEORIES TO FACTUAL PROPOSITIONS

A. LEGAL THEORIES ARE ABSTRACT SHELLS

The earth probably did not tremble for you when you read that you should probe time line stories pursuant to legal theories. What other source would you use—theories of skeletal structure as set forth in Gray's Anatomy? However, you may feel at least a small tremor when you realize that legal theories are largely ephemeral. Most legal

---

2. For example, at one time a landlord's failure to maintain leased premises in a habitable condition was not a theory that would defeat a suit for eviction. In most states, it now is.

theories, be they criminal or civil, common law or statutory, are abstract shells which are not themselves provable. At a minimum, provable legal theories consist of bundles of elements. The elements are necessary to give content to legal theories. For example, if you were asked what evidence you would offer to prove "breach of contract" or securities fraud, you would have to first ask what legal requirements you must satisfy to establish each legal theory. The legal theories standing alone are simply housings for elements, not concrete guides to proof.[3]

B.　ELEMENTS THEMSELVES ARE LEGAL ABSTRACTIONS

Elements establish the requirements of legal theories. Nevertheless, elements themselves remain legal abstractions. As a result, mere identification of elements is not a sufficient guide to case-specific questions.

For example, assume that a client's time line story focuses on his near-decapitation by an exploding kitchen appliance. Prior to theory development questioning, you identify potentially applicable legal theories, such as negligent manufacture of goods, breach of warranty, and strict liability on a theory of defective design. You then proceed to enumerate requisite elements. For example, for "strict liability/defective design", the elements are:

1.　The defendant introduced a product into commerce.

2.　The product when introduced contained a design defect.

3.　The design defect was the actual cause of damages.

4.　The design defect was the proximate cause of damages.

5.　The design defect resulted in damages.[4]

As is apparent, these elements tell you nothing about what you must prove with respect to your specific client's situation. They tell you nothing about the kitchen appliance, its design, the client's injuries and other damages or how the appliance was introduced into commerce. The elements are so broad that they can apply to an infinite number of stories. Indeed, elements are intentionally broad and abstract, for it is impossible to draft a specific rule for each situation that might arise in the context of a given legal element.[5] Thus, abstract

---

3.　Certain legal theories, primarily invoked by defendants, tend to constitute exceptions to the "abstract shell" character of legal theories. Such legal theories consist of but one element, so that the theory and the element are identical. For example, "statute of limitations" and "alibi" are single element theories. However, plaintiffs too may need to prove "one element" theories. For example, a plaintiff may allege that for purposes of diversity jurisdiction, a defendant is a citizen of a particular state. Or, plaintiff may allege that a certain entity is a corporation.

4.　See American Law Institute, Restatement of Torts, 2d § 402A and Comment (1965); 63 AmJur 2d, Products Liability §§ 528–577 (1989).

5.　For example, "citizenship" for purposes of diversity jurisdiction is a combination of geographical residence and intent. Obviously it is impossible to draft rules for every combination of factors that would govern determination of citizenship.

elements alone are not adequate guides to the "facts" that either you or an adversary may attempt to establish at trial, or to the questions you might ask to develop evidence of such facts.

The key to effective theory-development questioning is converting such abstract legal elements into factual propositions that meld events in time line stories with legal theories and their elements. Once an element is restated as a factual proposition, you know what facts will establish that element in a client's specific case. In turn, once you delineate factual propositions, you can then think concretely about what evidence in the existing story, and what potential evidence, is likely to establish the facts you need to prove.[6]

C. RESTATE ELEMENTS IN FACTUAL TERMS

To understand the process of converting a legal theory into a set of factual propositions, assume that you represent Wilson. During time line questioning, you learned that Wilson was injured when the brakes in Wilson's car failed, causing Wilson's car to collide with another vehicle. Wilson's time line story of this misadventure is as follows: (1) On June 10, Wilson brought Wilson's car to Goodstone Service Center to purchase two new tires. (2) Goodstone's manager stated that the car needed new brakes. (3) Wilson authorized Goodstone to do a brake job. (4) The brake job took longer than anticipated, and Wilson was without a car for two days, which caused Wilson hardship, including being late for work, needing friends to pick up children, etc. (5) During the week after picking up the car on June 12, Wilson noticed that the car pulled to the left when Wilson braked. (6) Wilson was returning to Goodstone on June 17 to have the brakes checked when, approaching a red light at an intersection, Wilson put on the brakes and they failed totally. (7) Wilson's car collided with the rear end of another car at a speed of about 35 mph. (8) Wilson was in the hospital with head injuries for three days, incurring medical costs of about $12,000; over $3000 in damage was done to Wilson's car. (9) Wilson was contacted by the insurance company for the driver of the car Wilson collided with and was asked for a statement.

With litigation in the offing, you adjourn the interview to think about theory development questioning. The time line story suggests a number of potentially relevant legal theories by which Wilson might recover for damages. Such principles include Goodstone's negligence, fraud and breach of warranty. For purposes of this discussion, focus on the negligence theory. In abstract terms, one element of this theory is "breach of the duty of reasonable care." Restated as a factual proposition tailored to Wilson's story, this element might read as follows:

> "Goodstone breached the duty of reasonable care to Wilson, in that Goodstone failed to check the master brake cylinder when it repaired the brakes on Wilson's car."

---

6. In addition to substantive legal theories, you may have to prove miscellaneous facts such as jurisdiction and a litigant's corporate status as part of a lawsuit. Moreover, you may want to formulate factual propositions relating to credibility.

Unlike the abstract version of "breach of duty of reasonable care," the factual proposition indicates concretely what you must prove on Wilson's behalf to satisfy that legal element. Thus, by restating the legal element in factual terms, you learn what specific facts you need to prove the abstract legal concept. In turn, knowing what you have to prove allows you to identify what evidence might establish the factual proposition. Comparing the abstract element to the restated factual proposition, doesn't the latter tend to be much more suggestive of the potential evidence you might use to prove breach of the duty of reasonable care? For example, in the context of the abstract element, did you think that evidence that an old master brake cylinder was in Wilson's car following the mishap might be evidence tending to prove "breach of duty of reasonable care?" In this way, as this example illustrates, factual propositions, because they explicitly state what it is you need to prove, promote identification of an array of items of potential evidence.

Identifying potential evidence ultimately translates into theory development questions. The list of potential evidentiary topics—e.g. old master brake cylinders—helps determine what questions you ask. For instance, the topic "old master brake cylinders" suggests questions such as:

    a. "Were you billed by Goodstone for inspection of the master brake cylinder?"

    b. "Were you billed for replacement of the master brake cylinder?"

    c. "When you picked up the car from Goodstone, were you given any parts which they said had been replaced?"

    d. "Before the accident, did the brake warning light in your car come on?"

D. DEVELOPING MULTIPLE FACTUAL PROPOSITIONS

Any single legal element may be satisfied by a virtually unlimited number of factual propositions. Across cases, this assertion is obvious: the factual proposition for the element of "formation of contract" that you might assert in one contract case, for example, will be very different from the one you might assert in another. Perhaps less obviously, you often assert multiple factual propositions for a single element in a single case. For instance, in a fraud case, you would have four different factual propositions for the element of "misrepresentation" if you contend that four different misstatements were made and relied upon. The variety of factual propositions that you may formulate for any given element simply follows from the fact that most elements are abstractions.

By the time of trial, perhaps you will assert only a single factual proposition to prove an element. But prior to trial, and especially when you are in the early stages of eliciting information, you often cannot be sure exactly what story might emerge at trial. Therefore, YOU ALMOST ALWAYS NEED TO DEVELOP MULTIPLE FACTUAL PROPOSITIONS FOR ELEMENTS BEFORE YOU BEGIN THEORY DEVELOPMENT QUESTIONING.[7]

To better understand the process of developing multiple factual propositions, assume that as Wilson's lawyer you are identifying potential evidence pursuant to the element, "breach of duty of reasonable care." As noted in subsection "C" above, this element might be satisfied by proving the factual proposition, "Goodstone failed to check the master brake cylinder."[8] But the following additional factual propositions might also satisfy this element:

> Goodstone breached the duty of reasonable care to Wilson, in that:
>
> 1. Goodstone failed to replace the brake fluid in Wilson's car.
>
> 2. Goodstone failed to properly install new brake linings.
>
> 3. Goodstone installed discs not designed for Wilson's model of car.

Especially if you are knowledgeable about cars, you might well be able to formulate additional factual propositions. But even the few alternatives above demonstrate how their development increases the scope of potentially relevant evidence. Propositions about master cylinders, brake fluid, brake linings and discs each may be established by different evidence, and hence each suggests different lines of inquiry. For example, evidence that stepping on the brakes caused Wilson's car to pull to the left or right might suggest a problem with the discs or linings, rather than with the master brake cylinder or the brake fluid. The same might be said about evidence that the brakes were smoking prior to the accident.[9]

Note: Sometimes, you will lack the experience to develop alternative propositions. For example, as the subject probably was not covered in law school, you may know little about potential causes of brake failure. Or, you might represent landowners who contend that a nearby dump contains illegal toxic wastes, and you may not be aware

---

7. We do not mean to imply that you must develop alternative factual propositions for every element in every cause of action. But rare will be the case in which you do not need to develop alternative propositions for at least one element. For example, in an action for breach of contract, you may never consider more than one story for formation of the contract, but may consider a number of possible stories of breach.

8. "Might be satisfied" is the correct term because "reasonable care" constitutes a normative standard. The trier of fact must decide whether failure to check the master brake cylinder, even if true, is unreasonable behavior on Goodstone's part. For a discussion of the differences between historical factual propositions and normative ones, see D. Binder and P. Bergman, *Fact Investigation: From Hypothesis to Proof* 7 (1984).

9. As this discussion suggests, your ability to develop factual propositions generally depends on your level of experience in the subject matter of a client's story. For further analysis of the role experience plays in identifying potential evidence, see sections 5, 6 and 7, *infra*.

precisely of how toxic waste problems manifest themselves. In such situations, you need to develop "industry knowledge" by involving an expert in the process of formulating factual propositions.[10]

Developing multiple factual propositions is often *the key* to thorough case preparation. Without identifying concretely what you want to prove, you lack guidelines for thinking about what evidence to search for. Just as there is no such thing as "negligence in the air," so too is there no such thing as "evidence in the air." Evidence proves past happenings, and you need to know, before you start to look, what past happenings you would like to prove. Aware of what you would like to prove, you in turn can focus your thoughts on the entire range of evidence to seek.

Seeking the fullest possible range of evidence from the outset also allows you to hedge your bets. If you limit your questioning to a single factual proposition, you are in trouble if down the road that solo proposition does not pan out with evidence. Searching feverishly for new factual propositions late in the game, you may instead be searching for a new client.

One reaction you might have to this advice is, "Why bother with multiple factual propositions? For each element, I'll just go with whatever factual propositions are suggested by a client's time line story." Of course you develop factual propositions directly suggested by a client's story. But you cannot limit yourself just to those propositions for at least three reasons:

a. Clients are often unaware of how events actually have transpired. For example, Wilson may have no idea why the brakes on the car failed.

b. Clients who think they are aware of how events took place may be mistaken. For example, Wilson's notion about why the brakes failed may be incorrect.

c. You may be unable to prove clients' versions of how events took place. For example, Wilson's car may have been damaged so badly in the crash that you cannot prove just what brake defect caused the mishap.

Thus, to assure that you seek the full range of potential evidence, you frequently must use your own experience and perhaps that gleaned through consulting experts to develop multiple factual propositions.

One note of caution: Judges and jurors do not award prizes to the side which produces the most factual propositions. Developing propositions to excess may prove the depth and breadth of your "industry knowledge" (e.g., that you are a master mechanic) as it drowns you in a sea of factual propositions. Do not be limited by the factual boundaries

---

10. An "expert" is not necessarily an individual; books are also sources of expertise. For further discussion of involving experts in the investigatory process, see Binder and Bergman, *supra* note 8, at 172–174.

contained in a time line story, but be reasonable in your creation of alternative ones.

E. PLAINTIFFS' AND DEFENDANTS' FACTUAL PROPOSITIONS

The process of converting legal principles into alternative factual propositions appears to respond to the way that plaintiffs' lawyers view the world. Plaintiffs normally pursue as many legal theories as are reasonably feasible, and they typically have the burden of proving each element of each alleged cause of action or criminal offense. Formulating a range of provable propositions, isolating the elements of each, restating elements in factual terms, and developing evidence pursuant to each therefore well serves plaintiffs' interests.

Perhaps for less obvious reasons, the process is just as important for defense counsel. First, it serves to remind defense counsel that pleadings alone are an insufficient guide to case preparation. Complaints typically do not specify the alternative factual propositions by which plaintiffs may attempt to prove their various theories. In the example above, the complaint will tell Goodstone only that it was allegedly negligent in servicing Wilson's car. Because Goodstone cannot attempt to negate every possible way in which its service might have been negligent, the process reminds Goodstone's counsel to learn the factual propositions Wilson is attempting to pursue. Elements such as "damages" and "reasonable care" are no less abstract for defense counsel than for plaintiffs' lawyers; consequently, defense counsel too must convert theories into factual propositions.

At the same time, defendants are very much like plaintiffs when it comes to establishing elements at trial. Defendants may not typically have the burden of proving elements, and they may not contest each and every element plaintiffs allege. But as to those elements defendants do contest, they usually not only contest plaintiffs' versions of events, but also offer their own affirmative stories. The notion of defendants "proving" elements might strike you as farfetched. Don't defense counsel merely negate plaintiffs' factual propositions? For example, wouldn't counsel for Goodstone simply formulate a factual proposition such as, "The failure to check the master brake cylinder was not the actual cause of the accident?"

Given the realities of trial, it is naive to think of defense counsel strictly as naysayers.[11] Defendants typically not only contest plaintiffs' versions of events but also offer their own affirmative versions. For example, Goodstone might attempt to prove that it did inspect the master brake cylinder. Or, if Goodstone concedes that it failed to do so, but contends that failure to check the master brake cylinder was not the cause of Wilson's mishap, it probably will try to prove what *was* its cause. Thus, Goodstone's counsel may develop one or more factual

---

11. Of course, in criminal cases defendants do occasionally sit silent at trial and argue the burden of proof, but except in criminal matters this tactic is fairly rare.

propositions, such as, "The actual cause of the accident was Wilson's failure to return the car to Goodstone for further servicing when Wilson noticed the brakes smoking on repeated occasions."

Still less are defense counsel naysayers when they allege affirmative defenses on which they have the burden of proof. For instance, if in a criminal case the defense relies on an alibi, the defense almost never limits itself to denying that the defendant was present at the scene of the crime. The defense will try to prove defendant's actual whereabouts, and it may even offer its own evidence as to the identity of the actual culprit. In such an instance, the defense might offer at least two factual propositions, such as: (a) "Defendant was actually in Miami Beach at the time of the robbery in Cleveland;" and (b) "The actual robber was Al Moore."

Hence, regardless of whether or not they have the burden of proving a theory, defense attorneys typically offer affirmative versions of events, and no less than plaintiffs' attorneys need to develop alternative affirmative factual propositions before embarking on theory development questioning.

5. USING FACTUAL PROPOSITIONS TO IDENTIFY POTENTIAL EVIDENCE

A. THE VALUE OF EXPERIENCE

The primary reason to develop multiple factual propositions before you begin theory development questioning is to enable you to identify a wide array of potential evidence. Identifying potential evidence pursuant to factual propositions keeps you squarely in the realm of fact, as you attempt to show that real world happenings establish the accuracy of your propositions. Naturally, legal rules do not disappear entirely when you identify potential evidence. You cannot identify potential evidence in blissful ignorance of what the rules of evidence *allow* you to prove.[12] But beyond the minimal constraints of evidentiary rules [13], you are largely in a factual realm.

Perhaps shaped by a law school education which emphasizes case law analysis, you may feel uncomfortable in a factual realm. Fortunately, to function in this factual realm you can rely primarily on a familiar source of thought and action: experience. Experience is the primary source for identifying evidence which tends to prove or disprove factual propositions. Often, all the experience you will need results from living life on a daily basis and observing and reading about

---

12. For instance, evidence rules greatly constrain your ability to offer character evidence. See Fed. Rule of Evid. 404.

13. We say "minimal" not to downplay the importance of evidentiary rules, but to recognize that evidence which may not be admissible at trial often has "nonlegal" value. For example, an adversary may settle to avoid the risk that questionable evidence may be admitted. Similarly, a party's moral attitudes may be affected by inadmissible evidence. Thus, you often may identify potential evidence without regard to its admissibility, and in that sense evidentiary rules are but a minimal constraint.

how others live. The kinds of familiar experiences you have undoubtedly internalized include such things as:

- how people typically behave

- how institutions typically behave

- how transactions commonly unfold

- how mechanical devices operate

- how people typically think

- how people normally react in emotional situations

How does experience enable you to identify evidence based on factual propositions? Based on our experiences, we expect that events usually proceed in recognizable patterns. Most of us accept, for example, that a bystander will be frightened when she or he witnesses a violent crime, that a stockbroker will stress the safety and growth potential of an investment when soliciting a potential purchaser for newly issued stock, that a person will be in a rush when late for an important meeting, and that a car may pull to the left or right when it is braked if its brakes are bad. Because we accept that events occur in recognizable patterns, we can identify a variety of features that are likely to have been part of past events. Thus, when you employ personal experience to identify potential evidence, you identify happenings that are consistent with a factual proposition. Proof of those happenings, in turn suggests the accuracy of a proposition.

For example, assume that a factual proposition you want to establish is the following: "Jones' identification of the robber is accurate in that Jones had an excellent opportunity to observe the robbery taking place." Knowing nothing about the robbery, you can undoubtedly use everyday personal experience to identify a number of items of potential evidence which would establish the accuracy of this proposition. You might include such matters as good lighting, a short distance between Jones and the robber, and Jones' seeing the robber for a measurable period of time.[14] You can identify such evidence not because of any experience you have had with Jones or robberies but because your everyday experience provides you with a pattern of factors that constitute "an excellent opportunity to observe."[15]

You are undoubtedly familiar with the process of reasoning from evidence to legal conclusions. Judges and jurors engage in it daily when weighing evidence pursuant to legal principles. Using experience

---

14. Of course, differences in personal experience may lead to different conclusions as to just what constitutes "good" lighting, a "short" distance, and the like. For example, some may find anything less than broad daylight a questionable basis for identification. Nevertheless, they would still be relying on their experience.

15. Note that you can readily call on experience even when you lack actual ex-

perience. Experience may be vicarious—you may never have been involved in a robbery, but you have read about robberies in books and newspapers and seen them re-enacted in movies and on television. Experience may also be analogous—you may never have been involved in a robbery, but you probably have experience observing people in other kinds of dangerous situations.

to identify potential evidence is simply the converse of this familiar process. Prior to theory development questioning, you begin with a conclusion (a factual proposition), and from that conclusion you identify evidence that is likely to have occurred if the conclusion is accurate. Instead of piecing together evidence to reach conclusions, you start with a conclusion and reason backwards.[16]

Experience also enables us to evaluate the credibility of stories. Because of the strength of our beliefs that events unfold in familiar patterns, we are inclined to disbelieve stories that depart from these patterns. For example, assume a client tells you, "True, I was running late on my way to meet the Queen to be the first person ever knighted on American soil. But I wasn't in a hurry." For most of us, the pattern of behavior for a person who is late for an important event is that the person will rush to get to the event. Most of us, therefore, would doubt the accuracy of the story. As an advocate in such a situation, you would have to use your experience to (a) recognize that the story is inconsistent with common experience and may not be believed, and (b) identify additional evidence demonstrating why general experience with the behavior of people who are late to important events is not applicable to this specific story.

Despite its importance, on many occasions everyday experience alone is not a sufficient source of potential evidence. Common experience may lead you to potential evidence about people in your client's general situation, but it may not tell you about factors that make each client's story unique. Therefore, to enable you to identify items of evidence tied to specific and unique factual propositions, you again often need "industry knowledge"—that is, experience in the underlying context of a dispute. If a client's matter grows out of a dispute over a shopping center lease, it behooves you to know something not just about leases in general but specifically about how shopping centers operate. If you represent a stockbroker who allegedly illegally "churned" an individual client's account, you must know not just about the stock market industry but about brokerage practices for non-institutional investors. If a client contends that she was negligently shot by a duck hunter, you must learn about duck hunting. Experience with the underlying circumstances giving rise to a client's problem is critical for identifying evidence tied directly to factual propositions.

Obviously, one reason that lawyers develop specialized practices is to accumulate experiences in a particular industry or way of life. But even specialization is no guarantee of subject matter experience. For instance, though you may specialize in "wrongful termination" matters, your experience with matters that originate in government offices may

16. Of course, this is the standard mode of reasoning found in many popular detective and mystery novels. See, e.g., A.C. Doyle, *The Silver Blaze* and *A Study in Scarlet*. See generally, U. Eco and T.A. Sebeok, Eds., *The Sign of Three: Dupin, Holmes, Peirce*" (1983).

be insufficient for a matter that arises in a restaurant. Even specialists, therefore, may need to call on experts.[17]

Experience, then, both in general and in the activity involved in a particular dispute, is the bridge that connects legal principles and real world events. Remember, each and every day, you use such experience to identify "evidence," if only subconsciously. Consider this sample dialogue:

Bo: "Why was Mr. Jones smiling when we got to school today?"

Jo: "Probably because we did real well on the test yesterday."

Thus, preparing for theory development questioning entails using the same thought processes you use in everyday life. Two organized approaches to applying experience to factual propositions are "Historical Reconstruction" and "Narrowing Generalizations." To employ those approaches, you must first understand the nature of circumstantial evidence.

B. CIRCUMSTANTIAL EVIDENCE

Potential evidence normally falls into one of three categories:

1. Direct Evidence

Evidence that establishes a proposition without the aid of an inference. In the Wilson/Goodstone hypothetical, the mechanic's admission at trial, "I never did look at the master brake cylinder," is direct evidence in support of the factual proposition involving negligence, "Goodstone failed to check the master brake cylinder." No inference (other than that the testimony is accurate [18]) is required to go from the mechanic's testimony to the truth of the factual proposition.

2. Circumstantial Evidence

Evidence that establishes a proposition with the aid of one or more inferences. For example, evidence that there are no tool marks on the screws of the master brake cylinder would constitute circumstantial evidence that the mechanic did not inspect the master cylinder. From the absence of tool marks, one can infer that the cylinder was not touched; from that, one can infer that it was not inspected.[19]

3. Credibility Evidence

Credibility evidence is a form of circumstantial evidence bearing on believability. For instance, evidence that Wilson has been recently

17. Note that an "expert" you consult to identify potential evidence can simply be a person who has experience that you do not. To learn about "restaurant practices," for instance, you would not need the advice of one who holds a graduate degree in restaurant management.

18. For purposes of defining evidence as "direct," evidentiary principles, generally

disregard the potential for the trier of fact to disbelieve the evidence. See Wright & Graham, Federal Practice and Procedure: Evidence § 5162, text and notes accompanying notes 21–23 (1990).

19. If this inferential chain strikes you as wrong, it may be due to the authors' lack of pertinent "industry knowledge" regarding brake repairs.

convicted of perjury would (in just about every jurisdiction) bear on Wilson's credibility. Similarly, evidence that because Goodstone was in financial distress its mechanics had to complete 50 brake jobs a day would bear on the believability of the mechanic's testimony that, "I thoroughly inspected the brakes on Wilson's car."

For a variety of reasons, most evidence that you either identify or offer at trial is circumstantial.[20] Circumstantial evidence, however, can prove or disprove a factual proposition only according to the strength of an underlying premise. That is, evidence has probative value only according to the strength of the premise which connects the evidence to a proposition. In the vast majority of cases, premises are generalizations about the behavior of people and objects. They are postulates about how people and objects sometimes, though not always, behave. The probative value of evidence, then, typically depends on the degree of accuracy of these underlying generalizations.

For example, assume that a factual proposition you are attempting to prove is, "Snider ran a red light and struck Mantle's car." Seeking to prove the accuracy of this proposition, Mantle's attorney calls Mays, who testifies, "I spoke to Snider 15 minutes before the collision, and he told me that he was very late for an important meeting across town." Mays' testimony is circumstantial evidence. And its probative value depends on a generalization such as, "People who are late for a meeting are likely to be in a hurry and thus to fail to stop for a red light." In the absence of such a premise (generalization), a trier of fact could make no inference connecting Mays' testimony about "lateness" and Snider's running the red light.

"Historical Reconstruction" and "Narrowing Generalizations" are methods of identifying potential circumstantial evidence. As you will see, each depends on your recognizing that a generalization connects an item of circumstantial evidence to a factual proposition. When you employ "historical reconstruction" you need not explicitly formulate a generalization; when you employ "narrowing generalizations," you usually must do so.

C. HISTORICAL RECONSTRUCTION

1. In General

Historical reconstruction is a method of reasoning by which you combine experience with chronology to identify potential evidence. The notion behind historical reconstruction is that most events are neither isolated nor random but they are part of larger sequences of events. For instance, most of us can predict the kinds of problems the owner of a small retail shop experienced when just starting out, and the activities of an apartment seeker who has two small children and who suddenly had to move. Experience can tell us not just how any discrete

---

20. For a discussion of the reasons that circumstantial evidence predominates, see   Binder and Bergman, *supra* note 8, at 81–82.

event may have unfolded, but how an entire sequence of events is likely to have unfolded.

With historical reconstruction, you adopt the attitude that a factual proposition is accurate. Then ask yourself, in essence, "If this proposition is true, what else also would probably have occurred?" The "what else" will be items of potential evidence which, if confirmed, become circumstantial evidence tending to prove the accuracy of the proposition.

As an illustration of historical reconstruction, assume that as counsel for Wilson, one factual proposition you have tentatively decided to pursue is that, "Goodstone failed to check the master brake cylinder when it repaired the brakes on Wilson's car." Prior to beginning theory development, you want to identify items of potential evidence which, if believed, would tend to prove the truth of this proposition.

To employ historical reconstruction, start from the premise that your proposition is accurate—Goodstone failed to check the master brake cylinder. Then, using everyday experience, think about what actions or happenings are consistent with failure to check a master brake cylinder. Probably even the most mechanically inept among us could identify such indicators as:

    a.   the mechanic's worksheet did not indicate that the mechanic had inspected the master brake cylinder;

    b.   Wilson was not billed for inspection of the master brake cylinder;

    c.   when Wilson picked up the car, the mechanic did not speak to Wilson about the condition of the master cylinder;

    d.   Goodstone mechanics are paid according to how many cars they repair per day.

Though you need not formally identify underlying generalizations when you engage in historical reconstruction, note that the potential evidence this technique identifies is circumstantial. And each item implicitly recognizes the existence of an underlying generalization. For example, the generalization underlying item "c" is something like, "A mechanic who inspects a master brake cylinder is likely to tell the car owner that he or she did so." The generalization supporting item "d" is something like, "A mechanic whose pay goes up the more cars she or he repairs is likely not to thoroughly inspect a car for latent problems, including a problem with the master brake cylinder." [21] Try formulating generalizations for items "a" and "b" on your own.

2. Chronology: Before, During and After

As you know, events which culminate in litigation typically take place over hours, days, months and even years. An alleged contract may follow lengthy negotiations; a traffic accident may happen after a

---

    21. We do not address the tactical question of whether you should, at trial, explic- itly identify underlying generalizations for judge or juror.

round of parties and social drinking; prolonged bitterness between a testator and a child may culminate in a will disinheriting the child. However, legal elements, and therefore factual propositions, nearly always bless particular moments in time with substantive importance.[22] For example, a factual proposition asserting that a party breached a contract typically focuses on the specific moment in time that the breach occurred. Similarly, a factual proposition asserting a testator's incompetency to make a will focuses on the testator's state of mind at the moment the will was signed. In a legal contest, then, the parties battle over whose version of substantively critical events is accurate.

However, events that occur "before" and "after" the substantively critical ones often determine which party's version of substantively critical events is believed. For example, a testator's behavior in the months preceding and following the signing of a will may well be determinative on the issue of testamentary capacity. From a party's conduct before, during and after a long course of negotiations, a trier of fact is likely to infer whether or not the party ultimately agreed to enter into a contract. Evidence that a defendant has a lengthy drug habit and left town the day after a robbery may produce an inference that the defendant committed a crime. Thus, circumstantial evidence describing what happened before and after, as well as during, substantively critical moments in time often determines the outcome of a trial.

Historical reconstruction encourages you to identify events that may have occurred before and after the substantively critical events. The usual question is, "If a factual proposition is true, what events are likely to have preceded or followed the substantively critical events?" For example, assume a factual proposition you are trying to prove is, "Testator P.J. Giddy was competent to make a will in that at the time he signed his will Giddy knew his children's names, ages and occupations." Potential "before" and "after" evidence suggesting that this proposition is true includes evidence that Giddy sent his children birthday and anniversary cards, telephoned them, and made statements to others about them both before and after the execution of the will.

Expanding the temporal scope of an interview through historical reconstruction typically expands the spectrum of potential sources of information. One goal of developing potential evidence is to learn of other people (or documents) that might either support your client or provide evidence of which your client is unaware. But often, the only people who can describe what occurred at a moment of substantive importance are the interested parties themselves. For instance, assume that a plaintiff investor seeks to establish that a defendant company knew its prospectus was false when issued. In that situation, only the company officials who prepared the prospectus may know what knowledge they had concerning the statements in the prospectus. Likewise, no one other than the drivers may claim to know how an accident occurred; and only a lawyer and a couple of strangers who

---

22. See Chapter 8, sec. 3(F).

acted as witnesses may have been present when a will was signed.   By identifying potential events at different points in time, you typically uncover potential sources of evidence other than the parties themselves.

3. Multiple Perspectives

When using historical reconstruction, try to re-create events from the perspectives of the different actors who might have had roles in those events.   Sometimes you will find that viewing events from the perspectives of different individuals leads you to think of potential evidence you might have overlooked had you been considering but one point of view.   For example, return to the factual proposition, "Goodstone failed to check the master brake cylinder when it repaired the brakes on Wilson's car."   The prior subsection briefly identified potential evidence that might support this proposition primarily from the standpoint of actions in which the mechanic might have engaged.

But further perspectives are possible.   You might, for instance, think about how Wilson was likely to have behaved during the incident. Is Wilson generally experienced with cars?   How do people who do have some expertise with brake repair describe a braking problem to a mechanic or service manager?   How about someone without such expertise?   Consider also the possible role of a Goodstone store manager.   What does experience suggest about the potential behavior of managers of automobile repair shops?   Why might such a manager pressure employees to complete a high daily volume of brake jobs?   For example, might a manager's job be on the line, or might there be competition among various Goodstone repair shops?   If so, what kind of memoranda might evidence such pressure?   Note that the store manager perspective produces not only new items of potential evidence but also another potential source of information (i.e., documents).

D. USING GENERALIZATIONS

Unlike historical reconstruction, the "using generalizations" approach to identifying potential evidence requires you to explicitly use generalizations.   Was any approach ever more aptly named?

To use this second technique, you again begin with an assumption that a factual proposition is correct.   Next, you incorporate that proposition into a generalization.   Lastly, you identify potential evidence by narrowing the generalization, either by adding "especially when" or "except when."   "Especially when" identifies potential evidence that tends to add credence to a factual proposition; "except when" identifies potential evidence that tends to lessen a generalization's credence.

For example, assume that a factual proposition suggesting Goodstone's negligence is, "Goodstone installed the wrong brake shoes when it repaired the brakes on Wilson's car."   Incorporating the "facts" in this factual proposition into a generalization, you might state, "Car mechanics sometimes install the wrong brake shoes in a car." This generalization may be "especially true" when

— the mechanic is in a hurry;

— the brake shoes that fit one model of car are quite similar to those that fit another;

— the mechanic is inexperienced;

— the mechanic is not closely supervised; and

— the mechanic is under the influence of alcohol or drugs.

On the other hand, the generalization may be true, "except when"

— the mechanic is an expert in brake repair;

— the car is owned by an important customer;

— the brake shoes come in a clearly marked package; and

— the brake shoes had to be specially ordered.

Note that sometimes, "except whens" are simply the converse of "especially whens." For instance, the mechanic being inexperienced makes it more likely that the mechanic would have installed the wrong brake shoes; the mechanic's being an expert makes it more likely that the mechanic would have installed the correct ones. However, other times you will identify potential evidence in the context of one option that you would not have if you thought only in terms of the other. For instance, when writing this section we identified the "important customer" item only in the context of "except when." Of course, as Wilson's attorney, your task would be to develop additional evidence that establishes the "especially whens" and negates the "except whens."

E. INCREASING THE "DEPTH" OF POTENTIAL EVIDENCE

Those prone to "winging it" with clients may think that the process of identifying potential evidence already described is about as far ahead as one could possibly imagine. However, during the planning process you can press identification of potential evidence still further. Subsequent interviews can truly "come alive" if you analyze items of potential evidence according to the same generalization-based processes already employed. For example, assume you have identified as potential evidence, "the mechanic was in a hurry." Do not contentedly stop here. Use "especially when" again, and say to yourself, "Mechanics are in a hurry, especially when . . . ." You may identify such items as, "when they are late for a date," "when they have many cars promised for the same day," or "when they get paid according to how many jobs they complete." In the alternative, you may say to yourself, "What is likely to be true before, during and after a mechanic is in a hurry?" Each layer of potential evidence that you identify will be richer in detail than the last.

The detailed topics that you identify through repeated use of the generalization processes will ultimately turn questioning into a search for concrete data rather than vague conclusions. For example, Wilson's affirmative answer to the question, "Did the mechanic seem to be in a hurry?" is nothing more than Wilson's conclusion. The answer may have little probative value, since what to one person is a "hurry" may to another be normal or even slow-paced. By contrast, Wilson's affirmative response to the question, "Did the mechanic say anything about having promised to complete too many jobs the same day?" (or ". . . that the mechanic was paid on a piecework basis?") is likely to be far more persuasive.[23]

F. MIRROR IMAGES

"Historical reconstruction" and "Using generalizations" both lead to the identification of circumstantial evidence through the use of generalizations. If later questioning establishes that the potential evidence you identified does exist, you may ask the trier of fact to engage in a reasoning process that is the mirror image of the one you used to identify the evidence in the first place. For example, if you uncover evidence that the mechanic who installed the brakes in Wilson's car was in a hurry because the mechanic had promised to complete too many repair jobs, you may later argue something like, "Mechanics who are in a hurry because they promise to complete too many jobs on the same day are especially likely to install incorrect brake shoes on a car." Such an argument asks the trier of fact to make an inference from a specific item of evidence (hurrying due to too many jobs) to a factual proposition (installation of incorrect brake shoes). The argument does so by asking the factfinder to rely on a generalization about the effect of hurry on the behavior of mechanics. When you originally identified the potential evidence, you used that same generalization, but moved in the opposite direction: you started with the conclusion (installation of incorrect brake shoes), and identified evidence (hurrying due to too many jobs) that would support its accuracy.

6. "INTERVIEWII INTERRUPTI"

The process of formulating alternative factual propositions and identifying potential evidence is designed to produce an array of topics to explore during theory development questioning. The end product is a list of concrete items of potential evidence, arranged according to factual propositions. Regardless of one's depth of knowledge of legal rules, few of us could achieve such a list immediately upon eliciting a time line story. Hence, the recommendation that you usually adjourn data gathering before conducting theory development questioning is

---

23. Note that applying the generalizations processes to potential evidence not only aids theory development questioning but also guides you to questions you might put to witnesses. For example, here you produce a number of items of potential evidence to pursue during informal or formal (e.g., deposition) questioning of the mechanic, other employees, or the Goodstone store manager.

premised on the need to identify precise topics of inquiry prior to actual questioning, not on any lack of legal expertise.

Should you as a matter of habit engage in the potential evidence identification process described in this chapter? Typically, yes. In its absence, whatever questioning you do after eliciting a time line will necessarily be quite incomplete.[24] Moreover, if a case matures at all, initial sloppy data gathering will almost certainly have to be extensively rehashed with a perplexed and possibly angry client at a later time. However, you can exercise judgment as to how extensively to pursue the process. For example, you may limit your pursuit in a "horizontal" manner, choosing not to develop the fullest possible array of factual propositions for each element, or at least postponing their development to a later time. Or, you may limit your pursuit "vertically," identifying potential evidence for all propositions, but not to the depth suggested in the chapter.

The approach you follow in a specific case is apt to be influenced by a variety of factors. For example, if you represent a plaintiff, you may want to delay extensive identification of potential evidence until you are confident that an adverse party intends to dispute your client's claim. If you represent a defendant, you may put to the side (for a time at least) factual propositions for elements the client seems prepared to concede.

Other factors include the time you have available to gather data before taking a required legal step, and a client's willingness to pay for your time.

7. CONCLUSION

In many of the best restaurants, customers see only the food that is served, not the helter-skelter of kitchen activity that goes into its preparation. The thoughts in this chapter are the equivalent of the kitchen activities in restaurants. Converting theories to elements, recasting elements in factual terms, and identifying potential evidence

24. One approach that some attorneys use in place of the sort of analysis we describe is checklists. As you probably know, checklists typically consist of information to seek in particular types of disputes. See, e.g. P.W. Kittredge, "Guideposts for the Investigation of a Negligence Case," 19 Prac.Law. 55, 58–62 (May 1973); L.S. Zubrensky, "Some Aids and Advice for Handling the Typical Personal Injury Case," 14 Prac.Law 43, 68–70 (Nov.1968); J. Kelner and F.E. McGovern, *Successful Litigation Techniques* § 4.04 (1981). While checklists can be useful, they typically have serious limitations. For example, many checklists are based only on abstract legal principles, and thus are not adequate guides to concrete topics that pertain to a specific client's story. Other checklists may apply to such specific factual circumstances that they are of little use outside their narrow scope: "What? You have a case involving a dead mouse in a bottle of Coca–Cola? Sorry—this checklist was designed for a case involving a dead bat in a bottle of 7–Up." Also, checklists typically describe types of information to seek without delineating the specific elements to which the information pertains. Hence, checklists may be of use, but they cannot substitute for your having a general approach to effective theory development questioning.

are thought processes that go on out of sight of clients. Clients will be aware only of the questions you ask. But just as the way that food is served affects a diner's enjoyment of it, so does the way you question affect the information you receive. The next chapter takes you out of the kitchen into the dining room as it considers theory development questioning techniques.

Chapter 10

THEORY DEVELOPMENT
QUESTIONING TECHNIQUES

* * *

1. L: All right, Pat [Wilson], since a few days have passed since our initial meeting, let me take just a few minutes to recapitulate what you told me. You've been very clear, and you have given me a good overall account. In brief, on March 12 you responded to a Goodstone ad that promised that all of their tires were slashed—tire prices, that is. You went in the next day: someone from Goodstone examined your old tires, and said that the wear pattern indicated a problem with your brakes. You agreed to a brake job and picked up your car two days later. As you were driving home your brakes failed, and you collided with a car ahead of you. You've been contacted by the insurance company that represents the driver of the other car, and the company is seeking to collect for injuries to its driver and his car. You've also contacted your insurance company. Are those the main points?

2. C: Yes, well, don't forget that I was injured and had to miss work for two weeks, and that my car was totalled.

3. L: Of course not. Your goal is not only not to pay anything yourself but also to recover for your own injuries and losses. The medical bills and your missing so much work have put a lot of pressure on your family, and you'd like the situation resolved as quickly as possible. Have any additional concerns arisen since we last talked?

4. C: I guess not, but I'm really anxious to get this over with.

5. L: I remember your explaining that time is important because you might be transferred out of town in the near future. You know I'll do my best. Has any new information come to your attention since our last meeting?

6. C: No.

7. L: All right. As you probably remember, when we last met we talked about the fact that your own insurance company will represent you in any claims the other driver has made against you, but that in seeking to recover from Goodstone I will be representing you. As far as recovering from Goodstone, there are a couple of legal theories that might be useful.

8. C: So you think I've got a pretty good chance? Does that mean you'll be able to take care of this quickly?

9. L: Well, it's still early days. I can't promise anything; after we talk today, we'll discuss more specifically where you stand legally and how you might proceed. As for how long it might take, again, I can't make any promises. A lot will depend on how strong our case turns out to be and the attitude of Goodstone's insurance company. I would hope that we could have it concluded within a year. I know that seems like a long time, but Goodstone's insurance company probably will be in no hurry to resolve your claim.

What I'd like to do now is go back through the events you've described and see if together we can flesh out the story a bit. This will enable me to explore my legal ideas, and perhaps come up with some new ones. After we're done, I'll try to give you a more precise assessment of how we might proceed. Do you have any other questions?

10. C: No, not at the moment.

11. L: All right. Let's go back . . .

* * *

1. BRIDGING THE TIME LINE AND THEORY DEVELOPMENT PHASES

The dialogue above marks the shift from time line to theory development questioning.[1] The brief summary of the time line story (No. 1) and mention of Wilson's principal concerns (Nos. 3 and 5) should give Wilson confidence in your capacity to listen and to understand Wilson's problem, encouraging Wilson to speak freely. You praise Wilson for providing a good account of events (No. 1), and you use the facilitator of "extrinsic reward" by suggesting that ensuing questioning will produce tangible results in the form of "a more precise assessment of how we might proceed." (No. 9) Wilson is asked about any new information or concerns (Nos. 3 and 5) and has an opportunity to ask questions. (No. 9)

1. For a fuller analysis of how you might begin follow-up interviews, see Chapter 7, sec. 5.

The dialogue is not a "model," and you might want to critique it in terms of what might be most comfortable for both you and a client. For example, No. 7 refers to "a couple of legal theories" but does not identify any. Would you be more specific? If so, how specific would you be? Would you also discuss your factual propositions? In addition, you do not disclose the potential evidence you seek. Would it be tactically wise or ethically proper for you to do so?[2] Also, the summary statement (No. 1) seems rather brief. How detailed do you think such a summary should be? Anything close to a complete rehash of a story seems pointless and unduly time consuming. Too little (e.g., "So, if I understand your story correctly, you've got some legal problems because of a brake job by Goodstone."), and a client may wonder whether you slept through the time line phase.[3]

Finally, as you will come to appreciate, during theory development you are likely to ask numerous closed questions in pursuit of potential evidence. The above preparatory explanation (No. 9) is silent about these variances. Do you think most clients would care to be informed of such information?

2. TWO IMPORTANT ASSUMPTIONS

Two important assumptions govern our approach to theory development questioning. First, theory development questioning is largely a search for details. Second, in order to elicit details, you typically need to focus a client's attention on discrete events. Consider each of these assumptions briefly.

A. THE PERSUASIVENESS OF DETAILS

Our first assumption is that discrete items of evidence—that is, a story's unique details—typically constitute its most persuasive evidence. For one thing, details link events with factual propositions. For instance, if a factual proposition concerns "speed," knowing only that an event consisted of "two cars colliding" tells you nothing about the extent to which the event proves or vitiates the factual proposition. Details such as skidmarks and their length, extent of damage to the cars, and one driver's being twenty minutes late to pick up a six-year-old child from school provide necessary evidentiary links to the factual proposition.

2. See, e.g., G. Bellow and B. Moulton, *The Lawyering Process* 261–264 (1978); M. Freedman, *Lawyers' Ethics in an Adversary System* 67–69, 71, 74–75 (1975). Cf. ABA Model Code of Professional Responsibility, DR 7–102(A), EC 7–26; ABA Model Rules of Professional Conduct, Rule 3.3, Rule 3.4(b) (1984).

3. When you summarize a story you risk altering it both in your mind and that of your client in an effort to enhance its legal effect. Many clients will not recognize or will be too timid to point out the subtle changes, but instead will adopt the altered story as their own. Problems are then likely to ensue as you probe for and a client tries to remember details pertaining to a story whose only reality is in your summary. Hence, even a summary requires care.

Moreover, details are critical to credibility. For example, a client's ability to describe just what portions of the cars were damaged and the extent of the damage usually helps convince a trier that the client recalls an event accurately.[4]

Similarly, details often are the key to a story's emotional impact. While events in and of themselves may have emotional appeal, details tend to magnify that appeal geometrically. For example, an event such as "Jack fell down and broke his crown" is likely to create sympathy for Jack. But add to that event details such as, "Jack suffered a six inch gash on his head that required 29 stitches to close and left a jagged scar," and you increase the emotional impact.

Lastly, the more details you elicit, the less likely you are to "fill in" with your own. As a result, a client's ultimate story more accurately reflects "what really happened," rather than what you assumed happened.

B. EVENTS ARE GATEWAYS TO DETAILS

Our second assumption is that events are the most efficient gateway to details.[5] That is, a client will usually be best able to recall details in the context of a specific occurrence. For instance, in the "speeding" example, a client will probably be better able to describe the extent of the cars' damage in the context of events such as "the collision" or "taking the car to the repair shop," than if you ask about damage in the abstract, without regard to a specific event.

3. SELECTING EVENTS

With factual propositions, items of potential evidence and time line events in hand, you have to decide which events to pursue during theory development. Almost certainly, you do not explore every time line event for potential evidence. In other words, if you imagine time line events as trees, you have to decide which trees to examine. Hopefully, you will also have other forests to attend to.

Obviously, you normally decide which events to pursue according to the factual propositions you are trying to establish. Factual propositions imbue some events with importance and render others seemingly irrelevant. For example, assume that in a case in which a client

---

4. For a discussion of the persuasive impact of details, see B.E. Bell and E.F. Loftus, "Degree of Detail of Eyewitness Testimony and Mock Juror Judgments," 18 J.Appl.Soc.Psych. 1171 (1988).

5. "Events" are temporally discrete occurrences. Events include physical activities (walking, firing a gun), conversations, or even non-occurrences (defendant's silence after receiving *Miranda* warnings.) Details are the unique and individualizing aspects of events (walking *hurriedly;* firing *3 shots in rapid succession*). Concededly,

you may at times find it difficult to distinguish an "event" from a "detail." For example, in the story of "Goldilocks," you may regard Goldilocks' sitting on the chair that was too soft as a separate event, or as a detail of a larger event. But as usual, abstract definitional purity is of little importance. If a factual proposition makes certain details important, and you believe that a clients' thinking of an occurrence as a separable event will enhance the client's memory, by all means treat it as such.

contemplates suit against a real estate broker growing out of the client's purchase of a home through the broker, one of your factual propositions is, "Broker misstated the condition of the roof." The client's time line includes these events: (a) on Sept. 1, client walked through the house for 10 minutes with only the seller present; (b) on Sept. 3, client walked through the house for an hour with the broker. Surely, the latter event is more likely to house important evidence than the former. Hence, you may choose to examine event (b), and ignore or delay examination of event (a).[6]

4.　WHY YOU CANNOT RELY ONLY ON A TIME LINE STORY AND A LIST OF POTENTIAL EVIDENCE ITEMS FOR THEORY DEVELOPMENT

Even if you accept these assumptions, you might expect this chapter to be a short one. "Theory development questioning is a snap," you might think. "Events are in the time line story; and I've got my list of potential evidence. I'll just remind a client of the important time line events, and ask closed questions seeking the potential evidence." Alas, things are usually not that simple, because of the following factors:

A.　TIME LINE STORIES FREQUENTLY CONTAIN "GAPS"

Because open questions do little to stimulate a client's memory, and because a client may not recognize an event's legal significance, clients frequently omit mention of events when telling a story during the time line phase. Thus, you need to give a client an opportunity during theory development to fill the resultant "gaps" in order to make a story complete and provide additional gateways for detail.

Filling gaps often requires that you make "topical" inquiries. That is, just as events serve as gateways to details, topics often serve as gateways to events. Topics are simply the subject matter areas determined by items of potential evidence. For example, assume that in a will contest case, one item of potential evidence is "Earhart (the decedent) told people he had a brother." One topic, then, is "conversations in which Earhart mentioned having a brother." Similarly, assume that in a criminal case in which Borden is accused of killing her parents, one item of potential evidence is "Borden had great love and affection for her parents." One topic in this case, then, is "Borden's love and affection for her parents."

Of course, all topics occur in connection with events. That is, if Earhart said something about having a brother, Earhart would have done so during a "conversation" event.[7] But a topic may arise during

---

6. Even within the universe of time line events imbued with importance by factual propositions, you may have further choosing to do. For discussion of considerations that you typically weigh when deciding the order in which to probe events, see sec. 12 *infra*.

7. A seeming exception occurs when you try to prove that something did *not* happen. That is, if a testator never said

many different events. The testator might have said something about
having a brother during a company picnic on May 22, while looking at
old pictures on June 8, or when going Christmas shopping on December
3. However, unless you first mention the topic "conversations in which
Earhart mentioned having a brother," the client may be unable to
recall such events.

B. TIME LINE STORIES TYPICALLY MASK EVENTS

An event most readily serves as a gateway to detail when it refers
to a discrete occurrence, and in so doing focuses a client's attention on a
sufficiently manageable chunk of time. Unfortunately, clients' time
line stories often tend to mask and blend together discrete happenings.
The masks behind which events tend to hide are "clumped events" and
"conditions and behaviors over time."

A "clumped event" is a group of sub-events that a client collective-
ly refers to as a single event. For instance, a client may say, "We had a
seven hour bargaining session with management." Outside a law office
the "session" would probably be viewed as a single event. But for
litigation purposes, the "session" as a whole may consist of too many
happenings for you to use it as the basis of a search for detail. You
probably can aid the client's memory by first breaking the clump into
more manageable chunks of sub-events (discussions of "seniority,"
"overtime," and "contracting out"), and then proceeding to probe the
chunks for details.

Statements of "conditions and behaviors over time" blend individual events into conclusory assertions that often do not refer to events.
For example, a client may say, "the roof leaked all winter," or, "Jean
was always getting angry with us." Such statements are devoid of
events which might serve as gateways for details. That is, they do not
refer to specific occasions on which the roof leaked or Jean got angry.
Hence, you generally need to tease out specific events underlying such
conclusions before seeking details.

C. YOUR ANALYSIS OF POTENTIAL EVIDENCE FREQUENT-
LY OVERLOOKS IMPORTANT DETAILS

Even thorough pre-theory development analysis of the type suggested in Chapter 9 is rarely sufficient to enable you to identify each
and every item of important potential evidence. One reason is simply
that, as suggested in subsections "A" and "B" above, the time line story
on which you base the analysis is almost certainly somewhat incomplete and conclusory. But more importantly, the past events underlying a dispute are typically so unique and unpredictable that unforeseen
details constituting important evidence are always lurking. While
closed questions might enable you to learn whether the potential

anything about having a brother, no such
event exists. Even in such situations, however, events are pertinent. You typically
try to show the various occasions during
which a topic *might* have arisen, but did
not.

evidence you have identified exists, they are of little use for uncovering evidence that you did not and could not foresee. Hence, even during theory development, you need to employ open questions to encourage clients to mention unanticipated evidentiary details.

D. SUMMARY

We have tried to suggest why you typically cannot rely on a time line story and a list of potential evidence items to uncover a client's complete story. Thorough theory development questioning requires you to fill gaps, break clumps and conclusory descriptions into manageable chunks, and encourage clients to mention unforeseen details. The remainder of the chapter examines techniques for carrying out these tasks.

5. T–FUNNELS: EXPLORING EXISTING EVENTS FOR DETAILS

The T-funnel questioning method is the principal technique for probing events for details.[8] T-funnels allow you to search an event both for potential evidence you have already identified *and* to encourage clients to recall additional evidentiary details that you have not.

The premise of the T-funnel technique is that your chance of efficiently learning all relevant evidence housed in an event is greatest if you ask open questions before barraging clients with closed questions. As you recall from Chapter 6, open questions give clients the freedom to discuss what they think is germane. Open questions elicit evidence from a client's own frame of reference, often producing evidence that your prior analysis of the potential evidence would never have led you to ask about.

However, you also know from Chapter 6 that responses to open questions are invariably incomplete. In large part because they stimulate memory, closed questions tend to elicit evidence that would go unstated in response to open questions, and thus often are necessary if you are to uncover the potential evidence that led you to pursue an event in the first place. The T-funnel method, which combines the advantages of open and closed questions, may be depicted as follows:

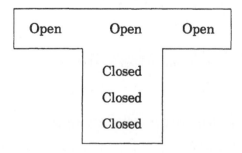

---

8. Focusing a person on an event more than once can enhance memory. See E. Scrivner and M.A. Safer, "Eyewitnesses Show Hyperamnesia For Details About a Violent Event," 73 J.Appl.Psych. 371 (1988).

In the diagram, open questions form the upper portion of the "T;" closed questions form the lower portion. As the diagram suggests, you begin to explore an event by asking open questions. Because the questions are open, the details you uncover may do more than furnish evidence in support of the factual proposition(s) you are pursuing. The details may also support other factual propositions, or even a story's credibility or emotional impact. Once a client's "spontaneous" memory seems exhausted, you turn to the bottom portion of the "T." [9] You ask closed questions derived by and large from your list of potential evidence.

Thus, if you believe an event may house three or four items of potential evidence that a client did not mention in response to open questions, each item will be the subject of a separate closed question.

Be aware, however, that using the T-funnel method is likely to demonstrate to you just how unaccustomed people are to supplying details. The persistence with which you may pursue details through T-funnels could stop a boisterous dinner party crowd dead in its tracks inside of five minutes. Thus, a client may become uncomfortable as you press for details that are alien to social discourse. In social discourse, perhaps because listeners usually want their turns at talking, reciting substantial detail is rude.[10] However, by continuing to use motivational techniques during theory development, and by explaining your need for details, you can generally assuage a client's discomfort.

By way of illustration, assume that you represent Dr. Rex, who is a defendant in a medical malpractice action. You are attempting to counter one of plaintiff Vee's factual propositions, which is, "Dr. Rex did not warn Vee of the potential dangerous side effects of Nembutal." A time line event mentioned by Rex is a conversation that Rex had with Vee in which the possible side effects of the medication were discussed. Now, during theory development, you want more information regarding this conversation. The upper part of the "T" might go as follows:

1. L: You mentioned earlier a conversation in which you discussed with Vee possible side effects of the medication you intended to prescribe. Do you recall that conversation?

2. C: Yes, I do.

9. Empirical evidence suggests that interviewers who use a large number of open questions often elicit more information than those who move right into closed questions. R.P. Fisher and R.E. Geiselman, "Enhancing Eyewitness Memory With The Cognitive Interview," 1 Practical Aspects of Memory: Current Research and Issues 37 (1988).

10. Moreover, details are usually unnecessary in social settings. On social oc-casions, listeners are generally more than willing to believe a story, and details are thus not needed to convince listeners that a story is accurate. For example, if in an ordinary social setting a storyteller says, "All of a sudden this car came out of nowhere," the listeners will probably fill in that the car was travelling at a high rate of speed. In litigation, an adversary is usually not so trusting.

3. L: Now, can you please tell me all you can remember about that conversation; give me as much detail as you can remember whether or not you think it's important.[11]

4. C: Well, after we reviewed the tests and the X-rays together, I told Vee that I was going to prescribe Nembutal. Vee asked me if there were any possible side effects of this medication. I told Vee, as I tell all of my patients, that there are always possible side effects with any medication, even aspirin or cough medicine. I told Vee that in terms of side effects noted in the literature in connection with this particular medication, there were a few reports of stuttering, rapid heart beat and digestive upset.

5. L: What else do you recall about this conversation?

6. C: Let's see. Oh yes—Vee asked to know more about these side effects, so I got out my Physician's Desk Reference and we reviewed the information on Nembutal together. As it happens, a recent medical journal had just published a short article on the medication, and I got it out and we looked that over also.

7. L: Your memory seems really clear. What else can you remember?

8. C: I remember Vee said that the information I had given him matched what a doctor friend of Vee's had told Vee. I remember that distinctly, because I didn't like the sense that Vee was checking up on me.

9. L: That's very helpful information. Please continue . . .

This is a classic example of "horizontal" "T" funnel questioning. All questions pertaining to the event—the conversation—are open. Note that in No. 8, you learn of evidence that you might not have thought to ask about on your own, an important benefit of open questions.

Next, moving into the lower portion of the "T," you ask closed questions seeking additional potential evidence. In the case of Dr. Rex, assume that the pertinent factual propositions is, "Dr. Rex thoroughly explained to Vee the potential side effects of Nembutal." Combining your own "industry knowledge" with an expert's advice, you have identified the following items of potential evidence as ones which, if they exist, would strengthen the factual proposition: Rex also told Vee that amnesia and sleeplessness are potential side effects of Nembutal and responded to questions by Vee about other potential side effects such as possible weight gain, decreased sex drive, and interaction with other drugs or foods. He also responded to Vee's questions about

11. The plea to include all details, whether or not the client thinks them important, can be useful. First, research shows that such an instruction can aid recall. See Geiselmen and Fisher, *supra* note 9, at 5. Second, a response to this request may provide you with details about which you would never think to ask.

alternative medications, and about where Vee might read about Nembutal. These items are the basis of the closed questions you might put to Rex in the lower portion of the "T": [12]

10. L: Let me ask you just a few more things about what may have taken place during your meeting with Vee. Do you recall saying anything about amnesia as a potential side effect?

11. C: I forget—you see, I once took Nembutal myself. Just kidding—no, I'm sure I didn't say anything about that; at least as of the time I prescribed it, that was not a side effect that had been noted in the literature, I don't believe.

12. L: Okay, how about sleeplessness; might you have mentioned that?

13. C: I forgot that—yes, I'm sure I did.

14. L: Now, might Vee have asked you about other side effects? For example, did Vee ask whether weight gain was a possible side effect?

15. C: No, I don't think so.

16. L: Might Vee have asked about the possible effect of Nembutal on Vee's sex drive?

17. C: No, I don't recall that.

18. L: How about its possible interaction with other drugs or foods?

19. C: Come to think of it, Vee said something about being on a megavitamin program, and Vee asked whether one could be on such a program and still take Nembutal.

20. L: That's helpful. Did Vee ask about whether there were alternative medications Vee might take?

21. C: _____

* * *

30. L: Those are the specific questions that I have. Is there anything else that you can remember about the conversation?

As you can see, the questions in the lower portion and the upper portion of the "T" both pertain to the same event—"conversation with Vee about side effects." However, the lower-T questions are closed and search for previously-identified potential evidence topics. Note, however, that the sequence concludes with an open question. Before leaving an event, you should usually give a client a last opportunity to recall a hitherto overlooked piece of data.

---

12. Note that an event may often house evidence pertaining to more than one factual proposition. For example, as Dr. Rex's lawyer you may believe that the conversation about side effects also houses information pertaining to Vee's symptoms and alleged damages. Efficiency suggests that when you target an event, you usually probe for evidence pertaining to all relevant factual propositions during vertical "T" questioning.

6. T–FUNNELS: SOME ADDITIONAL TECHNIQUES

The course of T-funnel questioning, like that of love, is not always smooth. Here are suggestions for handling situations you will frequently encounter.

A. "PARK" NEW EVIDENCE

As questions produce data, either in the upper or the lower portion of a "T," you will often be sorely tempted to ask about that new data before you exhaust the initial event which began the "T." If you follow that temptation, you may become sidetracked and neglect to return to the initial event. Instead, "park" new data until you complete questioning about the initial event. "Parking" data that emerges through T-funnel questioning is necessary if you are to explore important events fully.

To understand the importance of "parking," return to the exchange that took place during the open question portion of your interview of Dr. Rex:

7. L: Your memory seems really clear. What else can you remember?

8. C: I remember Vee said that the information I had given him matched what a doctor friend of Vee's had told Vee. I remember that distinctly, because I didn't like the sense that Vee was checking up on me.[13]

At the time Dr. Rex reveals this information, you have not yet finished asking about the event which is the initial subject of the "T," the conversation between Rex and Vee about side effects. Nevertheless, you continue the interview as follows:

9. L: Just what did Vee say this doctor friend had told Vee?

10. C: If memory serves, Vee said that he saw this doctor at a party, asked the doctor about Nembutal, and the doctor mentioned the same side effects that I did.

11. L: Did Vee mention this doctor's name?

12. C: Not that I can remember.

13. L: Did Vee say when this conversation took place?

14. C: Not exactly, but it seemed like no more than a couple of days before Vee came to my office.

15. L: Did Vee say anything about the specialty . . .

These questions have sidetracked you. Your initial topic was everything said by Rex and Vee about side effects. Before concluding

---

13. When a client can recall how he or she was feeling at a particular time, the recollection may enhance the client's overall memory. This will particularly be true if you ask your client to use the feeling to mentally recreate the scene. See text at *infra* note 14.

that topic, you begin pursuing an item of new evidence and end up talking about a completely different event.

Unfortunately, you may become so engrossed in the new topic that you never return to the original one. Even if you do remember to return to the original topic, the sidetracking might disrupt the client's paths of association. Better to "park" the new item until you have exhausted the original topic, and then probe the new item in it's own "T" sequence, as described in subsection "D" below.

Parking a topic might disappoint a client, especially one who under your persistent prodding has finally recalled what the client thinks is an important detail, only to have you ignore it. Undoubtedly, the client will not realize you are only parking the topic temporarily, and may think it will get lost in a tow-away zone. Hence, when you park a topic you might recognize a client's effort and explain that you will return to it. For instance, in lieu of becoming sidetracked in No. 9 above, you might have parked the topic with a statement such as the following:

9.   L: I'm glad you mentioned that. That's definitely worth pursuing, and I'll do so shortly. For the moment, let's stick with the initial conversation you had with Vee about side-effects. What else can you remember?

B. "KICK START" A CLIENT'S MEMORY THROUGH VISUALIZATION

Sometimes, clients can supply little information in response to open questions. This sort of dialogue may occur:

1.   L: Dr. Rex, please tell me all you can remember about the conversation with Vee about the potential side effects of Nembutal.

2.   C: I know that Vee and I talked about that for quite a while, but I just can't remember what we said.

Especially if in your heart of hearts you like to ask lots of questions, you may pounce upon the client's lack of recollection the way a vulture may pounce on a just-deceased fieldmouse, and begin firing closed questions. But open questions are too valuable to toss away at the first sign of client hesitancy. You may be able to stimulate a client's recollection by asking the client to form a visual image of a scene. Research indicates that people's memories are stimulated if questions first re-create the setting in which an event took place. The recreated scene is most effective if the client can recall the external environment and their own feelings and reactions.[14]

For example, after Dr. Rex's response in No. 2 above, you may proceed as follows:

14. See N.Y. Times, section B, p. 11 (Nov. 15, 1988); R.E. Geiselman and R.P. Fisher, "The Cognitive Interview Technique for Victims and Witnesses of Crime," 3–5 (1989) [Manuscript on file with authors.]

3. L: Perhaps it will help if you take a moment and try to picture the situation in your mind. Think about where the conversation took place.

4. C: It was in my office, which is separate from the examining rooms.

5. L: How were you seated?

6. C: I was at my desk, and Vee was seated across from me.

7. L: What time of day did the conversation occur?

8. C: I think it was in the late afternoon.

9. L: How were you feeling at that time?

10. C: Pretty calm.

11. L: All right, seeing yourself talking to Vee in your office, try to take on the feeling you had then and see if you can remember everything that you and Vee said to each other.

If the "mental image" route does not work, you may have to resort to closed questions. Remember, though, that a client's responses to a few closed questions may themselves jog a client's memory. Thus, you may try to boost yourself back into the horizontal portion of a "T" even if you have first asked a few closed questions. Moreover, if the "kick start" technique does not work in the upper portion of the T, you may have more success with it during the lower portion.

C. PRESS CLIENTS TO SEARCH THEIR MEMORIES

After horizontal "T" questioning, all clients at some point become unable to recall evidence. And, especially after an extensive open question dialogue, you may take a client's statement such as, "that's all I can remember," as a signal that you best move to the vertical portion of the "T" if you hope to uncover additional evidence.

However, the signal may be premature. You may suspect that with additional effort, a client can come up with more evidence in response to open questions. Thus, rather than retreat to closed questions, you might press the client to search her or his memory further. Consider the following directive:

> L: "I appreciate how much you've told me about that conversation. Frankly, what occurred during that conversation may be critically important. Keep trying to visualize the conversation, and see if you can recall anything else."

Such a statement marks the point at which both you as well as a client may become uncomfortable with T-funnels, as you press for information in a way that you do not in polite social conversation. But the statement does keep you in the upper portion of the "T," and in various ways attempts to motivate a client to continue to recall evidence. The statement indicates that you expect the client to recall additional evidence, praises the client and stresses the significance of the data. Also, it reminds the client to visualize the scene of the conversation.

The client's response may be one of frustration ("I've told you already, that's all I can remember.") or recall ("Come to think of it, there was one more thing . . . "). It is certainly not necessary to push every client to the point of absolute zero recall. Indeed, if you push too far, a client may provide false information in an effort to meet your expectation that she or he knows more than she or he has so far revealed. But given the benefits of open questions, you often do not want to accept automatically a client's first plea of lack of recall.

Summarizing the responses a client has given may aid an attempt to press a client to recall further details of an event. Remember that actively listening by reflecting content tends to motivate clients to go on, because the reflection indicates that you have heard and attended to what has been said. Thus, you might have phrased the above directive to Dr. Rex as follows:

> L: "I appreciate how much you've told me about that conversa-tion. Frankly, what occurred during that conversation may be critically important. So far, you've mentioned that you looked in the PDR, and told Vee that rapid heart beat and stuttering were potential side effects of Nembutal. Also, you talked about how Vee told you about a conversation with a doctor friend. Keep trying to visualize your conversation with Vee, and see if you can recall anything else."

D. USE T-FUNNELS CYCLICALLY AS YOU UNPARK DATA

When you complete T-funnel questioning for an event, you often have parked a few items of new evidence along the way. Most likely, you will want to probe at least some of these new items. To do so, use another "T!" Ask open questions about each new item, and follow with closed questions.

For example, recall that during the interview of Dr. Rex, you parked data concerning a conversation that Vee had with a doctor friend. You believe that this event may house evidence tending to show that Rex thoroughly discussed the potential side effects of Nembutal with Vee. Thus, you would call this event to Rex's attention, and probe it with a "T:"

(Upper portion of T, questions only):

> L: Now, you mentioned that at some point in the conversation, Vee mentioned speaking to a friend who is a doctor. Please tell me everything you remember about what Vee said about Vee's discus-sion with this friend.

> L: That's very helpful. Anything else you recall?

* * *

(Lower portion of T, questions only):

L: Did Vee mention the name of the friend?

L: Did Vee say that the friend mentioned that amnesia was a potential side effect?

L: Did Vee say that the friend mentioned any alternative drugs?

*   *   *

In turn, any topic Dr. Rex mentions in the course of *this* T-funnel sequence can become the subject of yet *another* T. For example, if Dr. Rex mentions that, "Vee's doctor friend told Vee that Pampredine was a possible alternative," you may later start a new funnel by asking, "Tell me all you can remember about what Vee told you about the doctor friend's recommendation of Pampredine as a possible alternative."

Like the image you see when you look in mirrors that face each other, you may think that T-funnel questioning will extend to infinity. Rest assured that is not so. You need continue the questioning only as long as the details you search for are important, and a client's memory holds out.

E. EXERCISE JUDGMENT

T-funnels are not as rigid in application as they might appear on paper. For example, in the course of theory development questioning, you may have to decide which event to probe next—an event that you had targeted for probing before you began theory development questioning, or one that you "parked" during T-funnel questioning. You will have to look to your reading of each client and sense of what is most critical in a given case, not to T-funnel "rules," to make such a choice. Also, no rules can tell you how extensively to press a client for answers to open questions. Moreover, we do not suggest that you subject every detail that a client mentions to full T-funnel analysis. T-funnels are simply a useful way of combining a client's awareness of historical events and your analysis of factual propositions to generate a story which is complete and persuasive.

While much remains for your judgment, we cannot over-emphasize the importance of using the T-funnel method. Failure to use it competently, usually by switching in midstream to a new event and neglecting to return to the original one, is often responsible for the most infamous of all lawyer-client colloquies:

Lawyer: Why didn't you tell me that before you got on the stand?

Client: Because you never asked me.

7. T–FUNNELS—EXAMPLES FOR REVIEW

To become more familiar with T-funnel questioning, consider the three sample theory development dialogues below. We provide analysis for the first two dialogues; the last we leave to your own thoughts.

Case No. 1:

Legal Theory: Fraud

Legal Element: Making false representations

Plaintiff's Factual Proposition: The car seller said that the car had been driven less than 15,000 miles.

Items of Potential Evidence—Salesperson said car had had only one prior owner; that it had been driven only for specific purposes, such as back and forth to work; that the prior owner did most of his or her driving with a different car; that the tires were original and still had most of their tread; that the interior was like new, etc.[15]

Events Appearing to House Relevant Evidence: Initial conversation with salesperson; conversation during test drive; post-sale conversation with salesperson on day the transaction was completed; taking car to mechanic for service, etc.

  1. L: Let's go back to your initial meeting with the salesperson. Tell me everything that took place during that meeting.

  2. C: She said that the car was in sound condition, that it had always been serviced regularly at their shop, and that it had less than 15,000 miles on it.

  3. L: What else happened?

  4. C: That's about it. Oh, she did say the car had just one previous owner.

  5. L: O.K., she mentioned sound condition, one owner, regular service, and the mileage; what else can you remember?

  6. C: That's all.

  7. L: I know it's difficult to remember, but I can see you're really trying. Try going back to the conversation in your mind's eye and picture yourself there with the saleswoman. Think very carefully, what else occurred?

  8. C: Well, I remember she told me to check the tires and notice how much tread was left on them. There did seem to be a lot of tread on them.

  9. L: Good, that's helpful. What else?

10. C: That's all, really.

---

15. Of course, the client's assertion that the car seller made the 15,000 mile statement provides direct evidence of the factual proposition. However, if the salesperson denies making that statement, potential evidence such as that listed above may provide helpful circumstantial evidence.

11. L: Did she say that the prior owner had only used the car for a specific purpose?

12. C: Yes, she said that the prior owner only used it to drive back and forth to work, only about 15 miles a day.

13. L: Did she say anything about a period of time when the car was not used?

14. C: No, not that I recall.

15. L: Did she say anything about how the interior showed that the car had not been driven much?

16. C: She did say something about that, but I think that was when I took the car for a test drive.

17. L: . . .

28. L: Is there anything else that took place during that initial meeting that we haven't talked about yet?

29. C: Not that I can recall.

Analysis:

This open-closed sequence is a genuine "model T." The upper portion of the T includes Nos. 1, 3, 5, 7 and 9; the lower portion consists of Nos. 11, 13, and 15. The sequence concludes with an open question. (No. 28)

Consider first No. 1. The question embraces the entire event, and does not confine the client to the specific factual proposition for which you are seeking evidence. Also, it asks for "everything that took place," not merely what was said. Next, note that in No. 5 you do not immediately accept the client's purported inability to remember more, but press the client for additional responses to open questions in two ways. No. 5 also employs the summary technique. In No. 7, you are *empathic* ("I know it's difficult to remember"); *recognize* the client's efforts ("I can see you're really trying."); and use *visualization* ("mind's eye . . . picture yourself there with the saleswoman."). However, you attempt not to press too far, and by moving to the lower portion of the "T" in No. 11 accept the client's lack of further recall. Finally, note that throughout the upper portion of the "T," you convey the *expectancy* that the client will remember additional evidence. For example, in No. 7 you ask, "What else occurred," not, "Did anything else happen?"

Throughout the entire discussion, you stay with the initial event—the initial meeting. Though the client does reveal specific items of evidence (e.g., Nos. 2, 4, 8, 12, 16), you do not become sidetracked into discussion of those items. You "park" these items, to await possible later T-funnel treatment.

Case No. 2:

Legal Theory: Fraud

Legal Element: Reliance

Plaintiff's Factual Proposition: Plaintiff relied on the salesperson's statement that the car had less than 15,000 miles on it.

Items of Potential Evidence: Plaintiff never repaired cars or took courses in car mechanics; didn't have car checked by an independent mechanic; car's interior and exterior were in good condition; plaintiff needed to buy a car quickly; car dealership was well established; salesperson was well-dressed and articulate, etc.

Events Appearing to House Relevant Evidence: Prior car stolen; seeing dealership ad on TV; seeing car on Sunday evening visit to car lot when it was closed; initial conversation with salesperson; conversation during test drive; conversation with salesperson on day the transaction was completed; etc.

1. L: You earlier told me that you first saw the car when you visited the dealership one Sunday evening, when it was closed. Can you tell me more about that?

2. C: I was wandering around the lot, and I started over to look at the car when I noticed another couple admiring it.

3. L: What led you to think they were admiring it?

4. C: They were smiling, nodding their heads up and down, and looking it over really carefully.

5. L: OK, please go on.

6. C: I walked over to look at the car and started talking to the couple.

7. L: Did they say anything about the car?

8. C: The woman said that she had test driven the car the day before and wanted her husband to see it. She said her cousin owned the same model car and really liked it.

9. L: Did you get this woman's name?

10. C: Yes, but I can't remember it. She was going to give me one of her business cards, but she was all out.

11. L: Did she tell you the name of the salesperson who she dealt with?

12. C: Yes, it was Renee Klein, the same saleswoman that I dealt with.

13. L: Did you ever ask Ms. Klein if she remembered this woman?

14. C: Yes, I felt kind of guilty because I ended up buying the car the woman was looking at. When I described the woman to Ms. Klein, she said she thought she knew who I was talking about, and that she had bought a different car.

15. L: Did Klein say what kind of car this woman ended up buying?

Analysis:

In this example, the original event is the client's visit to the used car lot. In No. 2 the client mentions seeing another couple, and you immediately narrow down to a specific detail about this couple. This glitch, if such it is, is minor. A narrow question or two for purposes of clarification may be helpful and need not derail a T-funnel sequence. You need not function like a machine. And, in No. 5 ("Please go on"), you do return to the original topic.

But then you do become sidetracked. Nos. 7, 9, 11, 13 and 15 pertain to the identity of a potential witness, not to the visit to the used car lot. Perhaps you will return to the initial event. However, once sidetracked, you may fail to return to the initial event, and so miss important evidence.

Case No. 3:

Legal Theory: Fraud

Legal Element: Knowledge

Plaintiff's Factual Proposition: Defendant knew that the car had more than 15,000 miles on it.

Items of Potential Evidence: Prior owner told defendant what car's mileage was; speedometer showed more than 15,000 before defendant offered car for sale; defendant knew that original tires, brakes, shock absorbers and etc. had been replaced by the original owner; etc.

Events Appearing to House Relevant Evidence: Initial conversation with salesperson; conversation during test drive; conversation with salesperson on day the transaction was completed; taking car to mechanic for service; taking car back to dealership for repair; taking car to mechanic; picking up car from mechanic after repairs were made; etc.

1. L: You told me earlier that after the problems developed and the place where you bought the car was unable to fix them, you took it to a mechanic a friend had recommended, and picked it up 3 days later. What happened when you picked up the car?

2. C: He told me that most of the problems had been caused by faulty prior repairs. He said wrong brake parts had been installed, and that the car had little power because improper replacement gaskets had been used.

3. L: That must have been really frustrating. What else do you remember?

4. C: Not too much else other than that he said the car obviously had a lot of miles on it. That really pissed me off.

5. L: I can understand how that would make you angry. But what you've just told me is useful; I'll come back to that in a moment. But for now try to think back to what else

happened when you picked up the car. Try to picture the scene in your mind. What went on?

6. C: We were standing just outside the cashier's office.

7. L: All right, you're outside the cashier's office. What else can you remember?

8. C: Really I don't remember anything other than paying the bill and driving away.

9. L: Okay, let's go back to the mechanic's comment about lots of miles. What did he say?

10. C: Just that the car had lots of miles on it. That's all I can remember.

11. L: Did he tell you how many miles he thought it had?

12. C: Not really.

13. L: Did he say what led him to think the car had lots of miles?

14. C: He mentioned that the wear on the brakes indicated the car had been used a lot.

15. L: Tell me more about the wear on the brakes.

16. C: He told me that they had been repaired a couple of times previously and that he had to replace parts that had already been replaced once before.

17. L: Did he say how long ago they had been replaced?

18. C: Not that I remember.

19. L: Okay, have you told me everything you can recall?

20. C: Yes.

21. L: Then let me ask you about the second time you took your car in for repairs . . ..

Please review this dialogue in light of the following questions:

1. In No. 3, was your use of active listening proper and effective? How about in No. 5?

2. In No. 5, were you correct in deciding to "park" the response about "a lot of miles?"

3. In Nos. 5 and 7, did you adequately employ visualization?

4. How does No. 9 operate to (a) cut off the top part of the original "T" too quickly; (b) eliminate the bottom part of the original "T;" and (c) unpark data and begin a new "T?"

5. In No. 9, how might you have used the summary technique to stay with the original "T?" Why might you have been better off doing so?

6. Recognizing that No. 9 starts a new "T," how do Nos. 11 through 17 sidetrack you from the new "T?"

7. Given that the original event was "picking the car up from the mechanic," what additional potential evidence, if any, might you have asked about in the lower portion of the original "T?"

8. BREAKING LARGE STORY CHUNKS INTO SUB–EVENTS

As you recall, clients often mask discrete events in "clumped events" and "conditions and behaviors over time." The T-funnel method does not readily adapt to such large chunks of stories because a client's attention is not sufficiently focused on a discrete event. Hence, before you begin to use T-funnels to probe clumped events and conditions and behaviors over time for details, you should first reduce large chunks to manageable sub-events. Techniques for doing so follow.

A. PROBING CLUMPED EVENTS

As you also recall, a clumped event is a series of events cloaked as a single occurrence. Since even the event of taking a single breath may be chronologically subdivided, obviously you need not try to atomize everything a client says. But when a client gives a clumped description of an important occurrence which took place over a span of time, attempt to parse the description into sub-events before you begin T-funnel questioning.

For example, assume that you represent The Dolinko Group, an advertising agency, in a breach of contract action against Aranella Corp. Dolinko contends that Aranella agreed to hire Dolinko to conduct an advertising campaign for Aranella's new "Instant Sushi" freeze-dried product. During time line questioning, Feris, a Dolinko Vice–President, tells you, "We made our presentation at a meeting on July 7," and goes on to describe a number of follow-up phone calls to Aranella's general manager. Just what took place during the July 7 meeting may provide important evidence tending to show that the parties ultimately entered into a contract. But since the meeting was lengthy, and probably consisted of sub-events (e.g., presentation of printed matter, video showing of sample television spot, discussion of costs and fees), begin by extracting the sub-events from the clumped "meeting" description before turning to T-funnel questioning.

The basic technique for piercing clumped events is the familiar one of eliciting a time line. Just as you ask clients to "start at the beginning" and use open questions to obtain a time line, so too do you elicit a "mini-time line" of a clumped event.

For example, to parse the "advertising presentation" clumped event, you may proceed as follows (questions only):

    1. "Think back to the start of the meeting, and step by step tell me everything you can recall happening."

    2. "After you described what campaigns the agency had done previously, what happened next? "

3. "Between the time you discussed costs for the TV ads and before you passed the drawings around, what else happened?"

By eliciting the mini-time line, you may uncover sub-events such as "description of previous campaigns," "discussion of costs for TV ads," and "passed drawings around." You may then T-funnel those sub-events which appear to house relevant evidence.

B. PROBING CONDITIONS AND BEHAVIORS OVER TIME

As you know, "conditions over time" are also composite groupings of discrete events. When a client says, "My back hurt for 6 months," or, "The architectural committee never paid attention to what the neighbors wanted," a client lumps together many discrete happenings into an overall assertion. Because such assertions do not refer to particular events, you will have difficulty eliciting details.

Thus, the key to probing conditions and behaviors over time is to develop a list of discrete events giving rise to the composite description. Often, you will not be able to uncover every such discrete event. For instance, the client with back pain could not possibly remember each moment that her back hurt. However, you can often uncover a few discrete events. The question you may ask is, "Can you remember any specific instances when (e.g., "you experienced back pain?" or "the architectural committee did not pay attention to the neighbors?"). In response, the back pain client may recall being unable to play softball at Uncle Harry's birthday picnic, and having to cancel a planned vacation; the other client may remember the meeting at which the architectural committee approved elevated solar panels on a roof.[16]

You may also use a time line to make a more directive search for events underlying a condition or behavior over time. That is, referring to time line events, you may ask whether a condition or behavior was a part of them. For instance, if three events in a client's time line are "renting a car," "talking to a witness to the accident on the telephone," and "talking to an insurance claims adjuster," you might ask whether the client specifically recalls back pain in connection with any of those events.

Once you have teased out events illustrating a condition or behavior over time, you then probe for details using the T-funnel method.

9. PROBING CONCLUSORY DETAILS

Clients often substitute conclusions or judgments for evidentiary detail. Conclusions characterize or judge data rather than describe it. For example, a client characterizes data by saying that "The meeting

---

16. A client's inability to identify such discrete events usually calls a client's credibility into question. For example, a trier of fact may not believe a client who says, "My back hurt constantly for 6 months," but who cannot recall more than one or two specific occasions on which it hurt.

was a *quick* one;" "Jan spoke in an *angry* tone of voice;" "Hilary *screamed* when her hamster died." [17]

To probe conclusions masking evidentiary detail, simply ask clients to relate the bases for their conclusions. For example, if a client states, "The robber became enraged when the alarm went off," ask what behavior of the robber led the client to that conclusion: "What did the robber do that leads you to say that he became enraged?" Similarly, if a client states, "The meeting was lengthy," you may ask: "How long was it?"

Unless you probe conclusions, you will fill in stories with information drawn from your own experiences. A client may consider a 10 minute meeting to be "lengthy," whereas after a few months of law practice you may regard any meeting of less than an hour as a quickie. And be warned that clients are prone to conclusions. To repeat, very little about everyday social discourse encourages people to describe happenings in great detail. Though this section may be small, the problem is large.

10. PROBING GAPS TO UNCOVER ADDITIONAL EVENTS

Another theory development task is to probe potential story gaps for additional events. You need to probe for gaps when you have identified potential evidence topics that may be housed in events which a client has not yet mentioned.

Two methods of searching gaps for omitted events are already familiar to you from Chapter 8 as time line questioning methods. You call a previously-disclosed event to a client's attention, and ask if anything happened before or after that event. Alternatively, you may remind the client of two events which "bookend" a period of time, and ask if anything took place during that intervening period. Even if you do some searching for possibly-omitted events during time line questioning, various reasons often lead you to do so again during theory development. For example, sometimes you do not realize the significance of a possibly omitted event until after you identify factual propositions and potential evidence. Or, you may believe that a client's recall has improved as a result of theory development questioning.

All well and good, you may say, but on what basis might you infer that a client has omitted mention of an event? Sometimes, your only basis will be an intuitive hunch. Other times, legal requirements may impel you to search for omitted events which must have taken place if a client is to succeed. For example, unless a client has filed a certain type of employment discrimination claim with governmental or administrative agencies, the client may be unable to proceed with a lawsuit.

Two other bases on which you often search for omitted events are:

---

17. As discussed in section 8, clients also refer to entire events in conclusory fashion, by using clumped events and conditions or behaviors over time.

"Normal Course" Events: In the course of telling a story, many people forget about routine, repetitive events. For instance, if you were asked, "What happened when you woke up?", you would probably not say, "I looked around the room." You would assume that such a "normal course" event was understood and jump to what you thought the questioner was interested in. Most of us live in worlds dominated by normal course events—always getting caught by the same red light on the way to work, routinely checking our electronic mail system when beginning the work day. And, if asked what we do on the way to work, or how we spend our working day, we are apt not to mention such routine, normal course events. They are so routine to us that we assume they could not be of interest to anyone else.

For the same reasons, clients typically omit mention of normal course events during time line questioning. Often, such omission is all to the good. You are no more interested in hearing about routine events than a client is in mentioning them. However, if important evidence is housed in a normal course event, a client's failure to mention the event may conceal the evidence.

If you intuit that a client has omitted mention of a routine event that may house important evidence, you may use a closed question to learn whether the event in fact took place. For example, a doctor-client describing a physical examination of a patient may not mention that she took the patient's blood pressure. If you think that the doctor did so, and that important evidence may be housed in that event, you may put the question to the doctor in closed form:

> "Doctor, after the office visit and before the surgery, did you order any tests run on Mr. Lipkis?" [18]

If the doctor confirms that she sent the patient for tests, you may then probe the test events for evidentiary detail through the T-funnel method.

Prior Knowledge of Events: Sometimes you know something about a client's story even before an initial meeting. A friend and/or former client who talks to you before referring a client may relate factual information to you. For instance, if you get a late night phone call to visit a client who has just been arrested, the caller may well provide you with details leading up to the arrest. Or, if you have represented an individual or entity previously, you may already know something of the client's procedures.

If a client omits mention of events your prior knowledge tells you probably occurred, you may use a closed question to bring such events to a client's attention: "I remember from my work on the Zolt matter that your company conducts annual evaluations of all employees in July. About that time, did you meet with Varat in connection with such an evaluation?"

---

18. Such a question does not constitute improper leading of a client, since the topic of the inquiry standing alone is merely preliminary.

Sometimes you may be tempted to conceal your knowledge of an event. For example, you may want to evaluate a client's truthfulness by whether the client reveals an event to you. But concealing your knowledge may mislead you both as to your client's credibility and story. Remember, it is always possible that it is your knowledge which is faulty, especially if it comes from a client's associate. On the other hand, you may at least want to delay inquiring about an omitted event which a client may find threatening or embarrassing.

11. TOPICAL INQUIRIES: DID "X" EVER HAPPEN?

Topical inquiries are an alternative route to uncovering additional events housing potential evidence. A topical inquiry asks, without reference to any event, whether a subject ever arose. You simply mention a topic and ask if a client can recall an event in which this topic arose. An inquiry typically takes the form of, "Did X ever happen?" Questions such as, "Did you ever see Warren with a gun," and "Did you ever tell Asimow that you own a second home?" are topical inquiries. They refer not to any specific happenings but to topics constituting items of potential evidence. The topical inquiry process operates as the mirror image of events-to-details questioning. Thus, just as events are frequently the gateway to details, so are topics often the gateway to events.

The level of concreteness or abstraction at which you mention a topic may affect how successful you are at stimulating a client's memory. For example, assume that you represent a will contestant, and are attempting to establish that the testator was incompetent to execute a will, in that he was senile. Employing a topical search, you ask the contestant whether she can recall "any indications of senility by your uncle." If the question elicits no information, the reason may be that "senility" is too abstract a term to stimulate the client's memory. You should therefore follow up with more specific topical inquiries: "Do you recall him forgetting his name?" "Do you remember him going out and being unable to find his way back home?"

Whether or not a client is able to recall events in which a topic arose, you should follow initial "Did X ever happen" questions by "taking the topic across the time line." Taking a topic across a time line focuses a client on specific time line events and asks whether a topic arose during each such event.

As an example of the topical inquiry process, assume that "discussion of planter warts" is a potential evidence topic in the Rex/Vee matter that Dr. Rex has not yet mentioned. The questioning may proceed as follows:

1. L: Do you recall ever speaking to Vee about planter warts?

2. C: Why, yes, come to think of it.

3. L: Can you tell me each occasion when you spoke to Vee about plantar warts?

4. C: I can recall one time, when Vee called me on the phone about a rash.

5. L: Can you recall any other times?

6. C: Hmm . . . No.

7. L: How about during Vee's first office visit, did the subject of plantar warts arise at that time?

8. C: No, not that I recall.

9. L: You mentioned that Vee called your office once and spoke to your nurse. Do you know whether the subject of plantar warts came up at that time?

10. C: Yes, I forgot about that.

11. L: How about the time that . . .

In this dialogue, No. 1 is a classic "Did X ever happen" inquiry. In Nos. 3 and 5, you continue this line of inquiry until the client's memory seems spent. Then, No. 7 takes the topic across events in the client's time line. When you employ this technique, you would not stop at every point in a time line, but only at those in which the topic is likely to have arisen. But though you may be selective, you cannot confine topical inquiries to "Did X ever happen." Such general inquiries compel clients to shuffle through all possible events to try to locate those involving a topic. Easy for computers, perhaps, but impossible for us lowly mortals. Remember, stories may include events occurring over periods of months or years. Hence, taking topics across time lines may enhance clients' memories by allowing them to focus on discrete blocks of time.

Note that in Nos. 5 and 11 you continue to search for additional events even though in Nos. 3 and 10 the client did recall an event. You "parked" the events in Nos. 3 and 10 to await later T-funnel inquiry. "Parking" is advisable because if you probe a topic immediately, you may neglect to complete a thorough search across events in which the topic may have arisen.

For reasons of efficiency, you might ask about two (or even more) topics of the general "Did X ever happen" variety before you take each across a time line. Then, when you do refer to specific time line events, you can ask whether each topic arose in connection with an event. That way, you need not take one topic across a time line, then do so with another, and so on. A client may become perturbed when you return to the same time line event for the 347th time.

For example, if two topics you want to pursue with Dr. Rex are discussions of plantar warts and psoriasis, you might begin with general topical inquiries: "Did you ever talk to Vee about plantar warts?" "Did you ever talk to Vee about psoriasis?" After concluding your general inquiries, you may take both topics across Rex's time line simultaneously: "During Vee's first office visit, did the subjects of plantar warts or psoriasis arise?"

In response to topical inquiries, a client is likely both to identify previously-unmentioned events, as well as to mention events that have already been discussed in some detail. You should probe the former in standard T-funnel fashion. But when you return to an event that has already been partially discussed, you might confine your questioning to the particular topic:

"You told me that you discussed plantar warts with Vee during the initial office consultation. We've already talked about that conversation a bit. Why don't you just tell me now what you can remember about the discussion of plantar warts during that conversation."

12. ORDER OF QUESTIONING

In contrast to time line questioning, you need not pursue story features chronologically. That is, you need not probe a potential gap before a clumped event, or an event before a condition over time, simply because the gap predates the clump and the event occurred earlier than the condition.

When thinking about the order of theory development questioning, you can begin by referring to your list of potential evidence. Factual propositions generally render some items of potential evidence more significant than others. Or, you may have a short time to prepare for a hearing on a preliminary injunction, and some of the potential evidence may particularly relate to the issues that will arise during the hearing. In either situation, it makes sense to first probe those events or gaps which are likely to house the greatest amount of significant potential evidence. Since you may not have the time, and your client may not have the resources, for you to probe every potentially relevant feature, you may begin with those events that seem the most evidentiarily promising.

Alternatively, recalling the discussion of motivational factors in Chapter 4, you may pursue a feature which a client is likely to perceive as relevant or feel comfortable discussing before one that may be ego-threatening or breach the etiquette barrier. Similarly, if you probe events or gaps that may contain evidence that is harmful to a client's cause (as surely you must do if you are to help clients reach realistic solutions), you may choose to search for helpful evidence before you look for the harmful.

Finally, do not dismiss chronology as a possible ordering principle. You may help the recall ability of some clients if you pursue events in roughly the same order that they occur on the time line.

13. EXPLORING CREDIBILITY

Thus far, the emphasis has been on theory development questioning with respect to substantive principles. That is, uncovering events and probing for details primarily produce evidence in support of factual propositions. But because substantive rights usually depend so heavily on precisely how historical events took place, a client's version of events is almost sure to be met by a competing version. Hence, you generally need to devote some portion of theory development to developing evidence pertaining to credibility.[19]

Of course, the dichotomy between "substantive" and "credibility" evidence is somewhat illusory. Without explicitly probing for credibility, you may develop evidence which allows you to make inferences about a client's credibility. For example, a client's ability to supply details during T-funnel questioning not only adds to the substantive story, but it also may bolster credibility by demonstrating that the client is observant and has an excellent memory. Likewise, credibility may be undermined if a client can recollect few details, or if details contradict the client's opinions and conclusions.

However, often credibility evidence is not embedded in substantive evidence. Instead, you must specifically search for credibility evidence. And compared to "substantive" theory development questioning, exploring credibility creates a greater risk of divisiveness between you and a client. Whereas probing for detail probably matches most clients' expectations about attorney-client interviews, a client may perceive your exploring credibility as implying distrust. In turn, such a perception may erode rapport and client confidence.

A. COMMON CREDIBILITY INQUIRIES AND WHY CLIENTS PERCEIVE THEM AS IMPLYING YOUR DISTRUST

In social milieu, listeners do not regularly challenge a person's veracity.[20] Thus, questions pertaining to credibility are unusual and may suggest that you personally doubt a client's story. Consider how some common credibility probes may have this effect:

1. Personal Background Questions

Various aspects of a client's personal background tend to affect credibility.[21] Such factors as a person's education, area of residence, and job duties may affect credibility even if they are completely unrelated to underlying factual issues. For example, the fact that a

19. Recall that one advantage of asking open questions during T-funnel questioning is that you may uncover credibility evidence that you would not have thought to ask about.

20. The challenge, if any, may come when the teller is safely out of range: "I didn't believe a word of Charlie's story last night." Charlie, of course, remains secure in the apparent acceptance of his tale.

21. See, e.g., P. Bergman, *Trial Advocacy in a Nutshell* 45–46 (2d ed. 1989); M. Berger, J. Mitchell, R. Clark, *Trial Advocacy—Planning, Analysis & Strategy* 282 (1989).

client is a business executive may enhance a client's credibility.[22] At the same time, a client's experience and training may influence a judgment as to a client's qualifications to speak as to the underlying factual issues. For example, the fact that a client is a bartender might add credibility in a case in which one factual concern is whether an individual was under the influence of alcohol.

To uncover personal background information beyond what you may gain through "chit-chat," you often must ask specific questions: "Tell me a bit about your educational background." "How did your experience as a bartender help you recognize that Bernard was under the influence of alcohol?"

At best, some clients perceive such questions as simply irrelevant. Others may think you are unduly prying, and still others may perceive you as challenging their stories.

2. Cause-and-Effect

Credibility is usually enhanced if a client can explain *why* events occurred as the client claims that they did.[23] For instance, the credibility of a client's statement, "I am certain they agreed to have the cement delivered on the 6th of July" will be aided if the client can explain her certainty: "That is my birthday."

On their own, clients may not explain why events took place as they contend. Hence, you may want to probe for cause-and-effect with specific inquiries: "How is it you can be certain that they agreed to the 6th of July?" A client, of course, may well understand such a question as implying that you doubt what the client has said.

3. Independent Evidence

A client's financial and/or emotional interest is an ever-present threat to the client's credibility. Hence, you routinely inquire whether more neutral witnesses and documents can confirm a client's version of important events or details.[24] For example, you might ask, "Was anyone else present when they stated that they wanted the cement delivered on July 6th?" or, "Do you have a memo, a letter or some other piece of paper indicating that delivery was to be on the 6th?" Again, such questions may lead a client to doubt your acceptance of a story.

4. Prior Statements

Statements made by a client which conflict with the client's testimony are admissible to impeach the client at trial; under certain circumstances, the conflicting statements are admissible for their truth. Hence, you commonly ask clients whether they have talked to anyone

---

22. We do not mean to imply that such factors necessarily *ought* to be indicative of credibility. However, they often are.

23. See, e.g., D. Binder and P. Bergman, *Fact Investigation* 140–141 (1984).

24. See, e.g., Bergman, *supra* note 21, at 42–44; H. Spellman, *Direct Examination of Witnesses* 100–101 (1968).

else concerning what happened, and, if so, what they have said.[25] Some clients perceive such questions as indicating your doubt as to their credibility.

B. TECHNIQUES FOR MAKING ROUTINE CREDIBILITY INQUIRIES

To overcome a client's possibly erroneous perception of mistrust, you may employ techniques such as the following:

1. Make a Straightforward Inquiry

You may choose to say nothing about the reason for a credibility inquiry unless a client verbally or otherwise questions the reason for it. That is, you may simply make straightforward inquiries of the kind illustrated in subsections 1–4 above. Only if a client questions your reason for making such an inquiry, or otherwise seems uncomfortable, do you explain your purpose.

2. Preface Inquiries with a Brief Explanation

An explanation may go as follows:

"In my experience, Mr. Eule, Mr. Liebeler will probably offer a very different version of the conversation and will undoubtedly deny that the subject of minimum pricing ever arose. Therefore, it will be very helpful if you can tell me how it is that you can remember so clearly that you and Liebeler discussed a minimum pricing policy. Remember, down the road we may have to convince a judge or an arbitrator that your recollection of the conversation is accurate, and anything you can remember that gives a reason for you to remember that the subject was discussed may be very helpful."

The explanation emphasizes that it is the opponent, not you, who might question the client's story. Thus, such an explanation may permit you to make a credibility inquiry without sacrificing rapport. Note also that you buttress the explanation with the motivational facilitator, "extrinsic reward" ("may have to convince . . . may be very helpful").

You need not habitually preface credibility inquiries with such an explanation. Keep attuned to a client's reactions during theory development and exercise judgment as to when an explanation may be helpful.

3. Tell a "War Story"

You implicitly tell a client of the importance of credibility inquiries by briefly describing how important such inquiries were in another client's situation. The "war story" generalizes the inquiry, and assures

---

25. See, e.g., F.L. Bailey and H.B. Rothblatt, *Fundamentals of Criminal Advocacy* 45 (1974). If a client responds that he or she has made a prior statement, do not confine your follow-up to a question such as, "Did you tell X the same thing that you've told me?" Such a question asks for a conclusion. Instead, focus a client's attention on the prior conversation and in T-funnel fashion elicit what was said.

the client that nothing in his or her story prompts the inquiry. For example, you might state:

> "A couple of years ago, I was representing a defendant in a criminal case. He had a perfectly good alibi, and luckily he told me that he had never mentioned it to the arresting officer. It turned out he had a good explanation for why he didn't mention it, but if I had not known that explanation ahead of time, I would have recommended that he accept a plea bargain. That taught me always to ask clients whether they have made any statements to anyone that in any way differ from what they have told me. So let me ask you whether you have told anyone anything different from what you have told me."

C. NON–ROUTINE CREDIBILITY INQUIRIES

Sometimes credibility inquiries are not so routine. If all or part of a story strikes you as implausible, if a story abounds with inconsistencies, or if a client was formerly a wooden puppet named Pinocchio, you have a special need to probe credibility issues. Such probes may eliminate your credibility concerns. For example, a client may offer an explanation that renders a seemingly implausible story plausible. Or, such probes may demonstrate that a client is mistaken or is fabricating. Approaches for making credibility probes of clients whose truthfulness you doubt are discussed in Chapter 14.

D. TIMING OF CREDIBILITY INQUIRIES

If a client is likely to perceive credibility inquiries as indicative of distrust, such inquiries may threaten the client's ego or run afoul of the etiquette barrier. Hence, you may want to postpone such inquiries until you are confident of your good rapport with a client. For instance, perhaps while discussing an event a client has mentioned important evidence whose credibility you wish to probe. Though piece-meal exploration of an event runs the risk of interrupting a client's memory train, you may decide to run that risk by postponing your credibility inquiry in order to avoid impairing rapport.

14. NOTE–TAKING

Note-taking tends to be an even greater concern during theory development than during the time line, for you typically elicit voluminous and detailed data. Keeping your head buried in a legal pad trying to record everything can well impair rapport.

Some lawyers resolve the dilemma with tape recorders. With a client's consent to tape an interview (which consent, by the way, should also be taped), you seemingly are free to focus your entire attention on a client. However, routine taping in lieu of note-taking presents at least two drawbacks. One, someone must transcribe the tape. This is time consuming both for the transcriber and for you as you later wade through an entire conversation. Second, notes are important *during* a meeting. In fact, conducting theory development questioning without notes is akin to trying to drive a car without a steering wheel.

For example, recall the technique of parking evidence that emerges during T-funnel questioning, and later making the parked evidence the focus of its own T-funnel. Without notes, you would find it nearly impossible to pursue this technique. Thus, if you do choose to mechanically record interviews, the recording should be in addition to, not in lieu of, note-taking.

As for the tension between taking notes and focusing attention on clients, most clients probably expect professionals to take notes. Such clients will not be put off by reasonable note-taking. Moreover, explanations may help. You may mollify a client who seems to be concerned about what you are writing with a statement such as,

> "I'm just making sure I have an accurate record of our discussion. In fact, later perhaps we can go over my notes together, and you can correct anything I've gotten wrong."

Remember too that you are not at the mercy of clients who reel off strings of detailed data. If your wrist becomes numb, or you suddenly realize that you have not looked at a client in 10 minutes, ask the client to pause while you catch up. Perhaps suggest a break, offer the client refreshment, and resume the conversation.

As during the time line phase, take down a client's own words as much as possible. The urge to substitute your own vocabulary for a client's is a strong one, particularly since yours is likely to be influenced by legal theories. Moreover, if you are like many attorneys, you will use your notes to prepare a "Memo to File" after a meeting has concluded. The Memo is typically more complete and orderly than notes. However, its preparation means that you usually have two chances to alter vocabulary: first when taking notes during a meeting, and second when you prepare the Memo. Changing words risks changing the meaning of a story. Moreover, using a client's own words may enhance your notes' usefulness for refreshing a client's recollection on the eve of deposition or trial.

Chapter 11

GATHERING INFORMATION FOR PROPOSED DEALS

* * *

Ms. Milford, your company wants to make a deal to purchase sportswear from the Guangzhou Clothing Cooperative if a way can be found to ensure that no money changes hands until you are satisfied that the clothing they produce meets your specifications. Do I understand your principal concern correctly?

Yes, that's it exactly. Their price is terrific and if they can deliver, it would be a great deal for us.

Okay, what I'd like to do this afternoon is get some preliminary information from you. I'll be interested in matters such as what terms you've already worked out with the Guanghzou representative, how you see the deal with Guanghzou functioning, what role you'd like me to play in helping you put this deal together and things like that. If we have time, I'll probably also get into some more specific details such as where a letter of credit might be established. When we finish today, I can then suggest where we should go from here. Do you have any questions before I start?

No. I'd like to get going, so fire away.

First, why don't you tell me . . . ..

* * *

1. FOCUSING ON PROPOSED DEALS

This Chapter and the next shift your attention from litigation to transactions. As is obvious, the term "transactions" encompasses a vast array of matters. On a general plane, transactions embrace personal and business agreements of all shapes and sizes [1] and estate planning.[2] Each of these categories itself embraces a wide variety of transactions. For example, business clients seek advice concerning proposed agreements with other persons, compliance with governmental regulations, and applications to government for licenses.

---

1. This includes matrimonial agreements of the pre- and post-nuptial variety.

2. Cf. L.M. Brown, "Planning By Lawyers," 15 Prac.Law. 70 at 71 (1969).

Within this vast array of potential transactions, Chapters 11 and 12 explore initial information-gathering only in the realm of proposed business deals between a client and at least one other party. Business planning is perhaps the largest single field of transactional activity,[3] and "deals" certainly account for a large portion of business planning work. An attempt to explore all varieties of business planning, let alone all other transactional matters, would overwhelm our attempt to focus on information-gathering and counseling skills. Thus, the type of information you typically need to gather in the context of proposed deals such as leases, partnerships, and employee agreements are the stuff of this Chapter. Techniques for gathering this information are explored in Chapter 13.

2. DO NOT A "DEAL–KILLER" BE

When a client comes to you with a proposed deal, one of your tasks is to gather sufficient information to expose its risks. Clients, however, usually focus on proposed deals' likely benefits, and they come to you for help in bringing deals to fruition. Because lawyers and clients often have a different focus, lawyers have gained the epithet, "deal-killers."[4] That is, many business people see lawyers as magnifying risks, jeopardizing deals by drafting and negotiating too aggressively, and killing deals by counseling them not to take risks.[5]

However, all business ventures entail risk, and businesswomen and men are by nature risk-takers. Some risks are financial: a transaction may not produce expected financial benefits. Other risks are legal: a non-competition clause in an employment contract may not be enforceable. Client-centeredness suggests that whether or not either type of risk is worth taking is ultimately for a client to decide. Helping clients evaluate and avoid risks is part of your professional role. But so is facilitating clients' legitimate business desires. As you gather information and counsel clients with regard to proposed deals, do not let your own sense of risk averseness overwhelm a client's desire to take normal business risks.[6]

3. Cf. E.O. Laumann and J.P. Heinz, "The Organization of Lawyers' Work: Size, Intensity, and Co–Practice of the Fields of Law", 1979 A.B.F.Res.J. 217, 225; D.O. Landon, "Lawyers and Localities: The Interaction of Community Context and Professionalism," 1982 A.B.F.Res.J. 459, at 466 Table 6.

4. Common types of lawyer behavior that are likely to kill deals are described by M.H. McCormack in *The Terrible Truth About Lawyers* (1987).

5. See McCormack, *supra* note 4, at 84–91, 111–112, 118–125; "A Businessman's View of Lawyers" 33 Bus.Law. 817, 825–826, 837–8 (1978).

6. The process of counseling described in Chapters 15–22 will help you understand how to discuss risks with a client once you have gathered information regarding them.

3. HOW PROPOSED DEALS TYPICALLY BECOME FINAL

You may be more familiar with the process by which litigation matters progress from initial interview through trial than the process by which a proposed deal moves from an initial interview to a concluded pact, since the latter process is largely unencumbered by statutes,[7] court rules and law school coverage. However, realizing how deals usually move forward will help you understand what information you need when a client seeks your help in connection with a proposed deal.

Typically, when a proposed deal is other than routine for a client, the process is something like the following.[8] In a first meeting, you preliminarily identify the problems a proposed deal presents and gather information of the type described in this chapter. Often you need additional meetings (perhaps conducted over the phone) to complete information-gathering. Therefore, an initial meeting might conclude with little more than tentative steps taken towards resolving potential problems and discussing a tentative structure for a proposed transaction.

When you have gathered sufficient data and understand the legal issues a deal presents, you frequently next prepare a draft agreement and send it to a client.[9] Afterwards, you and a client meet to review the draft.[10] That meeting usually produces a revised draft which you send to the other party. Negotiations may then begin with the other party's lawyer.[11] In preparation for these negotiations, you may again talk to a client and explore negotiation strategy.[12] The negotiations often require you to explore further revisions with your client. Eventually, the parties agree to terms and sign a written document.

7. Of course, tax rules, corporate codes and the like frequently affect the content of deals. But, by and large, they do not affect the process by which you help a client bring a deal to fruition.

8. When a client views a deal as routine, the process is quite likely to be more abbreviated. For example, owners of shopping centers routinely enter into lease agreements. Thus, if a shopping center owner comes to you to discuss a proposed lease to a new tenant in a going center, the process will be more attenuated than the one described here. Also, if a client is anxious to conclude a deal quickly, and most of its terms have been worked out before the client comes to you, the process will be likewise truncated.

9. In complex matters such as mergers and acquisitions, obtaining legal understanding may require considerable legal research.

10. Of course, when a client brings to an initial meeting a draft prepared by the other party, a follow-up meeting focuses on your suggested revisions to that draft.

11. Perhaps the parties themselves will be present. For some discussion of whether this is a good idea, see J. Ilich, *The Art And Skill of Successful Negotiation* 25–29 (1973); R.A. Wenke, *The Art of Negotiation For Lawyers* 10–11 (1985).

12. For a discussion of the importance and possible content of such a meeting, see D.G. Gifford, "The Synthesis of Legal Counseling and Negotiation Models: Preserving Client–Centered Advocacy in The Negotiation Context," 34 UCLA L.Rev. 811, 830–862 (1987); D.G. Gifford, *Legal Negotiation: Theory and Applications* 49, 184–200 (1989).

Thus, like litigation matters, proposed deals matters cannot be neatly segmented into "interviewing" and "counseling" stages. A client's need to make tentative decisions may require you to counsel before you have finished gathering information. Similarly, just when you think information-gathering is complete, negotiations may produce additional problems which require additional meetings. In sum, the ebb and flow of a typical deal involves you as an interviewer, counselor, drafter and negotiator, sometimes all simultaneously.

4. A TWO TIERED APPROACH TO INFORMATION GATHERING

Most lawyers classify themselves either as "litigators" or "business lawyers," giving many the impression that the twain never meet. To some extent, the impression is correct. Rights in litigated matters are highly dependent on which party's version of history a factfinder accepts, whereas historical details usually do not control a deal's outcome. Whatever parties' past dealings, they are generally free to reach any agreement they choose. However, and especially when it comes to the process by which you gather information, litigation and deals matters have similarities. That is, while the *kind* of information you gather may be very different, the *process* through which you acquire it is in some respects similar. Understanding this reality may advance your ability to apply in one field of lawyering the skills you have learned in the other.

Thus, in deals matters as in litigation, you typically begin by trying to preliminarily identify a client's problem.[13] Then, in either context you gather data using a two tiered attack. The first tier is more general, and it develops data that usually you must gather regardless of a client's specific type of problem. In litigation, the first tier explores time line events; in deals matters, it explores specific topics that are important in almost every transaction. Just as in litigation matters you elicit a time line regardless of substantive law issues, so too in deals matters do you elicit certain general data regardless of whether a client's problem involves a proposed lease of real property, a contemplated sale of a business, or a proposed employment agreement between a corporation and one of its executives.

The second tier develops detailed, substantively related data. In litigation, you pursue and examine events in an effort to prove or disprove factual propositions. In deals matters, you pursue topics relevant to the particular type of deal under review. Thus, second tier inquiries vary according to whether a deal involves lease of a building, formation of a partnership, or something else.

13. For a refresher on how to approach this task, see Chapter 7, sec. 4(C).

5. GATHERING LEGAL AND NONLEGAL INFORMATION

Business clients rarely hire you only as a scrivener to memorialize final agreements. Even if the parties have reduced some terms to writing, generally at the time you are consulted a deal is not yet finalized.[14] Hence, to help a client consummate a deal you need to do more than simply inquire about "where the deal stands now." To counsel a client, negotiate with another party if necessary, and draft language that so far as possible meets a client's needs and objectives, you must make additional inquiries.

Such inquiries often have a wide scope, as clients may ask you to help make both legal and nonlegal judgments. As you know, the world is not so neatly divisible.[15] And, lawyers and business clients frequently bandy the terms about without carefully defining them.[16] However, the terms do reflect attitudinal differences among clients. Some clients want you to restrict yourself to "legal" counseling; others ask for broader advice. Hence, brief examples of each may help you recognize the kinds of assessments you are often asked to facilitate.

To make legal assessments, you typically need to gather information relating to one or more of these categories:

(a) A proposed deal's validity: For example, if a deal is for an "exclusive dealership," you may have to gather information so that you can determine whether it might violate antitrust laws. Similarly, if a deal is for a tax-free exchange of property, your inquiries might be directed at whether the properties proposed to be exchanged are of "like kind."

(b) A client's intentions concerning his or her rights and obligations under a deal's terms: For example, assume that a client seeking to lease space for her retail business tells you initially that she has agreed to pay rent in the amount of "6% of gross sales." You might inquire whether she intends to pay 6% on the gross amount of credit card sales, or to deduct from gross the credit card company's charge.

---

14. As our friend Bill Rutter, President of The Rutter Group (a leading California organization in continuing legal education), has pointed out, clients sometimes come to you with what they think is simply a "tentative agreement," but which is in fact a fully enforceable contract. For example, a court may construe a "deposit receipt" in the purchase of a house or a "letter of intent" in the purchase of a business to be a binding contract. When a client seeks to further negotiate such a contract, the line between litigation and transaction matters is frequently obliterated.

15. Recall from Chapter 1, sec. 3 that solutions invariably produce a variety of non-legal ramifications.

16. See "A Businessman's View of Lawyers," 33 Bus.Law. 817, 824–25 (1978); D.N. Redlich, "Should a Lawyer Cross the Murky Divide?" 31 Bus.Law. 478 (1975); L.M. Brown and E.A. Dauer "Professional Responsibility in Nonadversarial Lawyering: A Review of the Model Rules," 1982 A.B.F.Res.J. 519, at 527–528.

(c) A client's intentions concerning her or his rights and obligations in the event of breach: For example, if a proposed deal is an installment sales agreement, you might inquire whether the client intends a single defective shipment to constitute a breach of the entire agreement.[17]

Nonlegal inquiries typically focus on practical ways of achieving a deal's purposes, and may even extend to its overall soundness.[18] For example, assume that Al Ford consults you about a proposed sales agreement pending with a Chinese production unit. Though he has some business experience, the deal would be Ford's initial entry into the international arena. Ford's concerns include how to have the goods inspected before they are shipped out of China. Though the concern may be "nonlegal," Ford would probably expect you to gather information about how the goods are to be manufactured and shipped so that you can draft a provision ensuring adequate inspection of the goods. Moreover, Ford may be sufficiently uncertain about doing business overseas that he seeks your counsel as to whether to go into it. If so, your inquiries are likely to extend into the deal's financial soundness, as well as into a variety of business and personal areas. For example, the discussion may concern whether the energy that Ford will devote to the new deal will unduly detract from his other business and personal endeavors.

When you are short of experience, you may feel uncomfortable when clients expect nonlegal advice.[19] But you are not without resources. Recall that in litigation matters, finding out about a client's problem prior to an initial meeting enables you to research relevant substantive law. In the same way, attempt to learn what a proposed deal entails before an initial meeting. Then you can speak to a lawyer who is familiar with deals of the type a client contemplates. In addition, especially when you are concerned about the financial ramifications of a deal, you might talk with professionals such as bankers, accountants or market analysts. Also, a wealth of practitioner-oriented books discussing particular kinds of deals, such as partnerships and real estate syndicates, are available. Finally, you may consult industry-specific books written for people working in the industry in ques-

---

17. See U.C.C. § 2–612.

18. Be aware that even within the group of clients who are sophisticated businesspeople and who deal with lawyers frequently, some will view your opening a discussion of whether it makes sense to go ahead with a deal as an attempt to substitute your business judgment for theirs, whereas others will welcome such a discussion. See "A Businessman's View of Lawyers," 33 Bus.Law. 817 (1978).

19. There is no duty to give non-legal advice. However, the ABA Code of Profes-

sional Responsibility EC 7–8 states that: "Advice of a lawyer to his client need not be confined to purely legal considerations;" and the ABA Model Rules of Professional Conduct Rule 2.1 states: "In rendering advice, a lawyer may refer not only to law but to other considerations as well, such as moral, economic, social and political factors, that may be relevant to the client's situation." Furthermore, the comment to Rule 2.1 states that technical legal advice may sometimes be inadequate.

tion.[20] If none of these sources are of avail, you may have to associate more experienced counsel or decline representation.[21]

Realizing that information-gathering about proposed deals embraces both legal and nonlegal concerns, turn next to the types of information you routinely have to gather in proposed deals matters.

6. THE FIRST TIER: GENERAL CATEGORIES OF DATA TO GATHER

The following subsections describe topics that you pursue for almost every proposed deal, regardless of how familiar you are with a client and the client's business. Though you may have pertinent "industry knowledge," you nevertheless need to gather information about these topics if you are to negotiate and draft an accurate, workable agreement. The discussion assumes that a deal is sufficiently large or non-routine to merit individualized analysis.

A. THE TERMS AND HISTORY OF THE PROPOSED DEAL

As you recall, clients typically consult you after a deal has been at least partially worked out. Therefore, routinely inquire about what terms have been agreed to. In addition, ask about the course of the negotiations leading up to the agreed-to terms, including what terms have been discussed but not yet agreed upon.

Knowing what terms have been agreed upon of course enables you to discuss an agreement's legality and soundness, and to identify ambiguities in the parties' understanding.[22] Perhaps less obviously, knowing the terms enables you to draft provisions that carry out the parties' understanding. All too often, attorneys neglect to learn precisely what parties have agreed to. As a result, a draft agreement may poison a negotiation by causing party A to think that party B is trying to change a deal without party A's consent.

Knowing the history of a proposed deal's negotiations, including what terms have been discussed but not yet agreed to, typically provides insight into such matters as both parties' objectives and their adversariness or cooperativeness. Thus, the history alerts you to problems that might arise during negotiation and that a client may want to address in a final agreement.

20. For example, if a client is considering a proposed restaurant deal, a book such as D.A. Dyer, *So You Want to Start a Restaurant?* (1981) would probably be of help.

21. See, e.g., ABA Code of Professional Responsibility, EC 2–30, EC 6–1, EC 6–3, EC 6–4, DR 6–101, DR 2–110; ABA Model Rules of Professional Conduct, Rule 1.1, Rule 1.16.

22. As an example of the type of ambiguity that might exist, assume that a client tells you that "deliveries will be on Thursdays." Do the parties intend that there be deliveries every Thursday, or only that if there are deliveries, they are to be on Thursday? Also, what constitutes "delivery"—dropping off goods to a common carrier, or a party's actual receipt? Note, however, that a too-ready willingness to find and eliminate ambiguity may render you a deal-killer. Sometimes parties prefer to leave terms vague and to trust to the future to work problems out.

Sometimes, a deal's history reveals that the parties have intentionally left terms open. It is not unusual for business people intentionally either to omit terms or leave them vague. They may be unable to agree on how to respond to a future contingency. They may prefer some deal to none at all and save to the future a decision on how to handle the contingency if it should arise. For example, parties to a sales contract may be unable to agree as to just what sort of manufacturing defect would represent a breach. But rather than hold up the deal because of the disagreement, they may prefer to resolve the problem when and if it arises.

Learning what terms have been agreed to or discussed is not necessarily a slam dunk. Clients may be uncertain about what has been discussed and what has actually been agreed upon. The uncertainty may be a product of wishful thinking. For example, a client's statement that "we've agreed to a five year lease" may reflect nothing more than the landlord's willingness to consider a five year lease. Or, the uncertainty may be caused by a client's naive assumption. For example, a client may state that in calculating gross sales for purposes of determining monthly rent, fees paid to credit card companies are to be deducted from the gross. However, the statement may reflect only the client's assumption and may not be a term to which the landlord has agreed.

B. TIMETABLE FOR FINALIZING A DEAL

Regardless of the type of deal, you typically need to learn by what date your client or the other party wants it finalized. If either is eager to conclude a deal quickly, your ability to develop options and to negotiate changes may well be constrained. To maintain good client relations, you must agree either to work within a timetable or discuss the possibility of changing it. The latter may raise a conflict of interest, as delay may be in your interest but not a client's.

That said, recognize that stated deadlines are sometimes false ones. "I need this concluded by tomorrow" is a phrase that may reflect a client's enthusiasm or anxiety rather than objective reality. Hence, if a deadline presents a problem to you, or you suspect a deadline may be a false one, everyone may benefit from your asking why a deadline is crucial.[23]

C. A CLIENT'S OBJECTIVES

Eliciting a client's objectives is the key to counseling clients about proposed deals and negotiating and drafting their final terms. On a general level, clients' goals vary between monetary and non-monetary, long-term and short-term.

---

23. Such an inquiry may reveal that a deadline has been imposed by the other party. If so, the deadline may turn out to be simply a ploy to pressure your client into signing the deal.

For example, assume that you represent a retail department store that wants to obtain an agreement with a clothing manufacturer. The department store hopes to achieve a long-term relationship with the manufacturer in order to promote and maintain a particular fashion image. Knowing of this objective, you might prepare a draft which allows the manufacturer considerable leeway in making deliveries and does not treat every failure to comply with design specifications as a breach of the agreement. In the absence of the store's desire to establish a long-term relationship, your draft might look very different.

Sometimes a client's objectives are such that a certain point becomes a "deal breaker." That is, an aspect of an agreement may be so important to a client's goals that the other party's failure to accede to it will prevent there being an agreement. For instance, a prospective executive may take the position that "if I don't have the final say in scheduling projects, I'm not going to work for them." Hence, knowing if any terms are potential "deal breakers" enables you to draft and negotiate with an eye towards holding a deal together.[24]

In addition to learning a client's objectives, it is also helpful to learn their basis. Knowing the basis on which a client has adopted a particular objective often helps you fashion multiple alternatives for achieving it. For instance, assume that the basis for a client's wanting to bring in a current employee as a partner is the client's desire to keep the employee's services. Knowing that reason may enable you to suggest ways that the client can induce the employee to stay in the business without making the employee a partner.

D. THE OTHER PARTY

It takes two to tango, and at least that many to conclude a deal. Information about "the other party" will help you finalize a deal. Who is the other party, and what does it do? What objectives does that party have? What terms, if any, does that party consider essential? What is the other party's financial condition? What is its reputation in the business community? For example, is it frequently involved in litigation?

Often, a client can provide information about such matters. In turn, you can use that information when considering how to word specific clauses and what negotiating approach to employ. For example, knowing that the other side has an urgent need for extrusions that only your client can manufacture quickly in sufficient quantity is likely to affect how favorably to your client you draft the agreement's terms.[25]

---

24. During an initial meeting, clients often are uncertain about their objectives, or think that points are deal-breakers when in fact the other party simply has not made a sweet enough offer. Moreover, during the course of negotiation, in reaction to another party's offers and demands or in response to changes in a client's own situation, a client's stated objectives may change. Thus, during initial meetings, *your* objective may not be so much to tie clients down to fixed objectives as it is to understand a client's present thinking.

25. But see C. Menkel–Meadow, "Toward Another View of Legal Negotiation: The Structure of Problem Solving," 31 UCLA L.Rev. 754, 764–804 (1984); R. Fish-

Moreover, the answer to such questions can help you respond to a client's inquiries about whether a deal is one with which she or he should go ahead. For example, assume that questions about the other party's business reveal that a deal would be its first outside its usual line of endeavor. Explicitly discussing that fact may help the client decide whether to go forward with the deal.

In addition to these specific types of questions, you should almost always ask clients more generally about their relationship with the other party. Has the other party dealt with your client previously? If so, how successful have those past dealings been? A client's answer may reveal that the client is somewhat distrustful of the other party, and is relying on you to draft an airtight agreement to keep the other party in line. If so, help your client recognize that the future may be fraught with difficulty. Given that the Ten Commandments seem to exercise little control over many people's behavior, a client needs to understand the limits of a written agreement. If a client depends on a legal document to insure that the other party will perform, the client should understand "going in" that making a deal may well be doing little more than "buying a lawsuit."

E. BUSINESS OPERATIONS

Knowing something about how a client's business developed and operates is often vital. Particularly when a deal is non-routine for a client, understanding a business' operations and history can shed light on such matters as a client's objectives and the deal's timetable. Moreover, that understanding may enable you to identify contingencies to address in a final agreement. For instance, assume that a proposed deal calls for a wholesaler to supply your client, a retailer, with goods over a two year period. Knowing how much inventory your client's business needs to have on hand and how long it takes your client to ship an order can help you discuss with the client the wisdom of a provision treating any delay in shipment by the wholesaler as a failure of contractual performance.

What part and how much of a business you need to learn about depends on a number of factors, including the sort of nonlegal advice a client seeks, a deal's size relative to the business, its routineness, and its likely economic impact on the business. For example, if a bank asks you to look over a security agreement in a routine loan transaction, you certainly will not go into the bank's history or its current operations. By contrast, assume that a client wants to purchase an existing business which will engage the client in a new line of endeavor. Now, you will probably need to understand how the client's business developed and currently operates, as well as how the "target company" operates.

er and W. Ury, *Getting to Yes* 41–57 (1981). Whether you intend to approach the negotiation as a problem solver or in a more traditional manner, knowing the other side's needs in going into the deal will often be critical.

Recognizing that what information about a business you need to gather necessarily varies from one deal to another, consider the following items developed by a group of business lawyers to assist in the development of an ABA skills training course.[26]

A. A description of the current business:

1. What does the company do, and how and where?
2. Who are the key employees and what does each do?
3. What is the company's current financial condition?
4. Who are the company's primary customers?
5. Who are the company's primary competitors?
6. What regulatory agencies commonly oversee the company's activities?

B. A brief history of the company.

Of course, even these items do not provide complete coverage of a business' operations. But they may serve as useful subjects for learning about a company's business operation.

F. HOW A DEAL WILL FUNCTION

Two of your principal tasks, which if overused will gain you a reputation as a "deal-killer," are to help a client structure a deal so that it fits into the client's business operations, and to guard the client against unwanted risks. To accomplish these tasks, you typically must learn how a proposed deal will function. For example, if a proposed deal calls for a client to make and deliver special goods, you will gather information about what will take place between the time the deal is finalized and the goods are delivered. If necessary, you might even walk through a plant and talk to the employees who will carry out the operations. Understanding the entire process will help you spot places where difficulties may arise and explore alternative ways the deal might function and what risk allocations, if any, should be addressed.

For instance, assume that a client brings you a proposed deal calling for it to manufacture and deliver resistors. In the course of reviewing the deal's functioning, you learn that some of the components the client will need to manufacture the resistors will be purchased overseas. You can then explore problems that might arise in the course of making overseas purchases. The discussion might aid you in advising the client how to word a material breach and *force majeure* provisions in order to protect the client.[27]

---

26. See D.A. Binder and C. Menkel–Meadow, *American Bar Association Lawyering Skills Program* (1982).

27. A *force majeure* clause is included in contracts to "protect the parties in the event that a part of the contract cannot be performed due to causes which are outside the control of the parties and could not be avoided by exercise of due care." *Black's* *Law Dictionary* (5th ed 1979). A *force majeure* clause is not limited to natural events; it may include events specific to the circumstances of the deal. For example, parties may agree that failure to deliver goods due to a third party labor strike does not constitute a breach of the contract.

Consider a second example. A client proposes to enter into a five-year lease to operate a restaurant in a shopping center. Eliciting information about how the restaurant will function, you learn that it will serve lunch and dinner, and that supplies will normally be delivered in the morning when other shops are open. Noting that the lease provides for unrestricted parking by customers and other tenants in the common areas and that the restaurant does not have access to a delivery dock, you and the client might consider altering the parking clause to ensure that deliveries can be received timely (e.g., seeking the establishment of a loading zone).

A description of a deal's functioning may not, of course, alert you to all potential pitfalls. However, it might well alert you to unique aspects of a client's situation that you might miss were you to rely only on standard deal-specific checklists.[28] Remember, by their very nature, checklists are meant to apply to whole classes of, say, long term leases and partnership agreements. By contrast, inquiries into a deal's functioning delve into each client's specific situation. Thus, while you may well use checklists, you should almost always supplement them with deal-specific questions such as, "Tell me a little bit about how your restaurant will operate?" and "Can you describe the manufacturing process for me?"

In addition to "walking through" a deal and using a checklist, with sophisticated clients do not overlook a very direct method of learning of potential problems a deal might create. That is, you might ask open-ended questions such as, "What potential risks do you see in this deal?" and "What can go wrong?" Though you may be very experienced, open questions may ferret out problems that you would have missed.

G. A DEAL'S ECONOMICS

Most clients, even non-profit corporations, view a proposed deal as a way to improve their economic positions. Therefore, the nonlegal advice you are called upon to give often concerns a deal's economic soundness. In turn, you have to gather information about a deal's economics. For example, examining a business' financial statement and any income and expense projections for a proposed deal will enable you and a client to discuss whether a client's financial projections are realistic.[29]

28. For more on the place of standard checklists in the gathering of information in a deals context see *infra* sec. 7.

29. This discussion assumes that you have the ability to read and interpret financial statements and documents. If you do not have this ability, you might nonetheless ask for the information with an eye toward having a colleague or a financial professional such as an accountant help you interpret the data. You might also consult books such as R.W. Hamilton, *Fundamentals of Modern Business* (1989); S. Siegel and D.A. Siegel, *Accounting and Financial Disclosure: A Guide to Basic Concepts* (1983).

7. THE SECOND TIER: DEAL–SPECIFIC INQUIRIES

In litigation matters, the equivalent of the shift from Tier One to Tier Two is the shift from time line to theory development. However, Tier Two topics for proposed deals are much less dominated by substantive principles than is theory development questioning. This is so because, as you know, in deals matters parties are generally free to establish whatever obligations they choose. For example, though UCC provisions may allocate the risk of loss of goods according to whether they have been identified to a contract,[30] the parties to an agreement are free to change that allocation if they wish.[31]

Tier Two topics primarily concern provisions covering obligations and risks typically found in the specific type of deal a client contemplates. For instance, shopping center leases commonly cover such potential obligations as payment of rent, purchase of insurance and maintenance of the premises. Risks commonly addressed in such leases include what will happen if the tenant defaults, dies or becomes bankrupt, or if the leased premises are destroyed or condemned by the government.[32] Such topics, then, are potential candidates for a Tier Two dialogue in a proposed shopping center lease deal.

Similarly, some of the obligations typically addressed in partnership agreements include capital contributions, partners' duties, distribution of profits, and payment of salaries. Risks commonly covered in such agreements include death or disability of a partner, transfer of partnership interests, and management disputes.[33]

Provisions which spell out parties' obligations over the life of an agreement are "operative provisions." They describe what each party must do. "Contingent" or "remedial" provisions address risks. They spell out the parties' rights and duties should a problem arise with the operative terms, say by breach by a party or interference by a third person or an outside force—e.g., a ship carrying goods identified to a contract is lost at sea.

Typically, the terms that a client mentions during a Tier One examination of "The Terms and History of the Proposed Deal" are operative terms. But just as typically, during Tier Two you will need to

---

30. See U.C.C. § 2–501.

31. Of course parties are not free to entirely disregard substantive law principles. For example, if two companies plan to form a joint venture and issue stock, various securities regulations have to be complied with and you need to gather information accordingly.

32. A compilation of standard provisions for particular types of transactions is beyond the scope of this book. Office form files, formbooks and checklists in books

targeted to practitioners are good sources of deal-specific topics. See, e.g., *Commercial Real Property Lease Practice* sec. 2.32 (Cal. CEB, 1976) (commercial real property leases); *Advising California Partnerships* (Cal. CEB, 2nd ed. 1988).

33. For a list of topics commonly covered in partnership agreements, see, e.g., J. Rabkin and M. Johnson, *Current Legal Forms With Tax Analysis* Vol. 1 (1989); *Advising California Partnerships* 2d 149–234 (Cal. CEB 1988).

explore both potential contingent terms and additional operative terms. For example, in a shopping center lease deal the parties may have agreed to one operative term, the amount of the rent, but may not have discussed either the tenant's obligation to purchase insurance (an additional operative provision) or what happens if the tenant merges with another business during the term of a lease (a contingent provision).

Nevertheless, a Tier Two dialogue typically does not embrace "all the operative and contingent provisions the parties have not yet agreed to but which might be part of the draft agreement." That view is overinclusive. Without a written draft agreement on the table, discussion of each and every possible provision that a final agreement might contain would be wasteful. You would inevitably discuss many topics which neither party to an agreement considers important. Moreover, subsequent review of the draft with a client would probably repeat much of the discussion. Hence, instead of discussing all possible Tier Two provisions, you must make a judgment about which topics merit discussion prior to preparing a written draft.[34] You will probably choose to discuss a topic if prior discussion with a client suggests the topic is an important one. Absent such a suggestion, you may well skip it. For example, assume that an important objective of a client seeking to enter into a partnership is to preserve the opportunity to devote time to non-partnership business activities. The client's concern may lead you to have a pre-draft discussion of an "outside activities" provision. But now assume that the client says nothing about wanting to engage in outside activities, and that what the client has said about the way the partnership's business will operate suggests that she or he will have little or no time to devote to outside activities. In the latter case, you may not bother to discuss an "outside activities" provision during Tier Two. Rather, as described in section 8 below, you can insert a provision such as an "outside activities" clause in the draft partnership agreement, and discuss it only when you review the agreement with the client.[35]

Discussion of a potential operative or contingent provision typically includes alternative approaches through which a client's goals might be accomplished. Return to the example of the partnership client whose objective was to have time to engage in non-partnership activities. Alternative methods of accomplishing this objective include permitting the client total freedom to engage in whatever outside activities she or he chooses, or permitting the client to engage only in activities that do

---

34. Your judgment may turn out to be incorrect. However, since review of a draft gives a client a second opportunity to discuss most topics you initially choose to omit, your exercise of judgment typically does not prevent a client from making important decisions.

35. Sometimes, as you know, a client will come to an initial meeting armed with a draft agreement that the other party has prepared. However, in most instances you will not have enough time during the initial meeting to study the agreement carefully enough to review adequately all of its provisions; at least one additional meeting will be necessary. For a discussion of how you might actually review the draft provisions with a client, see Chapter 22.

not compete with partnership business. Discussion of such alternatives enables you to prepare a draft that reflects a client's preferred approach.[36]

8. PREPARING A DRAFT AGREEMENT

As you have seen, some of a draft's provisions result from the data you gain through initial information-gathering. How do provisions that you do not discuss with a client during either Tier One or Tier Two find their way into a draft? Usually, they emanate from your knowledge of standard provisions for each particular type of agreement, together with your understanding of a client's likely needs. That is, you combine legal and "industry" knowledge with data gathered from a client to predict the choices a client is likely to find most satisfactory.[37] Those predictions typically produce two kinds of decisions.

First, you decide which obligations and risks, among all those that the agreement might cover, you will provide for in an agreement. For example, although a partnership agreement sometimes contains a provision concerning capital contributions in the form of property or services, you may choose to omit that provision in a deal where the parties have agreed to contribute cash.

Second, you decide what version of a provision to include in a draft. For example, if in the proposed partnership deal you decide to include a clause concerning "Interest on Capital Contributions," you must further decide whether the clause would provide for the payment of interest or indicate that no interest be paid.

When drafting an agreement, you almost certainly start with a form or two. Typical sources of forms are office files and standard form books. Realize, however, that forms are not fungible. For example, a form may reflect a buyer's rather than a seller's perspective; you should choose one which matches a client's. Also, because forms tend to carry language forward from one generation of lawyers to the next, forms may contain language that you do not understand. Rather than parroting language first used in a contract for the purchase of cotton gin parts in the 1800s, be sure you understand the purpose that each clause in a draft serves.

In all events, when reviewing a draft with a client, inform the client of your drafting decisions and explain that the client may want to make different choices.[38]

---

36. Helping a client to choose among alternative versions of a provision is a counseling task. Chapters 15–20 describe a basic approach to counseling; Chapter 22 explores the approach in the context of making decisions about alternative provisions in proposed deals.

37. Of course, in thinking about what a client is likely to find satisfactory, you will also consider the needs and desires of the other party: a client does not want you to be a deal-killer.

38. For more on post-draft counseling, please see Chapter 22.

Chapter 12

TECHNIQUES FOR GATHERING INFORMATION ABOUT PROPOSED DEALS

---

* * *

Ms. Pineda, how much capital have you and Lucero talked about initially putting into the partnership?

We've been talking about $15,000 each.

Why did you choose this figure?

Based on our experience in the retail clothing business, we figure we'll need at least $15,000 in inventory when we open the shop. We figured the expenses of leasing a shop and setting it up at around $10,000. So starting with $30,000 will give us a reserve if we need it.

OK, any other expenses you talked about?

Just how much we could afford to put into it, I guess. We're both very comfortable with this figure.

Did you talk about initial expenses for insurance and advertising?

Oh, yes. That will have to come out of the reserve.

Have you projected your income and expenses for the first year at least?

Here's what we've done . . .

* * *

1. INTRODUCTION

This chapter focuses on techniques for gathering information about proposed deals. To a large extent, the approaches and techniques are similar to those you use in litigation matters. For example, you often employ T-funnel questioning to probe thoroughly a client's wishes about specific terms of an agreement. Rather than re-explain those approaches and techniques, this chapter illustrates them in the deals context.

212

2. PRELIMINARY PROBLEM IDENTIFICATION

As with litigation matters, you typically follow the chit-chat portion of an initial proposed deal interview with preliminary problem identification. Of course, clients usually do not perceive deals as "problems" in the same way that they see disputes as problems. However, in a proposed deal matter you still begin by identifying:

(1) What brings a client to your office;

(2) What concerns a client has;

(3) What outcome a client wants to achieve;

(4) What potential solutions, if any, the client thinks might resolve the concerns.[1]

For example, assume that a new client, Mr. Hernandez, has come to see you. In an initial telephone conversation, Mr. Hernandez told you that he owns several medium-sized shopping centers, and that he has had some meetings with a possible important tenant for one of the centers. The preliminary problem identification conversation may proceed as follows:

1. L: Why don't we turn to what brought you in here today. Can you tell me more about the possible lease?

2. C: Gladly. I've had two meetings with the Vice President of Empire Grocery, one of the higher class grocery operations here in town. They're interested in a ten-year lease, and rather than just suggest my standard lease form, I thought maybe I should talk to you first.

3. L: I'll be glad to try to be of help to you. Perhaps you can begin by telling me what concerns you have that lead you to think your standard form lease may not be adequate.

4. C: Well, Empire would be an important tenant; the anchor space has been empty for over a year, and I'd really like to fill it. Of course, Empire realizes that, so I'm worried about my bargaining position. We've settled on the rent, that's not a problem. But there are a number of other things that affect the finances that have me concerned. I'm worried about things like who will pay for remodeling the space, when the rent will actually start and things like that.

5. L: What other concerns do you have?

6. C: We haven't settled on what hours they're going to be open. I'd like them open as late as possible, so that might be a problem. I guess that's about it.

---

1. For a refresher on why these topics constitute the heart of problem identification see Chapter 7, sec. 4(A).

7. L: I take it that if you could write your own ticket, you'd like the rent to start as soon as the lease is signed, and have them bear the costs of remodeling. But uppermost in your mind is to secure Empire as a tenant?

8. C: . . .

Here, you find out what brought the client to your office (Nos. 1–2) and what concerns the client has (Nos. 3–6). You then begin to find out what outcome the client wants to achieve (No. 7). The conversation enables you to learn about the problem from the client's perspective.

Note that the dialogue also produces information about some of the topics identified in Chapter 11 as belonging to Tier One. For example, Mr. Hernandez's responses alert you to the likelihood that he is seeking both legal and nonlegal advice. Moreover, his replies provide insight into his objectives: he wants to secure Empire as a tenant and to maximize the deal's financial soundness by seeking Empire's agreement to stay open late and by having Empire bear remodeling costs and start paying rent when the lease is signed. However, remember that at this point you only seek to preliminarily understand the problem from the client's perspective. Hence, further exploration of these and similar topics would occur only after the conclusion of preliminary problem identification.

3. PREPARATORY EXPLANATION

As described in Chapter 7, you typically follow preliminary problem identification with a Preparatory Explanation tailored to a client's unique situation. In Mr. Hernandez's case, your Preparatory Explanation may go as follows:

1. L: I think I understand what you would like to accomplish and your major concerns. Since a number of your concerns go to the financial aspects of the deal, what I'd like to do today is to get some general sense of the center and how it operates. Also, we should probably talk a little bit more about Empire and how it operates. I'll also want to know just what terms you and Empire have worked out so far, and any others that you've talked about but haven't resolved. If you feel ready to do so, we can also think about some possible specific lease provisions. Is there anything else you think we ought to cover?

2. C: No, that sounds like a full menu as is.

3. L: We can take as long as you'd like; I've got no other appointments this morning.

This explanation is likely to put Mr. Hernandez at ease because it indicates that you will cover what seems important. Indeed, you tell Mr. Hernandez that no time pressures exist. The explanation is short, and, in keeping with his apparent general sophistication, does not appear to be patronizing. Finally, note that though in a litigation matter a Preparatory Explanation typically alerts clients to differences between time line and theory development questioning patterns, this explanation does not differentiate between Tier One and Two. No distinction is made here because, as you will see, the questioning pattern for both tiers is largely the same; only the topics change.

4. TOPICAL INQUIRIES

Thus far, the approach to gathering information in a deals context looks much like that in a litigation setting. However, the usual approach in litigation combines chronological and topical inquiries, with the former typically preceding the latter. By contrast, as Chapter 11 stressed and the Preparatory Explanation above suggests, the usual approach in a deals context is topical. Hence, this chapter focuses on techniques for carrying out Tier One and Two topical inquiries.

5. ORDER OF INQUIRY

A. TIER ONE

Chapter 11 denominated as "Tier One" a number of topics that arise in almost every deals context. This section considers the order in which you might address those topics.

Following a client-centered approach, you typically start with whatever topic a client sees as most important. For example, if during preliminary problem identification a client repeatedly mentions his uncertainty about whether or not he should go forward with a deal, you might begin by discussing the client's objectives. On the other hand, if a client instead repeatedly mentions his anxiety to conclude a deal, you might begin by learning more about the parties' timetable.

If you are uncertain about a client's priorities, you might ask for clarification. For example, as part of a Preparatory Explanation, you might make a statement such as, "Over the next hour I'll ask you about the terms that have thus far been agreed to, find out a little bit more about how your business operates . . . . Do you have a preference about which topic you'd prefer to discuss first?" [2]

You may sometimes find it difficult to allow client interest to control topical order. For example, if a client is a new one, and the deal relates to a business of a type which is unfamiliar to you, you personally might prefer to start by gathering information about the client's business operations. However, unless you feel unable to carry out an interview without knowing how the client's business operates, you should attempt to follow the client's priorities. If the client wants

2. In most cases, you will not mention each and every Tier One topic. Usually, you will want to mention at least a client's objectives, and the terms thus far agreed to. When a client is a new one, you may also want to include the client's business operations, since knowing how a business operates may help you understand all other aspects of a deal and provide advice.

to talk about one subject when you are pursuing another, miscommunication is likely to occur and rapport is likely to suffer.

If your initial choice of topics grows out of a client's priorities, the order of the remaining topics is of secondary significance. Unless a client's preference is obvious, you may pursue the remaining topics in whichever order you think best.

B. TIER TWO

Tier Two topics, as you recall, are deal-specific. As set forth in Chapter 11, you generally do not have a pre-draft discussion of every topic that will ultimately find its way into an agreement. Nevertheless, you may order the topics you do choose to discuss according to each client's preferences. For example, assume that two clients have separate lease deals pending, and that in each matter you intend to have a pre-draft discussion of the rent formula, an option to renew, and insurance requirements. Different client interests might lead you in one deal to begin by discussing calculation of the rent formula, and in the other to begin with the option to renew. In the abstract, neither term is more important than the other, or than the insurance requirements. Instead, you choose a starting place based on the clients' differing priorities.

As in Tier One, if you are uncertain of a client's topical priorities, you might ask. In many cases, however, discussion of a client's objectives and the terms already agreed to by the parties makes a client's priorities abundantly clear, and specific requests are not needed.

C. INTERMINGLING TOPICS FROM TIERS ONE AND TWO

In litigation matters, the importance of chronology is such that time line questioning almost always precedes theory development questioning. Because questioning in deals matters is topically oriented, all Tier One topics may not necessarily precede those of Tier Two. The distinction between the tiers lies mainly in the ubiquitousness of the topics they incorporate; you inquire into Tier One topics in almost every deal, whereas Tier Two topics change from deal to deal. Nonetheless, not all Tier One topics are foundational to those of Tier Two. Especially if a client's priorities suggest that you do so, sometimes you may choose to discuss a deal-specific topic before one or more topics from Tier One.

For example, assume that a client in a pending lease deal is particularly concerned about the amount of rent. You may choose to talk about the rent formula (a Tier Two topic) before you talk about the parties' timetable or learn the extent to which your role extends to nonlegal matters (both Tier One topics). The touchstone should be a client's priorities, not a topic's classification as Tier One or Two.

That being said, some Tier One topics probably are foundational, and thus would almost always precede deal-specific topics. For example, you probably will discuss a client's objectives and the terms already agreed to before you move to deal-specific topics. Similarly, if you are completely unfamiliar with a client's business, you may regard learning about the business as foundational to Tier Two inquiries.

6. USING T–FUNNELS [3]

As you know, the T-funnel technique consists of pursuing a topic first with open questions, then with closed ones. No less than in litigation, this technique is extremely useful in the proposed deals context. It is useful for probing both Tier One and Two topics thoroughly.

First, consider how you might T-funnel a Tier One topic, "the other party." Your client is Serco, a company which intends to lease a large manufacturing building to the Bictel Corporation for 10 years; Bill McGeary is the Serco officer overseeing the deal:

1. L: Now that we've talked about the terms you and Bictel have worked out thus far, perhaps you can tell me something about Bictel. I find that if I know something about the other party before I start preparing an agreement, I can often phrase things in a way that makes negotiations go more smoothly. What can you tell me about Bictel's objectives in seeking this lease?

2. C: The company makes chemical food additives and it will have to invest in some modifications, particularly in the building's sewer design, to comply with environmental regulations. They don't want to make the investment unless they can amortize the costs over at least 10 years.

3. L: What other objectives might Bictel have?

4. C: Nothing else that I can think of.

5. L: Is there any reason in particular that Bictel wants to lease space in that part of town?

6. C: Actually, they've leased space in someone else's building for another of its business divisions about a half mile away, and I've heard that they're trying to sell a building they own on the other side of town. It looks like they're trying to consolidate their activities down there.

7. L: I know you've been talking about a ten-year lease, but do you think they may be interested in a longer or even more permanent arrangement?

8. C: Actually, in the back of my mind I've thought they may ultimately have some interest in buying the building.

9. L: I'll want to ask you more about that in a moment. But first . . .

---

3. For detailed discussion of this technique, see Chapter 10, sec. 5.

This dialogue is a T-funnel pursuit of the other party's objectives. Nos. 1 and 3 are open; Nos. 5 and 7 are closed. Note that No. 1 tells the client the purpose of your inquiry: "I find that if I know something about the other party before I start preparing an agreement, I can often phrase things in a way that makes negotiations go more smoothly." This comment provides an "extrinsic reward" and thus may motivate McGeary.[4]

McGeary's response in No. 8 might well have tempted you to become sidetracked, as it suggests that what started out as a straight lease may become a lease with an option to buy. However, you "park" the topic and indicate to McGeary that you will return to it, and in the meantime continue to pursue the original topic, "Bictel's objectives." Chances are, the topic "Bictel's interest in purchasing the building" will later be the subject of a separate T-funnel dialogue.

Next, consider how you might T-funnel the topic of the lessee's obligation to bear expenses, typically a Tier Two topic:

1. L: Mr. McGeary, you said earlier that Bictel has agreed that the lease will be a triple net lease. I'd like to clarify what costs Bictel will be responsible for during the lease term. Can you tell me what they will be?

2. C: Taxes, insurance and utilities.

3. L: What else?

4. C: Nothing; that's it.

5. L: How about maintenance costs? Anything there?

6. C: Not really. There is no regular maintenance of the building. But if they want some regular cleaning or trash service or anything like that, they'll have to provide it.

7. L: Any other costs you expect them to bear?

8. C: Well, of course they will be responsible for day to day repairs of things like lights and plumbing. If the transformer breaks down or the roof leaks, we'll take care of those things. But the day to day things are to be their responsibility.

9. L: Okay, Bictel will be responsible for day to day repairs. Any other costs whatsoever?

10. C: No.

---

4. As demonstrated throughout the book, you should routinely incorporate motivational statements into dialogues without waiting for clients to show signs of reluctance. Particularly if they have only infrequently dealt with lawyers in transactional matters, clients may not understand why you ask about the other party or other Tier One or Two topics. An explanation given at the outset, such as that in No. 1, thus provides motivation by telling a client an inquiry's purpose. Note that in litigation matters, explanations of a topic's relevance may raise difficult ethical concerns, as a client may read an explanation as an invitation to tailor his or her memory to the explanation. In transactional matters, where rights are rarely grounded in disputed versions of past events, explanations are far less likely to prejudice answers.

11. L: How about the costs of cleaning the building at the end of the term? Who is to bear those?

12. C: We hadn't discussed that but we'll want them to bear those as well. We want the place broom clean when they leave.

13. L: Off the top of my head that's everything I can think of. Can you think of any costs I've left out?

14. C: No.

Here, Nos. 1, 3, 7 and 9 are open questions on the topic of what expenses Bictel will bear. These open questions are interrupted by a closed question, No. 5. However, the effectiveness of the T-funnel technique does not depend on slavish adherence to an ideal order of open followed by closed questions. In addition to No. 5, No. 11 is the only other lower-T closed question, reflecting the fact that there were no other lease costs you could identify. As you do not become sidetracked, but rather stay with the initial topic of the tenant's expenses, you explore the topic thoroughly.

7. ELICITING A CHRONOLOGY

Because you typically gather information in a proposed deal setting topically rather than chronologically, a time line is often neither necessary nor useful.[5] Nonetheless, even in deals matters developing a chronology can be helpful. The following subsections illustrate specific instances where eliciting a chronology of events can be productive.

A. THE TERMS OF A PROPOSED DEAL

In a simple deal, a straightforward question such as, "What terms have you worked out thus far?" is all that is necessary to learn what terms the parties have already agreed to. In more complex deals, T-funnel questioning may be needed for you to elicit a deal's terms. That is, you might ask a number of open questions such as, "Are there any other terms you've agreed to?" followed by closed questions pertaining to the specific deal which is pending.

But when the parties have discussed terms a few different times, and those terms have changed, a client may have difficulty remembering just what has been agreed to. Even a T-funnel sequence may not fully jog a client's memory. If a client does exhibit memory difficulties, a time line dialogue may prompt his or her memory. Review the following example:

1. C: I know we talked about when and how the deliveries would be made, and about whether the price included shipping costs. But I guess I didn't take good notes, and now I just can't remember if we resolved those things.

5. For detailed discussion of the time line technique, see Chapter 8.

2. L: Don, as I mentioned before, we don't want to put something in a draft agreement that you and CIT have not agreed to; they might think we're trying to change the deal. How about a little different approach? Let's go through the three meetings you had with the CIT people one at a time. Tackling things this way sometimes helps people remember more details. Shall we try that?

3. C: Sure. But would it be better just to call up Bauman over at CIT?

4. L: We may end up having to do that. But we don't want them changing the deal on us either, nor do we want to give them the impression that we don't know what we've agreed to. So let's start with the first meeting. Where did that take place?

5. C: It was at their offices.

6. L: Can you picture yourself there and recall the scene?

7. C: Pretty clearly. It was in the afternoon; there were four of us in the room. I was sitting near a door.

8. L: How were you feeling?

9. C: A bit nervous; the deal is really important to us.

10. L: With that picture in your mind, why don't you start at the beginning and take me through the meeting step by step?

11. C: After the usual pleasantries, Bauman asked me to outline our proposal, and I did.

12. L: You've told me about that already, so you needn't do so again. Okay, what happened next?

13. C: . . .

30. L: That was very helpful. What about the second meeting; where and when did that occur?

As in litigation matters, breaking "clumps" into sub-events often elicits details that clients otherwise would be unable to remember. Your asking a client to place himself at the scene, and to remember both his physical and emotional state, may further enhance the client's memory.[6]

B. HOW A DEAL WILL FUNCTION

A time line that faces forward rather than backward is a useful technique for learning how a deal will function.[7] Knowing how a deal

---

6. Recall from Chapter 11, sec. 6(A) that sometimes, in addition to learning a proposed deal's terms, you also want to elicit information about the negotiations leading up to those terms. For example, you may want to know what terms the parties have intentionally omitted, and whether the negotiations have been friend-ly or antagonistic. Time line inquiries are often useful in such situations.

7. As you recall from Chapter 11, sec. 6(F), knowing how a deal will unfold is especially relevant when your role extends to giving nonlegal advice.

will function requires more than knowing that, e.g., "Shirtworld will deliver 12,000 T-shirts printed with the candidate's face and name to the Committee to Elect Dmitri Santorini." If you are to spot potential problem areas and give competent advice, you typically need an overview of how a deal will unfold over time. Consider, for example, the dialogue you might have with a representative of Shirtworld:

1. L: Barbara, I know basically what the deal is all about, but it will help me understand problems that might arise if you could walk me through it. Can you start from the point at which the deal is signed, and go step by step through what will happen?

2. C: Sure, though it's so routine for us by now that we hardly think about it anymore. The very first thing is we order the T-shirts from our overseas supplier, and then we prepare a silkscreen.

3. L: Do you have to do anything else before you prepare the silkscreen? [8]

4. C: Well, of course we have to meet with the customer and make sure that the design is one we can work with.

5. L: In this situation, what do you think that meeting will entail?

6. C: _____

9. L: All right, after the silkscreen is prepared, what will happen?

*   *   *

The step by step approach often enables you to identify potential problems that may arise in the course of carrying out an agreement. Once they are identified, you and a client can explore whether to address the problems in the final agreement. For example, learning that the T-shirts will be made overseas may prompt discussion of how the draft might address contingencies such as delays in overseas delivery and possible currency fluctuations.

Finally, through a chronology you learn intimate details of the T-shirt industry which you can lavish upon rapt audiences on social occasions.

C. "QUASI" TIME LINES

While not strictly time lines of events, chronological overviews can help you understand other topics related to proposed deals.

8. If you are knowledgeable about the T-shirt industry, you might realize that a meeting with the customer almost always takes place prior to preparation of the silkscreen. In that case, No. 3 in this dialogue might have been, "Will you meet with someone from the Santorini Campaign Committee before you prepare the silkscreen?" This narrow question is analogous to questions which emanate from your awareness of "normal course" events. See Chapter 10, sec. 10.

1. Business Operations

When you turn to the topic of how a client's business operates, you will in part ask here-and-now questions such as "What does the business do?," "What is its annual volume of sales?" and "Who are its major clients?" However, questions limited to present operations may not provide a true picture of a company. Knowing something about how the company has come to its present situation can provide insights into such concerns as a client's objectives and the problems a deal may create. A short chronological overview of a business' development, therefore, can increase your effectiveness as a counselor.

An open question such as, "Perhaps you can tell me a little about how the company has developed over the years" may be sufficient to elicit all the chronology you need. Sometimes, a client provides too brief a picture—e.g., "We started five years ago and we've been able to treble our gross sales in that period." Such a "quickie time line story" [9] is probably too sketchy to be useful. In such cases, consider a statement such as the following:

> "That must be very gratifying. It would give me a little clearer picture of that growth if you could go back to the beginning; tell me how your operations started out, and how they've changed."

Sometimes, you might also consider including a motivational statement in your instruction:

> "Having a picture of a company's development and the problems you've experienced along the way often helps me understand what you're trying to accomplish with the current deal and spot problems that we might address in the agreement."

While you might ask a few follow-up questions of the "What happened next" variety, it is unlikely that you will go step by step through a company's entire development. The goal is a general overview of a business' development, not a precise historical narrative.

2. Parties' Past Dealings

A chronology can also be helpful for learning about parties' past dealings. Again, a single open question may suffice to gather as much data as you need: "Tell me something about your past dealings with Kevin." And, if a client's response is too brief (e.g., "They've been fine."), you can press for further information with the approach depicted in the previous section. For example, you might say, "Michael, knowing a little bit more about how past deals with Kevin have worked out will help us think about how to draft the final agreement. For example, if Kevin in the past has insisted that the absence of a term meant there was no agreement about it, we'll have to be extra cautious when we draft this agreement. Can you go through the past deals you've had with Kevin and tell me about them?"

9. See Chapter 8, sec. 6.

8. CONCLUSION

Though you largely employ the same techniques in deals and litigation matters, information-gathering in deals matters is more wide-ranging and open. Litigation questioning is generally circumscribed by factual propositions growing out of events that have already taken place. What details does a client know about events made pertinent by a limited number of factual propositions all arising from a single time line story?

By contrast, deals matters look forward. Hence, inquiries in deals matters tend to be wide-ranging; what "might be" typically raises more possibilities than what "might have been." Most deals can be put together and can unravel in a variety of ways; no single story is controlling. How any deals story unfolds typically depends on how a client *wants* a story to unfold. That is, largely unrestricted by the past, a client is generally free to determine where he or she wishes to go, by what route and what risks are worth the trip.[10] Thus, successful information-gathering in deals matters typically features a substantial use of open questions to explore a client's views and expertise on a broad range of possibilities.

10. Again, a client's freedom is of course somewhat circumscribed by the other party's needs and desires.

Chapter 13

CONCLUDING CLIENT CONFERENCES

* * *

Mr. Martinez, we've gone about as far as we can today. As we've discussed, by forming a sub-chapter S corporation you and Richards can insulate yourselves from certain potential liabilities and yet be taxed as individuals. Under current tax law this can be a real advantage since individuals are taxed at a much lower rate than corporations. Do you have any other questions about that?

No. But you did say you'd be able to give me an idea of what your fees are likely to be for this.

Right. My standard fee for incorporating and setting up a sub-chapter S is a flat fee of $1500. The fee includes preparing Articles of Incorporation and By–Laws. Also, I'll file a disclosure form with the Commissioner of Corporations so the corporation may legally issue stock, and secure approval from the IRS for the corporation to operate as a sub-chapter S. If that fee is agreeable to you, I'll be delighted to undertake this work for you.

Well, it's a little more than I had in mind but I guess we can swing it. Will there be any other costs?

Yes, filing fees, probably not to exceed $200.

So the whole thing should cost less than $2000?

That's right. I understand this may be more than you had in mind, but I think you can see the tax advantages of operating as a sub-chapter S corporation.

Yeah, I have to keep that in mind. A top of $2000 sounds okay.

Good. As soon as you and Mr. Richards can decide on who the officers and directors will be, I'll need a list of their names and their business addresses. Within a week after I've got that, I'll prepare a draft of the Articles and By–Laws. Then, you can call or come in, and we can go over any questions you or Mr. Richards might have. If everything is satisfactory, I'll file them immediately. We should hear back from the Secretary of State about two weeks after that; then I'll take it from there. When do you think you can get those names for me?

By the end of the week. We've already been thinking about that, so it shouldn't take long. How long till the company is up and running?

You should be able to start operating in about four-five weeks from when you give me the names. Have you any other questions?

*   *   *

1. SPECIFYING "THE NEXT STEPS"

Social meetings often end on a vague note: "I'll give you a call sometime next week," or, "I'll talk to Jeannie, then get back to you." On the social level, failure to live up to such vague promises rarely carries serious consequences. In a professional context, however, developing satisfactory solutions to clients' problems often depends on actions being taken in a timely manner. Hence, you typically conclude client meetings by explicitly addressing three matters:

a. What actions you will undertake, and by when;

b. What actions a client will undertake, and by when; and

c. Remaining questions a client may have.[1]

Identifying the actions you will undertake typically fosters client confidence.[2] A client realizes that you are capable of and ready to take prompt action. A simple and straightforward statement is sufficient: "Within a week after I've got the names, I'll prepare a draft of the Articles and By-Laws. Then, you can call or come in, and we can go over any questions you or Mr. Richards might have. If everything is satisfactory, I'll file them immediately."

Articulating a client's responsibilities is also important. You typically need information beyond that which a client has available at a meeting, whether it be financial records, a copy of a contract, or, as in Martinez' case, the names of officers and directors. In the course of a meeting, you may have told a client something like, "I'll need you to get that information for me." Nevertheless, be sure to conclude by summarizing the tasks you expect a client to undertake: "Remember, you're to get me the projected earnings information by the end of the week." When tasks are numerous or complex, jot them down for a client to take home.

Carefully delineating a client's tasks avoids miscommunication and helps matters proceed expeditiously. It can also reduce a client's legal fees. For example, assume you are an estate planner and have prepared a client's inter vivos trust. The trust's effectiveness depends on property standing in the client's name being transferred into the trust. With your written instructions, the client can personally carry out the transfers, rather than paying you to do it. Finally, giving clients

---

1. Of course, one cannot always answer every client question. Often one can do no more than promise a response in the future. See *infra* sec. 3(A). Nonetheless, at least address each client question.

2. *Missouri Bar Prentice–Hall Survey* 65–69 & 75 (1963).

specific tasks is likely to increase their sense of involvement, again giving them more confidence in you.[3]

Finally, develop the habit of giving a client a last opportunity to ask questions. Perhaps you have neglected to answer a client's earlier question, or a client has forgotten whatever answer you did give. Or, your mentioning specific tasks may raise a new question or two. For these and undoubtedly many other reasons, invite questions just before concluding meetings.

2. CONCLUDING INITIAL MEETINGS: ESTABLISHING A PROFESSIONAL RELATIONSHIP

The remarks in section 1 above are appropriate for *all* meetings, including initial ones. But at the conclusion of initial meetings, you typically have to address a number of additional matters as well. The following subsections address these matters.

A. ESTABLISH AN ATTORNEY–CLIENT RELATIONSHIP

A couple may lead a long and happy life together without ever formally "tying the knot." But your ability to act on behalf of a client depends on formalizing the attorney-client relationship. Hence, before concluding an initial meeting, ascertain whether you have authority to act on a client's behalf.

The modern trend requires that authority to act be in writing.[4] Often, you mail a written fee agreement to a client rather than having a client sign it in person during an initial meeting. When you intend to mail a fee agreement, before concluding remind a client to expect it.[5] If you fail to do so, the sudden arrival of a formal fee agreement may take a client aback. If you have represented a client previously, the formality of a written agreement may seem unnecessary or even insulting. However, you may avoid discomfort by explaining that "the legal system" requires a written agreement.[6]

---

3. See D.E. Rosenthal, *Lawyer and Client: Who's in Charge?* 168–69 (1974); S.S. Clawar, *You & Your Clients* 20 (1988).

4. For a discussion of when written retainer agreements make sense, see J.W. McRae, "Clarifying Client Agreements", National Law Journal 14 (Dec. 5, 1983); G.R. Dillinger, "Your Outside Counsel Needs a Corporate Handbook", 71 A.B.A.J. 66, 66–68 (Nov. 1985); A. Windscheffel, "Fee Disputes and Fee Arrangements", 50 J.Kan.Bar Assoc. 230 (1981).

5. For a further discussion of the various matters that might be covered in a retainer agreement, see *Attorneys' Fees: Practical and Ethical Considerations* 51–65 (Cal. CEB 1984); Dillinger, *supra* note 4 at 68–70; McRae, *supra* note 4; D.G. Shekerjian, *Competent Counsel* 106–13 (1985); Windscheffel, *supra* note 4 at 232–234.

6. This is an example of the "absent third party" technique. For further discussion of this technique, see Chapter 14, sec. 7(B)(2)(b).

B. ESTABLISH A RELATIONSHIP'S PARAMETERS

Having authority to act on a client's behalf leaves open the question of just what it is you have authority to do. Unless you and a client are on the same wave length, misunderstandings may arise.

Sometimes you may interpret your authority more broadly than does a client. For example, you may believe you are authorized to pursue litigation when a client believes she hired you only for the limited purpose of researching her chance of success were she to file suit.

Other times, you may interpret your authority more narrowly. For example, a client may think that retaining you to pursue litigation obligates you to pursue an appeal; whereas, your understanding is that such service is beyond the scope of your obligation.

Thus, when you do enter into a formal attorney-client relationship, make sure you clarify its scope.

C. ESTABLISH A FEE ARRANGEMENT

An understanding as to fees should also be reached during an initial meeting.[7] Because you may be unable to establish a fee without an understanding of the scope of your obligation, a discussion of fee arrangements frequently arises near the end of an initial meeting. While the variety of fee arrangements defies setting forth a "typical" fee discussion, the following dialogue may help you verbalize fees:

1. L: We'll file an answer and thereafter defend this suit vigorously through trial, correct?

2. C: Exactly.

3. L: I'll want to meet with you at least once more to talk more specifically about how I think we ought to proceed. But earlier you asked about my fees, and I think I know enough now to give you a realistic estimate. I'll handle this on an hourly basis; my fee is $_____ an hour. I estimate that I'll need to spend about 60–80 hours prior to trial, though it could go higher if the other side files a lot of motions. My estimate includes taking or attending 3–4 depositions. Other fees will be court costs, costs of the deposition transcripts, and a few other miscellaneous costs for a pretrial total of $_____. I suggest an initial retainer of $_____; I'll bill you monthly if and when the retainer is used up. Does that sound OK?

---

7. Note that two areas which typically breed virulent disputes between lawyers and clients are fees and the scope of a lawyer's responsibility. See Windscheffel, *supra* note 4 at 231; E.H. Steele and R.T. Nimmer, "Lawyers, Clients and Professional Regulation," 1976 A.B.F.Res.J. 917, 950–56; D.N. Stern and J. Martin, "Mitigating the Risk of Being Sued By Your Former Client," 51 Okla.Bar J. 459, 462–63. (1980).

4. C: That's sure better than all at once. This is probably a
        dumb question, but I assume that if the case settles in just
        a few hours, I'd get the unused part of the retainer back?

5. L: Of course. You only pay for the time I actually spend. At
        the same time, remember that if they do push this to trial,
        the number of hours I have to spend may go way up. If
        that starts to happen, I'll let you know. One other thing
        that I'm ethically required to inform you of is that should
        you fall too far behind in your payments, I may have to
        withdraw as your counsel. I'm sure that won't happen,
        but it's something you should be aware of. Do you have
        any other questions?

6. C: No, we seem to have covered everything.

7. L: Great. Well, you've got your little list there of informa-
        tion I need. We'll meet again next week.

This brief dialogue sets out the specific work you will be undertaking and, based on your stated hourly fee, estimates its cost. In
addition, citing "ethical rules" rather than any personal doubt that the
client may pay, you explain the consequences of failure to pay your fee.
While such a discussion may strike you as "crass," as a professional you
are responsible for specifying fees.[8]

3. CONCLUDING INITIAL MEETINGS: GIVING A TENTATIVE ASSESSMENT

Often, you do not have enough information at the conclusion of an
initial meeting to fully assess a client's position or give detailed advice.
As a result, often you can do little more than provide a tentative
assessment and help a client decide whether a matter justifies your
services.

Unfortunately, however, clients sometimes expect definitive answers at the conclusion of initial meetings. Inexperienced clients in
particular often believe that the law provides clear answers and that
lawyers know which books contain them. Even relatively sophisticated
clients may be unrealistically hopeful of leaving an initial meeting with
a firm plan of attack in hand.

If such expectations are overly naive, you nevertheless must respond to them. Ignoring such expectations may damage a client's
confidence. Moreover, it is unfair, unprofessional and impolite for you
to absorb information like a sponge and give nothing back in return.
Clients should leave initial meetings with some insight into possible

8. See ABA Model Code of Professional
Responsibility, EC 2–19, 2–20 (1980); ABA
Model Rules of Professional Conduct, Rule
1.5 (1984); Center for Professional Responsibility of the ABA, *Avoiding Client Grievances* 1–3 (1988); Windscheffel, *supra* note

4 at 231–232. See generally, *Missouri Bar
Survey, supra* note 2, at 110–27. Frequently they will also want fee estimates. See
*Advocacy and Management in Complex Lit-
igation* 21–27 (Cal.CEB 1983).

resolutions. Unless you really cannot give one, a client is entitled to at least a tentative assessment of how things stand.[9]

The issue, then, is how to respond to a client's expectations in a way that both inspires a client's confidence and conveys your need for further information.[10] The suggestions below may be of help.

A. ADJOURNING WITHOUT AN ASSESSMENT OF RIGHTS

Clients who want to sue, or who have been sued, usually have an overwhelming "bottom line" interest in knowing whether they are going to "win." "Do I have a good case?" and "Can I get them to tear down the fence?" are questions of the sort they are likely to ask. While they may not talk about "winning," transactional clients usually have an equal "bottom line" focus. Illustrative questions include, "Will the exchange be tax-free?" and "Do you think they'll grant our license application?"

How might you respond when, because you lack either legal or factual knowledge, you are unable to provide even a tentative assessment? That is, while you believe yourself competent to handle a matter, you are too uncertain of applicable legal rules or of facts to assess realistically a client's position. You can neither reassure a client that her or his chances are good, nor warn a client that they are poor.[11]

In such situations, setting forth the legal parameters in which a client's problem arises and explicitly conveying your desire to provide help may maintain a client's confidence without overstating your analysis.[12] Consider this example.

Your client, Lowenstein, purchased a house from Aranella. A few months later, a wall developed significant cracks, apparently as the result of foundation shifting. Lowenstein does not recall Aranella ever saying anything about problems related to the walls or the foundation. In your judgment, Lowenstein's ability to recover against Aranella depends on showing that Aranella had actual or constructive notice of wall and/or foundation problems, but said nothing. However, Lowen-

---

9. You generally ought to make a tentative assessment even if a client does not think to ask something like, "How do things stand?"

10. Sometimes, even initial meetings conclude with clients making significant decisions. For example, the press of time may compel a client to make a decision based on sketchy data, or an interview may produce sufficient information to permit a decision to be made. The counseling process you might follow to help clients make decisions is the same, whether a decision is made in an initial or a later meeting; for a description of that process, see Chapters 15–22. This chapter assumes that a client is *not* making a significant decision during an initial meeting.

11. For a discussion of the propriety of presenting medical patients with unnecessarily pessimistic prognoses, see M. Siegler, "Pascal's Wager and the Hanging of Crepe," 293 New Eng.J. of Med. 853 (1975).

12. Obviously, we assume here that you have enough legal knowledge to describe the legal issues that are relevant to a client's problem. If this assumption is incorrect, perhaps you are not competent to handle that problem. See Steele and Nimmer, *supra* note 6, at 931–32; ABA Model Code, *supra* note 8, DR 6–101, EC 6–1, EC 6–3; ABA Models Rules, *supra* note 8, Rule 1.1.

stein has not provided you with sufficient data for you to assess whether Aranella had such notice. You conclude by telling Lowenstein:

> "Cases of this type are governed by the law of misrepresentation. One way to prove misrepresentation is to show that a seller said something that wasn't true.[13] As I understand it, Aranella said nothing about problems with the foundation or cracked walls. However, sellers may also be liable for misrepresentation even when they have said nothing about the condition of property. Sellers have a duty to disclose defective conditions of which they are aware. Thus, your ability to recover damages probably depends on our showing that Aranella was aware of the problems. At this point, I don't have enough information to know whether we'll be able to show that Aranella was aware. We've talked about having a home inspector go through the house and your talking to neighbors about things Aranella had said or repairs he made. When we've gotten that information, I'll be in a better position to let you know how strong your chances are. If it turns out that your chances of recovery are good, we can talk about what action you might take to recover some money.
>
> I really want to help you with this problem. It's very upsetting to buy a house that turns out to have a cracked foundation. I realize that you want to do something as quickly as possible, so I'll ask the home inspector I've worked with before, who really knows houses inside and out, to give this top priority. He'll probably call you tomorrow to arrange the inspection. In the meantime, you'll talk to the Jacksons and the Greens before the week is out. So we'll work on both fronts at once. All right?"

Without predicting the outcome of the factual investigation, this statement probably provides enough description of the law of misrepresentation to inspire Lowenstein's confidence that you know the parameters within which a solution might be found. Moreover, it indicates the type of investigation (home inspection; talk to neighbors) which will enable you to provide more specific advice. Also, the statement probably implies integrity. Implicitly, it contains the message, "I know certain things, but I'm willing to be up front about what I don't know." Finally, the explanation helps reassure Lowenstein by articulating explicitly your desire to help.[14]

---

13. For a discussion of the potential ethical problems involved in telling the client what needs to be proved to establish a case, see M.H. Freedman, "Professional Responsibility of the Criminal Defense Lawyer: The Three Hardest Questions," 64 Mich.L.Rev. 1469, 1478–1482 (1966); F. Chilar, "Client Self–Determination: Intervention or Interference," 14 St. Louis U.L.J. 604, 621–623 (1970). See also the graphic illustration of this problem in Robert Traver's *Anatomy Of A Murder* (1958); the illustrative portions can be found in A. Watson, *The Lawyer in the Interviewing and Counselling Process* 100–108 (1976). See also Chapter 10n 2.

14. Recall from Chapter 2, sec. 2(F) that explicitly conveying your desire to help is an integral part of a client-centered approach.

B. ADJOURNING AFTER PROVIDING A TENTATIVE AS-SESSMENT OF RIGHTS

Between the extremes of providing a client with a firm plan of attack, on the one hand, and inability to provide a tentative assessment, on the other, are matters in which you have enough data to make a tentative assessment. In such circumstances, state your assessment while emphasizing your need to do additional legal or factual research. Returning to Lowenstein's cracked foundation, assume that the client has given you enough information to predict that he will have some recovery against Aranella for misrepresentation. You might conclude by telling him:

> "Mr. Lowenstein, based on what you've told me about your conversation with Aranella's former next door neighbor, Gail Glikmann, and on what your contractor friend noticed about the foundation, I think there's a pretty good chance of recovery against Aranella. I do want to caution you, however, that we'll need to have an inspection by a licensed home inspector before I can be more certain.
>
> Also, you asked about your chance of recovery against the real estate agent, Dee Vorsay. Under recent legislation, realtors can be liable if they fail to disclose a significant defect of which they are aware, or could have become aware if they had conducted a reasonably diligent visual inspection. At this point, we don't know very much about what Vorsay knew, and I'm not sure whether the way that courts have interpreted the legislation will allow us to argue that a reasonably diligent visual inspection includes inspection of the foundation. I'll need to do some checking before our next meeting and get back to you on where you might stand with respect to Vorsay.
>
> I intend to do whatever I can to help. When we've nailed down the entire situation, let's talk about how best to proceed."

Here, you tell Lowenstein that "there's a pretty good chance" he can recover against the owner.[15] However, your prediction is qualified; you remind Lowenstein that you need additional information to make a more certain assessment. Note that this statement, unlike the earlier one, does not provide an overview of the law of misrepresentation. Since you do address the client's probable rights, abandoning the more abstract discussion probably is wise.

By contrast, you are unable to make a tentative assessment of Lowenstein's rights against the realtor. Hence, as in the previous subsection you do briefly articulate the controlling parameters, and explicitly express your desire to help.

C. ADJOURNING IN THE FACE OF UNCERTAINTY ABOUT POTENTIAL OPTIONS

Even when you can tentatively assess a client's rights, you may want to terminate an initial meeting without exploring possible solu-

---

15. When you have enough information to make a more definite assessment, you should generally couch a prediction in percentage terms. See Chapter 19, sec. 4(B).

tions to the client's problem. For one thing, you may not know what options are available. More commonly, while you might know about available options, you may lack the factual data which you need to help a client appraise which option is most likely to be satisfactory.

For example, assume that Phyllis Trimble and Bob Asimow consult with you about their new print shop venture. They want to know "whether we can run the business as a corporation." After some discussion, you recognize that incorporation is a valid option.[16] At the same time, you realize that other options are available which may in the long run be more suited to the clients. For example, they may be better off doing business as a partnership or a "subchapter-S" corporation. While these options are legally available, you need more information (such as projected income) before you can help the clients assess which option might be best. Thus, you want to defer consideration of courses of action until you have more data. You state as follows:

> "You initially asked whether you can do business as a corporation. Though we've had just a short time to talk, I think I can assure you that if you ultimately decide to do business in the corporate form, you can do so. However, before you decide to do business as a corporation, I think you ought to consider a couple of alternatives. One is a partnership; the other is a sub-chapter S corporation.
>
> Doing business as a partnership avoids the expense and time of forming a corporation and maintaining various types of corporate records. It may also, depending on your income, be disadvantageous from a tax standpoint. Doing business as a sub-chapter S leaves you with the messiness of doing business in the corporate form, but it can provide tax advantages.
>
> I really want to help you, but for you to make an intelligent choice between these options, we'll need more information than we've been able to gather today. What I'd like to do is set up another meeting. I'll ask you to bring . . .."

As in subsections (A) and (B), you lack the information to help the client decide on a course of action. However, you attempt to instill confidence by assuring the clients of your desire to help, and by identifying the parameters within which a solution is likely to be found.

D. GOOD NEWS, BAD NEWS

Often, tentative assessments convey either good news ("I think you've got a real good shot;" "I'm pretty sure that chocolate fudge cake is good for your heart;") or bad news ("Based on what you've told me today, there's some doubt whether Regency will have to agree to your subleasing the property to Explosives Inc.") In either event, you may need to be careful lest a client misinterpret your tentative assessment.

---

16. Of course, representing parties with conflicting interests would violate your fiduciary duties. In this matter, you should give Trimble and Asimow the opportunity to consult with separate counsel. ABA Model Rules, *supra* note 8, Rule 1.7; ABA Model Code, *supra* note 8, DR 5–105, EC 5–14, EC 5–15, EC 5–16; R.E. Mallen and J.M. Smith, *Legal Malpractice* § 12.2 (3d Ed.1989).

Consider first the happy dilemma of how to convey good news. Some clients are prone to hearing only what they want to hear. Therefore, such clients may not "hear" a caveat such as, "I'll need to do some research before we can talk about how to proceed with this matter." When clients do fail to hear, they may feel misled and angry if subsequent research alters the assessment.

As a result, you might be tempted to avoid all positive statements until you are certain of the accuracy of an assessment. However, such conservatism would needlessly frustrate clients and deprive them of assessments that they have a right to hear. Unless you believe a client is incapable of hearing a caveat, emphasizing the tentativeness of an assessment seems preferable to a policy against stating favorable tentative assessments at all. At the same time, unduly stressing a caveat may result in its trumping the good news, causing a client to wonder whether the news really is good.

With this dilemma in mind, consider the following example. Goldberg wants to sue Ambrose, the developer of a condominium building, to compel Ambrose to sell a condo unit to Goldberg. Goldberg contends that Ambrose refused to sell because of Goldberg's age. You state:

1. L: Ms. Goldberg, your case is covered by a Federal statute forbidding discrimination in the sale of housing. I'm happy to tell you that based on the information you have given me, I think a court is likely to order Ambrose to sell you the condo on the tentative terms that had been worked out between Ambrose and your broker, rather than simply ordering Ambrose to pay you money damages. However, before we reach a decision about how to best proceed, I want to check the latest court decisions in cases in which courts have been asked to order people like Ambrose to sell their property. I want to see as best I can what courts have actually been doing in cases like yours. How does that sound to you?

2. C: So you think I've got a good chance of owning the unit?

3. L: I think a court will look favorably on your situation and I very much want to help you. But I need to check the latest cases before I can tell you just how likely it is that a court will order Ambrose to sell you the condo. Do you understand why I need to read the latest court decisions?

No. 1 conveys both good news and a caveat. Recognizing that the news is good, No. 1 tells Ms. Goldberg you are happy for her. However, the client's response in No. 2 suggests that she may have heard only the favorable tentative decision, and disregarded the caveat. Thus, No. 3 asks her to confirm that she has heard the caveat. No. 3 is a question rather than a statement. Is it adequately phrased to prevent Goldberg's rose-colored glasses from being too deeply tinted?

Consider next the less happy problem of conveying bad news. To avoid prematurely dashing a client's hopes, you may (as with good news) contemplate an extreme position of delaying all negative statements until you are certain of their accuracy. After all, who among us does not prefer to postpone, if not avoid, telling clients that their positions appear weak? Again, however, such a cautious approach would deprive clients of assessments they have a right to hear. If prospects seem dim, clients should have the opportunity to discontinue your services.

A client generally will not ignore a caveat to a negative tentative assessment. However, you may be prone to "sugar coat" bad news to protect a client's feelings.[17] But if a client is to hear bad news, you must convey it directly. Indeed, consciously using a label such as "bad" may ensure that a client does not distort your message. At the same time, directness and empathy are not inconsistent. Thus, when you convey a negative tentative assessment, you may also empathize with a client's probable disappointment.

For example, assume you represent Mr. Pepper, who believes he was fired illegally by his employer, Data Corp. After talking to Mr. Pepper for an hour, your tentative assessment is that Pepper's chances of regaining his job or recovering damages are poor. Compare these statements:

Alternative 1

"Mr. Pepper, I know you want some idea of what your chances would be if you pursued a wrongful termination claim against Data. Wrongful termination is a relatively volatile area of law; court decisions tend to be conflicting and confusing. This can make it difficult to say where someone is likely to stand. In your situation, many factors are in your favor. You received regular raises, and your annual evaluations were positive. These are things that are important in a case like this. On the other hand, the courts consider strongly how long someone has worked for a company. You were at Data for four years, and while that's a good record, it's probably not long enough to prove an implied agreement that you could remain with Data as long as your work was good. Also, no supervisor ever told you that if you continued to do a good job, your future was secure. I wish I could be more positive at this point but I feel, based on what you've told me, that you have an uphill fight. I'm sorry; I wish I could be more encouraging.

I will be glad to do research and make sure I'm aware of the very latest court decisions. However, I would have to charge you for the time at my regular hourly rate; I'd estimate an additional fee of $_____. I wanted you to hear the down side before you told me to go ahead since you may be throwing good money after bad. What do you think you'd like to do? Have me check further or drop the matter?"

17. And perhaps your own purse?

Alternative 2

"Mr. Pepper, after listening to your story I can't be encouraging. I'd like to say I think things look good but in fact they don't. From what I can see now you probably don't have a case. Two facts probably kill your chances. The first is that you have been with Data for only four years. Courts usually hold that an employee must be with a company for a much longer period of time before they will rule that a company can terminate an employee only for good cause. The second fact is the absence of any statement to you by a supervisor that if you continued to do a good job your future was secure.

I realize my answer is not the one you were looking for. It's a terrible thing to be terminated by a supervisor you do not respect, especially when you've done good work. But I want to be absolutely straight with you, so as not to give you unrealistic expectations.

Now, some facts do cut in your favor, such as your annual promotions and evaluations. Thus, I can research the latest cases to see if there's any basis for a more optimistic prediction. This area of the law is constantly changing, and there may be developments I'm not aware of. However, I would have to charge you for the time at my regular hourly rate; I'd estimate an additional fee of $_____. I'd be glad to do that research because I'd very much like to help you. What do you think? "

While the "bottom lines" might be the same, Alternative 1 seems to "sugar coat" the bad news in a way that Alternative 2 does not. Alternative 1 sandwiches the bad news between favorable factors and willingness to engage in more research. Since some research suggests that people attend more to what they hear first and last than what they hear in between,[18] Alternative 1 may misleadingly soften the negative opinion. By contrast, Alternative 2 puts the negative assessment up front. Also, whereas Alternative 1 vaguely refers to an "uphill fight," Alternative 2 directly tells Pepper that as far as you now know, Pepper probably does not have a good case. Yet, Alternative 2 does not sacrifice empathy for directness. It clearly attempts to convey empathy with the client's probable feelings.[19]

One way to blunt the impact of bad news without misleading a client is to explore, through a counseling dialogue, other options for a client to consider. Often, when tentative bad news suggests that a client's favored alternative is unlikely, you will see legal or practical channels through which a client may be able to obtain a partial resolution of her or his problem. For example, assume that in Mr. Pepper's case, the discussion suggests to you that he might have a claim under Data's pension plan. You might begin to counsel Pepper by saying:

18. See, W.J. McGuire, "Attitudes and Attitude Change" in *The Handbook of Social Psychology* Vol. II, 272–3 (1985).

19. Each alternative assumes that you are familiar enough with the law and the facts to give "bad news." In the absence of such familiarity, you would have to defer giving advice.

Mr. Pepper, before you decide whether you want me to go forward on a possible wrongful termination claim, there's at least one other approach that may produce some money for you. It appears that Data's refusal to pay any pension benefits to you may well be illegal. While I have to check further . . . .[20]

As the song reminds us, clouds often have silver linings. Though the main news of the day be bad, you may often find a bit of good as well.

When a silver lining is not in sight, a client may construe a tentative assessment as a final one, and want to drop a matter. Naturally, a client is free to do so. However, as a client's decision is then both final and significant, a fuller counseling process may be appropriate. Chapters 15–22 explore this process.

E. ROOKIE NAIVETE AND TENTATIVE ASSESSMENTS

Giving even tentative assessments requires that you be somewhat conversant with legal principles and practical options relevant to a client's problem. However, during an initial meeting you generally will not have time to run to the library or the telephone to gain this familiarity. If you are to respond to a client's legitimate desire to know where he or she stands at the conclusion of the very first meeting, you must bring knowledge of legal principles and practical options to the meeting with you.

"Great in theory," you may say. "But I'm pretty new at this lawyer stuff. How do you expect me to have all this knowledge at my fingertips?"

That concern is a legitimate one. But as few attorneys, even very experienced ones, hold themselves out as experts in whatever problem a client may walk in with, neither should you. A pre-meeting phone conversation with a client, whether involving you, an associate, a secretary, or paralegal, usually can alert you to the nature of a client's problem. If the problem is situated in an unfamiliar area, research pertinent legal principles and practical options before the initial meeting. Of course, some risk always exists that a problem is very different than your initial information suggests. In most instances, however, having some preliminary information should allow you to do the research necessary for you to provide some form of tentative assessment.

20. For a discussion of ERISA claims see, 60A Am Jur 2d, "Pensions and Retirement Funds," Sections 1–1285 (1988).

Chapter 14

GATHERING INFORMATION FROM ATYPICAL AND DIFFICULT CLIENTS

1. INTRODUCTION

For the most part, client-centeredness assumes a spirit of good faith and cooperation between attorney and client. While clients may be subject to the lapses in memory and emotional travails that beset us all, they are responsive, interested in supplying information and honest. However, familiarity with human nature tells you that these assumptions do not describe the entire universe of clients. This chapter examines techniques for interviewing clients who present problem situations you frequently encounter when gathering information.[1]

2. RELUCTANCE TO DISCUSS PARTICULAR TOPICS

A situation which is perhaps closest to the assumption of "good faith and cooperation" concerns clients who are reluctant to discuss particular matters that arise in the course of discussion. This type of client is generally forthcoming and responsive, but changes noticeably when a topic which to the client is unpleasant or threatening comes along. This is a common reaction; you may recall from Chapter 4 that an advantage of open questions is that they enable clients to postpone mention of uncomfortable topics. Here, examine in a bit more detail how to respond to a client's reluctance to discuss certain topics.

---

1. Chapters 17–20 examine, in part, difficulties you are likely to encounter in counseling clients. For example, Chapter 20 explores, among other matters, how you might proceed when your client cannot make a decision or mispredicts a decision's likely outcome.

A. SOURCES AND INDICIA OF RELUCTANCE

Consider the following three hypothetical situations:

1. A client's matter involves a potential action for wrongful death based on medical malpractice. The apparent malpractice occurred when the deceased went into hospital for apparently routine surgery. The deceased's condition following the surgery grew progressively worse, and death occurred two weeks later. You are about to question the deceased's surviving spouse about conversations between the deceased and the principal doctor over the two-week period.

2. This client's matter is a civil suit for damages growing out of incidents of sexual molestation. The client is a parent of two young girls who were molested by a man who was their Sunday school teacher as well as a personal friend. You are about to talk to the client about a period of time when the client permitted the molester to live with the client and the children, before the girls revealed the incidents of molestation.

3. This client's matter concerns alleged fraud by a mortgage broker in connection with the sale of a house. Some years earlier the client had purchased a small house and had financed the purchase with a loan from a mortgage loan broker. After making payments for years, the client received a letter from the mortgage company stating that a "balloon payment" was owed, and that unless it were paid the company would foreclose on the house. The client has stated that the loan agent never said anything about a balloon payment, and you are about to probe the conversations that took place around the time the loan was taken out.

Why might these situations produce client reluctance? In the first example, in which a surviving spouse will be asked to recall conversations between a recently deceased spouse and an allegedly negligent physician, the surviving spouse may relive the emotional pain that followed the surgery. Recall that "trauma" is an inhibitor to the flow of information.[2] In order to avoid reliving the traumatic experience, the client may be reluctant to recall the details of the conversations.

Trauma may be involved in the second example as well, though here you may not directly probe acts of molestation. Asking the client about allowing a person who turned out to be a molester to live in the client's home may threaten the client's ego.[3] The client may well feel guilt and shame for failing to be more perceptive, and hence may try to avoid discussion of the topic.

Finally, ego threat may also be present in the last example. Fraudulent loan practices may not be as emotionally severe as child molestation. However, the client may well believe that you will regard

---

2. See Chapter 4, sec. 4(E).

3. For a discussion of the inhibitor of ego threat, see Chapter 4, sec. (A).

the client as stupid for not adequately investigating the loan deal, and be reluctant to discuss that part of the transaction.

In each example, therefore, client-centeredness requires sensitivity to potential client reluctance to discuss particular aspects of a transaction. However, to take it a step further, consider whether in any of the situations you might *anticipate* client reluctance. Anticipating client reluctance may affect your own behavior. When you feel confident that a topic will create reluctance, you may want to make a preparatory statement designed to cut off reluctance in advance. Otherwise, you must be content to respond to reluctance when and if it arises. Review again the three examples to explore how reasonable it would be for you to anticipate reluctance.

In the first two examples, the topics by their very nature suggest potential client reluctance. Death of a spouse and molestation of one's children by a close friend are extremely painful subjects. You therefore might anticipate that the clients will be reluctant to talk. But in the last example, is reluctance so easy to predict? If the client feels sheepishly guilty about being taken advantage of, the client may be reluctant to talk. On the other hand, if the client feels outrage because of having been taken advantage of, the client may not want to talk about anything else. Therefore, in the absence of clues that the client is anxious to avoid the topic—e.g., body movements indicating uneasiness; hesitancy to speak; silence; the client's changing the topic—you might reasonably not anticipate client reluctance in the last example.

B. TECHNIQUES FOR RESPONDING TO CLIENT RELUCTANCE

No matter whether you anticipate reluctance or become aware of it in the course of discussion, your choices are to (1) ignore the problem and press on with the topic; (2) postpone consideration of the topic until a future time when greater rapport or some other factor will overcome the client's reluctance; or (3) mention the problem of reluctance and seek to overcome it through discussion. In the abstract, no choice is inherently likely to be better than another. Considering such factors as a client's personality and your need for immediate discussion of a topic will at least insure that your choice is professionally responsible. Below, consider a few techniques for employing option No. 3, directly raising a client's reluctance.[4]

---

4. Professor Ellmann has argued that the use of techniques to overcome reluctance is manipulative because a client is not first made aware that remaining silent may be a better choice than divulging information. See S. Ellmann, "Lawyers and Clients," 34 UCLA L.Rev. 717 (1987). After all, sometimes the resultant data requires you to act against a client's interests. For example, if a client indicates an intent to commit a crime, you may be obligated to disclose this intention to the authorities. See, e.g., ABA Model Rules of Professional Conduct, Rule 1.6 (1984). Professor Ellmann's point that clients are encouraged to divulge information without understanding possible adverse reactions is correct. However, we believe the practice of encouraging clients to reveal information so that you can help them is a time honored one which you should continue. First, until the information is revealed there is no meaningful way to assess whether a revelation is helpful or harmful.

1. *Motivational Statements*

Motivational statements explicitly recognize or anticipate a client's reluctance and invite a client to talk about it. One type of motivational statement consists of two parts. The first part attempts to overcome the inhibiting factor by conveying *empathic understanding* of the client's anxiety or discomfort. The second part utilizes a *facilitator,* and typically points out the benefit the client is likely to gain by overcoming the inhibitor and discussing a topic openly.

For example, return to the client whose spouse recently died as the result of alleged medical malpractice. Assume you anticipate the client's reluctance to describe the deceased spouse's deathbed conversations with the physician, and you decide to make a motivational statement in advance. The motivational statement may be along these lines:

> "Ms. Bridges, I'd like to turn next to conversations your husband had with his physician after his surgery and before his death. I realize that this may not be easy for you; it may cause you to relive some very painful memories. But I'll be in the best position to help you if you tell me as much as you can recall."

Here you not only acknowledge that the topic will not be easy, but also identify a reason that it may not be easy: "it may cause you to relive some very painful memories." You may have chosen to omit this segment, since by including it you run the risk of playing "amateur psychologist." However, since just about everybody would agree that talking about the recent death of a spouse is likely to be painful, there is little risk to such a statement. As for the second, "reward," portion of the statement, it is a generic statement of potential benefit, not keyed in to this or any other client in particular. As such, you may employ this form of remark in most motivational statements.

Consider next the client faced with foreclosure. Assume that you do not anticipate client reluctance to discuss conversations with the mortgage loan broker. But after broaching the subject, you realize that the client seems uneasy and unwilling to talk about it. Since you did not anticipate reluctance, you may be unable to reflect the client's precise feelings. Hence, you might simply try to recognize the client's discomfort with a statement such as,

> "You look uncomfortable. It seems like something is bothering you."

This remark is empathic to a degree; it recognizes the client's discomfort. However, it may suggest criticism and therefore may make the client feel defensive. The client may respond in self-defense: "I don't feel uncomfortable. What makes you say that?" Or, the client's

---

Second, Professor Ellmann's point proves too much. All questions are intended to cause clients to reveal information. Surely no one would suggest that each should be preceded by a warning that a response may be harmful; such a result would surely paralyze all lawyer-client dialogue. See also, J.K. Morris, "Power and Responsibility Among Lawyers and Clients: Comment on Ellmann's 'Lawyers and Clients,'" 34 UCLA L.Rev. 781 (1987).

response may be vague: "I guess I'm just uncomfortable talking to a lawyer."

Hence, when a client seems uncomfortable, but you are uncertain of the reason, you may want to try other forms of motivational statements. One alternative is a *normalizing response*. A normalizing response tends not to make clients defensive because it spreads the client's feelings over a large group of clients. For example, you might say,

> "You seem a bit uncomfortable. You know, many people feel there are things they would rather not tell their lawyers. I understand that; after all, we do not know each other very well yet, and I can understand that many people find it difficult to confide in someone else who is a relative stranger. But only if I have all the information can I fully protect your interests."

Here too, you point out the client's discomfort. But by also stating that many people feel just as the client seems to, you avoid direct criticism. Again, you conclude with a generic statement of reward and a desire to help.

A second form of motivational statement you may use when uncertain of the basis of reluctance is a *request for corrective feedback*. Here, you take personal responsibility for a client's discomfort. A normalizing response puts the focus on the client; a request for corrective feedback places it on you. For example, again in the context of the foreclosure matter, you might say,

> "I have the sense there is some difficulty here. Perhaps something I've said has made you uncomfortable, or maybe even something that I've failed to say. Is there anything you want to tell me? I hope you'll let me know if I'm doing something that makes you feel uncomfortable."

Though a client's reluctance may have nothing to do with what you have said or failed to say, such a remark conveys empathy without making a client defensive. It may even encourage a client to describe the underlying source of concern: "No, it's nothing you've done. It's just that I think maybe I should have asked about a balloon payment, and I'm feeling kind of dumb."

2. Confidentiality

When utilizing motivational statements, you may also want to stress attorney-client confidentiality:

> "Remember, unless you tell me you're planning to rob a bank or something like that, everything you tell me is confidential. I cannot and will not divulge anything you say without your express permission." [5]

---

5. Hopefully, the humorous reference to bank robbery allows you to suggest that the attorney-client privilege is not unlimit- ed while still providing motivation. See ABA Model Rules, *supra* note 4, Rule 1.6.

3. *Changing the Pattern of Questions*

Facing a reluctant client, another option is to change your questioning pattern. If you have been using open questions, try a series of narrower ones; or vice versa.[6] As mentioned in Chapter 4, while open questions do motivate many people to provide narrative-type responses, there are clients for whom this is not true. Even clients who are generally forthcoming in response to open questions may become reluctant to talk about an anxiety-producing event. Such clients may respond better to narrow questions which can help ease a client into an event by eliciting information one step at a time. Narrow questions can remove some of the burden of disclosure by moving into a topic "bit by bit."

Assume, for example, you represent Charles Brown Inc., which is involved in a proposed deal to sell equipment to Gooddeal Inc. When through an open question you ask Brown to describe his prior relationship with Gooddeal, Brown hesitates and then says, "It's been okay; nothing to really talk about." Sensing reluctance, you choose to ease into the topic through narrow questions such as, "How many times have you dealt with Gooddeal?" "When was the first time?" and "What kind of a deal was that?" Perhaps in response to these specific questions, Brown may gradually reveal what is actually bothering him.[7]

Whether you move from open to closed questions, or the other way round, you may use a motivational statement as well. By way of example, return to the client whose children were molested by a close friend. Assume that your theory is that the church that employed the friend as a Sunday school teacher is liable for damages caused by acts of molestation committed on church property. You are concerned that evidence that the client permitted the molester to live in the client's home may in some way diminish the church's liability. However, you are not aware of any acts of molestation in the client's home. Well into theory development questioning, the client has been quite responsive to your questions. You now begin to question about the period of time the friend lived with the client:

1. L: Now, you indicated there was a period of time when Mr. Johnson came to live with you and the kids. Can you tell me more about that?

2. C: There's not much to tell. He just needed a place to stay; he asked if he could stay with us, so I said OK.

3. L: All right. Please continue.

4. C: That's really all. He stayed about 6 months.

6. Whether you approach reluctance through open or closed questions, you need to maintain a calm and respectful demeanor. If your tone of voice or body language suggests the topic makes you uncomfortable, the form of your questions will probably have little effect on your client's reticence.

7. Perhaps, for example, Brown's prior deals with Gooddeal have not gone well and Brown is afraid you will think him a fool for entering into another deal with Gooddeal. Of course, if this is the case it may be very helpful for you to understand why the prior difficulties arose.

5. L: Why don't you tell me all you can about how he came to live with you, and as much as you can remember about what went on during the period he lived with you.

6. C: Really, there's just not much I can remember. He was a close friend, or so I thought, and he needed a place to stay—that was all.

At this point, you realize that open questions are getting nowhere. Therefore, you change tactics:

7. L: Jean, so far you've been quite open with me and I really appreciate that; I'm sure it's not easy to talk about this with a stranger. I have the feeling there's probably more you can tell me about the period when Mr. Johnson lived with you. Maybe, in the light of what you later found out, you feel a bit guilty about allowing him to live with you. Or maybe this part of the story just doesn't seem important. I can understand that—many people know things they just feel should remain private. But I want you and the girls to get as much help as possible, and if I don't have all the information I won't be able to do the best job for you. Frankly, one of the hardest things about being a lawyer is learning information from the other side that I should already have been told by a client. Remember, whatever you tell me is confidential. So let me ask you this, who was it who first suggested that Mr. Johnson come to live with you.

8. C: He did.

9. L: Do you remember where and when he mentioned it?

10. C: Sometime in the spring, I remember it was around Easter. I had come to pick up the girls after Sunday School, and we just got to talking.

11. L: You're doing fine. Can you tell me as much as you can remember about the conversation?

The statement in No. 7 effectively combines many motivational techniques. You empathize with the client's feelings, make a normalizing remark, employ the "reward" facilitator, stress confidentiality and change from open to closed questions. Then, with the client seemingly becoming more responsive, No. 11 returns to a more open type of question.[8]

8. Though No. 7 seems generally effective, you may have concerns about it. Is the "kitchen sink" approach too lengthy, and perhaps intimidating? Is the remark that the client's guilt may be the cause of the reluctance too much of an attempt to play amateur psychologist?

3.   RELUCTANCE TO COMMENCE AN INTERVIEW

A type of reluctance which may seem strange to you is reluctance to commence an interview. This seems akin to phoning somebody and then having nothing to say. However, lawyers see this form of reluctance more often than you might think. For many people, whether it involves beginning a new social relationship, taking a new law course or starting out on holiday, beginnings are difficult. Moreover, sometimes clients do not come to see you entirely of their own volition; they are in your office physically, but not mentally. For example, estate planning clients frequently come only because their spouses insist they make a will. Similarly, a client who has a personal injury claim or a potential claim against a business partner may be able to gather enough momentum to enter your office, but not enough to be open and forthcoming with information. The following example from an initial meeting with a reluctant personal injury client illustrates how reluctance may manifest itself:

1.   L: Ms. Bryant, how can I help you?

2.   C: I'm just not sure . . .

3.   L: Can you tell me a bit about what brought you in here?

4.   C: It's kind of silly, really. A birthday party at a roller rink, I slipped . . . I'd just as soon not bother . . .

5.   L: Can you tell me a little bit more?

6.   C: It's my husband and friends really, they're pushing me . . . I just don't know . . .

A.   TECHNIQUES FOR GETTING STARTED

1.   Motivational Statements and Closed Questions

The motivational techniques described above are also effective with clients who are reluctant to commence an interview. Empathizing with a client's discomfort, making a normalizing remark and emphasizing confidentiality may help a client get started. Likewise, a shift to closed questions may take the conversational onus off the client at least temporarily. Especially if the questions seek non-threatening, statistical-type information, a client can ease into supplying data. For example, with the personal injury client above, you may ask questions such as:

Lawyer: At which roller rink did this occur?

Lawyer: What time of day did the mishap occur?

Lawyer: What date did this happen?

If you sense that a client's reluctance stems from uncertainty about whether to get enmeshed at all with a lawyer, statements such as, "Only if I have all the information can I adequately protect your interests" may further inhibit client cooperation. The client may feel that supplying information is a commitment to forging ahead before the client has decided to do so. To prevent this reaction, you may want to make a "reward" statement such as, "Only if I first have some basic information can we decide together whether it makes sense for you to go ahead."

2. Asking the Client to Ask Questions

Another motivational approach you can employ when reluctance appears at the outset of a meeting is to ask, "Perhaps you have a question or two you want to ask me?" Asking such a question may ferret out the reason for reluctance. However, be aware that many people are not comfortable asking questions. For example, many law students who have gone through job interviews say they are always uncomfortable when they are asked, "Do you have any questions about our firm?"

A method that may overcome this potential source of discomfort is to follow the general question with a *normalizing question*. In other words, have ready a question of the sort that is likely to have been asked by many past clients, and mention it to the reluctant client as an example of the type of question the client may have. Your dialogue may go as follows:

Lawyer:　Perhaps you have a question or two you want to ask me. For example, clients often want to know whether they are committed to going forward if they talk to me. Well, let me assure you that talking this over with me in no way obligates you to hire me or to go forward with this matter. I'd like to help and perhaps a good place to start is with your questions and concerns.

4. COMMUNICATING WITH AGED AND INFIRM CLIENTS

You may have difficulty getting information from some clients not because of reluctance, but because it is difficult for them to communicate. Common barriers to satisfactory communication include advanced age and medical infirmity. Certainly not every older person will have difficulty recalling and conveying information. But when the situation does arise, you want to be prepared to surmount it.

One skill you need to draw upon to interview and counsel clients with such difficulties is patience. What initially seems a client's marginal ability to respond may be little more than a relaxed style of speech. But when a client has genuine difficulty understanding and responding, you will need more than patience.

One simple technique is to ask closed questions. Clients who have difficulty communicating are more likely to respond to closed questions than open ones. However, you must be careful. The more difficulty a client is having, the more likely are you to ask questions that are leading. The leading questions may be unethical, and a client's responses may in turn mislead you.

Another technique is to speak to aged and infirm clients in surroundings comfortable to them. Thus, you may urge a client to come to your office with a close relative or friend. Or, you may hold the major portion of an interview in a client's home. Estate planning lawyers often interview clients in the presence of the client's personal physician.

If none of these techniques succeed, you may consider having a conservator or a guardian ad litem appointed for a client, and look then to that person as your client.[9]

5. RAMBLING CLIENTS

Perhaps every lawyer's worst fear is a rambling client, a client who views a question as little more than a momentary interruption in an excursion into details that seemingly have little to do with the problem at hand. There may be many reasons for lawyers' typically strong reactions to ramblers. Perhaps lawyers are uncomfortable with the feeling that they have lost control over an interview. Or perhaps ramblers simply consume too much of that most precious commodity, time. Finally, rambling may cut against the grain of those trained in the virtues of precision.

From clients' perspectives, a variety of factors may produce rambling responses. First, recognize that a client may actually be describing relevant, important data; only "premature diagnosis" stamps the description as rambling. Beyond that, clients may ramble because a topic is threatening, or because of a "greater need" to discuss their own subject. Finally, some clients, due to an emotional reaction to events or because of underlying personality factors, may have difficulty sticking to topics.

The initial decision is whether to respond to a client's rambling behavior. For instance, assume a client does respond adequately to questions, but in addition rambles into irrelevant areas. Would your tendency be to ignore the rambling responses or to attempt to confine the client in the future to relevant responses? Obviously no formula points to an unerring approach. Your judgment in an individual case will be based on such factors as time pressures, overall rapport, and the extent of the rambling. You may well decide to ignore the rambling. Indeed, even where a client's responses consist of little more than rambling you may choose to ignore it, perhaps on the theory that the client will eventually wear down and respond to ensuing inquiries.

9. Special considerations may also apply to gathering information from children. See N.W. Perry and L.L. Teply, "Interviewing, Counseling, and In–Court Examination of Children: Practical Approaches for Attorneys," 18 Creighton L.R. 1369 (1985).

When you decide to confront a rambling client, the following considerations may help. First, you may respond by empathizing with the client's concerns as evidenced in the rambling statements. Often, a client will ramble continuously about the same limited subject matter. Yet, aware that the topics have nothing to do with the client's legal concerns, you repeatedly fail to respond to what the client is saying. The dialogue resembles two ships passing in the night: you ask questions which are not answered, the client makes statements which are ignored. By simply empathizing with the client's concerns, you may satisfy a client's need to be heard and thereby diminish a client's tendency to ramble.

For example, consider this dialogue from a videotaped sample lawyer-client interview prepared in England.[10] In this demonstration, the client has come to see a solicitor about a divorce. The lawyer is questioning the client about the husband's earnings:

1. L: And before he was made redundant [laid off], you think he was earning a hundred and twenty pounds a week?

2. C: Yes.

3. L: Now, whose name is the rent book in?

4. C: Um, I think it's in both our names, but the rent gets paid from my husband's bank account on a standing order. And the thing is it hasn't gone through the last couple of months because we've had these letters from the council saying we're in arrears but all he does is throw them in the bin. And what I reckon is that he's going to take the car and sell it without telling me, and that's not on because it was my Mum's money what we used . . .

5. L: Yes, yes . . . hold on. The rent book is in both your names and your husband's been paying the rent, until recently, at any rate.

6. C: Yeah, but I don't reckon he's going to pay the arrears, and if he sells the car . . .

7. L: Right. Yes, well, if we're going to make quite sure that you are able to keep the flat, Mrs. Albert . . .

In this exchange, the client is clearly concerned about her car. Perhaps because the lawyer never acknowledges the concern, the client keeps returning to it. Consider the possible benefit of an empathic response by the lawyer such as:

"Mrs. Albert, I know how concerned you are that your husband not sell a car that belongs to both of you and that was bought with money that your mother gave you. I'd like to talk to you about that a bit later on. For the moment, however, let's concentrate on an even more pressing

10. The Law Society, "Solicitor/Client Relationship—Video 1", Ellis & Barton Productions Ltd. (1984).

concern, making sure you and your children can stay in your flat. Now, in that regard . . . . ."

Here, the lawyer acknowledges that the lawyer has heard the client's concern. Moreover, the empathic response includes the "reward" facilitators—if the client bears with the lawyer now, the lawyer will satisfy the client later; and by sticking with the lawyer's topic, the client will have her most pressing concern addressed. Though brief, this sort of response can greatly reduce a client's impetus to ramble. Note that following the empathic response, the lawyer simply proceeds with the interview.

If rambling persists despite your empathic response, you may employ a series of closed questions. Their limited focus of inquiry offers clients less opportunity to ramble. Once you get a client back on a non-rambling track, you may even revert to a more open questioning pattern.

A final approach, which you can use when speaking with talkative clients who you anticipate are likely to get off track, is to alert the client in advance to your need to interrupt. To apologize in advance, you might make a comment along the following lines.

"I want to apologize in advance for any interruptions I may make in our conversation if I feel we're getting off track. I don't like to interrupt but I find that in many instances it helps us use our time together more effectively."

Such an apology is usually well received. Typical client responses are, "You're right; I'm just so upset it's hard to stop myself" and "I know I'm a real talker, so go ahead and speak up when you need me to stop."

6. CLIENTS WHO ARE HOSTILE, ANGRY AND EXPLOSIVE

Sometimes clients' inner pressures escalate to the point that clients explode into fits of anger, hurt or hostility. In some clients, a fit takes the form of tears; in others, it takes the form of complaints, threats or accusations. Though you may think such fits are confined to inherently emotional matters such as child custody disputes, in fact outbursts are possible even in seemingly mundane settings.

For example, assume a client with whom you have enjoyed good rapport in the past owns a commercial building and seeks assistance about how to evict a tenant who is several months behind in rent. During the discussion, you learn that recently the client received a notice from the bankruptcy court that the tenant has sought protection from creditors pursuant to Chapter 11.[11] The dialogue then goes as follows:

11. See 11 U.S.C. § 101 et seq. (1988).

1. L: That's going to present some complications that we need to talk about. Once a debtor seeks the protection of the bankruptcy court, the court automatically stays any proceedings against the debtor. Before you can evict the tenant, you'll need permission of the bankruptcy court, which may not be granted.

2. C: What does that mean? When will I be able to get my back rent, and when will I be able to get this deadbeat out?

3. L: That's hard to say. We'll need to file two actions. First, we'll have to go to the bankruptcy court and get its permission. Then, we have to file an unlawful detainer action in state court . . .

4. C: WHAT THE HELL IS ALL THIS? WHO IS BEING PROTECTED ANYWAY? HE'S GOT MY MONEY, HE'S ON MY PROPERTY, AND THE BEST YOU CAN DO IS TELL ME IT'S HARD TO SAY. I'VE HAD IT WITH THIS FUCKIN' LEGAL SYSTEM. A FEW MONTHS AGO SOME OTHER TENANTS JUST ABOUT BURNED DOWN ONE OF MY BUILDINGS, THESE GODDAMN PUNKS SCRAWL GRAFFITI ALL OVER THE WALLS AND THE COPS AND COURTS DON'T DO A DAMN THING!

Here, the conversation was proceeding along smoothly when, out of the blue, something you said triggered the client to do his best impression of Mt. Vesuvius. Such eruptions are likely to leave you wondering, "Where on earth did that come from? Should I have seen it coming? What do I do now? Why did I go to law school anyway?"

Realize that you need not feel guilty for failing to predict sudden outbursts. After all, geologists have spent entire careers trying to predict earthquakes and volcanic eruptions, often without success. Sporadic and intense human behavior is often no easier to predict than seismic waves.

If you often cannot predict sudden outbursts, you can at least anticipate that some clients will suffer sudden losses of control. A client may, with some justification, feel that a problem is undeserved, unfair, outrageously expensive, difficult to escape and a "no-win" situation. Recognizing that it is very normal and understandable that a client may sometimes lose control helps you respond with skill and compassion.

First, recognize that at times clients may give off cues that an eruption is imminent. If you realize that a client is tired and on edge, you might initiate a short break. For example, perhaps you and a client have spent a good deal of time poring over a complex document, and you notice the client becoming impatient and cranky. You might say, "We've been at this awhile. I know I'm getting worn down. How about a short breather?"

If an outburst occurs without warning, active listening is a powerful skill for responding with compassion. You may not be able to immediately take away a client's hurt and anger, but you can let clients know that you understand and accept how upset they are feeling. For example, following the client's outburst in No. 4 above, you might have said, "I can understand your outrage. The bankruptcy laws seem to protect only the tenant at the expense of the owner." [12]

Another tactic is to allow a client a "cooling off" period following an emotional outburst. It is often unrealistic to expect that an active listening response will instantly defuse a client's anger and allow you to continue on as if nothing had happened. Offer a client a chance to relax with a soft drink or fruit juice.

Finally, help a client recover from an outburst by offering a face-saving, "normalizing" response. After an outburst, most clients feel sheepish, embarrassed or ashamed. As a result, some will try to make light of their discomfort. For example, the client above might say, "Well, my friends always say I have a short fuse." Control the impulse to tease back: "Short? More like invisible!" Instead, offer a response that generalizes and normalizes a client's feelings: "All of us blow up once in a while when we're under pressure," or "I know that many owners faced with your situation feel like they're being screwed over by the legal system." Then, re-affirm your desire to help: "When you're feeling ready, we can talk some more. I want to help you find every way we can to make the best of a bad situation."

Working with hostile, angry clients is neither easy nor pleasant. However, most clients respond to coping skills such as active listening, cooling off periods, normalizing replies, and affirmations of your desire to help.[13]

7. FABRICATION

One of the more vexing problems is talking to clients who you strongly suspect of lying.[14] Lying may be active or passive: a client may either supply false information, or withhold information.[15] Obvi-

12. Note that you need not, and probably could not, respond to all the ills apparently besetting the client. It is generally enough to respond to the immediate source of the client's complaint.

13. For detailed discussion of these as well as other techniques for coping with angry, hostile and explosive clients, see R. Bramson, "A Hostile–Aggressive Trio: German Tanks, Snipers and Explodiers," in *Coping With Difficult People* 8–37 (1981); J.E. Groves, M.D., "Taking Care of the Hateful Patient," 298 New Eng.J.Med. 883–887 (1978) (coping with "entitled demanders").

14. In considering the issue of whether a client is lying, recognize what psychological studies repeatedly show, namely that what people honestly think they perceive may be due in part to their self interest in having events come out a certain way. See, e.g., E.F. Loftus and J.M. Doyle, *Eyewitness Testimony: Civil and Criminal* § 3.08 (1987). While this phenomenon is of concern to lawyers, it is not one that involves fabrication. The client reports what she or he honestly believes to be true, though the client is in fact mistaken.

15. Although this problem perhaps arises more frequently in litigation than in deals matters, the problem is certainly not unknown in the latter area.

ously the line between a client who may be mistaken and who is lying, or one who is simply reluctant to supply information and one who consciously withholds it, is not a bright one. The matter is one of degree, rooted in a client's conscious intent. You have to rely on your judgment as to which side of the line a client's conduct falls.

A. INDICIA OF FABRICATION

Typically, the inhibitors of ego threat and case threat are the root cause of fabrication. Clients may lie in the belief (probably often correct) that truthful information will hurt their cause. They also may lie because they are ashamed or guilty about what really happened, or because they believe you would not respect them if you knew the true facts. Such feelings are not limited to clients: How freely do you share information that casts you in a negative light?

The bases upon which you might detect fabrication are the stuff of the literature of cross-examination, a full discussion of which is beyond the scope of this book.[16] Generally, inconsistencies are one clue to possible fabrication. A client's statement to you conflicts with what the client previously told somebody else; bad luck if the somebody else is a police officer. Or, a story may have internal inconsistencies—one portion does not square with another. For example, a client states at one point that he was driving late at night; at another point, he states that his car lights were not on.

Implausibilities also suggest fabrication. For example, in an actual case, a client testified, "James is fine now, but when I took his temperature, it was so high that it broke the thermometer." Common sense and experience suggest that the story is implausible. Not only are extremely high temperatures usually fatal, but also they rarely result in broken thermometers.

On other occasions, a story may conflict in some way with a more believable story. For example, a client tells you that a 6–month–old child's broken leg was caused by the child falling off a sofa onto a carpeted floor. The story conflicts with the medical expert, who concludes that the X-rays indicate a spiral fracture of the leg, and that spiral fractures can be caused only by a great deal of rotational force, not by a fall from a sofa.

These are some of the more common factors that are likely to lead you to suspect fabrication. Below, consider potential responses you might make.

B. RESPONDING TO SUSPECTED FABRICATION

Even an indirect suggestion that you suspect a client of lying can severely damage an attorney-client relationship. Therefore, first be reasonably confident of your diagnosis of fabrication. Movies have fostered an image of streetwise lawyers who can unerringly spot a lie

16. See, e.g., F.L. Wellman, *The Art of Cross Examination* (1931); T.A. Mauet, *Fundamentals of Trial Techniques* § 6.7 (1988).

and immediately force people to "come clean" with a statement such as: "Come on, nobody would believe that. I haven't believed something like that since I was 3 years old. Now, tell me what really happened." Most of us, however, are not blessed with such blinding certainty. Better to eliminate other possible explanations before leaping to the conclusion that a client is lying. After all, it may be that the third party, supposedly neutral witness, is mistaken, not your client. Perhaps the doctor in the spiral fracture case above misread the X-rays or picked up the wrong X-rays. Perhaps the client has made an honest mistake. You should at least consider such possibilities before you employ the following techniques.

1. Prevention

Hopefully, one benefit of a client-centered approach itself is reduced fabrication. The more rapport you have with a client, the less likely a client will lie. But in particular, three other devices may help to prevent fabrication. One is "topic avoidance." If you delay discussion of critical points which are most likely to lead to fabrication until after you have had a chance to build rapport, you may reduce the chance that a client will lie. Many criminal defense attorneys employ this technique, intentionally postponing discussion of what happened prior to an arrest until one or two meetings with their clients have taken place.[17]

A second device is "disclosure." By disclosing data already in your possession which is especially case or ego threatening, you lessen the risk that a client will deny its existence. This device is one frequently used by parents of young children. Assume that a father enters a room and finds an overturned beaker of milk in the middle of the living room rug moments after the father saw his six-year-old daughter Melinda playing in the living room. The father might confront Melinda with a question such as, "Melinda, did you spill the milk?" But that question is prone to elicit a defensive, deceitful response from Melinda. Instead, the father might say, "Melinda, it seems you've spilt that milk you were drinking. Why don't you tell me what happened." This remark discloses that the father already knows "the worst" and is likely to elicit a more honest response provided the father's tone of voice and body language indicate he is not threatening punishment.

You too will frequently be aware of negative information concerning clients. Perhaps you will know that a client seeking advice about a business venture has previously declared bankruptcy. Or, that a doctor who is a defendant in a wrongful death case has previously been discharged from the staffs of two hospitals. In each case, a question which puts the onus on the client to be the first to reveal the informa-

---

17. A number of criminal law specialists have mentioned this point to the authors on numerous occasions. However, the texts and articles we have examined are either silent on this point, or are perhaps contradictory. For an example of the latter, see F.L. Bailey and H.B. Rothblatt, *Fundamentals of Criminal Advocacy* 45 (1974).

tion may elicit an evasive, misleading or dishonest reply. Instead, a remark such as, "I understand you have had some problems in a couple of hospitals in the past. Can you tell me something about that?" may ease the client towards a full and forthright reply.

A "war story" is a third device you may employ to prevent fabrication. A war story is simply a tale drawn from your prior experience.[18] Sometimes, you tell a war story simply to entertain or impress a client with the depth of your experience. In this instance, you tell a war story to illustrate the pitfalls of dishonesty. For example, assume that you represent the owner of a restaurant who is applying for a liquor license. You are aware that the client has two "silent partners" ("Suds" McCalla and "Bugsy" Berenson) who are said to have ties to organized crime. Such information, if true, would in all likelihood prevent issuance of the liquor license. If you fear that the client will lie when asked about connections with Suds and Bugsy, you may tell a war story as follows:

> "I've handled a number of cases in which clients have sought liquor licenses, and issues concerning an applicant's associates arise frequently. Unfortunately, sometimes clients do not level with me completely, and information is concealed which, had I known about it earlier, could have been easily met and overcome. For instance, a couple of years ago a client of mine was seeking a liquor license, and there was some question about whether she had sold liquor to a minor in another state. When I asked her about it before we went before the Board, she assured me that she had never been licensed anywhere, that there must be some confusion. Then the Board came up with a record showing she had been licensed. As it turned out, she had signed the application in the other state simply to help out a friend; she never took an active role in the liquor business and had I known about it we could have explained what happened and she would have gotten her license. As it was, the license was denied, and by the time we could petition again, the business opportunity dried up.

> For the next few minutes I'll be asking you for information about your business operations because these applications for liquor licenses are pretty thorough. As we go through the application, be sure to tell me everything so if there's any problem in the offing we can try to think of ways to solve it."

Here, you tell a war story aimed at impressing the client with the need to be accurate. The message is that even if the information may be in some way negative, you may nevertheless produce a successful result. Thus, the war story is also motivational.[19]

---

18. If you are a newcomer to the legal profession, you may substitute an event that another attorney encountered for one of your own.

19. You could also combine disclosure with a war story. For example, here, after telling the war story, you might have disclosed that you knew about Suds and Bugsy.

2. Confrontation

When despite your best preventative efforts you are convinced a client is lying, and you want to uncover the actual facts, you must confront a client.[20] Available confrontational techniques range from indirect to direct, the latter consisting of an explicit statement of disbelief. Consider here four confrontational techniques, beginning with the most indirect.

a. Request for Clarification

A request for clarification phrases the confrontation in terms of your own confusion, rather than the client's misstatements. Explicitly point out what troubles you, and ask the client to clarify. For example, you might state,

> "I'm a bit confused. You've told me that minimum pricing was discussed at the meeting; but your own employee's memo summarizing the meeting makes no mention of that. Can you clarify this point for me?"

> * * *

> "I'm a little confused. According to the accident report, you told the officer you were going home at the time of the incident. But just a short time earlier, you told me that you were on your way to a doctor's appointment. Could you clarify this difference for me?"

Note that the requests for clarification do not overtly indicate your disbelief. And often, disbelief is premature. The first client may explain, "The employee had to leave the meeting for about 20 minutes to talk to the shop foreperson. Thinking back on it, that's when we talked about minimum pricing." The second may respond, "I was going home after the doctor's office and I guess I was nervous and just left out the part about the doctor."

b. The Omniscient Third Party

Another method of probing suspected fabrication while attempting to preserve rapport involves ascribing your need to broach a possible untruth to a non-present yet powerful and critically important third party. The third party is, of course, not present at your conversation and therefore is in no position to dispute the position you ascribe to it. Potential third party "whipping people" include opposing counsel, a judge, or even "law firm policy."

For example, you may take the role of opposing counsel, and ask the client why the client's version of events is more likely to be believed than the adversary's. By stressing that "this is what our opponent is going to say," you confront a client's story without personally indicating your disbelief. The tactic often impels a client either to provide

---

20. For a brief discussion of whether or not a lawyer will always want to obtain all the facts, see M.H. Freedman, "Profession-al Responsibility of the Criminal Defense Lawyer: The Three Hardest Questions," 64 Mich.L.R. 1469, 1471–72 (1966).

explanations (which you then investigate), or to admit that the original story was not entirely accurate.

Assume for instance that you represent a salesperson sued by a former employer for unlawfully taking that employer's customer list and using it on behalf of a new employer. The salesperson's story, which you find unbelievable, is that the salesperson did not take the customer list but has developed the customers on the salesperson's own. You may confront the client with the adversary's story as follows:

> "Pat, let's look at what the attorney for A. Co. (the former employer) is going to say. They will say that you worked for them for 14 years; that you were given monthly customer lists; that you agreed to turn over all customer lists to A. Co. if you left employment; that after you left you called on exactly the same customers you did when you worked for A. Co., and that you even showed one of these customers that you still had the A. Co. list. How are we going to overcome this story?"

A somewhat difficult variation of this technique is for you to ask a client to help you figure out what story an adversary is likely to present, and how to refute it. To establish an adversary's story, you typically need to work with a client by suggesting some possibilities. If a client has difficulty refuting the adversary's story, a client may understand the weakness of his or her own story, and perhaps tell a more truthful one. On the other hand, if a client too readily refutes an adversary's story, you may point out that the adversary is unlikely to rely on such an easily refuted story. Then, continue to work with a client to develop a story an adversary is more likely to tell. You may continue this process until you and a client arrive at a more realistic version. When the client cannot refute an adversary's ultimate story, the client may tell a more truthful version.[21]

A third variation of this technique is a mock cross examination. You question a client as though you were opposing counsel on cross. Often, until a role play exercise such as this forces a client to confront a story in a dynamic setting, clients do not face up to the obvious weaknesses in their false stories.

3. Silence

Alone or following the use of other techniques, silence can be a powerful indication of disbelief. Though you say little or nothing, your body language conveys your lack of belief and your expectation that a client will tell the truth. You need not have Shakespearian training to carry out this technique.[22] Direct eye contact, a facial expression that is both serious and indicative of disbelief, and perhaps a few shakes of the head are often more than sufficient.

---

21. If this technique seems to take unfair advantage of your power in an attorney-client relationship, remember that it is one you employ only when you strongly suspect fabrication.

22. Nevertheless, you may find this technique difficult to learn and employ. Most of us are not comfortable staring at another human being and waiting until the other speaks.

4. Direct Verbal Confrontation

Direct confrontation involves starkly telling a client that (a) a story is not believable and (b) why you disbelieve it. Consider this example:

> "Mr. Thomas, I simply do not believe what you are telling me. According to you, your brother failed to repay the $100,000 when it was due and you did not realize it until over a year later. People whose brothers owe them $100,000 by a certain date don't forget such a date for a whole year. I'd like the truth."

Directly confronting a client is difficult. A client may get angry, accuse you of misdeeds, and terminate the relationship. Thus, you should make such a statement only if you are quite certain a client is indeed lying. Keep in mind, however, that the statement's purpose is to help a client tell the truth. Therefore, your own conduct should be consistent with this goal. Your demeanor when making the statement, for example, should indicate your concern and desire to help. And, you might include a motivational statement, such as advising a client that the truth is likely to be in the client's best interest. In addition, you may let the client know that you will continue to accept the client even if the client admits to having lied. Thus, in the debt example above, you might have preceded the confrontational statement with a motivational statement as follows:

> "Mr. Thomas, I'd like to help you, and I think I can help you, but only if you are honest with me. Unfortunately, in my experience clients sometimes are less than totally honest. I'm used to that, and if it turns out that's occurred here it will in no way interfere with my willingness to help you. But frankly, I simply do not believe . . . ."

Do not expect results, if any there are, instantly. A client may need time before realizing that admitting to fabrication and telling a truthful story is in his or her best interests. Perhaps more meetings will take place before a client "comes clean." You may even have to repeat the motivational and confrontational statements. But short of terminating the attorney-client relationship, this is about as forceful as you can be when confronting a possibly fabricated story.[23]

Ultimately if a client sticks with a story and your suspicions continue, you will have to consider whether you need to withdraw as counsel.[24]

23. A decision to withdraw as counsel, particularly in litigated matters, is a complex matter beyond the scope of this text. For one perspective, see Freedman, *supra* note 18, at 1475–1478.

24. For a discussion of when a lawyer may withdraw, see ABA Model Rules, *su-* *pra* note 4, Rules 1.2, 1.16, and 3.3 and Comments thereto; ABA Model Code of Professional Responsibility, EC 2–32, DR 2–110, DR 7–102 (1980). But see, Freedman, *supra* note 18, at 1475–1478.

Part Four

DECISION-MAKING

Part Four (Chapters 15 through 23) explores the process of helping clients decide what solutions are most likely to resolve their problems. Chapter 15 explores the types of decisions that clients should have an opportunity to make, and your role in making clients active participants in the decision-making process. Chapter 16 describes a model for carrying out this client-centered role. Chapters 17 through 20 explore refinements in the basic model. Chapters 21 and 22, respectively, illustrate and analyze the model's use in the context of decisions that clients commonly face in litigation and deals matters. Finally, Chapter 23 briefly considers referral of clients to mental health professionals.

Chapter 15

THE NATURE OF THE COUNSELING PROCESS

* * *

From what you tell me, Mr. Rodale, your objective is to get DataCo's auditing department operating efficiently as quickly as possible. Is that right?

Exactly. We've got to start operating smoothly as soon as possible.

Well, from what you've said, it seems clear that DataCo has every legal right to terminate Ms. Hilary. She has repeatedly ignored warnings about getting her work done on time and, given the problems that her lateness has caused, there is certainly good reason to fire her. What you need to do, however, is determine whether you want to go ahead and terminate her or whether you want to follow some other course of action, such as suspending her or having her agree to resign in exchange for some kind of a severance package. From what you said so far, it does not appear as though the decision is going to be an easy one. Terminating Ms. Hilary seems to have a number of negatives attached to it, such as lowering morale in the audit division. Am I correct?

Yes; I guess that is the case.

Well, in that light, what I think we should do is to try to take a look at each of your options and try to figure out which one, on balance, will probably best accomplish your overall objective. Why don't we start by focusing on outright termination?

* * *

Ms. Biggs, has our discussion given you a picture of what options the partnership could follow in setting up a bank account and the pros and cons of each?

Yes, but I'm somewhat conflicted. On the one hand, I want to make sure that once the partnership is going Jean won't be able to make bank withdrawals of more than $2,000. On the other hand, I can see that asking for this kind of protective provision in our written agreement may really poison the negotiations and our future relationship. What option do you think I should choose?

* * *

258

1. INTRODUCTION

Numerous decisions are made as clients' matters move toward resolution. Some of these decisions involve resolution of the principal problems themselves: Should a settlement offer be accepted? Should a contract be signed, despite its failure to include an exclusive dealing provision? Often, however, decisions involve subsidiary strategies: Should discovery be undertaken immediately? Should the draft of a proposed agreement omit an arbitration clause? Who should prepare the draft—you or the other party?

This chapter explores issues that arise when you counsel and advise clients with respect to either type of decision. Those issues include:

    a.   Who, as between you and a client, should have the final say?

    b.   What decisions regarding the handling of a matter should you explore with a client?

    c.   With respect to decisions which require client consultation,

        1.   What information should you elicit from a client before a decision is made?

        2.   What information should you insure is available to a client before a decision is made?

        3.   When should you provide an opinion as to what decision should be made?

        4.   What criteria should you use in arriving at an opinion as to what decision should be made?

        5.   How fully must you counsel a client?

        6.   When, if ever, may you suggest that a client's decision is wrong?

Understanding these issues, and having some approach to resolving them whenever a decision looms, is critical. Answers to these questions define the counseling role and thus are at the heart of what it means to practice law.

2. COUNSELING AND ADVICE–GIVING DEFINED

Begin by considering the terms "counseling" and "advice-giving." They reflect related but quite different tasks. Usually you must both counsel and advise clients to help them make decisions.

Counseling

Counseling is the process by which lawyers help clients decide what course of action to adopt in order to resolve a problem. The process begins with identifying a problem and clarifying a client's objectives. Thereafter, the process entails identifying and evaluating the probable positive and negative consequences of potential solutions in order to decide which alternative is most likely to achieve a client's aims.[1]

Advice–Giving

Advice consists of your opinion. You may advise a client both about what consequences (legal and/or nonlegal) are likely to flow from alternative courses of action or about which alternative a client should adopt.

An example clarifies the distinction between these two forms of advice. Assume that you represent Snider, who is negotiating to lease space in a shopping center. The owner has indicated that she does not want to give Snider an option to renew the lease. Snider has to decide whether or not to insist on the option. Your opinion about whether or not Snider should insist on the option is an opinion about what course of action Snider should follow. Your opinion about how insisting on the option may affect upcoming negotiations constitutes an opinion about the likely consequences of selecting a particular course of action.[2]

Generally, when counseling you provide advice about consequences far more often than you do about which alternative a client should adopt.

3. AFFORD CLIENTS AN OPPORTUNITY TO MAKE DECISIONS

Inherent in the above definitions of advice-giving and counseling is the idea that clients should generally have the opportunity to make decisions.[3] This is not to say that you never venture your opinion about what course of action a client should adopt,[4] that you never make a decision without consulting a client,[5] or that you must always carry out a client's decision.[6] Our point is a more limited one. With respect to the many decisions that typically must be made as a matter progresses, usually you must give a client the opportunity to decide.

As a starting point, a client should have primary decision-making power because of the simple truth that *a problem is a client's problem, not yours.* For the most part a client, not you, will have to accept the immediate as well as the long term consequences of any decision. For example, deciding to take depositions may result in a client, not you,

---

1. This definition is a modification of that originally used by D.A. Binder & S.C. Price, *Legal Interviewing and Counseling: A Client–Centered Approach* 5 (1977).

2. Your obligation to counsel and advise is a reminder that you should not on your own represent a client whose matter requires expertise or experience that you do not have. See ABA Model Rules of Professional Conduct Rule 1.1 (1983) [hereinafter Model Rules]; ABA Model Code of Professional Responsibility DR 6–101(A)(1) (1980) [hereinafter Model Code].

3. See Sec. 4, *infra.*

4. For a discussion of when and how you might interject your opinions, see Sec. 6(D) and (E) *infra.*

5. For a discussion of what decisions might appropriately be made by lawyers see Sec. 4 *infra.*

6. See Sec. 6(E), *infra.*

expending thousands of dollars.[7]   Similarly, a client will receive the benefits or suffer the losses attendant to decisions to hire an expert, leave an arbitration clause out of an agreement, or accept a settlement offer.

Given that clients bear the brunt of decisions' consequences, clients presumptively should have the opportunity to determine what course of action to take.   Our society highly values each individual's right of self-determination, and you ought to abandon that value only in the face of strong reason for doing so.[8]   Because client autonomy is of paramount importance, decisions should be made on the basis of what choice is most likely to *provide a client with maximum satisfaction*.

Clients almost invariably are better able than you to assess which potential decision is most likely to be satisfactory.[9]   For one thing, as you recall from Chapter 1, resolving problems typically requires consideration of nonlegal consequences.   And clients are likely to be able to predict nonlegal consequences far better than you can.[10]   Moreover, even if both you and a client agreed precisely on the likely consequences of a decision, you would not necessarily weigh those consequences equally in making the decision.   The process of weighing consequences heavily depends on each person's unique values, and autonomy notions assign primary importance to a client's values.

The following example illustrates how decisions depend on subjective personal values.   Assume that you represent Kimmel, who has brought suit against Badger Outlets for wrongful termination.   The case has been pending for over a year, and Badger has now made a settlement offer of $35,000.   Your opinion is that if the case were to proceed to trial, Kimmel would be likely to recover at least $65,000.   At the same time, trial is still six months away, and there is a small chance that at trial Kimmel will recover nothing.   Should Kimmel accept the offer?

Your legal, "objective" point of view, balancing the "bird in the hand" of $35,000 against the risk of recovering nothing and the delay of trial, may be that the offer is acceptable.   But whether the offer is satisfactory to *Kimmel* depends on the importance Kimmel attaches to the likely consequences.   Choosing to settle will bring Kimmel

7. Even contingency fee lawyers who sometimes pay (albeit perhaps improperly) clients' litigation expenses should recognize that this statement is correct.

8. Some lawyers consider possession of a law degree a sufficiently strong reason to override client autonomy.   However, such a position fails to grasp fully how dependent most decisions are on nonlegal expertise and personal values.

9. A standard by which clients make decisions based on maximum satisfaction does not prevent your bringing to a client's

attention such important considerations as the interests of third persons, of society as a whole, or of your own interests.   Moreover, sometimes you may express disagreement with a decision even though you think it likely to provide maximum client satisfaction.   See Sec. 6(E), *infra*.

10. For example, a corporate executive having to decide whether to postpone a trial date will be far better able than you to predict how the delay may impact the company's financial planning and employee morale.

$35,000.[11] But how important is this cash to Kimmel? If Kimmel is wealthy, the answer may be, "not very." [12] Furthermore, there may be non-economic ramifications. As settling may eliminate Kimmel's opportunity to publicize the dispute, settlement may be very unattractive if Kimmel attaches importance to a public airing. Moreover, a decision will probably have an effect on Kimmel's state of mind. Is Kimmel worried about this case? Do thoughts of it wake Kimmel during the night? If so, perhaps Kimmel will place a high value on ending these worries and choose to settle. Or, will acceptance of the offer cause Kimmel to feel like a "chicken?" If Kimmel feels this way, settlement may adversely affect Kimmel's feelings of self esteem and give the settlement option little allure.

Clients' subjective assessments of likely consequences lie at the heart of determining maximum client satisfaction in transactional matters as well. Assume you represent Martino, the owner of several shopping centers, including a new mid-sized center. On Martino's behalf, you are negotiating a proposed lease with SafeBet Markets. Under the lease, SafeBets would become an anchor tenant in the new center. Per Martino's instructions, during negotiations with SafeBet you have repeatedly asked SafeBet's lawyer to agree to a lease provision obligating SafeBet to pay a pro-rata share of the maintenance costs for the upkeep of the center's common areas. Such a provision is typical in commercial leases in your area. During a prior negotiating session, SafeBet's lawyer has told you that a common areas clause is unacceptable to SafeBet. Tomorrow you are scheduled to have your final negotiation meeting with SafeBet's lawyer. In your opinion, there is only a small possibility that SafeBet will accede to the common areas provision. The decision to be made is whether or not to continue to insist on that provision.

One likely consequence of continued insistence on the provision is that SafeBet will break off negotiations, and as a result Martino will not acquire income from the lease. How important is it to Martino to obtain rent? If immediate additional income is important, or if Safebet's tenancy will encourage other potential tenants to lease space, the alternative of dropping the common areas clause will seem attractive.

However, if the fact that Martino dropped the demand for a common areas provision becomes generally known, Martino's bargaining position in future lease deals might be harmed. Future potential tenants might assume that if Martino did not require a common areas provision in a lease with SafeBet, Martino probably is in some way "desperate" for tenants. As a consequence, such tenants might contin-

---

11. For the sake of illustration, we put to the side questions of attorneys fees and costs.

12. Because the value of $35,000 must be made in terms of what value Mr. Kimmel attaches to the money, the decision about whether $35,000 is a fair figure cannot be made simply on the basis of whether the present discounted value of an eighty percent chance of $65,000 in six months is worth more or less than $35,000.

ually push Martino for concessions and make future lease negotiations difficult. How important is it to Martino to avoid this risk? If Martino believes that the absence of such a clause in SafeBet's lease will become generally known and therefore impact on future deals, Martino may conclude that maintaining the demand is of great importance.

While Martino might have to evaluate many other potential consequences before making a final decision about whether to drop the demand for a common areas provision, what should be clear is that an assessment of what choice is likely to produce maximum satisfaction for Martino requires Martino's subjective evaluation of the importance of the decision's likely ramifications.

As you can see, you cannot determine what decision is likely to lead to maximum client satisfaction through reference to an external standard. A rational choice can be made only by forecasting the likely economic, social, psychological and moral ramifications of a decision *and* determining their relative importance. While you may help a client identify a decision's likely ramifications only a client can determine their relative importance.

Moreover, as both examples illustrate, rarely are consequences either "all good" or "all bad." Virtually every decision entails trade-offs. For example, Kimmel's decision to settle in order to regain peace of mind may result in Kimmel's feeling a bit cowardly for having done so. Similarly, Martino's dropping the lease provision to gain a good tenant may produce anxiety about possible harmful effects on future negotiations. The trade-offs necessitated by almost all decisions reinforce the conclusion that only clients' subjective values can predict what decision is most likely to produce maximum satisfaction.[13]

As the above examples imply, the subjective factor of "risk aversion" often has a substantial impact on clients' decisions. When choosing a course of action, neither you nor a client can do more than predict *likely* consequences. Every decision entails a risk that predicted consequences may not occur. So, if Martino abandons the common areas provision, it does not follow automatically that SafeBet will sign the lease; or that if the lease is signed, Martino will receive the projected net income; or that Martino's future negotiating position will be damaged. These consequences are, to paraphrase Dickens, shadows of what *may* be, not what must be. Hence, by conceding to SafeBet, Martino indicates a willingness to risk a weakened bargaining position with future tenants. A "different" Martino, aware of precisely the same potential consequence, might not be willing to take this risk, and as a result might not concede to SafeBet. The fact that two clients can make the same predictions about consequences, yet make different

---

13. Clients' values, preferences and degree of risk aversion do not remain constant. Instead they change considerably over time as the client's life situation changes. Thus, a client who finds $85,000 an attractive offer today because of a need for capital may have an almost opposite reaction a few months later if the client's capital needs have since been met.

decisions depending on their willingness to run risks, is a strong factor in favor of clients being the primary decision-makers.

You might respond, "I realize that what is best for any client typically rests on subjective personal values which are unknown to me.[14] But that doesn't mean I shouldn't make decisions for a client. It just means that in addition to eliciting the 'facts,' I should also find out about each client's predictions and values." Such a response is not entirely without basis. As you will see, counseling does consist in part of asking clients about predicted consequences and personal values. However, in most instances such an inquiry will not give you a full understanding of a client's personal values. As noted elsewhere,

> "[I]t is often very difficult, if not impossible, for clients to precisely quantify the value they place on specific consequences. Thus, clients cannot usually say, even to themselves, such things as, 'On a scale from one to ten, getting $2500 now has a value of plus 5; avoiding the strain of trial has a value of plus 2; however, giving up the opportunity to obtain an additional $5500 has a value of minus 5;' etc. All that clients can usually do is give general statements of the value they place on the various consequences. Thus, clients can sometimes quantify consequences to the extent of labeling them as 'very important,' 'important,' 'not so important,' etc. However, this quantifying process does not usually allow clients to distinguish between consequences which they see as fitting into the same general category of importance. Thus, typically, clients cannot distinguish between two or three consequences, each of which they see as 'important,' 'not so important,' etc. This inability to distinguish between consequences is particularly pronounced when the consequences are of different types. For instance, a client typically cannot distinguish between an 'important' economic consequence and an 'important' psychological consequence. When asked to rank or weigh the relative importance of such consequences, clients will typically say such things as 'I can't say which is more important. Getting an additional $1500 is important, but it's also important that I not be under a lot of stress. My friends say go for the additional money, but they don't have to face testifying in court. I can't say which is more important; they're both important.' " [15]

Moreover, what is true about conveying values and preferences is also true with respect to conveying risk averseness. Most clients have a difficult time articulating precisely the degree to which they are willing to risk possible losses to achieve possible gains. Thus, they may say such things as, "I'm just not sure how willing I am to get SafeBet as a tenant if it means I have to sign a lease waiving my right to have SafeBet contribute its pro-rata share of the maintenance costs." Cli-

---

14. An exception to some degree may exist in the case where you have represented a client over a long time and know that client extremely well. In such a situation, assuming no recent major changes in a client's life situation, you may well have a fairly good idea about many of a client's values and preferences.

15. See Binder & Price, *supra* note 1, at 149.

ents' typical inability to express accurately their subjective thoughts about their willingness to take risks is another reason that you must give clients the opportunity to decide what course of action to follow.

Finally, even if you could become fully conversant with a client's value and preference structure, you perhaps ought not be trusted to make important decisions because of potential conflicts of interest. When it comes time to make decisions, your interests and those of a client frequently are adverse. For instance, in making decisions about what provisions to include in a deal, lawyers often want to include a great many more contingency provisions than do clients.[16] Lawyers often want clients to insert such provisions in agreements not only to protect the client but also to make sure that if the contingency ultimately does arise, the lawyer cannot be sued for malpractice.[17] Clients, on the other hand, are often more interested in making a deal than in being fully protected if an agreement should ultimately break down. Clients often predict that insistence on a contingency provision may kill the deal and they are therefore willing to drop the provision and take the risk that the contingency will not arise.[18]

Other common examples of potential lawyer-client decision-making conflicts include whether to accept an offer, whether to take depositions, and whether to call a witness to testify. In each of these instances, what may be financially beneficial or convenient for a lawyer may conflict with what is financially best for a client.

That lawyers and clients often have conflicting interests suggests once again that decisions ought to remain in a client's hands. Even if you could determine a client's values and preferences, the temptation to decide the matter in a way which advances your personal interests is reason to allow a client to make the ultimate choice.[19]

---

16. For a discussion of contingency provisions, see Chapter 11, sec. 7. For a discussion of lawyers' tendency to be more risk-averse than clients, see Chapter 11, sec. 2.

17. More cynical commentators may suggest lawyers' insistence on covering "all possible contingencies" also arises from lawyers interests in more legal fees.

18. For an interesting description of this phenomenon see the Los Angeles Times' description of the negotiations between the San Diego Padres and Bruce Hurst. *Los Angeles Times*, Dec. 9, 1988, Part III, at 1.

19. The reality is that lawyers often do put self-interest before clients' interests. In a survey of recent developments in legal ethics published by The Georgetown Journal of Legal Ethics, a full 110 pages were devoted to attorney conflict of interest cases decided within a 12-month period. C.J. Bellini, L. Fisher, J.E. Gagliano, C.D. Grear, K.D. Head, J.M. Marrone, J. Reynolds, N. Ribaudo, R.R. Rothman & T.M. Zic, "Conflicts of Interest," 2 Geo. J. Legal Ethics 101 (1988). See also M. Spiegel, "Lawyering and Client Decision-making: Informed Consent and the Legal Profession," 128 U.Pa.L.Rev. 41, 87–100 (1979) ("Both theoretical and empirical evidence suggests . . . [that society's 'usual mechanisms' for controlling disloyal behavior— 'the market, legal regulation, and systems of norms'] do not effectively control the behavior of lawyers." Id. at 89.)

4. WHAT DECISIONS CAN YOU MAKE WITHOUT CONSULTING A CLIENT?

An emphasis on clients as primary decision-makers may suggest that clients should have the opportunity to make each and every decision. Some commentators, in fact, have urged such a position.[20]

However, the "client makes all the decisions" position is unworkable and, in fact, inconsistent with client-centeredness. If a client were to make every decision, you would have to inform a client each time a decision were necessary and engage a client in a discussion of potential options and consequences. Yet, as you recall, even a simple matter typically requires scores of decisions. Accordingly, you and your clients would have to be in nearly continuous communication.[21] Undoubtedly, most clients would not have the time, the desire or the financial resources to hire you under these conditions. Moreover, you would undoubtedly soon regard practicing law under such conditions as a sentence to a career of virtually continuous communication with a small number of clients.

If consultation about every decision is unacceptable, how might you decide what decisions to call to a client's attention? There is no easy answer to this question. In the past, some authorities attempted to draw a distinction between matters' "substantive" and "procedural" aspects. They suggested that lawyers should review with clients decisions affecting the objectives of representation, but need not do so with respect to decisions which only affected the means by which the objectives were secured.[22] Many courts continue to echo this ends-means distinction.[23]

---

20. See Spiegel, *supra* note 19, at 65–67.

21. See Model Rules, *supra* note 2. Rule 1.2 appears to suggest that consultation about each decision is required. The rule provides "[a] lawyer shall abide by a client's decisions concerning the objectives of representation * * * and shall consult with the client as to the means by which they are to be pursued." However, no legal scholar with whom we have spoken believes that the ABA actually advocates such a position.

22. M. Spiegel, "The New Model Rules of Professional Conduct: Lawyer–Client Decision Making and the Role of Rules in Structuring the Lawyer–Client Dialogue," 1980 Am.B.Found.Res.J. 1003, 1003–04. Cf. Spiegel, *supra* note 19, at 65–67.

23. See e.g., *Blanton v. Womancare, Inc.*, 38 Cal.3d 396, 404–05, 212 Cal.Rptr. 151, 156, 696 P.2d 645, 650–51 (1985); *Linsk v. Linsk*, 70 Cal.2d 272, 278, 74 Cal.

Rptr. 544, 548, 449 P.2d 760, 764 (1969). For similar cases in other jurisdictions, see 7A C.J.S. *Attorney & Client* § 193 (1980). See also, Speigel, *supra* note 19 at 49–65; M. Strauss, "Toward a Revised Model of Attorney–Client Relationship: The Argument for Autonomy," 65 N.C.L. Rev. 315, 318–21 (1987). Most court decisions involve litigation matters rather than transactional matters. How courts would explore the merits/tactics dichotomy in the transactional area is perhaps unclear. The Model Rules make a distinction between decisions affecting the objectives of the representation and the means of obtaining such objectives. The distinction is essentially the old merits/tactics line drawn by courts and used in the Model Code (See EC 7–7). However, as noted in note 21 *supra*, the ABA now appears to call for client consultation in both areas.

However, a moment's reflection suggests that drawing a meaningful line based on "ends" and "means" is often impossible.[24] For example, clients are often concerned both about what is achieved and how it is achieved. Assume that you represent a client charged with burglary, and a decision arises about whether or not to call the client's sister as an alibi witness. You believe the sister will make an excellent witness, but the client insists that she not be called because in the client's view testifying will cause the sister undue stress. Is the decision of whether to call the sister one of ends or means? If the client's objective is seen simply as avoiding conviction—winning the trial—the decision about calling the sister is arguably merely a question of tactics or means. However, if the client's objectives are seen as avoiding a conviction and also avoiding stress to the sister, both decisions involve objectives.

Asking a client early on to indicate what kinds of decisions he or she wishes to be consulted about has sometimes been suggested as an approach to the issue of when you need to consult a client.[25] However, this "waiver" approach too is typically inadequate. A client who is legally experienced may have a basis for making an informed choice about which decisions he or she wishes to be consulted on. You may therefore be justified in relying on that choice, at least when the client asks for frequent consultation.[26] When consultation occurs frequently, a client has repeated opportunities to reassess the decision about the kinds of issues on which he or she wishes to be consulted.

However, legally inexperienced clients usually cannot foresee the twists and turns that even relatively simple matters may take, and hence cannot know what decision points are likely to arise.[27] Accordingly you should probably not rely on an inexperienced client's waiver of decision-making responsibility.

Moreover, whether or not a client is experienced, the kinds of decisions a client wishes to be consulted about at one point in time are not necessarily the kinds of decisions the client will wish to be consulted about at some later time. As a client's life situation changes, and as a matter ages, the kinds of decisions which a client views as important and on which the client hence wants to be consulted may well also change. Thus, any initial guideline delineating when consultation is desired is a very soft decision which needs periodic review.

Hence, neither "ends-means" nor "prior waiver" adequately determine which decisions require client consultation. In our view, a

---

24. See Spiegel, *supra* note 19 at 52; Strauss, *supra* note 23 at 324; J.L. Maute, "Allocation of Decisionmaking Authority Under the Model Rules of Professional Conduct," 17 U.C.Davis L.Rev. 1049, 1061 (1984).

25. R.A. Epstein, "Medical Malpractice: The Case for Contract," 1976 Am.B.Found. Res.J. 87, 119–28.

26. If a client says consultation is necessary only in a narrow range of situations, a client's decision perhaps should be viewed as less binding. A case may take an unusual turn, or a client's life situation may change dramatically.

27. This lack will, of course, exist among both litigation and transactional clients.

different standard should apply. You ought to provide a client with an opportunity to make a decision whenever a lawyer using "such skill, prudence, and diligence as other members of the profession commonly possess and exercise," would or should know that a pending decision is likely to have a *substantial legal or nonlegal impact on a client.*[28]

This standard instructs you to consult a client if, measured by the presumed awareness of the legal community, a decision is likely to have a substantial legal or nonlegal impact on a client. Admittedly, the standard is not without its difficulties. For example, the standard may differ from one community to another. Also, it may burden a novice attorney with finding out whether experienced attorneys are likely to view a decision as one likely to have a substantial impact. However, the standard is one to which professionals are commonly held.[29] Moreover, it is client centered. It focuses on the likely impact on an individual client, rather than fuzzy distinctions between "ends" and "means."

Since helping clients resolve problems is a lawyer's major role, it is legitimate to require lawyers to be aware of clients' objectives and concerns throughout the attorney-client relationship. Moreover, many lawyers undoubtedly now gather information about clients' objectives and concerns. Finally, using a client-centered approach invariably elicits such information. For example, preliminary problem identification seeks to unearth objectives and concerns at the outset of a relationship. Hence, the standard is both fair and realistic.

Indeed, many lawyers undoubtedly comply with the standard in their everyday practices. When a decision may cause a substantial impact, many lawyers regularly consult clients about a wide variety of decisions that many would define as involving "means." For example, when decisions are likely to have a substantial legal or nonlegal impact, litigators often consult with their clients about matters such as continuances, filing of motions, taking of depositions, and negotiation strategy. Indeed, a lawyer might even consult a client as to the wisdom of asking a question on cross examination in circumstances where the impact of a

28. Normally the law defines an attorney's duty as one of using such skill, prudence, and diligence as other members of the profession commonly possess and exercise. See W. Prosser & W.P. Keeton, *The Law of Torts* 185–93 (1984); *Budd v. Nixen,* 6 Cal.3d 195, 200, 98 Cal.Rptr. 849, 852, 491 P.2d 433, 436 (1971). This standard is thought to impose an extra duty on lawyers beyond that imposed on ordinary people. Prosser and Keeton, *supra.* The extra burden is thought to exist because it is assumed that lawyers possess special knowledge that lay persons do not. However, if lawyers in the exercise of their professional tasks are not very thorough, the standard of "using skill etc. commonly possessed" may only provide an escape

hatch for the slovenly. For example, what if most lawyers are so focused on gathering "legally salient information" that they fail to learn facts which would suggest that common decisions such as the granting of continuances and the inclusion of standard boiler plate language in agreements may produce severe adverse nonlegal ramifications? Could the lawyer who fails to acquire information that would make him or her aware of such ramifications avoid liability because most members of the profession also typically fail to gather such data? The questions are ones we leave for others to resolve.

29. See Prosser & Keeton, *supra* note 29, at 185.

critical admission might be undercut by an explanation, and the lawyer believes that the client may know whether the witness will give that explanation.   Likewise, when substantial impact decisions arise in transactional matters, lawyers discuss with their clients such issues as how to word provisions, which side will draft the agreement, and what negotiation strategy to pursue.[30]

An example will illustrate how you might apply a "substantial impact" standard in practice. Assume that you represent Gower "Tower of Power" Bower, a financially independent professional basketball player nearing the end of his career with the Smeltics. Gower is in the "option" (last) year of his current contract; you are negotiating an extension with the Smeltics. Gower's primary goal is a three year contract which would allow him to continue to receive his salary for three years even if he were injured or let go. (The Smeltics, he knows, have a history of not re-signing former stars to save money once they are somewhat past their prime.) Gower would like a raise in his $800,000 per year salary, but is willing to forgo an increase in favor of a three-year deal. He is anxious to conclude the negotiations as quickly as possible, since a career-ending injury is always a possibility.

Early in the negotiations, the Smeltics' attorney asks that Gower consent to a thorough physical examination. Should you or Gower make this auxiliary decision? The standard allocates the decision to Gower if its consequences are likely to have a substantial impact on him. Here, the outcome of the physical might well determine whether the team makes a multiyear offer. Thus the decision is likely to have a substantial impact, and the decision is one for Gower to make.

The Smeltics' attorney next reminds you that the team's usual policy is not to negotiate in midseason. However, the team is willing to negotiate with Gower if a new contract can be signed within two weeks. You understand that if Gower does sign quickly, he will probably not be eligible to benefit financially from royalties from a pay TV contract that you expect the Smeltics to conclude before next season. If he were to sign a new contract *after* the Smeltics signed a pay TV contract, Gower would probably receive a salary bonus in the range of $5000 to

---

30. Little data exists which indicates the kinds of decisions lawyers typically examine with their clients. However, two small surveys by UCLA law students (K. Bresnahan and B. Kuyper, "A Survey of Lawyers Who Have Corporate Clients" (1989); R. Gomez and G. McKenzie, "A Survey Measuring Client Satisfaction" (1989)) (on file with authors) indicate that at least lawyers working with large corporate clients (annual revenues in excess of twenty million dollars) review a wide variety of decisions with the corporate representatives with whom they are working. The studies indicate that these reviews occur with some frequency in both litigation and transactional matters and in matters which are deemed routine (a matter a client commonly engages in or is commonly confronted with) as well as non-routine (a matter that endangers the viability of, or has a major impact on, the corporation). While the studies do not show why the lawyers consulted their clients, we assume they did so either because of clients' requests and/or the lawyers' recognition that their clients input was important. An earlier survey of members of the Florida Bar indicated that at least in litigation matters, client consultation was generally infrequent. See J.P. Reed, "The Lawyer-Client: A Managed Relationship?" Acad. Mgmt.J. 67, 76–77 (Mar. 1969).

$10,000. Our standard would probably permit you to decide whether to open negotiations immediately. Given that a three year deal is worth at least $1.6 million more than a one year deal, and that Gower has told you of his desire to conclude negotiations quickly, the decision is not likely to have a substantial impact on him.[31]

Analyzing the likely impact of a decision in light of Gower's actual situation, rather than using vague distinctions such as "ends" and "means," seems to us to be the best way to allocate decision-making responsibility. And, since it looks to impact on a client, the standard almost surely satisfies rules governing your duty to allow clients to make decisions.[32]

5. EFFECT OF THE "SUBSTANTIAL IMPACT" STANDARD ON "LAWYERING SKILLS" CONCERNS

You may worry about whether a standard obligating you to consult a client whenever a decision is likely to have a substantial impact unduly interferes with your exercise of professional skills. For example, if a decision to pursue a certain line of questioning on cross is likely to have a substantial impact, are you therefore obligated to consult the client regarding cross examination questioning strategy?

Clients, recognizing their own lack of expertise, undoubtedly assume you will make such decisions, and do not expect to be consulted about them. By analogy, consider that a plumber does not consult a customer as to what type of wrench to use on a stopped drain. The customer's act of hiring the plumber indicates the customer's desire for the plumber to make those decisions which are in the plumber's traditional domain. Similarly, a client's decision to hire you is tacit willingness for you to make lawyering skills decisions free from consultation. Thus, such matters as how you cross examine, write briefs, or phrase contingency clauses are generally for you alone to decide, even though they may have a substantial impact. They involve primarily the exercise of the skills and crafts that are the special domain of lawyers.

However, "lawyering skills" are often not a sufficient excuse for failure to consult a client. When a decision is likely to have an impact beyond that normally associated with the exercise of lawyering skills and crafts, the "substantial impact" standard obligates consultation. For example, consider these situations:

    a.   A witness you are considering calling on behalf of your client is the client's boss.

---

31. This is to say that the standard might not *require* you to permit Gower to make the decision. You might, of course, choose to apply your own stricter standard and make a decisional pass to Gower.

32. See, e.g., Model Rules, *supra* note 2, Rule 1.2 & 1.4.

b.   You are considering phrasing a contingency clause in a purposely vague manner because you do not think the other party will agree to the precise language your client desires, and the vague wording may at a future date be interpreted in your client's favor.

c.   You are considering whether to remove an action from state to federal court.

d.   You are considering whether to defend an action vigorously, as opposed to simply countering the plaintiff's moves.

You probably should consult a client in each of these situations. The decisions carry impacts beyond those normally associated with the use of professional skills and crafts.

Thus, in "a," developing case-in-chief may usually lie entirely within your professional judgment. But calling a client's boss raises sensitive issues beyond those normally associated with direct examination. Hence, the need for client consultation.

Similarly, in "b," the question of how to phrase the contingency clause is not simply one of professional craft, but of risk averseness, of a client's willingness to live with uncertainty. That decision too does not involve primarily the craft of legal writing, but may have a substantial impact on the client's position in the event the contingency arises. Hence, the need for consultation.

In "c," whether an action is tried in state or federal court is likely to have many effects, such as what evidentiary rules apply and when the action may come to trial. Again, even though the decision rests in part on the exercise of professional judgment, the potential impacts suggest the need for client consultation.

Finally, in "d," costs to a client may be very different depending on how vigorously a suit is defended. Costs, of course, are the type of impact which very much suggest the need for client consultation.

Admittedly, knowing when an impact is beyond that normally associated with the exercise of professional skills and crafts will often be difficult. We make no pretense that our line is a bright and unwavering one. However, we do think that the "ends"–"means" test leaves far too many decisions in an attorney's hands alone. The four examples above may help you understand why many "lawyering skills" decisions require client consultation.[33]

33. Note that the fact that a decision requires client consultation does not mean that the consultation is necessarily lengthy. As you will see in Sec. 6(C) *infra*, the extent of the counseling obligation varies, depending, among other factors, on the "complexity of the decision." Hence, if you think that the decision to remove a case to federal court, for example, is so apparent that it lacks complexity, you might satisfy your obligation with a statement such as, "We have the opportunity to remove this case to federal court, where it will come to trial within a year. You've said you want to get to trial as soon as possible. I see no added costs or other disadvantages of removing the case. Do you see any problem with removing it?"

6. YOUR ROLE IN THE COUNSELING AND ADVICE–GIVING PROCESS

Once you have undertaken to review a decision with a client, what role should you play in the counseling and advice-giving process? [34] Primarily, your role is to explore with a client, with respect to each such decision, alternative courses of action and their likely consequences. Only after such an exploration can a client evaluate which choice is most likely to provide maximum satisfaction. Consider therefore the process of helping clients explore choices and outcomes—i.e., the process of counseling.

A. EXPOSE CLIENTS TO ALTERNATIVES AND CONSEQUENCES

When lawyers think of counseling and advising clients, they tend to think in terms of information flowing from lawyer (expert) to client (non-expert). Indeed when courts and professional bodies such as the American Bar Association talk in terms of legal obligations in the counseling field, they speak principally in terms of disclosure: information a lawyer must provide to a client.[35] However, for a client to meaningfully consider alternatives and likely consequences, you must both elicit information from a client as well as provide it. Succinctly stated, counseling is a two-way street.

1. *Information to Elicit From Clients*

Because lawyers tend to view counseling as a process only of providing advice, the subject of what information to elicit from clients is perhaps the most neglected and counter-intuitive topic in counseling. Consider, therefore, what information you might try to elicit and the importance of an informational flow that moves from client to you.

a. *Client Objectives*

To help a client choose an alternative that is most likely to provide maximum satisfaction, you invariably need to understand a client's objectives. What is a client trying to accomplish? Solutions can be identified and assessed only in light of a client's overall objectives, and these objectives, of course, are known only by your client. Therefore, you should ask a client to articulate major goals and objectives.[36]

---

34. We assume that your role remains the same regardless of whether you bring a decision to a client's attention or a client comes to you asking for advice on how to resolve a decision.

35. See also Model Rules, *supra* note 2, Rules 1.4 & 2.1.

36. On some occasions a client may have difficulty articulating objectives and you will need to spend time helping your client clarify what they are. See T.L. Shaffer, *Legal Interviewing in a Nutshell*, Ch. 3 (1976). For a discussion of how you might accomplish this task, see Chapter 17, sec. 2. In other instances a client's initial objectives will have to be clarified or modified in light of new information that comes forth during the counseling process. See Chapter 17, sec. 3.

b. Potential Solutions

You almost always must ask clients for their thoughts about potential solutions. Since problems are rarely purely legal, clients will often have excellent ideas about possible solutions. For example, in thinking about alternative ways to frame particular lease provisions, a client's experience in leasing other properties may lead to potential solutions that you would never have thought of.

c. Potential Consequences

Similarly, you almost always must ask clients what consequences they can foresee. Your legal expertise is insufficient to allow you to predict all of the consequences specific to a client's individual situation. For example, in counseling a client about whether to include an insurance-funded buyout provision in the buy-sell terms of a partnership agreement, you usually will not know your client well enough to determine all the likely economic, social and psychological consequences that might follow from selecting such an arrangement. You therefore need to ask the client about the probable ramifications of including such a provision.

d. Questions and Concerns

Finally, you must continually ask clients whether they understand what you are saying and whether they have questions and/or concerns. Solutions are likely to be optimal only to the extent clients understand their likely results. And clients are likely to feel comfortable with results only to the extent they understand what is being discussed and feel that particular solutions meet as many of their concerns and needs as possible. Continually encouraging clients to raise concerns and questions enables clients to arrive at solutions that are finely tailored to their concerns.

2. Information to Provide to Clients

Since counseling is a two way street, recognize the verbal traffic that needs to flow from you to client.

a. Potential Solutions

You typically need to propose solutions because you will see solutions that a client cannot. Your knowledge of legal doctrine is one resource you will draw on to fashion possible solutions. For example, in a litigation matter you may suggest pursuing injunctive relief or punitive damages, potential solutions of which a client may be unaware.

You will also draw upon your professional experience, awareness of human behavior and "industry knowledge" to fashion possible solutions. For example, you may through your practice with real estate matters be able to offer for a client's consideration various rent-fixing formulas that are used in connection with the leasing of commercial buildings.   Similarly, your experience in the criminal justice system may allow you to propose a diversion alternative that, by including a particular type of community service, permits a client to avoid a jail sentence.

Finally, note that sometimes your ability to see additional solutions is a product not of greater knowledge, but of greater emotional distance from a problem.

b.   Potential Consequences

Obviously, you advise clients of the likely legal consequences of proposed solutions.   For example, if an estate planning client is trying to choose between an individual and a corporate trustee, you would advise the client that a court is likely to hold a corporate trustee to a higher standard of care than an individual.

But perhaps less obviously, often you also advise clients of potential nonlegal consequences.   The same factors that enable you to see solutions that a client does not also enable you to see additional nonlegal consequences.   For example, you may point out to a corporate executive that litigation may require numerous employees to devote substantial time and effort to discovery.   Similarly, if a client doing business as an individual is deciding whether to incorporate, you may point out the ongoing monetary and time costs which arise from the numerous governmental reports that corporations must file.

B.   PROVIDE AN OPPORTUNITY TO EVALUATE OPTIONS AND CONSEQUENCES

Once potential solutions and their likely consequences are on the table, you help clients evaluate which solution appears most satisfactory.   As you recall, which solution is "best" rests on subjective factors unique to each client.   Value preferences, degree of risk aversion, and a sense of which consequences are most important are some factors a client usually thinks through in choosing a "best" solution.

For example, in the Gower–Smeltics matter, assume that two of the options Gower and you have identified are opening negotiations immediately on a three-year contract at the same salary and forgoing negotiations until after the season concludes.   Assume further that among the likely consequences identified by you and Gower are the following: if Gower waits until after the season to negotiate a contract, "plus" consequences include the possibility that as a free agent open to competitive bidding from different teams, he will be offered an increased salary; and enhanced post-career opportunities resulting from the added publicity the competitive negotiations produce.   On the "down" side, delay in signing a new contract subjects Gower to the risk that an injury will reduce or end his career before he can sign a new contract; and may suggest that he is disloyal to the team and its fans.[37]

---

37. Remember from Chapter 1, sec. 4(A) that all potential solutions carry with them both positive and negative consequences.

During the process of evaluating the options, you need to afford Gower the opportunity to weigh the likely consequences. Which consequences seem most likely to occur, and which are most important to Gower? How risk averse is Gower, and what are his personal values? Only through engaging in such a process can Gower make a decision that is most likely to satisfy him.

C. THE EXTENT TO WHICH YOU MUST COUNSEL CLIENTS

How far does the obligation to discuss options and alternatives with a client extend? The question has at least two sub-parts. First, must you try to counsel a client with respect to every possible option and its likely consequences? If not, what is the extent of your obligation to develop and explore options and consequences? Second, must you continue a counseling dialogue until a client actually understands the options and consequences? If not, how far towards actual understanding need you go?

In our view, the extent of the obligation to explore a decision with a client should be governed by the following standard:

> **In counseling clients, lawyers should provide clients with a reasonable opportunity to identify and evaluate those alternatives and consequences that similarly-situated clients usually find pivotal or pertinent.**

Consider what this standard entails.

1. "Pivotal or Pertinent Alternatives and Consequences"

Limiting a lawyer's obligation to identifying and evaluating "pivotal or pertinent" alternatives and consequences recognizes that it is virtually impossible to explore all possible alternatives and likely consequences. "Pivotal" alternatives and consequences are those which might alter or change a client's decision. For example, assume that a client is negotiating a purchase of knives from a Chinese manufacturer, and that the manufacturer insists that it be paid upon delivery to a carrier in Shanghai. The client is willing to agree to this arrangement provided a way can be found to inspect the goods before they are shipped. However, the client has no offices in China and knows no one in China who could inspect the goods on his behalf. Accordingly, the client is considering abandoning the deal. An opportunity to have the goods inspected by an independent inspection company in China would be a "pivotal option" because it would make or break the client's decision to go ahead with the deal.

"Pertinent" alternatives and consequences are those which a client would want to know about even though the information would not alter the client's decision. Assume that one likely consequence of using an independent Chinese company to inspect goods is a two week delay in the knives' delivery. Assume further that this consequence is not one which would cause the client to reject the option. Nonetheless, the client would like to know about the possible delay in order to arrange work schedules for his employees. This consequence would be a "pertinent" one.

The standard requires, as you can see, that you know about options and consequences that clients dealing in matters of the kind under discussion typically find significant. Thus, if a client is involved in leasing space in a shopping center, you need to know something about options and ramifications of commonly available shopping center lease transactions. Likewise, if a client is attempting to settle a wrongful termination case, you need to be aware of settlement alternatives that are ordinarily available to resolve such disputes, and their usual consequences.[38]

2. "Similarly–Situated Clients"

The term "similarly-situated clients" takes into account clients' individual characteristics. Such characteristics include a client's apparent level of intelligence, sophistication,[39] and emotional involvement.[40] You should counsel not according to the needs of your most or least able clients, but according to the apparent individual makeup of each client.

3. "Reasonable Opportunity to Identify and Evaluate"

The standard does not require that clients be made aware of *all* pivotal or pertinent alternatives and consequences. You need only provide clients with a *reasonable opportunity* to identify alternatives and consequences. A standard of reasonableness, as you know, rarely permits clear lines to be drawn. Rather, reasonableness must be derived from an exploration of the unique facts of an individual setting.[41] Here are common situational factors that may help you consider what constitutes a "reasonable opportunity." [42]

38. These examples should remind you of Chapter 1's notion that you need to understand the context in which clients' problems are embedded.

39. By sophistication we mean level of experience in the area under consideration.

40. The standard of "similarly situated clients" is a reasoned mid-line position. To one side are standards that are too lax. Such standards might include "options and consequences that a reasonable client might find pertinent," or "alternatives and ramifications that practicing lawyers using the skill and prudence of the procession might find apropos." A reasonable client standard is not adequately tailored to the needs of individual clients. The practicing lawyer standard is inadequate because lawyers too often fail to pay sufficient attention to nonlegal matters. See *supra* note 29 and *infra* note 41. To the other side is a requirement that a lawyer must help the client examine and consider "all pertinent" choices and potential consequences; such a requirement would be too burdensome. In adopting the standard of "options and consequences that similarly situated clients find pertinent," we recognize that the standard is not free from ambiguity. For example, how does one know what "similarly situated" means until one has spent a considerable period of time with the client and learned who he or she "really" is?

41. Use of "reasonableness" clearly permits defenders of "informed consent" to paste the "ambiguity" label on us as well. We would respond by pointing out that our standard requires only that the *opportunity* must be reasonable, and is not ambiguous in terms of whether a client must have actual understanding.

42. In choosing the standard of a "reasonable opportunity," we consciously avoid using the common legal standard which

One important factor is a decision's likely impact. The greater a decision's potential legal or nonlegal impact, the greater the amount of time and effort a "reasonableness" standard demands you devote to counseling.[43]

Another common factor is an alternative's complexity. An alternative may be complicated either due to complex legal doctrine, or due to the complexity of alternatives and consequences. The more complex a potential solution, the greater counseling effort must you make.

Third, if a client is apparently quite intelligent, well informed and emotionally uninvolved, reasonableness may require a reduced counseling effort.

Time concerns are also relevant to reasonableness. If circumstances dictate that a problem must be resolved in a relatively short period of time, then reasonableness permits less counseling.

A client's willingness to explore a problem and to pay for your time also affects reasonableness. A client who has the time and money to explore a matter, but who is unwilling to do so, may be "reasonably" counseled according to his or her willingness, at least when a client is intelligent and experienced. However, it may be unreasonable to make a reduced counseling effort if a client faced with an important and complex problem is unable to explore alternatives and consequences only because the client cannot pay your full hourly fee.[44]

4. A "Reasonable Opportunity" Standard Is Preferable to a Subjective Standard

Note that the standard defines counseling in process terms rather than in terms of the results of that process. That is, you comply with the standard as long as a client has a reasonable opportunity to evaluate alternatives, even if a client does not in fact fully understand each alternative. Thus, you might well wonder whether the standard is as client-centered as one which required actual client understanding.

requires that a lawyer conduct himself or herself with such "skill, prudence, and diligence as lawyers of ordinary skill and capacity commonly possess and exercise." See R.E. Mallen & V.B. Levit, *Legal Malpractice* 317 (2d ed. 1981). First, to the extent that pronouncements such as the Model Rules reflect the current practices of the profession, the pronouncements seem to ignore the reality that to effectively counsel clients a lawyer must elicit information as well as provide it and must also provide clients with an opportunity to identify values and risk preferences. See e.g., Model Rules, *supra* note 2, Rule 2.1. Second, the little empirical data that we can find on the subject suggests that lawyers often do ignore the foregoing essential parts of the counseling process and other important practices as well. See e.g. A.

Sarat & W.L. Felstiner, "Law & Strategy in the Divorce Lawyer's Office," 20 Law & Soc'y Rev. 93, 96 (1986); G. Neustadter, "When Lawyer and Client Meet: Observations of Interviewing and Counseling Behavior in the Consumer Bankruptcy Law Office," 35 Buff.L.Rev. 177, 228–30 (1986).

43. Especially at an early stage of a matter, you may not know enough about a client to determine how significant a problem is. In case of doubt, you should probably err on the side of thorough counseling.

44. The issue of when a lawyer may be obligated to service clients who can no longer afford to pay raises significant ethical questions. For a discussion of such questions, see *Lawyers' Manual on Professional Conduct* (ABA/BNA) 41:307–08 (1985).

However, a standard based on "actual" client understanding would necessarily be subjective. You would have to ensure that each and every client, not a mythical "reasonable" client, have "actual" understanding. Such a requirement would create enormous problems.

For example, consider how a subjective standard might handle client unawareness of real but insignificant consequences of decisions. Assume that a client has to decide whether to file suit in state or federal court. The client does not realize that filing in federal court may require somewhat more travel time when and if the client has to make court appearances, because the federal courthouse is located fifteen miles farther from the client's home. A subjective test may require that the client be informed of this consequence because without the information the client may lack complete understanding. However, as the information seems neither "pivotal" nor "pertinent," under our standard it is not a consequence of which the client must be informed.

Similarly, how would a subjective standard treat the case of a client who is aware of a consequence, but who may not fully appreciate it? For example, suppose a client is aware that proceeding to trial will be stressful, but has little concept of just how stressful the trial will be. This client seemingly does not *completely* understand the likely consequences of rejecting a settlement offer and proceeding to trial. However, as long as the client has had a reasonable opportunity to consider how stressful trial might be, the process-oriented standard is satisfied.

A subjective standard would also have difficulty with the extent to which clients must understand how the consequences of a decision reflect their values. For full understanding, is it enough for a client to assess consequences within the specific problem context, or must a client also assess consequences according to her or his overall value system? [45] For example, an owner of a commercial building realizes that a particular rent-fixing formula will result in increased rent, and that a tenant will probably accept that formula because the tenant is unsophisticated. Within the specific problem context, a decision to impose the rent-maximizing formula undoubtedly satisfies one of the client's values: to obtain a high rent. But does the owner fully understand the consequences of making this decision if the owner does not also consider whether the decision violates an overall personal value: not to take unfair advantage of others? [46]

45. For a discussion of this issue, see R.R. Faden & T.L. Beauchamp, *A History and Theory of Informed Consent*, 265–66 (1986); R. Dworkin, *Law's Empire* 166 (1986).

46. To help answer such questions, some commentators have looked to the "informed consent" standard by which courts evaluate whether doctors have adequately counseled their patients. See, e.g., C.J. Peck, "A New Tort Liability For Lack of Informed Consent in Legal Matters", 44 La.L.Rev. 1289 (1984); Spiegel, *supra* note 19; Strauss, *supra* note 23. Insofar as using an "informed consent" standard would push lawyers towards making clients real partners in the decision-making process, we agree with its philosophy. However, we do not find the informed consent standard helpful. For one thing, there is tremendous controversy about what types of information, and how much

Problems of full client understanding to the side, our process standard responds to the realities of law practice. Only rarely, if ever, will you have the time and clients have the desire, time or money to fully and completely evaluate all potential alternatives and consequences.[47] A standard that focuses on your own counseling behavior, and speaks of reasonableness rather than a client's unknowable mental state, is consistent with these realities.

Thus, a process standard is the best method of ensuring that clients are as knowledgeable as possible of the full range of available options and likely consequences before they make decisions. Defenders of "full understanding" or "informed consent" standards may consume paper as they debate just what constitutes that shadowy mental state, but their definitions provide little guidance as to what you should do when you sit down to help clients resolve problems.

D. RESPOND TO CLIENTS' REQUESTS FOR ADVICE ABOUT WHICH ALTERNATIVE TO CHOOSE ON THE BASIS OF CLIENTS' VALUES

During counseling, clients often ask for advice about what they should do. They do so for a variety of reasons, ranging from simply wanting you to confirm their own choice to feeling such inner conflict that they cannot make a decision. Client-centered counseling places maximum value on client decision-making. How, then, do you respond to clients who ask for advice about what to do? Can you respond in a way that is consistent with clients' making decisions based on their subjective values?

A radical view of the client-centered approach might lead you to reject requests for advice in order to avoid influencing decisions. However, that view demeans clients' ability to make independent judgments; deprives clients of the opportunity to get advice from a person who has professional expertise and emotional distance from a problem; and may well defeat the expectations of most clients. We therefore reject such a radical position.

However, though you may ultimately provide a client who asks for it with your opinion, you should do so only after you have counseled a client thoroughly enough that you can base your opinion on the client's subjective values, not on your own. A short example may illustrate how you may tailor your opinion to a client's subjective values. Assume that a client, Ms. Gilliger, consults you about terminating an employee. The potential options you have discussed are firing the

of each type, must be disclosed to satisfy the standard. See Faden & Beauchamp *supra* note 45, at 30. For another, there is great uncertainty as to what degree of understanding a client would have to have before a decision could be said to be "informed." Id. at 235–329: "But what does it mean for a person to understand? There is no consensus answer or approach to this question in philosophy or psychology . . ." Id. at 249.

47. For a detailed and rich discussion of all the issues that might have to be resolved to accomplish full understanding, see Faden & Beauchamp, *supra* note 45, at ch. 7, 8, 9, and 10.

employee, and asking the employee to resign upon several months' severance pay. When evaluating these options, the consequences which Gilliger deemed most important were (1) supporting the supervisor who gave the employee a poor evaluation; and (2) avoiding a lawsuit by the employee. Gilliger asks for your opinion about what she ought to do. Given the values Gilliger espoused during the counseling dialogue, you would probably advise her that the severance pay option seems best. For example, you might tell her, "In my opinion, you'd be better off with the severance pay option, since it would both support the supervisor and minimize the risk of a lawsuit." [48] You may personally feel that it is wrong to "pay off" an employee simply to avoid a lawsuit, but your opinion should reflect the client's values, not yours.[49]

While clients may reveal their values during any phase of your representation (e.g., during theory development questioning), typically a thorough counseling dialogue is necessary to provide understanding of a client's values. As clients evaluate options and consequences during the counseling process, they reveal the values on which you may frame your opinion. Hence, you should be extremely hesitant to give an opinion until you have counseled a client thoroughly.

Sometimes, of course, a client's request for your opinion is a request for advice based on *your* personal values. Such a request may seek the benefit of your experience. For example, Ms. Gilliger might ask, "What would you do if you were making this decision?" Or, a client may seek your "moral" judgment.[50] A client who has decided to disinherit a child, for example, might ask you if you think he or she is "doing the right thing." For the reasons noted above, client-centered lawyering suggests that you provide such clients with opinions based on your personal values.[51]

48. On the other hand, had Gilliger emphasized her desire to "make an example of the employee to all others, no matter what the cost," you might well have suggested the firing option.

49. After you give an opinion based on a client's values, a client may press you further: "Is that what you would do if you were in my place?" In these circumstances, you might appropriately regard the question as a request for an opinion based on your personal values. That is, the client's question really is, "What factors do you think are most important?" Again, providing an opinion is consistent with client-centered lawyering. If you regard clients as autonomous individuals, you must respect their desire for your opinion. However, you ought not baldly state your opinion. When a client asks for what you personally would do if you were in the client's place, you should first take a client through a full counseling dialogue, to help a client realize what their own values are in the specific problem context. That dia-

logue alone may clarify a client's thoughts enough that the client no longer needs to know what decision you personally would make. However, if a client continues to seek your personal opinion, you may state what your decision would be as well as the values upon which you base it. By first eliciting a client's values and then stating your own, you help a client realize that to the extent the client's values differ from yours, so might a client's decision. For example, had Ms. Gilliger asked for your personal values, you might have responded, "Frankly, if it were me, I'd fire the employee outright. I personally do not like to pay off people who have done a bad job. However, since you strongly want to avoid a lawsuit, you may not want to do what I would do."

50. For a discussion of the moral aspects of client problems, see Chapter 1, sec. 2.

51. In some instances, you may have difficulty determining whether a client is

E. INTERVENING IN CLIENTS' DECISIONS

Client-centeredness assumes that clients are capable of making intelligent and morally acceptable choices.[52] However, these assumptions are less than universally correct. Therefore, when a client makes a decision which you believe is wrong, can you, without violating notions of client centeredness, present your contrary view? This section examines two differing circumstances in which you might label a client's decision wrong, and explores whether in each situation it is appropriate for you to mention your disagreement.[53] The first circumstance arises when a client makes a decision which you view as erroneous because the client has misjudged the likely outcome. The second circumstance arises when a client makes a decision which you view as morally wrong, even if correct in its assessment of the likely outcome.[54]

1. Client Misjudges Likely Outcome

Consider first the circumstance in which a client selects an option which, in your view, will not produce the client's desired outcome. As you recall, a major argument for allowing clients to make their own decisions is that clients are usually in a better position than you to predict consequences. In some instances, however, clients may make choices that appear to you to mispredict the likely outcome despite their greater familiarity with a situation.

The following example illustrates apparent client misprediction. Mr. and Mrs. Benizi have been married for 17 years, and they have two children, ages 12 and 10. Mr. Benizi left his family and took up residence with his 28–year–old lover. He has filed for divorce, and Mrs. Benizi has retained you to represent her. Mr. Benizi makes a marital settlement proposal which you believe will provide Mrs. Benizi with far less than she would receive if the matter went to trial. Mrs. Benizi and you have discussed the "trial" option, and the likely consequences of accepting Mr. Benizi's offer. Mrs. Benizi states that she realizes she might do better by going to trial, but nonetheless has decided to accept the offer. She asserts that accepting the offer will cause her husband to realize what a wonderful person she is and therefore to return to the marriage.

In this circumstance, Mrs. Benizi probably has much greater familiarity with Mr. Benizi and his likely reaction than do you, and arguably is in a much better position to predict her husband's response. None-

asking for advice based on a client's values or yours. For a discussion of how you might make this determination and of techniques for offering advice based on your personal values, see Chapter 20, sec. 2(B); note 49, *supra*.

52. See Chapter 2, sec. 1.

53. Our focus in this section is primarily on a general attitude towards interven-

tion. For the most part, we save for Chapter 17 a discussion of specific techniques you might employ once you decide to intervene.

54. Of course, your disagreement could be founded on some combination of these two grounds of assessment.

theless you might believe that Mrs. Benizi's prediction is erroneous: Husbands who leave their wives usually do not return because their wives accede to divorce proposals. Thus, you need not accept Mrs. Benizi's decision to accede to her husband's offer. Rather, you may point out to her that her forecast is probably wrong, and that it is unlikely to produce the result she wants.[55]

Far from being isolated events, mispredictions such as Mrs. Benizi's are common. Research suggests that people routinely employ fallacious reasoning strategies.[56] And because legal problems are often anything but routine, clients' emotional reactions are likely to further cloud their predictive capacities. Hence, mechanistic acceptance of clients' forecasts will often fail to produce a satisfactory solution. Of course, when you do point out a client's erroneous prediction, couch your comments in a way that maintains a client's self-esteem. A client must be able to "hear" what you have to say.[57]

2. A Client's Arguably "Immoral" Preferences

More difficult considerations come into play when you disagree with a decision because you do not approve of the values embedded in a client's choice. When a client such as Mrs. Benizi mispredicts the likely consequences of a decision, you may base your disagreement on logic and experience. But when a client makes a decision based on value preferences which conflict with yours, you cannot ground your disagreement in a client's illogical thinking. Disagreement asserts, if only implicitly, that your values are more important than a client's. And unless a client's decision violates the law or is clearly immoral, principles of client autonomy suggest that client values prevail.

Nonethless, even though a client's decision may be legally valid and not clearly immoral, client centeredness sometimes allows you to express values that conflict with a client's. You do not completely surrender your autonomy by becoming a lawyer. Some clients may even appreciate and benefit from knowing about competing values.[58] However, client centeredness does impact both how often and the way in which you ought to phrase your value preferences.

55. You should be hesitant to voice your disagreement if you recognize that your predictive data base is little better than a client's.

56. For a detailed account of common predictive errors, see A. Tversky & D. Kahneman, "Judgment Under Uncertainty: Heuristics and Biases," in D. Kahneman, P. Slovic, A. Tversky, *Judgment Under Uncertainty: Heuristics and Biases* 3–20 (1982); R. Nisbett & L. Ross, *Human Inference: Strategies and Shortcomings of Social Judgment* 228–48 (1980).

57. Pointing out such an error in a manner that allows your client to hear what you have to say requires substantial

interpersonal skill. For a discussion of how this task might be approached see Chapter 20, sec. 4(A).

58. Indeed, the Model Code indicates that many clients will appreciate knowing that their values conflict with yours. See Model Code, *supra* note 2, EC 7–8. See also, T.L. Shaffer & R. Elkins, *Legal Interviewing and Counseling in a Nutshell*, 290–319 (2d ed. 1987) (Arguing that since lawyers' morals always affect the decision making process, lawyers should articulate and expose these influences in order to achieve client self-determination and openness in the lawyer-client relationship.)

With respect to the way in which you voice your views, client autonomy demands that you take care not to state your values so forcefully that you override clients' capacities to make their own decisions. Moreover, as a tactical matter, you must exercise discretion when stating value preferences if you hope to influence a client's decision. Thus, what you tell a client with whose values you disagree is likely to be very different from what you tell a client who mispredicts the consequences of a decision. You may explicitly tell the mispredicter that he or she is probably "wrong." But since a client whose values differ from yours is not "wrong," you often must use language that recognizes rather than denigrates a client's values. Only if you recognize the legitimacy of a client's values is a client likely to "hear" you.

The following example illustrates how a client's decision may rest upon value preferences with which you disagree, and how you might intervene in such situations. Assume that you represent Magic Properties, a large development company. Magic owns a factory leased to Community Corp., a corporation initially financed by the Small Business Administration. Community employs and retrains approximately 100 low income wage earners. Bob Lynn, Magic's Vice President for property management, has consulted you because Community has fallen behind in its rent. Though Community pays rent each month, its payments are invariably late and incomplete. Thus, although the lease calls for a monthly rent of $4,000, Community commonly remits only $3,500. At present, Community is $10,500 in arrears in its rent. You have reviewed Magic's options and their likely consequences with Lynn, and he has decided to institute suit to terminate Community's lease and recover past due rent. Magic will then be able to relet the factory at substantially higher rent. Lynn has indicated that Magic is not greatly concerned about the $10,500 arrearage, but in the interests of its employees and shareholders wants to make the factory more profitable.

You have no doubt that Lynn's prediction about Magic's ability to gain more income from the property is correct. Hence, his decision is neither logically nor legally "wrong." However, in your view his decision is morally wrong. Even with Community paying only $3500 per month, Magic derives a positive cash flow from the factory. You believe that Magic's desire for additional income from the factory is outweighed by the good that Community accomplishes by employing and retraining low income workers. In these circumstances, may you suggest to Lynn that he has made the wrong choice? [59]

A "yes" response is consistent with client centeredness and professional autonomy. Your interest in furthering what you perceive as society's interests through your law practice allows you to raise your moral concerns. You can do so by first recognizing the legitimacy of

---

59. Of course, when the action a client proposes to take is illegal or even runs the risk of being found illegal, you must point such illegality out to the client. See Model Rules, *supra* note 2, Rule 1.2(d); Model Code, *supra* note 2, DR 7–102(A)(7), 7–106(A) & EC 7–5.

Lynn's values: "Maximizing Magic's profits and protecting its share-holders are important considerations." Then, you can ask Lynn to consider how Community promotes the social good, how his decision is likely to affect Community, and whether Community's interests in this instance ought to trump Magic's. However, if Lynn rejects your position, you should allow his views to prevail unless you either intend to ask Lynn to seek other counsel or to withdraw if ethical rules permit you to do so.[60]

"Frequency" raises the difficult question of how often you voice disagreement over values. Over the course of a matter, a client may make a number of decisions that contradict your personal values. In the Magic Properties case, for example, Lynn might want you to pursue a "leave no prisoners" litigation strategy, while you think the public interest is better served when attorneys adopt a less aggressive approach. Similarly, Lynn may ask you to draft a new lease agreement leasing the space formerly occupied by Community to any one of a number of organizations (e.g., a producer of chemicals which increase pollution, a pro- or anti-abortion group, the local branch of the Socialist Party, etc.) with whose values you disagree.

Do you voice personal values whenever clients make decisions which concern you morally? A "yes" response is likely to turn you into something of a "moral know-it-all," regularly converting client dialogues into morality plays. Undoubtedly, few clients want attorneys to conduct regular moral check-ups. Hence, while we have no line by which to measure how frequently you voice moral concerns, we do believe that you should do so sparingly. Moreover, if you do raise moral concerns and a client rejects them, your choice again is to accede to the client, to ask a client voluntarily to seek other counsel, or to withdraw.

3. Other Lawyer–Client Value Conflicts

a. Risk–Averseness

The common stereotype of lawyers as nay-sayers who want to throw cold water on all sorts of clever plans [61] suggests that you and a client may differ as to whether a client should proceed in the face of an uncertain future. From your perspective, clients about to enter into deals or to precipitate litigation often resemble high school lovers who are determined to wed: They unduly minimize the risk that something will go wrong. But from a client's perspective, you may be too ready to recommend against a decision because uncertain contingencies may ultimately sour it.

In part, a client's desire to press forward in the face of uncertainty may reflect misprediction of the likely outcome. For example, the high

---

60. Strauss, *supra* note 23, at 333; Model Code, *supra* note 2, at DR 2–110(B) & (C); Model Rules, *supra* note 2, at Rule 1.16.

61. See R.J. Ringer, *Looking Out for Number One* 197–204 (1977): M.H. McCormack, *The Terrible Truth About Lawyers* 111–12 (1987).

school lovers may erroneously believe that few marriages end in divorce. But often, a client recognizes the same risks that you do but disagrees about whether the risk is worth taking. In such situations, whose values ought to prevail?

As when you and a client have different moral views, a client's values are paramount and under most conditions ought to prevail. Of course, during the discussion of likely outcomes you can inform a client of risks and the likelihood that they will occur.[62] Moreover, absent an indication that a client does not welcome your input, you may give your opinion that a risk may not be worth taking. But ultimately, the decision is a client's.[63]

For example, assume that your client is Jerry Bilt, Vice President of Landview Corp., which is negotiating to buy several acres of land from Donner Development Co. Landview plans to construct a housing tract on the land. Donner refuses to include in the proposed sales agreement a clause protecting Landview should all or part of the land, because of soil conditions or otherwise, prove unbuildable. Bilt, relying on a study conducted by a Landview soils engineer, is anxious to purchase the land and begin construction. You might point out the advisability of a review by an independent soils engineer and Landview's lack of recourse should all or part of the land prove unbuildable. But if Bilt has confidence in Landview's own soils engineer, perhaps because of his prior experience with the engineer, and wants to proceed with the purchase, you should honor his decision. The risk is what many lawyers and business people would call a "business risk." [64] Unless Bilt has grossly mispredicted the likelihood that the land will be unbuildable, the risk is Landview's to take.[65]

b. Interference With Professional Skills

Lawyer and client autonomy clash most directly when a client's decision conflicts with a lawyer's standards of professional practice. For example, a litigation client may want to refuse an adversary's first request for a continuance, when your steadfast practice may be to grant such requests. Or, a client may desire to make a legal argument in a

---

62. Documenting such advice in your file may forestall later malpractice claims.

63. We of course would make exceptions for clients who are not fully competent. Model Code, *supra* note 2, EC 7–11, 7–12.

64. See "A Businessman's View of Lawyers," 33 Bus.Law. 817, 825 (1978); J.D. Donnell, "Reflections of Corporate Counsel in a Two–Way Mirror," 22 Bus.Law. 991, 1001–03 (1967).

65. In many cases, you may find it difficult to determine whether your disagreement with a client's decision emanates from a client's having mispredicted likely consequences or from a client's being less risk-averse than you. You may tend to combine the two criteria, believing that "the reason the client wants to go ahead is because the client is mispredicting the consequences." Because misprediction may result in your explicitly telling a client that you believe the client is wrong, do not treat disagreement as a problem of misprediction without solid evidence. For example, unless you have some expertise in soils engineering, or unless Bilt's statements indicate that he has misunderstood the report of Landview's soils engineer, you probably should not regard his desire to go forward with the purchase as a problem of misprediction.

trial brief which you think extremely tenuous and not worth making. Similarly, a client in a deals matter may want to accept language which you consider vague and poorly drafted. In each case, acceding to the client's request seems to compromise your personal standards, and may harm your reputation within the bar and thus affect your ability to gain and represent future clients. For example, if the poorly drafted agreement winds up in litigation and becomes known to other lawyers and potential clients, you may lose future business.

If attorneys were nothing more than "hired guns," the short answer to such conflicts would be that since the clients' desires are neither illegal nor immoral, you are powerless to raise your disagreement. However, as a professional, you have an interest independent from that of clients in how you conduct your practice. Undoubtedly, then, you could advise a client that a decision conflicts with your practice norms and urge the client to change it.[66] As you do so, however, remember that a client may have legitimate reasons for asking you to engage in conduct that you regard as compromising your professional standards. Thus, even as you urge a client to change a decision, recognize the legitimacy of the client's values: "Your not wanting to give them a continuance is perfectly understandable; it keeps maximum pressure on them. My problem with that response is that I almost always grant a continuance to an adversary when the adversary's lawyer is in trial and cannot answer within the statutory time. Frankly, I expect and almost always receive the same courtesy from other attorneys. In the light of what I've just said, would you like to reconsider your decision?"

4. *Refusing to Implement a Client's Choice*

You may advise a client that a decision mispredicts outcomes, may be immoral, does not take sufficient account of risks, or conflicts with your professional standards.[67] If a client holds fast to a decision despite your opinion, how might you respond?

Your immediate reaction might be, "I'll withdraw." Even after thinking about the impact on your pocketbook, you may hold to that reaction. However, be aware that ethical rules may constrain your ability to withdraw. As this book concerns how to create and maintain effective lawyer-client relationships, exploring when rules might permit withdrawal when those relationships deteriorate is beyond its scope.[68]

---

66. For a greater exploration of conflicts concerning professional standards, see Spiegel, *supra* note 19, at 113–20.

67. Indeed, some decisions may conflict on more than one ground. For instance, you may regard representing Magic in its unlawful detainer suit against Community both as immoral and in conflict with your professional standards.

68. For discussion of when withdrawal is proper, see Model Rules, *supra* note 2, Rule 1.16; Model Code, *supra* note 2, DR 2–110, 5–102, 5–105. See also Model Rules, *supra* note 2, Rules 1.2 comment 7 & Rule 1.6 comment 14.

Chapter 16

IMPLEMENTING THE BASIC COUNSELING APPROACH

* * *

Bob, we've created quite a list of the advantages of insisting upon personal guarantees from Metal Beams' officers. But let's think for a moment about the possible negatives. An obvious one is that it increases the chances that Metal Beams won't go for the deal. Do you think that is a serious risk?

I just don't know. Metal's president, Marsh, has been around a long time and he may be really offended if we start talking about personal guarantees. It's hard to know how he'll react.

So one con of asking for the guarantees is that we run a somewhat undefined risk of offending Marsh at the outset.

I guess that's right, but, on the other hand, if we don't have the guarantees the size of our financial risk is pretty big and the board may be unhappy.

Okay. On the con side of forgoing the personal guarantees is both an increased financial risk and the risk of making the board unhappy. Things sure seem to be piling up in favor of asking for the guarantees. But let's think for just a moment about other negatives if you insist that Metal's officers sign personal guarantees.

It might cause them to look elsewhere for future deals. We know they have other projects in mind and if things go well with this deal, we'd like to have a shot at those other projects as well.

How likely is it that if you insist on guarantees in this deal, it will influence Metal Beams in the future?

Well, knowing Marsh, I think there is some chance of that.

Okay; anything else you can think of?

* * *

The counseling approach described in Chapter 15 consists of four steps:

1. Clarifying a client's objectives;

2. Identifying alternative solutions;

287

3. Identifying the likely consequences of each alternative;

4. Helping a client decide which alternative is likely to be most satisfactory.

This Chapter explores techniques for implementing this approach when counseling "typical" clients. Chapters 17 through 20 explore refinements in the approach, as well as techniques for counseling "non-typical" clients. For example, they consider techniques for counseling clients who are unwilling to think through options, or who are unwilling to make decisions, or who make decisions based upon unrealistic predictions. Finally, Chapters 21 and 22 recognize that you cannot fully apply the model each and every time a client faces a decision. These chapters therefore illustrate how you might modify the approach in the contexts of typical decisions arising during litigation and proposed deals matters.

1. THE IMPORTANCE OF NEUTRALITY

Effective counseling usually requires the appearance of neutrality; that is, the appearance that you have no favorites among available alternatives.[1] Even when you counsel clients who are ready, willing and able to make their own decisions, neutrality often is important. Such clients may resent your suggesting, by word or by conduct, that one alternative is more meritorious than another. Assume, for example, that each time a client mentions a possible advantage of option A, you mention a possible disadvantage. The client may believe that you are arguing against the selection of option A, and resent what he or she perceives as your attempt to influence the decision. That resentment may block the client's hearing your later efforts to impart information objectively.

Similarly, the appearance of neutrality encourages clients to disclose all relevant information, especially when you counsel clients who by nature defer to experts and authority figures.[2] If your behavior indicates that you favor a particular solution, such clients will often be unwilling or perhaps unable to think through alternatives and consequences themselves, and they might be reticent to verbalize those that they do identify. As a result, such clients will not participate actively in the resolution of their problems.

Accordingly, strive to maintain an appearance of impartiality throughout the counseling process.[3] If you do not, clients may not hear

---

1. Note that you are neutral only with respect to specific options. As the book's emphasis on the value of rapport makes clear, you certainly need not be neutral with respect to broader matters such as your interest in clients and your willingness to help resolve their problems. And, as you recall, you may not be neutral when a client's decision raises moral concerns. See Chapter 15, sec. 6(b).

2. A well-known sociological text refers to such people as "other-directed people." See D. Reisman, *The Lonely Crowd—A Study of the Changing American Character* pp. 9, 19–25 (1950).

3. Two scholars have pointed out that consistently maintaining such an appearance may be impossible. T.L. Shaffer and J.R. Elkins, *Legal Interviewing and Counseling* 73 (2d ed. 1987).

what you have to say and may fail to express their own thoughts fully. Either circumstance may prevent clients from having a reasonable opportunity to consider pertinent alternatives and consequences.

2. PREPARATORY EXPLANATION: THE PRELIMINARY STEP

As you may recall, a Preparatory Explanation can alert clients to what to expect during an ensuing discussion. Such an explanation tends to build rapport and to encourage a client's full involvement in the subjects under discussion.[4] Hence, you typically ought to preface a discussion of any major decision with a Preparatory Explanation.

Usually, an explanation can be relatively brief. Consider this example:

1. L: Jan, next you need to decide who you want to appoint as the guardian for your children should something happen to you. What we can do is talk about the two kinds of guardians for which the law provides, what sorts of qualities you are looking for in a guardian, and possible candidates. Maybe you already have someone in mind. Even if you do, I'll ask you to consider all possible candidates and the pros and cons of each. This will give you a solid basis for whatever decision you ultimately make. Does that make sense?

2. C: Sure, although I'm pretty sure that James and Kim are the people I want.

3. L: Great; it sounds like you've already given some thought to this issue. So let's start by talking about . . . .

Assuming that Jan is a "typical" client, this explanation seems adequate. It identifies the decision which requires consideration (naming a guardian) and states that objectives (qualities of a guardian), alternatives (possible candidates), and consequences (pros and cons) will be explored. This description gives even a relatively inexperienced client a preview of what to expect. Of course, sometimes a single description of the process may not be adequate, and you may have to re-explain it as you approach the various steps.

Also, note that you encourage a counseling dialogue even though Jan may have reached a tentative decision. Counseling in the face of a client's preliminary decision is consistent with neutrality. Your purpose is not to undermine Jan's tentative decision, but to make sure that Jan has a reasonable opportunity to consider which choice is most likely to be satisfactory.[5] Hopefully, Jan will understand your state-

---

4. For discussion of the purpose of preparatory explanations, see Chapter 7, sec. 6.

5. Remember that your obligation under the counseling standard is to provide clients with a reasonable opportunity to consider pertinent and pivotal alternatives and consequences. See Chapter 15, sec. 6.

ment in No. 1, "Even if you do, ..." as indicating that you accept any choice that Jan ultimately makes.

3. STEP ONE: CLARIFYING OBJECTIVES

Jan, like most clients, cannot know which choice is most likely to be satisfactory unless Jan first understands the available options. For example, Jan cannot make a sensible decision about a guardian unless Jan knows that a guardian of the person is different from a guardian of the estate, and that they may be different people.

However, options are often not apparent until clients first understand and verbalize their objectives. For example, assume Jan states, "It's really important to me that the children continue to be raised in the same religion." That objective might make some guardianship possibilities apparent even as it eliminates others.[6] Hence, the first step in a counseling dialogue often consists of exploring a client's objectives.

Remembering that preliminary problem identification includes an inquiry into clients' objectives,[7] you might think that by the time counseling rolls around a further inquiry into objectives would be unnecessary. However, a discussion of objectives during an initial interview is typically not a substitute for Step One. For one thing, a client's objectives may well have changed since preliminary problem identification.

Moreover, during initial interviews, the focus is necessarily on *overall* goals; that is, goals related to clients' principal or core problems. But as matters progress, you invariably counsel clients with respect to myriads of subsidiary decisions. The subsidiary decisions typically concern implementation of whatever overall course of action a client has chosen to resolve her or his principal problem. Since a client's overall objectives often are not applicable to subsidiary decisions, you may have to elicit a client's specific objectives as you counsel with respect to individual subsidiary decisions.

For example, during an initial meeting you learn that a corporate client's overall goal is to raise capital to build a new plant. After some meetings with you, the client decides to raise the capital through a public sale of stock. In the course of determining how best to accomplish the sale, the client will likely face a number of subsidiary decisions, such as when to go public, what underwriter to use, what disclosures to make in its prospectus, and whether to issue preferred or common stock. The client's overall goal of "raising capital" is probably not directly applicable to these subsidiary decisions. That is, knowing that the client's objective is to "raise capital" does not fully illuminate what the client's objectives may be with regard to choosing an under-

---

6. Sometimes further goals emerge later in a counseling dialogue. For example, when discussing the likely consequences of a particular option, a client may discover additional goals. In turn, the new goals may lead to additional alternatives.

7. See Chap. 7, sec. 4(A).

writer, timing the public sale, etc. Thus, as the need to counsel with respect to subsidiary decisions arises, during Step One remember to elicit a client's specific objectives.[8]

Commencing counseling by exploring a client's goals is inherent in a client-centered approach. By starting with a client's objectives, you avoid treating a problem solely as a legal matter, and you continue to identify a problem from a client's perspective.

Usually, you begin clarifying a client's objectives by employing open questions similar to those found at the top part of a T-funnel.[9]

The following example is illustrative:

1. L: Claire, the next thing we have to talk about is which underwriter you want to handle the offering. Have you talked this over with the Board?

2. C: No, I wanted to meet with you before I go to the Board.

3. L: I'll be glad to give whatever help I can. Why don't you start by telling me your objectives?

4. C: Obviously, a major objective will be selecting an underwriter that will give us the best price. Given where our stock is selling now, my thinking is to get a guarantee of at least $24.00 a share. Also, given the competitive nature of the industry, speed is absolutely essential; I'd want an underwriter who will guarantee to complete the offering within 60 days.

5. L: Given what you've told me about the competition you're facing, I understand why that is so important. Any additional objectives I should know about?

6. C: Well, in recent years I've become increasingly concerned about interference from institutional investors. I'd like to use a firm that will be able to target sales to individual investors.

7. L: All right. Anything else?

8. C: I think that's about it.

9. L: Fine. Let's think about some underwriters who might meet these specifications . . . ..

No. 3 alerts the client to talk about objectives. If you sense that a client may be reluctant to discuss objectives, you might motivate the client to do so by including in your alert a "reward" statement such as, "When objectives are clear, I find that it is easier to come up with a solution that makes the most sense."

---

8. When an implementing decision is particularly legal in character, you and not a client may be the one who identifies what objectives may be achieved by making that decision. For example, it often makes little sense to ask clients what objectives they can attain by taking depositions rather than sending out interrogatories. See Chapter 17, sec. 4.

9. For a review of the T-funnel approach see Chapter 10, sec. 5.

In T-funnel fashion, Nos. 3, 5 and 7 are open questions. Note, however, that No. 9 is not a lower-T narrow question searching for "other possible objectives." Instead, you move on to a discussion of options. Unless a client fails to mention an objective that you think most similarly-situated clients would have, the ones that a client mentions will be sufficient to start the process. If other objectives are lurking, they will invariably emerge in the course of the counseling dialogue. In this case, however, were you an experienced securities lawyer, you might have recognized that maintaining a relationship with a previously-used underwriter might have been one of Claire's objectives. If so, you might have said in No. 9, "If I recall, you used Merrill Shearson for your previous offerings. Is it important that you continue to do business with them?"

4. STEP TWO: IDENTIFYING ALTERNATIVES

Once a client's objectives are out in the open, the *second step* is to identify alternatives. For example, assume that Jim owns a business and consults you regarding how to reestablish harmony in a poorly-managed department. You can start this step with a brief preparatory alert: "Okay, Jim, let's turn to what choices might help you attain your objectives." Then, you typically should take the lead in articulating options. For example, you might state, "Jim, the options I see are to fire Mr. Frankel [the manager], to transfer him to a different department, or to give him what we call a 'golden handshake.' "

Clients often are frustrated if you begin Step 2 by asking a client for alternatives they have thought of. A client may doubt your competence, reacting internally something like, "Why in the hell are you asking me about options; that's what I hired you for." Furthermore, when you do finally voice your thoughts, a client may feel you are "playing games." A client may well wonder why you did not reveal your thoughts in the first place.[10]

Of course, a client's greater familiarity with a problem's context may enable a client to identify options you might never have thought of. Therefore, after mentioning alternatives you have thought about, be sure to invite a client's thoughts on other alternatives.[11] For example, you might ask Jim, "These are the alternatives I see. You probably have some others in mind and I'd like to hear them. Please bring up any possibility you see since, in the end, the decision has to be one with which you feel comfortable."

10. Sometimes, a client may in earlier discussions have identified an option or two. For example, Jim might have suggested the possibility of firing the employee. In such instances, you might show "recognition" by identifying an option as one a client first mentioned: "Jim, as you mentioned earlier, one option is to fire Mr. Frankel. The others I see are . . . ."

11. Similarly, clients who are overly-deferential to authority figures may not mention an option unless you specifically invite them to do so. The upshot of your failing to invite options may be that perfectly sensible options never come to light, and that the client does not fully pay attention to those you identify.

However, if a client is far more likely than you to know about available options, or if the client has already indicated that he or she has a particular solution in mind, you might start Step Two by asking the client to lead off the identification of options. Assume for example that you are defending a client who operates a small business and who has consulted you about whether to borrow money in order to make a settlement offer. The client will probably understand that he or she should have many more ideas about possible funding sources than you, and thus should not be put off by your looking first to the client for ideas. For instance, the client knows what lending institutions she or he has dealt with, which relatives and friends might be "hit up," and the like. Thus, you might start Step 2 by saying something like,

> "Now that we can see that a settlement offer of $50,000 might make sense, let's get back to your questions about borrowing the $50,000. Let's start with the possibilities you see. What sources might be able to lend you all or some of the money?" [12]

Whether you or a client begins the identification of options, you might be tempted at Step Two to preface the mention of specific options with a grand discourse on the legal theories and issues embedded in a client's problem. For example, in an estate planning matter you may be inclined to expand on the intricacies of the Rule Against Perpetuities, and in a litigation matter on the chances that a hearsay statement will qualify as a "declaration against interest." The temptation may spring either from a belief that such discourse is likely to be helpful or from a desire to impress a client. In any event, unless a client indicates a desire for such information, we urge you to limit your remarks at this stage to simply identifying the various options you see. A prefatory "lecture," unconnected to particular options, is abstract and thus often serves only to mystify, frustrate and confuse. Save legal analysis for your law professor friends, or for Step Three, where it may be relevant to demonstrate how legal rules affect the consequences which are likely to attach to various options.

5. STEP THREE: IDENTIFYING CONSEQUENCES

With potential options identified, the *third step* is to identify the likely consequences of each. Since, as you know, solutions carry nonlegal consequences, you must explore likely nonlegal as well as legal consequences. For example, if a decision concerns whether to include a buy-out provision in a proposed agreement, your discussion of this option must focus on both the likely legal and nonlegal consequences of including the buyout provision.

12. Whether you start with your alternatives or those of a client, you discharge your role as a client centered counselor. Under both approaches, you actively involve a client in the process of exploring potential solutions.

A. THE NECESSITY TO PREDICT

Assessing consequences involves a prediction of what is likely to occur in the future. For example, a common question that arises in assessing consequences is how a third person will respond to a particular offer. In such circumstances, one cannot "know" what the response will be; rather, the best one can do is make an educated guess or prediction.

Predictions are statements of probability. Scientists ascertain probability by observing the same phenomena over time and measuring outcomes. For example, by observing the effects of a general anesthetic on a population of patients over time, medical researchers can predict that death will occur in a given percentage of cases. The data (experience) collected in arriving at an overall percentage can be called a data base.

The predictions that you and your clients make almost always center on people's behavior for which accurate data bases are not available. Human behavior is so complex that it does not lend itself to mathematical or statistical analysis.[13] For example, one cannot predict with certainty that an impeached witness will not be believed, or that an owner of property will be so put off by a "lowball" offer that the owner will cease negotiations. Any data bases you and a client have individually acquired for predicting future consequences have usually been arrived at by a highly selective and intuitive process in which seeming similarities tend to mask important differences, and thus introduce uncertainty into your data base.[14]

However, those imperfect data bases are often all that you and your clients will have available for making predictions. The question, then, is on whose data base should a prediction be made—yours or a client's?

B. PREDICTING LEGAL CONSEQUENCES

Predicting legal consequences is the essence of providing "legal advice." As you would imagine, responsibility for predicting legal consequences rests primarily on you. A client expects you to have a better data base for predicting such matters as how a jury is likely to rule, what legal consequences attach to doing business as a corporation

---

13. But, see generally, 66 B.U.L.Rev. 377 (1986) (Symposium issue: "Probability and Inference in the Law of Evidence").

14. Predictions about human behavior rely on the generalization process described in Chapter 9. For example, your prediction as the attorney for a prospective tenant that proposing a clause in a shopping center lease agreement maintaining the rent at a fixed amount over the five year period of the lease will cause the landlord to reject the tenant is based on a generalization such as, "Shopping center owners who receive proposals from prospective tenants barring increases in rent over a five year term usually refuse to continue negotiations with the tenants." Research indicates that predictions based on generalizations about human behavior are fraught with error. See R. Nisbett & L. Ross, *Human Inference: Strategies and Shortcomings of Social Judgment* 77–89 (1980). See generally, D. Kahneman, P. Slovic & A. Tversky, *Judgment Under Uncertainty: Heuristics and Biases* (1982).

rather than a sole proprietorship, how getting a trademark might protect a company's product, and whether a corporation's omission of information from a securities prospectus might subject the officers to criminal or civil liability.[15]

C. PREDICTING NONLEGAL CONSEQUENCES

Nonlegal consequences, as you know, consist of the likely economic, social, psychological, political and moral ramifications that may flow from adopting a particular solution. And just as you generally have the better data base for predicting legal consequences, a client often has the better data base for predicting nonlegal ones. Clients often know better than you the likely economic effects on their companies when employees have to take time away from their regular duties to participate in discovery and prepare for trial; the likely social effects of suing a defendant that has a high-profile, exemplary reputation in the community; and the likely psychological effects of accepting settlement offers after having previously stated to friends that they would go "all the way to trial." Therefore, you often rely on clients to predict nonlegal consequences.[16]

At the same time, your own experiences may enable you to predict (or at least inquire about) nonlegal consequences. For example, when it comes to recognizing how the business operations of a retail merchant whose rent is tied to the Consumer Price Index might be affected by fluctuations in the Index, or psychological consequences such as the potential degree of stress that a long trial can create, you may contribute valuable insights to a client's thinking about nonlegal consequences.

D. ORGANIZING THE DISCUSSION OF CONSEQUENCES

Turn now to techniques for counseling clients with respect to likely consequences.

1. Review Options Separately

Many people have difficulty solving problems because they cannot focus on discrete options and their attendant advantages and disadvantages. Just as simultaneous input from competing sources can immobilize a robot, so are clients often immobilized by failing to attach discrete

---

15. Occasionally you may seek a client's prediction about legal consequences. Clients with legal problems often consult friends and business acquaintances who have had similar problems. Clients sometimes find the experiences of their lay peers very persuasive, and tend to consider those experiences a foolproof data base from which to predict their own legal outcomes. On occasion, a client will (privately, at least) disbelieve a legal prediction you make that conflicts with a friend's experience in a similar matter. Thus, if a client appears to be skeptical about your legal prediction, you may want to find out if he or she has a contrary one. Then, if you think a client's prediction is based on a wrong or a too-limited data base, you may at least discuss why your predictions differ from the client's.

16. This point underscores the statement in Chapter 15, sec. 6(A) that counseling is a two way street and that information must flow from the client to you as well as in the other direction.

consequences to specific options. Thus, once Step Two has placed available options on the table, you should begin Step Three by focusing on a specific option.

2. Ask a Client to Choose a Starting Place

To maintain a client centered approach, ask clients which option they want to discuss first. For instance, you might say, "Peter, it appears that our options are either to demand reinstatement plus back pay, or to offer to resign on the condition of a suitable severance package. Which option would you prefer to discuss first?"

This approach builds on the advantages of neutrality, as you leave to a client the choice of which option to discuss first. It also tends to motivate a client to participate actively, since the client can select whichever option seems most appealing.

3. Adopt the Role of Information Seeker

After a client selects an option, you generally continue to place a client in the figurative limelight by asking the client to identify the pros and cons of that option. Again, beginning with a client's thoughts preserves neutrality: you do not implicitly discard an option by mentioning sixteen "cons" as opposed to one "pro." Also, you continue to encourage a client's full participation. If you begin by describing the pros and cons that you see, a client may unwittingly be content with your description on the grounds that "you're the expert." [17]

You can seek a client's thoughts about consequences in one of three ways. You can ask a client only about advantages, about both advantages and disadvantages, or only about disadvantages. For example, if the option a client chooses to select first is whether to include an arbitration clause in a proposed agreement, your choice of questions includes:

    1. "Why don't you start by telling me what advantages you see of including an arbitration clause?"

    2. "Great. What are the pros and cons you see of including such a clause?"

    3. "Okay, maybe we should begin with your outlining what problems you see in including an arbitration provision."

Normally, question 1 or 3 is superior to question 2. Remember, people usually have an easier time thinking of one topic at a time. As between 1 and 3, the former ("advantages") is probably the better choice. A client's choosing to discuss an option usually reflects that client's positive orientation toward it. Therefore, to ask first about

---

17. Remember this is a general approach, not a recipe to follow slavishly. For example, if a client is extremely naive, nervous, or unfamiliar with the legal system, you might well consider begining the discussion of pros and cons yourself. Simi- larly, if a client indicates interest in legal consequences, of if you think legal consequences will predominate in a client's thinking, you may begin by predicting legal outcomes. For a discussion of how you might do this, see Chapter 19, section 4.

advantages is often to see a matter from a client's perspective. However, if during Step Two (identification of alternatives) a client indicates concerns with an alternative, you may ask the client to begin by describing its potential "downsides." Thus, if initially the client above had said, "I'm not sure about arbitration; the last time we were in arbitration we got burned," starting with question 3 may make sense.

The familiar T-funnel questioning pattern is well suited to obtaining a client's full input. Through open questions, you attempt to uncover all the consequences a client can identify. Then, through closed questions, you see if a client "recognizes" other possibilities.[18] The topics you select for your closed questions are consequences that similarly situated clients commonly find pivotal or pertinent.

Consider this example of T-funnel questioning to elicit the consequences a client foresees. Assume that your client, Doug, is exploring who he should appoint in his will as guardian for his children, ages seven and five. Doug's alternatives are his sister, Helen, and his brother, Bob. The option Doug has selected to discuss first is his sister.

1. L: Doug, what are the advantages you see in appointing Helen?

2. C: Well, she will be able to spend more time with the children and also the children know her better.

3. L: Those are important points; I can see you've given this careful thought. What other advantages do you see?

4. C: I think it'll be less of an economic imposition on her than it would be on Bob.

5. L: What else do you see as a positive reason for naming Helen?

6. C: She's more interested in education than Bob is, so I think she'd be more concerned about their school work.

7. L: I understand your making education a top priority. To summarize, then, it seems that Helen will spend more time with the children, is closer to them, is financially better off and will be more concerned with their schooling. What other advantages do you see?

8. C: That's about it.

9. L: Okay. Here are some other factors you may want to consider. Any differences as far as ability to manage the children's assets might be concerned?

10. C: Well, Helen's not so great with money matters, but her husband has a lot of experience in that area.

18. Using closed questions to suggest additional possible consequences does not require you to make predictions about the likely consequences of a client's decision. Rather their use takes advantage of your expertise and experience to initiate a discussion of consequences a client ought to at least consider. For a discussion of how you might meld in the consequences you foresee, see section 6 *infra*.

11. L: All right. How about in terms of allowing the children to maintain their current friends and contacts?

12. C: Well . . ..

Nos. 1, 5, and 7 are open questions giving Doug the opportunity to list all the reasons he can think of. No. 3 gives recognition, and No. 7 includes an active listening response and the familiar summary technique.

Nos. 9 and 11 demonstrate the turn to closed questions. Choosing consequences commonly relevant to selecting a guardian (friendships and money management ability), you search for other consequences the client might want to evaluate. Note that the closed questions do not specifically seek pros or cons. That is, No. 9 identifies the topic "managing assets." It does not ask, for example, "Would ability to manage assets be a pro of choosing Helen?" The latter type of question may suggest that Helen is a better money manager, rendering it non-neutral.

Since the closed questions do not specifically seek pros or cons, clients' responses may be unclear as to how they regard a consequence. For example, in No. 10, it is not at all clear that Doug considers Helen's being not so great with money matters a con of choosing Helen. If you are uncertain, you may ask a clarifying question that converts an ambiguous response into a pro or con.[19]

4. *The Cross Over Phenomenon*

Despite the seeming orderliness of a T-funnel approach, rarely will it be possible or desirable to systematically run through every alternative individually, taking up pros and then cons. Rather, clients tend to "cross over" from one alternative to another. Within a single alternative, they often jump back and forth between "pros" and "cons."

Several factors account for clients' tendency to "cross over." Comparing "pros" and "cons" naturally leads people to cross over. For instance, examine Doug's response in No. 6, "Well, she is more interested in education than my brother is and I think she'd be more concerned about their school work." Doug is thinking about both his brother and his sister. And, as is often the case, the "pro" of one alternative is the con of another, and vice versa. The "pro" for the sister (attention to children's education) is simultaneously the "con" for the brother (less attention to children's education). Hence, the very asking of questions concerning "pros" and "cons" invites clients to make comparisons and to cross over.

Similarly, your organizational efforts notwithstanding, clients tend to stray back and forth on the "pros" vs. "cons" ledger within the context of a single alternative. Many clients state a "con" of an alternative almost in the same breath as they state a "pro." For

19. For a discussion of conversion techniques, see Chapter 19, sec. 2(A).

instance, Doug may say, "Helen will look after the kids' education, but I've got to say that she's not the world's best disciplinarian." A "pro" of Helen is offset immediately by a "con." Of course, Doug can cross over further by also shifting to the "Bob" option: "Helen will look after the kids' education, but I've got to say that compared to Bob, she's not the world's best disciplinarian."

5. *Responding to Client Cross Over*

The inevitability and frequency of cross over may entice you into abandoning any thoughts of an organized exploration of consequences. However, while cross over means that you must modify an "ideal" counseling dialogue, you should not abandon orderliness altogether.

The risk of cross over is that you fail to unearth all salient consequences. Crossing over is akin to the danger of "sidetracking" that you encounter when probing events for details.[20] As clients jump back and forth, both of you are likely to lose track of how thoroughly consequences have been exhausted.

How might you achieve a balance between the spontaneity of crossing over and the thoroughness of T-funnels? You may begin a discussion of consequences with a T-funnel approach. That is, ask open questions at the outset solely about either the pros or cons of a single option. When a client crosses over, you may either stay on the original side of the ledger (e.g., "cons of Option A," if that is the point with which you began), or ask about the side to which the client has crossed over (e.g., "cons of Option B,"). Exercise your judgment about whether to return to the original point or to follow the client's cross over in light of the principle of neutrality: do not return or follow simply to further discussion of your favored option. Moreover, if you do return to the original side of the ledger, you may further a neutral stance by expressly acknowledging through active listening the points the client mentioned during the cross over. Finally, when open questions cease to elicit consequences, you may systematically subject each option to lower-T questioning to learn whether other potential consequences that you have thought of are present. As you begin the lower-T questioning with respect to each option, you may want to summarize the pros or cons already on the table, depending on which side of the ledger you intend to focus on. The example below explores this flexible approach.

Assume that you represent a commercial shopping center developer, Montoya Realty. On Montoya's behalf, you have been negotiating a lease with Exotic Electronics under which Exotic would rent two thousand square feet in a corner shopping mall from Montoya for 5 years. All but one of the terms of the proposed lease have been worked out. The exception is that the officers of Exotic refuse to sign personal guarantees unless Montoya modifies the rent requirements. At present the proposed lease calls for Exotic to pay an amount equal to 5% of Exotic's yearly gross sales, but in no event less than $4500 per month.

20. See Chapter 10, sec. 6(A).

Exotic's officers, however, are willing to sign personal guarantees only if the minimum monthly provision is reduced to $3000. You are now consulting with Alfredo Gomez, a Montoya vice president who is in charge of the property. Both you and Gomez agree that the only way to get the personal guarantees is to accede to Exotic's demand to reduce the minimum monthly rent. The options you have identified together are: (1) Insist on the guarantees and reduce the rent; (2) Drop the demand for guarantees and go ahead with the deal at the $4500 monthly rent figure; and (3) Terminate negotiations with Exotic and lease the space to Radio Hut, which is willing to lease the property at $3,800 minimum monthly rental as against 7% of gross sales.

1. L: Alfredo, which of these options shall we discuss first?

2. C: Let's talk about insisting on the guarantees. That's what I prefer.

3. L: What do you see as the advantages of going that route?

4. C: Well, if they sign a guarantee they will have a real incentive to make sure the business turns a profit. I know $1500 a month may not be that much, but if you think in terms of a 5 year lease, there is real incentive for them to pay attention to the operation. And since most of our money comes from the percentage of gross, I want a tenant whose top management will pay attention to what is going on. If we take Radio Hut we just won't get that.

5. L: Okay; so a downside of Radio is that the attention to operations may not be as great and hence your income may be less. What else is an advantage in having the guarantees?

6. C: It's the kind of customers that Exotic will attract to the center. The quality of Exotic's merchandise is better than Radio Hut's and therefore the kind of customers they will attract will have more money to spend in all the stores.

7. L: So another pro of having Exotic is that they'll attract customers with more money than will Radio Hut and that means there is another negative in Radio's column.

8. C: We have to be careful though. Radio Hut has a big name; it's certainly bigger than Exotic's. Radio, therefore, may attract more customers.

9. L: That's a plus for Radio. Do you see others?

10. C: There probably is less worry about whether they are giving us correct figures regarding gross sales. Radio is a national company; they use standardized accounting procedures. If things get tough, they are probably less likely to fudge.

11. L: So another pro for Radio is that their sales figures are likely to be more reliable, and hence it will be easier to know if the percentage rent figures are correct.

12. C: Exactly.

13. L: Anything else working in Radio's favor?

14. C: Not that I can see at the moment.

15. L: How about going ahead with Exotic without any personal guarantees? What advantages there?

16. C: It's hard to think of any. A promise of a bigger minimum is important only if they do poorly and I don't think that is going to happen. If I did, we wouldn't be talking with them. To me the guarantees are the key. That gets top management focused on this store and that's exactly what is likely to make the operation quite profitable.

17. L: So without a guarantee, there's lack of management incentive.

18. C: Right. Also . . ..

[Further upper-T dialogue omitted.]

40. L: Anything else you can think of that would be a negative of making a deal with Radio Hut?

41. C: Not really.

42. L: Okay, now that we've talked about each of the options, let's make sure that we've considered all the possible consequences of each. Maybe we can start by finishing up the option of insisting on personal guarantees from Exotic's officers. As far as the "pros" of that option go, so far we listed your belief that top management will pay close attention to business operations and that Exotic is likely to attract more affluent customers. Now, another one that may be so obvious that you didn't bother to mention it is that personal guarantees offer extra protection should Exotic itself default on the rent. Would you agree?

43. C: Sure.

44. L: All right. Now let me ask you some additional questions about potential advantages of insisting on guarantees. Should Montoya decide to sell the shopping center during the term of Exotic's lease, would having guarantees make a sale more attractive?

45. C: Given the size of the center and the variety of tenants and lease provisions, I don't think so.

46. L: Would having guarantees in this instance help your negotiating stance with respect to other prospective tenants?

47. C: Probably it would—that's a point I hadn't considered.

48. L: OK, we'll list that as another pro. How about . . ..
[Further lower-T dialogue concerning "pros" of Exotic
omitted.]

54. L: Now let's turn for a moment to the possible "cons" of
insisting on personal guarantees. So far, we don't seem to
have anything down. Can you think of any?

55. C: Not right off; I guess that's why I kind of favor this option.

56. L: And maybe that's the option you'll end up with. But just
to make sure, let me play the Devil's advocate and ask you
a couple of questions. Might insisting on guarantees
poison your long-term relationship with Exotic?

57. C: Well . . .

This dialogue illustrates structure and flexibility. No. 1 asks the
client which option he wants to discuss first, and No. 3 pursues the
advantages of the client's favored option. No. 5 stays with the topic of
advantages of the initial option, even though Gomez concluded No. 4
with a negative of a different option. This choice to stay with the
original option seems sound. As the option was the one the client
initially favored, failure to switch does not seem to represent an overly-
structured response. Moreover, the decision not to switch does not
violate neutrality principles since No. 5 first acknowledges the client's
cross-over (Okay; so a downside . . . ").

No. 7 also acknowledges a cross over to a negative of choosing
Radio. But when the client in No. 8 switches from the pros of Exotic to
the pros of Radio, you follow the switch. Doing so abandons a systematic examination of the pros of leasing to Exotic in favor of the pros of
renting to Radio. This switch too seems appropriate. On three occasions the client has switched from the initial option of Exotic to Radio,
and in addition has crossed over to the pros and cons of Radio.
Arguably this switch indicates the client's considerable interest in
thinking about Radio, and neutrality suggests that for the moment you
discard a structured approach.

Having switched to the advantages of Radio in No. 9, you stay with
this topic until in No. 14 the client indicates he can see no more
advantages. In Nos. 8 and 10 the client identifies pros favoring Radio,
which Nos. 9 and 11 acknowledge. However, in acknowledging these
pros, you do not cross over to note Gomez's implied negatives of
selecting Exotic. Is this failure a mistake? Probably not. You need
not note a cross over each and every time a client's articulation of a
consequence implies such. Acknowledgement of the consequence the
client does note—e.g. "Radio therefore may attract more customers"—
seems sufficient to maintain the appearance of impartiality.

No. 15 brings in the third alternative (waiving a request for
personal guarantees) not because of any cross over by the client and
before completely examining the pros and cons of the two alternatives
already under discussion. You may regard this switch either as prema-

ture or as consistent with neutrality. Neutrality is sometimes best served when you touch on each alternative before systematically exhausting a single option. Alternatively No. 15 might have been phrased something like the following:

> You've mentioned three pros for Radio; so it seems you have some feelings in that direction. We may need to explore your feelings in that direction in more detail later. For now, let's consider the option of going ahead with Exotic without any personal guarantees. What advantages do you see for that?

This response seems more empathic to the client's point of view and therefore may make it easier for the client to switch to the Exotic alternative.

Nos. 40 through 42 mark the transition to lower-T systematic review of each option. No. 42 summarizes the previously identified advantages of one option, and then asks about possible additional advantages of that option. (Nos. 44 and 46 continue in that same vein.) No. 54 turns to the "cons" of the same option. However, since no "cons" emerged in the earlier conversation, you begin the search for cons with an open question. When still no cons emerge, you turn to a closed question (No. 56). No. 56 maintains neutrality by indicating that inquiries about possible disadvantages do not imply rejection of the option. It then asks about a specific possible disadvantage. In similarly thorough fashion, you would ultimately turn to the other options, and the "pros" and "cons" of each.

Finally, compare Nos. 44 and 46 with Nos. 9 and 11 in the "Doug" dialogue (pp. 297–298). In Nos. 9 and 11, you simply identify a category and ask which way it cuts. In Nos. 44 and 46, by contrast, you subtly suggest two reasons that having guarantees might be a pro. Thus, the latter set of questions is less neutral than the former. On the other hand, Gomez's response in No. 45 is clear that he does not regard the lack of guarantees as a con, whereas Doug's response in No. 10 is more ambiguous. Hence, somewhat non-neutral questions such as Nos. 44 and 46 may be more likely to produce unambiguous responses than neutral questions such as Nos. 9 and 11. In the abstract, then, you have a choice as to which form of closed question to use. Realize that, in some circumstances, suggesting that a factor is a pro or a con may bias a response by indicating your own preference. In Gomez's case, given the substantial discussion of consequences which preceded the questions, Nos. 44 and 46 appear not to be overly suggestive.

6. Discuss Consequences You Foresee

As you undoubtedly recognize, a Step Three discussion of likely consequences includes advising clients of potential legal and nonlegal consequences that you foresee. If, as will usually be the case, you first ask a client to predict consequences, you might then either (1) integrate the consequences you foresee into the client's discussion, or (2) wait until the client concludes and supplement the client's list with your own.

Deciding between these two approaches itself requires you to predict likely consequences of each approach. The "pros" of "integrating" include more equal participation in a discussion by you and a client, and a greater opportunity to have on one plate, as it were, all the consequences of a particular option. Also, if a client's consideration of a consequence rests heavily on what the legal outcome is likely to be, postponing a legal prediction is unrealistic. For example, most clients cannot evaluate the merits of a settlement offer unless they know the likely outcome of a trial. Hence, when you ask a client to discuss the "pros" or "cons" of accepting a settlement offer, you would almost certainly integrate your prediction of the likely outcome of trial into the discussion.[21]

The "cons" of integrating include the risk of influencing a client's decision by jumping in quickly with your own predictions and giving an impression that a client's predictions are not as well-informed as yours. These cons seem particularly apt to occur if your predictions require lengthy explanation.

The "pros" of delaying your predictions until after a client is "predicted out" are pretty much the converse of the cons stated above. Delaying your own predictions indicates serious interest in a client's ideas. Also, if both you and a client see the same consequence, allowing the client to state it may promote a client's confidence that he or she can play an important role in solving a problem. The main "con" of delay is the danger that your later discussion of consequences makes a client feel "sandbagged." That is, a client may feel manipulated if you implicitly brush off the client's attempts at prediction with a lengthy catalogue of your own predictions.

On balance, we tend to favor the integrationist approach. Not only does it make you and a client joint partners in a search for a solution, but also it seems a more natural conversational style. Especially since a discussion of consequences is likely to be rather frenetic, with much crossing over among topics, steadfastly delaying your predictions is likely to sound artificial. If your overall approach is consistent with client centeredness, interspersing your predictions among those of a client is unlikely to run roughshod over client autonomy.

To get a clearer sense of how you might integrate your predictions into Step Three, return to the discussion with Doug, the client who is attempting to choose a guardian. Doug's options are his sister, Helen, and his brother, Bob. Assume that one legal consequence of Doug's selecting Bob is that Bob, a nonresident, would have to post a bond. (The dialogue picks up with a repeat of No. 11.)

21. The implicit message of law school to the contrary, remember as noted in Chapter 1 that many client decisions are *not* dominated by legal consequences. For example, neither Doug's selection of a guardian nor Gomez's choice of tenants hinges primarily on legal consequences.

11. L: How about in terms of allowing the children to maintain their current friends and contacts?

12. C: Well, again, Helen seems best on this one. She lives close to us; the kids could go to the same school. Bob, on the other hand, lives out of state. The kids, however, seem to like Bob more, even though they know Helen better. It's tough; maybe the move wouldn't be too upsetting.

13. L: Perhaps in the long run the children might feel more comfortable with Bob?

14. C: That's a real possibility. He's further away but they relate better to him. Maybe I've been trying to avoid facing this fact.

15. L: Doug, I sense this is isn't an easy choice to make, and I'm glad we are taking the time to go through it. Your conclusion, however, is that while a pro of choosing Helen is that the children could maintain their current contacts, an even stronger pro is that in the long term the children will feel more comfortable dealing with Bob. Is that right?

16. C: I think that's right.

17. L: There is one legal point I should throw in here; I'm not sure how important it is. It concerns the necessity to post a bond. Because your brother lives out of state, the court is probably going to require him to post a bond if he is appointed guardian. It's to ensure that if he were to mismanage the kids' money or run off with it, the kids won't be left empty handed.

18. C: What exactly is a bond?

19. L: It's the same as an insurance policy; what happens is that for a premium an insurance company issues a policy which says in effect that if the guardian takes or mismanages the children's money, the insurance company will pay.

20. C: Well, I trust my brother. Does he have to post a bond?

21. L: I'm afraid it's quite likely. Under our state's law, you can waive bond for a resident, but with nonresidents the court has discretion to require bonds and they usually do. That distinction may not make sense but that's the way things are. A bond would cost about one and one half percent of the total value of the property. The bond premium would be paid out of the money you left to the children.

22. C: So it would cost about $2,000 a year, right?

23. L: Correct. Therefore a disadvantage of appointing your brother would be the extra cost of about $2,000 each year. Correspondingly, an advantage of choosing your sister is that it would save about $2,000 a year.

24. C: Are there other legal requirements that might make a difference?

25. L: Not really. Whoever is guardian would have to hire a lawyer to file an account with the court once a year. An account is a written statement outlining what income the children received during the year from their property and what expenses the guardian incurred. It is a simple document and probably could be prepared for about $400 or $500 a year. It would be required of whoever was appointed as guardian. I guess, however, I should ask you if it would be a problem for your brother to hire a local lawyer given that he lives out of state?

26. C: I don't think so, so long as he doesn't have to come here. Would he have to do that?

27. L: No, it could all be done by mail. Okay; with the legalities of posting bond and filing an accounting in mind, let's go back to the practical pros and cons. What else do you see as a pro . . ..

No. 11 is a question exploring consequences that Doug foresees. No. 13 is an appropriate attempt to clarify the client's ambiguous response in No. 12. The first sentence of No. 15 is an active listening response to the client's apparent discomfort; the second sentence notes that each alternative has a pro and that the pro favoring Bob is the stronger. This clarification is likely to help Doug sort out his apparent discomfort. That you do not go further in No. 15 and note a cross over to cons seems okay. Only unthinking rigidity would require you to verbally note each lurking cross over.

No. 17 is a shift from the client's predictions to yours, integrating your forecasts into the discussion. You insert the prediction at a point where the client is discussing a related topic—i.e., the children living out of state. Because the insertion is "naturally" connected to a topic already under discussion, Doug is likely to view the insertion as neutral.[22] Arguably, switching from Doug's prediction (that the children will be happier with Bob) to a con of selecting Bob (the expense of a bond) may lead Doug to think that you are rejecting his position. However, the previous active listening response and the comment, "I'm not sure how important this is" should eliminate any inference of rejection.

No. 18, "What exactly is a bond?," is a reminder that even a common legal term may constitute jargon.[23] Fortunately, Doug's ques-

---

22. Of course, a dry transcript does not permit a full assessment of neutrality, especially since non-verbal cues such as body language and facial cues often undercut verbal messages. For instance, holding your nose while continuing to ask a client for pros of an option probably suggests rejection of the client's input.

23. Jargon in this context refers to the many legal abstractions to which your training and experience gives content, but which are often meaningless to clients. For example, think about how you might explain what the following terms mean: "cause of action;" "trust;" "deposition;" and "security interest." If you have diffi-

tion spurred an explanation (No. 19). In No. 25, by contrast, you anticipate the need to explain what an "account" is without forcing Doug to ask.

No. 21 illustrates how advice-giving often requires both legal and nonlegal knowledge. Legal expertise signals a need for a bond; nonlegal expertise allows you to indicate its economic costs.

No. 23 summarizes with a cross over. Nos. 25 and 27 continue to integrate legal with nonlegal predictions. Finally, No. 27 summarizes the legal aspects of guardianship and then returns to the client's forecasts.

This sample is, of course, not a model for every situation. However, hopefully it helps you begin to understand how you and a client can work together to explore likely consequences.

7. Charting Alternatives and Consequences

We **strongly recommend** that during a Step Three discussion, you make a written chart of the advantages and disadvantages of every option. While you might organize such a chart in any number of ways, we illustrate one simple way in the context of the Montoya–Exotic hypothetical. As you recall, in that hypothetical Alfredo Gomez was considering three options: 1. Reducing the monthly rent to $3000 and obtaining personal guarantees; 2. Keeping the monthly minimum at $4500 and waiving the guarantees; 3. Leasing the space to Radio Hut rather than to Exotic. In this situation, you might prepare a chart as follows: [24]

Exotic Guarantees		Exotic Waive Guarantees		Radio Hut	
Pro	Con	Pro	Con	Pro	Con

Writing down consequences as they emerge is very important. First, a chart is often essential for carrying out the goal of fully exploring each alternative. Because of cross over, a discussion of alternatives and consequences rarely proceeds in a straightforward manner. Without a written record, it is hard for both you and a client to remember what territory has already been covered. Also, seeing consequences in writing may stimulate both you and a client to recall additional ones.

culty, it is because these terms refer more to concepts than to physical realities. You must be able to understand and communicate the underlying meaning of such terms if you are to counsel effectively.

24. For another method of preparing a chart, see R. Dinerstein, "Client–Centered Counseling: Reappraisal and Refinement" 32 Ariz.L.Rev. 501 (1990).

A chart may not only foster a discussion of consequences, but it may also facilitate a client's ultimate decision. Many clients are unable to hold in mind each of the pros and cons of a variety of alternatives. Psychologists, for example, have determined that most people can hold no more than seven facts in their mind at one time.[25] Hence, a written record drawing together the various options and their respective pros and cons can help clients get full and balanced views before making a final determination.

Even a complete chart will not enable every client to make a decision immediately. Thus, you may want to make a chart "to go," so the client can mull over the consequences with others at home or in the office. Often, such mulling over will produce a decision without the need for further input from you. Once a decision is made, the chart becomes a reference point that enables clients to recall the bases of their decisions, obviating the need for many frenzied phone calls in which clients try to recall why they decided as they did.

6. STEP FOUR: MAKING A DECISION

With alternatives and consequences fully flushed out, you and a client are ready for *the fourth step,* making a decision. Often, you need do no more than ask for a client's choice:

Lawyer: Doug, we've gotten everything out. Who do you want to name as your first choice of guardian, Helen or Bob?

Client: All things considered, I guess I'll go with . . . ..

However, the conversation may not always proceed this smoothly. Sometimes you may have to re-review the options and their likely consequences, perhaps asking a client to think carefully about how likely a consequence really is and how much importance a consequence carries as you do so. Referring to a chart and summarizing its contents will often help you carry out the re-review:

"Alfredo, you seem a little uncertain now as to whether you really want to insist on personal guarantees from Exotic's officers. It may help if we review what we've talked about here today. Let's look over this chart, and see if it helps . . . .."

Other times, as noted, some clients respond by asking for time to "think it over." Assuming time permits, such clients can be given a chart, a handshake, and another appointment.

Recall from Chapter 15 that sometimes clients ask for your opinion about what to do, and sometimes make decisions in which you feel a need to intervene. Approaches for handling each of these situations are explored in Chapter 20.

25. See Miller, "The Magic Number Seven, Plus or Minus Two: Some Limits on Our Capacity for Processing Information," 63 Psychological Rev. 81 (1956); Simon, "How Big Is a Chunk," 183 Science 482 (1974).

Chapter 17

REFINING AND TAILORING STEP ONE: CLARIFYING OBJECTIVES

* * *

Peiguo, I'm glad I caught you in. I've just spoken with the lawyer for Genesco; they're quite interested in your proposal. Genesco's lawyer indicated, however, that they probably couldn't go for an all cash purchase. The lawyer wanted to know whether you'd have any interest in part cash and part stock. The lawyer says that Genesco is doing quite well and that if you're interested at all in stock you can look at Genesco's books.

I don't know. I was originally thinking about cash. You know I had that real estate deal with Han Properties cooking. But last week Han told me they are not sure they can get the necessary financing. So I really don't know what to say.

Okay, Peiguo, let's assume for a moment that things don't work out with Han. In what way would that affect your need for cash from the deal with Genesco?

* * *

1. INTRODUCTION

The techniques explored in Chapter 16 presuppose clients who are "ready, willing and able." For example, clients can explain their goals, make decisions without depending on you to tell them what to do, and arrive at decisions that you consider appropriate. Chapter 16 also presupposes that clients' objectives and options (as well as the consequences of those options) remain static as matters progress, and that decisions are made independently of each other.

These presuppositions made it possible to model basic counseling techniques, but they did so by oversimplifying the world of attorney-client relationships. As we all know, people are often undecided about their objectives or find it difficult to express them adequately. Others have difficulty making decisions, perhaps because they are faced with too many choices or because changing circumstances constantly alter their sense of decisions' acceptability. And other people make decisions with which you disagree.

This chapter and the next three examine this more complex world, and attempt to suggest techniques for tailoring counseling techniques to clients who in some way are less than "ready, willing and able." As you will see, we do not pretend to have sure-fire methods that overcome all obstacles. Moreover, we recognize that the four step process described in Chapter 16 and elaborated upon in these chapters does not capture the full dynamic of counseling. For instance, it is folly to think that a discussion of objectives always precedes identification of options. Similarly, counseling is typically cyclical rather than linear. Rather than moving in a lock step fashion through the four steps, you often have to glide back and forth among them. For example, a discussion of consequences (Step Three) may cause a client to realize that she or he has additional objectives, and necessitate a return to Steps One and Two.

Mindful of our inability to capture the cyclical dynamics of counseling, we continue to organize the discussion of "tailoring" techniques according to the four-step counseling model. The suggestions may further your capacity to help clients arrive at satisfactory solutions in a changing and complex world.

This chapter begins the examination of this more complex world. It explores techniques for dealing with three issues that commonly arise during Step One—Clarifying Objectives.

2. VAGUE OR UNARTICULATED OBJECTIVES

As Chapter 16 noted, eliciting objectives whenever you and a client begin exploring a decision typically helps you shape options to a client's specific goals. Sometimes, however, clients are either unsure about their objectives, or they are unable to articulate them. Consider these examples:

Estate Planning Matter

Lawyer: What objectives do you have in mind in wanting to avoid probate?

Client: I'm not really sure; I guess I just want everything to go smoothly when the time comes.

Litigation Matter

Lawyer: What are your objectives in wanting to sue the insurance company?

Client: They really screwed me, and all I know is I want to make them pay for everything I've been put through.

In these examples neither client has stated clear objectives. Their thoughts are too vaguely expressed to suggest specific approaches for accomplishing their goals. For example, does the will client want to prevent a certain person from inheriting? Save taxes? Just what does she or he mean by "everything to go smoothly?" As for the litigation client, does she or he want a public airing through trial? Something other than or in addition to money damages?

You may think these scenarios unlikely because you would have clarified a client's objectives during the initial phase of interviewing. However, you typically do not press clients to articulate specific goals when they first describe problems to you. Even vaguely expressed goals such as those above can enable you to begin to understand a problem from a client's perspective. But when you turn to counseling a client about particular decisions, your ability to fashion options usually requires a more precise statement of goals.

When clients are vague about their goals in response to open questions, consider suggesting possible goals by using closed, lower-T questions based on your experience with similarly-situated clients. For example, you might say to the will client, "Many people nowadays come to lawyers to avoid probate because they want to avoid lawyers' fees and costs associated with probate. Would this be one of your goals?" [1]

Occasionally, a client may be so unfocused that even your efforts to suggest options is fruitless. For instance, the will client may respond, "It's just so hard to say, especially since I won't be around anyway." Pressing a client to come up with objectives may require more than a client is capable of giving at that moment. Thus, the best approach may be to move on to Step Two without a clearer statement of objectives. Often you will find that a discussion of consequences during Step Three finally stimulates clients to clarify their goals. Thus, when the will client learns during Step Three about the fees that are a consequence of probate, the client may at that time articulate the goal of avoiding probate.

3. UPDATING CLIENTS' OBJECTIVES

Whenever you and a client consider a decision, you may be inclined to skip Step One and move directly to identifying options because previous discussions have familiarized you with a client's objectives. However, clients' objectives frequently change. For example, as clients' life situations change, or as they mull over problems with friends, or as situations arise that a client did not fully appreciate when an earlier decision was made, they are apt to change their objectives. Clients often react differently when events actually occur than when the events are but abstract shadows of things to come. Thus, as new decisions arise, you generally should pause to check whether a client's objectives have changed.

1. Especially if you doubt a client's legal sophistication, you may also want to inquire during Step One whether the client understands what probate is and briefly explain it, if necessary.

Consider this example. Assume that a client ("Felice") has come to you for advice on how to bring another person ("Clara") into a take-out food business ("Broccoli Heaven") that Felice has previously run by herself. You learn during the initial interview that Felice's principal objective is to maximize profits by expanding into a sit-down restaurant. She also wants to continue to devote full time to the take out business, and therefore to leave all decisions concerning the sit-down operation to Clara. During a second discussion, you and Felice explore how she might formalize her venture with Clara. Felice's options include entering into a partnership, starting a corporation, or continuing as a sole proprietor and hiring Clara to manage the sit-down operation. You might begin the discussion assuming that you know Felice's objectives, and immediately turn to her options. However, unbeknownst to you, Felice's objectives may well have changed since the initial interview. If so, the new objectives may alter the wisdom of the available options or suggest additional ones. Thus, you should start out with an "objectives check-up" along the following lines:

1. L: Felice, since we last talked I've had a chance to check on a few matters, and we can now talk about the ways you can operate the expanded business. First, though, let's make sure I correctly understand your major objectives. If I remember from our first meeting, you want to expand the operation in order to maximize its profitability, and to do this in a way that leaves you free to spend all your time on the take-out end of the business. Do I have it right?

2. C: Actually, I've been thinking about that. Since we met initially, I've become a little worried about Clara. She has a lot of experience, but as I've talked to her over the past couple of weeks I've seen that her ideas don't always match mine. I've got a reputation for doing things a certain way, and I don't want to lose all control over the sit down part of the business. I'd still like her to be responsible for the sit-down service, but I want to have some oversight on what she does.

As you see, the "update" itself is straightforward—you simply refer to whatever previously-articulated objectives appear relevant to the decision you are about to discuss. Had Felice's objectives been unchanged, you could have quickly proceeded to the Step Two discussion of options.

Here, however, the client announces changed objectives. Faced with new objectives, you may not be ready to proceed to Step Two; indeed, you may have to postpone the counseling session to another date to give you time to consider how the new objectives affect the available options. Before doing so, though, probe the new objectives. On the one hand, they may be sufficiently similar to the initial ones that you can proceed to Step Two without delay. On the other hand, the new objectives may be but the tip of an iceberg; a client may have a radically different view of his or her problem. When a client voices changed objectives, your inquiry may proceed along these lines:

3. L: Well, I'm glad we stopped for a moment to make sure we're on the same track. Given what you've learned recently, you now want to make sure that the business arrangement allows you to exercise some say in sit-down operations, correct?

4. C: Exactly. I'd rather keep some control. I don't want to face a situation where the horse has already left the barn.

5. L: Besides wanting to maintain some say in how the sit-down business operates, have your objectives changed in any other way?

6. C: No. I still strongly favor going ahead with a sit-down operation, and I'm still comfortable working with Clara.

7. L: Well, I think that we can structure into whatever form of organization you choose a way for you to have some say in the sit-down business. Why don't we look at those options now . . .

No. 3 notes the changed objective. No. 5 is an open question which gives the client an opportunity to disclose further changes. When none are forthcoming, No. 7 moves the dialogue to Step Two, signaling your belief that this change does not require much retooling of options.

Continuation of the Felice–Clara hypothetical may illustrate the cyclical manner by which objectives produce decisions whose attempted implementation in turn leads to changed objectives. Assume that during the second discussion, Felice decided to bring Clara into her business as a full partner. A few days later, you meet with Felice to discuss a draft partnership agreement. When you reach the portion of the agreement providing for partners' capital accounts, Felice tells you that she wants to have money available for non-partnership investments, and that therefore the agreement should provide for each partner to maintain small capital accounts of only $15,000. Later, during negotiations, Clara's lawyer states that Clara wants to be sure that Felice is committed to the financial success of the partnership, and therefore insists that each partner maintain a capital account of $35,000. Thereafter, once again you talk to Felice about the capital accounts provision. When you do so, check to see whether Felice's financial objective has changed. Perhaps in response to Clara's insistence that Felice prove her financial commitment, Felice might alter that objective.[2]

2. In this example, the potential cause of a changed objective is an event peculiar to the transaction itself: the response of another party. In reality, causes are diverse, and may have nothing to do with the specific matter for which you have been hired. For example, if Felice has earned large sums of money on outside investments since deciding to commit only $15,000 to the partnership, or if those outside investments have turned sour, she may want or need to rethink her financial objectives.

4. MODIFYING STEP ONE WHEN IDENTIFYING OBJECTIVES OF "IMPLEMENTING DECISIONS"

As you realize by now, your typical role during Step One is to ask clients what objectives they have in mind. You generally need to switch roles, however, when a client is faced with an "implementing decision."

"Implementing decisions" concern options and steps lawyers commonly use to help clients carry out their previously selected courses of action. For example, if a client has chosen to litigate, implementing decisions include taking depositions, sending interrogatories, and hiring experts. Similarly, if a client has decided to do business in the partnership form, implementing decisions include such options as arbitration, method of accounting and buy-out clauses. Finally, in an employment agreement, implementing decisions encompass provisions for non-direct compensation such as use of a company car, country club membership, and season tickets to the local ballet company.

Because implementing decisions usually require legal expertise to appreciate, it often makes little sense to ask clients what their goals are with respect to them. That is, unless clients are experienced or sophisticated, they will not be familiar enough with depositions, interrogatories and buy-outs to specify what objectives those devices might enable them to attain. Hence, when you identify implementing steps and options, tell clients what objectives they can attain by opting for those steps or options.

For example, unless Felice were quite sophisticated, you would not say, "Felice, one option you have is to include an arbitration clause in the partnership agreement. What objectives might such a clause fulfill?" Felice would probably not know enough about an arbitration clause to know what objectives it might help her attain. Hence, when telling Felice about the option of an arbitration clause, you would tell her the objectives such a clause would fulfill.[3]

The dialogue that accompanies your identifying implementing decisions is usually quite simple. The following examples are illustrative:

"Felice, let's think about whether the partnership agreement with Clara should contain an arbitration clause. Arbitration clauses are usually put into agreements in order to provide a means of more quickly and cheaply resolving disputes rather than going to court."

3. We assume that an implementing decision which must be made is one which is likely to have a substantial legal or nonlegal impact on a client, and to have an impact beyond that normally associated with the exercise of lawyering skills and crafts and therefore is one the client should have an opportunity to make. If it is not likely to have a substantial legal or nonlegal impact you need not counsel with respect to it, and the concerns examined in the text are irrelevant. See Chap. 15, sec. 4.

"Mr. Xiao, what I'd like to talk with you about is whether to go ahead with a series of four depositions. The depositions I have in mind are those of DongTian Corp.'s chief engineer and the three people who operate under her. The main objective I have in mind is to obtain the history of how they designed their computer, and what alternative design possibilities they considered. This information will be important in establishing that the computers you bought had design defects."

* * *

Following such explanations, you might choose either to (a) further explain a client's options, or (b) move into a Step Three discussion of consequences. For example, you might describe arbitration clauses to Felice in more detail, or you might ask her what she sees as the advantages of having an arbitration provision. In either event, having yourself mentioned the objectives, you have modified Step One.

Notwithstanding the above discussion, sometimes you may assume that a technical action is familiar to a client, either because the client is experienced or sophisticated, or because the action is one that most people are likely to know about through daily life. In such instances, you need not modify Step One, but instead can ask clients to articulate their objectives. So, if you are drawing up an employment agreement on behalf of a client who is familiar with such agreements, you might explore the client's objectives by asking, "What might you accomplish by including a non-competition clause in the agreement?" Or, if a client has young children and wants you to draft a will, you could tell the client, "One decision you have to make is who to name as the guardian of the children. What objectives would you hope to achieve in appointing a guardian?"

Likewise, a client may demonstrate familiarity by mentioning a technical action. When a client mentions a technical action, you may infer that the client is familiar with it and has particular purposes in mind.[4] So, if Felice on her own asks about including an arbitration clause in her partnership agreement, you could ask, "What goals do you hope to achieve with such a clause?"

---

4. This is not always the case, however. For example, so widely advertised are "living trusts" that a client may well tell a lawyer that "I'd like a living trust" without having any real understanding of what the term means.

Chapter 18

REFINING AND TAILORING STEP TWO: IDENTIFYING ALTERNATIVES

* * *

Linda, the studio is definitely interested in your script. You've told me that you don't want just to sell your script, that one thing you want to make sure of is that the movie is faithful to what you've written. I know this is your first script, but perhaps you have some ideas about what kind of control might give you the protection you want?

Up to this point, I've always done writing for other people. So I'm not too sure how to go about this.

Well, generally there are two areas in which control is sometimes exercised by a writer. One is casting approval. I'd say we have two options when it comes to casting approval. One is for you to have the right to participate in the casting process; the other is for you to approve a final list from which the leads will be chosen. I think that the studio might be open to either possibility. With respect to supervision of the final cut, it's almost unheard of for a first-time author such as yourself to get final cut approval. But given the extraordinary success of your novel, I think that asking for final cut approval will at least produce a counter-offer. Do you have any other possibilities in mind when it comes to control?

* * *

1. INTRODUCTION

This chapter explores issues that arise during Step Two, when you and a client work together to identify potential solutions. As even experienced clients typically expect you to provide them with realistic alternatives, identifying alternatives is a principal counseling function. It often requires you to combine knowledge of legal rules and processes with awareness of the intricate real-world settings in which clients' problems arise. Thus, this chapter explores issues relevant to your framing both legal and nonlegal alternatives. Moreover, either on their own or in response to your questions, clients often propose

316

alternatives. Hence, the chapter concludes with a discussion of responding to clients' proposed alternatives.

2. SUGGEST ONLY THOSE ALTERNATIVES WHICH APPEAR PIVOTAL OR PERTINENT TO AN INDIVIDUAL CLIENT'S CIRCUMSTANCES

Many problems have a large number of potential solutions. For example, among the potential solutions to most litigation problems are trial, mini-trial, arbitration, mediation, and settlement. Within the "settlement" option you might identify a myriad of options. Similarly, among the potential solutions for a transactional problem involving a client's need for capital are public and non-public stock offerings, public and non-public bond offerings and loans from a variety of institutional and individual sources. As you counsel, do you have to mention every possible option every time a problem to which it might apply arises?

Common sense and our counseling standard dictate that you not befuddle a client with all possible options. Recall that the counseling standard requires only that you provide a client with a reasonable opportunity to consider those alternatives that a "similarly-situated client" would find pivotal or pertinent. In other words, the standard asks that you take a client's individual circumstances and goals into account when presenting a client with alternatives.

Thus, it probably makes little sense to suggest the alternative of a "living trust" to a client whose quite modest estate will not go through probate. Similarly, if you represent a tenant faced with an unlawful detainer complaint, it may be useless to suggest mediation when a client informs you that a landlord wants to evict every tenant and convert a building to condominiums. Finally, it is often fruitless to suggest modifications in a franchise agreement when representing an individual seeking a franchise from a multinational franchisor. In each instance, alternatives which are available in the abstract probably make no sense in the individual circumstances.

3. DEVELOP FAMILIARITY WITH RELEVANT "INDUSTRIES" TO IDENTIFY A VARIETY OF OPTIONS

Much of your effectiveness as a counselor depends on your ability to present clients with a variety of options. Within limits, the more options that are on the table, the more likely that a client will find a satisfactory one. Of course, you reap no benefits by dazzling a client with a potpourri of options removed from clients' concerns. On the contrary, a variety of options is helpful only if you have carefully listened to each client's individual objectives and have developed alternatives that respond to them.

Developing options is the aspect of law practice which is often both the most creative and satisfying, and the one you are least likely to learn about in law school. To develop a variety of alternatives that meet clients' individual objectives, you must be familiar with the context (the "industries") in which those concerns arise. By way of illustration, assume that you have three clients. One is a supplier of industrial gloves and similar safety equipment who is being threatened with eviction from a warehouse in an industrial park, and who seeks advice about restructuring the rent called for in the lease. The second is an elementary school principal who seeks advice about formulating appropriate disciplinary rules and procedures. The third is a married couple who want to draft wills for the purpose of naming a guardian for their two young children. In each case, your ability to formulate potential solutions requires some knowledge of the following:

a. General operation of the "industries" touching upon a client's problem: For the industrial supplier, relevant industries include warehouse and industrial parks operations; for the principal, elementary school education and discipline; for the parent, child-rearing practices and guardianship functions.

b. How a client specifically operates within these industries: For example, how do the glove and safety equipment supplier and the industrial park operator conduct their businesses; how does the school run its educational program and respond to disciplinary problems; what child-rearing practices does the couple follow?

c. Generally-available alternative solutions in the particular problem area: For the industrial supplier, you will need to be familiar with alternative forms of industrial park or commercial rent provisions; for the principal, codes of conduct and disciplinary procedures that schools have developed; for the married couple, standard guardianship provisions.

Examining two of these clients' problems from a closer perspective may demonstrate how the foregoing types of knowledge connect to potential solutions. Assume that Swapco is the tenant which has leased a warehouse in an industrial park. Swapco shares a loading dock with another tenant. The owner is pressuring Swapco for back rent and has threatened to begin eviction proceedings. Melinda, Swapco's president, admits owing rent. But she states that the landlord has failed to provide tenants with security protection and has provided inadequate dock access, and that under these conditions Swapco cannot make a profit.

In this situation, standard options for Swapco include taking its chances at trial should the owner commence eviction proceedings; paying the back rent; renegotiating the agreement; or moving voluntarily to a new location, perhaps pursuant to a negotiated agreement in which the owner forgives all or part of the back rent.

However, familiarity with the three areas noted above can help you to identify additional potential solutions. Assume that Melinda is willing to have Swapco remain a tenant if the security and docking problems can be resolved. Your knowledge of (a) warehouse operations and security systems generally; (b) Swapco's security problems and the industrial park's particular security operation, and (c) alternative security systems available on the market might enable you to create proposals for solving Swapco's security problems. Likewise, your knowledge of (a) warehouse loading and unloading procedures and traffic patterns in industrial parks generally; (b) Swapco's receiving and delivery procedures, and (c) typical lease provisions concerning dock access might enable you to create proposals concerning additional loading docks and access routes, and staggered delivery hours (e.g., setting specific hours for Swapco and its dock-mate to load and unload). Finally, your knowledge of (a) rent calculations in industrial parks and of accounting procedures; (b) Swapco's financial condition; and (c) typical commercial and industrial rent formulas might enable you to devise alternative rental formulas (e.g., lower monthly minimum rent combined with a percentage of net or gross income) that might protect Swapco while it is having economic difficulty and also protect the landlord once the industrial park problems are solved and Swapco becomes more profitable.

As for the married couple who wants to nominate a guardian, assume that their first choice for guardian is the husband's brother and his wife, who themselves have a toddler. With respect to housing, the clients' objectives include allowing their children to have as "normal" a home life as possible after the clients' deaths. A standard option in this situation is for the clients' children to move into the guardians' home.

Again, awareness of the relevant "industries" may enable you to develop additional options. For example, familiarity with (a) the housing "industry;" (b) the clients' and the proposed guardians' current housing arrangements and financial conditions; and (c) generally-available provisions relating to housing of wards might enable you to develop such additional options as the guardians' moving into the clients' home during the wards' minority, enlarging either the guardians' or the clients' home using funds from the clients' estate, or selling both the guardians' and the clients' home and buying a larger home.[1]

In both the Swapco and the guardianship matters, note that (as is frequently the case) the various options are neither compelled nor forbidden by legal rules.[2] All are allowable; their usefulness depends

---

1. Note that it may take a number of counseling sessions for all of these alternatives to emerge. For instance, based on an initial discussion with the will client, you may prepare and send out for review a draft will which contains some "basic" guardianship provisions. Then, reviewing the draft with the client in a later meeting, you may point out alternative ways of accomplishing the goals of the guardianship.

2. Of course, in some matters legal principles will torpedo or limit particular options. For example, if a non-competition clause attempts to bar an employee from pursuing her or his occupation for 20 years, such a clause would probably be invalid. However, rarely will legal principles *mandate* particular options.

on the extent to which they help the clients meet their objectives. Your ability to identify such options does not come from knowledge of legal rules. Rather, your ability emerges from familiarity with the broad situational backdrops within which the clients' problems arise, the clients' particular methods of operation within that situational backdrop, and the range of options which attorneys (and perhaps others) have developed to resolve them.

Thus, no matter how extensive your knowledge of legal principles, you are not prepared to counsel unless you are familiar with the "industries" relevant to a problem. Many years ago, it was the custom for newly-admitted lawyers to gain such experience through "mentors." While the economics of the modern practice of law have relegated mentors to the endangered species list,[3] other sources of experience thrive. Sometimes, you can pick up necessary familiarity from clients. For example, Melinda can probably tell you about Swapco's security practices and, indeed, may even know something about alternative security systems. Practitioner works and formbooks may provide information about particular industries. Other times, of course, you may need to consult an expert, even to find out what the relevant "industries" are.[4] The expert may be another lawyer who specializes in a particular field.[5] Coming from a variety of sources, familiarity with how the real world operates is the catalyst for many of the alternatives you identify, and is necessary for you to be a competent counselor.[6]

Clients usually have more familiarity than you both with the "industries" in which their problems arise and with their own operations within that industry. Indeed, an experienced client may know about generally-available provisions of which you are unaware. Therefore, you might ask why, during Step Two, you should bother to ask clients to tell you about relevant industries and their own operations.[7] It might strike you that it would save time and money simply to ask clients for the alternatives they see.

That viewpoint does have some validity: as you know, the counseling model anticipates that during Step Two you solicit potential solutions from clients. However, you cannot rely totally on their solutions. Though clients' "industry" knowledge may be greater than yours, you

3. See, e.g., J.S. Elson, "The Case Against Legal Scholarship or, If The Professor Must Publish, Must the Profession Perish?" 39 J.Leg.Ed. 343, 353 n. 32 (1989).

4. For example, an expert might alert you to the need to learn about life insurance before you draft a partnership buy-sell agreement.

5. One reason that lawyers specialize is the need to be familiar with relevant industries in addition to doctrinal principles.

6. We hope this discussion demonstrates that gaps in substantive knowledge are not the only cause of the sense of inadequacy that often pervades newly-admitted lawyers. Gaining familiarity with relevant industries, not doing additional legal research, may be the method by which you can overcome such feelings.

7. At least with transactional matters, you usually begin to elicit "industry" information during information-gathering. See Chapter 11, sec. 6. Even if you have done so, and in any event during the counseling phase in most litigation matters, you almost always have additional "industry" discussion.

may be more creative when it comes to using that knowledge to develop solutions. Likewise, clients may be too emotionally involved in their own problems to identify a variety of solutions. Finally, clients may be reluctant to suggest solutions, thinking that those are "legal matters" best left to the legal expert. Hence, you need to work with clients to develop familiarity with relevant industries and apply that familiarity in the service of potential solutions.

A sample dialogue illustrates how "industry" discussions might play out in actual counseling settings. Assume that you are talking with Melinda, Swapco's president, about the possibility of renegotiating the lease to include provisions requiring the owner to provide Swapco with adequate access to its loading dock. The dialogue might proceed as follows:

1. L: Melinda, let's see if we can develop some ideas that we can suggest to the owner to take care of the dock access problem. I know from my previous experience working with industrial park matters that most owners don't like to commit themselves to specific rules regarding loading dock access. It's difficult to set up rules that don't prejudice some tenants, and it's also difficult to monitor specific parking and access rules. But if I can learn a bit more about your particular situation, maybe we can come up with possible solutions. Tell me a little more about your loading dock situation.

2. C: I'm one of the smaller operations in the park. Most of our customers are small companies and even individuals, who come in throughout the day in cars and pickup trucks to pick up merchandise. Our edge on our competitors is that we deal in smaller quantities and give personal service. But a lot of the time customers can't get in and out of our dock because large lorries waiting to get into Maxwell Industries' warehouse just to the east of us line up and block access to our dock. Once these big rigs get lined up, it's impossible to get them to move; the line is just too long and trucks can't back up. I know we've lost a lot of business because smaller customers especially just don't like the hassle.

3. L: That's got to be really frustrating. When I visited your warehouse last week, I probably came in like your customers, off of Hanley and then turned on to Bolas where the dock is located. I noticed that Logan also accesses the industrial park. Could your customers reach you by entering on Logan?

4. C: Yes, but they'd have the same problem reaching my dock. The line of trucks on Bolas would still prevent access.

5. L: How many trucks does it take to block off your access?

6. C: Well, when four large rigs are in line, which isn't at all unusual, our access is pretty much cut off. Sometimes as many as seven or eight trucks line up, and the line doesn't move for fifteen or twenty minutes.

7. L: Could the trucks line up on Logan, and not proceed to a warehouse until space was free on Bolas?

8. C: That might be an idea, but I think the police will hassle the truckers if they were to wait out there—I'll have to think about that a bit more.

9. L: If the lorries lined up on Hanley, would that disrupt traffic there?

10. C: No, the trucks could be angled in such a way on Hanley that they stay within the industrial park and then move on to Bolas once there is space available.

11. L: Okay, that's a possibility we might work with. Can you think of any others?

12. C: Not really.

13. L: Well, let me try one other. Suppose lines were painted on Bolas such that the trucks waiting to go to Maxwell's were instructed to leave a space in front of your dock. Would truckers pay attention to such lines?

14. C: I'd like to think about that. You know, we might even be able to do the painting. I remember seeing that done someplace.

No. 1 refers to your experience in industrial park matters, mercifully saving you from reading a lengthy dialogue about industrial parks. Though you probably learned something about the client's operations during earlier information-gathering, in No. 1 you seek additional information specifically related to Swapco's dock access problems. In No. 3 you make an active listening response, and suggest one possible option. When the client nixes that suggestion, you elicit more information in No. 5, and in No. 7 suggest a second alternative. No. 9 again seeks information. In No. 11 you confirm an option suggested by the client in No. 10 and then ask the client if she can see other options. When the client cannot add to the list, No. 13 suggests a third option which the client embellishes upon in No. 14. Later, in Step Three, you and client can review the pros and cons of the options outlined in Nos. 7, 10 and 13.

4. BRIEFLY DESCRIBE ALTERNATIVES WITH WHICH CLIENTS MAY BE UNFAMILIAR

Hopefully, industry knowledge, practitioner works, or other sources enable you to propose at least one potential option to a client during Step Two. But if a client is to participate actively in a Step Three discussion of an option's likely consequences, you often have to do more during Step Two than simply identify an option by its legal label. Consider conclusory recitals of alternatives such as:

1. "One option is to go to trial."

2. "An alternative I've thought of is to include a non-competition clause in the partnership agreement."

3. "Jim, we might give Mr. Frankel what we call a 'golden handshake.'"

Just as one cannot think about the pros and cons of purchasing a particular make of exercise bicycle without knowing something about its features, a client cannot assess the likely consequences of an alternative without some awareness of its characteristics. Thus, if in Step Three a client is to have a hand in thinking through consequences, in Step Two you should accompany the mention of an unfamiliar alternative with a brief description of its primary features.

Among the factors you might consider in deciding whether an alternative is likely to be unfamiliar to a client are a client's level of sophistication and the community's general familiarity with the alternative. Refer to the three alternatives above. Regardless of a client's sophistication, a community's general awareness of trials means that you would not generally have to describe what a trial is. Indeed, most clients will perceive an explanation as unnecessary and condescending. By contrast, many people are likely to be unfamiliar with non-competition clauses and golden handshakes. Thus, unless a client's background suggests that he or she knows what these options are, you probably should briefly describe them. For instance, in the second and third examples above you might have said,

2. "A non-competition clause is a provision which prevents an employee from competing directly against you as soon as he or she leaves your employ."

3. "Just to explain, Jim, a 'golden handshake' is a substantial retirement bonus that you can offer to an employee like Frankel to encourage him to leave quickly and voluntarily."

You may readily agree that it makes sense to describe unfamiliar alternatives during Step Two. But difficulties arise when you consider just how extensive a description should be. Describe too much, and you defeat the purpose altogether. Just as the would-be purchaser of an exercise bicycle would probably not be interested in and would be confused by a description of the specifications of the ball bearings in the wheel, so is a client's thinking about consequences unlikely to be aided, for example, by a lengthy description of the features of golden handshakes. First, a lengthy description is likely to be confusing. It all too often turns into abstract legal discourse which causes a client to think, "How does any of this affect what I should do?" Second, elaborate description may portray you as an option's non-neutral advocate.

For instance, assume that you describe a non-competition clause in terms such as, "A non-competition clause is a means by which you can restrict where, for how long, for what type of employer and in what capacity Woods may work after leaving your employ. Courts will enforce a non-competition clause if it is tailored to protect your legitimate interests while not unfairly limiting Woods' ability to earn a living. Of course, what the job market looks like when Woods leaves, and what kind of work Woods is capable of, and the time period for which we seek to restrict Woods will all have an impact on a court's decision." Such a dissertation may display your legal acumen, but it undoubtedly will create in a client's mind more questions than it answers.

Seeing the dilemma, you may respond that the better approach is to do nothing more than identify alternatives in Step Two, and to save *all* description for Step Three. For example, you might choose to simply tell a client during Step Two that one alternative is a non-competition clause. Then, if and when the client states during Step Three that she or he wants to talk about the non-competition clause alternative, you can engage the client in a full discussion of consequences.

However, such a response is short-sighted. If you lay out only bare alternatives in Step Two, a client will almost always choose to talk first about an unfamiliar alternative during Step Three:

Lawyer: Which option would you like to discuss first?

Client: You said something about a non-competition clause. I'm not really sure what that is, so let's talk about that one first.

By not providing *any* description in Step Two, you in effect dictate the agenda of Step Three, and thus influence a client's decision. Leaving a client completely in the dark about an unfamiliar option almost guarantees that during Step Three it will be the first option discussed, even if a client has no real interest in it. Moreover, starting Step Three with an elaborate description of an unfamiliar option impairs your opportunity to maintain neutrality by having a client begin by describing the advantages or disadvantages of the option of most interest to the client.

For all these reasons, the step of "identifying alternatives" requires brief description of options with which a client is likely to be unfamiliar.[8]

5. IMPART AN ALTERNATIVE'S LIKELY LEGAL OUTCOME

In addition to briefly describing unfamiliar options, during Step Two you should also pithily explain an option's likely legal outcome.

---

8. Of course, if a client requests additional description, you should provide it. In general, elaborate description is typically better left to Step Three. But as pointed out in the introduction to Chapter 17, counseling is a dynamic process, and you often have to move back and forth between the steps.

For example, if "going to trial" is an option, state its likely legal consequence:

> "I think the most likely outcome of trial is that we'll recover the contract price in its entirety along with attorney's fees; I think there's a less than 20% chance that we'll get an award of punitive damages."

Similarly, if an option is "not disclosing in the SEC offering statement of IBN Corp. that IBN's president owns the building which IBN is leasing," state the likely legal consequence of failing to make that disclosure: "Frankly, I think that the SEC is very strict on potential conflicts of interest, and is very likely to require disclosure of that information." [9]

Clients need to have some sense of an option's likely legal outcome if they are to have a reasonable opportunity to identify consequences during Step Three. That is, unless a client knows what the outcome of a trial or of failing to disclose in an SEC statement is likely to be, the client cannot even begin to compare alternatives during Step Three. For example, unless a client knows the likely outcome of trial, the client cannot begin thinking about the comparative pros and cons of trial versus accepting a settlement offer.

Mentioning an option's legal outcome frequently gives rise to the dilemma explored in the previous section. Typically, options have a range of possible legal outcomes. For example, the option of trial often involves a range of potential outcomes, from "the best possible" to "the worst possible." Moreover, factors such as the probative worth and admissibility of evidence may affect each potential outcome. Attempting to describe each possible outcome and the factors tending to produce it is likely to confuse a client and portray you as an option's advocate. Thus, limit your description to an option's most likely legal outcome, and save nuances for Step Three. [10]

6. FRAME OPTIONS NEUTRALLY

As you know, maintaining neutrality is vital to promoting client autonomy. What may be dismaying, then, is how easily you can influence clients' responses without intentionally doing so.

Social scientists have long known that the way in which a question is asked can influence an answer. Perhaps the best known example is that of the "Kinsey Reports," which were an empirical investigation into American sexual mores. [11] Questions asking people *if* they engaged in oral sex or homosexual activity were far less likely to uncover the

---

9. Note that the prediction about trial is phrased as a percentage ("less than 20% chance"); the prediction concerning the SEC is more vaguely phrased ("very likely"). Lawyers often adopt the latter phraseology. See Chapter 19, sec. 4(B) for a discussion of why statements of percentage tend to enhance client understanding.

10. Again, should a client request further description during Step Two, you should provide it.

11. See R.L. Gorden, *Interviewing Strategies, Techniques and Tactics* 212–220 (1969).

extent of the behavior than questions asking people *how often* they engaged in the activity. The second type of question implies that the questioner expects that the respondent has engaged in the sexual activity and thus will not think ill of the respondent for confirming it.

Current social science research suggests that questions can influence responses even in relatively impersonal areas. For example, describing an option in terms of "gain" may elicit one reaction from a client, while describing that same option in terms of "loss" may elicit another. In general, people are far more likely to choose an option they think will result in gain than one they think will produce loss, even if the two options actually produce the same outcome.[12]

For instance, assume that in the Swapco scenario, Swapco's current monthly rent is $2000. Melinda hopes to renegotiate the rent to $1000; the owner offers to reduce it to $1500. As Melinda's attorney, you might describe the owner's offer in one of these two ways:

    a.   "By accepting the owner's offer, you gain $500 a month off your current rent."

    b.   "By accepting the owner's offer, you lose $500 a month off our original proposal."

Research suggests that Melinda is more likely to accede to the owner's offer phrased as it is in "a" rather than "b."

Awareness of how you may inadvertently influence clients need not make you paranoid about every word you utter. Rather, understanding that absolute neutrality is probably impossible may underline the importance of following a generally client-centered approach. Such an approach can minimize, if not eliminate, your influence.

7. EVALUATE CLIENTS' IMMEDIATE REJECTION OF ALTERNATIVES

One situation that commonly arises during Step Two is a client's immediate rejection of an alternative. For example, imagine that part of the Swapco dialogue had proceeded as follows:

    7.   L: Could the trucks line up on Logan and not proceed to a warehouse until space was free on Bolas?

    8.   C: I think the police will hassle the truckers if they wait out there—that'll never work.[13]

Your first reaction may be that client centeredness requires you to acquiesce in the client's rejection and consign the rejected alternative to the "Graveyard of Unwanted Options." And, especially if a client's

12. See for example, A. Tversky and D. Kahneman, "The Framing of Decisions and the Psychology of Choice," 211 Science 453 (Jan. 1981).

13. Of course, instead of rejecting an alternative as soon as you identify it, a client may reject it when you try to examine its pros and cons during Step Three. In most situations, however, how you respond does not depend on when a client happens to reject an alternative.

rejection is stated vehemently and accompanied by valid reasons, that initial reaction may be proper. For example, assume that when you suggest someone as a possible guardian, the client responds, "I've thought about him, but honestly he would not give the children any religious training whatsoever, and there is no way I could accept him." This client has evidently considered the option, knows a critical likely consequence, and finds it personally unacceptable. Arguably the client has had a "reasonable opportunity" to consider the alternative, and you may let well enough alone.

However, automatic acquiescence in clients' rejections is not always consistent with client-centered lawyering. Clients may reject alternatives out of hand for a variety of reasons. They may mispredict an option's likely outcome. For example, Melinda may immediately reject the Logan Street option because she is mistaken about the likely police reaction to trucks lining up on Logan.

Or, a client may fail to understand an option because you have neglected to describe it in sufficient detail. For example, Melinda may reject the Logan Street option because you omitted to explain that part of that option is convincing the city to provide a waiting area for trucks on Logan.

Also, clients may reject options because they are convinced that much better solutions are just over the horizon. For example, perhaps every option you suggest strikes a client as too expensive, and the client is sure that a cheaper alternative is out there somewhere.[14]

Finally, clients may reject alternatives for reasons that cause you moral or ethical concerns. For example, Melinda may reject an alternative because she hopes to force the tenant at whose dock trucks usually line up out of business. Melinda believes that the tenant's practice of delivering food and clothes to the needy attracts homeless people to the site.[15]

When clients reject options because of misprediction, lack of full understanding, or mistaken faith in the existence of "better" alternatives, they have usually not had a "reasonable opportunity" to make a decision. Similarly, a rejection based on reasons which raise moral concerns may mean a client has not had a "reasonable opportunity" to decide; in addition, it may also interfere with your moral autonomy. In each situation, therefore, you may temporarily shelve a discussion of rejected options in the interest of maintaining rapport, but resurrect them later. How and when you resurrect rejected options often depends on the basis for the rejection.

14. This reaction is common when clients are faced with situations in which each option is perceived to be a "loser." For a discussion of techniques useful in helping clients faced with "lose-lose" situations see Chapter 20, sec 3(A).

15. There may be many other reasons for clients' precipitous rejection of alternatives; we do not pretend to have catalogued them all.

For example, if a client indicates that she or he does not fully understand an option, you may follow a rejection with an immediate explanation.   For instance, after Melinda's response in No. 8, you might say:

> "That's a good point, but I should have explained that option in more detail.   Logan is pretty wide near the industrial park, and part of my idea is to convince the city to widen Logan to provide a truck waiting area.   We can talk more about this option in a little bit." [16]

If you think a client is simply hoping for a better solution, you may choose not to bring up a rejected option until a future counseling discussion, when other alternatives have not panned out.[17]   Finally, you may treat problems of misprediction or immorality according to the suggestions in Chapter 20.

8. RECAST CLIENTS' INADEQUATE ALTERNATIVES

As you recall, during Step Two you typically invite clients to propose alternatives.   However, when they accept an invitation, your client-centered attitude and skills are occasionally sorely tested by the impracticality or unavailability of suggested alternatives.   For example, a tenant-client who has not suffered legally cognizable damages may propose filing suit to compel a landlord to consent to a sublease.   Or, an employer may want you to draft a non-competition clause that "will tie Ramseyer to my company forever."   Or, a client who wants her entire estate to go to a charity may insist on a no-contest clause to prevent a will contest by her disinherited child.   Assuming the inadequacy of each of the suggestions, how might you respond?

Generally, you best serve clients by taking inadequate proposals off the table quickly.[18]   Assuming a client makes an inadequate suggestion during Step Two, you should generally derail it before moving on to Step Three.   To do so, respond empathically and then explain the reason for your rejection:

1. L: Mr. Even, those are my suggested options.   Have you thought of any additional ones?

2. C: After what they've done to me, I really want to sue the jerks.

3. L: They've caused you enormous aggravation, and I can understand your desire to sue.   Unfortunately, were we to file suit, the other side would have it thrown out immedi-

---

16. If you are unsure of the reason a client has rejected an option, clarify rather than guess at the reason: "You've said you don't want to even consider the Logan Street option.   Might I ask you why?"

17. Of course, if a client continues to reject an option, your counseling burden is satisfied.   Remember, your burden is to provide a "reasonable opportunity," not to insure client consideration of every feasible option.

18. Be wary, however, of rejecting a client's proposed alternative out of hand.   What strikes you at first as fanciful may simply reflect a client's greater imagination or willingness to take risks.

ately, and the court might require you to pay their legal fees. I don't think filing suit is an option we should consider.

At the same time, recognize that clients' suggestions often reflect legitimate objectives. When that is so, after making an empathic response to indicate that you understand their objectives, look for other solutions. Depending on who has greater "expertise," you might either suggest a different option which responds to those objectives, or ask a client to think of other possibilities. For example, in Mr. Even's case you might continue with No. 3 as follows:

3.　However, it's clearly very important that you be able to sub-lease the property. Can you think of anything we can offer to the landlord to persuade it to accept Prager Co. as a subten-ant?

In the above example, you ask for the client's suggestions. Howev-er, when you have greater expertise, you typically suggest the options. For example, you may respond to the client who wants to disinherit the child as follows:

Given the circumstances you've described, I can understand why you want your property to go to the Environmental Federation, and your desire to prevent a will contest. But simply putting a no contest clause in your will may not prevent your child from contesting it. If you leave everything to charity, the child has nothing to lose by contesting the will. And the legal fees your executor will incur if your child does contest will reduce the amount that goes to the charity. Therefore, one option to consider is to leave the child enough in your will to make the child reluctant to contest the will. We can talk about that in a bit. But before we do, do you see any other ways of perhaps preventing a contest?

9.　USE THE STEP THREE DISCUSSION OF CONSEQUENCES TO IDENTIFY ADDITIONAL ALTERNATIVES

Alternatives typically emerge through a cyclical process. Step Two identifies a limited number of alternatives whose likely consequences emerge during Step Three. Often, a Step Three discussion identifies concerns which necessitates a return to Step Two for further alterna-tives that respond to those concerns. Moving back and forth between Steps Two and Three may continue over a period of time until a client makes a decision.

For example, assume that you are counseling a civil defendant who is considering whether to offer a negotiated settlement prior to trial. The client's interest in resolving the matter quickly may lead in Step Two to the alternatives of (a) offering a cash payment of $50,000; and (b) offering a cash substitute, a two-acre parcel of real estate the client owns that has a market value of approximately $50,000, but in which the client has a basis of only $35,000. As you and the client examine the consequences of these alternatives, the client may realize that a consequence of giving up the real estate is forgoing its future appreciation. As a result, protecting future appreciation may become a new goal which leads to identification of additional alternatives. For example, a new alternative might be an offer which consists partly of cash and partly of some other non-cash asset, or of half of the real estate.

Because counseling usually does not proceed in linear fashion, you need not feel compelled to put every possible alternative on the table before moving from Step Two to Step Three. On some level, of course, stating every potential alternative is impossible. That is, a cash offer might be $10,000, 10,001, etc. Similarly, a trust provision may provide for periodic payments to a beneficiary beginning at age 25, 26, and so forth. Moreover, having too many alternatives on the table at one time may overload a client's circuits and hinder rather than facilitate a client's thinking.[19]

Hence, be content during Step Two with identification of a limited number of alternatives which respond to a client's initial objectives. The Step Three discussion of those alternatives may produce yet further objectives which necessitate a return to Step Two.

10. USE CHANGED CIRCUMSTANCES TO IDENTIFY ADDITIONAL ALTERNATIVES

Counseling is dynamic not only in the sense that clients often realize new objectives as they discuss consequences, but also in the sense that problems often take on new complexions as matters progress. As you know, new characteristics may arise because the outside world changes, or because of clients' changed attitudes or perceptions. Thus, the commercial office building owner who initially insisted on an extremely lessor-oriented lease may become more accommodating as changed economic conditions leave the building half occupied. Similarly, the client who was four sails to the wind in favor of defending a suit vigorously when it was first served may, months or even years later, develop the attitude that the suit is not worth defending. Thus, until a decision has been finally implemented, a client may voice objectives which require re-analysis of a decision you had thought was behind you.[20]

Such a re-analysis generally entails returning to Steps Two and Three. Often, fresh alternatives emerge in response to the changed circumstances. Too, an alternative which emerges might be one which a client has previously rejected. The dialogue may go something as follows:

19. See I.L. Janis and L. Mann, *Decision Making: A Psychological Analysis of Conflict, Choice, and Commitment* 22 (1977); S. Ellmann, "Lawyers and Clients," 34 UCLA.L.Rev. 717, 730 (1987).

20. See D.G. Gifford, *Legal Negotiation: Theory and Applications* Chap. 11 (1989).

1. L: Willie, I sent you the draft of the will and asked you to look it over. I'll go over it with you, but first do you have any questions?

2. C: Well, like I wanted, the will leaves everything to the Federation. But seeing it written out has made me more uncomfortable about leaving it so much money and disinheriting Eddie completely.

3. L: What has made you uncomfortable?

4. C: Well, I'm still worried about his gambling, and I'm afraid that he'll throw everything away. But I read recently that a lot of big charities spend almost as much money on fundraising as they do on their work. Plus I read that last week the Federation has put a lot of effort into something about spotted owls, and that's just not a big deal to me. So I'm just not too sure anymore.

5. L: You've really given this a lot of thought. You might remember that when we first talked I mentioned the possibility of your leaving some of your money to Eddie in trust, but after we talked about it you decided to disinherit him instead. Now that you have some concerns about the charity, perhaps we should think about a trust again. Does that make sense?

6. C: Yes. I'm a bit hazy on what you said before, so . . .

Chapter 19

REFINING AND TAILORING STEP THREE: IDENTIFYING CONSEQUENCES

* * *

(Fade in) Linda, you have the two options, casting approval and final cut approval. Which would you like to talk about first?

Probably the final cut. From what you said when you described what final cut approval means, that sounds pretty good.

Fine. Let me just ask you, what advantages do you see to being able to approve the final cut?

I guess that's when the producer and director decide what the audience actually sees. So since more people will probably associate my name with the movie than with the book, I should have some influence.

So one advantage of participating in the final cut is being able to protect your name and reputation. Any others?

Not that I can see.

How about disadvantages?

Well, here's something I just thought of. I wouldn't want time on the movie to interfere too much with the new novel I'm working on. How much time might it take?

That's difficult to predict, since so much depends on things like the shooting schedule and when the studio plans to release it. But your concern is valid, and I'll note that a possible disadvantage of participating in the final cut is interference with your current work. Any other disadvantages that you see?

What if the critics don't like the movie? If I've participated in the final cut . . . (Fade out)[1]

* * *

1. Since this example concerns "showbiz," it seemed fair to present a fantasy dialogue. In reality, few writers, espe-cially novices, have contracts with final cut or casting approval provisions.

1. INTRODUCTION

Once alternatives are on the table, during Step Three you and a client flush out their likely legal and nonlegal consequences. This chapter examines frequently-needed refinements in the flushing-out process, and it explores methods of facilitating clients' understanding and participation.

2. RESPONDING TO CONSEQUENCES A CLIENT FORESEES

The two subsections below briefly discuss issues that commonly arise when clients identify consequences.

A. CONVERT CONSEQUENCES INTO PROS AND CONS

As you recall, the counseling standard calls for clients to have a reasonable opportunity to understand alternatives' likely pros and cons. However, a client's mention of a consequence may leave you uncertain about whether a client regards it as a pro or a con of an option. In such instances, asking follow-up questions which convert consequences into the language of pros and cons helps clients evaluate options. The following examples illustrate the conversion process:

Case No. 1:

Lawyer: So you'd first like to talk about the option of going to trial?

Client: Yeah. And from what I've read, going to trial means this thing won't be resolved for a long time.

Lawyer: That's possible. But just so I understand, do you regard keeping this matter unresolved for some time an advantage or a disadvantage?

Case No. 2:

Lawyer: What do you see as the advantages of requesting a variance from the zoning board?

Client: Primarily, I can start the business in the location that I think is best. But another thing to think about is will the local homeowners' association get involved if I ask for a variance.

Lawyer: You think the homeowners' association might oppose the request?

Client: Yes.

Lawyer: So the possibility of getting into a fight with them is a potential disadvantage of seeking a variance?

Client: I'd say so.

In each case you ask follow-up questions to clarify your uncertainty about whether a consequence is a pro or a con.[2]

B. ASCERTAIN A CLIENT'S DATA BASE

Consider the following dialogue:

1. L: Mr. Derian, do you see any disadvantages of coming back to Woods with a proposal for a five-year employment contract?

2. C: I'm afraid that if we do that, she'll break off negotiations and look elsewhere.

Here, in line with the suggestions in Chapter 16, you have asked a client to predict nonlegal consequences, and Derian has done so. But whether Derian has *correctly* predicted a consequence of making the proposal depends in part on the quality of Derian's data base. Only if Derian has an adequate data base is the potential disadvantage one which should weigh heavily at the time a decision is made.[3] Thus, if you are uncertain of the quality of the data base on which a client bases a prediction, you may want to explore the nature of that data base in more detail. Whether you confirm the quality of a data base or reveal its paucity, the dialogue usually advances a client's understanding.

In the above example, you might continue as follows:

3. L: Woods' breaking off negotiations is certainly not what you want to happen. But why do you think that's what Woods will do?

4. C: Just my general sense, I guess. I've been in the high-tech industry for a while now, and in most of the companies I'm aware of, the entrepreneurial types who run them don't like to tie themselves down to long-term contracts.

5. L: And 5 years is considered a long-term contract?

6. C: Things change so fast in this business that anything over a year is long-term.

7. L: Do you know whether Woods has the same attitude towards long-term contracts as other entrepreneurs in the field?

8. C: I assume so.

9. L: Of course, we can lay out specific reasons that could justify Woods giving you a five-year contract. But even if Woods doesn't go along with it, do you know anything about her

---

2. Of course, sometimes follow-up questioning will be unnecessary, because the prior context will have made it clear how a client regards a consequence.

3. Remember, inferential errors in prediction are common. See sources cited in Chapter 16nn. 13–14. Moreover, recognize that predictions will never achieve scientific certainty. Even when a prediction is based on the past behavior of the individual whose behavior is being predicted, the typical infrequency of past behaviors and the likelihood of unique circumstances, makes prediction perilous.

specifically which leads you to think that she'll break off negotiations as opposed to countering?

10. C: Nothing specific, just a hunch. I don't really know her very well.

11. L: Can you think of any way of finding out more about how she's likely to respond to a five-year proposal?

12. C: Not really.

Here, when you inquire in No. 3 about Derian's data base, Derian responds in terms of industry practice generally (No. 4). Then, you follow up by asking whether the "entrepreneurial type" generalization applies to Woods (No. 7) and Derian's basis for thinking that Woods is likely to break off negotiations (No. 9). As this example demonstrates, exposing a client's data base can involve more than simply asking for the basis of a prediction. Typically, inquiries seek information about the previous actions of (a) the group of which the person whose behavior is being predicted is a member, and (b) the specific person whose behavior is being predicted.

In this example, you learn that Derian's data base is limited to awareness of characteristics of a group of which Woods is a part—high tech entrepreneurs. Also, Derian has little or no data base on the precise issue under discussion: whether Woods will break off negotiations. Therefore, you might want to consider whether additional data is needed for Derian to have a reasonable opportunity to make a decision. For example, you might consider contacting (or asking Derian to contact) other sources to check on the accuracy of Derian's assertions about industry norms and Woods personally. However, depending on factors such as the amount of time and money a client is willing to devote to a decision and the importance of the prediction to the decision, the most you might be able to do is inform the client of a prediction's shakiness. Assuming in the Woods matter that you decide not to probe further, a statement conveying the shakiness of the prediction may be helpful:

13. L: We'll list that one possible disadvantage of proposing a five-year contract is that Woods might break off the negotiations. However, we'll put an asterisk next to it to remind ourselves that we don't have much hard evidence to support the prediction. Would you agree with that?

3. HELPING CLIENTS RECOGNIZE NONLEGAL CONSEQUENCES

Chapter 16 pointed out that while you typically begin a Step Three probe for nonlegal consequences with open questions, you typically use lower-T, closed questions to search for additional potential consequences.[4] The following subsections briefly explore the bases upon which you commonly formulate the closed questions.

A. "INDUSTRY KNOWLEDGE"

Just as knowledge of the industries in which a problem is situated often suggests options, so too is such knowledge commonly the basis of closed questions seeking additional potential consequences. Though clients may in general be more expert than you when it comes to predicting economic, social and psychological consequences, using your industry knowledge often enables you to help clients recognize consequences that they do not foresee in response to open questions.

For example, assumè that in the above example, Derian is a computer programmer and analyst, and Woods is the President of an architectural company which uses computers to generate building plans. Woods has offered Derian an employment contract which is terminable by either party "at will." In the course of discussing that offer, Derian has suggested countering with the alternative of a five-year contract.

In response to open questions, Derian states that the potential "pros" of a five-year contract are security at a very good salary (economic and psychological consequences) and the opportunity to develop contacts with people who are very knowledgeable about Woods' state-of-the-art software design (social and economic consequences). The only potential "con" Derian foresees, based on Derian's conversations with former associates of Woods, is that Woods may respond by breaking off negotiations (uncertain negative economic, social and psychological consequences).

Computer industry knowledge may enable you to ask closed questions prompting Derian's recognition of additional social, economic and psychological pros or cons. In the economic realm, for example, you might ask how being in building design work for five years might impact on Derian's future employability. Within this topic, you might ask how working for Woods for five years might affect Derian's ability (1) to handle different computer languages, (2) to work in areas other than computer-aided design, (3) to develop and market new applications, and (4) to stay abreast of changes in hardware and software design. Such topics would become the basis of closed questions searching for economic pros and cons that Derian has not mentioned.

B. EVERYDAY EXPERIENCE

Everyday experience also is a good source of closed questions searching for additional potential social, economic and psychological consequences of decisions. At times, "knowledge of an industry" and everyday experience may overlap and lead you to identify similar potential consequences. However, the latter often enables you to identify consequences that the former does not.

4. See Chapter 16, sec. 5(D)(3).

For example, assume that you represent Whittington, a stockbroker who is charged with a securities-related offense which, even upon conviction, is unlikely to result in loss of license. Whittington has been offered a "plea bargain," and must decide whether to accept it or proceed toward trial. Everyday experience may enable you to ask Whittington about potential consequences of accepting the plea bargain, such as (a) the likely attitudes of Whittington's clients, family members, co-workers and friends (economic and social consequences); (b) the likely effect on Whittington's self-esteem (a psychological consequence); and (c) Whittington's potential sense of regret in future years if Whittington pleads guilty rather than pressing for complete acquittal (a psychological consequence). Without your prompting through a series of closed questions, such consequences may remain locked in Whittington's "data base," never intruding into Whittington's conscious awareness.

4. ARTICULATING LEGAL CONSEQUENCES YOU FORESEE

Predicting legal consequences is almost always your responsibility. And as set forth in Chapter 18, during Step Two you typically pithily state an option's most likely legal consequence when you first mention it. For example, if "go to trial" is an option, you might point out that the most probable result is "to recover $35,000 in damages." The following subsections examine how, during Step Three, you might articulate legal consequences in addition to "the most probable result."

A. LEGAL SUB-PREDICTIONS

Predictions about legal outcomes are often amalgams of sub-predictions. Understanding the factors you typically take into account when predicting a legal outcome should enable you to give clients more accurate predictions.

In litigation matters, sub-predictions may include (a) how a factfinder is likely to resolve disputed issues of fact; (b) how a court (trial or appellate) is likely to resolve unsettled questions of law; and (c) how a trial judge is likely to exercise discretion.

As to (a), parties dispute how historical events took place. Hekyll claims he had an oral agreement with Jekyll; Jekyll denies it. The State claims that Yeazell robbed a bank; Yeazell asserts an alibi. Marks claims that he became disabled after being struck by a car driven by Spencer; Spencer contends that Marks is not disabled and that whatever disability Marks has pre-existed the collision. In such cases, a prediction about legal outcome rests largely on a sub-prediction of how a factfinder is likely to resolve conflicting evidence.[5]

5. Much of your prediction will grow out of your analysis of how strongly parties' competing evidence tends to prove or disprove factual propositions, the topic of Chapter 9. For a somewhat different type of analysis termed "Litigation Risk Analysis," see M.B. Victor, "How Much Is a Case Worth?" Trial 48 (July, 1984).

As to (b), even when historical events are largely undisputed, parties disagree as to what legal rule ought to apply to those events. For example, assume that you represent a client seeking a jury trial in a bankruptcy matter. Prediction of a legal outcome would rest primarily on a sub-prediction about how a court is likely to resolve the currently unsettled legal question of whether a bankruptcy referee, who is not an "Article III" judge, can hold a jury trial.[6]

Finally, as to (c), even when the law and the facts are clear, a matter's outcome may rest on a judge's (or jury's) exercise of discretion. Judges, and sometimes juries, often have wide latitude when it comes to specific outcomes.[7] For example, after conviction a defendant may be sent to prison or placed on probation. Likewise, a probate judge usually has discretion as to how large a family allowance to award a decedent's family. Finally, a judge (or jury) has discretion to decide what damages are appropriate to award an injured civil litigant by way of punitive damages. In each of these cases, a prediction would involve a sub-prediction of how discretion is likely to be exercised.

Predictions about legal outcomes in transactional matters also often rest on sub-predictions. The sub-predictions tend to fall largely into categories (b) and (c) above, since factual issues usually have not ripened in transactional contexts. For example, since every provision of a proposed agreement is a potential gleam in a litigator's eye, you may need to predict whether a court will uphold a non-competition clause in an employment agreement. In turn, that prediction may rest on a sub-prediction about how a court is likely to interpret its language, a sub-prediction falling into category (b), above. And, in a matter in which a client seeks a liquor license for a restaurant located in a primarily residential area, you may need to predict whether the Alcoholic Beverage Control Board will issue the license. Since the Board is likely to have discretion, the prediction falls primarily into category (c) above.

When a transactional matter is subject to review by a government agency, additional sub-predictions may be required. To the extent you predict the outcome of agency review, the sub-predictions mirror those above. But in addition, you sometimes need to make sub-predictions about the likelihood of agency review itself. Typically, such sub-predictions consist of whether an agency will review a matter, and if so, when. For example, assume that a client is concerned about whether an exchange of property will qualify as a tax free exchange. If the client wants to claim that the exchange is tax free, you may need to make the usual sub-predictions about what conclusion an audit will reach and what consequences will ensue if the IRS finds that the exchange was taxable. But in addition, you may have to make sub-

6. See *In re Ben Cooper, Inc.*, 896 F.2d 1394 (2d Cir.1990).

7. Of course, an appellate court may overturn the result if it finds an abuse of discretion.

predictions about whether the IRS is likely to audit the return, and when.[8]

B. STATE PREDICTIONS IN PERCENTAGE TERMS

Given the inherent riskiness of predictions, you may be inclined to take refuge in vague terminology. For example, you may say that, "We've got a pretty good shot at a not guilty verdict," or, "I don't think a copyright violation claim would hold up."

Vague terminology is more likely to create misimpressions than inform. If you tell a client that she has a "pretty good shot" at winning, she may think she has a 90% chance of success. Meanwhile you, knowing in your own mind that the case was somewhat of an uphill fight from the outset, meant that she had a 40% chance of winning. Hence, without suggesting more certainty than you really feel, you can enhance client understanding by describing legal outcomes in percentage terms. Compare these assertions:

1. "There's a small chance that if we go to trial, you'll recover punitive damages." vs. "There's a small chance, about 10%, that if we go to trial you'll recover punitive damages."

2. "I'm reasonably certain that the Board will approve the request for a variance." vs. "I'm 90% certain that the Board will approve the request for a variance."

Whether in litigation or transactional contexts, statements of percentage are more tangible than vague assertions and are more to clients' liking.[9] Unless you reduce a discussion to specific figures, chances are excellent that clients will misunderstand the prediction you had in mind. (At least they will 64% of the time!) [10]

C. IDENTIFY A RANGE OF PREDICTIONS

If clients are to have a reasonable opportunity to decide, they need to know more than an option's "most likely outcome." Thus, during Step Three, you must inform clients of other possible results that are somewhat less likely. For example, assume that you have told a client who must decide whether or not to go to trial that the "most likely result" of trial is that the client will have judgment entered against him in the amount of $76,000. A reasonable opportunity to decide requires that you inform the client that the worst likely judgment that might be entered is $104,000, and that the best he can expect to do is to have judgment entered against him in the amount of $25,000.[11]

8. See B. Wolfman & J.P. Holden, *Ethical Problems in Federal Tax Practice* 161–172 (1985).

9. See "A Businessman's View of Lawyers," 33 Bus.Law. 817 (1978).

10. Recognize that even using percentages cannot overcome all communication barriers. For example, your interpretation of "a 70% chance" may vary from a cli-

ent's. However, language is inherently ambiguous. See G.E. Myers and M.T. Myers, *The Dynamics of Human Communication* 122–125 (1988). Using percentages can reduce, not eliminate, ambiguity.

11. Beyond the boundaries set by the "worst likely" and the "best likely" outcomes are the extremes of the "best possible" and "worst possible" outcomes. These

Though you might think of a range of possible outcomes principally in connection with litigation, transactional matters too often produce ranges. For example, you might tell a builder whose application for a building permit is subject to an environmental impact report that "the most likely" outcome is that the city will require the builder to pay for widening the street; the "best likely" result is that the builder will share those costs equally with the city; and the "worst likely" result is denial of the permit. Similarly, the most likely result of a prospective employee's proposing a 5 year employment contract may be that the employer makes a counter-offer. The best likely result may be that the proposal is accepted; the worst likely may be that the employer cuts off negotiations.[12]

Outcomes in addition to the "most likely" ones also should be described in percentage terms. For instance, you might tell the prospective employee that "The best we can hope for is that Varat will accept our offer, but I'd say the chances of that are pretty small, probably around 30%. Of course, at worst Varat may cut off negotiations altogether, but I'd say the chances of that happening are even smaller, about 10%."

You may sometimes believe that using a specific percentage conveys more certainty than you really feel. In such situations, using numbers permits you to describe a range-within-a-range. If you are not exactly sure how small the chance is that Varat will cut off negotiations entirely, you might say "the chances of that happening are even smaller, about 10–20%." As long as you do not opt for too much elasticity ("the chances of that are somewhere between 10 and 90%"), figures are more meaningful than vague terms such as "pretty good."

D. CHARACTERIZE LEGAL PREDICTIONS AS ADVANTAGES AND DISADVANTAGES

At this point, you may be wondering how to integrate an analysis of legal predictions into a Step Three dialogue. You do so by characterizing potential outcomes as either advantages or disadvantages. That is, the "best likely" outcome of an option is an advantage, the "worst

extremes may be only a theoretical possibility in one case, and a realistic consideration in another. For example, consider two personal injury cases in which you represent the plaintiffs. In the one, punitive damages in the amount of a million dollars may be a theoretical possibility, but extremely implausible; whereas in the other, punitive damages in that amount may not be "likely," but nevertheless an outcome within the realm of reason. In the first case you would not mention that the "best possible outcome is that you'll be awarded punitive damages in the amount of $1 million;" in the other, you might well make such a statement. Recognize, however, that in a few circumstances you may be required to mention extreme possibilities, even though the chances of their occurring are remote. See (criminal cases where defendants try to set aside guilty pleas; check the law as to civil cases.) Finally, note that in any given matter, an extreme possibility may be synonymous with a likely one. For example, the "best likely" outcome may also be the "best possible" one. Thus, in a criminal case, "not guilty" may constitute both the "best likely" and the "best possible" result.

12. The fact that these predictions involve non-legal outcomes does not alter the need to present a client with a range of possible outcomes.

likely" is a disadvantage, and the "most likely" may be one or the other, depending upon how it compares to the most likely outcome of other options.[13]

Example One—Transactional Matter

Assume that your client is a builder who is considering the options of (a) applying for a permit to build an office complex in a highly developed area; and (b) applying for a permit to build the complex in a less congested area. Assume further that the "most likely" outcome of option "a" is that the builder will receive a permit subject to having to pay for street widening and provide excess parking. The "best likely" outcome is that the city will grant the permit without restrictions; and the "worst likely" is that the city will deny the permit. You might discuss these consequences as follows:

1. L: One advantage of going ahead with the application is that you retain a slim chance, no more than 20%, that the city will grant the permit without restriction. A disadvantage is that you take a very small risk, 10% or less, of having the city deny the permit altogether, and you will have wasted time and money. However, as I told you earlier, the most likely result is that the city will grant the permit, but it will require you to pay for street widening and to provide excess parking. I think the chances are at least 70–80% that the city will impose these requirements.

2. C: Why do you think that? This office complex will be a great asset to the community, and I don't think the city should create all these roadblocks.

3. L: I appreciate how much time and money you've spent designing this building. But a local ordinance gives the City Planning Office the power to review building applications and impose various conditions, and as you know in recent times that Office has been under pressure from homeowner and consumer groups to manage growth. Based on the street widening and excess parking requirements that have been imposed on other applications in the central district, I think it likely that the same requirements will be applied to your project.

   By comparison to the other site that you are considering, would you see this result as an advantage or disadvantage?

4. C: Frankly, while these requirements would increase costs on the front end, both might end up as advantages. Wider streets and more parking may enhance the overall attractiveness of the building and allow us to charge higher rents. On balance, it seems better than the other site. But what are the odds there?

13. For a discussion of integrating legal predictions into a Step Three examination of consequences, see Chapter 16, sec. 5(D)(6).

5. L: One advantage of site "b" is that there is a 0% chance that the city will deny your application. By choosing "b," therefore, you avoid the 10% risk with site "a" that you will spend money and time pursuing an application which is ultimately turned down. At the same time, a disadvantage of "b" is that by going ahead with the site "b" application, you give up the 20% chance that the city will grant the permit for site "a" without restrictions. The most likely outcome of going with site "b", I'd say as high as 90–95%, is that the city will grant a permit without imposing restrictions. I assume you regard this as an advantage?

6. C: Well, sure. But this discussion has helped me realize that the economics of the deal probably outweigh whatever legal requirements the city imposes. By building in the central district . . .

In this dialogue, No. 1 characterizes the "best likely" and "worst likely" outcomes as a pro and a con respectively. When you mention the most likely result, the client, in No. 2, questions the basis of the prediction. In No. 3 you make an active listening response and a sub-prediction, explaining the rule and the past actions of the Planning Office which give rise to the prediction.[14] In No. 4, the client characterizes the "most likely" result as an advantage, and he then "crosses over" to the other option. In No. 5, you point out how the options mirror each other. That is, an advantage of one option is a disadvantage of another. Here, for example, the site "b" option carries no risk of disapproval, but gives up the chance that site "a" will be approved without restriction.[15] In No. 5 you also identify the "most likely" result of option "b," and based on the earlier discussion characterize it as an advantage. In No. 6 the client agrees, and he recognizes that whatever the legal outcome, nonlegal consequences will play the major role in decision-making.

14. In the absence of the client's specific request, you probably would not have disclosed the sub-prediction. Clients tend to be bottom-line oriented, and often do not want an exposition of the reasoning leading to predictions. Of course, even if you do not verbalize sub-predictions, they are necessary to the prediction that you do verbalize. Finally, had the client not only questioned the prediction but indicated skepticism, you might have asked if the client had a contrary legal prediction in mind and explored its basis. See Chapter 16 n 15.

15. In general, no "magic words" spell victory or defeat for carrying out any of the techniques described in this book. However, in our experience you can greatly facilitate client understanding of comparative pros and cons of options by pointing out that with respect to the "best possible" outcome, one option allows a client to "retain" the chance that the outcome will occur, while another option "gives up" that chance. Conversely, with respect to the "worst possible" outcome, you may point out that one option "creates a risk" that that outcome will occur, while another option "avoids the risk."

Example Two—Litigation Matter

Assume that your client, Meadow, has brought suit for fraud in the sale of a house. The complaint alleges that the sellers concealed certain defects in the property, and seeks damages in the amount of $90,000, and punitive damages in an unspecified amount. After some of the usual pretrial skirmishes and discovery proceedings have taken place, the defendant offers to settle for $35,000. Meadow's options are to (1) accept the offer; (2) make a counter-offer [16]; or (3) proceed to trial. You believe that the "most likely" result of trial (a 70–75% chance) is that Meadow will recover $53,000 in general damages and nothing by way of punitive damages.[17] You believe there is only a 10% chance of the "best likely" result, $90,000, and again little chance that Meadow will be awarded punitive damages. On the downside, you believe that there is a very small chance—about 10%—of the "worst" likely result, Meadow recovering nothing.[18] As to settlement, the most likely result of Meadow's accepting the offer is of course the 100% chance that Meadow will realize $35,000. Should Meadow reject the offer, you believe that the "worst likely" result nearly coincides with the most likely one, because there is but a small chance, about 10–15%, that the other side will reduce or withdraw its offer. The "best likely" result of rejection is about a 30% chance that another, higher offer will be made before trial, perhaps around $40,000.

Examination of a simple diagram illustrates that the advantages of one option are typically the disadvantages of another:

TRIAL ALTERNATIVE	SETTLEMENT ALTERNATIVE
70–75 percent chance of $53,000. (Most Likely)	$35,000
Advantages Retain ten percent chance to recover $90,000. (Best Likely)	**Advantages** Avoid ten percent chance of receiving nothing. (Worst Likely)
Disadvantages Take ten percent chance of recovering nothing. (Worst Likely)	**Disadvantages** Give up ten percent chance to recover $90,000. (Best Likely)

[F5540]

16. To simplify the discussion, we omit further discussion of the counter-proposal option.

17. To simplify the discussion, we omit mention of attorney's fees and other costs. In an actual discussion, you would work through the calculations necessary to convert "gross" figures to "net."

18. Note that in situations when a client may come away completely empty-handed, the "worst likely" and the "worst possible" outcomes overlap completely.

As you see, by way of example, one advantage of trial (Meadow retains about a 10% chance of recovering $90,000) is a disadvantage of settlement (Meadow gives up the 10% chance to recover $90,000). Similarly, one advantage of settlement (Meadow avoids the 10% risk of recovering nothing) is a disadvantage of trial (Meadow takes a 10% chance of recovering nothing).

Again, a sample dialogue may help you think about how to discuss consequences with clients:

1. L: Why don't we turn to whether to accept their settlement offer or proceed toward trial? Which option do you want to talk about first?

2. C: Trial, definitely.

3. L: I know how anxious you are to testify about what happened, so I've reviewed the case thoroughly. As I've said the most likely outcome of trial, about a 70% chance, is that you'll recover $53,000. That's not a figure I picked out of the air—it covers repair of the cracked foundation and structural problems in the house related to it. At the same time, I think there is close to a 0% chance you'll be awarded punitive damages.

4. C: But I really got screwed. Why wouldn't I get punitive damages?

5. L: Remember that punitive damages are designed to punish. Jurors have lots of discretion in awarding them, subject of course to review by the judge. In this case, because we admit that the sellers gave you ready access to the house, and you hired a home inspection service to prepare a report prior to the sale, I think it unlikely that you'll get punitive damages.

6. C: And why only the $53,000 figure?

7. L: That's my best estimate of how the jurors are likely to resolve the conflicts in the experts' testimony. Our expert will testify to the cracks in the foundation, and their likely cause. Their expert will testify that there's nothing wrong with the foundation but frankly I think the jurors will believe our expert. I'm basing the $53,000 figure primarily on that factor. The other damages relate to problems with the roof and the front and back yard. Our expert's testimony cannot tie those problems to the foundation, and I think there is little evidence that the sellers were aware of those problems. That's why I place the chance of recovering $90,000 at only about 10%.

8. C: Well, I must say it's not as good as I hoped for.

9. L: I understand your disappointment. But let's talk more about trial—what do you see as the advantages of rejecting the offer and proceeding to trial?

10. C: Well, it sounds like I'll get more money than they're offering. And at trial I could do even better than $53,000, right?

11. L: That is another possible advantage, that you retain the 10% chance that you'll recover as much as $90,000.

12. C: One thing about settlement, it puts money in my pocket much sooner. So I guess that's an advantage of settling. Aside from the delay, is there any other reason why I shouldn't go to trial?

13. L: A disadvantage of trial we have to keep in mind is that you could come away empty-handed. Lawyers always remind clients that trial is never a sure thing. However, given the strength of our expert, I'd say the chance of losing is slight—maybe 10–15%.

14. C: That doesn't sound too bad. However, there's something else that might be a disadvantage. It just came up last week. I've been contacted about a job offer out of state . . .

Abundantly willing to follow the counseling model, in No. 1 you ask Meadow which option she prefers discussing. In No. 3 you make an active listening response, then remind Meadow of the likely outcome of trial, the option Meadow chose to discuss first. (Remember, you would have mentioned the likely outcome when presenting the trial option during Step Two.) Sub-predictions are the subject of Nos. 4 through 7. The sub-predictions involve the trier's exercise of discretion (No. 5) and factual uncertainty (No. 7). In No. 9 you empathize with Meadow's disappointment, and ask what she sees as the advantages of the trial option. When Meadow in No. 10 mentions the chance of getting more money, in No. 11 you restate that chance in percentage terms as an advantage. In No. 12 Meadow crosses over, both to disadvantages and to the settlement option. You partially cross over by describing a disadvantage of trial in No. 13. The dialogue concludes with Meadow in No. 14 about to mention a nonlegal disadvantage.

E. ENSURING THAT CLIENTS HEAR YOU

In everyday life, you have undoubtedly experienced numerous conversations in which thoughts pass by each other like ships in the night. You are talking about one thing; a friend is talking about something else. Much the same thing can happen during counseling. You may mention a consequence, only to have a client respond to some different point entirely.[19]

Since any technique will fail unless a client attends to what you say, be alert for indications that a client has not heard you. Apart from repeating yourself, or speaking louder, one technique you may

19. Usually, the point is one which the client has already made at least a half dozen times despite your repeated efforts at active listening.

find useful is to ask a client to repeat what you have said. That way, you will know that you have been heard, even if you cannot be certain that you have been understood.

For example, assume that at No. 13, the previous dialogue with Meadow had gone as follows:

13. L: A disadvantage of trial we have to keep in mind is that you could come away empty-handed. Lawyers always remind clients that trial is never a sure thing. However, given the strength of our expert, I'd say the chance of losing is slight—maybe 10–15%.

14. C: I'm still really bothered about not getting punitive damages. If ever there was a case where someone should get punitive damages, this is it.

15. L: I understand how angry you are; you've made that point before. But I want to make sure that you realize there's a 10–15% chance that we'd come away with nothing after a trial. Just to make sure that you understand the situation, why don't you tell me what I said about coming away with nothing after trial?

While the request in No. 15 may initially strike you as patronizing, such requests are sometimes needed for you to feel confident that you have been heard.

Chapter 20

REFINING AND TAILORING
STEP FOUR: DECISION MAKING

* * *

I really appreciate all the time you've spent with me going over this, but I still can't decide between taking what they've offered and going to trial. What do you think I ought to do?

* * *

1. INTRODUCTION

If you have engaged a client in a full counseling dialogue, together you and a client will have identified objectives and visually linked pros and cons to specific options. Such a process provides a client with a reasonable opportunity to decide, and, more often than not, a client in fact makes an implementable decision. This chapter examines processes that do not run quite so smoothly.

One issue that commonly creates bumps in the course of decision-making is how to respond to clients who ask for your opinion about what they should do; section 2 below addresses that issue. Another issue concerns what to do when clients who seek to make decisions on their own are unable to do so; suggestions for coping with this scenario are in section 3. Recognize, however, that both issues may arise in the course of a single discussion. For example, clients who seek to make their own decision may be unable to do so, then ask for your opinion, and after you give it still be unable to decide. Hence, the fact that we address the issues separately does not imply that they are necessarily independent of each other.

2. CLIENT REQUESTS YOUR OPINION

Responding to client requests for your opinion about what to do primarily concerns not whether, but how and when you give it.[1]

---

1. As you may recall from Chapter 15, we define advice-giving broadly to include both advising of consequences and advising which option a client should choose. The discussion in this section is limited to the latter meaning.

A. GIVING ADVICE BASED ON CLIENTS' VALUES

When you give an opinion, client-centeredness suggests that you usually do so on the basis of each client's unique mix of values and attitudes towards the consequences at stake.[2] Thus, if a client asks for your opinion early on, you should normally withhold it until after you have engaged the client in a thorough counseling dialogue. However, explain your desire to postpone giving your opinion in an empathic manner which indicates that you are aware of the client's request and will respond to it. A dialogue conveying such an explanation may go as follows:

> Lawyer: Next, Diana, why don't we turn to the question I asked you to think about, whether to insist on a personal guarantee from the officers?

> Client: I've been thinking about it a lot, and I'm still not sure what to do. What do you suggest?

> Lawyer: I hate to sound like a lawyer, but there's not one right answer. A lot depends on the unique circumstances of your situation. What I suggest is this. Let's discuss the likely pros and cons both of having and not having personal guarantees. We'll even prepare a chart of the likely consequences. If you still want my opinion after we've done that, I'll certainly give it to you. But by postponing my view, I'll be able to take what you say into account in giving you my opinion. Does that sound all right?

> Client: Sure.

Sometimes clients will not agree to a counseling dialogue. For example, after the explanation above, instead of "Sure," Diana might have said,

> Client: That sounds like it'll take some time, and frankly I don't want to devote the time or money to it. You're a lawyer, and I'm sure you've come across these situations lots of times. I'll go along with what you think is best.

Here, the client refuses the invitation to go through the counseling process, and again asks for your opinion. Should you give it? The answer depends on whether the client has had a "reasonable opportunity" to make the decision.[3] That, in turn, entails consideration of, among other things, the relative importance of the decision in the framework of the client's problem and the content and extent of your

---

2. This comment assumes that the client wants to know what you would do if you were in the client's shoes. Sometimes, of course, a client wants to know what decision you would make on your own behalf, given your own values and preferences; as to that possibility, see subsection (3) below. Usually, you will be able to make a judgment based on the entire context about which form of opinion a client wants. If you are unsure, ask.

3. See Chapter 15, sec. 6(C).

prior discussions with Diana. Assuming you believe that Diana has had a reasonable opportunity to decide, you might respond as follows:

Lawyer: I'm not sure that I know what's best. But you tell me if I'm wrong. My sense is that your primary objective is for this deal to go through and that you feel the company itself is pretty solid. If I'm right about those things, probably you're better off not insisting on personal guarantees. Is that a decision you're comfortable with?

Note that you couch the advice in terms of the client's apparent values, invite the client to disagree if you have the values wrong, and conclude by giving the client room to have the last word. Thus, when you do give advice, you do so as much as possible based on the client's values.[4]

In a second type of scenario, clients make (or renew) requests for your opinion after a thorough counseling dialogue has taken place. In these situations, you are at least confident that a client has had a reasonable opportunity to decide. The advice-giving dialogue might proceed as follows:

Client: I know we've gone round and round on this, but I just can't decide. What do you think I ought to do?

Lawyer: Well, I agree that it's time to cut bait on this one. In the abstract, either decision might be proper, so primarily my advice grows out of what you've said as we've talked. I know your accountant has advised you to get personal guarantees, and I don't want to come between you and her. You can tell me if I'm wrong, but what you've indicated is that your primary objective is for this deal to go through, and that you feel the company itself is pretty solid. Also, you have some fear that insisting on guarantees might sour this deal and spoil future business opportunities. Based on these feelings, I think you'd be best off not insisting on personal guarantees. Does that seem sound?

As you can see, the advice remains tied to the client's values. But since a full counseling dialogue has already taken place, you have a richer data base from which to operate, and can give advice on what the client has actually said.

B. OFFERING OPINIONS BASED ON YOUR PERSONAL VALUES

Chapter 15 pointed out that clients may ask for and are entitled to receive opinions based on your own personal values.[5] That is, they want to know what you personally would do if you faced the same decision as they do.

---

4. See Chapter 2, sec. 2(D); Chapter 15, sec. 6(D).

5. Chapter 15, sec. 6(D).

Assume that a client asks, "What would you do personally?" or, "I want to do what's right. Do you think I'm doing the right thing?" These questions are ambiguous in terms of what sort of reply the client expects. You should ask a question such as the following to clarify the ambiguity:

"Just so I'm clear, do you want to know what I'd do if I were in your shoes, or what I would personally do, given my own values and objectives?"

In response, a client may say one or the other, or both. In any event, when a client does want to know what you personally would do, be sure to mention the values and attitudes on which you rest your decision. That way, clients can compare their attitudes to yours when deciding how much weight to give your opinion.

For example, assume that you represent an employer who has to decide which form of non-competition clause to include in a contract proposal to a prospective employee, Huber. One option is a very restrictive clause which has an 80% chance of being held invalid; the other is a less restrictive provision which is in all likelihood valid. The latter provision would give Huber far more opportunity to seek other employment should Huber cease working for the employer after signing the contract. The client asks, "Which clause would you personally choose if you were in this situation?" You might respond,

"That's pretty difficult to say—I've never been in this exact situation. But in my experience people often go along with what they agree to. Also, I'm pretty willing to take risks, and here I'd be willing to take the risk that Huber will live up to the agreement rather than try to defy it and risk being sued. So based on that, I'd choose the more restrictive language. Now you may feel differently, in which case you might not want to do what I would do."

This statement tells the client that your opinion is based on your experience with how people generally behave and your willingness to take risks. The client can then compare her or his beliefs with yours and decide how much stock to put in your opinion.

3. CLIENT IS UNABLE TO DECIDE

Lucia Blanco consults you with respect to a will. No more than five minutes after the start of the initial interview, you learn that she is in a quandary over whether to have a will or a inter vivos trust. Several conversations later, Blanco has in hand a detailed chart of both options and their likely consequences. You then get a telephone call from her: "You know, I just can't decide whether to go with a will or an inter vivos trust."

As this scenario suggests, even a substantial review of options does not always break the logjam of indecision. The subsections below discuss three techniques for doing so—clarifying conflicting feelings, rating consequences and providing your opinion.

A. CLARIFYING CONFLICTING FEELINGS

Frequently, indecision stems from the fact that all available options have pros and cons, and having to settle on only one option creates internal conflicts. The conflicts may involve "win-win," "win-lose," or "lose-lose" feelings.[6]

In *win-lose* conflicts, clients have both positive and negative feelings about the same option. For example, a client may say, "Settling puts cash in my pocket now, but I don't want my family to think I was afraid to go to trial." Or, a client may say, "I like the security of a five-year lease, but this business changes so fast I hate to lock us in to this location."

In *lose-lose* conflicts, clients have primarily negative feelings about all available options. For instance, a client may say, "If I settle now, I get practically nothing. Trial involves delays and lots of expenses. Either way, I get ripped off." Or, a client may say, "I can operate my studio where I want to only under such restrictions that it's almost impossible to stay in business, or I can operate it in a completely different part of town. You call that a choice?"

In *win-win* conflicts, clients have primarily positive feelings about all available options. Conflict arises because accepting the pros of one alternative means giving up the pros of another. For example, a client says, "If I proceed towards trial, I will get no less than $30,000, and possibly as much as $70,000. If I accept their settlement offer, I get $22,000. Frankly, when I first came to see you I never thought I'd get as much as $10,000. I don't know what to do." Or, a client may say, "By granting the lessee an option for a second five-year term, I have the advantage of including a rent escalation clause based on today's tight rental market. But by not giving an option, I can take advantage of what might be an even tighter market five years down the road. I'm not sure which route is better."

Because each type of conflict may create a belief that no single alternative is satisfactory, conflicting feelings often create indecision. By explicitly and empathically identifying the conflict, you can help clients understand that conflicts are inevitable and thereby enable them to make decisions. Sometimes explicit recognition of a conflict alone prompts a decision. If not, you may follow identification of conflict by suggesting that clients re-think their options in the light of the clarified feelings. Consider these examples:

---

6. As the old cliche about optimists seeing cups as half full and pessimists seeing them as half empty reminds us, clients' conflicting feelings may arise as much from their own reactions to situations as from situations themselves. For example, one client may see having to decide between two possible guardians as a "win-win" situation, while another sees it as "lose-lose." This reality hearkens back to our repeated emphasis on the predominance of subjective personal values. See, e.g., Chapter 15, sec. 3.

Win–Lose

Client: I like the security of a five-year lease, but this business changes so fast I hate to lock us in to this location.

Lawyer: You feel that a five-year lease will enable you to make definite plans, but at the risk of not being where the action is five years down the road. It seems like you can't have both security and absolute flexibility . . .. Given this conflict, do you want to think again about the pros and cons of each option?

Lose–Lose

Client: If I settle now, I get practically nothing. Trial involves delays and lots of expenses. Either way, I get ripped off.

Lawyer: Neither choice is appealing. You're going to feel like a victim of the judicial system whether you settle or go to trial . . .. Perhaps we should re-examine the options, and try to figure out which alternative will make you feel less ripped off.

Win–Win

Client: If I proceed towards trial, I will get no less than $30,000, and possibly as much as $70,000. If I accept their settlement offer, I get $22,000. Frankly, when I first came to see you I never thought I'd get as much as $10,000. I don't know what to do.

Lawyer: Compared to your initial expectations, you feel like a winner whichever option you choose. However, you have some doubts about which alternative will work out better in the long run . . .. Maybe by looking at the alternatives again, you can try to figure out which one seems more satisfactory.

B. RATING CONSEQUENCES

Most clients cannot assign precise values to consequences.[7] For example, a client usually cannot say, "The risk of getting nothing if we try the case is a minus 8 on my Scale of Satisfaction, whereas the chance of settling now for $15,000 is a plus 5." However, asking clients to revisit and rate consequences typically enables them to distinguish more generally between "more" or "less" important consequences, and finally to make decisions.

For example, consider the client who is having trouble deciding between the "win-win" options of (a) settling for $22,000 and (b) going to trial and receiving $30,000 and possibly $70,000. A "rating conse-quences" dialogue might proceed as follows:

7. See Chapter 15, sec. 3.

1. L: Sometimes, Mr. Kuperberg, it helps if clients identify which consequences are more important to them. Let's go back over the ones we've listed to see which ones you think are really important. We've got our two options of settlement or trial; which do you want to start with?

2. C: Trial, I suppose. We started with that one before, so maybe it'll bring me luck.

3. L: Fine. Now, of course one advantage of trial is retaining the 20% chance that you'll recover as much as $70,000, or almost $50,000 more than they're offering. Does this advantage strike you as an important one?

4. C: Well, I don't have to tell you what that kind of money would mean to my family. I know the chance of that is slight, but if it happens, it could really make a difference. I'd say that's pretty important.

5. L: On a 1–5 scale, with five being the most important, how many points would you give it?

6. C: I guess, I'd give it a three.

7. L: Ok. I'll mark down three plus marks on our little chart here. Now, another advantage is that going to trial will teach them a lesson, make them really understand what they did wrong. How important is this one?

8. C: When we first started all this, it was really important. It still is, but seeing what I've put them through so far makes actually going to trial seem not so important.

9. L: It's a less important advantage than the chance of recovering $70,000?

10. C: Definitely.

11. L: All right, what do you say we give that a plus one? Now, another advantage . . ..

The rating of consequences may continue through the advantages and disadvantages of different options. Eventually, you arrive at a question such as,

Lawyer: Now, Mr. Kuperberg, maybe you can look at each option according to the importance of its advantages and disadvantages. See if that helps you decide which alternative seems best.

While the rating process may seem long and tedious, indecisive clients often benefit from the concreteness of this approach.

C. OFFERING ADVICE TO BREAK LOGJAMS

Some clients fail to reach decisions despite your repeated efforts to help them do so. Among other factors, either their personalities or the thorniness of their problems make it very difficult for some clients to make decisions. Often, undecided clients will ask for your opinion, which returns you to the discussion in section 2 above. But even if they do not, offering your opinion in an effort to break a decisional logjam is consistent with client-centered lawyering. Hearing your opinion often leads clients to make decisions, even if they do not always follow your advice.

The propriety of offering your unsolicited opinion follows from the simple truth that indecisive clients do not have a choice between "decision" and "no decision." In most instances, a non-decision is itself a decision. Thus, refusing to intervene when a client is unable to decide does not preserve client autonomy, but rather may produce a decision with which a client is unhappy. For example, assume that a client has to decide whether or not to take a series of depositions. The client's inability to decide is the equivalent of a decision not to take the depositions. Similarly, in a transactional context a client may be undecided about whether to propose including an arbitration clause in a contract. Indecision is the equivalent to there being no arbitration clause.

Offering advice to break a decisional logjam is typically a two-step process. First, enhance a client's willingness to listen to your opinion by pointing out explicitly that a non-decision is by default a decision:

> "Jean, we've got to submit our contract proposal by 5:00 tonight. I know we've talked about this at length, but do you understand that if you can't decide whether to include an arbitration clause in the contract, that's the same as saying that we won't put one in?"

Second, state your opinion relying on your understanding of the client's values:

> "Since we can't escape making a decision of one sort or the other, let me give you my advice. As we talked, whenever I pointed out that some people promote arbitration as a relatively inexpensive and quick way to resolve disputes, you always mentioned a couple of cases you heard of where arbitration was just about as expensive as going to court and where a person was shafted by an unfair arbitrator, and frankly there is some validity to what you say. My sense is that you really feel uncomfortable with an arbitration provision, and therefore I would advise you against it. Maybe I've misread you, but does that make sense?"

As you see, your statement in this context differs little from when a client asks for your opinion. Your advice is tailored to the client's articulated values and attitudes, and you invite the client's response.

D. INABILITY TO OFFER ADVICE TO BREAK LOGJAMS

This chapter has advised you to offer opinions about what clients should do when they ask for your opinion, and when your opinion may break a logjam. However, sometimes you may decline to offer an opinion despite a client's request for it and the existence of a logjam. Typically, the reason you decline is that you lack a valid basis for providing an opinion.

You have two possible bases for offering an opinion: (1) a client's values; and (2) the values you personally would favor were you making the decision. If a client's conflicting expression of values gives you no fair sense of what choice is most likely to be satisfactory, you cannot readily rest an opinion on a client's values. And, if one or more available options' likely consequences are unpredictable, you may feel that you lack the data base to state what you personally would do were you in a client's situation. Thus, you may lack both possible bases for offering an opinion and be left holding only a "no opinion" bag.

When you decline to provide an opinion, realize that your reluctance may frustrate a client. Hence, explain why it is you cannot give advice, empathizing with the client's plight as you do so. At the same time, clarify the "default" position—that is, state what will happen if a client is unable to make a decision. Finally, encourage a client to give the matter further thought.

For example, assume that during counseling, Amy, a company executive, has repeatedly expressed conflicting feelings about granting an option for a 15–year lease renewal to a prospective tenant. Though you have tried to clarify her conflicting feelings and to specify which consequences are most important, she is unable to decide. Moreover, you feel that the decision is primarily a "business" one about which you lack a data base for predicting the likely outcome. Your "advice" to Amy might be limited to something like the following:

"Amy, it doesn't appear that you've been able to come to a decision on this. And I can understand your hesitancy. From what you've said, they're likely to be a model tenant, and it would be beneficial to your company to have a quarter of the space leased. But as you've also pointed out, giving that long an option has the potential disadvantage of tying up the property, and might make it difficult to sell if that's what your company decides to do down the road. I'd give you my opinion if I had a strong feeling as to whether the risk is worth taking. But you and the company have to live with any decision, and frankly it's not one I feel I have the expertise to make. I can tell you that your failure to agree to an option will probably cause them to walk away from the deal, so you probably want to come to some decision. What I suggest is this. I'll tell them we need another day or two to get back to them. Meanwhile, you can talk it over with some other people at the company, and get back to me."

You may make similar statements in a litigation context. For example, assume that you have counseled Brice with respect to his conflicting feelings about whether to institute suit against Oliver, a customer. In response to Brice's question about what you think he ought to do, you might say something along these lines:

"Brice, that's really a question I can't answer. On the one hand, recovering for the damages Oliver has caused you is very important, given your company's need for capital. On the other, apparently other customers on whom you depend will be very upset if you proceed with a lawsuit. It's a tough call, and I just don't know enough to advise you what to do. You have to live with the decision, and I can do no more than make sure you are aware of each option's likely consequences. Believe me, if I had a strong opinion about what you ought to do, I'd give it to you. Of course, if in the end you are unable to make a decision, that's the equivalent of deciding not to sue Oliver. Why don't you think about it? If you decide to file suit, call me and I'll take it from there. Just remember, as I indicated to you, to contact me before May 30, or it'll be too late to file a lawsuit."

4. CLIENT REACHES A DECISION WITH WHICH YOU DISAGREE

As you recall, you may want to intervene in decisions either when you think a client has mispredicted a decision's likely outcome or has made a morally wrong decision.[8]

A. MISPREDICTION

When a client mispredicts a decision's likely outcome, your intervention does not conflict with client autonomy, but rather seeks to assure that clients make decisions based on realistic predictions. Chapter 15 gives the example of Mrs. Benizi who in a dissolution of marriage decides to accept her husband's very low property settlement proposal on the theory that her acceptance will signal to Mr. Benizi what a fine person she is and induce him to return to the marriage. Assuming that you have a substantial enough data base to realize that Mrs. Benizi has mispredicted the likely outcome of her decision, pointing out the error can enable her to make a decision based on a more realistic prediction.

When you call a misprediction to a client's attention, help a client "hear" you by empathically acknowledging a client's objective. Then, inform a client what you think the likely outcome will be, stating your data base. Finally, make your point in a way that does not overwhelm a client's will. Pounding your desk, or threatening to replay recorded summaries of "Famous Southern Reporter Opinions" until a client changes a decision are inappropriate. For example, to call a misprediction to Mrs. Benizi's attention, you might say:

"I understand that your principal desire is to reunite with your husband. I have communicated that thought to his attorney a number of times, and perhaps he will change his mind at some later time. But in my view, by agreeing to his property settlement offer, you hurt yourself financially without in any way making it more likely that he'll want to resume the marriage. I doubt that his feelings towards you would change according to whether or not you accept his offer. Of course, I don't know your husband, but in my experience people in your husband's situation just don't behave like that. If ultimately you decide to accept the offer, then, of course, that is what we'll do. But I think you ought to recognize that there's only a very slight chance, no

8. Chapter 15, sec. 6(E).

more than about 5%, that accepting it will influence your husband to come back. Would you like some more time to think about this?"

This statement empathizes with the client's ultimate objective, points out why you believe that her decision is unlikely to accomplish it, and invites her to examine other options.[9] At the same time, it reassures the client that the decision is hers to make and that you will abide by it.

Whenever you ask a client to reconsider a decision which you think is based on a misprediction, keep in mind that what appears to you as a problem of misprediction may simply reflect a client's greater willingness to take risks. That is, a client may understand that the chance that a decision will produce her or his desired outcome is slight but decide to take it anyway. For example, Mrs. Benizi might say, "I know that the chance that accepting this offer will make my husband want to come back to me is a slim one. But I want to take it." Similarly, you may think that a client who decides to include a legally questionable non-competition clause in an employment agreement is mispredicting how the court is likely to rule on the clause's enforceability. Again, however, the client may simply be more willing to take a risk than you are.

Since every misprediction is potentially a difference in risk averseness, you should typically give clients the opportunity to distinguish between prediction and risk averseness. For example, you might tell Mrs. Benizi:

"If you recognize that accepting your husband's offer has only a slight chance of bringing him back, but decide to take that risk, you are entitled to do so. My main concern is that you not accept the offer on what seems to me an erroneous assumption that doing so is likely to bring him back."

These pious words and client centeredness aside, on some occasions you are likely to be very uncomfortable with a client's decision that seemingly bucks overwhelming odds.[10] For example, you would undoubtedly be troubled by Mrs. Benizi's giving up large amounts of property and income, possibly hurting her children, because of the slight chance that accepting the offer will restore her marriage. On such occasions, your instinct may be to do more than point out the risk. You may want to add your opinion that, according to your personal values, the risk is not worth taking. For instance, you might tell Mrs. Benizi,

---

9. The statement does nothing more than invite the consideration of other options, because presumably none of the options are likely to accomplish the client's ultimate objective. Had there been such an option, the statement could have referred to it.

10. As previously stated, you do not intervene in a client's decision merely because a client is willing to take a risk that you are not. See Chapter 15, sec. 6(E)(3)(a).

"Frankly, Mrs. Benizi, if it were me, I would not take this risk. I'd have too much to lose, both for myself and my children, to take this small a chance."

Some cynics might interpret such a statement as a fundamental concession to the traditional role of lawyers as experts who tell their clients what is best.[11] However, most prescriptive theories, the client-centered one included, run into specific situations in which applying them would be absurd. Your human desire to help cannot be completely subservient to any grand theory. To say that clients are in the best position to make decisions is not to say that those decisions are always correct. Thus, when risks seem far out of proportion to likely gain, giving a client an opinion based on your values is proper. Besides, perhaps in the end, theory wins. If Mrs. Benizi decides, in the face of everything, to take the risk, you must generally accept her decision.

B. "IMMORAL" DECISIONS

Communicating moral disagreement rests partly on the notion that many clients appreciate having the opportunity to reconsider decisions whose negative moral implications you call to their attention. In addition, communicating moral disagreement also rests partly on notions of autonomy—yours. You have an autonomous right to voice disagreement with decisions with which you morally disagree.[12]

A number of techniques can help ensure that clients "hear" your moral point of view. First, acknowledge openly that a client's views are legitimate. Second, avoid using the term "moral." The term itself may suggest to clients that you are calling them immoral and prevent them from "hearing" you, and typically you can refer both to a client's and to competing social values without labeling any of them as "moral." Finally, indicate that the final choice is a client's to make.[13]

For example, assume that you represent Ari, the owner of a shopping center, who has filed suit against Diana, the owner of an adjoining shopping center. The suit claims that Diana damaged Ari's business by erecting a fence along the property line that divides the two shopping centers, cutting off car access from one of the city's main commercial thoroughfares into Ari's center. Since filing of the suit, Diana has offered to tear down the fence, which was built because troublemakers attracted to a bar in Ari's center were harassing customers and employees in Diana's center. (The businesses in Diana's center cater largely to senior citizens.) Diana asks that after the fence is torn down, Ari share in the cost of a private security service for both shopping centers. Ari has decided to reject Diana's offer, knowing that with the small rents of the traditional shops in Diana's center, the costs of a prolonged suit will probably compel her to sell the center. Ari

---

11. See Chapter 2, sec. 1.

12. See Chapter 15, sec. 6(E)(2).

13. As noted in Chapter 15, sec. 6(E)(4), on some occasions your moral disagree-

ment may be so strong that you seek to withdraw.

hopes to buy it, evict the present tenants, and convert the center to an extension of his more upscale concept.

Assume further that you agree that Ari's prediction is likely to be correct: prolonging the suit may well force Diana to sell. However, Ari's decision disturbs you on moral grounds. The fence, though perhaps improperly erected, was erected for understandable motives. Moreover, Diana's shopping center is one of the last areas of the city that caters to senior customers. In this circumstance, you might say to Ari something along these lines:

> "Ari, I fully understand your desire to maximize the profitability of your center. Your goal of buying Diana's center is an important and legally legitimate one. But I'm asking you to reconsider her offer to tear down the fence if you will drop the lawsuit and share the costs of a security service. Her center caters to an older group of people who don't have many other places to go in this city. So what you decide to do affects not only Diana, but also the seniors for whom the center is a main activity. I hope you'll take some more time and think through your decision again."

This statement recognizes the legitimacy of Ari's values, and without using the term "moral" conveys your disagreement with his decision and expresses competing values.[14]

5. CLIENT'S MIND IS MADE UP BEFORE COUNSELING

If you place indecisive clients at one end of a continuum, then clients who are certain of what they want to do even before counseling begins are at the other. For example, an estate planning client may walk in your office and announce at an early stage, "I know just what I want to do, and that's leave everything to my youngest daughter. Can you write that up for me?" Or, a litigation client may reject an opponent's settlement offer out of hand. If you know enough about a matter to realize that a client's decision involves a misprediction or "immorality," you may respond as set forth above. But what if you lack the data base for reaching such a conclusion? Indeed, what if you think a client's choice is a perfectly valid one? What burden do you have to make sure that every decision which is a client's to make is preceded by a counseling dialogue?

A standard that requires you to give clients a "reasonable opportunity" to make decisions suggests that you must afford clients a chance to evaluate decisions. The ABA Code of Professional Responsibility adopts the same approach. The Code urges lawyers to initiate decision-making dialogues and to exert their best efforts to ensure that clients are aware of relevant considerations before making decisions.[15] Thus,

---

14. If Ari sticks to his decision, you would have to decide whether you would seek to withdraw as his attorney assuming you could properly do so. For whatever it's worth, the authors would seek to withdraw in this case.

15. Model Code, *supra* note 10, at EC 7–8.

your initial concern is how to go about initiating a counseling dialogue with a client who seems not to want one.

In general, you may initiate such dialogues directly or obliquely. With a direct approach, you seek a client's agreement to participate in counseling. You may enhance the chances of agreement by empathizing with the client's stated desire, acknowledging the client's right to make the final decision, and citing rules laid down by an "absent 3rd party." For example, assume that you represent McGee, the litigation client who does not want even to discuss the adversary's offer of settlement. When you tell McGee about the offer, McGee responds, "That's not at all what I had in mind. I'm not letting those bastards get off this easy, and I don't even want to talk about it." While you do not think that McGee's rejection is necessarily wrong, you do believe the offer is significant enough that McGee ought to consider it seriously. Using a direct approach, you might tell McGee something like this:

> "I understand your wanting to punish them for the injuries you've suffered. And after we discuss their offer a bit, you, of course, have the final word and can reject it. But this offer is a significant improvement over their previous one, and I think you owe it to yourself to at least consider it. Also, to fulfill my obligation as a lawyer I have to discuss with you some of the consequences of accepting and not accepting this offer before you reach your final decision. Can we talk now or can get together sometime soon?"

This statement empathizes with McGee's desires, emphasizes McGee's right to have the final say, and supports the need for a dialogue by mentioning an obligation created by an "absent 3rd party." [16] Your goal is McGee's agreement to discuss the decision.

Using an oblique approach, you simply sashay into a counseling dialogue without ever asking a client to agree to do so. While some may find this technique "manipulative," it is nothing more than an attempt to carry out your ethical responsibilities. Moreover, the fact that a client has a preconceived decision in mind does not mean that the client is dead set against discussion.

In the oblique approach, you again empathize with a client's objective and emphasize that the client has the final word. However, instead of seeking explicit agreement, you simply proceed to counseling. For example, return to the will client, Littleton, who states, "I know just what I want to do, and that's leave everything to my youngest daughter. Can you write that up for me?" You might respond:

> "You must be very close to her. I'm glad to tell you that you are perfectly free to leave all your property to one child if that is what you wish. And, of course, you have the final say in how to leave your property. But tell me a little bit about what lead you to this decision."

This statement opens up discussion of the decision without Littleton's agreement to do so. However, at least until Littleton objects,

---

16. In other situations, "law firm policies" or "my supervisor's practice," among other sources, can serve as "absent 3rd parties."

assuming that Littleton has absolutely no interest in counseling seems incorrect.

Direct and oblique approaches are quite capable of failure. Thus, McGee might reply, "I really don't want to talk about it. My mind's made up." And, Littleton might respond, "I really don't think you need to know that. I just want you to write the will." Do you press further, with a statement such as, "I understand that you don't want to talk about it. But I have an obligation to make sure that before you decide, you have considered all available options."

Note that having to press a client to consider other options is typically not a problem when a client's desired option cannot be obtained. For example, consider this dialogue:

Client:　I want a trust that'll allow me to control my property until I die and still avoid paying any estate taxes.

Lawyer:　Given the size of your estate, I'm afraid that's not going to be possible. But some other possibilities that could reduce your taxes might be of interest to you. Shall we talk about those?

In such situations, a client has little choice but to consider other options. But when the desired options are attainable, pressing a client to participate in counseling is more problematic. In some instances, the initial direct or oblique approach may be sufficient to afford a client a "reasonable opportunity to decide." But where a decision is critical, or the underlying issues are complex, giving a client a "reasonable opportunity" may require you to press further.[17]

---

17. When clients resist counseling, some lawyers write "CYA" letters in an effort to avoid malpractice claims. See T. Brown, *How to Avoid Being Sued by Your Client* 42–44 (1981). In general, we think this practice is likely to drive a wedge in your relationship with clients, and that a "note to the file" recounting your efforts is usually sufficient.

Chapter 21

THE COUNSELING MODEL AND LITIGATION

1. INTRODUCTION

This chapter explores how you might apply the counseling principles explored in Chapters 15–20 to typical decisions that arise in the course of litigation. Using a hypothetical case, the chapter explores decision-making at three different stages of a lawsuit. Admittedly, the hypothetical oversimplifies reality; we cannot capture the richness and complexity of counseling in a few pages of text. However, examining counseling "snapshots" as the case unfolds over time may further your understanding of how common variables affect a client's having a reasonable opportunity to decide.[1] The variables include:

(a) a client's level of intelligence, experience, sophistication and emotional involvement;

(b) changed circumstances;

(c) time pressure;

(d) a client's willingness to spend the time or money to engage in a counseling dialogue; and

(e) the apparent relative importance of a decision in the context of a client's overall problem.

Stated differently, this chapter provides an opportunity for you to reflect on how you might modify the tasks embedded in the four-step counseling process to clients' unique interests, needs and personalities.

2. A CASE STUDY: VITIS v. LINUS HAULING CO. AND INDUSTRIAL RESOURCES CORP

George Vitis is a 48–year–old married man with two children. Until having recently been fired, he was President of Linus Hauling Co., a rubbish disposal company which is a division of Industrial

---

1. See Chapter 15 sec. 6(C)(3).

Resources Corp. Linus' business consists of picking up and disposing of solid waste. Before coming to Linus, George was a Vice President of one of Linus' competitors, Dumpright. In his capacity as a Dumpright VP, George had consulted you on several occasions about contract and labor matters.

George came to see you shortly after he was "sacked" by Linus. His sacking was supposedly due to his poor management and a corresponding drop in Linus' revenues. However, George believes that he was fired because of actions he took after he learned that Linus was regularly engaged in dumping Class II (toxic waste) materials into Class I landfills authorized only for non-toxic materials. He reported his discovery to Industrial's President, and not long afterwards he was terminated.

George is a college graduate who majored in engineering; he is articulate and intelligent. He is very concerned about environmental damage caused by illegal dumping, and he is angry and humiliated about the way Linus treated him. After his termination, because George and his wife need two incomes, George took a job as a Vice President with another Linus competitor, Cleanfill Co. While his pay and status with Cleanfill are somewhat lower than at Linus, George feels no pressure to obtain immediate relief.

Assume that under the law in your jurisdiction, dumping Class II materials into Class I landfills is unlawful, and that proof that George was fired for disclosing an illegal business practice would establish the tort of "wrongful termination."

3. "SNAPSHOT 1": WHETHER TO FILE SUIT

During the initial interview, George related the information summarized above and gave you copies of various documents which substantiated that Linus was illegally dumping Class II material. He also said that what he really wanted was to get his job back, as he believes that without reinstatement few high level executive positions will be open to him. At the conclusion of the initial meeting, George agreed to hire you for the limited purpose of analyzing his legal position and advising him what he might do. It was understood that should George want to proceed further, a new fee arrangement would be necessary. You asked George to return in two days to discuss the results of your research and analysis.

Your research revealed two options for *compelling* Linus to rehire George: (1) court order, and (2) the order of your state's Unlawful Employment Practices Agency (UEPA), which is charged with resolving cases of employment discrimination. A court, but not the agency, would have the power to award compensatory and punitive damages in addition to reinstatement. In addition, George could seek reinstatement through voluntary alternative dispute resolution processes such as negotiation, arbitration and mediation.[2]

Your opinion is that George's story, if believed, establishes the tort of wrongful termination. Moreover, you have learned that the UEPA is backlogged and unlikely to investigate George's case for at least a year. In addition, the UEPA is subject to political pressure, and it frequently clears disputes off its docket by simply advising complainants to file suit rather than awaiting action by the UEPA.

George has returned for the follow-up meeting. After introductory pleasantries, the conversation proceeds as follows:

1. L: George, I've been thinking about your problem with an eye to what seem to me are your two main objectives: getting your job back and halting Linus' illegal dumping. Do I have those right?

2. C: I'd only add that if I can't get my job back, I want those bastards to pay for what they've put me through. Pardon my French.

3. L: Your anger is quite understandable; you needn't apologize. Now, as you know, what we need to do now is go through your options. The one option that responds to all of your objectives is litigation. Only a court can compel Linus to rehire you and to stop its dumping practices, and award damages. The litigation option gives us at least two ways to go. We could file the complaint and immediately undertake extensive discovery, or we could file a complaint with an eye toward bringing the case to trial primarily on the basis of the information you have already given me. An alternative to litigation, of course, is to file a complaint with the Unlawful Employment Practices Agency. As you know from your experience at Dumpright, the UEPA can't award damages or order Linus to halt illegal dumping; but it can order you reinstated. Finally, we can approach Linus and see if they are interested in negotiating a settlement. Here, too, there are at least a couple of possibilities. I could prepare a complaint and mail it to Linus' counsel, indicating that it will be filed and served unless they open meaningful negotiations immediately. Or, we can indicate our interest in negotiations without sending a complaint.

4. C: Well, talking about negotiation probably is a waste of time. I tried to talk to them when I was getting the ax, but no one paid any attention. Let's forget about that. Also, I know enough about the UEPA to know that that's likely to be a giant waste of time. In fact, when I was at Dump-

---

2. For a summary of alternative dispute resolution processes, see S. Goldberg, E. Green and F. Sander, *Dispute Resolution* 7–14 (1985).

right, we'd love it when an employee would go to the UEPA; we knew that would probably be the last we'd hear of the matter. It may save attorney's fees, but you get what you pay for.

5. L: I guess that leaves us with litigation. Which sounds best to you—the fast or slow approach?

6. C: What do you think my chances are based on the information I've already given you?

7. L: With the documents you've got, together with your testimony, I think the chances are good, probably at least 70%, that we'll be able to prove that illegal dumping was going on. We'd still have to prove the connection between the dumping and your firing, and as to that issue it's simply too early for me to say. So we'll need some discovery on that issue at least, but we can get that within the context of a slow approach.

8. C: What's this slow approach likely to cost?

9. L: In part, that depends on how aggressively Linus litigates this. Even under the slow approach, I'd say you're looking at thirty to forty hours on my part, and potentially a lot more if they file motions and start taking depositions, in essence forcing us into a fast approach.

10. C: I'm not liking this—it's starting to sound as expensive as I thought it would be.

11. L: There's no question that a disadvantage of litigation in any form is its expense. Also, as you know litigation often takes two or three years, and, hence another disadvantage is that the problem is not resolved quickly. On the other hand, litigation has some advantages that we ought to keep in mind.

12. C: I agree. A suit could really put pressure on Linus to settle. I know Resources' officers wouldn't want their depositions taken with regard to the dumping. The Board might well take a dim view of what's been going on. Also, Resources is considering offering additional stock and a suit might make underwriters think twice.

13. L: Okay. A suit has the disadvantage of expense, but the advantage of immediate pressure.

14. C: I think that's right, but I'm still worried about the money.

15. L: That information about a new stock offering is potentially very important, and it means that at some point we ought to talk more about it. But given your financial concerns, perhaps you have other options in mind?

16. C: One thought I've been mulling over is to contact someone I know in the mayor's office. I'm not sure that will work,

because hauling companies have a lot of political clout. Also, I've been thinking about approaching someone in the media with my story. What do you think about those things?

17. L: I think we should talk about both of those possibilities, in addition to litigation in either the aggressive or passive mode. It may help to take these up one at a time. Which do you want to talk about first?

18. C: Well, I'm pretty familiar with litigation already, and the expenses are worrisome. Also, I'm a bit dubious about the political route. So I guess that leaves the media. What are your thoughts?

19. L: Before we get too far, let's think carefully about what an approach to the media might look like. First, how does going to the media tie in to your goals of stopping the dumping and getting reinstated and reimbursed for what you've been through?

This dialogue illustrates how you may integrate three steps of the counseling model into a discussion without having to rigidly follow the model. Step One (articulating objectives) is just where the model suggests it should be, at the beginning (No. 1). As for Step Two, you both identify options (No. 3) and ask the client to do so (No. 15). However, note that your asking the client to identify the options he sees does not take place until after a partial Step Three discussion of advantages and disadvantages (e.g., Nos. 11–13). Step Three is evident in the discussion of the pros and cons of the two approaches to litigation (Nos. 11–15). However, that discussion is truncated. While you and George do identify a few pros and cons, before flushing the litigation options out thoroughly you return to Step Two by asking the client for the options that he sees (No. 15). The "bottom line," though, is that the discussion seems neutral and focused on the elements of the model. That it is non-linear is not a weakness, but rather a concession to the dynamics of actual conversations.

The dialogue also gives you a chance to examine some of the refining and tailoring techniques described in Chapters 17–20. First, the dialogue demonstrates how you might modify the model according to a client's apparent level of intelligence, experience and sophistication. In No. 3, you place a great many options on the table in a relatively short span of time. You mention two levels of litigation, the UEPA and two levels of negotiation.[3] Given a client with less experience or sophistication, a reasonable opportunity to decide might lead you to have fewer options in the air at one time. Likewise, your description of the options is quite terse. For example, you say nothing

3. Note that though "voluntary" alternative dispute resolution methods are potentially available, you say nothing about them. Presumably, the failure to do so reflects your judgment that at least at this time, those options are not pivotal or pertinent to George's situation. See Chapter 18, sec. 2.

about the procedures or powers of the UEPA. Again with a less informed client, you might need to more fully explain these matters.

In addition, the dialogue highlights the issue of how to respond to a client's immediate rejection of proposed options. In No. 4, George immediately rejects the UEPA and negotiation options, and in No. 5 you apparently acquiesce. The dialogue does not continue long enough to demonstrate resuscitation of one or both of the rejected options. However, resurrecting at least the negotiation option would seem vital to ensuring that George has a reasonable opportunity to decide. His apparent level of experience and sophistication may lead you to acquiesce in his rejecting the UEPA out of hand, since his prediction meshes with your research. But his rejection of negotiation may be a case of misprediction based on an inadequate data base.[4] Perhaps George was so emotionally involved when he attempted to talk with people at Linus and Resources that his approach to negotiation did not fully test their receptivity. Moreover, you should recognize that a not-yet mentioned disadvantage of litigation is that once the claim of illegal dumping becomes a matter of public record, George's leverage for achieving a settlement is substantially diminished.[5] Both of these reasons militate in favor of resuscitating the negotiation option before George makes a final decision.

Other refining and tailoring techniques from Chapters 17–20 are also evident in the dialogue. Using percentage terms, you make a sub-prediction as to how a trier is likely to resolve a factual dispute (No. 7). Though you do not indicate the most likely outcome of trial, given your lack of information about the reason that George was fired, your omission is understandable. You also ask George which option he wants to discuss first (No. 17); and convert consequences into advantages and disadvantages (Nos. 11 and 13).

Finally, the dialogue also demonstrates how other client-centered techniques suggested in the book factor into counseling. You are empathic (No. 3); you immediately respond to the client's questions to the extent you are able (e.g., Nos. 7 and 17); and attempt to give the client some idea of the fees involved in discovery should he choose to litigate (No. 9).

4. "SNAPSHOT 2": WHETHER TO TAKE A DEPOSITION

After you fully explored possible solutions with George, he decided to proceed by suing Linus and Resources.[6] However, since he has only moderate savings, he has asked you to proceed judiciously and to notify him as your time approaches thirty hours.

---

4. For further discussion of misprediction, see Chapter 19, sec. 2(B).

5. In some circumstances, however, threatening to "go public" with information about illegal activity in order to exact a settlement may constitute extortion. See 31A AmJur 2d, "Extortion, Blackmail and Threats" § 31 (1989).

6. For convenience, we hereafter refer to the defendants as "Linus."

You have now filed suit on George's behalf; the suit seeks George's reinstatement, an injunction against illegal dumping, and compensatory and punitive damages. Linus moved to dismiss, and when the motion was denied, filed an answer denying George's claims. The case is in the discovery phase.

You decided first to undertake brief discovery to cement the factual proposition, "Linus dumped Class II materials into Class I dumpsites during the nine months George worked for Linus," [7] and to that end deposed Linus' principal dispatcher, Alison Anderson. During Anderson's deposition, the name of Ken Karst came up repeatedly, and you believe he might provide important evidence of illegal dumping. However, it also came out in Anderson's deposition that Karst is a substantial customer both of Cleanfill and Linus. Recognizing that involving Karst in George's lawsuit against Linus may have an adverse impact on George's job with Cleanfill, you decide to consult with George over the phone about taking Karst's deposition:

1. L: George, I'd like to talk to you about deposing Ken Karst. Last week I took Alison Anderson's deposition. Things went well; she was clearly trying to protect Linus, but I think I got some good evidence of illegal dumping activities. I'm calling because in her testimony, Anderson mentioned Karst's name a couple of times. My belief is that Karst will be able to verify that Linus officials offered to dump Class II materials into Class I fills. However, from what Anderson said, I surmise that Karst is a substantial customer both of Linus and Cleanfill. I'm worried that taking his deposition will involve Karst in your lawsuit. If Karst resents that, he might retaliate by taking his business away from Cleanfill, and that might hurt your position. That's potentially a big disadvantage of taking Karst's deposition, and so I thought I'd better talk to you before going ahead with it.

2. C: Thanks, I appreciate the call. How important do you think his testimony will be?

3. L: As someone who is outside the company, I'd say it's likely to be important. As I told you earlier we have about a 70% chance of proving that illegal dumping was taking place. I think an outsider's evidence would really cement our position.

4. C: Besides taking his deposition, what else could we do?

5. L: Well, we always have the option to do nothing right now, or I could talk to him informally. Another possibility is that we could find some other outsider, not a customer of

7. For more on factual propositions, see Chapter 9, sec. 4.

Cleanfill, who might know about Linus' illegal dumping practices. Do you know anyone?

6. C: No. Of course I know a lot of people I dealt with when I was at Linus, but nobody offhand who knows anything about the illegal dumping.

7. L: Let's keep the possibility of someone else in the back of our minds. You might think of any friends you have at Linus who might put you on to someone. Meanwhile, can you think of any other options?

8. C: I can't. It seems to me that whether you talk to Karst informally or take his deposition, he may get angry because it's not his affair. What do you think?

9. L: Not knowing anything about Karst, it's difficult to say if there's any advantage in proceeding in one way rather than the other. I was hoping you might be able to give me some insights.

10. C: From what I know of him, he's a pretty touchy guy. I've heard talk that he's got a real temper. If we can avoid it, I'd like to leave Karst alone.

11. L: Here's one thought. Do you know Karst well enough to talk to him and ask if he'd be willing to talk to me informally or to have me take his deposition?

12. C: I know him slightly but I'd feel uncomfortable talking to him about my situation. I know it might help the case for me to talk to him, but I'm worried about what might happen. I'm still new at Cleanfill, and I just don't know what to do. What do you think?

13. L: At this point I'm not sure either. Lets talk a bit more. On a scale from one to five with five being the highest, how important is to you at this time to avoid the risk of upsetting Karst?

14. C: Pretty high.

15. L: Say a three or four?

16. C: I'd say a four.

17. L: Okay, how important is it for you at this point to know whether Karst knows about the illegal dumping?

18. C: Not that important now. Maybe it's a two.

19. L: Are you willing at this point to take a risk that we won't be able to find some other outsider who knows about the dumping and that eventually Karst may not be available to testify or may not know anything?

20. C: I'm not sure.

21. L: Back to our scale; how important is it to you to avoid that risk by talking with Karst now?

22. C: I guess not too important. I guess for now we should put talking to Karst on the back burner.

In this dialogue, the topic of discussion is an "implementing decision:" whether to depose Karst.[8] And, as the model suggests is typically the case with implementing decisions, you begin by identifying the objectives (No. 1). Then, when you identify the deposition option in No. 1, you also mention a potential disadvantage of the option. Thus, No. 1 deviates from the model in two respects. You, not the client, open up the topic of pros and cons; and you do so before getting all the options on the table. However, you called George specifically to talk about taking the deposition, and the disadvantage you mention in No. 1 motivated the call. Hence, the deviation responds to the realities of everyday conversation and seems acceptable.

In Nos. 5, 7 and 11, you adhere to the model by mentioning additional options and asking George if he can add any. Note that No. 5 includes what you may think of as a "search for an option." That is, deposing an outsider other than Karst is an option only if you or George are aware of such an outsider. When neither of you can identify someone, this option is temporarily shelved.

With respect to Step Three, the dialogue does identify some potential advantages (No. 3) and disadvantages (No. 1) of speaking to Karst. However, you do not identify, nor press George to identify, additional pros and cons. Furthermore, you do not attempt to distinguish between the pros and cons of talking with Karst as compared to the pros and cons of taking his deposition. Instead, you seem content to rely on George's potentially superficial data base (No. 10) to conclude that the potential disadvantage that motivated your phone call is likely to occur.

With respect to Step Four, you facilitate George's making his own decision by using the rating technique referred to in Chapter 20.[9] In Nos. 13, 15, 17 and 21, you ask Karst to assign degrees of importance to potential consequences. However, at best the consideration of the potential consequences was brief.

Despite George's sophistication and experience, and the fact that the decision is at the moment an interim one, the adequacy of the counseling here is dubious. The interim decision may, in fact, become final if neither of you can identify another outsider who knows of illegal dumping and if Karst becomes unavailable. Moreover, you neither address nor invite George to address the important subject of potential advantages of taking Karst's deposition now. For example, might having his testimony alter Linus' bargaining position? In combination with the other shortcomings identified in the analysis above, you may not have provided George with a reasonable opportunity to decide.

8. Because under the circumstances taking Karst's deposition may have a substantial impact on George's position at Cleanfill, you consult with him.

9. See Chapter 20, sec. 3(B).

5. "SNAPSHOT 3": WHETHER TO SETTLE

George's case against Linus progressed swimmingly. You deposed an "outsider" other than Karst who provided strong evidence that Linus was engaged in illegal dumping. In addition, you located company memos suggesting that George was fired in retaliation for making noise about illegal dumping. Though trial is still six months away, you regard the case as nearly complete and very strong, and the opportunity to air the facts in a public setting and getting a large judgment brought a smile to your face during unguarded moments.

The smile suddenly faded when George phoned a couple of days ago, telling you excitedly that he had just been hired to run a waste disposal company in another state. He therefore does not want to get his job back at Linus, nor does he have any continuing interest in enjoining Linus' illegal dumping. While he wants as favorable a financial settlement as you can arrange, he states that his primary objective is to conclude the matter quickly, if possible before he leaves town in a couple of weeks. You asked George to come in and see you, and the discussion goes as follows:

1. L: George, I must say you're looking and sounding better than at any time since I've known you. Congratulations on the new position—I'm delighted for you.

2. C: Thanks, the whole family is excited. They're especially looking forward to getting out of these cold winters.

3. L: I know you've got a lot to do, so let's get right down to business. When we spoke yesterday, you told me that you wanted to drop the lawsuit, get as much cash as you can and forget about everything else. Do you still feel that way?

4. C: Yes. I want to concentrate all my energy on the new position, and I want to put all this behind me. It's been a strain on all of us.

5. L: Yes, remember we talked about that before you decided to go ahead with the lawsuit in the first place. It's more stressful when it's you personally involved in a suit, instead of the company. Does anyone at Linus know about the new job?

6. C: Not that I know of, but I suppose it's going to come out sooner or later. It's a pretty small network of companies.

7. L: That could be important. Once Linus knows you've taken a new position out of state, our leverage is bound to go down. Linus' counsel will realize that you are no longer interested in being rehired and that you probably are not anxious to disrupt your new position by preparing for and sitting through trial. So Linus' finding out that you're taking a new job and moving hurts our bargaining posi-

tion. With that in mind, let's think about the two options
I see—(1) begin negotiating with Linus at once or (2) sitting
tight for five months until the mandatory settlement conference to talk settlement. As you know, the mandatory
usually takes place about a month before trial is scheduled
to start, and it's a time when parties normally talk settlement. But before we discuss these, do you see any other
alternatives?

8. C: No, not unless you can.

9. L: No, so let's talk about the two options we do have. Which
one do you want to talk about first—negotiating now or
waiting until the mandatory?

10. C: The first one, because I'd love to have this whole mess
behind me as soon as possible.

11. L: OK, we'll make a little chart; you know how fond I am of
them. And first off, we'll list that an advantage of negotiating now is that assuming Linus comes up with a figure
that you're willing to accept, you'll be able to put the
whole case behind you sooner. Any other advantages that
strike you?

12. C: Well, is there a possibility they'd offer more now than they
will closer to trial? After all, we're probably saving them
some attorney's fees by settling earlier.

13. L: George, that's a good thought, but your taking a new job
really complicates things. Is it fair to say that the longer
we wait, the more likely Linus will find out about your
new position?

14. C: Sure. In fact the annual Waste Convention is in a couple
of months. I'm not planning on going, but Linus always
sends someone, and they may find out then.

15. L: Then we'll have to list that a disadvantage of waiting until
the mandatory is the increased chance that Linus will find
out about your new job and therefore make a lower offer.
The other side of that coin is that an advantage of trying
to settle now is a reduced likelihood that Linus will find
out about your leaving. On the other hand, opening
negotiations now may lead Linus' counsel to smell a rat.
After all, we have no particular reason to negotiate now,
and so counsel may suspect that you're anxious to settle.
So a disadvantage of going ahead now is the risk that you
will be perceived as anxious to settle and therefore get a
lowball offer. So it's kind of a lose-lose situation: either
way, we run a risk of getting a lowball offer, but at this
point we can't really tell which risk is greater.

16. C: Seems like I've got everything to lose and nothing to gain
by waiting.

17. L: You may be right. However, an advantage of waiting is that, as far as I can see, it requires no further activity on your part. They've already taken your deposition, and you've gone through all the files. I realize that you can't entirely close the matter in your mind. But, at least as far as your daily life is concerned, I don't think you'll have to do anything more. And that would allow us to talk settlement at a more natural time and lead them to think that the case is likely to go to trial. Even if they know you don't want to be rehired, they may still be plenty worried about the punitive damages and the injunction.

18. C: Look, I understand all this; as an executive, I have to make decisions in the face of uncertainty all the time. I want to try to settle this now, and if the money is reasonable, I want to get out. I don't care about nickels and dimes at this point. I'm willing to give up some money. I want to recover what I've got into this case, plus my salary differential. Is that reasonable?

19. L: That's a decision only you can make. But let me tell you what I think would happen if the case were to go to trial. In terms of money, the salary differential by the time of trial will be about $65,000. I'd say the chances of that verdict are quite good, in the range of 80–90%. As for punitive damages, some of these company memos about why they need to fire you are pretty inflammatory. I'd say the chances are at least 60% that you'll be awarded punitive damages in the neighborhood of $50,000; there's some chance, maybe around 20%, that the punitives could go as high as $100,000. Also, I think there's almost a 100% chance we'll get the injunction to stop the illegal dumping, and about a 70% chance the court would order you rehired.

20. C: What I could get at trial sounds good, but if I can recover fees and costs, plus the $65,000, I'd be happy.

21. L: I think that's something I could negotiate towards now. Of course, if Linus doesn't come back with that, we'll have to talk again. But for the moment, you understand that you'd be giving up the 60% chance of getting $50,000 in punitive damages, as well as the injunction. Are you comfortable with that?

22. C: Well, I think so.

23. L: I want to stress that the decision is yours to make. But given the rather sudden change of direction, I want to make sure you've had a chance to think through the ramifications carefully. I know of your concern for the environment. How do you feel about giving up the injunction claim?

24. C: I can't say that doesn't bother me. But at the same time, I see no reason why the burden of stopping it should rest with me. I plan to turn over my records to the local authorities, and hopefully they'll pursue Linus.

25. L: Do you have any personal friends, or maybe people you left behind at Linus, who you may feel you've let down by dropping the suit?

26. C: Not really. I'm sure they expect me to do what's best for me and my family in the long run.

27. L: Any other ramifications that you can see that we haven't talked about?

28. C: Not that I can see.

29. L: Do you see any advantages at all in holding out for more than $65,000?

30. C: Look, like anyone else, I'll take more if you can get it. But I want to put all this behind me, and I'll be perfectly happy with the $65,000.

31. L: Okay. Our bottom line will be $65,000, plus the fees and costs.

32. C: Great.

Here, changed circumstances create a new set of objectives, which in turn necessitate a thorough examination of options and consequences. The dialogue covers two decisions: (1) negotiating now or later; and (2) how much to accept by way of settlement.

As to the "negotiate now" decision, you check objectives (No. 3), and identify two options and ask George for others (No. 7). You do not describe what each option entails, but given George's experience such an explanation is surely unnecessary. Moreover, you demonstrate neutrality by asking George which option he prefers to discuss first (No. 9). Then, Nos. 11–18 demonstrate a rather full discussion of likely consequences, leading to the decision (No. 18).[10] Together with George's background and the length of time he has lived with the lawsuit, your discussion with George seemingly provides him with a reasonable opportunity to consider pivotal and pertinent alternatives and consequences.

On the other hand, recognize that the discussion omits mention of a potentially important option: not settling at all and going to trial. You accept George's decision to settle and limit the discussion to timing and settlement amount. But among other things, trial might have publicly aired Linus' environmental sins and prompted action with respect to other environmental hazards. Does your omission therefore deprive George of the opportunity to consider a pivotal or pertinent option and

10. The discussion of consequences, though thorough, is not as extensive as it might be. For example, you do not ask George about whether negotiating now has any disadvantages.

consequence? Even if it does not, should you have raised the alternative and its potential consequences to give George an opportunity to reflect on the morality of his decision? [11]

Next, consider the discussion of the settlement offer decision. To help ensure that George has had a reasonable opportunity to decide you did the following:

(a) stressed that the decision is for George to make (Nos. 19 and 23);

(b) gave George an opportunity to compare the trial and negotiation options by predicting both the most likely and the best likely outcome of trial in percentage terms (No. 19); [12]

(c) searched for potential nonlegal disadvantages of accepting $65,000 (Nos. 23–30); [13] and

(d) afforded George a chance to consider the advantages of an additional option—holding out for a higher settlement amount (No. 29).

From the perspective of those who advocate a "problem-solving" approach to negotiation, the settlement offer discussion is perhaps troubling. Presumably, such advocates would want to develop such matters as what needs George is attempting to satisfy in arriving at his figure, and whether options besides "more money" and "less money" might be available.[14] However, the dialogue omits both a Step One discussion of objectives related to a settlement figure and a Step Two discussion of additional options. Hence, those who espouse a problem-solving approach to negotiation are likely to believe that George has been deprived of knowing about a pivotal or pertinent option, and therefore he has not had a reasonable opportunity to decide on a settlement offer.

11. No. 23 contains a germ of broader environmental concerns. However, arising as it does in the context of discussing possible terms of settlement, it seems insufficient to identify the trial option and its likely attendant advantages.

12. While you say nothing about the worst likely outcome of trial, as George seems hellbent on settlement anyway, he probably has not been deprived of learning of a pivotal or pertinent consequence.

13. Note that the search for nonlegal disadvantages is an inverted T-funnel. That is, you ask closed questions (No. 25) before an open one (No. 27). While this compromises the counseling model, it seems a minor digression in the overall dialogue.

14. See, e.g., C. Menkel–Meadow, "Toward Another View of Legal Negotiation: The Structure of Problem Solving," 31 UCLA L.Rev. 754 (1984).

Chapter 22

THE COUNSELING MODEL AND PROPOSED DEALS

* * *

Miriam, today we are going to go over the buy-sell agreement I've prepared for the company. Did you have a chance to read through the copy I mailed to you?

I spent almost two hours with it. It looks terrific. You've really thought of everything. I'm quite pleased but I do have a couple of questions.

I'm glad you're happy. Why don't we start with your questions?

* * *

1. THE SCOPE OF THIS CHAPTER

This chapter explores the counseling model in the context of proposed deals.[1] It assumes that, as suggested in Chapter 11, you and a client have had one or more meetings leading to your producing a draft document which you have sent to the client for review. You now meet to review the draft. Such a post-draft meeting typically entails a counseling dialogue in which you explain a draft's provisions, give a client the opportunity to consider alternative provisions, and encourage the client to decide which alternative is most likely to be satisfactory.[2] Of course, subsequent negotiations may require further counseling dialogues and new decisions.[3]

1. Although this discussion occurs in the context of reviewing proposed commercial agreements, the discussion is equally applicable to discussion of settlement agreements in litigation. Likewise, except for those parts of the discussion which focus on negotiation, the discussion also applies to the review of documents in the estate planning context.

2. As pointed out in Chapter 11, a similar, though typically more attenuated, dialogue often takes place before preparation of a draft. However, the most significant counseling usually takes place after a draft has been prepared.

3. For the most part, how you counsel is independent of which party's lawyer drafts a proposed agreement. However, for ease of understanding, this chapter assumes you are the drafter.

As in Chapter 21, we explore the counseling model through the use of illustrative case studies. That chapter's proviso that such studies cannot capture the richness and complexity of counseling applies here as well. Nonetheless, the studies may further your understanding of how you might adapt the counseling model in the light of such variables as a client's sophistication, experience, risk averseness, willingness to pay and the time available. Stated differently, we hope this chapter helps you understand how, within a deal's domain, clients' unique interests, needs, backgrounds, personalities and particular circumstances influence how you counsel to afford a client a reasonable opportunity to decide.

Counseling about deals generally has two dimensions: discussing the adequacy of individual provisions of a draft agreement and discussing the underlying wisdom of the deal itself. We use the first case study, "PSD Corporation," to explore counseling with respect to individual provisions. We use the second, "Snacks Sixth Avenue," to examine how counseling principles apply to a discussion of a deal's wisdom.

2. CASE STUDY NO. 1: PSD CORPORATION

Your client is PSD Corporation, whose representative is Andrea Paul, PSD's president. PSD is a small corporation which develops and markets software programs. PSD has been your client for the past two years and you are familiar with its operations, officers and directors.

In an initial meeting pertaining to a proposed new deal, Andrea told you that PSD is developing a software program for use by lawyers. The program is one which lawyers, aided by paralegals, can use to track evidence and documents during the discovery phases of a lawsuit. Although other evidence programs are available, Andrea believes that PSD's program will be considerably more sophisticated than any now on the market. PSD has been working on its program for about five months and anticipates that it will take at least eighteen to twenty months to complete the program and the documentation. The initial marketing phase will then take another six months. PSD is very excited about the project and wants to retain the services of its lead programmer, Rhonda Fleming, until the programming and the initial marketing phases are complete. Andrea has talked with Fleming about Fleming's committing herself to the project for that twenty-four-month period, and Fleming has indicated interest provided that she is given a free hand in developing the program and is adequately compensated. No specific terms of compensation have been discussed, but Fleming's current salary is $54,000 per year. Fleming has indicated that before she commits herself to any formal agreement, she wants a lawyer to look it over.

During the initial meeting, you also described alternative approaches which PSD might use to tie Fleming to PSD for the duration of the project—i.e., at least twenty-four months. Among the options you reviewed were signing Fleming to an employment contract which provided a salary increase, giving Fleming some equity interest in PSD, and giving Fleming some equity interest in any income PSD derived from the marketing of the evidence program. After you and Andrea batted the various options around, Andrea decided that PSD did not want, for various reasons, to give Fleming an equity position in PSD, although it might be willing to give her some interest in income PSD derived from the program. Andrea's favored approach was an employment contract with a salary increase.[4] At the discussion's conclusion, Andrea said she thought PSD should offer Fleming a salary increase to $64,000 per year.

Four days after meeting with Andrea, you prepared a draft agreement and mailed it to her.[5] Your cover letter asked Andrea to read the agreement and to then set up a meeting so that the two of you could discuss it. Today you are meeting with Andrea to review the agreement. The proposed agreement is twenty pages in length and contains clauses regarding the following:

(1) The contract term and Fleming's duties,

(2) Fleming's compensation, including provisions providing incentives and covering inflation,

(3) PSD's ownership of all program codes and copyrights developed by Fleming while working on the project,

(4) Fleming's limits on outside computer activities during the duration of the project,

(5) PSD's right to terminate Fleming under various circumstances,

(6) Fleming's rights should PSD breach the agreement,

(7) PSD's and Fleming's obligation to arbitrate any disputes,

(8) Unfair competition by Fleming after termination (e.g., trade secrets and customer lists clauses),

(9) PSD's obligation to indemnify Fleming with respect to lawsuits concerning the inadequacy of the program,

(10) PSD's entitlement to liquidated damages in event of Fleming's breach,

(11) Notices required to each party,

(12) Choice of Law.[6]

---

4. Obviously you would have used the counseling model to help your client reach this decision. In the interest of time, however, we have omitted the dialogue leading to it.

5. As you recall from Chapter 11, follow-ups to initial meetings normally are preceded by your sending a client a draft agreement to review.

6. For a discussion and exploration of provisions commonly found in employment agreements see J. Rabkin & M. Johnson, 5 *Current Legal Forms With Tax Analysis* (1989); *Advising California Employers* 215 et seq. (Cal. CEB 1981).

3. PREPARING TO REVIEW AN AGREEMENT

Preparing to meet with a client to discuss a draft agreement usually requires you to make three determinations: (a) Which provisions it makes sense to discuss; (b) Which omitted or alternative versions of provisions it makes sense to discuss [7]; and (c) In what order to discuss the provisions. Consider briefly each of these tasks.

A. DECIDING WHICH PROVISIONS TO DISCUSS

A primary counseling goal is to give a client a reasonable opportunity to decide if a draft's provisions are satisfactory.[8] In many cases, achieving this goal may not require that you review each and every provision in a draft. One reason is that the sheer length of some agreements defies individual consideration of each provision. But in addition, some operative and contingent terms may be so apparent or unimportant in the context of a particular deal that no review seems warranted. For example, in the PSD matter, consider the clauses pertaining to the agreement's duration (two years) and the giving of required notices. The first may be so plain to Andrea, and the second so unimportant, that absent questions from Andrea, you would plan not to review them with her.[9]

Similarly, certain contingency provisions may come into play only under circumstances you think extremely remote. For example, many commercial leases contain provisions governing the parties' rights in the event that a portion of the leased premises is condemned through eminent domain.[10] Assume that a client desires to lease a warehouse for a year; that the landlord's twelve page proposed lease contains an eminent domain provision; and that you put the chance that a governmental agency will exercise its eminent domain powers over the leased premises during the term of the lease at less than 5%. Here, too, absent a client's questions, you may plan not to review the provision.

Often, however, determining whether to review a provision with a client is not so obvious. When preparing to review a draft, you may have to evaluate factors such as a provision's apparent importance, the client's prior opportunity to review it, the client's sophistication, the client's prior experience, the client's willingness to pay, and the time

---

7. Note that for the most part you face these same issues even if the agreement is one which has been drafted by the other side. As to task (b), while you may not know whether the other party has "consciously" chosen to omit a provision, in looking over the other party's draft you still need to think about whether to inform a client about the possibility of including a provision the other party has omitted.

8. For a more detailed discussion of this standard, see Chapter 15, sec. 6(C).

9. Be warned, however, that even a provision apparently so benign as one requiring that notices of breach "be given within 10 days" may in a particular context merit individual review. A client may not have thought through whether, given the client's business practices, a 10–day notice period provides adequate time to discover a problem and report it.

10. See, e.g. *Commercial Real Property Lease Practice* §§ 3.98–3.109 (Cal. CEB 1976).

available for discussion. When in doubt, you might involve the client in the decision-making process. Consider the following dialogue:

1. L: Andrea, let's turn our attention to the agreement I sent you. Have you had a chance to go over it?

2. C: I spent about an hour last night looking through it, and it's just the kind of thing I had in mind. I'm particularly glad you put in the provision about arbitration. I've been involved in arbitrations many times, and I really think that's the way for a company like PSD to go. If problems arise, we want to stay out of court.[11]

3. L: Good. As I recall, PSD has never used employment contracts but you're familiar with them, correct?

4. C: Right. We used them with consultants when I was with FastPro.

5. L: Well, does it make sense then to limit ourselves to talking over those provisions about which you have questions or concerns and those on which I feel I need your input?

6. C: Absolutely. I'm counting on you to know what's important and what's not. As I said, I've looked at this thing and if our discussion skips something that I want to know about I'll ask you. If we go over everything, it's going to take too much time. I really don't want to devote more than an hour or so to this. I think we can skip the stuff regarding her rights if we fire her and in fact all the clauses starting with number 6. I'm willing to leave those things to you.

7. L: I appreciate that; I monitor our hourly charges as closely as you do. Which ones would you like to talk about?

8. C: My only interests are numbers 2 and 5; the ones on compensation and our rights to terminate her.

9. L: Good—those are on my list too.

Here, in No. 6, Andrea indicates that she wants to talk only about two provisions. Would acceding to her "waiver" deprive her of a reasonable opportunity to explore the agreement's other ten provisions?

Without knowing more about Andrea, her objectives, the nature of the deal, and the details of the parties' prior discussions, and actually reading the draft, you have an inadequate basis to answer the question. For example, without knowing the specific terms of the liquidated damages provision and Andrea's experience with such provisions, no

---

11. Without an express indication that a client understands arbitration, you would have to take the initiative to discuss the clause with her. Clients often think they understand provisions when in fact they do not. For example, a client may have a general sense of what arbitration is, yet not understand its bypassing of a jury and its finality.

conclusion about your obligation to discuss those provisions with her is possible.[12]

Nonetheless, the dialogue may help you understand how preliminary discussions with a client can help you develop information from which to judge which provisions to discuss.[13] Of course, any judgment must be a preliminary one since subsequent discussion may lead to greater or lesser review than you or a client initially contemplated.

B. ALERTING CLIENTS TO OMITTED OR ALTERNATIVE VERSIONS OF PROVISIONS

As you know, rarely during pre-draft information-gathering do you discuss every potential provision. As a result, you often rely on your own judgment, rather than on any overt discussion with a client, in deciding whether to include certain provisions in a draft.[14] The upshot is that almost every draft omits provisions that potentially might be included in a final agreement. For example, the PSD draft omits common provisions such as PSD's right to terminate the agreement in the event of merger, and Fleming's obligation to mitigate damages in the event of PSD's breach.[15]

Similarly, almost any provision included in a draft typically results from your choice among possible alternative versions of the provision. For example, one common alternative to the cash salary provision in the PSD draft is compensation in addition to cash, such as a car or an expense account. Therefore, before meeting a client to review a draft, you must decide which if any of the omitted or alternative versions of a provision a client should know about if a client is to have a reasonable opportunity to come away with a satisfactory agreement.

By and large, the factors to consider when determining which omitted or alternative versions of provisions to review with a client are the same as those you think about in the context of included provisions. Given a client's experience, objectives, the type of deal, and the parties' prior discussions, you evaluate factors such as how important an omitted or alternative version of a provision would likely be, the client's sophistication, the client's prior experience, the client's willingness to pay, and the time available for discussion.

In addition, you should factor in a client's reaction to an included provision to help you decide whether to mention an omitted or alterna-

12. For further discussion of this point, see sec. 4(A) *infra*.

13. Inquiries such as that just illustrated, of course, will sometimes give you little help. Clients sometimes respond by telling you they have been too busy to read anything and wish to discuss only a very limited number of provisions. Such responses often put you face to face with a client whose mind is mostly made up and who wants to rely on you for most of the decision making. In such circumstances if you believe your client may not have had a reasonable opportunity to explore all the important decisions, you might try some of the approaches described in Chapter 20.

14. For discussion of the factors you typically rely on when deciding on which provisions to include in a draft, see Chapter 11, sec. 8.

15. For sources of common employment agreement provisions, see note 6 *supra*.

tive version of a provision. For example, assume that Clause 5 of the PSD draft agreement obligates PSD to employ Fleming for two years. If Andrea were to indicate that the two-year term could be a problem if PSD were to abandon the evidence tracking system project, you probably would then suggest alternative versions of Clause 5, such as one giving PSD the right to terminate the agreement in such event.

When you do decide to mention an omitted or alternative version of a provision, you may say something like the following:

> "Andrea, while we're looking at the compensation clause, let me mention an additional possibility since you seem to think that the amount of the salary might not be a sufficient inducement to Fleming. We might include a provision giving her the use of a company car, or an expense account, or perhaps a bonus. I can explain how this kind of provision might work and what the tax consequences would be, if you are interested. Do you want to talk about these ideas?"

As this statement suggests, you typically mention an omitted or alternative version of a provision in connection with the included provision to which it is most closely tied. That practice facilitates clients' understanding the impact of adding an omitted provision or adopting an alternative one.[16]

C. ORDER OF REVIEW OF PROVISIONS

As noted in Chapter 7, you typically begin follow-up meetings by asking clients about their current concerns.[17] Through a client's response to such a question, you are likely to learn whether any of a draft's terms are particularly worrisome. When counseling a client about the agreement you ought to give priority to any provisions which a client mentions as a concern. When a client voices no special concerns, you may order a review however you think most effective and efficient. For example, you may go through provisions in numerical order or according to their importance.

4. TOPICS TO EXPLORE WHEN COUNSELING ABOUT A DEAL'S INDIVIDUAL PROVISIONS

Law schools pay scant attention to how you might counsel clients with respect to the adequacy of provisions typically found in deals agreements. Nor do practitioner-oriented works tell you what subjects you need to cover in order to explore a provision's adequacy.[18] This section is an attempt, perhaps a very rudimentary one, to fill this void. We describe here the topics that typically are relevant to a client's

16. Making a list of consciously omitted provisions will help you remember to mention the provisions at pertinent times.

17. See Chapter 7, sec. 5(B).

18. Practitioner-oriented works often do a splendid job of setting out the potential content of a myriad of provisions for use in various types of deals. However, to our knowledge they say little or nothing about how to walk clients through the subjects that must be examined before a client has a reasonable opportunity to determine a provision's adequacy.

decision as to whether a provision is adequate. As we describe the topics, we also mention how they relate to the four-step counseling model. However, we largely save for section (E) below a more detailed analysis of how you might integrate the topics into a counseling dialogue.

A. A PROVISION'S MEANING

No matter how concise and attentive to laypeople's vocabulary a draft is, clients frequently find provisions confusing. Yet to avoid embarrassment, clients may not volunteer their lack of understanding. Hence, any doubt in your own mind about whether or not a client understands a provision should prompt you to explain it.

Because it is often the abstract quality of provisions that confuses clients,[19] a useful way of explaining a provision is providing a concrete example or two of how it works. For example, assume that you have decided to review paragraph 9 of the proposed agreement between PSD and Fleming with Andrea. That provision reads as follows:

> PSD shall, to the maximum extent permitted by law, indemnify and hold Fleming harmless against expenses, including reasonable attorneys' fees, judgments, fines, settlements, and other amounts actually and reasonably incurred in connection with any action or proceeding brought against Fleming by any third person arising by reason of Fleming's employment by PSD. PSD shall advance to Fleming any expenses to be incurred in defending any such proceeding to the maximum extent permitted by law.[20]

To explain this provision, you might proceed as follows:

> Lawyer: Andrea, let's look at paragraph 9 for a minute. In essence, this clause provides that should someone sue Rhonda as the result of her work for PSD, possibly because of an alleged defect in the software, PSD will pay for her legal defense and also will pay any judgment entered against her by a court. Also, if she settles any such suit and the settlement is a reasonable one, PSD will also pay that.

Absent questions from Andrea, this statement probably adequately explains the meaning of paragraph 9. The contingency seems a remote one, and Andrea is apparently sophisticated and experienced. Of course, you might have given a more detailed explanation. For example, you could have pointed out that Fleming might be sued for reasons

---

19. See, e.g., G.E. Myers and M.T. Myers, *The Dynamics of Human Communication: A Laboratory Approach* 124–5 (5 ed. 1988). Cf. J.B. White, "The Invisible Discourse of the Law: Reflections on Legal Literacy and General Education," 54 Col.L. Rev. 143 (1983).

20. Recognize that the clauses used in this and other illustrations are not intend-

ed as "models." Our focus is on the counseling process rather than the specific language of potential provisions. For the most part, in actual practice, provisions tend to be more precisely worded than our illustrative provisions.

other than defects in the software and clarified what a "reasonable" settlement might be. But on balance, the concrete examples in the explanation in all likelihood give Andrea a reasonable opportunity to understand the provision.

Note that the explanation takes it as a given that *some* version of indemnity clause is appropriate and does not include a legal justification for the provision. For example, you do not launch into an explanation of the law's "default position" with respect to indemnity. That is, you do not explain what indemnity obligation PSD might have in the absence of an indemnity clause. Unless a provision is legally controversial, or a client asks a question which indicates she or he wants a glimpse of what was missed by not attending law school, choosing not to explore the role of indemnity provisions seems valid. Clients tend to be more interested in a provision's "bottom line"—what it means—than in whatever legal reasoning underlies its use.

Finally, note that an explanation of a provision is a partial description of its consequences, and therefore it relates to the third step of the counseling model.

B. A PROVISION'S ADEQUACY FROM YOUR CLIENT'S PERSPECTIVE

After explaining a provision, the next step in the review process typically involves helping a client assess its adequacy. Generally, a provision provides benefits for one party and imposes burdens on the other. You seek, therefore, to help clients predict whether a provision's benefits are adequate, or its burdens too steep.

For example, on the benefits side, you might help Andrea predict whether tying Fleming to PSD for two years is likely to allow PSD to develop and market its software program. Similarly, you might ask her whether the restrictions on Fleming's outside computer activities adequately ensure that Fleming's time and energy will be mainly directed toward PSD's project.

On the burdens side, you might help Andrea assess whether PSD can live with the contingency provision requiring PSD to indemnify Fleming. In another case, you might ask a client who is about to lease space in a small commercial shopping center whether he or she can comply with a provision which requires remaining open twelve hours a day. Clients often fail to evaluate carefully their ability to comply with a burdensome requirement, particularly when it is contingent on some future occurrence. You therefore need to encourage clients to think through the adequacy of contingency provisions which impose burdens.

Inquiries into a clause's adequacy can be quite straightforward. Consider the following examples.

Is The Protection Adequate?

1. L: Andrea, paragraph 1 requires Fleming to work full time for PSD on the evidence program for two years. You need

to think about whether PSD will need Fleming for more than two years. Realistically, is the project going to be finished and in the market place within that time?

2. C: I really think eighteen months should do it, so I'm quite comfortable with two years.

* * *

12. L: Great. How about paragraph 8? What this paragraph means is that should Fleming quit before the two-year period expires, she could not develop programs in the legal field for another company or free lance for herself for six months plus a period of time equal to that remaining on her contract. Will this restriction give PSD adequate protection from competition by Fleming should she leave before the end of the contract?

13. C: I think so. We have a couple of other people working for Fleming on the project. I think we'd be all right.

Nos. 1 and 12 combine the tasks of explaining a provision's meaning and inquiring about its adequacy. Since each provision is intended to provide the client with benefits, the questions encourage her to assess the protection they provide.

Are The Burdens Bearable?

1. L: Andrea, let's talk about paragraph 2. This paragraph commits PSD to pay Fleming a monthly salary of $3500 plus bonuses of $2,000 if certain aspects of the source code are completed by July 1, Jan. 1 and April 2. Is PSD going to have any problem at all meeting those financial requirements?

2. C: I'm sure we won't.

3. L: Good, because paragraph 6 says that if PSD breaches the agreement in any way, Fleming can at her option terminate the contract. So, if PSD were not to pay Fleming's salary or give her the incentive payments called for by paragraph 2, Fleming would be free to walk away from PSD.

4. C: What happens if we are a few days late with a payment?

5. L: Well, the provision says that any failure on PSD's part must be material. A couple of days shouldn't be a problem, but if payments get much later than that, especially the monthly salary payments, or if PSD were continually late, then that might constitute a "material" breach giving Fleming a right to end the contract. Do you have any reason to think that PSD is going to have any difficulty complying with its obligations under paragraph 2?

6. C: No. We are in good financial shape. I just don't see a problem.

Your review of the provisions which impose burdens on PSD again both explain the provisions and assess their adequacy.

Note that in part, a discussion of a provision's adequacy is a Step One inquiry into a client's objectives with regard to a particular provision. For example, in the context of the discussion of paragraph 8 in the first dialogue, Andrea verifies that one of her objectives is to protect PSD against direct competition when Fleming leaves. Moreover, both dialogues demonstrate that an assessment of adequacy relates to the Step Three notion of "pivotal" and "pertinent" consequences.[21] For instance, in the second dialogue Andrea learns that repeated failure to pay Fleming's salary when due is likely to allow Fleming to abrogate the deal.

Client Dissatisfaction With a Provision

In the examples above, the client was pleased with the draft agreement. Alas, that will not always be so. Matching objectives against a provision's consequences, a client may be dissatisfied with a provision. Such dissatisfaction typically requires you or a client to develop new alternatives. Indeed, sometimes the dissatisfaction produces entirely new objectives as well. Consider this dialogue:

1.   L: Andrea, next let's look briefly at paragraph 5. In essence it says that PSD can fire Fleming if she fails to perform in any way or in any way breaches the agreement. Is this adequate to meet your needs?

2.   C: The one problem I see is that it may not go far enough. We don't want to be stuck with Fleming if for some reason we decide to abandon the evidence software project.

3.   L: Do you anticipate that PSD might want to do that?

4.   C: Not really, but in this business that is always a possibility. For example, someone may beat us to market.

5.   L: I see your point. If you want to, we could add a clause saying that if PSD chooses to sell or abandon the evidence tracking project during the two-year period, PSD shall have the right to cancel the contract. Would that give you what you need?

6.   C: I think it would.

7.   L: Assuming we add this provision, how do you think Fleming will react?

8.   C: . . .

Here, Andrea is dissatisfied with the draft of paragraph 5. That dissatisfaction is the vehicle for her mentioning a new objective (No. 2). Aware of that objective, you mention another alternative (No. 5), the

---

21. For a discussion of pivotal and pertinent consequences, see Chapter 15, sec. 6(C).

consequences of which you then begin to explore (No. 7). As is often the case, Andrea's dissatisfaction implicates all of the steps in the counseling model.

C. A PROVISION'S ADEQUACY FROM THE OTHER PARTY'S PERSPECTIVE

Part of assessing a provision's adequacy is evaluating its likely effect on the other party, both in terms of negotiating a final agreement and the parties' long-term relationship. For example, a provision may give your client all the protection in the world, but insisting on such protection may offend the other side or cause it to walk away from the deal.[22] If such risks exist, they are ones for a client to take or avoid.[23] Thus, even when a client is satisfied with a provision, the reasonable opportunity standard often requires that you inquire about its potential effect on future negotiations and relations,[24] and when appropriate raise the possibility of altering it.[25]

For example, assume that you are exploring paragraph 8 with Andrea:

> 1. L: Andrea, we're agreed that paragraph 8's language prohibiting Fleming from engaging in any other computer programing work during the two years of the contract meets PSD's objective that Fleming devote full attention to PSD's project. However, just to be safe, let's take a minute to talk about Fleming's likely response. Before we submit the draft to her let's at least consider whether it might anger her in some way. After all, there's no point alienating Fleming if we can avoid it.[26]

> 2. C: I agree, so long as we don't give up anything we need.

22. See M.H. McCormack, *The Terrible Truth About Lawyers* 111–112, 84–87 (1987). Even if you succeed in winning such one-sided provisions, you may find later that this was a pyrrhic victory. See, Ibid at 142–145 ("lopsided deals don't last").

23. See Chapter 15, sec. 6(E). We assume here that omission of the provision would not violate the law or create a situation that you would find so morally objectionable that you would feel compelled to withdraw as counsel.

24. If the proposed agreement being reviewed has been drawn by the other side, the comments in this section apply to any revisions you suggest be sent back to the other side.

25. Some lawyers believe you need not explore this topic on a paragraph by paragraph basis. They say that so long as a client has read an agreement, you can simply ask a client if the client believes that any of the provisions are likely to harm the negotiations or the parties' ultimate relationship. Such an inquiry may cause a client to identify potentially troublesome provisions. But it is highly unlikely that the question will cause a client's mind to run through each of the agreement's paragraphs. The client's response therefore will be based on less than a complete review. We made the same point with respect to making topical searches by taking a topic across the time line. See Chapter 10, sec. 11.

26. Whenever you ask a client to think about the other party's likely reaction, make sure the client understands that he or she, rather than the other party, is your primary concern. If you begin to examine this subject without prior explanation, a client might doubt your loyalty.

3. L: I understand. What problems, if any, is Fleming likely to have with a requirement that she not do any outside work?[27]

4. C: Well, I think she does do some programing with a couple of other people on weekends. She might not want to give that up.

5. L: What does that work entail?

6. C: I'm not sure but it has something to do with education of school children.

7. L: Okay; so Fleming may have some objection to giving up that work. Do you think we should leave the provision as it is or make some changes in it, such as to allow her to spend a limited time, say on weekends, working on outside projects?

8. C: I'm not sure we ought to do that. Lots of us have started spending some weekend time at the office, and especially as we get close to marketing the program, I'd hate for her contract to say that she has a right not to work on weekends.

9. L: Can you see any alternative that would allow her to continue with some outside work and still protect PSD?

10. C: I can't think of anything. Besides, the way the clause reads now allows us to start at a strong place; if she wants to change it let her bring it up. Don't forget she is getting a $10,000 raise in this deal.

11. L: Certainly with that kind of raise, PSD ought to have first call on her activities. But since you've said that Fleming's current activities are not a problem for you, how about itemizing the specific outside work Fleming is now doing, and providing that she can continue to do that work? That provision might help us in negotiations by allowing us to point out that the agreement is drafted with both parties' interests in mind.

12. C: It sounds fine now, but the outside work may become a problem down the road.

13. L: How likely is that?

14. C: I really can't say.

15. L: All right, one con of allowing her to continue with her present activities is that there's an undefined risk that those activities may conflict with your future needs. Do you see any other cons?

16. C: Well, ...

27. Lawyers sometimes examine the other party's perspective through role playing, with a client playing the other party. We are again indebted to Bill Rutter for pointing this out.

This dialogue demonstrates that examining a provision from the other party's perspective often involves each step of the counseling process. No. 1 includes a Step One inquiry as to whether one of Andrea's objectives is not to anger Fleming. Andrea agrees that it is (No. 2), and mentions that Fleming might be unhappy with the provision in its draft form (No. 4). The conflict between Andrea's objective and the impact of the provision leads you to a Step Two examination of possible alternatives (Nos. 7 and 11), and a Step Three discussion of likely "pivotal" and "pertinent" consequences (No. 10; Nos. 12–15).

No. 11 shows the inevitable relationship between examining a provision from the other party's perspective and negotiation strategy. In No. 10, Andrea takes a traditional stance toward negotiation, stating that standing by the draft may be advantageous as it allows PSD to "start at a strong place." In response, you set forth an alternative that might meet both PSD's and Fleming's needs (No. 11); Nos. 12–15 begin to examine the consequences of this "problem solving" approach.[28]

D. INTEGRATING THE TOPICAL INQUIRIES INTO THE FOUR STEP COUNSELING MODEL

We now explore to what extent modifying the four step counseling model in a discussion of a deal's individual provisions is consistent with giving a client a reasonable opportunity to decide.

For a change of pace, assume that your client is Fleming rather than PSD. Last week you met with Fleming for the first time and gathered basic information about her proposed deal with PSD. You learned that PSD has offered Fleming a two-year employment contract at an annual salary of $64,000. Fleming, who is 29, has been a computer programmer for seven years and has done work on PSD's evidence tracking program since coming to the company six months ago. Fleming is quite happy with the financial terms of PSD's offer, but she has never signed a formal contract of any kind and has not tried to read through PSD's proposal. Accordingly, at the conclusion of the meeting, it was agreed that both you and Fleming would review the

28. For discussion of traditional and problem-solving approaches to negotiation, see, e.g., S. Goldberg, E. Green, F. Sander, *Dispute Resolution* 19–89 (1985); C. Menkel–Meadow, "Toward Another View of Legal Negotiation: The Structure of Problem–Solving, 31 UCLA L Rev. 754 (1984). Note that many lawyers have traditionally regarded negotiation strategy as strictly a matter of "professional craft," and thus not a matter requiring client consultation. However, as the text suggests, a client may not have a reasonable opportunity to choose an alternative unless the client is aware of its potential impact on negotiation strategy. Indeed, whenever a provision places a burden on the other party that the other party has not agreed to, the provision's potential impact on fu-

ture negotiations is a consequence that you should typically discuss with a client.

In addition to asking a client to assess a provision's potential impact on negotiations, client-centeredness also suggests that you often consult a client with regard to other issues of negotiation strategy. Such issues might include whether in general to take a "cooperative" or "competitive" approach to the negotiations; whether you or the client should conduct the negotiation; and if it is you, whether the client should be present. Remember, a client may know the other party far better than you do. For further discussion of counseling dialogues with respect to negotiation, see D.G. Gifford, *Legal Negotiations: Theory and Applications* 55–72; 184–200 (1989).

proposed agreement and then meet to discuss it. The discussion focuses on paragraph 4, which reads as follows:

"During her employment by PSD Fleming shall devote her full energies, interests, abilities, and productive time to the performance of her duties under this agreement and shall not, without PSD's prior written consent, engage in any computer activities or services of any kind for herself or any other person or entity which services are designed to produce financial benefit for Fleming or any other person or entity."

The dialogue is as follows:

1. L: Rhonda, it's nice to see you again. Any new developments since we last met?

2. C: Not at all.

3. L: I've gone over PSD's draft and I think I understand what PSD is proposing. Have you had a chance to go through the agreement since we last met?

4. C: I read through it, but frankly I'm not sure I understand it all. I understand that it's for two years and I would get $64,000 a year plus a cost of living raise in the second year. Also, I understand the fringe benefits stuff. But all that stuff about what happens if I leave and things like that is somewhat confusing.

5. L: As I recall you've never been involved in a contract such as this, so I can see why you may have some questions. What we will do today is go through each section, and I hope that by the time we're through you'll have a good picture of what's involved. But before I get started, are there any particular clauses you'd like to talk about?

6. C: Well, I'm not sure I understand paragraph 4. Does it mean that I can't do any other programing work while I'm working for PSD?

7. L: It does seem to say that, and we will certainly talk about that one. Are there other provisions that particularly concern you?

8. C: Not specifically.

9. L: OK, then why don't we start with paragraph 4. What it says is that while you work for PSD you can't, without PSD's consent, engage in any outside computer work with the intent of making money for you or anyone else. In other words, you can't do any programing with the intent that it will immediately or eventually bring you money. From what you've said, these restrictions present problems. Why don't you tell me what they are?

10. C: At home on the weekends, I've been working on a program with a couple of friends. It's a tutorial program for use with high school students in helping them learn econom-

ics. We've made quite a bit of progress on it and should have a prototype done in four to six months. Our plan is to market the program as soon as we beta test the proto-type. Also, once in awhile I get a chance to do some independent consulting work which I do on weekends to pick up some extra money. So if I couldn't do these things, then I'm not sure I'd want to sign the contract even though it gives me a $10,000 raise.

11. L: You want to keep your opportunities for additional income open.

12. C: Exactly; I don't want to compete with PSD, and I understand they are entitled to a full week's work. But what I do on the weekends or at night is my own business.

13. L: There are a number of ways we might try to work this situation out. Let me list some for you and then see if you have some other ideas. You might try to get PSD to agree that you can continue with your current activities. After all, you've been doing this kind of work right along and they are obviously happy with you. Or, since stopping those activities will cost you money, you might ask for a bigger raise than $10,000. With respect to either option, you might approach Paul informally or we might go back to them in a more formal way by revising this paragraph. Do you see any other possibilities?

14. C: Not really, unless I just go ahead and sign. What do you think I should do? I'm not sure how to handle this situation.

15. L: I can understand why you'd like some advice on this, and I want to give you all the help I can. Signing the agreement as it stands is an option we can talk about. But before I can give you an opinion about what option might be best, we'll need to talk some more. Let's talk a bit about each of these approaches and try to figure out the possible advantages and disadvantages of each. After we've done that it may become clear how you should proceed. Let me list the choices on this piece of paper so we can keep track of the possible pros and cons. Let's start with the possibility of their agreeing to your keeping on with your current activities. What do you see as positive about such an approach?

16. C: That seems like the most friendly approach; certainly it's less antagonistic than asking for more salary. The company's pretty new and I'm uncomfortable asking for more money, especially since they are already offering me a $10,000 raise.

17. L: So going back to them about maintaining the status quo has the advantage of keeping matters on a friendly and informal basis and avoids the discomfort you may feel about asking for more money. What other advantages do you see for seeking to keep up your current outside activities?

18. C: It's better than asking for more salary because I don't have to try and figure out how much more would be fair and because I really want to continue my outside work. I really like the tutorial project. I want to continue working on it because I think it's a valuable idea. Also, the consulting lets me work on various projects and keeps me from going stale.

19. L: I can see you really want to maintain your outside activities. A real disadvantage to asking for more money and giving up all your outside work would be the loss of variety in your work life. Any other advantages you see to keeping the outside work?

20. C: It's an approach that I feel comfortable with. In fact, as I think about this matter, I really don't want to ask them for more money. They're being generous, and I wouldn't feel comfortable asking for more money. They'll just get pissed and things will get messy. I just don't want to risk that.

21. L: Well, you know PSD better than I do, so maybe we should drop that idea. So let's talk about how to approach PSD. What about a formal approach of redrafting the agreement to provide that you can continue working on the tutorial program and do consulting on the weekends and presenting that redraft to them? What advantages might that have over your just going to Paul informally?

22. C: None that I see. It presents the same problems. If I bring this up, then the whole thing is likely to become unraveled. I like the idea of the $10,000 annual raise, I like the company. It's not that I'm afraid PSD may back away from the deal. They need me more than I need them. The problem is that once Paul finds out about my extra work she'll always be looking over my shoulder to make sure I'm working on the PSD project. If that happens, a great work situation will go down the tubes. Instead of being able to work independently, someone will always be checking on what I'm doing. I wish this damn language weren't in here. If it weren't I could just sign this thing and get on with my life.

   Maybe, I should just sign the agreement and continue with my present practice. They don't know what I'm doing now and they are not likely to find out. What happens if I sign, continue with my work and then they find out?

23. L: That probably would give PSD the right under paragraph 5 to terminate your contract. Now, the agreement contains an arbitration clause. Therefore, you'd have to file an arbitration claim if you believe that PSD had improperly terminated you. [Explanation of arbitration provision omitted] There is a small possibility, say ten percent or so, that an arbitrator might find the clause invalid because it placed an unreasonable restriction on your activities. If an arbitrator were to hold that, then if PSD fires you and you file an arbitration claim, you'd have a right to damages under paragraph 6. You would be entitled to any difference in salary between what you were being paid by PSD and your new job. You would, of course, have to try to get a new job and I guess from what you've told me that wouldn't be a problem. But as I said, the chances that an arbitrator would find the clause invalid and therefore rule in your favor are quiet slim.

24. C: I just don't think PSD will fire me even if they find out about my extra work. They need me; that's why they're offering me the $10,000 raise. The longer I work on the project the more they'll need me. Unless it's illegal or something, I'd just as soon sign the deal as it is and take my chances. That way I get the raise and there is no hassle about extra work. What do you think about that?

25. L: I'm not sure you should run the risk. In my experience people are best off facing problems before they arise. Why run the risk? If they fire you in the middle of the contract, where will that leave you?

26. C: I'm great at what I do. I'd find another job quickly. Maybe not at $64,000 a year but certainly for close to what I'm making now. And furthermore, I'm sure they are not going to fire me. They really need me. The more I think about this the more I realize that the best thing to do is sign the agreement and not worry about this paragraph.

27. L: Rhonda, if you do that and they fire you, at best you'll have to sue them if you want to enforce the contract. If it were me I wouldn't put myself in that situation. I'd face the situation now and rest easy at night.

28. C: I know this possible arbitration claim bothers you but unless there are some other serious problems with this agreement, I'm just going to let sleeping dogs lie and sign. Really, I feel comfortable with that.

29. L: Okay. As long as you understand what the risk is, I guess I can't say anything else. Let's see if there are other

> problems, perhaps there won't be. Why don't we start with paragraph 1. What this says is . . ..

Nos. 1 and 2 properly start the follow-up meeting by inquiring about new developments and reporting on your actions.[29] In No. 3 you ask Rhonda whether she has read the agreement. This question is clearly appropriate. Through the response in No. 4, you learn that your client has not read the agreement thoroughly and seems uncertain about the meaning of many of its provisions. Hence, affording her a reasonable opportunity to decide probably requires you to conduct a thorough review, and your comment in No. 5 reflecting your decision to review each clause seems correct.[30]

No. 5 is a brief Preparatory Explanation of your intent to review each provision. The explanation may defuse any uncertainty on your client's part about what the conference will entail. Nos. 5 and 7 ask the client to identify troublesome provisions. As you recall, at the beginning of a conference you typically should give a client an opportunity to express concerns.[31] As Rhonda expresses concern only about paragraph 4, (No. 6), you sensibly start your review with that paragraph (No. 9).

As suggested in the earlier subsections, No. 9 starts the review by briefly explaining the clause's likely legal effect without getting caught up in legal abstractions. You also inquire as to its adequacy by asking whether it creates an undue burden. The active listening response (No. 11) encourages Rhonda to identify additional burdens. In describing the burdens she sees (Nos. 10 and 12), Rhonda is concurrently outlining her objectives with respect to paragraph 4. Thus Nos. 9 and 11 simultaneously uncover burdens and undertake the Step One task of identifying objectives. Your move in No. 13 to Step Two—potential alternatives—cuts off further objectives that Rhonda might have. Might you have asked an additional question such as, "Are there any other difficulties you have with paragraph 4?"

No. 13 begins the Step Two discussion by identifying possible alternatives you see. Given Rhonda's apparent inexperience with employment contracts, starting with alternatives you see seems appropriate.[32] You propose that PSD either permit her to continue her current activities or compensate her for giving them up. You also indicate that PSD might be approached either formally or informally. Certainly the alternatives are not the only ones which you might have mentioned. For example, another alternative is leaving Rhonda free to do her own work on weekends. However, you cannot mention all possible alternatives [33] and your choices seem to cover the basic approaches. Note also that you explain each alternative, and maintain

---

29. For a review of these ideas see Chapter 7, sec. 5.

30. This assessment assumes no problems of time, money or client willingness to review the document.

31. See Chapter 7, sec. 5.

32. See Chapter 16, sec. 4.

33. See Chapter 18, sec. 2.

neutrality between them. Finally, you ask Rhonda if she sees any additional options.

In No. 14, Rhonda indicates that she sees an additional option—to sign the agreement as it stands. She then asks for your opinion about which of your options to follow. In No. 15 you acknowledge the viability of her suggested option. Then, since any opinion you give should be based on a client's values,[34] you tell Rhonda that you will need to talk further before giving her any advice. To ameliorate her possible disappointment, you include an active listening remark ("I can understand . . .") and expressly articulate your desire to help.[35] Moreover, by telling Rhonda that "it may become clear how you should proceed," you leave open the possibility that she may be able to make the decision herself. You then move to a Step Three examination of the pros and cons of the options.

As you can see, the dialogue in Nos. 13–15 fails to comport fully with the counseling model. After Rhonda contributes a new option (No. 14), you fail to ask her if she sees any others. Also, at the conclusion of No. 15 you instruct Rhonda to start with the "status quo" option, rather than asking her which option she prefers to discuss first. Remembering that paragraph 4 is the one of most concern to Rhonda, you might conclude that these shortcomings deny her a reasonable opportunity to explore all pivotal and pertinent options. However, with five options already on the table, and Rhonda expressing uncertainty, perhaps your decision not to troll for additional ones is sensible. On the other hand, your starting with one of your own options is more questionable. Perhaps you have ceased to be neutral and have shown a personal preference for one option.[36]

Nos. 15–19 start to follow Step Three of the counseling model. No. 15 asks Rhonda about the pros of the "status quo" option. Although her mention in No. 16 of not asking for more money crosses over to a con of a different option, No. 17 keeps Rhonda focused on the pros of the status quo option. Moreover, Nos. 17 and 19 both incorporate active listening responses; the former reflects content, the latter reflects both content and feelings. No. 17 "converts" the consequences Rhonda identifies to advantages. No. 19 acknowledges Rhonda's cross over by converting it to disadvantages,[37] but returns Rhonda to the pro side of the ledger by searching for additional advantages.

In No. 20, Rhonda rejects the "ask PSD for more money" option. She gives two reasons for doing so: (1) her own discomfort and (2) not wanting to risk messing up the deal. In No. 21, you accept her decision. However, given Rhonda's background how confident could

---

34. See Chapter 15, sec. 6(D).

35. See Chapter 2, sec. 2(F).

36. Such a preference is at least understandable from a psychological standpoint. You may feel you have been of no help if the client simply signs the proposed draft. However, ethical rules demand that you put a client's interests above your own. See ABA Model Rules of Professional Conduct. Rule 1.7(b); ABA Model Code of Professional Responsibility, EC 5–1, EC 5–2.

37. See Chapter 19, sec. D.

you be that Rhonda has an adequate data base to predict correctly that "things will get messy?" For that matter, "messiness" is a vague term; after further discussion it might turn out that PSD would seriously consider a counter-proposal. Hence, No. 21 may too readily accept Rhonda's rejection. Given Rhonda's concern over paragraph 4, a reasonable opportunity to consider the option might at least have prompted you to inquire about the adequacy of her data base.[38] Consider this approach:

> "Rhonda, I can tell you want to avoid angering PSD and that this is an important goal. But I want to make sure that your asking for more money if you have to give up the outside activities really will create hard feelings on PSD's part. Why do you feel they would get angry if you ask for more money to make up for the extra income and satisfaction you lose if you have to give up your present outside work?"

This comment might cause Rhonda to examine her data base and reconsider her decision.[39] Alternatively, she might stick with her decision, reasoning that though she has little or no data base for predicting that a demand for a bigger raise will create hostility, she nevertheless does not want to take the risk. With misprediction put to the side, and no question of immorality, the issue becomes one of whose sense of risk averseness prevails. And as you know, absent special circumstances,[40] you should not push a client to take a risk the client chooses not to.[41]

Return again to No. 21. Here you turn to the alternative of presenting PSD with a revised draft which permits Rhonda to continue her current outside activities, and ask her what advantages she sees. In No. 22, Rhonda indicates dissatisfaction with any approach that discloses her outside activities to PSD. Stating that PSD is not aware of her extra work, Rhonda returns to her previously-broached option of signing the agreement as is. After brief discussion, Rhonda chooses this option (No. 28), and you concur with her choice (No. 29).

You may find the discussion leading up to Rhonda's final decision troublesome. It demonstrates how use of a few counseling techniques does not necessarily provide a client with a reasonable opportunity to decide. On a positive note, you do convert the chance that an arbitrator will invalidate the restriction to percentage terms and you explain what result would ensue were she to prevail (No. 23). Moreover, if Rhonda's question at the end of No. 24 can fairly be interpreted as a

---

38. See Chapter 19, sec. 2(B).

39. Even if her decision does not change, you have at least afforded her a reasonable opportunity to consider the matter.

40. Such circumstances include a client's choice raising moral concerns and a situation where a client is likely to incur a major loss for little gain. See Chapter 20, secs. 4(A) and (B).

41. See Chapter 20, sec. 4(A). The situation here is the opposite that you will usually encounter in the deals setting. The more typical situation is represented by Nos. 25–29 in the Rhonda dialogue—the client wants to take a risk which you believe is not warranted.

request for your personal opinion, you do give her the benefit of that opinion (No. 25).[42]

Yet, the dialogue manages to miss most of the underlying concerns of the counseling model. Perhaps as a result, the client's choice may be both immoral and based on mispredictions. Rhonda decides that the "sign as is" option is most likely to achieve her objective of continuing her outside work on the basis of a number of predictions: that she will not be found out; that if she is, she will not be fired; and that if she is fired, she will quickly land a comparable job somewhere else. Despite Rhonda's apparent inexperience with how PSD might react to counter-proposals, you question none of these assertions. Instead, you meekly assume that her data base for making each is adequate.

Your failure to question Rhonda's data bases also means that potential "cons" go unexamined. You neither ask Rhonda in open fashion what downsides she might see, nor do you use closed questions to raise possible downsides. For example, you might have asked, "Will needing to hide your outside activities be a daily source of worry for you?" and "Would future job opportunities be hurt if you are fired by PSD?"

Additionally, you allow Rhonda to make what is arguably an immoral choice without so much as a whimper. Rhonda intends to sign the agreement and ignore its restriction on outside activities. Even though there is a 10% chance that an arbitrator would hold the restriction invalid, Rhonda's proposed course of action is deceptive. Engaging Rhonda in a discussion of this moral concern may well be necessary if she is to have a reasonable opportunity to consider all "pivotal" and "pertinent" consequences of her choice.[43] For example, you might have said, "I realize that the outside activities are very important to you, and I appreciate your desire for diversity. But I have some concern over your signing the agreement intending not to comply with paragraph 4. How do you feel about that?" [44]

Finally, recognize that instead of engaging Rhonda in a fuller counseling dialogue, you attempt to dissuade her from her intended path by trying to convince her that the risks (of being found out and fired) are not worth taking. When Rhonda asks for your opinion about whether she should sign, without clarifying her question you interpret it as one seeking to know what you personally would do, and you respond that she should not run the risk (No. 25). However, Rhonda clearly views the risks as minimal (No. 26). Against this backdrop,

---

42. See Chapter 20, sec. 2(B). As there suggested, perhaps it would have been better had you first asked a question to find out whether Rhonda wanted your personal opinion.

43. In addition, you will want to consider withdrawing should Rhonda insist on going ahead with her choice.

44. See Chapter 20, sec. 4(B). However, some lawyers would have no qualms about allowing Rhonda to sign the agreement despite her stated intention to disobey its restriction on outside activities.

your pushing her not to run the risks (No. 27) seems a blatant attempt to substitute your sense of risk averseness for hers.[45]

In the end, then, the dialogue probably does not provide Rhonda with a reasonable opportunity to make a decision about paragraph 4. Admittedly, the four-step counseling model need not be slavishly adhered to in reviewing each and every provision of an agreement. But here, given (a) the importance of paragraph 4 to Rhonda; (b) her inexperience; (c) the paucity of hard data that PSD would react negatively to an alternative proposal; and (d) Rhonda's contemplated deception and its attendant risks, the number and the severity of the deviations from the model are unacceptable.

On the other hand, note that you at least do attend to the topics you typically need to explore when counseling a client about an individual provision. You explain its meaning (No. 9) and explore its adequacy and that of potential alternatives from Rhonda's perspective (Nos. 9–27). The one topic that gets rather short shrift is examining a provision from the other party's perspective. But the reason for that is understandable. When the other party prepares a draft, you need to examine that party's perspective only when a client wants to offer an alternative. Here, Rhonda's accepting PSD's version of paragraph 4 largely obviated the necessity to explore PSD's likely reaction.

5.   COUNSELING CLIENTS ABOUT A DEAL'S OVERALL WISDOM

The discussion thus far has focused on counseling clients about a proposed deal's individual terms. As mentioned in Chapter 11, however, sometimes clients seek advice about a deal's overall wisdom. Or, as some might say, a client asks a "Go–No Go" question.[46]

As may be apparent, the counseling model applies to "Go–No Go" decisions. No matter if the question is "Should I sign this lease" or "Is this the right time to bring in a partner?" or some other global sort of question, you examine alternatives and consequences in light of the client's objectives. This section examines how variables such as a client's background and circumstances might lead you to adapt the counseling model to the "Go–No Go" context.

A.   CASE STUDY NO. 2: SNACKS SIXTH AVENUE

You represent Josef Thrush. For the last three years, Josef has been running a catering business out of his house, mostly catering birthday and anniversary parties in people's homes. You represented him in connection with the initial licensing of his catering business, and you have consulted with him from time to time as problems arose regarding employees, payments from customers, and the like.

---

45. See Chapter 15, sec. 6(E).

46. This term is borrowed from James C. Freund although used in a slightly dif-

ferent way from that used by Mr. Freund. See J.C. Freund, *Lawyering: A Realistic Approach to Legal Practice* 268 (1979).

A couple of weeks ago, you got a phone call from a very excited Josef. He told you that for some time he had been thinking of stopping the catering business in favor of opening up a restaurant. By having a restaurant, he hopes to realize a more steady income. While he realizes that a restaurant might not be immediately profitable, he thinks that a restaurant in a newly located site soon would be profitable, and would offer a great potential for growth.

The site Josef has located is the Sixth Avenue Shopping Center, a block-long collection of upscale shops. A restaurant site is currently vacant in the Center, and Josef has begun lease negotiations with Arthur Crenshaw, the Center's manager. Josef believes that the people who tend to patronize the Center's shops will be at acted to his style of cuisine. Josef's discussions with Crenshaw resulted in Crenshaw giving Josef a written lease proposal. After telling you all this, Josef said that he is anxious to get started, but he asked you to look over the lease proposal "just to make sure I'm not signing my life away." He mailed it to your office and made an appointment to meet with you in two days so that you could review the lease with him.

Based on the phone conversation and review of the lease, you understand the parties' preliminary agreement to be as follows: Josef and Crenshaw have agreed to a five-year lease for rent of $108,000 per year ($9000 per month) minimum, as against 7% of gross annual sales. The lease term would start in two months from signing, giving Josef time to make some modest capital improvements. The lease is "net, net, net," meaning that Josef would have to pay for repairs, real property taxes and assessments, and fire insurance. In addition, Josef would be obligated to pay a pro-rata share for maintenance of the Center's common areas. From what Josef told you, you know that last year, taxes for the site were $3600, and the maintenance cost was $400 per month.

B. SHOULD JOSEF ENTER INTO THE LEASE?: "GO–NO GO"

You are now meeting with Josef to review the lease proposal. He remains very anxious to open a restaurant in the Center. However, from your prior dealings with Josef, you realize that while he is excellent at planning and preparing menus, he is not always as careful in making business decisions as he might be. On a couple of occasions that you can remember, Josef has made quick decisions which he has in hindsight regretted. Hence, you think it important for Josef to have a chance to consider whether it makes sense for him to open up his restaurant in the Sixth Avenue Center at all. This portion of the discussion goes as follows:

    1. L: Josef, I've looked at the lease, and there's a couple of ways we can go here. Either we can just go through the lease and make sure you are comfortable with its provisions, or we can spend a few minutes first talking about whether this deal makes sense for you at all.

2. C: Well, I'm pretty committed to it. But if you think it's a big mistake, I guess I should know about that.

3. L: I'm not suggesting that at all; in fact, I don't have enough information to begin to make that judgment. I'm sure you've given it a lot of thought, so it might be helpful if you and I took a few minutes to look at the forest before we focus on the trees.

4. C: The trees? Does the lease say I'm paying for those too? I wouldn't be surprised—it seems like I have to pay for everything else in that Center.

5. L: Hopefully, your restaurant will be a smash and it'll be worth it. But it does sound like you have some concerns about the financial commitment you'd be making by signing this lease, so maybe we ought to talk briefly about it. I understand your thinking that a restaurant can provide steadier income than a catering business and also that it might provide a greater opportunity for growth. But tell me, have you explored other possible sites for the restaurant?

6. C: No, I figured you'd ask that. I assume there's lots of other places around town where I could open my restaurant, but this one just seems perfect. The clientele and the types of businesses that the Center has will fit in perfectly with my restaurant operation. Also, it's in a growing market, and the location would be very convenient for me and my employees. I don't really want to look elsewhere.

7. L: You've obviously thought carefully about the advantages of this location. Are there any other pros you can think of?

8. C: The parking is good. Also, most of the shops are open late, and people are usually around there after dark. That's important because I want to have both a dinner and a lunch crowd.

9. L: It sounds like an ideal spot. Any other advantages?

10. C: No. What else could I ask for?

11. L: Let's look at it from the other side—any disadvantages that you see?

12. C: No, only I wish the rent weren't so high.

13. L: Is there any room to negotiate further on that?

14. C: I don't think so. Crenshaw was definite; standard rent in the center is $3.00 a square foot minimum, against a percentage of gross. And 7% is a pretty standard percentage for restaurants.

15. L: So the options really are to accept this deal or to keep the catering business going until some other opportunity comes along?

16. C: Yes, but I'm not really interested in looking elsewhere. Also, my goal when I began catering was to go into a restaurant, and I just feel the time is right.

17. L: Then let's talk about what you see as the major potential drawback, the cost of the lease. For the first year at least, the minimum cost is $116,400. That includes rent, real property taxes and common areas maintenance, assuming the latter two don't increase. And if your annual gross is higher than $108,000, 7% of the excess belongs to the Center. So what we should do is approximate as closely as we can your other likely operating expenses, compare expenses to expected income, and see what the bottom line might look like. Have you projected income and expenses?

18. C: Yes. I was given access to the books of the restaurant that used to be in that location. It was making money and would still be in operation if the owner hadn't died. Over the last two years, it grossed about $290,000 per year; expenses averaged around $210,000. I'm going to put about $20,000 into modernizing the place, and together with my style of cuisine, I figure I can do at least $400,000 gross the first year, and $450,000 the second year. That's based on an average price per meal of around $5.50 for lunch and $9.50 for dinner. I know what other restaurants in the area are charging and these prices are reasonable. If I do 160–180 meals a day, I'll reach that gross.

19. L: How about the expenses side?

20. C: Because I pay my employees very well and need a couple more people than the old restaurant, and also to take care of unexpected expenses, I added 35% to the expenses of the old restaurant; that amounts to about $280,000. Plus if I'm serving more meals, my food costs will be higher, say $40,000. So I'm looking at about $320,000 in expenses the first year.

21. L: Have you calculated the number of seatings for both lunch and dinner?

22. C: I really didn't get that specific.

23. L: I think that might be worthwhile; it's one of the biggest differences between being a caterer and running a restaurant. When you cater a party you know in advance how many meals you'll be serving but in the restaurant business the most realistic way to think about likely income is in terms of number of meals per day. How many square

feet of seating are available and how many customers can you serve at one time?

24. C: The entire restaurant is 3000 square feet; the layout gives me about 1500 square feet for seating. It'll hold around 60–70 people at once.

25. L: All right. How many meals a day do you figure to serve at lunch, and how many at dinner?

26. C: At lunch, I can probably count on two seatings. At least for the first year, let's figure one seating for dinner.

27. L: Working through those figures it seems like your income projections are based on two full seatings at lunch and a full seating at dinner almost every day. Is that realistic?

28. C: I guess I didn't get down to that level of detail. I mainly made my projections based on the old restaurant, and assuming I could do better.

29. L: Unfortunately, the books can't tell us how many meals the restaurant served. Perhaps it would be worthwhile to think through the likelihood that you can serve this many meals per day, especially in the opening months. Also, I'm wondering about your cost projections. Your costs may be different from those you encounter in the catering business and from those incurred by the former tenant. Have you actually worked through all of your costs?

30. C: I pretty much relied on cost figures from my business. I guess I haven't really worked the numbers.

31. L: I'm certainly not an expert on food and restaurant costs, but it does seem to me that you ought to work through the numbers a bit more. Costs for things like utilities and insurance are likely to differ from those in your catering business. Can you work the numbers through by yourself, or would you be better off going through those with your accountant?

32. C: I'll think about that. But I'm glad we're doing this. I guess I liked the location so much that I got carried away. I can see that it makes sense to do some more specific projections on both the income and expense side.

33. L: Why don't you do that, and then we can talk further. If the deal makes economic sense, and probably it will, then there are some other factors to think about, such as how much time you'll need to devote to the restaurant and whether your time commitment is going to take you away from other things you are now able to do.

34. C: I've thought about those things. I'm pretty comfortable with the time commitment. I've got a great chef who wants to continue working with me and take on more

responsibility. She'll be able to share a great deal of the supervision, so I should have enough free time.[47]

35. L: So going with the restaurant is not a disadvantage in terms of time?

36. C: No. It's actually an advantage because I should have more time on the weekends. The restaurant would be closed on Sundays; I hate having to work Sundays, but in the catering business, that's a big day.

37. L: Sundays free sounds great. Okay, at this point here's what I suggest. You sit down either with or without your accountant and run more specific projections. Call Crenshaw, let him know of your continued interest and see if he'll commit to holding the site open for you for a week or so. Then, if the finances make sense, we can get back together and go through some of the specific provisions in the lease. There's a few other financial matters we'll want to try to control in connection with potential increased costs under the lease. For example, as the lease now reads, increased property taxes will be passed on to you. And under current tax laws, if the center is sold, its assessed value will undoubtedly go up. We can talk about adding a clause to the lease to protect you from some kinds of tax increases. We can also talk about the wording of specific provisions once you decide the deal as a whole makes sense. Does that seem okay?

38. C: Sounds good to me. I appreciate the advice—I didn't really think about actual seatings, but I can see that I have to. When can we meet again?

39. L: Just about any time you like . . .

As you can see, Josef has experience in the food service industry. Thus, he is somewhat familiar with food costs and the expenses of meal preparation, as well as with how to price meals to customers. But his experience is as a caterer and not a restauranteur. At the same time, he may be a bit impetuous. He has found a location that apparently will enable him to realize his goal of operating a restaurant and he does not want to consider other possible locations. Thus his mind is partially made up. In the light of these individual circumstances, do you give Josef a reasonable opportunity to decide whether to go forward with the deal?

This question is germane only because Josef agrees to talk about the practical viability of the deal. Josef initially asked you only to "look over" the lease proposal and therefore was perhaps interested in nothing more than your views on its individual provisions. Because

---

47. This comment suggests that as is undoubtedly usually the case in the restaurant business, the chef's role in Josef's decision is critical. Hence, before Josef makes a final decision to "Go," you would want to delve into the terms of any deal between Josef and the chef, and what might happen if the chef leaves.

business people often resent your giving what they see as business advice [48], you sensibly ask whether Josef wants to talk about whether the deal makes sense (No. 1). Josef's mild acquiescence (No. 2) opens the door to the Go–No Go discussion.[49]

Step One of this discussion is quite truncated. In No. 5 you make but passing reference to Josef's overall objectives and make no effort to update them. Surely a question or two about new or changed objectives would not have been out of line. On the other hand, perhaps your limited exploration is sufficient as only "a couple of weeks" have gone by since Josef explained his objectives to you.

Turning to Step Two, apart from the question at the end of No. 5, you concur in Josef's limiting the alternatives to opening a restaurant in the Sixth Street site. The brief mention of staying in the catering business (No. 15) is not supported by any examination of its consequences. Moreover, you mention but do not push Josef to explore alternative locations for the restaurant (Nos. 5–6). Finally, you fail to mention other possibilities, such as a shorter lease with renewal options or your client's distributing "Josef's Gourmet Cuisine" in pre-packaged form in upscale food stores and markets. For all intents and purposes, then, the Step Two discussion is a "one note" dialogue.

The Step Three discussion explores a number of likely consequences, particularly financial ones. In Nos. 7 and 9, you convert Josef's reasons for wanting to open a restaurant in the center to advantages and search for additional ones.

In No. 11 you begin the search for disadvantages. Though Josef sees none (No. 10), his concern about the high rent sets the agenda for the rest of the discussion. First, you check the data base for his assertion that the rent is fixed (No. 13). Then, in Nos. 17–32 you help Josef focus on the possibility that the deal may not "pencil out." As the dialogue demonstrates, consideration of a single consequence may be quite extensive. You first elicit the data base for Josef's financial predictions. (Nos. 18–22) Then, in Nos. 23–29, you bring to bear your knowledge of restaurant financing and accounting procedures to suggest that more financial information is needed for Josef to make a better informed prediction of the deal's likely financial consequences. From experience, you know that the restaurant industry typically calculates gross sales in terms of numbers of seatings per day.[50]

Moreover, you also briefly explore potential non-financial consequences, such as time commitment (Nos. 33–36).

48. See Chapter 11, note 15.

49. The timing of a "Go–No Go" discussion often varies from that depicted in this example. For example, such a discussion may follow, or be interspersed with, a discussion of a deal's individual provisions. Among the reasons for clients belatedly wanting to discuss a deal's underlying wisdom are dissatisfaction with an individual provision that becomes manifest only after discussion of that provision, negotiating demands made by the other party, and changed circumstances in the client's life.

50. See, D.A. Dyer, *So You Want to Start a Restaurant?* 37–39 (Rev. ed 1981).

At the end of the day, Josef recognizes that his calculations may be both incomplete and overly optimistic and decides that, either on his own or with his accountant, he will make more precise calculations before going further. Hence, the "Go–No Go" discussion never reaches Step Four.

Despite the truncated search for goals, the focus on a single alternative and consideration of a limited set of consequences, the dialogue seems to give Josef a reasonable opportunity to explore the "Go–No Go" decision. First, you do not accept his predilection to enter into the lease. Securing his permission to expand the scope of the discussion allows you to begin to educate Josef about the likely financial consequences of leasing the restaurant.[51]

In this context, initially focusing almost entirely on the financial viability of the single option enhances, rather than detracts from, Josef's opportunity to decide whether to go ahead with the lease deal. The limited focus results in Josef's realizing that he lacks the data to predict whether going forward is likely to allow him to achieve his goal of having a steadier income.

Of course, the limited focus would have been more troublesome had Josef had adequate financial and marketing data. Had the data been adequate to show that the deal was financially viable, or had Josef wanted to take the risk of not getting more precise data, allowing Josef to enter into the lease without giving him the opportunity to examine other alternatives and consequences might well have fallen below the "reasonable opportunity" standard. For example, had Josef decided to open the restaurant without having an opportunity to consider such matters as whether the restaurant would have to remain open on Sundays for Josef to make as much as a restauranteur as he does as a caterer, or without your reviewing the chef's commitment to the restaurant, Josef probably would not have had a reasonable opportunity to make the "Go–No Go" decision.[52]

Note, however, that the dialogue is not completely decision-free. In addition to deciding to make more financial calculations, Josef decides to hold off further negotiations until he has more financial data. Also, Josef accepts your suggestion in No. 37 that he call Crenshaw and seek a commitment to hold the site open. Neither decision is subjected to a counseling dialogue. As to the former, you do not examine the consequences of delay. And as to the latter, you do not give Josef the opportunity to consider and evaluate other possible options, such as saying nothing to Crenshaw or purchasing an option for a longer period than a "week or so."

51. See Chapter 20, sec. 5.

52. Remember that the standard only requires you to afford Josef the *reasonable opportunity* to consider the pertinent and pivotal alternatives and consequences.

There is no requirement that you insist that Josef consider these matters if he does not want to do so. See Chapter 15, sec. 6(C).

Consider, therefore, whether the lack of a counseling dialogue about holding off negotiations and what to tell Crenshaw is appropriate. Arguably these decisions are rather insignificant. The delay may be no more than a week and talking with Crenshaw appears to be a simple matter. Moreover, Josef is somewhat experienced and familiar with Crenshaw. You make your suggestions explicit and give him the opportunity to voice disagreement. You might reasonably expect that Josef would be aware of and would raise negative consequences if there were any.

However, the decisions may be quite important. For example, the financial analysis may take longer than "a week or so," and the delay may result in someone else leasing the restaurant site. Moreover, the opportunity you give Josef to voice disagreement may mean little if he is unaware of or blind to any potential downsides. For example, he may have no idea whether other people are interested in the space. Balanced against these risks, reasonable opportunity may dictate spending a few moments on potential consequences such as: "Do you see any problems with a delay?" or "Do you know if anyone else is interested in the space?"

Chapter 23

REFERRING CLIENTS TO
MENTAL HEALTH
PROFESSIONALS

This chapter explores the process of referring clients who are under severe stress to mental health professionals. Such clients typically experience difficulty making decisions not only about case-related matters but also about matters involving day-to-day life.[1]

For example, a client involved in a personal injury action may desire your advice not only about a case-related matter such as whether or not to hire an investigator but also about what to do about a range of day-to-day problems which have cropped up since the client was disabled and lost his job and created severe stress. The client wants to know whether or not to borrow money from family members, what kind of disability income is available, whether or not it makes sense to move to a smaller home, and what kind of job opportunities might be available to a disabled person. In such a case, you may want to refer the client to a mental health professional because you believe that obtaining the advice and support of a professional such as a social worker, psychologist, or psychiatrist is likely to ease the client's difficulties.

1. REFERRALS FOR HELP IN RESOLVING DAY–TO–DAY PROBLEMS

Clients under severe stress often turn to you for help. Sometimes you can provide the necessary help simply by listening empathically and making a few practical suggestions. However, in many instances you lack both the time and expertise to provide assistance that would help reduce a client's stress. When this is so, it can be to the mutual

---

1. Sometimes you also refer a client to a mental health professional for an evaluation of a client's mental state when that mental state is itself an issue in a case. Though the referral process may be similar to that described in this chapter, this chapter does not address such referrals.

benefit of both the client and you to refer the client to a mental health professional.

A. PREPARING TO MAKE A REFERRAL

Typically a client will more readily accept a suggestion to consult a mental health professional if you refer the client to a specific person (or office) who is immediately available and whose general procedures you can describe. Therefore, if possible, do the following before you broach referral.

First, find a qualified professional willing to accept a referral. The kind of referral you make varies according to a number of factors, including how severely distressed a client appears to be, the nature of the problems involved, and a client's financial condition. If you are uncertain about what kind of mental health professional might best assist a client, contact sources such as another lawyer, a local university mental health clinic or a local or state community mental health clinic, a crisis intervention center, or a suicide prevention center. Local or state psychological, psychiatric, or social work associations also might be of assistance.

Second, when you have obtained the name of a specific person or agency, contact the professional and verify that counseling is currently available including, if possible, specific dates and times. Additionally, obtain a description of what the counseling process will entail so that you can subsequently communicate this information to the client.[2]

B. MAKING A REFERRAL

With a referral in hand, your next step is to help a client understand the need to talk to a mental health professional. The following suggestions may help:

1. Explain what aspects of a client's current situation indicate a need for referral. An explanation might point out that a client appears to be under a great deal of stress, that the client seems to spend a great deal of time talking about day-to-day problems, and that the client seems to be continually seeking advice about how to handle these problems.

2. Empathize with the client's current situation and dilemmas, but point out that you lack the time and expertise to discuss and help resolve the problems.

2. Because the process of finding a qualified mental health professional may become lengthy, you may think that a client, not you, should have the burden of making the search. However, placing the burden on a client would make it far less likely that a client will actually end up talking to a mental health professional. And, if the professional's intervention is at all successful, the time you spend preparing to make a referral is likely to be far less than the time you would otherwise have spent listening to a client repeatedly unload his or her day-to-day living problems on you. What if a client declines a referral? As the client did not authorize your search, you will probably be unable to bill for your time.

3. Explain that being under stress is not abnormal and that many people benefit from counseling. In outlining the potential benefits, you can point out that counseling can reduce stress, that the counselor may be able to help the client make decisions, and that the counselor may be able to refer the client to other specialized sources of help in the community (e.g., vocational guidance, day-care centers, rehabilitation programs, self-help programs).

4. Empathize with a client's discomfort about seeing a counselor.

5. Explain what the counseling will entail and that you can arrange a specific first appointment at a time convenient for the client.

To consider how you might communicate such an explanation, review the following examples:

Case No. 1:

Ms. Peters is a 37–year-old woman with two children. She has initiated divorce proceedings after ten years of marriage. Her children are upset about the divorce, and one of the children is currently in trouble at school for fighting and truancy. Her husband's parents are calling her daily and haranguing her. Her babysitter has just quit, and she has no one to watch the children while she is at work. She doesn't know whether or not to quit her job, or to try to find another babysitter. Further, she cannot decide what items of personal property she is willing to allow her husband to keep. She talks about her problems incessantly and almost to the exclusion of everything else. She cries often.

She keeps calling you under the pretext of discussing the case, but then quickly switches to a discussion of day-to-day problems. You have tried to be empathic, but really do not have the time or the expertise to advise her how to handle her child's school problem or whether or not to keep working. You sense that with mental health counseling, Ms. Peters might be able to resolve her day-to-day problems, as well as her problems with the property settlement agreement.

1. L: Ms. Peters, it seems you're facing a lot of problems you weren't really expecting. Your child is having problems at school, your in-laws are hassling you, and now the babysitter has quit. All of these problems seem to be causing you a great deal of stress. Many clients in similar situations have also been quite upset and didn't know where to turn for help. You've called me a number of times and I only wish I could be of help in some way. Unfortunately, I really don't have the time or training to help you with these problems, but I do know of some professionals who do. Many clients have benefited from counseling, and I think it could be helpful for you to talk to someone now.

2. C: I don't think I'm that sick. You know, I don't think there's anything wrong with me. It's just his parents are impossible and won't leave me alone, and now the school is

calling about Dennis. I just don't know what to do with all of this, and I just can't decide what property I should have.

3.   L: You're right. You really do have too many things happening at one time. It's a lot to cope with, and it's very normal to experience a great deal of stress in the face of problems like these. I wish I could offer some helpful suggestions, but I can't. However, Dr. Klein, at the Reed Clinic on Broadway, near 6th, has counseled a number of people going through divorces. I think she could help you make some of the decisions you're facing, and also help with Dennis and your in-laws. She specializes in counseling families and children; that's why I thought she'd be the right person for you to talk to. I'm pretty sure I can call and arrange an appointment for you. Shall I go ahead?

4.   C: I don't know. I think I should handle these problems myself.

5.   L: I can understand how you might want to handle this alone. Many people feel reluctant to seek help from a counselor. I guess I've also seen how upset you've been in the last few weeks and really think that you could benefit from some outside advice and support. Dr. Klein would probably meet with you for one hour per week and you could discuss some of your personal concerns. In addition, she could contact Dennis' teacher and the school counselor. I think she would be quite helpful. Would you like me to call for an appointment for you?

6.   C: I guess so, but how much will this cost?

7.   L: Dr. Klein sees people on a sliding fee basis. You can discuss your financial situation with her at the first meeting. She will likely set a fee that is quite manageable for you.

Analysis:

In general, you adequately follow the suggested guidelines. In Nos. 1 and 3, you articulate those aspects of Ms. Peters' situation that indicate the need for a referral. You express empathy for her dilemma, but also indicate that you lack both the time and expertise to provide help for her many problems. In No. 3, you point out that it is quite normal to experience stress, and that counseling can be beneficial. In No. 5, you empathize with the client's discomfort about seeking counseling. Additionally, in Nos. 3, 5 and 7, you point out the ready availability of counseling, and explain briefly what the counseling will entail.

Assume that Ms. Peters remains adamant that she is not interested in seeing Dr. Klein or any other counselor. Would you then intervene and try to convince her to see a counselor? Examine the following possibilities:

Alternative 1: Ms. Peters, I think you're making a mistake. You've got so many problems now, and the way to straighten them out is to see someone like Dr. Klein. I'm going to call and arrange an appointment for you.

Alternative 2: Ms. Peters, I'm disappointed to hear you're not interested. You have a lot of problems right now, and you're under a lot of stress. Many clients have been helped by counseling, and I think you could benefit from it also. If you change your mind, please call and I'll go ahead and make an appointment for you.

Alternative 3: O.K., Ms. Peters. I wanted to make the suggestion, but certainly you are free to make your own decision. I'd like to give you this paper with Dr. Klein's phone number and address so if you change your mind you can call her and set up an appointment. I've already spoken with her and I know she can give you an appointment on Tuesday, Wednesday or Thursday afternoons.

Client autonomy may be less of a concern when the issue is whether a client should see a mental health professional than it is when a client selects a course of action for resolving a problem. After all, the usual purpose of referring a client to a mental health professional is to help a client achieve autonomy. Nevertheless, some may find Alternative 1 offensive. Others may find Alternatives 2 and 3 too weak. In the end, you must make your own judgment, informed by your assessment of a client's needs and your attitude towards client autonomy, about how to respond when a client refuses referral to a mental health professional.

Case No. 2:

Bernard Sossin was arrested for embezzling funds from the insurance company by which he was employed. Although he has told his wife, Rhoda, about the arrest and the loss of his job, he has been unable to "break the news" to his children, Ruth and Adam. Without income, his debts are mounting. He is determined not to go into bankruptcy, at least until after his trial, which is set for 90 days hence. In addition to the concern he feels about telling his children, Mr. Sossin is worried about what to say to his social acquaintances and how to handle his financial situation. He is considering withdrawing his children from private school. He would like to get a temporary job but has no idea how to do so. He is especially uncertain of how to explain why he now needs a job. He is mulling his problems over continually and has started to drink. He calls you at least twice a week, supposedly to talk about the case. However, Mr. Sossin always turns the conversation to the subjects of his children, his lack of a job, and his worries about facing his friends. You have decided to end this meeting with Mr. Sossin by recommending he seek counseling to help him cope with his problems.

1. L: Bernie, there is something I'd like to discuss with you. You've called me a number of times this past week to discuss your concerns about your family, your job situation, and what to tell your friends. You seem to want to talk about these problems a lot, and they seem to be causing you a lot of stress at this time. I'd like to help with these problems, but they're really out of my area of expertise. It's not just the job, or what to tell the kids, we've been over that. Right now the real problem, as I see it, is all the stress you're under. You've got all of this plus the worry of the trial, so I can understand why you're so preoccupied with your problems. I'd like to make a suggestion. There is a Dr. Bolberg who has an office in this building. He has counseled a number of people with problems similar to yours, and I think he could help you.

2. C: Look, you know how I feel about shrinks. No way. I know I've been drinking a little too much, but what do you expect? I'll stop being such a pain in the ass, but you gotta admit I'm really in a mess.

3. L: Hey, I knew you wouldn't like the idea of seeing a counselor, but there's really nothing wrong with doing it. One doesn't have to be sick to need some help. You've got enough problems for two or three people to handle, and counselors often know about resources that I'm not at all aware of. Do yourself a favor, let me call Dr. Bolberg and arrange an appointment. It can't hurt and it might help.

4. C: I fail to see how lying on a couch and going on and on about my mother is going to help me now.

5. L: Listen, you've been watching too much T.V. I'm not talking about five years of intensive psychoanalysis. Dr. Bolberg will meet with you once or twice a week and talk to you directly about the problems you raised with me. I think he'll be able to help you feel a lot better in a short period of time. Unless you say no, I'd really like to give him a call. I think it would help.

Analysis:

In reviewing the foregoing example, consider the following:

1. In No. 1, do you do an adequate job of pointing out the factors indicating that a referral may be helpful? Why or why not?

2. In No. 3, are you empathic about the client's discomfort about seeing a counselor? Why or why not?

3. Do you do an adequate job of explaining what the counseling will entail? Why or why not?

4. What other things might you have said to facilitate this referral?

2. CONCLUSION

Suggesting that a client consult a mental health professional is often difficult. You may feel that merely mentioning the subject will cause a client to become angry, or at least uncooperative, and rupture the lawyer-client relationship. Admittedly, the referral process outlined here is no guarantee that ruptures in the lawyer-client relationship will never occur. However, referrals are often necessary. The suggestions above may be a useful starting point for thinking about when and how to make a referral.

*

Index

References are to Pages

†